Database Performance Tuning and Optimization
Using Oracle

Springer
New York
Berlin
Heidelberg
Hong Kong
London
Milan
Paris
Tokyo

Sitansu S. Mittra

Database Performance Tuning and Optimization
Using Oracle

With 214 Illustrations

 Includes CD-ROM

 Springer

Sitansu S. Mittra
Senior Principal Engineer and Database Management Specialist
Computer Sciences Corporation
5 Cambridge Center
Cambridge, MA 02139
USA
mittra4@aol.com

Library of Congress Cataloging-in-Publication Data
Mittra, Sitansu S.
    Database performance tuning and optimization : using Oracle / Sitansu
  S. Mittra.
       p. cm.
    Includes bibliographical references and index.
    ISBN 0-387-95393-0 (alk. paper)
    1. Database management. 2. Oracle (Computer file). II. Title.
  QA76.9.D3 M579   2002
  005.75′85—dc21   2002070558

ACM Computing Classification (1998): C.4, E.1, E.2, H.2, H.3, H.4

ISBN 0-387-95393-0   Printed on acid-free paper.

© 2003 Springer-Verlag New York, Inc.
All rights reserved. This work may not be translated or copied in whole or in part without the written permission of the publisher (Springer-Verlag New York, Inc., 175 Fifth Avenue, New York, NY 10010, USA), except for brief excerpts in connection with reviews or scholarly analysis. Use in connection with any form of information storage and retrieval, electronic adaptation, computer software, or by similar or dissimilar methodology now known or hereafter developed is forbidden.
The use in this publication of trade names, trademarks, service marks, and similar terms, even if they are not identified as such, is not to be taken as an expression of opinion as to whether or not they are subject to proprietary rights.

Printed in the United States of America.

9 8 7 6 5 4 3 2 1   SPIN 10857938

www.springer-ny.com

Springer-Verlag New York Berlin Heidelberg
A member of BertelsmannSpringer Science+Business Media GmbH

*To my family
— Pranati, Partha, and Ansuman —
for their unwavering support
during my solitary sojourn into
the intricacies and excitement
of the database world*

Preface

Scope

The book provides comprehensive coverage of database performance tuning and optimization using Oracle 8i as the RDBMS. The chapters contain both theoretical discussions dealing with principles and methodology as well as actual SQL scripts to implement the methodology. The book combines theory with practice so as to make it useful for DBAs and developers irrespective of whether they use Oracle 8i. Readers who do not use Oracle 8i can implement the principles via scripts of their own written for the particular RDBMS they use. I have tested each script for accuracy and have included the sample outputs generated from them.

An operational database has three levels: conceptual, internal, and external. The conceptual level results from data modeling and logical database design. When it is implemented via an RDBMS such as Oracle, it is mapped onto the internal level. Database objects of the conceptual level are associated with their physical counterparts in the internal level. An external level results from a query against the database and, as such, provides a window to the database. There are many external levels for a single conceptual level.

The performance of an OLTP database is measured by the response times of the database transactions. The response time depends on the efficiency of all three levels. A query on a well-designed conceptual level can run slowly if the SQL formulation of the query is poorly done, or if the database objects involved in the query are fragmented, or if a table used by the query has excessive chaining. Likewise, a well-formulated query can run slowly if the design of the conceptual level is bad. Such examples abound in database applications. The book addresses each level separately by focusing first on the underlying principles and root causes of problems and then offering solutions, both on a theoretical level and with Oracle SQL scripts with sample outputs.

Even if all three levels of a database are kept properly tuned, its performance may suffer due to other factors. For example, the CPU may remain pegged at or very near to 100%, the memory may be inadequate causing excessive paging and swapping bordering on thrashing, disk controllers may be inefficient, etc. These factors are outside the realm of the database and, therefore, are not treated in this book. Some discussion of tuning the CPU and the memory as a part of the internal level of a database appears in Chapter 6.

The theory of relational databases as propounded by Codd has its foundation rooted in mathematics. Consequently, database topics can often be discussed using the mathematical language and notations. Due to the inherent precision of such language I have used it in my treatment of database topics, whenever appropriate.

Overview of the Book

The book consists of 12 chapters grouped in three parts, five appendices, and an index. Each part starts with an overview of the part and a brief description of each chapter included in the part. Each chapter starts with a list of topics and an overview and ends with a list of key words used in the chapter, a section on references and further reading, and exercises, where appropriate.

Part 1: Chapters 1 to 3

Part 1, Methodology, consists of Chapters 1 to 3 that cover the methodology aspect of database performance tuning and optimization. The goal of Part 1 is to establish a sound conceptual framework for identifying tuning issues and taking a well-planned approach to address them. As such, it is primarily theoretical in nature and avoids, as far as practicable, references to any particular RDBMS. The methods and principles discussed in this part can be applied to any RDBMS with which the reader works.

Chapter 1, Database Application Development, contains a detailed discussion of the five phases of building a database application starting with the information requirements analysis, continuing through logical and physical database designs, and ending in database implementation. This is a one-time effort. When the database becomes operational, its ongoing maintenance phase begins. The issues of performance tuning happen primarily during this phase, although initial performance checks are done during the development. This chapter is targeted primarily for the developers and the system analysts.

Chapter 2, Performance Tuning Methodology, describes the three levels of a database and emphasizes that a database must be well tuned at all three levels in order to run optimally. It provides the methodology for performance tuning. Both the DBAs and the developers will benefit from this chapter.

Chapter 3, Tuning the Conceptual Level of a Database, explores a variety of issues underlying the tuning process of the conceptual level. It covers three major areas: denormalization, partitioning of tables and indices, and data replication among multiple locations of a database. The primary readers of this chapter are the developers.

Part 2: Chapters 4 to 10

Part 2, Oracle Tools for Tuning and Optimization, consists of Chapters 4 to 10 that cover the Oracle tools for monitoring the performance of a database and tuning and optimizing its internal and external levels, as needed. This part is specific to Oracle 8i with a glimpse into Oracle 9i in Chapter 10. It is intended for the DBAs. The goal of Part 2 is to provide the underlying tuning principles and a repertoire of Oracle tools to implement these principles. Chapters 4 to 7 discuss the tuning of the internal level and Chapters 8 to 9 that of the external level. Chapter 10 describes several features of Oracle 8i not covered in the earlier chapters and gives an overview of several tuning features of Oracle 9i.

Chapter 4, Internal Level of an Oracle Database, introduces the structure of the internal level comprising an instance and a database. The instance consists of a set of memory-resident data structures and a set of background processes. The database consists of a set of disk-resident data structures, namely, the tablespaces, tables, indices, etc.

Chapter 5, Tuning of Disk-Resident Data Structures, discusses in detail the tuning principles of the components of an Oracle database. Fragmentation and chaining are two major areas that the DBAs need to track and address for tuning. Ample scripts are provided to implement the tuning principles.

Chapter 6, Tuning of Memory-Resident Data Structures, discusses in detail the tuning principles of the System Global Area (SGA) of an Oracle instance and the administration and optimization of the background processes. The chapter includes separate sections dealing with the tuning of the CPU and memory-related objects. Ample scripts are provided to implement the tuning principles.

Chapter 7, Oracle Utility for Tuning and Optimization, involves a detailed discussion of the two Oracle diagnostic tools, UTLBSTAT and UTLESTAT, that collect detailed statistics during a data collection period specified by the DBA and generate a report containing an analysis of the collected statistics along with recommendations for improvement, as needed. The chapter includes detailed directions for interpreting the output and for taking corrective actions to address the deficiencies identified in the output.

Chapter 8, Optimization of the External Level of a Database, introduces the mathematical theory underlying the query optimization process. This is followed by a detailed treatment of Oracle's optimization tools such as EXPLAIN PLAN, SQLTRACE and TKPROF, and AUTOTRACE.

Chapter 9, Query Tuning and Optimization Under Oracle 8i, discusses the rule-based and the cost-based optimizers, various joining techniques, and the use of hints in queries to suggest specific query execution plans.

Chapter 10, Special Features of Oracle 8i and a Glimpse into Oracle 9i, covers several special features of Oracle 8i pertaining to performance tuning and optimization that were not covered in the earlier chapters. It closes with an overview of some of the features of Oracle 9i.

Part 3: Chapters 11 and 12

Part 3, Contemporary Issues, consists of two chapters that discuss two specific contemporary issues, namely, the tuning principles of data warehouses and of Web-based databases. Although the design principles of an OLTP database are different from those of a data warehouse or a Web-based database, their tuning principles are substantially the same. In this part we capture only those tools and techniques that are unique to these two special types of databases.

Chapter 11, Tuning Data Warehouses at All Levels, starts with a discussion of the design principles of a data warehouse and identifies the structural differences between an OLTP database and a data warehouse. It then introduces the data loading principles for a data warehouse. The chapter closes with a discussion of the tuning principles for a data warehouse at the internal and the external levels.

Chapter 12, Tuning Web-Based Databases, starts with an introduction to the three-tier and n-tier architectures of client-server applications with emphasis on the Web-based applications. The Oracle product OAS is discussed in detail and an overview is offered of Oracle's new product iAS. The chapter closes with a discussion of the tuning principles for a Web-based database at the internal and the external levels.

Appendices A to E

The five appendices discuss several DBA issues, although they are not directly related to performance tuning and optimization. They are included here to make the book useful for addressing issues outside the realm of performance monitoring and tuning.

Appendix A, Sizing Methodology in Oracle 8i, contains the algorithms and two C programs for estimating the storage space needed for tables, indices, and tablespaces during the physical design phase, as discussed in Chapter 1. The two C programs implement the sizing algorithms. Sizing of the tables, indices, and tablespaces constitutes the capacity planning activity which is extremely important for smooth and optimal operation of a database.

Appendix B, Instance and Database Creation, contains detailed instructions for creating an Oracle instance and an Oracle database under UNIX. Sample files such as init.ora, config.ora, etc. are included as attachments to clarify the steps. Inexperienced DBAs often find the creation of an instance quite a formidable job because of the following two reasons:

- Various files and directories must be properly set up before the instance can be created.
- After the database is created, its tablespaces, tables, indices, views, user roles and privileges, etc. must be created within the database.

Appendix C, Instance and Database Removal, offers a similar step-by-step methodology to drop an instance and its associated database.

Appendix D, Database Refresh with Transportable Tablespaces, provides a methodology for refreshing an existing database with data from another database with identical structure. The transportable tablespaces introduced in Oracle 8i are used for this purpose. The appendix also includes the procedure to determine if a set of tablespaces is transportable.

Appendix E, Mathematical Foundation of Relational Databases, contains relevant mathematical materials that were used by Dr. Codd to establish the relational database theory on a sound mathematical foundation. He introduced relational algebra and relational calculus as the two alternative but equivalent mechanisms for query languages and query processing. The later sections of the appendix contain discussions of three data structures, namely, linear linked list, search tree, and hash tables, as the underlying mechanisms for sequential, indexed, and direct search of relations in a database. Appendix E is included primarily for the mathematically inquisitive readers. A graduate level course normally labeled as discrete mathematics in the current day computer science curricula will provide adequate mathematical preparation to understand this appendix. But a lack of understanding of this appendix will not interfere with reading and using the rest of the book.

The key words appearing at the end of each chapter and each appendix are combined into a single comprehensive index for the whole book. It is included at the end of the book.

Unique Features

The book offers several unique features that distinguish it from other books with similar titles and scope that are currently available in the market.

(a) *Three Levels of a Database*: A clear knowledge of the three levels and their mutual relationships is crucial to the understanding of database operations and performance tuning issues. Chapter 2 explains this background information with examples and emphasizes that a database must run optimally at each level for overall optimal performance. Also, tuning may have to be done at multiple levels to resolve a problem.

(a) *Ideal Mix of Theory and Practice*: Throughout the book I have described the underlying principles for handling database performance and then included Oracle SQL scripts to implement these principles. This is the standard error-fixing methodology for software and database problems. One first localizes a problem, then finds the root cause(s), and finally corrects it. My treatment allows the reader to understand the principles and then apply them to other RDBMSs besides Oracle.

(a) *Web Based Databases*: In today's software industry n-tier ($n \geq 3$) architecture with the database residing on the nth tier is very common. The principles of database design and performance tuning remain largely the same in such applications. However, a few nuances need to be clarified. Chapter 12 addresses that area.

(a) *Complete Instructions for Creating an Instance and a Database*: From my own experience I have found that creating an Oracle instance often poses a more serious problem than running a script to create the database. Creation of an instance involves an understanding of the disk storage structure, defining the initialization parameters properly, and setting up the necessary directories. Appendix B contains a complete set of instructions to implement a database and all its objects.

(a) *Mathematical Foundation of Relational Databases*: Dr. Edgar Codd established the relational database theory on a sound mathematical foundation. He introduced relational algebra and relational calculus as the two alternative but equivalent mechanisms for query languages and query processing. Appendix E contains the relevant mathematical materials along with the three data structures that are used for sequential, indexed, and direct searches of a relational database.

(a) *References and Further Reading*: Titles included in this section at the end of each chapter will help the more inquisitive readers in finding additional materials relevant to the topics. Some of the references offer an alternative approach to handle the performance and tuning issues.

(a) *Exercises*: The exercises at the end of each chapter are optional. Occasionally they introduce topics that are an extension to the main body of the text. But they are intended primarily for students and instructors when the book is used as a text for a database course. In today's educational systems often colleges and universities offer certificate courses in specialized areas such as performance tuning of Oracle databases. The exercises can then be used as assignments for the students.

Reader Community

The book assumes an understanding of relational database concepts and a familiarity with Oracle. Some knowledge of college-level mathematics will be helpful. Thus, it is not intended for the beginners. It is designed primarily for database professionals such as DBAs, developers, and system analysts with two to three years of experience in the development, implementation, and maintenance of relational databases using some RDBMS, preferably Oracle. A junior DBA or a developer can use the scripts of the book under the guidance of a senior DBA or developer. The principles and tools presented here arise out of my personal experience with Oracle and several other RDBMSs (e.g., SQL Server, INGRES, LOGIX, RIM, etc.) that I have used since 1983. I have been using them regularly as a part of my current and previous positions as a senior Oracle DBA, Data Architecture Group Manager, Development and Architecture Manager, and QA Manager, in industry. In addition, I have taught graduate-level database courses at Boston University, Northeastern University, and Wentworth Institute of Technology. I have used the collective experience from these activities in writing this book. The scripts and their sample output included in the book were written over several years as my ideas shaped up through academic and industrial experience.

Colleges and universities do not offer full semester courses dealing with database performance and tuning per se. Usually such materials are included in other database courses at an advanced level, in the certificate and state-of-the-art programs offered for the industry professionals, or simply as courses in continuing education programs. The book can be used as a text for such courses. The instructors can use the exercises at the end of each chapter as student assignments. Some of the exercises explore new topics not discussed in the accompanying chapters. These can be used as group projects for the students.

In order to keep the book self-contained I have avoided the use of any third party tools. The only software being used is Oracle 8i RDBMS along with SQL*Plus and PL/SQL. Almost all of the scripts included in the book are completely portable between UNIX and NT and can be used in any Oracle 8i installation under either operating system. The scripts are collected into a separate CD that is included with the book.

Some readers will read the book from beginning to end. Others will use it as a reference and utilize the tuning guidelines and accompanying scripts to resolve specific problems. Possibilities are quite varied.

Acknowledgments

I got much valuable information from Oracle MetaLink (accessible through the web site http://metalink.oracle.com). I was able to resolve several issues and clarify concepts with the help of the information. In addition, I benefited from phone conversations with members of the Oracle Technical Group in response to TARs that I opened with Oracle. I am highly impressed with the courtesy, promptness, and professionalism of the Oracle technical staff.

I acknowledge the friendly support of the staff of Springer-Verlag to make the publication of the book a success. In particular, I thank Wayne Yuhasz, the Executive Editor of Computing and Information Science, Wayne Wheeler, the Assistant Editor of Computing and Information Science, and Robert Wexler, who converted the whole manuscript into the format needed for publication.

Sudbury, Massachusetts, USA Sitansu S. Mittra
July 2002

Contents

Preface vii

Part 1 Methodology 1

1 Database Application Development 3
    Outline 3
    Overview of the Chapter 3
    1.1 1970s Software Technology Era 4
    1.2 Role of the Database in SDLC and SMLC 6
    1.3 Enterprise Modeling 7
    1.4 Logical Database Design 11
    1.5. Physical Database Design 15
    1.6 Database Implementation 18
    1.7 Database Maintenance 20
    1.8 Naming Guidelines for Database Objects 20
    Key Words 25
    References and Further Reading 26
    Exercises 27

2 Performance Tuning Methodology 29
    Outline 29
    Overview of the Chapter 29
    2.1 Three Levels of a Database 29
    2.2 Optimization at Each Level 31
    2.3 Process and Metric for Performance Tuning 33
    Key Words 38
    References and Further Reading 38
    Exercises 39

3 Tuning the Conceptual Level of a Database 41
    Outline 41
    Overview of the Chapter 41
    3.1 Three Versions of the Conceptual Level 42

3.2 Performance Issues at the Conceptual Level 43
3.3 Denormalization of the Conceptual Level 43
3.4 Optimal Indexing of Tables.. 47
3.5 Integration of Views into Queries 48
3.6 Partitioning of Tables and Indices 48
3.7 Data Replication 52
Key Words 52
References and Further Reading 53
Exercises 54

Part 2 Oracle Tools for Tuning and Optimization   55

4 Internal Level of an Oracle Database   57

Outline.. 57
Overview of the Chapter 57
4.1 Components of the Internal Level.. 58
4.2 Oracle Instance 59
4.3 Oracle Database 67
4.4 Internal Level Tuning Methodology 70
4.5 Oracle Data Dictionary... 70
4.6 V$ Views and X$ Tables 74
4.7 Initialization Parameters for an Oracle Database 77
Key Words 79
References and Further Reading 80
Exercises 80

5 Tuning of Disk Resident Data Structures   81

Outline.. 81
Overview of the Chapter 81
5.1 Disk-Resident Data Structures 82
5.2 Performance Tuning of Disk-Resident Data Structures... 82
5.3 Baseline of Disk-Resident Data Structures.. 82
5.3.3 Segments with Information on Extents... 86
5.4 Changes to Database Schema... 95
5.5 Data Block Structure 96
5.6 Used Space Fragmentation at the Segment Level 96
5.7 Severity of Free Space Shortage 101
5.8 Free Space Fragmentation at Tablespace Level 105
5.9 Row Chaining and Row Migration in Tables.. 110
5.10 Performance Tuning of Rollback Segments.. 115
Key Words 134
References and Further Reading 135
Exercises 135

6 Tuning of Memory-Resident Data Structures — 137
- Outline — 137
- Overview of the Chapter — 137
- 6.1 Memory Resident Data Structures — 138
- 6.2 Performance Tuning — 138
- 6.3 Data Block Buffers — 139
- 6.4 Redo Log Buffer — 146
- 6.5 Shared SQL Pool — 148
- 6.6 Background Processes — 156
- 6.7 Tuning the Memory — 166
- 6.8 Tuning the CPU — 175
- 6.9 Pinning Packages in Memory — 176
- 6.10 Latching Mechanism for Access Control — 178
- Key Words — 184
- References and Further Reading — 185
- Exercises — 186

7 Oracle Utility for Tuning and Optimization — 189
- Outline — 189
- Overview of the Chapter — 189
- 7.1 Scope of Oracle Utilities — 189
- 7.2 UTLBSTAT and UTLESTAT Utilities — 190
- 7.3 Location and Function of the Utility Scripts — 190
- 7.4 Procedure for Running the Utilities — 203
- 7.5 UTLBSTAT/ESTAT Performance Report Analysis — 204
- 7.6 Comprehensive Tuning Plan for Internal Level — 224
- 7.7 Performance Tracking — 224
- 7.8 Tuning Activities — 225
- Key Words — 226
- References and Further Reading — 226
- Exercises — 227

8 Optimization of the External Level of a Database — 229
- Outline — 229
- Overview of the Chapter — 229
- 8.1 Contents of the External Level — 230
- 8.2 Principles of Query Optimization — 230
- 8.3 Query Optimization in Oracle — 232
- 8.4 Optimal Indexing Guidelines — 235
- 8.5 Methodology for Optimal Indexing — 239
- 8.6 Implementation of Indices in Oracle — 245

8.7 Tools for Tracking Query Performance 263
Key Words 279
References and Further Reading 280
Exercises 281

9 Query Tuning and Optimization Under Oracle 8i   283

Outline 283
Overview of the Chapter 283
9.1 Oracle Query Performance 283
9.2 Query Tuning in Oracle: General Principles 284
9.3 Query Tuning in Oracle: Cost-based Optimizer 292
9.4 Query Tuning in Oracle: Rule-based Optimizer 299
9.5 Tuning of Join Queries 301
9.6 Statistical Forecasting for Tracking Performance 310
Key Words 312
References and Further Reading 312
Exercises 313

10 Special Features of Oracle 8i and a Glimpse into Oracle 9i   315

Outline 315
Overview of the Chapter 315
10.1 Scope of the Chapter 316
10.2 Evolution of Oracle Through Versions 8 and 8i 316
10.3 Partitioning of Tables and Indices 317
10.4 Materialized Views 323
10.5 Defragmentation via Local Tablespace Management 325
10.6 LOB Data Type Versus LONG Data Type 332
10.7 Multiple Buffer Pools in the SGA 333
10.8 Query Execution Plan Stability via Stored Outlines 338
10.9 Index Enhancements 342
10.10 Query Rewrite for Materialized Views 346
10.11 Online Index Creation, Rebuild, Defragmentation 347
10.12 ANALYZE versus DBMS_STATS 348
10.13 Optimization of Top_N Queries 351
10.14 Glimpse into Oracle 9i 352
Key Words 357
References and Further Reading 357

Part 3 Contemporary Issues   359

11 Tuning the Data Warehouse at All Levels   361

Outline 361
Overview of the Chapter 361
11.1 Advent of Data Warehouse 362

11.2 Features of Data Warehouse	362
11.3 Design Issues of Data Warehouse	363
11.4 Structure of Data Warehouse	365
11.5 Proliferation from Data Warehouse	366
11.6 Metadata	368
11.7 Implementation and Internal Level	369
11.8 Data Loading in Warehouse	371
11.9 Query Processing and Optimization	374
Key Words	382
References and Further Reading	382
Exercises	383

12 Web-Based Database Applications   385

Outline	385
Overview of the Chapter	385
12.1 Advent of Web-Based Applications	386
12.2 Components of Web-Based Applications	387
12.3 Oracle Application Server (OAS)	389
12.4 Database Transaction Management Under OAS	393
12.5 Oracle Internet Application Server (iAS)	394
12.6 Performance Tuning of Web-Based Databases	394
12.7 Tuning of Internal Level	395
12.8 Tuning of External Level	397
Key Words	397
References and Further Reading	397
Exercises	398

Appendices   399

Appendix A Sizing Methodology in Oracle 8i   401

Outline	401
Overview of the Appendix	401
A1. Transition from Logical to Physical Database Design	401
A2. Space Usage via Extents	402
A3. Algorithms for Sizing Tables, Indices, Tablespaces	403
A4. STORAGE Clause Inclusion: Table and Index Levels	407
A5. Sizing Methodology	407
A6. RBS, SYSTEM, TEMP, and TOOLS Tablespace Sizing	408
Key Words	411
References and Further Reading	411

Appendix B Instance and Database Creation   413

Outline	413
Overview of the Appendix	413

    B1. Preparation 413
    B2. Instance Startup... 416
    B3. Database Creation 417
    B4. Creation of Users, Roles, Privileges, Schema.................................... 417
    B5. Miscellaneous Informational Items.. 418
    Attachments 418

Appendix C Instance and Database Removal   **433**
    Outline... 433
    Overview of the Appendix 433
    C1. Preparation 433
    C2. Locating the Components.. 434
    C3. Removing the Components 436
    C4. Verification 437

Appendix D Database Refresh with Transportable Tablespaces   **439**
    Outline... 439
    Overview of the Appendix 439
    D1. Database Refresh Process.. 439
    D2. Detailed Methodology with Scripts 440
    D3. Time Estimates 444
    D4. Internal Consistency 445
    Key Words 447

Appendix E Mathematical Foundation of Relational Databases   **449**
    Outline... 449
    Overview of the Appendix 449
    E1. Relational Database Systems Foundation Pillars............................... 450
    E2. Relation.. 450
    E3. Functional Dependency 451
    E4. Query Languages 453
    E5. Relational Algebra: Prescriptive Query Languages........................... 454
    E 6. Primitive and Derived Operations 458
    E7. Closure Property for Relational Algebra... 459
    E8. Relational Calculus: Descriptive Query Languages 460
    E9. Tuple Relational Calculus.. 462
    E10. Domain Relational Calculus.. 464
    E11. Equivalence Theorem for Algebra and Calculus 465
    E12. Data Structures for Search Algorithms 467
    E13. Linear Linked List... 467
    E14. Search Tree.. 469
    E15. Hash Table... 472

E16. Performance Metrics 477
Key Words 478
References and Further Reading 479

Index **481**

Part 1
Methodology

Part 1 consists of three chapters that cover the methodology aspect of database performance tuning and optimization. The goal of Part 1 is to establish a sound conceptual framework for identifying tuning issues and taking a well-planned approach to address them. As such, it is primarily theoretical in nature and avoids, as far as practicable, references to any particular RDBMS. The methods and principles discussed in this part can be applied to any RDBMS with which the reader works.

Chapter 1, Database Application Development, contains a detailed discussion of the five phases of building a database application starting with the information requirements analysis, continuing through logical and physical database designs, and ending in database implementation. This is provided as a basis for the subsequent discussions involving performance tuning.

Chapter 2, Performance Tuning Methodology, describes the three levels of a database and emphasizes that a database must be well tuned at all three levels in order to run optimally. The chapter describes two metrics that are used for measuring database performance.

Chapter 3, Tuning the Conceptual Level of a Database, explores a variety of issues underlying the tuning process of the conceptual level. Since this level is built during the logical database design, it is essentially independent of any RDBMS. Consequently, I have included this chapter in Part 1.

I have used Oracle 8i as the RDBMS in giving specific implementation bound examples, if needed. A case in point is a tuning example appearing in Section 2.3.1.

1
Database Application Development

Outline

1.1 1970s Software Technology Era
1.2 Role of the Database in SDLC and SMLC
1.3 Enterprise Modeling
1.4 Logical Database Design
1.5 Physical Database Design
1.6 Database Implementation
1.7 Database Maintenance
1.8 Naming Guidelines for Database Objects
Key Words
References and Further Reading
Exercises

Overview of the Chapter

The chapter provides a perspective on the role of relational databases in software development and its performance issues during software maintenance. During the 1970s two major innovations appeared in the software industry:

- Introduction of relational databases as an improvement over the files and non-relational databases, both of which were cumbersome to use, and
- Structured methodology that later became known as the software development life cycle process.

E.F. Codd was the inventor of the former and several contributors such as Yourdon and Constantine, Gane and Sarson, and Jackson formulated the latter. Database development is an integral part of the software development life cycle (SDLC) and software maintenance life cycle (SMLC). It consists of five phases, the first four of which encompass SDLC and the last one occurs under SMLC. A detailed discussion of each phase is offered in the chapter as a foundation for introducing the subsequent topics in the following chapters. The chapter concludes with a detailed set of naming guidelines for database objects.

1.1 1970s Software Technology Era

The 1970s saw two major innovations in computer software technology:

- Relational database system, and
- Software development life cycle (SDLC).

Relational Database System

Up to the early 1970s only nonrelational data models were used for databases in the form of hierarchical, network, or inverted file systems. Dr. E.F. Codd, at that time a member of the IBM Research Laboratory in San Jose, California, first introduced the theory of the relational data model in his paper, *A Relational Model of Data for Large Shared Data Banks* (see [3]). Subsequently he published several papers between 1970 and 1973 formulating the relational database technology consisting of the principles of database design, detailed syntax and examples of the query language, and database administration issues. He introduced the query language as a nonprocedural language based on two separate but logically equivalent mathematical paradigms of relational algebra and relational calculus. Appendix E offers a discussion of these two paradigms along with other mathematical topics underlying relational database systems. The query language commands fall into two major categories, Data Definition Language (DDL) and Data Manipulation Language (DML). Being a mathematician himself, Codd founded the entire theory of relational database systems on mathematics. The first commercially available relational database management system (RDBMS) was INGRES, marketed in 1979 by Relational Technology, Inc. This was followed shortly by ORACLE, marketed in the same year by Relational Software, Inc., which was later renamed Oracle Corporation. The INGRES query language was based on relational calculus, and that of ORACLE primarily used the relational algebra.

In 1982 the American National Standards Institute (ANSI) asked its Database Committee (X3H2) to develop a proposal for a standard relational database language. The X3H2 proposal was finally ratified by ANSI in 1986 resulting in ANSI SQL, popularly called SQL/86, as the industry standard for query languages using a hybrid of the two paradigms of relational algebra and relational calculus. The International Organization for Standardization (ISO) accepted SQL/86 in 1987. This standard was extended in 1989 to include an Integrity Enhancement Feature and was called SQL/89 or SQL1. In 1991 a group of vendors known as the SQL Access Group published a set of enhancements to support the interoperability of SQL/89 across different operating systems. Subsequently, ANSI and ISO jointly published a revised and greatly expanded version of SQL/89. This became a ratified standard in late 1992 under the name of International Standard ISO/IEC 9075:1992, Database Language SQL (see [5]). Informally, it was called SQL/92 or SQL2.

From mid-1992 efforts had been underway to formulate and publish the next set of enhancements to SQL/92. By 1998 over 900 pages of specifications had been written under the name SQL3. In the U.S.A. the entirety of SQL3 was being processed as both an ANSI domestic project and as an ISO project. In late 1999 these specifications were ratified under the name SQL:1999, which became the next update of SQL/92. Informally SQL:1999 is still referred to as SQL/3 [6, p. 423] and is the current version of the SQL specifications.

Software Development Life Cycle (SDLC)

Throughout the early 1970s MIS applications were developed using a variety of mostly ad hoc methodologies. By the mid-1970s several parallel efforts started to build a uniform methodology to develop applications. Three separate schools of thought were organized by Yourdon and Constantine, Gane and Sarson, and Jackson. Their approaches were similar so that by the late 1970s an integrated methodology emerged and was called the software development life cycle or SDLC. Under this methodology an application development consists of five distinct phases, as described below (see [9]):

(a) Problem definition and feasibility study,
(b) Requirements analysis,
(c) Preliminary system design,
(d) Detailed system design, and
(e) System implementation, maintenance, and evaluation.

These five phases are grouped into three logical categories: *analysis* consisting of (a) and (b), *design* consisting of (c) and (d), and *implementation* consisting of (e) alone. Strictly speaking, maintenance and evaluation under (e) fall outside the SDLC, which ends with the installation of the application as an operational system. After an application is installed, it enters the maintenance phase which is governed by a methodology similar to SDLC and is called the software maintenance life cycle or SMLC (see [11]).

The analysis category is guided by the keyword WHAT, i.e., what functions will the application provide for the end users. Its end product consists of a logical system specification (also called functional requirements document) that describes in detail the tasks that end users will be able to do when the system becomes operational. The design category is guided by the keyword HOW, i.e., how the functions described in the logical system specification will be implemented. The end product here is called the physical system specification that describes the architecture of the proposed system, screen formats with samples, report formats with samples, the logical design of the database, the process flow and logic, required hardware and software tools, architecture of the application, resource estimates, etc. This document is a "paper" system built in response to the logical system specification. The implementation category consists of converting the "paper" system into an "electronic" system and ends with a successful acceptance test by end users.

More than 25 years have elapsed since the SDLC was first introduced in the information industry for the purpose of building applications. Various technologies have appeared since then such as object-oriented design and programming, first two-tier and then n-tier ($n > 2$) client server architecture, Web-based design, event-driven programming instead of logic-driven programming, etc. Although the tools used for building applications in each of these areas are widely different, SDLC still remains the underlying methodology.

The main differences between SDLC and SMLC arise from the focus: SMLC operates with an existing application, whereas SDLC builds a new application. The salient points of difference are listed below.

- An SMLC job is initiated by a software maintenance request form, whereas an SDLC job starts as a new application development.
- SMLC deals with a code and a database that are already in existence and need modification, whereas SDLC involves a new code and database.
- The analysis and design phases of SDLC are much longer and require in-depth discussion with the end users, whereas they are much simpler in SMLC.

1.2 Role of the Database in SDLC and SMLC

Any application deals with two distinct but related items, *data* and *process*. A process in a generic sense accepts data as its input and transforms it into information, which is the output from the application. Data and process can be kept separate as in a relational database application, or can be integrated into objects as in an object-oriented paradigm. SDLC can be used as the underlying methodology in either case. For the former, the relational database manages the data that are accessed by programs to produce reports and graphics. For the latter, an object-oriented database is needed. A relational DBMS such as Oracle 8i offers both features for the database side.

The processes are coded as programs, modules, functions, procedures, etc. and interact with the database. In a relational database environment the processes are kept separate from the data, whereas in an object-oriented environment the two are encapsulated into classes that have two components: data and method. A *class* can be thought of as a template that can have multiple runtime versions called *objects*. Individual processes in an object are executed by passing *messages*, which are the object-oriented versions of function and procedure calls used in a relational database environment.

In a client-server application the database resides on the server. In a two-tier client-server application all end-user functions are executed on the client. Each client request for data retrieval or update is executed on the server under the control of the RDBMS residing there. Data validation can be split between the client and the server or may be done on the server alone. In an n-tier ($n > 2$) client server application the client requests are handled by the first $n - 1$ tiers, called the client and the application tier(s), and all database transactions, i.e., data retrieval and update requests, are done on the nth or the most remote tier. Typically the client tier, which is often called a thin client, is equipped with a Web browser that sends client requests to the application tier(s). The application server processes the client request and returns the result to the client tier. It contains code to handle complex business logic such as transaction management, fault tolerance, scalability, and sharing/reusing code modules. In no case does a client access the database server tier directly.

The analysis and design phases of the SDLC and SMLC result in the following database tasks,

(a) Enterprise modeling,
(b) Logical database design,
(c) Physical database design,
(d) Database implementation, and
(e) Database maintenance.

Except for (a) and (b), the remaining activities require the use of a specific RDBMS. The database performance and tuning principles are related to activities covered under (b) through (e) and need an RDBMS for their implementation.

1.3 Enterprise Modeling

The starting point of any data modeling is a pool of data elements that are collected during the analysis phase of the SDLC. They are gathered from source documents such as data entry forms, data entry screen captures, and reports, and also during the interviews with the end users as a part of the requirements collection process. The data elements at this stage are often at group levels. For example, a data element called Customer Address contains several primitive data elements such as Street Number, City, State, Zipcode, etc.; Employee Name typically has at least three parts: First Name, Middle Initial, and Last Name, and so on. Therefore, the data modeler begins with

Step 1: Identify as much as possible the primitive data elements and decompose the group level data elements into their component primitive data elements.

1.3.1 Entity, Relationship, and Attribute

The next task is to bring order into this data pool chaos by grouping the data into separate sets such that each set consists of data elements representing an atomic concept such as person, place, object, event, etc. The guiding principle here is not to mix two or more atomic concepts into a single set. Therefore, the data modeler performs

Step 2: Create distinct sets of data elements from the pool such that each set represents an atomic concept.

The sets thus created do not normally have common data elements among them. Since the data in a database must be related to one another, the data modeler needs to create links among the sets, which leads to

Step 3: Create additional sets, as needed, so that distinct atomic sets are linked by them. Such link sets do not represent atomic concepts. Instead, they relate two or more atomic concepts.

Steps (1) through (3) are iterative in nature in that a final enterprise data model results after several attempts with the three steps.

In 1976, Peter Chen proposed an entity relationship (ER) model to formalize these steps (see [2]). Each atomic set is called an entity, and each linking set a relationship. Thus, an enterprise data model consists of entities and relationships. The component data elements of entities and relationships are called attributes.

A database transaction involves accessing one or more records located among one or more entities and relationships in the database. There are two types of transactions: retrieval, which is READ ONLY access, and update, which is WRITE access and is of three types—insert a new record, modify an existing record, or delete an existing record. Thus, a transaction requires searching for record(s) matching a given set of criteria. This is facilitated by creating keys in entities and relationships. A *key* is defined as a set of attribute(s) in an entity or a relationship such that given a value of the key the search returns either no record or only one record. When multiple sets of attribute(s) qualify for a key, each set is called a *candidate key*. One of them is designated a *primary key* and the rest are called *alternate key(s)*.

1.3.2 Types of Relationships

Two entities A and B, say, can be related to each other in one of three possible ways: one to one (1:1), one to many (1:N), and many to many (M:N). If a given value of the primary key of A matches that of only one record in B, then A and B are related in a 1:1 manner. If a given value of the primary key of A matches that of one or more records in B, then A and B are related in a 1:N manner. Finally, if a given value of the primary key of A matches that of one or more records in B and vice versa, then A and B are related in an M:N manner. In this case, a new relationship R, say, can be created such that A and R as well as B and R are each related in a 1:N manner. The data modeler thus performs

Step 4: Determine how different entities are related and replace each M:N type of relationship with two distinct relationships each of type 1:N. As a minimum, each relationship contains the primary keys of both linked entities as attributes.

1.3.3 Recursive Relationship

A recursive relationship can best be described as an M:N type relationship of an entity with itself. It is called recursive because a query involving such an entity makes many passes through the entity before returning the solution. For example, consider a COURSE entity:

```
COURSE (Course Number, Course Description, Prerequisite
Course Number)
```

Here a given course can have many prerequisites and can itself be a prerequisite of other courses. In order to find a complete list of all prerequisites of a given course, a query first finds the prerequisite of that course and then the prerequisite of each prerequisite and so on until there are no more prerequisites. This entails a recursive search process through all the members of the COURSE entity.

1.3.4 Vector-Valued Attributes

An entity may contain vector-valued attributes. For example, consider the following Student entity,

```
STUDENT (ID, Name, Major, Course Number, Grade)
```

with the sample data values shown in Figure 1.1.

ID	Name	Major	Course Number	Grade
112	Sheila Martin	History	HIS231, ENG224	B+, A-
563	Biman Basu	Math	MA423, COMP367, BI201	A, A, C+
632	Len Frankinson	Physics	PHY342	D

FIGURE 1.1: STUDENT Entity with Vector-Valued Attributes

The attributes, Course Number and Grade, of the first two records are vector valued since more than one value is recorded there. In general, an RDBMS cannot process such records. Consequently, the data modeler needs to perform

   Step 5: Break down each vector valued attribute into multiple records, each containing a single value from the vector and repeat the remaining attributes.

The student entity then will appear as shown in Figure 1.2.

ID	Name	Major	Course Number	Grade
112	Sheila Martin	History	HIS231	B+
112	Sheila Martin	History	ENG224	A-
563	Biman Basu	Math	MA423	A
563	Biman Basu	Math	COMP367	A
563	Biman Basu	Math	BI201	C+
632	Len Frankinson	Physics	PHY342	D

FIGURE 1.2: STUDENT Entity Without Vector-Valued Attributes

However, Oracle 8i supports a datatype called VARRAY that can handle vector-valued attributes.

1.3.5 Supertypes and Subtypes

Two or more entities can have several common attributes and a few distinct attributes. For example, an organization can have different types of employees such as Salaried, Contract, and Wage-Based. All of them have many common attributes such as Name, Address, Date of Birth, Hire Date, Department, etc. But a salaried employee has Annual Salary, a contract employee has Contract Amount, and a Wage-Based employee has Hourly Wage as their respective unique attributes. In such a case, the data modeler creates a *supertype* called EMPLOYEE containing all the common attributes, and three *subtypes* called SALARIED EMPLOYEE, CONTRACT EMPLOYEE, and WAGE BASED EMPLOYEE. Each subtype contains the primary key, Social Security Number, of the supertype EMPLOYEE, and all the distinct attribute(s) of that subtype. For example, SALARIED EMPLOYEE may contain only two attributes: Social Security Number and Annual Salary. Figure 1.3 shows this situation, where ISA stands for "is a supertype of". Thus, the data modeler completes the enterprise model with

Step 6: Identify entities that can be classified as supertypes and subtypes and separate them into distinct entities such that each subtype is a supertype and each supertype is one of the subtypes.

These six steps complete the enterprise modeling and produce a data model that works as the starting point of the next phase, the logical database design.

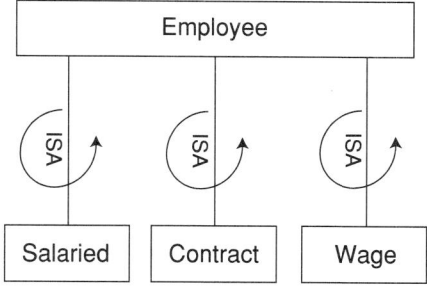

FIGURE 1.3: Subtype and Supertype

1.4 Logical Database Design

This phase starts by performing the following conversions, almost mechanically, from the enterprise data model.

- All the entities and relationships become tables and their respective attributes become the columns of the corresponding tables.
- The primary key of an entity becomes the primary key of the corresponding table.
- The primary key of a relationship consists of the primary keys of the entities linked by the relationship.

Functional dependency and normalization are driving principles for refining the logical database design. A set of columns B, say, in a table T is *functionally dependent* (FD) on another set of columns A, say, in T if for a given value of A we always get *only one* set of values of B. Thus, any non-PK column in a table is functionally dependent on the PK of the table. *Normalization* is the mechanism by which each table is made to represent an atomic entity. The level of atomicity depends on the specific normal form to which a table belongs. There are six normal forms defined in a progressively restrictive manner: first, second, third, Boyce-Codd, fourth, and fifth. For logical design purposes it is enough to strive for a database with all of its tables in the third normal form.

1.4.1 Normal Forms

The three normal forms are described below with examples.

First Normal Form (1NF)—A Table Is in 1NF if It Satisfies the Following Four Conditions

- There are no vector valued attributes.
- There are no duplicate rows.

- All values of a column belong to the domain of that column.
- The order of rows and columns is immaterial.

The second condition cannot be enforced without a PK for the table. Theoretically, therefore, a database can contain tables that are not even in 1NF. In practice, however, that does not happen since a PK is usually defined for a table at the time of its creation.

The STUDENT entity shown in Figure 1.2 is an example of a table in 1NF.

Second Normal Form (2NF)—A Table Is in 2NF if It Satisfies the Following Two Conditions

- It is in 1NF.
- Exactly one of the following three possibilities holds:
  —PK consists of a single column,
  —PK consists of all the columns, or
  —every non-PK column depends on the entire PK.

The table STUDENT (Figure 1.2) is not in 2NF. Its PK is (ID, Course Number). But the non-PK column Major depends only on the part ID of its PK and not on Course Number. STUDENT can be decomposed into three separate tables, each in 2NF, as shown in Figure 1.4.

```
STUDENT (ID, Name, Major)
COURSE (Course Number)
GRADE (ID, Course Number, Grade)
```

FIGURE 1.4: 2NF Tables STUDENT, COURSE, and GRADE

Figure 1.5 shows the entity relationship diagram for the above 3-table database.

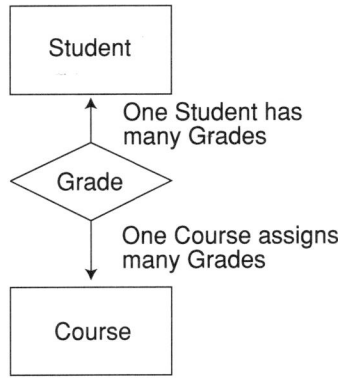

FIGURE 1.5: E/R Diagram for Three-table Database

Third Normal Form (3NF)—A Table Is in 3NF if It Satisfies the Following Two Conditions:

- It is in 2NF.
- It has no *transitive dependency*.

As an example, each table in Figure 1.4 is in 3NF.

A table has *transitive dependency* (TD) if a non-PK column functionally depends on another non-PK column without involving the PK. TD is undesirable because, theoretically, a table with TD can cause update anomalies by incurring loss of information. In reality such a phenomenon rarely occurs, if at all. Consequently, we practice denormalization for performance reasons, if needed, by allowing one or more 3NF tables to degenerate into 2NF or even 1NF tables.

1.4.2 Tasks for Logical Database Design

The five important tasks of this phase are as follows.

(a) Ensure that each table is in the third normal form (3NF). For performance reasons it may be necessary later to do some denormalization. But the logical database should start with all 3NF tables.
(b) Assign to each column in each table a data type and a size according to the specifications of the RDBMS that will be used later during the physical database design phase.
(c) Formulate all data validations that can be enforced in the next phase through declarative constraints, i.e., clauses such as REFERENCES, CHECK, etc. of the data definition language (DDL) commands for creating or altering tables. REFERENCES involves the principle of referential integrity discussed below in Section 1.4.3. CHECK ensures the entry of a discrete or continuous range of valid values for column(s).
(d) Formulate additional data validation algorithms that cannot be enforced through declarative constraints. These are implemented through triggers, procedures, and functions using proprietory procedural languages such as PL/SQL in Oracle or through host language interface programs using embedded SQL such as Pro*C, Pro*COBOL, etc. in Oracle.
(e) Formulate additional indexing requirements besides the declaration of primary keys, if known at this point in time.

1.4.3 Referential Integrity

The principle of referential integrity involving foreign keys plays a crucial role in Step (c), Section 1.4.2 above. The principle is stated as follows.

One or more columns in a table T constitute a foreign key (FK) of T if they match the primary key (PK) or a unique key (UK) of a table S, where T and S can be the same or different tables. A value of FK can be inserted or modified in T only if its matching PK or UK in S already contains that value. A value of the PK or UK of S can be deleted only if there are no matching FK values in T.

In most cases, tables T and S are different. For example, in Figure 1.4, GRADE.ID is an FK in GRADE matching STUDENT.ID as the PK of STUDENT. They are two different tables. Now consider the table SUBJECT given below.

```
SUBJECT (Course Number, Course Description, Prerequisite
Course Number)
```

Here Course Number is the PK of SUBJECT. But Prerequisite Course Number must always match Course Number. Hence Prerequisite Course Number is an FK matching the PK Course Number of the same table. Such tables are called *self-referencing* tables.

Based on the principle of referential integrity the tables in a database are divided into two categories, validation and transaction. A validation table contains the valid column values for the matching columns in transaction table(s). If a new data value in a transaction table does not match an existing data value in a validation table, then it cannot be entered, thereby ensuring data integrity. On the other hand, if a transaction table contains data matching row(s) in the corresponding validation table, then the row(s) in the validation table can be deleted only after the corresponding row(s) in the transaction table have been deleted. This phenomenon is called *cascading* of updates and deletes. To cascade an update, a change made in a validation table is propagated to all the related transaction tables. To cascade a delete, when a row is deleted from a validation table, all rows in all transaction tables depending on the deleted row are also deleted. If the RDBMS does not support the cascade option through DDL, it should be enforced via triggers.

1.4.4 Data Dictionary

During the enterprise modeling and logical database design a lot of information is generated about the structure of the proposed database. A *data dictionary* provides a central repository to document the work done during Phases (1) and (2), and is often described as a database about a database, or a meta database. It should preferably be built with a CASE (Computer Aided Software Engineering) tool such as ERwin, Power Designer, Oracle Designer, etc. although some desktop RDBMS software such as Microsoft Access can also be used.

A CASE tool automatically builds the data dictionary as the enterprise data model is created. If, however, RDBMS software is used to create the data dictionary, the following structure is recommended.

As a minimum, the data dictionary should consist of the following three tables to document the structure of the database for the application.

a. COLUMN   (Column Name, Column Description, Column Format, Data Source, Load Procedure, Validation, Comment)
PK = Column Name.

This table is a master list of all distinct columns in all tables in the database. Data Source provides the origin of a column and Load Procedure describes how that source value will be captured and converted, if necessary, to its current destination. Validation contains rule(s) for ensuring data integrity via FK - PK and FK - UK relationships, CHECK constraints, or update-driven triggers. The Comment column is a catch-all for capturing any relevant information for a column.

b. TABLE   (Table Name, Table Description, Table Type, Rowsize, Rowcount, Comment)
PK = Table Name.

This table is a master list of all distinct tables in the database. Rowsize is counted as the total number of bytes in each column in the table. Rowcount is an estimate of the number of rows in the table. These two data elements are used for sizing the database in Phase (3), physical database design.

c. TABLE vs. COLUMN   (Table Name, Column Name, PK - UK, FK, CHECK)
PK = (Table Name, Column Name).

This is a linking table connecting COLUMN with TABLE. Since a TABLE can contain many COLUMNs and a COLUMN can belong to many TABLEs, their relationship is M:N. This table captures this relationship. When a COLUMN belongs to many TABLEs, usually one of them contains its source values and the rest contain copies of the source values. The two columns, PK - UK and FK, capture that information and are used along with the Validation column of the COLUMN table to enforce referential integrity.

1.5. Physical Database Design

From now on the activities are RDBMS bound. Each RDBMS has its own internal storage structure that must be taken into consideration in designing the physical database. Accordingly it is assumed here that Oracle 8i is the RDBMS used. All subsequent discussions are based on this assumption.

1.5.1 Transition from Logical to Physical Design

The transition from logical to physical database design involves the mapping of the logical data structures onto physical disk storage. This requires the sizing of tables, indices, and tablespaces. The internal storage requirements of these database objects are properly estimated in order to assign values to their initial and next extents. Appendix A contains detailed algorithms and two C programs to estimate data storage requirements.

Oracle partitions the physical disk space of a database into a hierarchy of components: tablespace, segment, extent, and block. A database consists of multiple tablespaces, which are logical concepts. Each tablespace spans one or more physical disk files that are explicitly assigned to it. A tablespace consists of many segments such as table, index, temporary, rollback, etc. Thus, a segment is a logical concept and is mapped onto multiple chunks of physical storage areas called extents. The extents belonging to a segment need not be contiguous. Each extent, however, consists of multiple contiguous blocks, which are the lowest indivisible units of disk space. See Figure 1.6.

An Oracle block can be of size 2, 4, 8, 16, 32, or 64 K with 2 K being the default, where K = 1,024 bytes. A segment consists of an *initial* extent and many *next* extents with the total number of extents not exceeding a parameter called *maxextent*. The default value of the maxextent depends on the operating system and the block size. For most operating systems the default values are given by the following table.

Block Size	Maxextent
2K	121
4K	249
8K	505
16K	1017

However, these default values can be overridden by the database designer. Also, maxextent can be set at UNLIMITED. This option, which became available with Oracle 7.3, allows the maxextent to reach the value 2,147,483,645. This is an enormous number and should be used with caution and be monitored regularly, since it can lead to a system crash if a disk becomes full by continued allocation of extents during long transactions containing inserts, updates, or deletes.

When a database object is created, its initial extent is made available to store the data belonging to the object. When this extent becomes full, the next extent is made available to the object. This process continues until one of two things happens, either the maxextent value is reached for the object, or the tablespace in which the object has been created no longer contains contiguous blocks that equal the size of the required extent. In that case, the DBA needs to allocate additional disk files to the tablespace via the command

ALTER TABLESPACE ... ADD DATAFILE...

Besides the tablespaces for tables and indices, an Oracle database contains the SYSTEM tablespace, rollback tablespace consisting of rollback segments, temporary tablespace containing the temporary segments, tablespaces created for users, and tablespaces for tools, if needed. Each of them must be sized properly for efficient database operation. Appendix A discusses these sizing issues in depth.

1.5 Physical Database Design

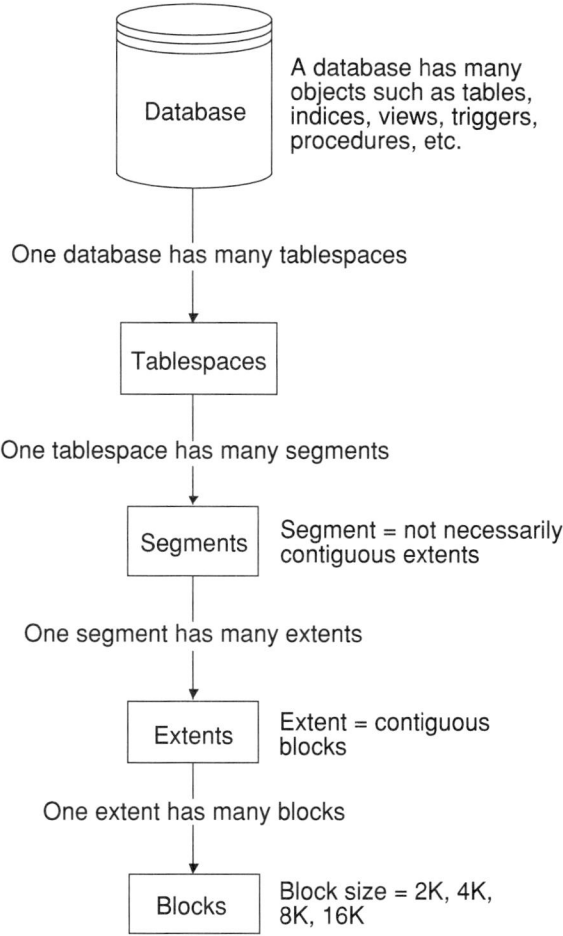

FIGURE 1.6: Hierarchical Storage Structure of Database

1.5.2 Tasks for Physical Database Design

The tasks under the physical database design, therefore, consist of the following.

(a) Decide on the unique and nonunique indices needed for each table. This depends on the reporting needs and may not be fully known at this stage. The best possible estimates will suffice. Remember that all the PKs, UKs, and FKs have already been determined during the logical database design.
(b) Estimate the total storage space needed for each table and each index including the PKs and FKs.
(c) Estimate the initial and next extents for each table and each index.

(d) Estimate the total storage space needed for each tablespace containing the tables and indices.
(e) Estimate the total storage space needed for the rollback tablespace, temporary tablespace, user tablespace, and tools tablespace.

Capacity planning for a database is critical before implementing it. Various algorithms are available for this purpose. Appendix A contains a detailed procedure with examples for sizing tables, indices, and tablespaces.

Depending on the future growth of a database in production an appropriate archiving policy should be considered at this stage. The policy is guided by business and legal requirements for the organization, e.g., how long the data need be available online, how much storage is currently available, what type of storage, disk or tape/cartridge, will be used, etc. Periodic archiving, purging of old data from the current database, and saving them in archived storage are standard components of an archiving policy. Such archiving keeps tables at a manageable size and thereby improves performance. The archived data can be accessed whenever necessary, e.g., to meet legal issues, perform analysis for business trends, etc.

1.6 Database Implementation

This phase involves the creation of script files for implementing the database and all of its components that have already been designed during the logical database design and sized during the physical database design. Appendix B contains detailed step-by-step instructions covering the issues discussed below.

Preparation

Create all the requisite directories for various system files such as initSID.ora, configSID.ora, listener.ora, etc. and destinations of datafiles for tablespaces, where SID is the instance name.

Instance Creation

Using Server Manager in line mode and connecting as internal, perform the following tasks.
- Start up the instance via the initSID.ora file.
- Using the CREATE DATABASE command create the redo log file groups and the SYSTEM datafile.

Database Creation

Using Server Manager in line mode and connecting as internal, create the
- Data dictionary (Oracle catalog) in SYSTEM tablespace;

- First rollback segment available online;
- Additional tablespaces
  - Rollback tablespace(s) for additional rollback segments,
  - Temporary tablespace for temporary segments,
  - Tablespace(s) for data tables,
  - Tablespace(s) for indices of the data tables,
- TOOLS for the tables created and used by database tools;
- USERS for database objects to be created by users during tests.

Creation of Users, Role, and Privileges

Using Server Manager in line mode and connecting as internal, create all user accounts with appropriate roles and privileges.

Schema Creation

Log in as a DBA privileged user other than SYSTEM/MANAGER and then create all tables, indices, constraints, triggers, procedures, functions, and packages. Maintain the proper order in creating tables with constraints so as to enforce the referential integrity via PK – UK/FK relationships. Thereby all the database objects in the schema are owned by this DBA privileged user instead of by SYSTEM.

An internally consistent database structure with all of its data validation routines has now been implemented. We next need to validate this structure through data loading to populate all the tables.

Database Loading

Database loading is affected by several factors such as the sizes and numbers of tables and indices, the order of loading tables linked by PK – UK/FK relationship to maintain referential integrity, triggers, functions, and procedures, etc. For loading very large tables it is recommended that indices be dropped and later recreated after the loading is complete. If the order of input data does not match the order of the referential integrity constraints, all FK constraints should be disabled before the loading and then be enabled after the loading is complete.

- Perform necessary data conversions, if appropriate, to prepare clean data for populating all the data tables.
- Data can be loaded manually through data entry screens by data entry operators or automatically through program control or some bulk data loading utility such as SQL*Loader from Oracle.

The above steps should be implemented through scripts, as far as possible. Appendix B contains a complete set of scripts and procedures for this purpose.

1.7 Database Maintenance

Unlike the first four phases which are one-time developmental tasks, database maintenance is a set of ongoing tasks that are performed by the DBAs regularly and routinely to ensure data integrity, security, proper backup and recovery, and overall database tuning and performance. These tasks affect the three levels of a database known as external, conceptual, and internal that are described in Chapter 2. The following are the major tasks in this phase.

(a) Monitor the performance at the internal level by checking tablespace fragmentation, chaining of rows in tables, proper sizing of tables and indices, proper allocation of extents to them, sizing of the system global area (SGA) and its components, and computation of various hit ratios. In addition, periodically run the Oracle diagnostic tools UTILBSTAT and UTLESTAT and examine the generated report REPORT.TXT to track overall database performance. To allow running the utilities UTILBSTAT and UTLESTAT, you need to set the initialization parameter TIMED_STATISTICS=TRUE either at the system level via the initSID.ora file, or at the session level via the command

```
ALTER SESSION SET TIMED_STATISTICS=TRUE;
```

(b) Monitor the performance at the external level by tracking and improving query performance through EXPLAIN PLAN and other utilities, and rebuilding indices as appropriate.

(c) Monitor the performance at the conceptual level by validating the database structure after any changes to it caused by denormalization, partitioning of very large tables, data replication, etc. This process ensures that the database has not suffered any loss of information content.

(d) Set the initialization parameter AUDIT_TRAIL=TRUE in the initSID.ora file so that the AUDIT option can be turned on for selected tables to monitor user transactions against them.

1.8 Naming Guidelines for Database Objects

As the conceptual level is built, some naming conventions should be used to maintain uniformity among the names of the database objects. Although such a policy has no bearing on the database performance, it helps in standardizing policies and procedures in a database installation. The guidelines described below for eight database objects can be used if no naming policy exists:

- Database,
- Column,
- Table,
- View,

- Index,
- Tablespace,
- Synonym, and
- Sequence.

Sections 1.8.1 through 1.8.8 describe the naming guidelines for the above objects.

No guidelines are provided for naming packages, procedures, functions, and triggers, because these are programs rather than data objects. Normally, such objects are named so as to indicate their purpose. Examples are UPDATE_CUSTNO, CHECK_BALANCE, etc.

CASE tools such as ERwin or Oracle Designer often use their own default naming conventions. In such cases, the following guidelines may not always be applicable.

1.8.1 Database

1. A database name will be the same as the application name in capital letters followed by _DB. Example: ORDER_DB.
2. If multiple databases are used in an application, then the application name will have suffix starting with 1 followed by _DB. Example: ORDR1_DB, ORDR2_DB, ORDR3_DB, etc.

1.8.2 Column

1. A column name will be expressive enough to indicate the data element it represents. Example: STATUS, COLOR, etc.
2. If a column name has multiple parts, each part will be connected to another by an underscore (_). Example: SUPPLIER_NO, PART_CITY, etc.
3. Column names using generic descriptors like name, description, number, etc. will be prefixed with the table name. Example: SUPPLIER_NAME instead of NAME, PART_DESCRIPTION instead of DESCRIPTION, etc.
4. A column representing a date will have two or more parts, where the last part will be DATE. The remaining part(s) will indicate the type of the date being named. Example: SHIPMENT_DATE, INVOICE_CREATION_DATE, etc.
5. The data type of a column will be in uppercase. Example: NUMBER, DATE, etc.
6. If the data type is followed by a size indicator, then these conventions will be used:
    - Single number size indicator: data type, one blank space, left parenthesis, number, right parenthesis, Example: CHAR (6), NUMBER (5)
    - Paired number size indicator: data type, one blank space, left parenthesis, first number, comma, second number, right parenthesis, Example: NUMBER (4,1).

1.8.3 Table

1. The table name will be expressive enough to indicate the contents of the table. Example: SUPPLIER, PART, etc.
2. If a table name has multiple parts, each part will be connected to another by an underscore (_). Example: DETENTION_PAYMENT_DETAIL, AMTRAK_SHIPMENT, INBOUND_CAR_LOCATOR_MESSAGE, etc.

1.8.4 View

1. A view based on a single table will have the same name as the table followed with a suffix _V (V for view).
2. The name of a view based on multiple tables will consist of the component table names connected by #(s) and followed with a suffix _V. If thereby the name exceeds 30 characters (Oracle restriction on names), then the component table name(s) will be abbreviated meaningfully to comply with the 30-character restriction. Example: SUPPLIER#PART_V, SHIPMENT# AMTRAK_SHIPMENT_V, etc.

1.8.5 Index

The standards will handle four types of indices: PK, FK, unique, and nonunique. An index can be single or composite. There can be only one PK for a table.

1. The PK of a table will be named PK_(table name).
   Example: PK_SUPPLIER = SUPPLIER_NO   single index
   PK_SHIPMENT = (SUPPLIER_NO, PART_NO)   composite index.

The PRIMARY KEY clause of the CREATE TABLE command will not be used to create the PK of a table since it does not allow the assignment of a selected name to the PK. Instead Oracle assigns a default name of the form SYS_Cnnnnn (e.g., SYS_C00972), which is very obscure. The PK will be created via the clause

```
CONSTRAINT PK_(name) PRIMARY KEY (column(s))
```

of the CREATE TABLE command.

2. The FK will be named FK_(column name(s)). If the FK is based on multiple columns, the column names will be connected by #(s).

   ```
   Example: FK_ SUPPLIER_NO, FK_ PART_NO,
   FK_PAYMENT_ID#PAYMENT_HISTORY_ID, etc.
   ```

The REFERENCES clause of the CREATE TABLE command will not be used to create the FK(s) in a table since it does not allow the assignment of a selected name to the FK. Instead Oracle assigns a default name of the form SYS_Cnnnnn (e.g., SYS_C00972), which is very obscure. The FK will be created via the clause

1.8 Naming Guidelines for Database Objects

```
CONSTRAINT FK_(name) FOREIGN KEY (column(s))
REFERENCES table (column(s))
```

of the CREATE TABLE command.

3. If a given set of column(s) appears as FKs in multiple tables, the naming convention of step (2) becomes ambiguous. To avoid this ambiguity, each FK- name will have a suffix with an underscored numeral starting with 1 and incremented by 1 such as _1, _2, _3, etc.

    Example: FK_UNIT_ID#UNIT_HISTORY_ID_1,
               FK_UNIT_ID#UNIT_HISTORY_ID_2, etc.

4. A unique index will be named UNQ_(column name(s)). If the index is based on multiple columns, the column names will be connected by #(s).

    Example: UNQ_ SUPPLIER_NAME, UNQ_ FACILITY_ID,
               UNQ_PAYMENT_ID#PAYMENT_HISTORY_ID, etc.

The UNIQUE clause of the CREATE TABLE command will not be used to create the unique index in a table since it does not allow the assignment of a selected name to the index. Instead Oracle assigns a default name of the form SYS_Cnnnnn (e.g., SYS_C00972), which is very obscure. The unique index will be created via the CREATE UNIQUE INDEX command.

5. If a given set of column(s) appears as unique indices in multiple tables, the naming convention of step (4) becomes ambiguous. To avoid this ambiguity, each UNQ- name will have a suffix of an underscored numeral starting with 1 and incremented by 1 such as _1, _2, _3, etc.

    Example: UNQ_UNIT_ID#UNIT_HISTORY_ID_1,
               UNQ_UNIT_ID#UNIT_HISTORY_ID_2, etc.

6. A nonunique index will be named IND_(column name(s)). If the index is based on multiple columns, the column names will be connected by #(s).

    Example: IND_ SUPPLIER_NAME, IND_ FACILITY_ID,
               IND_PAYMENT_ID#PAYMENT_HISTORY_ID, etc.

7. If a given set of column(s) appears as nonunique indices in multiple tables, the naming convention of step (6) becomes ambiguous. To avoid this ambiguity, each IND- name will have a suffix of an underscored numeral starting with 1 and incremented by 1 such as _1, _2, _3, etc.

    Example: IND_UNIT_ID#UNIT_HISTORY_ID_1,
               IND_UNIT_ID#UNIT_HISTORY_ID_2, etc.

1.8.6 Tablespace

A database consists of many tablespaces and each tablespace is made up of one or more datafiles. Tablespaces are the mechanisms by which logical database objects such as tables, indices, rollback segments, etc. are mapped onto the physical storage structure. These tablespaces are normally used in a database:

- System,
- Data,
- Index,
- RBS (rollback segments),
- TEMP (temporary segments),
- Tools, and
- Users.

Except for the System tablespace, there can be one or more of the remaining tablespaces depending on the size and complexity of the database.

1. *System*: The System tablespace will be named SYSTEM and will contain only Oracle's data dictionary tables (owned by SYS), the V$ views, and the System rollback segment.
2. *Data*: If the database contains both dynamic transaction tables and relatively static validation tables, then there will be at least two tablespaces called DATA_TRANS and DATA_VALS for these two types of tables. Additional tablespaces, if needed, will be named DATA_TRANS1, DATA_TRANS2, DATA_VALS1, DATA_VALS2 etc.
3. *Index*: If the database contains both dynamic transaction tables and relatively static validation tables, then there will be at least two tablespaces called INDEX_TRANS and INDEX_VALS for the indices created on these two types of tables. Additional tablespaces, if needed, will be named INDEX_TRANS1, INDEX_TRANS2, INDEX_VALS1, INDEX_VALS2 etc.
4. *RBS*: If a single rollback tablespace is needed, it will be named RBS. If multiple rollback tablespaces are needed, they will be named RBS_1, RBS_2, etc.
5. *TEMP*: The temporary segment will be named TEMP. If certain users of an application require much larger temporary segments than the rest of the application's users, then a separate temporary segment will be created for them under the name TEMP_USER.
6. *Tools*: Many Oracle and third party tools store their data segments in the SYSTEM tablespace because they store them under the SYSTEM database account, which has the SYSTEM tablespace as its default tablespace. To avoid this situation, the SYSTEM account's default tablespace will be named TOOLS and its quota will be revoked on the SYSTEM tablespace. If multiple TOOLS tablespaces are needed, they will be named TOOLS_1, TOOLS_2, etc.

If a database shows a lot of activity against the TOOLS tablespace, then the indices for these tools' data tables should be moved to a different tablespace. This tablespace will be named TOOLS_IND. If multiple TOOLS_IND tablespaces are needed, they will be named TOOLS_IND1, TOOLS_IND2, etc.

7. *Users*: If users are allowed the privilege of creating database objects in the test database during the test phase, users' quotas on other tablespaces will be revoked and their default tablespace will be named USERS.

1.8.7 Synonym

A *synonym* is a name assigned to a table or a view that may thereafter be used to refer to it and is created via the CREATE SYNONYM command.

The name of a synonym will be the same as the name of the table or view to which it refers but without the owner as a prefix. Example: SMITTRA.SUPPLIER table created by SMITTRA will have synonym SUPPLIER, OPSUSER.SUPPLIER#PART_V view created by OPSUSER will have the synonym SUPPLIER#PART_V, etc.

1.8.8 Sequence

A *sequence* is used to generate unique integer values for primary keys with data type NUMBER or NUMBER (integer) (e.g., NUMBER (6)) and is created via the CREATE SEQUENCE command.

The name of a sequence will be the same as the name of the PK it sequences and will be of the form SEQ_(PK name).

Example: SEQ_PK_PART refers to the sequence that assigns unique integer values to the primary key PK_PART comprising the column PART_NO of the PART table.

Key Words

1:1 relationship	cardinality
1:N relationship	cascading
1NF	chaining
2NF	class
3NF	client-server application
alternate key	conceptual level
archiving	Data Definition Language
atomic concept	data dictionary
attribute	Data Manipulation Language
block	data validation
candidate key	database transaction

declarative constraint
denormalization
entity
extent
extent, initial
extent, next
external level
first normal form
FK
foreign key
function
functional dependency
functionally dependent
hit ratio
Integrity Enhancement Feature
internal level
key language, nonprocedural
logical record
mapping
maxextent
message
method
normalization
optimization
package
PCTFREE
physical record
PK, see primary key
primary key
privilege
procedure

process
recursive relationship
referential integrity
relationship
relationship, many to many
relationship, one to many
relationship, one to one
retrieval
role
SDLC
second normal form
segment
SGA
SMLC
software development life cycle
software maintenance life cycle
subtype
supertype
System Global Area
tablespace
third normal form
transaction, types of
transitive dependency
trigger
tuning
UK
unique key
update
validation table
vector-valued attribute

References and Further Reading

1. D. K. Burleson—*High Performance Oracle Database Applications*, Coriolis Group Books, 1996.
2. P. P-S. Chen—*"The Entity-Relationship Model—Toward a Unified View of Data"*, ACM Trans. on Database Systems, vol. 1, 1976, pp. 9–36.
3. E. F. Codd—*"A Relational Model of Data for Large Shared Data Banks"*, Comm. ACM (June) vol. 13, no.6, 1970.
4. M. J. Corey, M. Abbey, and D. Dechichio—*Tuning Oracle*, Oracle Press, 1995.
5. C. J. Date—*A Guide to the SQL Standard*, third edition, Addison-Wesley, 1994.

6. C. J. Date and H. Darwen—*Foundation of Future Database Systems: The Third Manifesto*, second edition, Addison-Wesley, 2000.
7. K. Loney—*Oracle 8i DBA Handbook*, Oracle Press, 2000.
8. F. R. McFadden and J. A. Hoffer—*Modern Database Management*, Benjamin/Cummings, 1994.
9. S. S. Mittra—*Structured Techniques of System Analysis, Design, and Implementation*, John Wiley & Sons, 1988.
10. S. S. Mittra—*Principles of Relational Database Systems*, Prentice-Hall, 1991.
11. S. S. Mittra—"A Roadmap for Migrating Legacy Systems to Client/Server," *Journal of Software Maintenance*, Summer, 1995.
12. E. Yourdon—*Managing the Structured Techniques*, Yourdon Press, 1986.

Some prior database experience is needed in order to understand the topics discussed in this chapter. McFadden and Hoffer [8] and Mittra [10] provide ample coverage of such materials. Codd's paper [3] is regarded as a classic in relational database systems. It introduces and builds the entire theory and application of RDBMS with mathematics as its foundation, which was Codd's goal. The terms *relation*, *tuple*, and *attribute* have their origin in mathematics, and the same applies to *functional dependency* and *transitive dependency*. Under his leadership the IBM System Research Institute built System R, the very first RDBMS, although it was never marketed for commercial use. SDLC and SMLC are tangentially related to the database application development process. Mittra [9] offers adequate coverage of the related concepts. Mittra [11] discusses how SDLC and SMLC are used in a client-server environment. Yourdon [12] deals with the structured methodology from a management perspective. Also, any textbook dealing with systems analysis and design can be used to gain additional information in this area. The five-phase approach to database development is fairly standard in industry, although the exact packaging of tasks in each phase is somewhat open-ended. I have given my own view here. McFadden and Hoffer [8, Chapters 3, 5] discuss this topic in a more descriptive manner. Burleson [1, Chapter 1] discusses the enterprise modeling and logical database design at length as a preparation for database tuning. An efficient physical database design requires a solid understanding of the architecture of the underlying RDBMS that is used for implementing the database. I have assumed here Oracle as the RDBMS and described the storage structure accordingly. Additional discussion of Oracle-specific concepts and algorithms related to physical design, implementation, and maintenance of databases are available in Corey et al. [4] and Loney [7].

Exercises

The Philanthropy Foundation, Inc. (PFI) is a Boston-based nonprofit agency that awards grants for philanthropic activities to organizations in the U.S.A. and abroad. Started in 1966 as a small five-member private business it has now grown into a company with over 100 employees. PFI operates with these four goals:

- Invite organizations worldwide to submit proposals for receiving PFI grants;

- Evaluate grant proposals to determine if they are worthy of funding by PFI;
- Award grants for up to five years to successful applicants in multiple annual installments;
- Conduct careful periodic scrutiny of each grant, usually several times during the first two years and then once a year prior to renewal.

PFI's current Grant Management System (GMS) is a three-tier client-server application running on a Compaq Proliant computer under UNIX and Oracle 8i. GMS captures data via interactive data entry screens and bulk data load through file transfer. The output from GMS consists primarily of reports, although files containing snapshots of its database are sent periodically to other agencies with similar goals. However, GMS has to be redesigned and its database restructured to handle the potential workload of PFI. Two options currently under review by PFI management are a distributed database and a data warehouse for report generation.

Assume that through an initial round of enterprise modeling you have designed the following five entities with a partial list of their attributes for the upgraded version of GMS, which is called Grants Award, Management, and Evaluation System (GAMES).

```
RFP (ID, Name, Description, Start Date, End Date, Special
Clause,....)
APPLICANT (ID, Name, Address, ....)
AWARD CONTENT (ID, Project Name, Start Date, End Date,....)
GRANTEE (ID, Name, Line of Business, Years in Business,....)
GRANT SCRUTINY (Award_ID, Grantee_ID, Scrutiny Date,
Findings,....)
```

Assume that the GAMES enterprise model will consist of many more entities than those listed above. You will need expertise in SDLC to complete this exercise. Conduct the first two phases of the database application development process for GAMES as follows:

(a) Prepare a complete list of entities, relationships, and their respective attributes. Ensure that you have resolved all issues, as applicable, related to vector valued attributes, recursive relationships, and subtype supertype relationships.
(b) Prepare an entity relationship diagram for the proposed enterprise model.
(c) Ascertain that each entity and each relationship are in 3NF. If not, convert each non-3NF object into a 3NF object.
(d) Identify all PKs, UKs, FKs, and CHECK constraints.
(e) Identify any additional data validation algorithms for your model.
(f) Prepare a data dictionary using any CASE tool or RDBMS software. Do NOT use a word processor to prepare the data dictionary.

2
Performance Tuning Methodology

Outline

2.1 Three Levels of a Database
2.2 Optimization at Each Level
2.3 Process and Metric for Performance Tuning
Key Words
References and Further Reading
Exercises

Overview of the Chapter

The chapter describes a conceptual framework within which any tuning activity should be performed. A database operates at three separate but connected levels: conceptual, internal, and external. Its performance depends on the optimization of all three levels. Continuous monitoring of each level becomes an ongoing task for the database group in an organization when an application becomes operational. The chapter discusses with an actual case study a three-step methodology for conducting a performance tuning exercise. It ends with an overview of several distinct tuning items needed at each level in the form of a checklist.

2.1 Three Levels of a Database

The architecture of a database consists of three distinct but interrelated levels: conceptual, internal, and external. The database operates at all three levels and may show poor performance due to deficiency at one or more of these three levels.

The *conceptual level* involves a representation of the entire information content of the database and, as such, is the most important in a database application. The conceptual level is defined here to include ALL structural information about all database objects belonging to the database. From a logical design standpoint it includes the definitions of tables, indices, constraints, views, triggers, procedures, functions, packages, synonyms, etc. From a physical design standpoint it contains the specifications of tablespaces, datafiles, and the storage clauses of all tables and indices. To sum up, the conceptual level provides all the details for implementing a database. One only needs to write the DDL commands and programs to convert the conceptual level into an operational database. Since the conceptual level is independent of implementation, it can be developed using only pseudocode. But a data dictionary built with a CASE tool is the best vehicle for building such a conceptual level. As an example, the CASE tool Oracle Designer offers such a facility. One can draw an E/R diagram with Oracle Designer and start to build at the entity-attribute level, and then gradually make a transition to the logical design and then to the physical design phases. Oracle Designer captures all the information in its repository and can also generate all the script files from it with which the developers or the DBAs can then implement the database.

The *internal level*, also called the physical level, is the one closest to the physical storage, where the data contents of the conceptual level are stored on disk files. In addition, the internal level contains a set of memory resident data structures that Oracle calls the System Global Area, and a set of background processes. Similar to the conceptual level, there is only one internal level. The rows of the tables in the conceptual level are often called *logical records*, and their counterparts at the internal level are called *physical records*.

The *external level* is closest to the users. It is concerned with the way in which the users view the data for their own use. Thus, different users access different external levels of the database. The user can be an end user, a database developer, or a DBA working on some specific query generation. Each external level consists of a subset of the conceptual level. In this sense, the latter can be regarded as a set-theoretic union of all possible external levels. Hence, for a given database, there can be many external levels, but only one conceptual level. Some authors call it the logical level.

The tools used for building the external levels are SQL-based and can be GUI type or executed at the command line. In an n-tier ($n \geq 3$) client-server architecture the GUI type external levels normally reside on the application tier(s) comprising levels 2 through $n - 1$. They access the database residing on the database server at the nth tier through the intervention of application programs. But the external level of any user accessing the database through the command line interface resides on the database server at the nth tier. An example is a DBA who wants to test the performance of a query and types the query directly at the SQL prompt.

During the five-phase database development process discussed in Chapter 1 the conceptual level is designed starting with the enterprise modeling (Phase (1)) and continuing through the logical database design (Phase (2)). The external levels are directly related to the reporting needs of the users. Hence their design starts during the logical database design (Phase (2)) and continues through the physical database design (Phase (3)). The internal level is designed during the physical database design (Phase (3)). All three levels as designed are then implemented during the database implementation (Phase (4)). The performance monitoring and tuning of the database at all three levels are conducted during database maintenance (Phase (5)).

The three levels communicate with one another through sets of mappings (see [4, Chapter 1]), as shown in Figure 2.1:

1. External to conceptual level mapping, and
2. Conceptual to internal level mapping.

The first mapping defines the correspondence between a particular external level and the conceptual level. It maps each column referenced in the external level to its counterpart in the conceptual level. Since there are many external levels but only one conceptual level, this mapping is many-to-one. The second mapping specifies how the columns in the conceptual level map onto their stored counterparts in the internal level. Since each logical record maps in a one-to-one manner to a physical record, this mapping is one-to-one.

The external/conceptual level mapping ensures the *logical data independence*. As the database grows, it may become necessary to modify the conceptual level by adding new data structures. But such changes do not affect the existing external levels. New external levels can be generated to utilize the modified conceptual level. Similarly, the conceptual/internal level mapping implements the *physical data independence*. This means that the internal storage structure for database objects can be changed without affecting the conceptual level. Internally, the DBMS keeps track of the actual storage locations of all objects. Application programs using the conceptual level need not be changed at all. The DBMS will provide the necessary connections to run such programs under the changed internal level.

2.2 Optimization at Each Level

At the Oracle International User Week conference in 1989 I presented a paper with a rather unusual title, "Efficiency * (Database Design + Query Formulation) = Improved Performance" (see [3]). I offered a justification of the "equation" used in the title by discussing with actual timing examples the improvement that occurred by tuning database applications at all three levels. The performance is typically measured by the response time experienced by the users. The response time, for our discussion, is defined as the time elapsed between the instant when the user presses the Enter key or clicks on the mouse and the instant when the first character of the system's response (e.g., desired output, error message, etc.) appears on the screen. This response time depends on all three levels. A well-designed conceptual level that currently operates in an inefficient internal level such as a highly fragmented set of tablespaces or a high amount of table chaining results in high response time. Similarly, an external level containing poorly designed queries run against a well-tuned internal level leads to poor response time. Hence optimization is needed at each level.

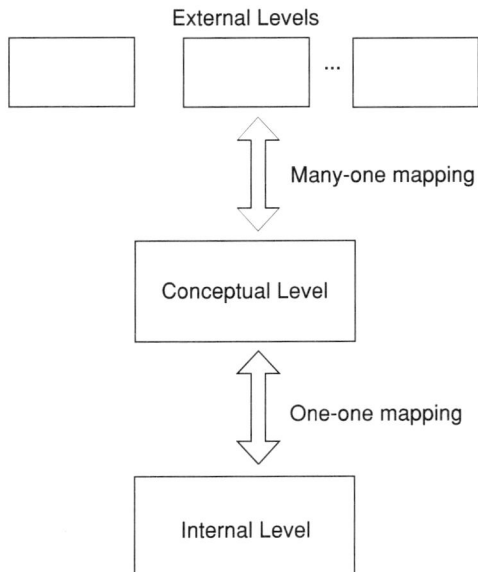

FIGURE 2.1: Mapping Among Levels

2.2.1 Conceptual Level

Since the starting point of a database application is the conceptual level, the optimization process should start here. If the five-phase database development process described in Sections 1.3 through 1.7 are followed properly and are well documented in the data dictionary as outlined there, then the resulting conceptual level is optimized for performance, when implemented. If, however, some queries at the external level require five or more joins due to normalization necessitated by 3NF tables, then some level of denormalization may be needed for performance reasons. This should be the only deviation from the normalization principle.

Two other measures adopted for improving performance are partitioning of the conceptual level, as allowed under Oracle 8i, and data replication. Very large tables may be partitioned into separate smaller fragments for parallel processing and conceptual levels may be copied at different locations through data replication to reduce network traffic in a distributed database. But these two measures do not interfere with normalization.

2.2.2 Internal Level

As noted in Section 2.1, the conceptual level is implemented through a one-to-one mapping onto the internal level. If the internal level is properly designed according to the guidelines described in Sections 1.5 and 1.6, it starts at an optimal stage. But fragmentation of used space of the tables and of free space in their respective tablespaces can occur due to improper sizing. *Fragmentation* occurs when the extents of a table are not contiguous, or when the free space of a tablespace consists of many small sets of noncontiguous extents instead of a few large sets of contiguous extents. It degrades database performance because a single table with many noncontiguous extents is scattered over many small isolated fragments. Therefore, a data search may have to traverse many fragments to access the required data.

Chaining and *migration* of rows (see Section 5.9) in a table can occur due to inserts and updates of records when its PCTFREE parameter is set incorrectly or when columns with VARCHAR2 data types that were initially NULL start getting updated with nonnull values. Excessive chaining degrades performance because retrieval of chained data involves following a chain of pointers, which is slower than retrieving physically contiguous data. Tables with LONG or LONG RAW data types deserve special attention since they almost always cause chaining. Adequate planning during the physical database design discussed in Section 1.5 is required to handle such issues. Constant monitoring of such phenomena during database maintenance is needed to keep the internal level optimized.

2.2.3 External Level

Query optimization is the tuning mechanism for the external level. A given query can usually be implemented in multiple ways. The query optimizer in an RDBMS functions as follows (see Sections 8.2 and 8.3).

- Formulates one or more internal representations of the query using relational algebra or relational calculus, the two underlying mathematical formalisms for representing queries;
- Converts the representation(s) into a single equivalent canonical form that can be processed more efficiently;
- Selects an optimal access path, often called the execution plan for the query, to implement the query.

This improvement in implementation strategy is called *query optimization*. The strategy applies to both interactive and embedded forms of SQL. The latter is used in programs written in procedural languages such as PL/SQL and host language interfaces such as Pro*C, Pro*C++, Pro*COBOL, etc. Query optimization strives to minimize the response time for the query or maximize the throughput.

2.3 Process and Metric for Performance Tuning

A database application is developed subject to pre-established performance requirements described in terms of response time. When the application goes into production, these requirements are regularly monitored and maintained through *database tuning*. Tuning is an ongoing iterative activity intended to be proactive rather than reactive in addressing performance issues. Most of the performance problems are but symptoms of some underlying root cause(s). Tuning efforts should, therefore, be focused on identifying and fixing these flaws instead of only providing a temporary solution to a problem. The DBA needs to start where the symptoms first appear, but must take a global view of the system and recognize that tuning should occur at all three levels. The paradigm of fixing software bugs provides a close analogy.

Let us suppose that we have a modular program with a calling module and several nested called modules. An error message appears in the calling module and is related to a called module, say f_k. This module in turn calls another module, say f_n. The programmer has to fix the root cause in f_n to remove the bug. Then he or she must ensure that no new bugs have been introduced as a result of the fix. When we analyze this process the following three-step principle emerges.

(a) Localize the problem by starting at the location where the problem surfaces for the first time and trace it to its root.
(b) Fix the root cause and test to ensure that the problem does not reappear.
(c) Look for any adverse side effects caused by the fix. If they exist, fix them one at a time until they are all gone.

2.3.1 A Tuning Example

A word of caution! The example discussed below assumes a good level of knowledge about the internal and external levels of a database. If the reader lacks such knowledge, the example will not be very meaningful. Please note, however, that the different chapters of the book cover all these materials. Therefore, the reader may want to revisit this example to understand its contents after completing Chapters 1 through 8.

Now to the example! I was working with an Oracle8 database comprising some 70 tables and 300 indices including primary and foreign keys. Some of the tables contained millions of rows and the entire database at production level would comprise some 200 gigabytes of storage. One developer was running a view based on five joins involving 6 tables and was getting very poor performance. When she complained to me about the situation and asked me for a suggestion, my first reaction was to go for denormalization to reduce the number of joins. We often find that the query performance starts to degrade when the number of joins exceeds four. However, I regard denormalization as the last resort, because it changes the structure of the conceptual level and can have adverse side effects that may not be uncovered and resolved very easily. Therefore, I proceeded with my three-step principle as follows.

(a) Localize the problem and trace it to its root.

Since the long response time was caused by the query, I used the EXPLAIN PLAN utility with SET AUTOTRACE ON to derive and analyze the execution plan of the query (see Section 8.7 and its subsections). Nothing of a glaring nature appeared there. The query was using a *driving table* with full table scan and was accessing all the other tables in indexed search, as expected. No additional indexing would help. So, the root cause was not there.

Next I wanted to find the level of chaining (see Section 5.9) in the tables, if any. Note that one has to ANALYZE a table to get its chaining level. So, I ANALYZEd each of the six tables with the COMPUTE STATISTICS option. Then I queried the Oracle data dictionary view DBA_TABLES to retrieve the values of three of its columns, NUM_ROWS, CHAIN_CNT, and AVG_ROW_LEN, for each of the six tables. The driving table that was being searched sequentially had the statistics:

```
NUM_ROWS = 10,003
CHAIN_CNT = 9,357
AVG_ROW_LEN = 8,522
```

The driving table had 93.5% (= 9,357/10,003) chaining, which is excessive. Almost every row was being chained! The reason was not difficult to find. The database was using blocks of size 8 K (=8,192 bytes), whereas an average row needed 8,522 bytes to be stored. Hence almost every row had to be chained to a second data block for storage. So, indeed I found the root cause!

(b) Fix the root cause and test to ensure that the problem does not reappear.

I could not fix the root cause by increasing the data block size. One assigns the data block size at the time of creating the database and it cannot be changed short of recreating the database. So, I looked at the columns of the offending table and found one column with its data type as LONG. Since Oracle allows a LONG data type to be of size up to two gigabytes, the reason for such excessive chaining became obvious.

I split the driving table P, say, into parts, P1 and P2. P1 contained all the columns except the column with the LONG data type, and P2 contained only the primary key of the original table and the column with the LONG data type. P1 and P2 were related in a PK/FK relationship that was maintained by referential integrity. The view that started this whole range of tuning investigation did not use the column with the LONG data type and, therefore, was reformulated with P1 replacing the driving table P.

I ran the query with SET TIMING ON and got an average of two seconds as the running time, which was well within the performance goal.

(c) Look for any adverse side effects caused by the fix.

This was a clean solution since an adverse effect could arise only from using the table P2 mentioned above. All queries that used P before but did not need the LONG column were reformulated to use P1. Any query that needed the LONG column and one or more column(s) from P1 were formulated using both P1 and P2 with a join via P1.PK and P2.PK. Those happened to be rare occasions and did not cause any problem.

2.3.2 Block Access Time as Metric

Tuning goals are always set in measurable terms so that it can be verified objectively if the goals have been met. A database transaction involves data retrieval and update. Since data reside within a data block in auxiliary storage, every transaction requires access to a block. The data must be fetched in memory for processing. Since the memory access time is enormously fast, the time needed for any computation on the data inside a block resident in memory is negligible compared to the time needed for transferring the data from auxiliary storage to memory. The *block access time* for data needed by a query is defined as the time to fetch those data from auxiliary storage to memory. Let

t_b = block access time for data needed by a query
t_r = response time for that query.

Then,

$t_r = O(t_b)$, where O stands for the order of magnitude.

Since t_b is much simpler to compute compared to t_r, we shall use t_b as the metric for measuring performance. Tuning activities are guided by the goal of reducing t_b as far as practicable. As we show in the succeeding chapters, t_b is affected by a variety of factors such as hit ratios, memory utilization, query design, logical database design, fragmentation of free space, chaining and migration of rows in a table, etc. Each of these issues needs to be addressed.

Since it is easier to rectify flaws during the development and test phases instead of the production phase, Oracle recommends that a new application should be tuned in the order (see [5, pp. 1–8]):

- Design,
- Application Code,
- Memory,
- Auxiliary storage,
- Contention, and
- Operating System.

If the application is already in production, the order of the above six steps should be reversed. Normally, the first two steps are the responsibility of the system architects and the developers, and the last four are that of the DBAs. We should strive for an environment where the two groups work together.

2.3.3 Preliminary Checklist of Tuning Activities

The following is a preliminary checklist of tuning activities at each level.

Conceptual Level

- Denormalization
- Partitioning of Very Large Tables
- Data Replication in Distributed Database

Internal Level

- Data Storage

Two main reasons for inefficiency of data storage are fragmentation of tablespaces, and chaining and migration of rows in tables.

- Memory Usage

Here the goal is to make data available in memory instead of retrieving them from the disks since the data transfer rate for memory is an order of magnitude faster than that from auxiliary storage.

External Level

- Data Retrieval

Oracle's EXPLAIN PLAN utility (see Section 8.7.1) allows the developer to examine the access path and to determine whether any changes should be made in indexing the table(s) involved, reducing the number of joins, etc. The *selectivity* of an indexed column determines if a full table scan is preferable to an indexed search.

- Data Update

If a large table is heavily indexed besides its PK, it may be worthwhile to drop all the indices before starting the bulk update. It really depends on the number of rows and the time and convenience of dropping and creating the indices. Since Oracle rearranges the B*-tree for each index with an update of the indexed table, the process becomes very slow for bulk updates. As a rule of thumb, if the data load with indices takes longer than 10 minutes or so, then I drop the indices first, load the data into the table, and then create the indices for the updated table. Bulk deletes are best handled through the TRUNCATE command. Although this command uses rollback segments to handle adjustments to the segment header and to the data dictionary, the rollback segment space used is very small. Hence the error of rollback segments being too small does not arise. Also, TRUNCATE retains all the structural information of the table such as grants, indices, and constraints. In addition, DELETE does not reclaim the space occupied by the deleted records. But TRUNCATE with its default DROP STORAGE option deallocates all the extents of the table except its INITIAL extent.

Key Words

access path	logical design
auxiliary storage	logical record
cache memory	mapping, conceptual to internal level
canonical form	
CASE	mapping, external to conceptual level
chaining	
client-server architecture	N-tier
conceptual level	optimization
Data Definition Language (DDL)	Oracle Designer
data dictionary	parallel processing
data replication	partitioning
data transfer rate	PCTFREE
database, distributed	physical data independence
datafile	physical design
denormalization	physical record
driving table	primary key
execution plan	pseudocode
external level	query optimization
fragmentation	referential integrity
full table scan	response time
host language interface	selectivity
indexed search	System Global Area
internal level	tablespace
join	unique key
logical data independence	

References and Further Reading

1. M. J. Corey, M. Abbey, and D. Dechichio—*Tuning Oracle*, Oracle Press, 1995.
2. K. Loney—*Oracle 8i DBA Handbook*, Oracle Press, 2000.
3. S. S. Mittra—"Efficiency * (Database Design + Query Formulation) = Improved Performance", *Proceedings of International Oracle User Week—Methodology*, pp. 187–190, 1989,.
4. S. S. Mittra—*Principles of Relational Database Systems*, Prentice-Hall, 1991.
5. *Oracle8 Performance Tuning Workshop: Student Guide, Volume 1*, Oracle Corporation, 1998.
6. D. E. Shasha—*Database Tuning: A Principled Approach*, Prentice-Hall, 1992.
7. J. D. Ullman—*Principles of Database and Knowledge-Base Systems*, Volume I, Computer Science Press, 1988.

Mittra [4, Chapter 1] contains a good discussion of the three levels of a database. The notion of optimizing the database performance at each level was introduced in Mittra [3] at an international Oracle User Week Conference. The performance and tuning methods of databases at all levels are covered in Corey et al. [1] and Loney [2]. These topics are explored in significant detail in the rest of the book. Shasha [6, Chapter 1] describes how tuning activities can be handled in a systematic well-planned manner. Ullman [7, Chapter 6] discusses the physical data organization from a mathematical viewpoint and explains the basis of using block access time as a metric for tuning.

Exercises

1. The dictum of "Divide and Conquer" is often used as a principle in solving problems in various disciplines including computer science.

    a. Can you use this principle to handle database performance tuning?
    b. How would it differ from the three-step methodology described in Section 2.3?

2. Use the database that you designed for GAMES (Exercises in Chapter 1).

    a. Using structured English or pseudocode describe the external levels below:
        - List of all grantees in Argentina, India, and Japan for their projects dealing with the establishment of eye clinics in their countries;
        - List of all project names with respective start and end dates that received "adverse" findings on scrutiny.
    b. Identify the entities referenced by each external level above.

3. Refer to the entity RFP in the GAMES database of Chapter 1. Assume that you have created a table RFP matching this entity under Oracle. The following questions apply to this Oracle table RFP.

    a. Can you think of any column in RFP that should have the LONG data type? If so, how would you split RFP into two separate tables to avoid the kind of problems described in Section 2.3.1?
    b. Can you think of more than one column in RFP that should have the LONG data type? Since the table RFP can have only one column with LONG datatype, how would you resolve the problem?
    c. Repeat parts (a) and (b) above for the table GRANT_SCRUTINY matching the entity GRANT SCRUTINY in its structure.

4. A tuning action mostly results in some structural change of the database. For example, a new index may be created, size of next extents may be changed, a new tablespace may be created, etc. As a result, some or all of the three levels of the database may change.

    a. How will you ensure that the three levels will still continue to be mutually consistent?
    b. What tools (e.g., CASE tool, desktop DBMS, spreadsheet, etc.) do you need to implement your proposal?

3
Tuning the Conceptual Level of a Database

Outline

3.1 Three Versions of the Conceptual Level
3.2 Performance Issues at the Conceptual Level
3.3 Denormalization of the Conceptual Level
3.4 Optimal Indexing of Tables
3.5 Integration of Views into Queries
3.6 Partitioning of Tables and Indices
3.7 Data Replication
Key Words
References and Further Reading
Exercises

Overview of the Chapter

The chapter takes an in-depth look at the performance issues that are caused by an inefficient conceptual level of a database. Several techniques are discussed here.

The conceptual level undergoes changes as an application migrates from development to test to production. The database starts with only 3NF tables, but may need to be denormalized if queries involve joins of many tables. Often such queries have high response times. A denormalized database leads to fewer joins. However, denormalization leads to extra redundancy of data among tables. Special effort is needed to synchronize the data values among these tables for data consistency.

The principle of optimal indexing requires that in addition to the primary key any other index should be created only if so dictated by query processing requirements. Indexing in most cases speeds up retrieval, but slows down updates, i.e., insert, delete, and modify operations. Views and especially nested views may be integrated into queries to improve response time.

Very large tables in a database can be partitioned to allow parallel processing of data yielding lower response time. Only tables and indices can be partitioned dynamically into smaller components under Oracle 8i. All partitions have the same logical attributes (e.g., column names, data types, etc.), but may have different physical attributes related to storage. The partitions of an index need not match those of the table to which the index belongs. The partitions can be implemented at the time of creating the tables or indices, or can be added later.

Data replication applies to a database that resides in multiple sites, as with a distributed database. It reduces network traffic generated by queries accessing data from multiple sites. The query is processed with the local replica of the database, as far as practicable. Oracle 8i offers two types of data replication, basic and advanced. Basic replication provides at each remote site read-only replicas of tables selected for data replication. Advanced replication extends the features of basic replication by allowing updatable replicas at remote sites.

3.1 Three Versions of the Conceptual Level

A database application progresses through three versions: development, test, and production. The conceptual level remains at its initial version when the development activities start. But it undergoes almost continuous changes during development. As the developers build different components of the application, they experiment with the tables and indices, create views as needed, introduce new constraints for data validation through referential integrity and CHECKs, etc. These changes end when the application is ready for test. The version of the development database at this point is frozen and is migrated to the test database. Thus, the conceptual level of the test database becomes a replica of that of the development database at this instant, although the data contents of the two versions may differ.

During the test phase problems may be uncovered that may lead to further changes to the conceptual level of the test database. This may become an iterative process that ends when the application passes the user acceptance test. The version of the test database at this point is frozen and becomes the basis of the production database. Thus, the conceptual level of a database undergoes several version changes and is finalized when the application goes into production.

As a part of the SDLC methodology (see Section 1.2), changes to the conceptual level are made only to the development version. Therefore, if changes are needed during the test phase, the database is migrated to the development environment, changes are made to it, and then the application is reinstalled in the test environment with the changed conceptual level. If changes are needed after the application is operational, the application maintenance staff makes the changes in an isolated support environment and then reinstalls the application with the changed conceptual level.

3.2 Performance Issues at the Conceptual Level

As indicated in Section 2.2, performance issues manifest themselves in the form of high response time that is unacceptable to the users. During the development phase the developers and the DBAs jointly address such issues by tuning all three levels of the database. The improved response time is then demonstrated during the test phase. The conceptual level can be tuned through these activities:

(a) Denormalization of the schema to reduce the number of joins in ad hoc queries and reports;
(b) Creation of new indices or modification of existing indices to force indexed search of tables instead of full table scans, where appropriate;
(c) Integration of views into queries to avoid long-running SELECT statements involving views;
(d) Partitioning of very large tables to take advantage of parallel full table scans or to access only some partitions instead of accessing the entire tables;
(e) Data replication for copying the same conceptual level at multiple locations to reduce query processing time and to avoid failed updates when communication links to some of the remote sites are down. Each of the above items involves a change in the conceptual level, which, therefore, must be updated with each change. If ERwin or any other similar CASE tool is used, such changes are automatically migrated to the relevant scripts for schema creation.

We now discuss each of the above items separately.

3.3 Denormalization of the Conceptual Level

We first explain denormalization with an example and then discuss its advantages and disadvantages.

3.3.1 Denormalization Explained

The development database is designed initially with the goal of making all tables in third normal form (3NF). As a result, data are scattered over many tables. But the user view of the database is geared towards running ad hoc queries and generating reports. It is not surprising for a 3NF-only database to use joins of 6 or more tables to create a report or a view. Normally, response time starts to degrade when more than 4 tables are involved in a multi-table join. I have seen queries involving over 12 tables take 18 to 20 minutes to produce the result. That is unacceptable in an OLTP environment. An Oracle expert once remarked to the effect that no production database can run in only 3NFs. Let us examine why a large number (> 4) of joins leads to poor performance.

A join is a binary operation. When n (> 2) tables are joined in a query, Oracle designates one of them as the *driving table* and performs a full table scan of it to start the first join. The resulting row set is labeled a *driving set* and is joined with the third table to produce the next driving set. This process is repeated $n - 1$ times to exhaust the n tables and return the final result. Depending on the availability and selectivity of the indices in the tables and the sizes of the driving sets, the query uses indexed search and/or full table scans. The actual query processing and optimization are discussed in Chapters 8 and 9. But the concept of denormalization can be understood without knowing the details of query processing.

The response time of a join query can improve if we can reduce the number of joins in the query. To do that, we eliminate one or more tables by bringing their relevant columns into another table. Thereby we degenerate 3NF tables into 2NF or even 1NF tables and allow transitive dependency to enter into such tables. This is called *denormalization*, which is incorporated at the conceptual level and thereby enforced at the internal level. We strive for improving query performance at the cost of introducing possible update anomalies. However, an update anomaly is more of a theoretical issue than an operational reality for a database with tables below 3NF. Hence denormalization rarely causes loss of data through updates.

Chris Date has offered a slightly different view of denormalization. Date recommends that denormalization should happen "at the physical storage level, not at the logical or base relation level" [3, p. 5]. This means that the mapping between the conceptual and the internal levels need not be one-to-one (see Section 2.1). One possible implementation of this principle is through clustering. See Section 8.6.5 for a discussion of clusters.

3.3.2 An Example of Denormalization

Let us take an example of denormalization. Figure 3.1, A five-table database, shows the schema involving five tables, CUSTOMER, TRANSPORT_ROUTE, ROUTE_PLAN, ORDER, and STATE. The business situation is as follows.

```
CUSTOMER (CUSTOMER_ID, CUSTOMER_NAME, ....)
        /*   Master List Of Customers    */
ORDER (ORDER_NUM, ORDER_VALUE, CUSTOMER_ID, SHIPPING_ADDRESS_1,
SHIPPING_ADDRESS_2, SHIPPING_ADDRESS_3, CITY, STATE, ....)
        /*   Master List Of Orders    */
TRANSPORT_ROUTE (ORDER_NUM, ROUTE_ID,....)
        /*   Link Table Of ORDER and ROUTE_PLAN */
```

FIGURE 3.1: A Five-Table Database

3.3 Denormalization of the Conceptual Level

```
ROUTE_PLAN (ROUTE_ID, ORIGIN_CITY, ORIGIN_STATE, DESTINATION_CITY,
      DESTINATION _STATE, TRANSPORT_COST, ....)
      /* Master List Of Route Plans  */
STATE (STATE_CODE, STATE_NAME, ....)  /* Master List of States  */
```

FIGURE 3.1 (*continued*): A Five-Table Database

A CUSTOMER places an ORDER for one or more items. Each ORDER is tied to a TRANSPORT_ROUTE, which follows a ROUTE_PLAN. Two of the columns in the ROUTE_PLAN table are ORIGIN_STATE and DESTINATION_STATE, which are validated through its validation table STATE. For the customer named Acme Corporation, a developer wants to determine the name(s) of state(s) through which all orders exceeding $100,000 from that customer will be transported. She uses the following logic for this query.

(a) Select the customer;
(b) Select the order;
(c) Select the order's transport route;
(d) Select the route plan for the route;
(e) Select the state(s) through which this route will go.

Accordingly, she writes the following query.

```
SELECT STATE_NAME FROM CUSTOMER, ORDER, TRANSPORT_ROUTE,
ROUTE_PLAN, STATE WHERE
    CUSTOMER_NAME = 'ACME CORPORATION' AND
    ORDER_VALUE > 100000 AND
    CUSTOMER.CUSTOMER_ID = ORDER.CUSTOMER_ID AND
    ORDER.ORDER_NUM = TRANSPORT_ROUTE.ORDER_NUM AND
    TRANSPORT_ROUTE.ROUTE_ID = ROUTE_PLAN. ROUTE_ID AND
    ROUTE_PLAN.ORIGIN_STATE = STATE.STATE_CODE AND
    ROUTE_PLAN.DESTINATION_STATE = STATE.STATE_CODE;
```

As we can see, the query involves a five-table join and may perform poorly. We can modify the database design to reduce the number of tables to four, as shown in Figure 3.2, and the number of joins to two. The above query now can be reformulated as a three-table join:

```
SELECT STATE_NAME FROM ORDER, TRANSPORT_ROUTE,
ROUTE_PLAN WHERE
    ORDER.CUSTOMER_NAME = 'ACME CORPORATION' AND
    ORDER_VALUE > 100000 AND
    ORDER.ORDER_NUM = TRANSPORT_ROUTE.ORDER_NUM AND
    TRANSPORT_ROUTE.ROUTE_ID = ROUTE_PLAN. ROUTE_ID;
```

The database has been denormalized in that both ORDER and ROUTE_PLAN are now in 2NF and have transitive dependency. We sacrifice normalization to improve performance.

```
CUSTOMER (CUSTOMER_ID, CUSTOMER_NAME, ....)
      /* Master List Of Customers  */
ORDER (ORDER_NUM, ORDER_VALUE, CUSTOMER_ID, CUSTOMER_NAME,
SHIPPING_ADDRESS_1, SHIPPING_ADDRESS_2, SHIPPING_ADDRESS_3, CITY,
STATE_CODE, ....)
      /* Master List Of Orders   */
TRANSPORT_ROUTE (ORDER_NUM, ROUTE_ID, ....)
      /* Link Table Of ORDER and ROUTE_PLAN */
ROUTE_PLAN (ROUTE_ID, ORIGIN_CITY, ORIGIN_STATE_CODE,
ORIGIN_STATE_NAME,
DESTINATION_CITY, DESTINATION STATE_CODE, DESTINATION STATE_NAME,
TRANSPORT_COST,     ....)
      /* Master List of Route Plans  */
```

FIGURE 3.2: A Four-Table Database

3.3.3 Pros and Cons of Denormalization

On Line Transaction Processing (OLTP) applications update tables through online transactions performed by the users. The GUI front-end accepts input data and transfers them to the database residing on a remote tier. Data validation is maintained through referential integrity, triggers, and stored procedures. Tables in third normal forms perform well under this environment.

A decision support system (DSS) or a data warehouse (see Chapter 11), on the other hand, poses a different type of demand on the database. Here joins of five or more tables can occur frequently to produce reports needed by users. Denormalization reduces the number of component tables by combining them, thereby improving the response time. This is the advantage of denormalization.

But denormalization has its downside too. Three major disadvantages of denormalization are extra storage needed for the database, extra redundancy of data in the database, and possible change of existing code due to change(s) in the conceptual level. As shown in Section 3.3.2, the denormalized database eliminates the table STATE by including the State_Name with the State_Code in the table ROUTE_PLAN and in all other tables using State_Code. Thus, instead of being stored in only one table STATE, the column State_Name is now stored in many tables. This leads to the need for extra storage space for the database. The extra redundancy of data is caused by the repetition of the same column(s) in multiple tables. As a result, when such redundant columns are updated, the updates must be propagated and synchronized among several tables. For example, if a new state, say, Puerto Rico with a code PR, is added to USA, then State_Name = Puerto Rico must be added to all tables where State_Code = PR appears. Synchronizing multiple updates is a constant challenge for maintaining data integrity in a denormalized database. Finally, all the programs that currently use the column STATE.State_Code and retrieve STATE.State_Name through referential integrity must be modified to suit the denormalized version of the conceptual level where the table STATE no longer exists.

In view of the above considerations, denormalization as a performance tuning option should be considered very carefully. Long-running reports against an OLTP database should preferably be generated as batch jobs or be scheduled during off-peak hours. Then the response time does not become an issue and the conceptual level need not be denormalized. On the other hand, if such jobs are to be run during the peak hours of an OLTP database operation, then appropriate denormalization may be necessary.

An alternative approach to using a single OLTP database for both OLTP and DSS applications is to create two different instances such that one instance caters to OLTP requirements and the other is geared towards batch DSS needs. The two instances will then have two different parameter files matching the application needs. Each application will start up with the parameter file that suits the application requirements. However, this option involves the internal level of the database which is discussed in Section 4.7.

3.4 Optimal Indexing of Tables

Indices are created for faster data retrievals when queries search for data using indexed columns. Barring some special situations involving low *selectivity* (see Section 8.4.1) of indexed columns, an indexed search is faster than a full table scan when the table contains over 500 rows. Oracle allows a variety of indices such as B-tree, bitmap, and reverse key, and creation of index-organized tables and clustered tables. They are all related to the efficiency of data access from indexed tables. We discuss all of them along with selectivity and other related issues in Chapters 8 and 9 where query processing and optimization are covered. Here we discuss how tables should be indexed optimally at the conceptual level.

A table need not have an index at all. It can be created without even a primary key, if so desired by the developers. Of course, then there will be no built-in checks against allowing duplicate rows into the table. It is recommended that initially each table should have its primary key. Since indexing imposes overhead and slows down updates, any additional indexing must always be adequately justified. Only those columns should be indexed that are used in existing queries and reports. This means that indexing should match the query execution plans.

Oracle distinguishes between a primary key and a unique index:

- A table can have at most one primary key, but can have multiple unique indices on different columns;
- A primary key enforces the NOT NULL constraint on its column(s), but a unique index does not. One can insert at most one new row or modify at most one existing row with NULL value(s) assigned to uniquely indexed column(s).

As always, each piece of indexing information must be recorded at the conceptual level.

3.5 Integration of Views into Queries

A view is often called a virtual table since it does not have any storage of its own, although it resembles a table in structure. Oracle stores only the definitions of the views in its data dictionary. Any query involving views executes them dynamically at the time of processing the query by using their stored definitions. Views can be nested in that one view can be defined in terms of another view and this level of nesting can be continued. When a query involving multiple-level nested views is processed, the topmost parent view is populated first and then all the descendent views are processed according to their order of ancestry. Depending on the sizes of the component tables and the complexity of the view definitions, the query processing time can be high. In such cases, performance often improves when one or more of the views are removed and their definitions are incorporated into the query itself. See Section 9.2.7 for further details.

Views can be used for security of a database and also to insulate applications from changes in the conceptual level. For example, suppose that several applications use a view V_ACCOUNT to access the table ACCOUNT. As a security measure, the view includes only those columns of ACCOUNT that the application users are allowed to see. Later the conceptual level changes and the table ACCOUNT is split into two tables, ACCOUNT1 and ACCOUNT2, say. To accommodate this change, only the definition of the view V_ACCOUNT need be changed at the conceptual level. But the individual applications need not change their individual codes since the new view is still called V_ACCOUNT.

3.6 Partitioning of Tables and Indices

When a table becomes very large, say, containing over 10 million rows and occupying 10 GB in storage, its management becomes very difficult. Any query using such a table tends to be slow. In particular, if such a table is accessed via a full table scan, the performance degrades heavily. Partitioning of such a table and its associated indices can be done to improve performance. As an example, consider the ORDER table of Section 3.3.2. For a large company with 100,000 customers, say, and each customer placing an average of 10 orders each month, we estimate an average of 12 million records added to ORDER each year. The table can easily occupy several gigabytes of storage. Partition then becomes a serious option to consider for performance improvement. Besides improving the query performance partitioning also reduces the execution times of analyzing tables and rebuilding indices.

3.6.1 Partitioning Explained

Partitioning breaks up a table or an index dynamically into two or more components. In essence, it creates an extra layer of granularity between a table or an index and its data. The table (index) is called a *partitioned table (index)* and each component is called a *partition*. Partitioning addresses the key problem of supporting very large tables and indices by allowing their decomposition into smaller and more manageable pieces. Oracle 8i only supports partitioning for tables and indices. It does not support partitioning of clustered tables and their indices, nor of the snapshots.

All partitions of a table or an index have the same logical attributes, although their physical attributes can be different. For example, all partitions in a table have the same column names and data types, and the same constraint definitions, and all partitions in an index have the same index column names with data types. However, the storage specifications and other physical attributes such as PCTFREE, PCTUSED, INITRANS, and MAXTRANS can vary for different partitions of the same table or index. Each partition is stored in a separate segment. It is highly recommended that each partition be stored in a separate tablespace. Thereby one gains the following three advantages.

(a) The impact of damaged data in a given partition stays confined within that tablespace and datafile.
(b) Each partition can be backed up and recovered independently of the rest.
(c) The DBA can balance the I/O load by mapping partitions to disk drives and thereby avoid contention among the partitions.

At the time of creating the conceptual level of a database, one or more tables and indices may be designated as candidates for partitioning. Alternatively, partitioning can be implemented after the conceptual level is in place by altering the candidate tables and indices. In either case, it is regarded as belonging to the conceptual level of a database, which must be updated with each creation or alteration of a partition.

3.6.2 Implementation of Partitions

Table Level

If partitioning is planned during the conceptual level design, it is implemented with the option of PARTITION BY RANGE added to the CREATE TABLE statement. If it is implemented after a table has been created, one uses the ALTER TABLE command with the option of ADD PARTITION. An existing partition on a table can be changed via any of the six commands:

- DROP PARTITION,
- MODIFY PARTITION,
- MOVE PARTITION,
- RENAME PARTITION,

- TRUNCATE PARTITION, or
- SPLIT PARTITION.

The CREATE TABLE statement for a partitioned table specifies:

(a) Logical attributes of the table, such as column and constraint definitions;
(b) Physical attributes of the table specifying defaults for the individual partitions of the table;
(c) Partition specification which includes:

- The table-level algorithm used to map rows to partitions based on the values of the partition key, and
- A list of partition descriptions, one for each partition in the table

Each partition description includes a clause that defines supplemental, partition-level information about the algorithm used to map rows to partitions. It also includes, optionally, a partition name and physical attributes for the partition.

Partitioned tables cannot have any columns with LONG or LONG RAW data types, LOB data types (BLOB, CLOB, NCLOB, or BFILE), or object types.

Index Level

Partitioning is done for indices in the same way as it is done for tables, i.e., either by the CREATE INDEX command with the PARTITION BY RANGE clause, or by the ALTER INDEX command with the ADD PARTITION clause. An existing partitioned index can be changed with the five options for modification, DROP, MODIFY, MOVE, RENAME, and TRUNCATE, as listed above for tables.

It is not necessary to partition the indices of a partitioned table. An index should be partitioned only if it is large enough to justify partitioning. An index on a partitioned table may be created according to the same range values as were used to partition the table, or with a different set of range values. In the former case the table and its associated indices are said to be *equipartitioned*. Such a choice often improves query performance since data and their indices are accessed on the same range of values. Also, an index that is equipartitioned with its table is easier to implement (see [1, pp. 187 – 189]). However, the tablespace of a table partition should be placed on a different drive than that of its associated index partition to avoid data contention problems, because a data table and its index table are accessed together during an indexed search.

See Section 10.3 for additional information on partitions.

3.6.3 An Example of Partitioning

Let us suppose that the table ORDER of Section 3.3.2 is partitioned on the column ORDER_VALUE, which has the data type NUMBER. We create the partitioned table as follows:

3.6 Partitioning of Tables and Indices

```
CREATE TABLE ORDER     /*  pseudocode   */
(ORDER_NUM NUMBER,
ORDER_VALUE NUMBER,
....
)

PARTITION BY RANGE (ORDER_VALUE)
   (PARTITION ORDER_VALUE_1 VALUES LESS THAN (10000)
   TABLESPACE DATA_PARTITION_1,
   PARTITION ORDER_VALUE_2 VALUES LESS THAN (100000)
   TABLESPACE DATA_PARTITION_2,
         ....
   PARTITION ORDER_VALUE_N VALUES LESS THAN (MAXVALUE)
   TABLESPACE DATA_PARTITION_N);
```

ORDER is partitioned into N pieces, each piece being stored in a separate tablespace. We can now define a partitioned index on ORDER_VALUE that is equipartitioned with ORDER as follows.

```
CREATE INDEX IND_ORDER_VALUE ON ORDER (ORDER_VALUE)
/*  pseudocode    */
LOCAL
   (PARTITION ORDER_VALUE_1
   TABLESPACE INDEX_PARTITION_1,
   PARTITION ORDER_VALUE_2
   TABLESPACE INDEX_PARTITION_2,
   ....
   PARTITION ORDER_VALUE_N
   TABLESPACE INDEX_PARTITION_N);
```

Due to equipartitioning it is not necessary to specify the VALUES LESS THAN clause. A locally partitioned index inherits these properties from its equipartitioned table.

The same query formulated against the denormalized database in Section 3.3.2 can now be run using the partitioned table ORDER with its equipartitioned index on ORDER_VALUE. Oracle places a CHECK constraint on each partition. When the above query runs with the condition "ORDER_VALUE > 100000", Oracle finds out the partitions where the matching data reside, i.e., the partitions ORDER_VALUE_3 through ORDER_VALUE_N, and processes the query only against those partitions. This speeds up the query when the ORDER table becomes very large.

3.7 Data Replication

An application running in a distributed database system accesses data residing in multiple locations. One of the databases is the local database and the rest are remote. In a purely distributed configuration each data element resides in only one database and any query involving remote database(s) uses the network to send requests and receive results. This can put a severe burden on the network during peak traffic times and degrade database performance. In a sense, an attempt to run a distributed database application without any data replication among sites is similar to building a database with only 3NF tables. Both are theoretically sound and desirable, but are often found impractical in a production environment.

Data replication alleviates this problem just as denormalization addresses the problems with 3NF-only tables in a database. In both cases, we compromise the theory for practical gain. *Replication* is the process of copying and maintaining database objects in multiple locations constituting a distributed database environment. It improves performance since alternate data access options exist. A query uses a remote database only when not all of the data it needs are available at the local replica of the database. Also, the application continues to run when the local server fails but the other servers are available with the replicated data.

Oracle supports two types of data replication: basic and advanced. *Basic replication* provides at each remote site read-only replicas of tables selected for data replication. All such replicas originate from a single master table, which is updatable. Queries involving only data retrieval are run against the local replicas to avoid network access regardless of network availability. However, queries involving updates must access the single master table via the network. Once updated, the master table replicates its contents at all remote sites. Oracle implements basic replication by using read-only table snapshots. *Advanced replication* extends the features of basic replication by allowing updatable replicas at remote sites. Thereby, queries involving both data retrieval and data update can be processed at the local site. Oracle database servers supporting these sites automatically synchronize the replicas to ensure global transaction consistency and data integrity.

Data replication changes the conceptual level of a database. Additional information about the replication sites and the types of replication must now be maintained at this level.

Key Words

1NF	CHECK (constraint)
2NF	conceptual level
3NF	contention
acceptance test	data consistency
advanced replication	data dictionary
basic replication	data integrity

data replication
data warehouse
database, distributed
decision support system
denormalization
denormalized
driving set
driving table
equipartitioned
full table scan
I/O load
indexed search
indexing, optimal
network traffic
OLTP
On Line Transaction Processing
Oracle Designer

parallel processing
partition
PARTITION BY RANGE
partitioned table (index)
partitioning
primary key
referential integrity
response time
SDLC
segment
selectivity
stored procedure
tablespace
triggers
update anomaly
view

References and Further Reading

1. M. R. Ault—*Oracle8 Black Book*, Coriolis Group Books, 1998.
2. S. Bobrowski—*Oracle8 Architecture*, Oracle Press, Osbourne McGraw-Hill, 1998.
3. C. J. Date—"The Birth of the Relational Model, Part 2 of 3," *The Intelligent Enterprise*, November 1998.
4. K. Loney—*Oracle 8i DBA Handbook*, Oracle Press, Osbourne McGraw-Hill, 2000.
5. D. E. Shasha—*Database Tuning*, Prentice-Hall, 1992.

Very few books discuss conceptual level tuning. Loney [4, p. 163–170] contains some materials about the three versions of a database. Cursory references to denormalization appear in [1] and [5], but no examples are given. Partitioning is treated in detail with examples of sample SQL code in [1, Chapter 5], [2, Chapter 7], and [4, Chapter 12]. In particular, [4] contains SQL commands with syntax for creating and modifying partitions. Data replication is treated as a network traffic issue in both [2, Chapter 11] and ([4, Chapter 16]. Shasha [5, Chapter 4] compares denormalization with the clustering of tables and indices as possible modes of tuning the conceptual level. However, clustering is not offered by all RDBMS vendors. Oracle supports clustering. Denormalizaton, on the other hand, is independent of the RDBMS used. Date [3, pp. 4–5] wants denormalization only at the physical level.

Exercises

1. As a tuning method denormalization does not go well with updates. Why? Can you identify update situations where denormalization is less harmful?
2. Read the reference Shasha [5] cited in References and Further Reading above. Explore clustering as a tuning option for the conceptual level. Describe your findings with actual examples of both denormalization and clustering.
3. Using your own experience as a database professional describe situations where partitioning helped to improve response time.
4. Identify the disadvantages of overindexing tables in a database.
5. How will you implement denormalization *after* a database application has gone into production?
6. Repeat Question 5 for partitioning.

Part 2
Oracle Tools for Tuning and Optimization

Part 2 consists of seven chapters that cover the Oracle tools for monitoring the performance of a database and tuning and optimizing its internal and external levels, as needed. This part is specific to Oracle 8i with a glimpse into Oracle 9i in Chapter 10. The goal of Part 2 is to provide the underlying tuning principles and a repertoire of Oracle tools to implement these principles. Chapters 4 to 7 discuss the tuning of the internal level and Chapters 8 and 9 that of the external level. Chapter 10 describes several features of Oracle 8i not covered in the earlier chapters and gives an overview of several tuning features of Oracle 9i.

Chapter 4, Internal Level of an Oracle Database, introduces the structure of the internal level comprising an instance and a database. The instance consists of a set of memory-resident data structures and a set of background processes. Their tuning principles are treated in detail in Chapter 6, Tuning of Memory-Resident Data Structures. The database consists of a set of disk-resident data structures, namely, the tablespaces, tables, indices, etc. Their tuning principles are treated in detail in Chapter 5, Tuning of Disk-Resident Data Structures. Chapter 7, Oracle Utility for Tuning and Optimization, involves a detailed discussion of the two Oracle diagnostic tools UTLBSTAT and UTLESTAT.

Chapter 8, Optimization of the External Level of an Oracle Database, introduces the mathematical theory underlying the query optimization process. This is followed by a detailed treatment of Oracle's optimization tools such as EXPLAIN PLAN, SQLTRACE and TKPROF, and AUTOTRACE. Then, Chapter 9, Query Tuning and Optimization Under Oracle 8i, discusses the rule-based and the cost-based optimizers, various joining techniques, and the use of hints in queries to suggest specific query execution plans.

Chapter 10, Special Features of Oracle 8i and a Glimpse into Oracle 9i, covers several special features of Oracle 8i pertaining to performance tuning and optimization that were not covered in the earlier chapters. It closes with an overview of some of the features of Oracle 9i.

4
Internal Level of an Oracle Database

Outline

4.1 Components of the Internal Level
4.2 Oracle Instance
4.3 Oracle Database
4.4 Tuning Methodology for Internal Level
4.5 Oracle Data Dictionary
4.6 V$ Views and X$ Tables
4.7 Initialization Parameters for an Oracle Database
Key Words
References and Further Reading
Exercises

Overview of the Chapter

The chapter offers an in-depth discussion of the internal level of an Oracle database. The internal level consists of two parts: instance and database. The instance consists of a set of data structures residing in memory and a set of background processes. The database consists of the datafiles residing in auxiliary storage. Each instance is defined by the init<instance name>.ora file containing its initialization parameters. A database can support multiple instances with each instance defined by its own parameter file.

Oracle provides static views in the data dictionary and the dynamic performance views, popularly called V$ views, to monitor the performance of both the instance and the database for an application. The X$ tables underlie the V$ views. A sound understanding of the scope of these tables and views is necessary for performance monitoring and tuning. The chapter closes with a description of these views and tables.

4.1 Components of the Internal Level

The internal level of a database consists of a set of background processes and a set of data structures some of which reside in memory and the rest in auxiliary storage. The RDBMS and the operating system work hand in hand to create and maintain the internal level. The memory resident data structures and the auxiliary storage disk files are dependent on the operating system. Hence the installation procedure of the database is always operating system specific. Once the database is created, all the physical data structures and the background processes become operational.

Memory Structures and Background Processes

All the memory structures reside in the *System Global Area* (SGA), which consists of three main components:

- Data block buffers,
- Redo log buffers, and
- Shared SQL pool.

Each component occupies a block of storage in the memory called the memory cache. The *memory cache* is a preallocated memory area that Oracle reserves for the specific purpose of holding frequently accessed blocks of data. Thereby Oracle eliminates the need for bringing those blocks from disk files each time they are requested. This reduces disk I/O and improves performance. Since the SGA is limited in size, Oracle uses a caching algorithm called *least recently used* (LRU) to manage the blocks residing in the memory cache. Under LRU, a block is retained in the cache according to the time span since the block was last requested. As a result, the most recently used (MRU) blocks stay in the cache longer and the least recently used blocks are swapped out to disk files to make room for newly requested blocks.

A *process* is a memory-resident executable program that is currently running. An Oracle *background process* runs automatically in the background triggered by special internal events. These events are mostly determined by values of the initialization parameters (see Section 4.7). Depending on the database configuration chosen, there can be up to 11 background processes. They are called SMON (system monitor), PMON (process monitor), DBWR (database writer), LGWR (log writer), CKPT (checkpoint), ARCH (archiver), RECO (recoverer), SNPn (snapshot, with "n" representing a letter or a number), LCKn (lock for parallel server option, labeled 0 through 9), Dnnn (dispatcher, labeled 000 through 999 depending on the SQL*Net V2 multithreaded server architecture), and Snnn (server, labeled 000 through 999 depending on the pre-SQL*Net V2 connection). These processes together handle a variety of housekeeping jobs to keep the database running smoothly. As a minimum, five of them, namely, SMON, PMON, DBWR, LGWR, and CKPT, are required in running an instance.

The SGA and the background processes together constitute an *Oracle instance*. Section 4.2 describes the function of each structure and each background process of the Oracle instance in more detail.

Auxiliary Storage Data Structures

The auxiliary storage contains these data structures.

- Datafiles for tablespaces,
- Redo log files,
- Control file (binary),
- Trace files, and
- Alert log file.

The first three files constitute an *Oracle database*. Section 4.3 describes in more detail the function of all five data structures listed above. Figure 4.1 shows the structure of the internal level.

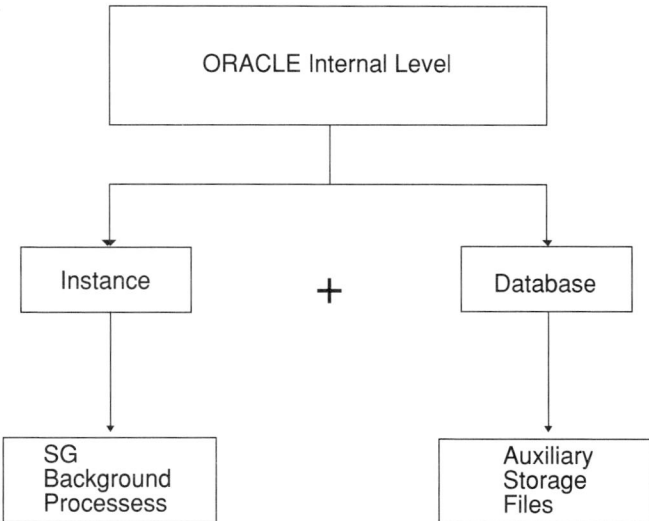

FIGURE 4.1: Oracle Iinternal Level

4.2 Oracle Instance

An Oracle instance is a mechanism to access an Oracle database. Using the initialization parameter file init<instance name>.ora, the instance opens one and only one database.

Multiple instances can map onto a single database. The number of instances that can be associated with a given database is determined by the value of MAXINSTANCES in the CREATE DATABASE command. Sections 4.2.1 and 4.2.2 describe respectively the memory structures and the background processes that together constitute an Oracle instance.

When an instance is started, Oracle creates the operational background processes. When the database is mounted, it is available for DBA activities only. Next as the database is opened, all the physical structures become operational. At this time, the database becomes available to all users. Installation is a separate process that may not actually create a database or open an instance.

4.2.1 Memory Structures

The memory resident structures of an Oracle instance reside in the System Global Area. The size of the SGA can be found as follows:

```
SQL> select * from V$SGA;
NAME                    VALUE
------------------      ----------
Fixed Size                  69616
Variable Size            75911168
Database Buffers         81920000
Redo Buffers               278528
```

A *transaction* in an Oracle database is defined as a logical unit of work that executes a series of SQL statements such as INSERT, UPDATE, and DELETE to update objects. The transaction begins with the first executable INSERT, UPDATE, or DELETE statement in the logical unit and ends either by saving it via COMMIT or discarding it via ROLLBACK. Although a retrieval operation involving the SELECT command does not update any object, it can be regarded as a transaction in an extended sense that includes data retrieval. A database transaction, retrieval or update, has the following features.

(a) It needs data from segments such as tables, indices, clusters, etc.
(b) An update transaction must be recorded in some log file so that in case of a system crash before the transaction is committed or rolled back, the database can be recovered and data integrity can be maintained.
(c) The locations of the needed data elements are available from appropriate views of the Oracle data dictionary. The parsed and compiled form of the query used by the transaction should be stored in some location for later retrieval, if needed. If the same query is reused, it need not be recompiled.

The SGA is a location in memory that is divided into three main components, called data block buffers, redo log buffers, and shared SQL pool corresponding respectively to the features (a), (b), and (c), listed above.

Data Block Buffers

These buffers constitute a cache in the SGA. Each buffer holds only one data block read from the data segments such as tables, indices, and clusters residing on disk files. Rollback segment data blocks are also read into here. The size of the cache in number of blocks is determined by the initialization parameter DB_BLOCK_BUFFERS. Since this value is much smaller than the size of the data segments, it cannot hold the contents of all these segments. In managing the space within these buffers Oracle uses the principle of moving to disk files the least recently used blocks that have changed. Thereby when a new data block cannot fit into these buffers, the least recently used blocks are written back to disks. New data blocks occupy the freed space. Thus, the most recently used data blocks are kept in memory.

At any given time, there can be one or more of the following three types of buffers in the cache.

- *Free* buffers have the same image on disk and in memory and are available for reuse.
- *Dirty* buffers have a different image on the disk compared to that in memory. These buffers must be written to disk by the background process DBWR.
- *Pinned* buffers are currently being accessed.

At any given time, the data block buffers may hold multiple copies of the same data block from the disk. Only one current copy of the block exists, but additional copies of that block may be made to construct read-consistent views of data using rollback information to satisfy queries.

Redo Log Buffers

Redo log entries describe the changes that are made to the database by INSERT, UPDATE, DELETE, CREATE, ALTER, and DROP commands. Thus, they are related to the update transactions alone. Oracle server processes copy redo entries from the users' memory space to this area in cache memory for every DML and DDL statement. Later these entries are written to the redo log files (see Section 4.3 below) by the background process LGWR. The size of this cache area is determined by the initialization parameter LOG_BUFFER.

Oracle 8i allows the option of NOLOGGING with the parallel INSERTs, direct SQL loads under SQL Loader, CREATE TABLE AS command, and CREATE INDEX with PARALLEL or NOPARALLEL commands. When NOLOGGING is used, Oracle logs in the redo log buffer only the DDL commands to create the objects but not the data underlying the object. LOGGING is the default option. Also, one can create indices with the NOPARALLEL or the PARALLEL option. NOPARALLEL is the default that signifies serial execution. The option "PARALLEL n" causes Oracle to select "n" as the *degree* of parallelism. This means that n query servers are used to create the index.

The redo log buffer is a circular buffer. Redo entries that have already been written to the redo log files are overwritten by new entries. LGWR normally writes fast enough to ensure that space is always available in the redo log buffer for new entries.

Shared SQL Pool

The shared SQL pool consists of three main parts: library cache, dictionary cache, and user global area (UGA). Its size is determined by the initialization parameter SHARED_POOL_SIZE.

- Library Cache

The *library cache* contains the execution plan and the parse tree for SQL and PL/SQL statements that are executed in the course of a transaction. This includes queries, triggers, functions, procedures, and packages. If another transaction subsequently uses the identical statement, it is not parsed again. Instead the query optimizer uses the execution plan and the parse tree residing in the shared SQL pool. The hashed location of the execution plan in the library cache is computed by using the ASCII code of each of the first 64 characters appearing in the query. If the first 64 characters of two queries hash to the same location, then their complete texts are used in this hashing process to determine if they still hash to the same location. As a result, two equivalent queries hash to the same location in the library cache only when their formulations are identical including cases. Thus, the following two statements are not identical.

```
SELECT CUST_ID, NAME FROM CUSTOMER;
select CUST_ID, Name FROM CUSTOMER;
```

See Section E15, Appendix E, for a discussion of hash tables and hashing. The space in the library cache is managed by the LRU algorithm.

- Dictionary Cache

The Oracle data dictionary stores information about all the database objects in the database. When information is needed about any of them, the relevant portion of the corresponding data dictionary views are read into a cache area in memory called the *dictionary cache*.

- User Global Area (UGA)

If an application uses the multithreaded server (MTS), information on user sessions and cursor states is stored in the *user global area* (UGA). User session data includes sort areas and private SQL areas.

Figure 4.2 shows the structure of the SGA in an Oracle instance.

4.2 Oracle Instance

<pre>
                    Shared Global Area

   ┌─────────────┬─────────────┬──────────────────────┐
   │   │   │ Shared SQL Pool   │
   │ Data   │ Redo   │ – Library Cache   │
   │ Block   │ Log   │ – Dictionary Cache │
   │ Buffers   │ Buffers   │ – UGA   │
   │   │   │   │
   └─────────────┴─────────────┴──────────────────────┘
</pre>

FIGURE 4.2: Memory Structres in Oracle Instance

4.2.2 Background Processes

One can obtain a complete list of the background processes running in an Oracle instance as follows.

```
COLUMN DESCRIPTION FORMAT A30
SELECT NAME, DESCRIPTION FROM V$BGPROCESS ORDER BY NAME;
```

A partial output is shown below.

```
NAME              DESCRIPTION
----              -----------
ARCH              Archival
CKPT              checkpoint
DBW0              db writer process 0
DBW1              db writer process 1
DBW2              db writer process 2
DBW3              db writer process 3
DBW4              db writer process 4
DBW5              db writer process 5
DBW6              db writer process 6
DBW7              db writer process 7
DBW8              db writer process 8
DBW9              db writer process 9
LCK0              MI Lock Process 0
LCK1              MI Lock Process 1
LCK2              MI Lock Process 2
LCK3              MI Lock Process 3
LCK4              MI Lock Process 4
LCK5              MI Lock Process 5
LCK6              MI Lock Process 6
LCK7              MI Lock Process 7
LCK8              MI Lock Process 8
LCK9              MI Lock Process 9
LGWR              Redo etc.
```

System Monitor (SMON)

When the database is started, SMON

- Performs instance recovery, as needed, using the online redo log files;
- Cleans up the database by eliminating transactional objects that are no longer needed; and
- Coalesces each set of contiguous free extents in a tablespace into a single large free extent if PCTINCREASE is positive.

Process Monitor (PMON)

PMON cleans up when a user process fails by freeing up the resources that the process was using. For example, when a process holding a lock on a resource is killed, PMON releases the lock and makes the unlocked resource available for other users.

Database Writer (DBWR)

DBWR manages the contents of the data block buffers and the dictionary cache as follows.

- Performs batch writes to transfer the changed ("dirty") data blocks in data block buffers to datafiles in auxiliary storage;
- Transfers contents of the data dictionary from the SYSTEM tablespace to the dictionary cache; and
- Transfers data from the dictionary cache to the SYSTEM tablespace according to the LRU principle if the dictionary cache runs out of space.

Under Oracle 8i an instance can have multiple DBWR processes running at the same time. This improves performance by minimizing contention within the DBWR during large queries that span multiple datafiles. The number of DBWR I/O slaves that can run simultaneously at a given time is determined by the initialization parameter DBWR_IO_SLAVES. Alternatively, one can set up to 10 DBWR processes via the initialization parameter DB_WRITER_PROCESSES (see Section 6.6.1).

Log Writer (LGWR)

LGWR operates the same way with transaction logs as DBWR operates with the data blocks. Every database transaction that does not use the NOLOGGING option is written to the redo log buffers. LGWR then periodically transfers in batch mode the contents of the redo log buffers to the online redo log files and triggers the checkpoint event described below. If these files are mirrored as redo log file groups, then LGWR writes to each member of the group simultaneously. As with the DBWR process, an instance under Oracle 8i can have multiple LGWR processes running at the same time. The number of LGWR I/O slaves that can run simultaneously at a given time is determined by the initialization parameter LGWR_IO_SLAVES. See Section 6.6.2 for more details.

Checkpoint and CKPT Process

Checkpoint is an event that triggers the DBWR process to wake up and write all the changed data blocks since the previous checkpoint to the datafiles. CKPT is a background process that updates the datafile headers and the control files to record the checkpoint event. Thereby it ensures an instance recovery. These three initialization parameters can be set to control the frequency of checkpoints:

- LOG_CHECKPOINT_INTERVAL,
- LOG_CHECKPOINT_TIMEOUT,
- LOG_CHECKPOINTS_TO_ALERT.

In essence, the scheduling of checkpoints involves some tradeoff. Checkpoints occurring more frequently make instance recovery run faster, because datafiles, redo logs, and control files are synchronized more often. But it entails the risk of degrading the performance of the database for online users.

Archiver (ARCH)

An Oracle instance can run in ARCHIVELOG mode or in NOARCHIVELOG mode, which is the default. Under the latter option, when one redo log file becomes full, LGWR writes to the next redo log file, and continues this process until the last redo log file is full. Then, LGWR writes to the first redo log file overwriting its contents. If the instance runs in ARCHIVELOG mode, the contents of a redo log file are copied onto a tape or a disk file before LGWR is allowed to overwrite its contents. This archiving function is performed by the background process ARCH. In this case, the database recovery from a disk crash can be done quickly and online since no transactions are lost.

An instance can be made to run in ARCHIVELOG mode by issuing the command

```
ALTER DATABASE ARCHIVELOG;
```

The automatic archiving is started by setting the initialization parameter LOG_ARCHIVE_START to the value TRUE. Under Oracle 8i multiple ARCH I/O slave processes can run at the same time, thereby improving performance. The number of ARCH I/O slaves that can run simultaneously at a given time is determined by the initialization parameter ARCH_IO_SLAVES.

If an instance runs under ARCHIVELOG mode, three background processes, LGWR, CKPT, and ARCH, need to be properly coordinated. LGWR writes sequentially in batch the contents of the redo log buffer to the online redo log files. It then causes DBWR to write to the datafiles all of the data blocks that have been modified since the last checkpoint. When DBWR is finished with its task, CKPT is invoked. Then, CKPT updates the datafile headers and control files to record the checkpoint. The frequency of invoking CKPT is determined by the initialization parameter LOG_CHECKPOINT_INTERVAL. ARCH performs the archiving function by making a copy on a disk device of each online redo log file before overwriting it. As a result, a delay occurs if ARCH is busy archiving while LGWR and CKPT wait for overwriting the already full online redo log file. It is a tradeoff situation. But I always recommend ARCHIVELOG mode so that the database can be recovered from media failure. EXPORT/IMPORT only protects from instance failure.

The delay caused by ARCHIVELOG mode can be addressed as follows. Until the system becomes stable, set LOG_CHECKPOINT_INTERVAL to a value that enforces a checkpoint uniformly distributed over the entire file. For example, suppose that each redo log file is 50 MB. Compute a value for the parameter LOG_CHECKPOINT_INTERVAL to enforce a checkpoint at every 10 MB level, say. Then there will be five uniformly distributed checkpoints for each redo log file. When the system is deemed stable and, therefore, crashes very rarely, set LOG_CHECK-POINT_INTERVAL to a value larger than the online redo log file, thereby forcing a checkpoint to coincide with a log switch, which happens only when the redo log file is full. This will minimize the contention among LGWR, CKPT, and ARCH processes.

Snapshots (SNPn)

SNP processes refresh snapshots and scheduling of internal job queues. The suffix "n" can be a number or a letter to signify each distinct SNP. The total number of SNPn processes is determined by the initialization parameter JOB_QUEUE_PROCESSES.

Recoverer (RECO)

RECO is used only for distributed databases to resolve failures. It accesses the distributed transactions that are suspected to have failed and resolves the transactions by commit or rollback.

Lock (LCKn)

LCK processes are used only when the Oracle Parallel Server option is used. Here the suffix "n" ranges from 0 to 9. The processes LCKn are used for inter-instance locking. The total number of LCKn processes is determined by the initialization parameter GC_LCK_PROCS.

Dispatcher (Dnnn)

Dnnn processes are part of the multithreaded server (MTS) architecture. They help in minimizing resource needs by handling multiple connections. These are created at database startup based on the SQL*Net configuration and can be removed or additional processes can be created while the database is open.

Server (Snnn)

Server processes are created for managing those database connections that require a dedicated server.

Figure 4.3 shows a schematic view of an Oracle instance.

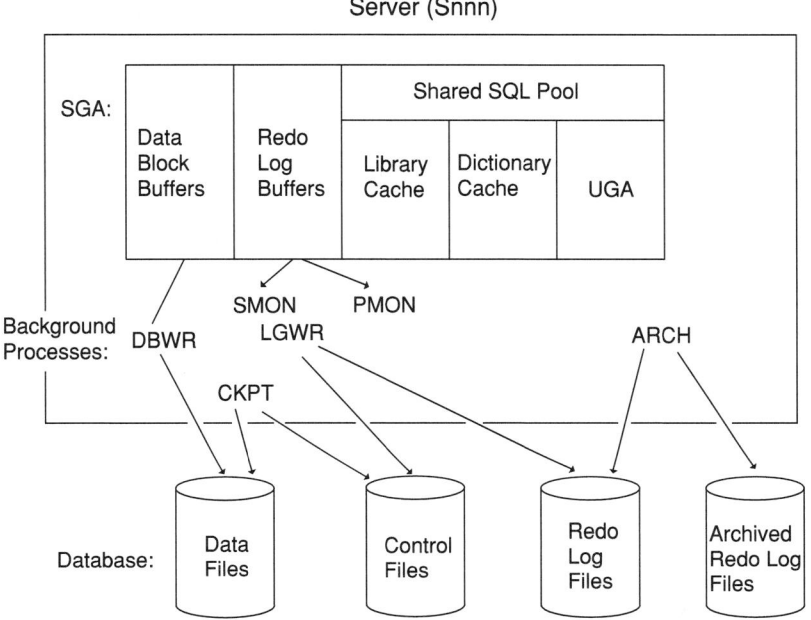

FIGURE 4.3: Functions of Background Processes

4.3 Oracle Database

An Oracle database consists of the first three of the five files:

- Datafiles for tablespaces
- Redo log files
- Control file (binary)
- Trace files
- Alert log file.

All of these files reside on auxiliary storage as external data structures. They are created during and after the Oracle instance corresponding to the database has been created. Each one is now described below.

Datafiles for Tablespaces

One of the building blocks of an Oracle database is a set of logical data structures called tablespaces. Each tablespace is mapped onto one or more datafile(s), which are physical disk files. Cary Millsap, formerly of Oracle Corporation, formulated an architecture for the tablespaces that is called the *Optimal Flexible Architecture* (OFA). It offers a minimal configuration that is scalable. The purpose of the OFA is to optimize the performance of a database operation by separating its tablespaces by their types and activities. Since all other database objects reside within their respective tablespaces, the configuration created by the OFA optimizes database performance.

The basic OFA consists of the tablespaces with their contents listed below:

- SYSTEM: Data dictionary views, V$ views, SYSTEM rollback segment;
- DATA: Data tables for the application;
- INDEX: Indices created on all the data tables in DATA;
- TOOLS: Objects created by Oracle and other third party vendors;
- RBS: Rollback segments;
- TEMP: Temporary segments ; and
- USERS: Objects (tables, indices, views, etc.) created by the end users.

The basic OFA is extended to handle more complex databases by including the two additional tablespaces:

- DATA_2: The data tables usually fall into two categories, dynamic for transactions and static for validation; DATA_1 (new name of DATA) holds the former and DATA_2 the latter; and
- INDEX_2: Two separate tablespaces, INDEX_1 (new name for INDEX) and INDEX_2 to hold the indices for data tables in DATA_1 and DATA_2 respectively.

Additional tablespaces may be added if necessary.

Redo Log Files

When a database transaction occurs, it is recorded temporarily in the redo log buffers. Subsequently, LGWR writes them to external disk files called redo log files. These files are used to recover the database transactions in case of media crash. There must be at least two such files. But Oracle recommends that there be two or more groups of redo log files with each group containing two mirrored redo log files residing on separate disks. If asynchronous I/O is enabled, LGWR writes to both members of a group simultaneously. Otherwise, LGWR writes serially. These files are cyclical in nature; i.e., when one file is full, LGWR writes to the next file and continues the process until all the redo log files are full. Then, the first file is overwritten only after it has been checkpointed or has been archived in case the database runs in ARCHIVELOG mode.

Since the members of the same group are placed on different disks, the transactions are saved even when one of the disks crashes.

Control File

This is a binary file and is not human readable. It contains control information about all the files in the database. The file is used for maintaining the physical architecture and internal consistency of the database, and for any database recovery operation. This file is vital for the database in that a database cannot start without its control file. For this reason, it is recommended that multiple, say, three, copies of the control file be kept on three separate disk devices. In case of media crash at least one copy will hopefully survive to bring the database back into operation.

Trace Files

There are two types of trace files: the background process trace file and user process trace file. Each background process running in an Oracle instance keeps a trace file to record significant events encountered by the process. There are as many trace files as there are running background processes. These files are used for uncovering the cause of major failure of the database. A user process trace file can be generated by server processes at user request to display resource consumption during statement processing.

The location of the background process trace file is determined by the initialization parameter BACKGROUND_DUMP_DEST. Its default values under UNIX and NT are respectively $ORACLE_HOME/rdbms/log and %ORACLE_HOME%\Rdbms80\Trace.

The location of the user process trace file is determined by the parameter USER_DUMP_DEST. Its default values under UNIX and NT are respectively $ORACLE_HOME/rdbms/log and %ORACLE_HOME%\Rdbms80\Trace. The size of the user process trace file is determined by the initialization parameter MAX_DUMP_FILE_SIZE. User process tracing can be enabled at the instance level by setting the initialization parameter SQL_TRACE to TRUE. Alternatively, tracing can be enabled at session level by the command

```
ALTER SESSION SET SQL_TRACE=TRUE;
```

All trace files have .TRC as the extension.

Alert Log File

This file is a chronological log of messages and errors that occur while an Oracle instance is running. It records the commands and results from execution of those commands for major events in the operation of a database. Examples of alert log file entries are creation and alteration of tablespaces and their datafiles, redo log switches, instance startups, recovery from media crash, etc. An instance will abort if entries cannot be made to the alert log file.

The alert log file has the extension .LOG. Its location is determined by the value of the initialization parameter BACKGROUND_DUMP_DEST. Its default values under UNIX and under NT are respectively $ORACLE_HOME/rdbms/log and %ORACLE_HOME%\Rdbms80\Trace.

Figure 4.4 shows the contents of an Oracle database.

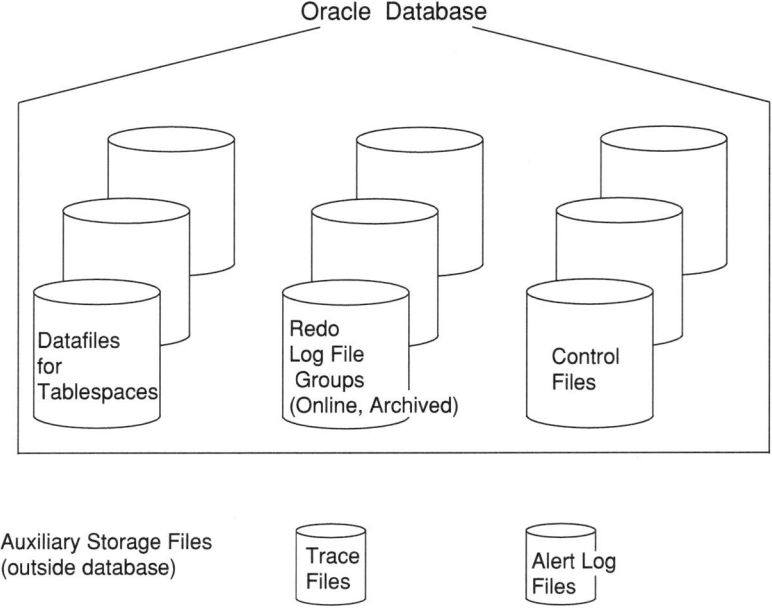

FIGURE 4.4: Oracle Database and Files

4.4 Internal Level Tuning Methodology

The internal level is tuned at both of its components, the instance and the database.

The primary information about the instance is available from the V$ views. They are called dynamic performance views because they are continuously updated when a database is open and in use. They contain data about the performance of the memory structures and internal disk structures. See Section 4.6 for the descriptions of the V$ views, and Chapters 6 and 7 for details about instance tuning methodology using these views and the two Oracle utilities, UTLBSTAT and UTLESTAT.

The primary information about the database is available from the static data dictionary views described in Section 4.5. See Chapter 5 for further details about database tuning methodology using these views.

4.5 Oracle Data Dictionary

Oracle maintains an extensive set of views that contain very detailed information about the internal level of each Oracle database running under that installation. Descriptions of the views belonging to the data dictionary are found in two views, DICT and DICT_COLUMNS. DICT lists the views with their descriptions. DICT_COLUMNS lists each view with its component columns and their descriptions. Figures 4.5 and 4.7 contain two scripts for querying DICT and DICT_COLUMNS respectively to show the kind of information that is available from them. Figures 4.6 and 4.8 contain partial listings of the sample output from these scripts. The data dictionary views belong to three major categories, ALL, DBA, and USER with the names of the views starting with prefixes ALL_, DBA_, and USER_ respectively.

Views prefixed with USER_ contain information on all database objects owned by the account performing the query. Those with the prefix ALL_ include the information in USER_ views as well as the information about objects on which privileges have been granted to PUBLIC or to the user. The views prefixed with DBA_ are all inclusive in that they contain information on all database objects irrespective of the owner.

```
REM  Listing of all views in Oracle Data Dictionary
REM  Script File Name: My_Directory\Data_Dictionary_Tables.sql
REM  Spool File Name:  My_Directory \Data_Dictionary_Tables.lst
REM  Author:           NAME
REM  Date Created:     DATE
REM  Purpose:          Information on Data Dictionary views about
REM                    any Oracle database
REM
REM

COLUMN TODAY  NEW_VALUE xTODAY NOPRINT FORMAT A1 TRUNC

TTITLE LEFT xTODAY -
    RIGHT 'Page ' FORMAT 999 SQL.PNO -
    CENTER 'Oracle Data Dictionary Views ' SKIP 2
BTITLE 'Script File: My_Directory Data_Dictionary_Tables.sql|Spool
    File: My_Directory \Data_Dictionary_Tables.lst'
COLUMN TABLE_NAME HEADING 'Table|Name' FORMAT A25
COLUMN COMMENTS FORMAT A50 WORD WRAP

SET LINESIZE 78
SET PAGESIZE 41
SET NEWPAGE 0

SPOOL   My_Directory \Data_Dictionary_Tables.lst

SELECT TABLE_NAME, COMMENTS, TO_CHAR (SysDate, 'fmMonth ddth, YYYY')
    TODAY FROM DICT
    WHERE TABLE_NAME NOT LIKE '%$%'
    ORDER BY TABLE_NAME;

SPOOL OFF
```

FIGURE 4.5: Script for Querying DICT View

Figure 4.6 contains a partial listing of the output from the script.

```
May 17th, 2001        Oracle Data Dictionary Views      Page 1
Table
Name                              COMMENTS
------------------------          --------------------------------
ALL_ALL_TABLES                    Description of all object and
                                  relational  tables accessible to
                                  the user

ALL_ARGUMENTS                     Arguments in object accessible to
                                  the user

ALL_CATALOG                       All tables, views, synonyms,
                                  sequences accessible to the user

ALL_CLUSTERS                      Description of clusters accessible
                                  to the user

ALL_CLUSTER_HASH_EXPRESSIONS      Hash functions for all accessible
                                  clusters

ALL_COLL_TYPES                    Description of named collection
                                  types accessible to the user

ALL_COL_COMMENTS                  Comments on columns of accessible
                                  tables and views

ALL_COL_PRIVS                     Grants on columns for which the
                                  user is the grantor, grantee,
                                  owner, or an enabled role or
                                  PUBLIC is the grantee
```

FIGURE 4.6: Data Dictionary Views (Partial List)

```
REM   Listing of columns in all views in Oracle Data Dictionary
REM   Script File Name: My_Directory
      \Data_Dictionary_TableColumns.sql
REM   Spool File Name: My_Directory\Data_Dictionary_
      TableColumns.lst
REM   Author:         NAME
REM   Date Created:   DATE

REM   Purpose:   Information on Data Dictionary views and their
REM              columns
REM
REM

COLUMN TODAY   NEW_VALUE xTODAY NOPRINT FORMAT A1 TRUNC

TTITLE LEFT xTODAY -
     RIGHT 'Page ' FORMAT 999 SQL.PNO -
     CENTER 'Oracle Data Dictionary View/Columns ' SKIP 2
```

FIGURE 4.7: Script File for Querying DICT_COLUMNS View

4.5 Oracle Data Dictionary

```
BTITLE 'Script File:My_Directory\Data_Dictionary_TableColumns.sql|
       Spool File: My_Directory\Data_Dictionary_TableColumns.lst'
COLUMN TABLE_NAME HEADING            'Table|Name' FORMAT A25
COLUMN COLUMN_NAME HEADING           'Column|Name' FORMAT A25
COLUMN COMMENTS FORMAT A50 WORD WRAP

SET LINESIZE 78
SET PAGESIZE 41
SET NEWPAGE 0

SPOOL   My_Directory \Data_Dictionary_TableColumns.lst

SELECT TABLE_NAME, COLUMN_NAME, COMMENTS,
       TO_CHAR (SysDate, 'fmMonth ddth, YYYY') TODAY
       FROM DICT_COLUMNS
       WHERE TABLE_NAME NOT LIKE '%$%'
       ORDER BY TABLE_NAME, COLUMN_NAME;
SPOOL OFF
```

FIGURE 4.7 (*continued*): Script File for Querying DICT_COLUMNS View

Figure 4.8 contains a partial listing of the output generated by the script file shown in Figure 4.7..

```
May 17th, 2001        Oracle Data Dictionary View/Columns      Page 1
Table                 Column
Name                  Name                  COMMENTS
--------------        ----------------      --------------------------

ALL_ALL_TABLES        AVG_ROW_LEN           The average row length,
                                            including row overhead

ALL_ALL_TABLES        AVG_SPACE             The average available free
                                            space in the table

ALL_ALL_TABLES        AVG_SPACE__           The average freespace of
                      FREELIST BLOCKS       all blocks on a freelist

ALL_ALL_TABLES        BACKED_UP             Has table been backed up
                                            since last modification?

ALL_ALL_TABLES        BLOCKS                The number of used blocks
                                            in the table

ALL_ALL_TABLES        BUFFER_POOL           The default buffer pool to
                                            be used for table blocks

ALL_ALL_TABLES        CACHE                 Whether the table is to be
                                            cached in the buffer cache
```

FIGURE 4.8: Data Dictionary Views with Columns (Partial List)

ALL_ALL_TABLES	CHAIN_CNT	The number of chained rows in the table
ALL_ALL_TABLES	CLUSTER_NAME	Name of the cluster, if any, to which the table belongs
ALL_ALL_TABLES	DEGREE	The number of threads per instance for scanning the table
ALL_ALL_TABLES	EMPTY_BLOCKS	The number of empty (never used) blocks in the table

FIGURE 4.8 (*continued*): Data Dictionary Views with Columns (Partial List)

4.6 V$ Views and X$ Tables

The V$ views are based on X$ tables, which are memory structures that hold instance information. As a result, they are available only when the instance is in a NOMOUNT or MOUNT state. However, a few V$ views such as V$DATAFILE are not available when the database is in a NOMOUNT state. The view V$FIXED_TABLE contains a complete list of the X$ tables. The view V$FIXED_VIEW_DEFINITION contains a complete list of all the V$ views along with the SELECT statements that define them. The X$ tables and, therefore, the V$ views are populated at instance startup and cleared at instance shutdown. Consequently, if a database runs under 7 x 24 coverage, these views gather information from the very first time when the instance started. The V$ views contain timing information if the initialization parameter TIMED_STATISTICS is set to the value TRUE.

Unlike the DICT view in the data dictionary (see Section 4.5) there is no master table that contains the name and description of each V$ view. The view V$FIXED_VIEW_DEFINITION lists the V$ views with their definitions in the form of SELECT statements.

The Oracle utilities UTLBSTAT and UTLESTAT collect statistics for a user specified time interval by accessing the V$ views. See Chapter 7 for further details.

4.6.1 V$ Views

Figure 4.9 contains a script for querying the view V$FIXED_VIEW_DEFINITION and prints a list of all such views with their respective definitions.

4.6 V$ Views and X$ Tables

```
REM  Listing of all V$ views in Oracle Data Dictionary
REM  Script File Name: My_directory\V$_Tables.sql
REM  Spool File Name:  My_directory \V$_Tables.lst
REM  Author:           NAME
REM  Date Created:     DATE

REM  Purpose:          Information on V$ views about dynamic
                       performance
REM
REM
COLUMN TODAY   NEW_VALUE xTODAY NOPRINT FORMAT A1 TRUNC

TTITLE LEFT xTODAY -
    RIGHT 'Page ' FORMAT 999 SQL.PNO -
    CENTER 'Oracle V$ Views ' SKIP 2
BTITLE 'Script File: My_directory \V$_Tables.sql|Spool File:
    My_directory \V$_Tables.lst'
COLUMN VIEW_NAME HEADING 'V$ View|Name' FORMAT A25
COLUMN VIEW_DEFINITION FORMAT A50 WORD WRAP

SET LINESIZE 78
SET PAGESIZE 41
SET NEWPAGE 0

SPOOL My_directory \V$_Tables.lst

SELECT VIEW_NAME, VIEW_DEFINITION, TO_CHAR (SysDate, 'fmMonth
        ddth, YYYY') TODAY
    FROM V$FIXED_VIEW_DEFINITION
    ORDER BY VIEW_NAME;
SPOOL OFF
```

FIGURE 4.9: Script File for Querying V$FIXED_VIEW_DEFINITION View

Figure 4.10 contains a partial output from running the script file shown in Figure 4.9.

```
May 17th, 2001             Oracle V$ Views              Page  29
V$ View
Name                    VIEW_DEFINITION
---------               --------------------------------------------
V$ARCHIVED_LOG          select RECID , STAMP , NAME , THREAD# ,
                        SEQUENCE# , RESETLOGS_CHANGE# ,
                        RESETLOGS_TIME , FIRST_CHANGE# , FIRST_TIME ,
                        NEXT_CHANGE# , NEXT_TIME , BLOCKS ,
                        BLOCK_SIZE , ARCHIVED , DELETED , COMPLETION
                        TIME from GV$ARCHIVED_LOG where inst_id =
                        USERENV('Instance')
```

FIGURE 4.10: V$ Views with Definitions

V$ARCHIVE_DEST	select ARCMODE, STATUS, DESTINATION from GV$ARCHIVE_DEST where inst_id = USERENV('Instance')
V$BACKUP	select FILE# , STATUS , CHANGE# , TIME from GV$BACKUP where inst_id = USERENV('Instance')
V$BACKUP_CORRUPTION	select RECID , STAMP , SET_STAMP , SET_COUNT , PIECE# , FILE# , BLOCK# , BLOCKS , CORRUPTION_CHANGE# , MARKED_CORRUPT from GV$BACKUP_CORRUPTION where inst_id = USERENV('Instance')

FIGURE 4.10 (*continued*): V$ Views with Definitions

4.6.2 X$ Tables

Oracle provides very scanty documentation about the X$ tables that underlie the V$ views. These tables store up-to-date information about database activities since the last startup. The tables cannot be updated or dropped. As they reside in memory, there is very limited access to them, which makes them very difficult to use. Also, unlike the data dictionary views and the V$ views, the names of the X$ tables are very cryptic and do not give any indication of their contents. The SELECT statement is the only command that can be run against them. An error occurs if one attempts to grant the SELECT privilege on these tables to another user. As a result, SQL*Plus reporting commands cannot be executed on the X$ tables. However, one can use a "bypass" procedure described in Figure 4.11 to create views from two tables, x$kcbrbh and x$kcbcbh, and then execute SQL*Plus reporting commands against these views.

```
Purpose: grant access to select from x$ tables owned by SYS
$ > svrmgrl
Oracle Server Manager Release 3.0.5.0.0 - Production
(c) Copyright 1997, Oracle Corporation. All Rights Reserved.
Oracle 8i Enterprise Edition Release 8.1.6.2.0 - Production PL/SQL
Release 8.1.6.2.0 - Production
SVRMGR> connect sys/change_on_install
Connected.
SVRMGR> create view query_x$kcbrbh as
     2> select * from x$kcbrbh;
Statement processed.
SVRMGR> create public synonym x$kcbrbh for query_x$kcbrbh;
Statement processed.
```

FIGURE 4.11: Procedure to Create Views from X$ Tables

```
SVRMGR> grant select on query_x$kcbrbh to system;
Statement processed.
SVRMGR> create view query_x$kcbcbh as
    2> select * from x$kcbcbh;
Statement processed.
SVRMGR> create public synonym x$kcbcbh for query_x$kcbcbh;
Statement processed.
SVRMGR> grant select on query_x$kcbcbh to system;
Statement processed.
```

FIGURE 4.11 (*continued*): Procedure to Create Views from X$ Tables

Now, we can write script files using SQL*Plus commands to query the views x$kcbrbh and x$kcbcbh. See Figures 6.7 and 6.8 for two examples of such script files.

4.7 Initialization Parameters for an Oracle Database

In Sections 4.2 and 4.3 we have seen several initialization parameters. The initialization parameter file is a text file containing a list of parameters and their respective values that determine and manage the internal level of an Oracle database. Each parameter comes with a default value, some of which can be modified by the DBA to improve the performance. The parameter file name is init<instance name>.ora. However, the DBA can change the file name, if desired. Oracle allows multiple instances to be associated with the same database. When the database is started, the particular instance is identified by its associated parameter file. Thus, a given database can be used for an OLTP application during the day and for a reporting application with plenty of batch jobs during the night. The DBA creates two separate parameter files with different values of the same parameters to suit the particular application. For example, the parameter PROCESSES can be set to a high value for the OLTP and a low value for the batch. The rollback segments can be sized differently for the two applications. Batch jobs typically need much larger rollback segments due to their long transactions compared to OLTP jobs.

Oracle provides an init<instance name>.ora file with three options, SMALL, MEDIUM, and LARGE, for the size of the application determined by the number of concurrent users. For almost any production database use the option LARGE.

Some of the tasks that a DBA can perform using the parameters in the initialization parameter file are listed below:

- Optimize performance by adjusting the sizes of the memory-resident data structures such as the shared SQL pool, data block buffers, etc.;
- Set up various limits for parameters for the entire database such as the total number of processes running at any given time, maximum number of database users, etc.;
- Specify the names and configuration of the rollback segments; and
- Enable runtime statistics collection via UTLBSTAT and UTLESTAT.

Values of the updateable (also called variable) parameters can be changed at any time by editing the parameter file. But the new values will take effect only after the instance is shut down and then restarted. The only exception to this rule is the set of dynamic parameters. They can be changed as follows via ALTER SESSION or ALTER SYSTEM command while the instance is running:

```
ALTER SESSION SET parameter = value
ALTER SYSTEM SET parameter = value
```

The contents of a parameter file can be displayed by invoking the Server Manager and typing

```
SHOW PARAMETERS
```

Alternatively, the script file in Figure 4.12 can be used to display the contents of a parameter file.

```
REM      Initialization Parameter Listing for EXAMPLE Database
REM      Script File Name:   My_Directory\INIT_ORA.sql
REM      Spool File Name:    My_Directory \INIT_ORA.lst
REM      Author:             NAME
REM      Date Created:       DATE
REM      Purpose:            Information on all parameters in
REM                          init<instance name>.ORA file in EXAMPLE
                             database
REM
REM
COLUMN TODAY     NEW_VALUE xTODAY NOPRINT FORMAT A1 TRUNC
TTITLE LEFT xTODAY -
       RIGHT 'Page ' FORMAT 999 SQL.PNO -
       CENTER 'Initialization Parameter Listing ' SKIP 3
BTITLE 'Script File: My_Directory \INIT_ORA.sql|Spool File:
       My_Directory \INIT_ORA.lst'
COLUMN NAME HEADING 'Parameter|Name' FORMAT A20
COLUMN VALUE HEADING 'Parameter|Value' FORMAT A14
COLUMN ISDEFAULT HEADING 'Default|Value' FORMAT A6
COLUMN DESCRIPTION HEADING 'Parameter|Description' FORMAT A35
SET LINESIZE 78
SET PAGESIZE 41
SET NEWPAGE 0
SPOOL My_Directory\INIT_ORA.lst
SELECT NAME, VALUE, ISDEFAULT, DESCRIPTION,
       TO_CHAR (SysDate, 'fmMonth ddth, YYYY') TODAY
       FROM V$PARAMETER
       ORDER BY NAME;
SPOOL OFF
```

FIGURE 4.12: Script for Listing Initialization Parameters

Figure 4.13 shows a partial listing of the contents of the parameter file.

```
May 17th, 2001    Initialization Parameter Listing for EXAMPLE Database    Page 1
Parameter                 Parameter          Default     Parameter
Name                      Value              Value       Description
----------------------    --------------     --------    --------------
always_anti_join          NESTED_LOOPS       FALSE       always use this
                                                         anti-join when
                                                         possible
audit_trail               TRUE               FALSE       enable system
                                                         auditing
b_tree_bitmap_plans       FALSE              TRUE        enable the use
                                                         of bitmap plans
                                                         for tables w.
                                                         only B-tree
                                                         indexes
blank_trimming            FALSE              TRUE        blank trimming
                                                         semantics
                                                         parameter
cache_size_threshold      480                FALSE       maximum size of
                                                         table or piece
                                                         to be cached (in
                                                         blocks)
checkpoint_process        TRUE               FALSE       create a
                                                         separate
                                                         checkpoint
                                                         process
```

FIGURE 4.13: Partial Listing of init<instance name>.ora File

Key Words

alert log file
ARCH
ARCHIVELOG
background process
checkpoint
CKPT
control file
data block buffer
data dictionary
database transaction
datafile
DBWR

initialization parameter
instance
LGWR
library cache
log switch
memory cache
Optimal Flexible Architecture
redo log buffer
redo log file
rollback segment
SGA
shared SQL pool

SMON
temporary segment
trace file
UGA

user object
V$ view
X$ table

References and Further Reading

1. E. Aronoff et al.—*Advanced Oracle Tuning and Administration*, Oracle Press, 1997.
2. M. R. Ault—*Oracle8 Black Book*, Coriolis Group Books, 1998.
3. K. Loney—*Oracle 8i DBA Handbook*, Oracle Press, 2000.
4. R. J. Niemiec—*Oracle Performance Tuning*, Oracle Press, 1999.

Loney [3, Chapter 1] offers a good discussion of the Oracle instance and the database. Also, Loney [3, Chapter 3] discusses the Optimal Flexible Architecture introduced by Oracle Corporation. A good treatment of the V$ views, the X$ tables, and the initialization parameters can be found in Aronoff et al. [1, Chapters 3 and 7] and Ault [2, Chapter 9]. Niemiec [8] is almost encyclopedic in nature. Most of its chapters are labeled with the target readers such as Beginner Developer and Beginner DBA, Developer and DBA, DBA, and Advanced DBA. Specifically, Niemiec [8, Chapter 4] discusses the initialization parameters from a tuning aspect.

Exercises

The exercises given below identify some of the areas not specifically covered in Chapter 4 and should be considered an extension of the text.

1. A *user schema* in a database is defined as a collection of all database objects owned by the *user*. The data dictionary view DBA_TABLES contains information about all tables created by all the users of the database. How can you query DBA_TABLES to extract information about all the tables created by a particular user?
2. Which of the following two statements is true? Why?
   a. An instance can be associated with multiple databases.
   b. A database can be associated with multiple instances.
3. Which of the following two statements is true? Why?
   a. A log switch enforces a checkpoint.
   b. A checkpoint enforces a log switch.
4. The *init.ora* file is created for an instance. How does the instance identify its database?
5. How can you tell by looking at the *init.ora* file whether a database runs in the ARCHIVELOG mode?
6. What is the difference between an alert log file and a user trace file with respect to the information content of the files?

5
Tuning of Disk Resident Data Structures

Outline

5.1 Disk-Resident Data Structures
5.2 Performance Tuning of Disk-Resident Data Structures
5.3 Baseline of Disk-Resident Data Structure
5.4 Changes to Database Schema
5.5 Data Block Structure
5.6 Used Space Fragmentation at the Segment Level
5.7 Severity of Free Space Shortage
5.8 Free Space Fragmentation at Tablespace Level
5.9 Row Chaining and Row Migration in Tables
5.10 Performance Tuning of Rollback Segments
Key Words
References and Further Reading
Exercises

Overview of the Chapter

The chapter covers the performance tuning and optimization of the components of an Oracle database, primarily the segments and the tablespaces. The monitoring and tuning of the storage space are addressed at two levels: the used space of the segments and the free space in the tablespaces. After discussing the underlying monitoring and tuning principles the chapter includes a large number of SQL scripts to implement these principles. The sizing and the number of the rollback segments are covered in detail with a special emphasis on the Oracle error ORA-01555: "snapshot too old."

5.1 Disk-Resident Data Structures

As noted in Section 4.3, the Oracle database consists of a set of data files residing in auxiliary storage as disk files. They include the data files used by various types of tablespaces such as the data, the index, the rollback, the system, the temporary, etc. Performance tuning is needed primarily for the data, index, and rollback tablespaces. The temporary segment residing in the temporary tablespace grows and shrinks depending on the database activities. For example, when a large sort takes place, the temporary segment may use most of its space. But the space is made available when the sort operation is finished. The system tablespace should contain only the Oracle data dictionary, the V$ views, and other Oracle internal objects. The DBA can enforce that no user-defined objects reside in the system tablespace (see Section 5.3.8). Consequently, the performance tuning activities for the disk-resident data structures are aimed almost exclusively at the data, index, and rollback tablespaces.

5.2 Performance Tuning of Disk-Resident Data Structures

The space used by the data structures in auxiliary storage falls into two categories: used space at the segment level and free space at the tablespace level. The performance is affected by fragmentation of both. So, the DBA needs to follow a systematic procedure to track the fragmentation and take corrective action. The following five steps establish such an approach.

- Establish the baseline of the database (Sections 5.3 to 5.3.7).
- Monitor all changes to the database at the schema level and update the conceptual level accordingly. The conceptual and the internal levels must always match on schema, i.e., tables, indices, views, constraints, functions, procedures, packages, package bodies, sequences, and synonyms (Section 5.4).
- Monitor used space fragmentation at the segment level and take corrective action (Sections 5.6 to 5.6.2).
- Monitor free space fragmentation at the tablespace level and take corrective action (Sections 5.7 and 5.8).
- Monitor row chaining and migration of tables and take corrective action (Sections 5.9 to 5.9.2).

Fragmentation of tables, indices, and tablespaces, and chaining and migration of tables are causes for poor performance.

5.3 Baseline of Disk-Resident Data Structures

The data structures maintained in auxiliary storage, i.e., disk files, that are subject to fragmentation are: tablespaces, tables, and indices. After the database stabilizes, run the set of scripts given in Sections 5.3.1 through 5.3.7 to establish the baseline for the stored data.

5.3.1 Datafile Location and Size

```
REM  Data File Listing for EXAMPLE Database
REM  Script File Name:    My_Directory\DATAFILE.sql
REM  Spool File Name: My_Directory\DATAFILE.lst
REM  Author:              NAME
REM  Date Created:        DATE
REM  Purpose: Information on operating system level datafiles used
REM           by the tablespaces in EXAMPLE Database
REM
REM

COLUMN TODAY      NEW_VALUE xTODAY NOPRINT FORMAT A1 TRUNC

TTITLE         LEFT xTODAY -
    RIGHT 'Page ' FORMAT 999 SQL.PNO -
    CENTER 'Data File Listing for EXAMPLE Database'  SKIP 4
BTITLE 'Script File: My_Directory\DATAFILE.sql|
       Spool File: My_Directory\DATAFILE.lst'

COLUMN TABLESPACE_NAME HEADING 'Tablespace|Name' FORMAT A16
COLUMN FILE_NAME HEADING 'File|Name' FORMAT A45
COLUMN BLOCKS HEADING 'File Size in|Oracle Blocks' FORMAT
    999,999,999

BREAK ON TABLESPACE_NAME SKIP 1

SET LINESIZE 78
SET PAGESIZE 41
SET NEWPAGE 0
SPOOL My_Directory\DATAFILE.lst

SELECT TABLESPACE_NAME, FILE_NAME, BLOCKS,
    TO_CHAR (SysDate, 'fmMonth ddth, YYYY') TODAY
    FROM SYS.DBA_DATA_FILES
    ORDER BY TABLESPACE_NAME, FILE_NAME;

SPOOL OFF
```

FIGURE 5.1: Script for Datafile Location and Size

Figure 5.2 shows the sample output from the script file shown in Figure 5.1.

84   5. Tuning of Disk-Resident Data Structures

```
May 17th, 2001    Data File Listing for EXAMPLE Database    Page 1
Tablespace        File                                      File Size in
Name              Name                                      Oracle Blocks
----------        ----------------------------              ------------
EXPLORE_DATA      D:\ORANT\DATABASE\USR2ORCL.ORA            50
                  D:\ORANT\DATABASE\USR3ORCL.ORA            2,560
ROLLBACK_DATA     D:\ORANT\DATABASE\RBS1ORCL.ORA            2,560
SYSTEM            D:\ORANT\DATABASE\SYS1ORCL.ORA            10,240
TEMPORARY_DATA    D:\ORANT\DATABASE\TMP1ORCL.ORA            1,024
USER_DATA         D:\ORANT\DATABASE\USR1ORCL.ORA            1,536
Script File:  My_Directory\DATAFILE.sql
Spool File:   My_Directory\DATAFILE.lst
```

FIGURE 5.2: Datafile Listing for EXAMPLE Database

The report shows that EXPLORE_DATA has two datafiles allocated to it, and the other four tablespaces have one datafile each.

5.3.2 Tablespaces with Information on Extents

```
REM    Tablespace Extent Listing for EXAMPLE Database
REM    Script File Name:    My_Directory\TABLESPC.sql
REM    Spool File Name: My_Directory \TABLESPC.lst
REM    Author:              NAME
REM    Date Created:        DATE
REM    Purpose:             Information on the tablespace extents
                            in EXAMPLE database
REM
REM
COLUMN TODAY   NEW_VALUE xTODAY NOPRINT FORMAT A1 TRUNC

TTITLE LEFT xTODAY -
       RIGHT 'Page ' FORMAT 999 SQL.PNO -
       CENTER 'Tablespace Extents for EXAMPLE Database'    SKIP 4
BTITLE 'Script File: My_Directory \TABLESPC.sql|
       Spool File: My_Directory\TABLESPC.lst'
COLUMN TABLESPACE_NAME HEADING 'Tablespace|Name' FORMAT A16
COLUMN INITIAL_EXTENT HEADING 'Initial|Extent' FORMAT 999,999,999
COLUMN NEXT_EXTENT HEADING 'Next|Extent' FORMAT 999,999,999
COLUMN MAX_EXTENTS HEADING 'Max|ExtentS' FORMAT 999,999,999,999
```

FIGURE 5.3: Script for Listing Tablespaces with Extent Information

5.3 Baseline of Disk-Resident Data Structures

```
BREAK ON TABLESPACE_NAME SKIP 1

SET LINESIZE 78
SET PAGESIZE 41
SET NEWPAGE 0

SPOOL My_Directory\TABLESPC.lst

SELECT TABLESPACE_NAME, INITIAL_EXTENT, NEXT_EXTENT, MAX_EXTENTS,
       TO_CHAR (SysDate, 'fmMonth ddth, YYYY') TODAY
       FROM DBA_TABLESPACES
       ORDER BY TABLESPACE_NAME;
SPOOL OFF
```

FIGURE 5.3 (*continued*): Script for Listing Tablespaces with Extent Information

Figure 5.4 shows the sample output from the script shown in Figure 5.3.

```
May 17th, 2001       Tablespace Extent Listing for EXAMPLE Database      Page 1
Tablespace           Initia                      Next                Max
Name                 Extent                      Extent              Extents
-----------          ---------                   --------            --------
EXPLORE_DATA         516,096                     5,120,000           505
ROLLBACK_DATA        40,960                      40,960              505
SYSTEM               16,384                      16,384              505
TEMPORARY_DATA       40,960                      40,960              505
USER_DATA            40,960                      40,960              505
        Script File: My_Directory\TABLESPC.sql
        Spool File: My_Directory \TABLESPC.lst
```

FIGURE 5.4: Tablespace Extent Listing for EXAMPLE Database

The report shows the size of the initial and next extents of each tablespace in bytes. Each tablespace can claim up to 505 extents depending on available space in its datafile(s).

5.3.3 Segments with Information on Extents

```
REM     Segment Extent Listing for EXAMPLE Database
REM     Script File Name:   My_Directory\SEGEXTN.sql
REM     Spool File Name: My_Directory\SEGEXTN.lst
REM     Author:         NAME
REM     Date Created:       DATE
REM     Purpose: Information on initial, next, and max extents of
REM              segments (tables and indices) in EXAMPLE Database
REM
REM
COLUMN TODAY    NEW_VALUE xTODAY NOPRINT FORMAT A1 TRUNC

TTITLE          LEFT xTODAY -
      RIGHT 'Page ' FORMAT 999 SQL.PNO -
      CENTER 'Segment Extents for EXAMPLE Database '  SKIP 4
BTITLE 'Script File: My_Directory\SEGEXTN.sql|
      Spool File: My_Directory\SEGEXTN.lst'
COLUMN TABLESPACE_NAME HEADING 'Tablespace|Name' FORMAT A12
COLUMN SEGMENT_NAME HEADING 'Segment|Name' FORMAT A20
COLUMN INITIAL_EXTENT HEADING 'Initial|Extent' FORMAT 999,999,999
COLUMN NEXT_EXTENT HEADING 'Next|Extent' FORMAT 999,999,999
COLUMN MAX_EXTENTS HEADING 'Max|Extents' FORMAT 999,999,999,999

BREAK ON TABLESPACE_NAME SKIP 2

SET LINESIZE 78
SET PAGESIZE 41
SET NEWPAGE 0

SPOOL My_Directory\SEGEXTN.lst

SELECT TABLESPACE_NAME, SEGMENT_NAME, INITIAL_EXTENT, NEXT_EXTENT,
      MAX_EXTENTS, TO_CHAR (SysDate, 'fmMonth ddth, YYYY') TODAY
      FROM DBA_SEGMENTS WHERE
      SEGMENT_TYPE = 'TABLE' OR SEGMENT_TYPE = 'INDEX'
      AND TABLESPACE_NAME != 'SYSTEM'
      ORDER BY TABLESPACE_NAME, SEGMENT_NAME;

SPOOL OFF
```

FIGURE 5.5: Script for Listing Segments with Extent Information

Figure 5.6 shows a partial listing of the report against the EXAMPLE database.

```
May 17th, 2001      Segment Extents for EXAMPLE Database        Page 1
Tablespace       Segment         Initial         Next            Max
Name             Name            Extent          Extent          Extents
----------       ----------      ----------      ----------      --------
USER_DATA        BONUS           10,240          10,240          505
                 CALL            10,240          10,240          505
                 CALLER          10,240          10,240          505
                 CALL_CSR        10,240          10,240          505
                 CSR             10,240          10,240          505
                 CUSTOMER        10,240          10,240          505
         Script File: My_Directory\SEGEXTN.sql
         Spool File: My_Directory\SEGEXTN.lst
```

FIGURE 5.6: Segment Extent Listing for EXAMPLE Database

Figure 5.6 provides the same information for segments that Figure 5.4 provides for tablespaces.

5.3.4 Segments with Information on Extent Allocation

```
REM  Tablespace, Segment, and Extent Listing in EXAMPLE Database
REM  Script File Name:  My_Directory\SEG_FRAG.sql
REM  Spool File Name:   My_Directory \SEG_FRAG.lst
REM  Author:            NAME
REM  Date Created:      DATE
REM  Purpose:   Information on tablespace segments and their
REM  associated extents created on all objects in EXAMPLE database.
REM  Note:   Segment = Table, Index, Rollback, Temporary
REM

COLUMN TODAY    NEW_VALUE xTODAY NOPRINT FORMAT A1 TRUNC

TTITLE LEFT xTODAY -
    RIGHT 'Page ' FORMAT 999 SQL.PNO -
    CENTER 'Tablespace Segment and Extent - EXAMPLE Database'
    SKIP 4
BTITLE 'Script File: My_Directory \SEG_FRAG.sql|
    Spool File: My_Directory\SEG_FRAG.lst'
COLUMN TABLESPACE_NAME HEADING 'Tablespace|Name' FORMAT A15
COLUMN SEGMENT_NAME HEADING 'Segment|Name' FORMAT A25
COLUMN SEGMENT_TYPE HEADING 'Segment|Type' FORMAT A8
COLUMN EXTENT_ID HEADING 'Ext|ID' FORMAT 999
COLUMN EXTENTS HEADING 'Ext' FORMAT 999
COLUMN BLOCKS HEADING 'Blocks' FORMAT 999,999
```

FIGURE 5.7: Script for Listing Segments with Extent Allocation

```
BREAK ON TABLESPACE_NAME SKIP 3 ON SEGMENT_TYPE SKIP 2 -
    ON SEGMENT_NAME SKIP 0
SET LINESIZE 78
SET PAGESIZE 41
SET NEWPAGE 0

SPOOL My_Directory\SEG_FRAG.lst

SELECT a.TABLESPACE_NAME, a.SEGMENT_TYPE, a.SEGMENT_NAME, EXTENTS,
    a.BLOCKS, EXTENT_ID, b.BLOCKS,
    TO_CHAR (SysDate, 'fmMonth ddth, YYYY') TODAY
    FROM DBA_SEGMENTS a, DBA_EXTENTS b
    WHERE
    a.TABLESPACE_NAME = b.TABLESPACE_NAME    AND
    a.SEGMENT_TYPE = b.SEGMENT_TYPE          AND
    a.SEGMENT_NAME = b.SEGMENT_NAME          AND
    a.TABLESPACE_NAME != 'SYSTEM'
    ORDER BY a.TABLESPACE_NAME, a.SEGMENT_TYPE, a.SEGMENT_NAME,
EXTENT_ID;

SPOOL OFF
```

FIGURE 5.7 (*continued*): Script for Listing Segments with Extent Allocation

Figure 5.8 shows a partial listing of the sample report from the EXAMPLE database,

May 17th, 2001		Tablespace Segment and Extent - EXAMPLE Database				Page 1
Tablespace Name	Segment Type	Segment Name	Ext	Blocks	Ext ID	Blocks
---	---	---	---	---	---	---
ROLLBACK_DATA	ROLLBACK	RB1	2	150	0	25
			2	150	1	125
		RB2	2	150	0	25
			2	150	1	125
		RB3	2	150	0	25
			2	150	1	125
		RB4	2	150	0	25
			2	150	1	125
		RB5	2	150	0	25
USER_DATA	INDEX	PK_EMP	1	5	0	5
		SYS_C00532	1	5	0	5
		SYS_C00535	1	5	0	5

FIGURE 5.8: Extent Allocation for Segments

```
USER_DATA        TABLE      BONUS       1       5       0           5
                            CALL        1       5       0       5
                            CALLER      1       5       0           5
                            CALL_CSR    1       5       0           5
                            CSR         1       5       0           5
                            CUSTOMER    1       5       0           5
                 Script File: My_Directory\SEG_FRAG.sql
                 Spool File:  My_Directory \SEG_FRAG.lst
```

FIGURE 5.8 (*continued*): Extent Allocation for Segments

and provides a complete map of the extents allocated to each segment. For example, the rollback segment RB1 has two extents comprising 150 blocks of storage (one block = 2,048 bytes). This space is taken from the datafile D:\ORANT\DATABASE\ RBS1ORCL.ORA of size 2,560 blocks assigned to the tablespace ROLLBACK_DATA (see Figure 5.2). The two extents are identified by their Extent IDs of 0 and 1. Similarly, the segment CALL has one extent of size 5 blocks and with Extent ID of 0. This space is taken from the datafile of the tablespace USER_DATA containing the segment CALL. Oracle always assigns sequential values to Extent IDs starting with 0.

5.3.5 Table Structure Listing

```
REM     Table Structure Listing for EXAMPLE Database
REM     Script File Name:   My_Directory\TBL_STRC.sql
REM     Spool File Name:    My_Directory\TBL_STRC.lst
REM     Author:             NAME
REM     Date Created:       DATE
REM     Purpose:            Complete listing of tables with their
REM                         column names and data types in EXAMPLE
REM                         Database
REM
COLUMN TODAY     NEW_VALUE xTODAY NOPRINT FORMAT A1 TRUNC
TTITLE LEFT xTODAY -
    RIGHT 'Page ' FORMAT 999 SQL.PNO -
    CENTER 'Table Structures in EXAMPLE Database' SKIP 4
BTITLE 'Script File: My_Directory\TBL_STRC.sql|
    Spool File: My_Directory\TBL_STRC.lst'
COLUMN S_TABLE HEADING 'Table Name' FORMAT A20
```

FIGURE 5.9: Script for Listing Table Structures

```
COLUMN COLUMN_NAME HEADING 'Column Name' FORMAT A25
COLUMN COL_DATA HEADING 'Column|Size' FORMAT A20
COLUMN NULLABLE HEADING 'Null?' FORMAT A6

BREAK ON TABLE_NAME SKIP 1

SET LINESIZE 78
SET PAGESIZE 41
SET NEWPAGE 0

SPOOL My_Directory\TBL_STRC.lst

SELECT a.TABLE_NAME S_TABLE, COLUMN_NAME,
    DATA_TYPE || '(' || DATA_LENGTH || ')' COL_DATA, NULLABLE,
    TO_CHAR (SysDate, 'fmMonth ddth, YYYY') TODAY
    FROM DBA_TABLES a, DBA_TAB_COLUMNS b
    WHERE a.TABLE_NAME = b.TABLE_NAME
    ORDER BY 1;

SPOOL OFF
```

FIGURE 5.9 (*continued*): Script for Listing Table Structures

Figure 5.9 gives the table structure listing and Figure 5.10 shows a sample report for EXAMPLE database.

```
May 17th, 2001     Table Structures in EXAMPLE Database      Page 1
Table Name         Column Name        Column Size           Null?
------------       -----------        ---------------       -----
AUDIT_ACTIONS      ACTION             NUMBER(22)            N
                   NAME               VARCHAR2(27)          N

DBMS_ALERT_INFO    NAME               VARCHAR2(30)          N
                   SID                VARCHAR2(30)          N
                   CHANGED            VARCHAR2(1)           Y
                   MESSAGE            VARCHAR2(1800)        Y

INCEXP             OWNER#             NUMBER(22)            N
                   NAME               VARCHAR2(30)          N
                   TYPE#              NUMBER(22)            N
                   CTIME              DATE(7)               Y
                   ITIME              DATE(7)               N
                   EXPID              NUMBER(22)            N
```

FIGURE 5.10: Table Structures in EXAMPLE Database

Each table in Figure 5.10 is listed with its column names, column data types, and an indication if a column can remain blank.

5.3.6 Index Structure Listing

```
REM    Index Listing for EXAMPLE Database
REM    Script File Name:   My_Directory\INDXRPT.sql
REM    Spool File Name:    My_Directory \INDXRPT.lst
REM    Author:             NAME
REM    Date Created:       DATE
REM    Purpose:            Information on index names and structures
REM                        used in tables in EXAMPLE Database
REM
REM
COLUMN TODAY      NEW_VALUE xTODAY NOPRINT FORMAT A1 TRUNC

TTITLE            LEFT xTODAY -
     RIGHT 'Page ' FORMAT 999 SQL.PNO -
     CENTER 'Index Listing for EXAMPLE Database '     SKIP 4
BTITLE 'Script File: My_Directory\INDXRPT.sql|Spool File:
     My_Directory\INDXRPT.lst'
COLUMN TABLE_NAME HEADING 'Table|Name' FORMAT A20
COLUMN INDEX_NAME HEADING 'Index|Name' FORMAT A20
COLUMN COLUMN_NAME HEADING 'Column|Name' FORMAT A20
COLUMN COLUMN_POSITION HEADING 'Column|Position' FORMAT 999
COLUMN COLUMN_LENGTH HEADING 'Column|Length' FORMAT 9,999

BREAK ON TABLE_NAME SKIP 1 ON INDEX_NAME SKIP 0

SET LINESIZE 78
SET PAGESIZE 41
SET NEWPAGE 0

SPOOL My_Directory\INDXRPT.lst

SELECT TABLE_NAME, INDEX_NAME, COLUMN_NAME, COLUMN_POSITION,
COLUMN_LENGTH,
     TO_CHAR (SysDate, 'fmMonth ddth, YYYY') TODAY
     FROM DBA_IND_COLUMNS
     ORDER BY TABLE_NAME, INDEX_NAME;

SPOOL OFF
```

FIGURE 5.11: Script for Listing Index Structure

Figure 5.11 gives the index structure listing and Figure 5.12 shows a partial report for the EXAMPLE database.

```
May 17th, 2001        Index Listing for EXAMPLE Database         Page 1
Table          Index        Column           Column           Column
Name           Name         Name             Position         Length
---------      ----------   ---------        -------          ------
CALL           SYS_C00709   CALL_ID          1                5
CALLER         SYS_C00698   CALLER_ID        1                10
CALL_CSR       SYS_C00696   CALL_ID          1                5
                            CSR_ID           2                10
CSR            SYS_C00700   CSR_ID           1                10
DEPT           PK_DEPT      DEPTNO           1                22
EMP            PK_EMP       EMPNO            1                22
EMPLOYEE       I_EMPLOYEE   EMPLOYEE_ID      1                22
               SYS_C00702   EMPLOYEE_ID      1                10
      Script File: My_Directory\INDXRPT.sql
      Spool File: My_Directory\INDXRPT.lst
```

FIGURE 5.12: Index Listing for EXAMPLE Database

Figure 5.12 shows, for example, that CALL_ID is a single column index in CALL, and (CALL_ID, CSR_ID) is a two-column composite index in CALL_CSR.

5.3.7 Constraint Listing

```
REM  Constraint Listing for EXAMPLE Database
REM  Script File Name:   My_Directory\CONSTRAINT.sql
REM  Spool File Name:    My_Directory\CONSTRAINT.lst
REM  Author:             NAME
REM  Date Created:       DATE
REM  Purpose:    Information on constraints created on all tables in
REM              EXAMPLE database
REM
REM

COLUMN TODAY     NEW_VALUE xTODAY NOPRINT FORMAT A1 TRUNC

TTITLE LEFT xTODAY -
    RIGHT 'Page ' FORMAT 999 SQL.PNO -
    CENTER 'Constraint Listing for EXAMPLE Database' SKIP 4
BTITLE 'Script File: My_Directory\CONSTRAINT.sql|
    Spool File: My_Directory\CONSTRAINT.lst'
COLUMN TABLE_NAME HEADING 'Table Name' FORMAT A12
COLUMN CONSTRAINT_NAME HEADING 'Constraint|Name' FORMAT A12
COLUMN CONSTRAINT_TYPE HEADING 'Type' FORMAT A4
COLUMN COLUMN_NAME HEADING 'Column Name' FORMAT A12
COLUMN COLUMN_POSITION HEADING 'Column|Position' FORMAT 999
```

FIGURE 5.13: Script for Listing Constraints

```
COLUMN DELETE_RULE HEADING 'Delete|Rule' FORMAT A12
BREAK ON TABLE_NAME SKIP 2
SET LINESIZE 78
SET PAGESIZE 41
SET NEWPAGE 0
SPOOL My_Directory \CONSTRAINT.lst
SELECT a.TABLE_NAME, a.CONSTRAINT_NAME, CONSTRAINT_TYPE,
    COLUMN_NAME, POSITION, DELETE_RULE,
    TO_CHAR (SysDate, 'fmMonth ddth, YYYY') TODAY
    FROM DBA_CONSTRAINTS a, DBA_CONS_COLUMNS b WHERE
    a.CONSTRAINT_NAME = b.CONSTRAINT_NAME  AND
    a.TABLE_NAME = b.TABLE_NAME
    ORDER BY TABLE_NAME, CONSTRAINT_NAME;
SPOOL OFF
```

FIGURE 5.13 (*continued*): Script for Listing Constraints

The script for listing constraints is provided in Figure 5.13, and Figure 5.14 shows a sample partial report for the EXAMPLE database, showing the constraints for each table. Unless the user gives a name for a constraint, Oracle assigns a name in the format SYS_Cnnnnnn, where n is an integer. The type of a constraint can be C for CHECK, P for primary key, R for foreign key, U for unique index, and N for the NOT NULL requirement. Thus, Figure 5.14 shows that CALL_ID is the single column primary key of CALL, (CALL_ID, CSR_ID) is the two-column primary key of CALL_CSR, CSR_ID is a foreign key in CALL_CSR, etc. We recall that this information matches the corresponding information from Figure 5.12.

```
May 17th, 2001         Constraint Listing for EXAMPLE Database  Page 4
Table        Constraint     Column                                Delete
Name         Name           Type     Name          POSITION       Rule
------       ----------     ------   ------        ---------      ------
CALL         SYS_C00707     C        CALL_ID
             SYS_C00708     C        CALLER_ID
             SYS_C00709     P        CALL_ID       1

CALLER       SYS_C00697     C        CALLER_ID
             SYS_C00698     P        CALLER_ID     1
```

FIGURE 5.14: Constraint Listing for EXAMPLE Database

```
CALL_CSR   SYS_C00694   C      CALL_ID
           SYS_C00695   C      CSR_ID
           SYS_C00696   P      CSR_ID       2
           SYS_C00696   P      CALL_ID      1
           SYS_C00705   R      CSR_ID       1         NO ACTION
CSR        SYS_C00699   C      CSR_ID
           SYS_C00700   P      CSR_ID       1
           SYS_C00706   R      EMPLOYEE_ID  1         NO ACTION
        Script File: My_Directory\CONSTRAINT.sql
        Spool File: My_Directory \CONSTRAINT.lst
```

FIGURE 5.14 (*continued*): Constraint Listing for EXAMPLE Database

5.3.8 User Objects in SYSTEM Tablespace

Oracle uses the SYSTEM tablespace to store database objects needed for database administration. No user objects should be stored in this tablespace. However, database objects created by any Oracle or third party tools use SYSTEM as the default database account and, therefore, any objects created by them use SYSTEM as the tablespace. To prevent this situation, designate TOOLS as the default tablespace for the SYSTEM account and reduce the quota of this account on SYSTEM tablespace to zero by running the following command.

```
alter user SYSTEM
quota 30M on TOOLS
quota 0 on SYSTEM
default tablespace TOOLS
temporary tablespace TEMP;
```

As a result, no database objects can be created by the SYSTEM account on the SYSTEM tablespace. Oracle's Optimal Flexible Architecture described in Section 4.3 recommends this policy.

Run the script in Figure 5.15 to determine if any user has SYSTEM as its default or temporary tablespace:

```
REM     SYSTEM tablespace used by users
REM     Script File Name:   My_Directory\SYSTEM_User_Objects.sql
REM     Spool File Name:    My_Directory\SYSTEM_User_Objects.lst
REM     Author:             NAME
REM     Date Created:       DATE
REM     Purpose:            Find if SYSTEM tablespace is used by any
REM                         user
REM                         as the default or temporary tablespace
REM
```

FIGURE 5.15: Script for Listing Users of SYSTEM Tablespace

```
COLUMN TODAY  NEW_VALUE xTODAY NOPRINT FORMAT A1 TRUNC
TTITLE LEFT xTODAY -
       RIGHT 'Page ' FORMAT 999 SQL.PNO -
       CENTER 'User Objects in SYSTEM Tablespace'     SKIP 4
BTITLE 'Script File: My_Directory\SYSTEM_User_Objects.sql|
        Spool File: My_Directory\SYSTEM_User_Objects.lst'
COLUMN USERNAME FORMAT A15
COLUMN DEFAULT_TABLESPACE HEADING 'Default|Tablespace' FORMAT A15
COLUMN TEMPORARY_TABLESPACE HEADING 'Temporary|Tablespace' FORMAT
       A15
SET LINESIZE 78
SET PAGESIZE 41
SET NEWPAGE 0
SPOOL My_Directory\SYSTEM_User_Objects.lst
select username, TO_CHAR (created, 'DD-MON-YYYY') "Created  ",
       default_tablespace, temporary_tablespace,
       TO_CHAR (SysDate, 'fmMonth ddth, YYYY') TODAY
       from dba_users where
       (dba_users.DEFAULT_TABLESPACE = 'SYSTEM'   or
       dba_users.TEMPORARY_TABLESPACE = 'SYSTEM')  and
       dba_users.USERNAME not in ('SYS', 'SYSTEM');
spool off
```

FIGURE 5.15 (*continued*): Script for Listing Users of SYSTEM Tablespace

If this script returns any user name, change its default or temporary tablespace to TOOLS via the ALTER USER command.

5.4 Changes to Database Schema

By running the script files listed in Sections 5.3.1 through 5.3.7 we get certain information about the database schema:

(a) Storage used by tablespaces and segments via their initial extents, next extents, and maxextents;
(b) Total disk storage allocated to the tablespaces;
(c) Actual configuration of the extents, i.e., contiguous or noncontiguous, allocated to the segments;
(d) Structures of tables and indices; and
(e) Listing of primary and foreign keys as table constraints.

As the database changes during production use, the above components also change. The DBA must track these changes by running the above script files on a regular basis. If the structure of any database object changes, it must be recorded at the conceptual level.

5.5 Data Block Structure

The data block is the lowest unit of storage for data. Its structure consists of three components:

(a) Overhead: It includes three parts, as described below:
- *Header* consisting of a common and a variable part that together contain such information as the block address, segment type, etc.;
- *Table Directory* containing information about the table(s) having rows in this block; and
- *Row Directory* containing information such as ROWIDs of the actual rows in the block using two bytes for each stored row. Since a ROWID is never reused, the space once allocated to store a ROWID is not reclaimed when that row is deleted;

(b) Row Data: This part of the data block contains the actual data in the table or index;

(c) Free Space: This part is reserved for inserting new rows or updating existing rows by replacing column(s) that were NULL before.

Two parameters, both of which are parts of the CREATE TABLE command, control the free space in a data block: PCTFREE and PCTUSED. PCTFREE (default = 10) sets the percentage of a data block that is reserved for possible updates of currently existing rows. PCTUSED (default = 40) sets the minimum percentage of a data block that can be used for row data plus overhead before new rows can be added to the block. PCTFREE and PCTUSED work together to optimize the space utilization within a data block. Also, PCTFREE + PCTUSED cannot exceed 100.

5.6 Used Space Fragmentation at the Segment Level

A segment is a table, an index, a rollback segment, or a temporary segment. When it is created, it is assigned a storage space S computed by the formula:

$$S = INITIAL + NEXT * (MINEXTENTS - 1)$$

If the segment is created without an initial extent and a next extent of its own, then those of its holding tablespace work as its default initial and next extents. As the segment gets populated, its allocated storage space S becomes full and another next extent is assigned to it for storage. The process continues as more and more rows are inserted into a segment. The extents allocated to a segment are never released for reuse until the segment is dropped or truncated. As a result, when rows are deleted from a table without dropping the table, the emptied space remains allocated to the table instead of being returned as free space to the holding tablespace. This phenomenon can make the used space in the table full of "holes". The analogy of Swiss cheese is often used to describe the situation. When a table is truncated, the option DROP STORAGE is the default. Consequently, a truncated table retains its structure, but releases its storage space for reuse. If it is necessary to retain the storage space of a truncated table instead of releasing it, then use the option REUSE STORAGE with the TRUNCATE command. This becomes useful if a table is truncated and immediately afterward is populated with new data. By using the REUSE STORAGE option Oracle avoids the overhead involved in first reclaiming the truncated space and then immediately allocating new space for storing the new data.

For each table, Oracle maintains one or more linked lists for free data blocks available within the extents allocated to the table. These blocks are used for INSERTs to the table. FREELISTS, a parameter of the CREATE TABLE command with a default value of 1, represents the number of these linked lists. Each INSERT statement refers to the FREELISTS to identify an available block.

5.6.1 Rules for Tracking Fragmentation

When the data belonging to a table are scattered over many noncontiguous extents, the used space of the segment becomes fragmented and the data retrieval takes longer. A rule of thumb is that a segment with 100 or more extents is starting to get fragmented and should, therefore, be examined for defragmentation. This leads us to the following rule:

(a) Run the script in Figure 5.7 regularly to monitor the number of extents ("Ext" column in Figure 5.8) allocated to each segment. Identify the segments for which this number exceeds 100.
(b) For each segment identified in step (a), run the script of Figure 5.16. Its output (see Figure 5.17 and its accompanying analysis below) lists each segment with all of its extents identified with their Extent_IDs, Block_IDs, and sizes in Oracle blocks.
(c) If the extents allocated to a segment are mostly contiguous, the performance may not suffer. Otherwise, corrective action is necessary.

```
REM    Used Space Extent Map for EXAMPLE Database
REM    Script File Name:    My_Directory\extent_contiguity.sql
REM    Spool File Name:     My_Directory \extent_contiguity.lst
REM    Author:              NAME
REM    Date Created:        DATE
REM    Purpose:             For each segment, list all its extents
REM                         by Extent_ID REM and Block_ID
REM    Note: Segment = Table, Index
REM
```

FIGURE 5.16: Script for Listing Used Space Extents

```
COLUMN TODAY  NEW_VALUE xTODAY NOPRINT FORMAT A1 TRUNC
TTITLE LEFT xTODAY -
      RIGHT 'Page ' FORMAT 999 SQL.PNO -
      CENTER ' Used Space Extent Map - EXAMPLE Database' SKIP 4
BTITLE 'Script File: My_Directory\ extent_contiguity.sql|
      Spool File: My_Directory\ extent_contiguity.lst'
COLUMN SEGMENT_NAME HEADING 'Segment|Name' FORMAT A25
COLUMN SEGMENT_TYPE HEADING 'Segment|Type' FORMAT A8
COLUMN EXTENT_ID HEADING 'Ext|ID' FORMAT 999
COLUMN BLOCK_ID HEADING 'Block|ID' FORMAT 99999
COLUMN EXTENTS HEADING 'Ext' FORMAT 999
COLUMN BLOCKS HEADING 'Blocks' FORMAT 999,999
BREAK ON SEGMENT_NAME SKIP 0 ON SEGMENT_TYPE SKIP 0 -
      ON EXTENTS SKIP 0
SET LINESIZE 78
SET PAGESIZE 41
SET NEWPAGE 0
SPOOL My_Directory\extent_contiguity.lst
SELECT a.SEGMENT_NAME, a.SEGMENT_TYPE, EXTENTS, EXTENT_ID,
      Block_ID, b.BLOCKS,
      TO_CHAR (SysDate, 'fmMonth ddth, YYYY') TODAY
      FROM DBA_SEGMENTS a, DBA_EXTENTS b
      WHERE
      a.SEGMENT_NAME = b.SEGMENT_NAME    AND
      a.SEGMENT_TYPE = b.SEGMENT_TYPE    AND
      a.TABLESPACE_NAME != 'SYSTEM'      AND
      a.SEGMENT_NAME NOT LIKE '%$%'
      ORDER BY a.SEGMENT_NAME, EXTENT_ID;
SPOOL OFF
```

FIGURE 5.16 (*continued*): Script for Listing Used Space Extents

The output from this script appears as Figure 5.17.

```
May 17th, 2001     Used Space Extent Map - EXAMPLE Database     Page 1
Segment          Segment                        Ext       Block
Name             Type           Ext             ID        ID        Blocks
-------          -------        -------         -----     ----      ------
BONUS            TABLE          1               0         307       5
CALL             TABLE          1               0         477       5
ITEM             TABLE          2               0         362       5
                                                1         367       5
```

FIGURE 5.17: Used Space Extent Map

```
PK_DEPT          INDEX        1         0         292          5
PK_EMP           INDEX        1         0         302          5
PRICE            TABLE        1         0         347          5
PRODUCT          TABLE        1         0         342          5
RB1              ROLLBACK     2         0           2         25
                                        1        2402        125
         Script File: My_Directory\extent_contiguity.sql
         Spool File: My_Directory\extent_contiguity.lst
```

FIGURE 5.17 (*continued*): Used Space Extent Map

When a segment has multiple extents, we can test if they are contiguous by using the following rule.

```
IF    (Block_ID) (n+1) = (Block_ID) n + (Blocks) n,
THEN  (Extent_ID) (n-1) and (Extent_ID) n are contiguous;
ELSE  (Extent_ID) (n-1) and (Extent_ID) n are not contiguous.
```

Here $(Block\_ID)_n$ is the nth Block ID within a given Ext ID, and $(Extent\_ID)_{(n-1)}$ is the nth Ext ID for a given segment, where $n = 1, 2, 3, \ldots$.

Looking at Figure 5.17 we find that the table ITEM has one extent with two blocks having the property

```
367 = (Block_ID) 2 = 362 + 5 = (Block_ID) 1 + (Blocks) 1
```

Hence its two extents with Extent_IDs 0 and 1 are contiguous. On the other hand, the rollback segment RB1 has two extents with the property

```
2402 = (Block_ID) 2 ≠ 2 + 25 = (Block_ID) 1 + (Blocks) 1
```

Hence its two extents with Extent_IDs 0 and 1 are not contiguous.

5.6.2 Corrective Action

The root cause of segment fragmentation is wrong sizing of the initial and next extents of the fragmented segments, primarily tables and rollback segments. Appendix A provides algorithms and C programs to compute the extent sizes of segments. One of the input parameters needed by the C programs in Appendix A is the ROWCOUNT of each table. Since this value is often not known during the initial sizing, an incorrect estimate of the INITIAL and NEXT extents may occur. The DBA, therefore, needs to monitor the rate of acquisition of new extents by the segments and then resize the NEXT EXTENTs, if necessary. A better estimate of the ROWCOUNTs of the tables is needed for this exercise. The following five-step methodology addresses the root cause of fragmentation.

(a) Perform a resizing of the table(s) and estimate the new value of the NEXT EXTENT for each table.

(b) Perform an export of the affected tables labeled table_1, table_2, ...,table_n, say, with the following specification

```
exp username/password file=expdat.dmp compress=Y grants=Y
indexes=Y tables=table_1,table_2,...,table_n
```

The command "exp" (short for Oracle's Export utility) exports all the n tables along with their respective indices and grants to a compressed file called expdat.dmp. The utility determines the total amount of space allocated to a table and then writes to the expdat.dmp file a newly computed INITIAL EXTENT storage parameter equal in size to the total of all the fragmented storage extents that were allocated to that table. As a result, the newly sized INITIAL EXTENTs of each table and its associated indices contain all the current data.

(c) Drop the tables table_1, table_2, ... ,table_n.

(d) Perform an import of the tables, table_1, table_2,..., table_n, with the following specification

```
imp username/password file=expdat.dmp commit=Y full=Y
buffer=1000000
```

The command "imp" (short for Oracle's Import utility) now imports the earlier exported tables with the new storage parameters. The option "full=Y" ensures that all the exported tables in expdat.dmp file are imported.

(e) For each imported table, run the command

`ALTER TABLE table_name STORAGE (NEXT size);`

where "size" is the newly computed value of the NEXT EXTENT for the table.

A few comments are in order here.

- The value of "buffer" in step (d) must be estimated according to the sizes of the tables being exported. It is usually set at a high value, say, over 200,000. Each "commit" occurs when the buffer becomes full.
- If the tables being exported do not contain columns of the LONG data type, then use the option "direct=Y" with the "exp" command. This speeds up the export process.
- Steps (c) and (d) imply that the tables, table_1, table_2, ... , table_n, are not available to the users between the instant when they are dropped and the instant when they are imported successfully. Consequently, for heavily used OLTP applications the above five-step procedure should be run when users do not access these tables, say, during late evenings (after 10 P.M.) or weekends. If the export dump file in Step (b) gets corrupted, then that step has to be repeated.
- If a table is very large, say, with millions of rows and occupying over 1 GB of space, its newly computed INITIAL EXTENT may not fit into its holding tablespace. In that case, proceed as follows.

- Using the script in Figure 5.18 find the largest chunk of contiguous blocks available in the tablespace.
- Create the table with its INITIAL EXTENT at about 70% of the largest chunk found above and its NEXT EXTENT as computed in Step (e).
- Run the "imp" command of Step (d) with the option "ignore=Y". This option causes the exported data from Step (b) to be imported into the newly created table without any problems regarding available storage. Also, it ignores error messages when the import utility finds that the table already exists.

5.7 Severity of Free Space Shortage

A segment gets its new extents from the free space belonging to its holding tablespace. Figure 5.18 contains a script along with its partial output showing the total amount of free space and the largest chunk of contiguous free space in each tablespace in a database.

```
SET LINESIZE 100
SET PAGESIZE 41
SET NEWPAGE 0
SELECT TABLESPACE_NAME TABLESPACE, ROUND (SUM (BYTES) / 1048576)
    "Free Space in MB",
    ROUND (MAX (BYTES) / 1048576) "Largest Contiguous Chunk in MB"
    FROM DBA_FREE_SPACE
    GROUP BY TABLESPACE_NAME;
OUTPUT:

TABLESPACE      Free Space in MB     Largest Contiguous Chunk in MB
----------      ----------------     ------------------------------
DATA_A                 8                            8
INDEX_A               52                           52
DATA_B                80                           40
INDEX_C              159                           10
DATA_D               100                          100
DATA_E                12                           10
RBS                  900                          270
SYSTEM                27                           26
TEMP                 995                          108
TOOLS                  9                            9
USERS                 10                           10
```

FIGURE 5.18: Status of Free Space in Tablespaces

Note that for DATA_B, INDEX_C, and RBS, the largest contiguous chunk is significantly smaller than the total free space available. This indicates some level of fragmentation of free space there. Since TEMP grows and shrinks depending on the database transactions at the time, the difference between the two columns (995 versus 108) may not be indicative of problems.

The DBA should track the usage of free space at the tablespace level and determine if more datafiles should be added to a tablespace before it runs out of its free space. Figures 5.19 and 5.21 contain two scripts that provide information that will help the DBA in this respect.

5.7.1 Free Space Left in Segments

The script shown in Figure 5.19 lists for each tablespace except SYSTEM the amount of free space in bytes for all the segments after the next largest extent is allocated.

```
REM    Free Space Left for EXAMPLE Database
REM    Script File Name:  My_Directory\Free_Space_Left_Segment.sql
REM    Spool File Name:   My_Directory\Free_Space_Left_Segment.lst
REM    Author:            NAME
REM    Date Created:      DATE
REM    Purpose:           Information on the amount of space left in
REM                       each tablespace after the next largest
REM                       extent of any segment in the tablespace is
REM                       allocated.
REM
COLUMN TODAY    NEW_VALUE xTODAY NOPRINT FORMAT A1 TRUNC
TTITLE   LEFT xTODAY -
     RIGHT 'Page ' FORMAT 999 SQL.PNO -
     CENTER 'Free Space Left in Tablespaces'   SKIP 4
BTITLE    'Script File: My_Directory\Free_Space_Left_Segment.sql
     Spool File: My_Directory\Free_Space_Left_Segment.lst'
COLUMN TABLESPACE_NAME HEADING 'Tablespace|Name' FORMAT A16
COLUMN SEGMENT_NAME HEADING 'Segment|Name' FORMAT A20
BREAK ON TABLESPACE_NAME SKIP 1 ON SEGMENT_NAME SKIP 0
SET LINESIZE 78
SET PAGESIZE 41
SET NEWPAGE 0
SPOOL My_Directory\Free_Space_Left_Segment.lst
```

FIGURE 5.19: Script Listing Free Space in Segments

```
select f.tablespace_name, segment_name,
      (max (f.bytes) - max (next_extent) ) "Bytes Left",
      max (next_extent) "Next Extent",
      TO_CHAR (SysDate, 'fmMonth ddth, YYYY') TODAY
   from dba_free_space f, dba_segments t
   where f.tablespace_name in
      (select distinct tablespace_name from dba_free_space)
      and t.tablespace_name = f.tablespace_name
      and t.tablespace_name != 'SYSTEM'
   group by f.tablespace_name, segment_name, next_extent
   order by 1, 2;
SPOOL OFF
```

FIGURE 5.19 (*continued*): Script Listing Free Space in Segments

Figure 5.20 shows a sample output from this script.

```
May 17th, 2001       Free Space Left in Tablespaces       Page 1
Tablespace        Segment                    Bytes           Next
Name              Name                       Left            Extent
-----------       -------------------        -------         --------
DATA              BUSINESS_DB                6592512         204800
                  KE_ORDER_RECONCILE         6592512         204800
                  KE_REJECT_DETAIL           6592512         204800
                  MES_ROLE                   6592512         204800
INDEX             AK_ERRCAT_ERROR_ID         7002112         204800
                  PK_BUSINESS_DB             7002112         204800
                  PK_CONST                   7002112         204800
                  PK_ERROR_CATALOG           7002112         204800
                  SYS_C00596                 7002112         204800
                  SYS_C00602                 7002112         204800
RBS               RBS_SMALL_01               1003520         1048576
                  RBS_SMALL_02               1003520         1048576
                  RBS_LARGE                  -3190784        5242880
Script File: My_Directory\Free_Space_Left_Segment.sql
Spool File: My_Directory\Free_Space_Left_Segment.lst
```

FIGURE 5.20: Free Space Left in Tablespaces

5.7.2 Free Space Unavailable

The script shown in Figure 5.21 is an exception report. It returns only those segments that cannot acquire the next extent within their tablespace(s) due to lack of free space.

```
REM    Free Space Unavailable for EXAMPLE Database
REM    Script File Name:    My_Directory\Free_Space_Unavailable.sql
REM    Spool File Name:     My_Directory\Free_Space_Unavailable.lst
REM    Author:              NAME
REM    Date Created:        DATE
REM    Purpose:             Information on tablespace(s) where free
REM                         space is NOT AVAILABLE for the next
REM                         extent of any segment in the tablespace(s)
REM
REM
COLUMN TODAY  NEW_VALUE xTODAY NOPRINT FORMAT A1 TRUNC
TTITLE LEFT xTODAY -
      RIGHT 'Page ' FORMAT 999 SQL.PNO -
      CENTER 'Free Space Unavailable in Tablespaces'  SKIP 4
BTITLE   'Script File: My_Directory\Free_Space_Unavailable.sql|
         Spool File: My_Directory\Free_Space_Unavailable.lst'
COLUMN TABLESPACE_NAME HEADING 'Tablespace|Name' FORMAT A16
COLUMN SEGMENT_NAME HEADING 'Segment|Name' FORMAT A20
COLUMN TABLE_NAME HEADING 'Table|Name' FORMAT A20
BREAK ON TABLESPACE_NAME SKIP 1 ON TABLE_NAME SKIP 0
SET LINESIZE 78
SET PAGESIZE 41
SET NEWPAGE 0
SPOOL My_Directory\Free_Space_Unavailable.lst
select s.tablespace_name, s.segment_name, s.next_extent "Next
     Extent",  f.free_bytes "Free Bytes", TO_CHAR (SysDate,
     'fmMonth ddth, YYYY')
TODAY
     from dba_segments s,
     (select tablespace_name,
     sum(bytes) free_bytes
     from dba_free_space
group by tablespace_name) f
where f.tablespace_name = s.tablespace_name
and s.next_extent > f.free_bytes;
SPOOL OFF
```

FIGURE 5.21: Script Listing Segments Unable to Extend

Figure 5.22 shows the output from Figure 5.21. Only one segment, RBS_LARGE, is unable to acquire the next extent due to lack of adequate free space. Ideally, when this script is run, the output should be "no rows selected." Otherwise, the DBA must take immediate measures such as adding more datafile(s) to the listed tablespace(s).

```
May 17th, 2001    Free Space Unavailable in Tablespaces    Page 1
Tablespace        Segment              Next                Free
Name              Name                 Extent              Bytes
---------         ----------           --------            --------
RBS               RBS_LARGE            5242880             2052096

     Script File: My_Directory\Free_Space_Unavailable.sql
     Spool File:  My_Directory\Free_Space_Unavailable.lst
```

FIGURE 5.22: Segments Unable to Extend

Comparing Figures 5.20 and 5.22 we note that the segment RBS_LARGE needs 5,242,880 bytes to extend. But the tablespace RBS has only 2,052,096 bytes of free space. The difference of –3,190,784 (=2,052,096 – 5,242,880) bytes is shown in Figure 5.20 as "Bytes Left" for this segment.

5.8 Free Space Fragmentation at Tablespace Level

Oracle stores the database objects in various tablespaces. Storage space is allocated to the tablespaces through the datafiles that are assigned to them when the tablespaces are created. Additional datafiles may be assigned subsequently if a tablespace needs more storage. As different database objects are created and populated within a given tablespace, its available free storage space gradually decreases. When the extents of segments within a tablespace claim free space through their initial and next extents, the tablespace starts to get fragmented. When a segment is dropped, its extents are deallocated and are marked as "free." But they are not automatically combined with neighboring free extents except in the two cases listed below. Thus, instead of containing few large contiguous extents a tablespace now contains many small contiguous or noncontiguous extents. The free space in a tablespace thereby consists of many "holes" or fragments, as shown in Figure 5.23. Reducing or removing these holes is the goal of free space defragmentation at the tablespace level.

We notice in Figure 5.23 that when tables A and B are created, the free space is not fragmented. The two initial extents of size 100 K each are allocated from the holding tablespace. After some growth of A and B fragments start to appear. For example, the free space chunk "Free 1" is smaller than 50 K and so cannot be used by the next extent of Table A. Thereby a "hole" appears in the free space available in the tablespace.

106   5. Tuning of Disk-Resident Data Structures

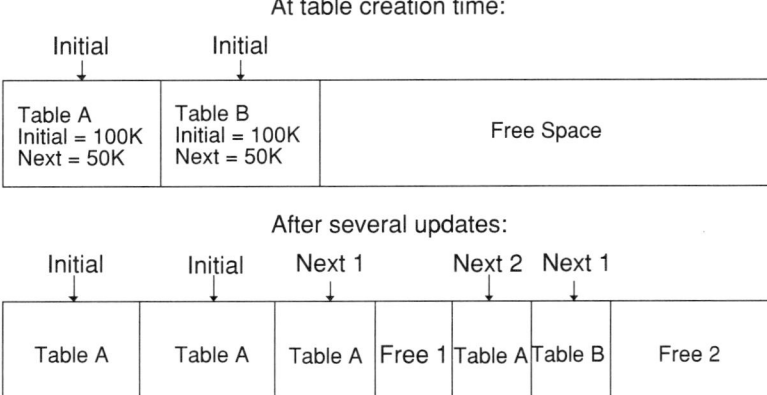

FIGURE 5.23: Fragmentation of Tablespace

There are some situations where two or more contiguous free extents are combined into a single large contiguous free extent.

1. If the PCTINCREASE storage parameter is positive, the background process SMON (System MONitor) automatically coalesces contiguous free extents into a single extent. However, we usually set PCTINCREASE = 0 while creating tablespaces to avoid combinatorial explosion of NEXT EXTENT sizes. A compromise can be made by setting PCTINCREASE = 1, the smallest positive integer, so that SMON can operate and, at the same time, the NEXT EXTENT sizes increase very slowly.
2. Starting with Oracle 7.3 we can use the command

   ALTER TABLESPACE tablespace_name COALESCE;

   to coalesce manually two or more contiguous free extents into a single free extent. Of course, it is necessary to establish via the procedure described below that the target tablespace indeed has many contiguous free extents.

We now describe a two-step procedure to reduce or eliminate tablespace fragmentation.

(a) Measure the level of fragmentation in each tablespace in the database.

Loney [2, p. 342–344] defined an index called the *free space fragmentation index* (FSFI) to determine the level of fragmentation. The index is given below:

$$\text{FSFI} = \text{sqrt}\left(\frac{\text{largest extent}}{\text{sum of all extents}}\right) * \frac{100}{(\text{number of extents})^{1/4}}.$$

5.8 Free Space Fragmentation at Tablespace Level

Ideally, FSFI should be 100. But as fragmentation occurs, FSFI gradually decreases. In general, a tablespace with FSFI < 30 should be further examined for possible defragmentation. Run the script in Figure 5.24 to calculate FSFI for each tablespace.

```
REM  Measure the level of free space fragmentation in tablespaces
REM  Script File Name: My_directory\FSFI.sql
REM  Script File Name: My_directory\FSFI.lst
REM  Purpose:          This script measures the fragmentation of
REM                    free space in all of the tablespaces in a
REM                    database and scores them according to an
REM                    index for comparison.
REM

COLUMN TODAY   NEW_VALUE xTODAY NOPRINT FORMAT A1 TRUNC

TTITLE LEFT xTODAY -
    RIGHT 'Page ' FORMAT 999 SQL.PNO -
    CENTER 'FSFI Index for EXAMPLE Database' SKIP 2
BTITLE 'Script File: My_directory \FSFI.sql|
    Spool File: My_directory \FSFI.lst'
COLUMN TABLESPACE_NAME HEADING 'Tablespace|Name' FORMAT A20
COLUMN FSFI FORMAT 999.99

BREAK ON TABLESPACE_NAME SKIP 0

SET LINESIZE 78
SET PAGESIZE 41
SET NEWPAGE 0

SPOOL My_directory \FSFI.lst

SELECT TABLESPACE_NAME,
    SQRT(MAX(Blocks)/SUM(Blocks))*
    (100/SQRT(SQRT(COUNT(Blocks)))) FSFI,
    TO_CHAR (SysDate, 'fmMonth ddth, YYYY') TODAY
    FROM DBA_FREE_SPACE
    GROUP BY TABLESPACE_NAME
    ORDER BY 1;

SPOOL OFF
```

FIGURE 5.24: Script to Compute FSFI

Figure 5.25 contains a sample output from the script. It shows that the tablespaces INDEX_B and PD_DATA warrant further investigation with respect to free space fragmentation since their FSFIs are below 30.

```
May 17th, 2001        FSFI Index for EXAMPLE Database    Page 1
        Tablespace
        Name                    FSFI
        -------------           ----------
        DATA_A                  74.56
        DATA_B                  75.26
        INDEX_A                 43.24
        INDEX_B                 27.90
        PD_DATA                 22.65
        ROLLBACK                73.59
        TOOLS                  100.00
            Script File: My_Directory\FSFI.sql
            Spool File: My_Directory \FSFI.lst
```

FIGURE 5.25: Tablespaces with FSFI

(b) List the File IDs, Block IDs, and the total blocks for each tablespace with FSFI < 30 and determine how many of their free space extents are contiguous.

Run the script in Figure 5.26.

```
REM    Free Space Listing for Tablespaces in EXAMPLE Database
REM    Script File Name: My_Directory\FREESPACE.sql
REM    Spool File Name   My_Directory\FREESPACE.lst
REM    Author:           NAME
REM    Date Created:     DATE
REM    Purpose:          Information on free space extents in all
REM                      tablespaces in EXAMPLE database
REM
REM
COLUMN TODAY   NEW_VALUE xTODAY NOPRINT FORMAT A1 TRUNC

TTITLE LEFT xTODAY -
    RIGHT 'Page ' FORMAT 999 SQL.PNO -
    CENTER 'Free Space List - EXAMPLE Database ' SKIP 4
BTITLE 'Script File: My_Directory\FREESPACE.sql|Spool File:
    My_Directory\FREESPACE.lst'

COLUMN TABLESPACE_NAME HEADING 'Tablespace|Name' FORMAT A15
COLUMN FILE_ID HEADING 'File ID' FORMAT 999
COLUMN BLOCK_ID HEADING 'Block ID' FORMAT 999999999
COLUMN BLOCKS HEADING 'Total|Blocks' FORMAT 999,999,999

BREAK ON TABLESPACE_NAME SKIP 2 ON FILE_ID SKIP 1
```

FIGURE 5.26: Script for Listing Free Space Extents in Tablespaces

```
SET LINESIZE 78
SET PAGESIZE 41
SET NEWPAGE 0

SPOOL    My_Directory\FREESPACE.lst

SELECT TABLESPACE_NAME, FILE_ID, BLOCK_ID, BLOCKS,
      TO_CHAR (SysDate, 'fmMonth ddth, YYYY') TODAY
      FROM DBA_FREE_SPACE
      ORDER BY TABLESPACE_NAME, FILE_ID, BLOCK_ID;
SPOOL OFF
```

FIGURE 5.26 (*continued*): Script for Listing Free Space Extents in Tablespaces

Figure 5.27 contains a sample output from the script.

```
May 17th, 2001        Free Space List - EXAMPLE Database       Page 1
Tablespace            File              Block                  Total
Name                  ID                ID                     Blocks
-----------           -------           ----------             --------
INDEX_B               3                     27                    125
                                          2527                     33
                                          2560                    776
PD_DATA               7                   6460                     45
                                         10260                     45
                                         10715                  4,646

         Script File: My_Directory\FREESPACE.sql
         Spool File: My_Directory\FREESPACE.lst
```

FIGURE 5.27: Free Space Extents in Tablespaces

The algorithm to determine contiguity of blocks is as follows.

```
    IF      within a given File ID,
            (Block_ID) (n+1) = (Block_ID) n + (Total Blocks) n,
    THEN    (Block_ID) (n+1) and (Block_ID) n are contiguous;
    ELSE    (Block_ID) (n+1) and (Block_ID) n are not contiguous.
```

Here $(Block\_ID)_n$ is the *n*th Block ID within a given File ID for a given tablespace, where n = 1, 2, 3, . . .

Looking at Figure 5.27, within File ID = 3, we have as follows.

$$2560 = (Block\_ID)_3 = 2527 + 33 = (Block\_ID)_2 + (Total\ Blocks)_2$$

Hence these two blocks are contiguous and should be coalesced via the command

```
ALTER TABLESPACE INDEX_B COALESCE;
```
No other blocks, however, are contiguous.

When free space contains contiguous blocks, they should be coalesced, as above. Otherwise, a tablespace level export and import need to be done to coalesce noncontiguous blocks. However, Oracle allows only full mode (FULL), or user mode (OWNER), or table mode (TABLES) exports. Therefore, one can do a table mode export for each table belonging to the fragmented tablespace, or a user mode export by OWNER of each table belonging to the fragmented tablespace. When Oracle imports data from the export dump file, the tablespace is substantially defragmented.

5.9 Row Chaining and Row Migration in Tables

Chaining and migration of rows occur in a table when a row cannot fit into a single Oracle data block. A table that undergoes frequent INSERTs or UPDATEs often has chained rows. Also, a table with a column having a LOB data type may have chaining when the data block size is smaller than the size of the data in the LOB column. Sections 5.9.1 and 5.9.2 discuss the chaining and the migration respectively.

5.9.1 Row Chaining in Tables

Chaining occurs in a table when a row physically spans multiple data blocks within an extent allocated to the table. Oracle then stores the data in the row in a chain of blocks by setting up pointer(s) linking the physically separated parts of the row.

In order to detect chaining in tables run the PL/SQL procedure, *examine_chaining.sql*, given in Figure 5.28. It contains a script file called *generate_analyze.sql* that ANALYZEs each designated table, COMPUTEs statistics, and LISTs CHAINED ROWS into the table called *chained_rows*. The Oracle utility UTLCHAIN.sql creates this table. If a table has chaining, the PL/SQL procedure calls another PL/SQL procedure, *selected_rows_proc.sql*, to return the count of chained rows in the table along with the ROWID of the first part of each chained row. Figure 5.29 contains this latter script file.

```
examine_chaining.sql

REM    Examine chaining in tables
REM    Script File Name:    My_directory\examine_chaining.sql
REM    Author:              NAME
REM    Date Created:        DATE
REM    Purpose:             Collect statistics via ANALYZE command and
REM                         list chained rows in tables.
REM
REM
```

FIGURE 5.28: Script *examine_chaining.sql*

```
SET FEEDBACK OFF
SET HEADING OFF

REM   Create the script GENERATE_ANALYZE.sql

SPOOL GENERATE_ANALYZE.sql

REM   Run UTLCHAIN.sql script before using this procedure.
REM   GENERATE_ANALYZE.sql script file ANALYZEs designated tables
REM   and COMPUTEs STATISTICS on each one of them.
REM
REM
SELECT 'ANALYZE TABLE ', TABLE_NAME, 'COMPUTE STATISTICS; '
      FROM DBA_TABLES
        WHERE TABLESPACE_NAME != 'SYSTEM';
SELECT 'ANALYZE TABLE ', TABLE_NAME, 'LIST CHAINED ROWS INTO
      CHAINED_ROWS;' FROM DBA_TABLES
        WHERE TABLESPACE_NAME != 'SYSTEM';
SPOOL OFF

SET FEEDBACK ON
SET HEADING ON
REM   Run the script GENERATE_ANALYZE.sql

START GENERATE_ANALYZE.sql

SET SERVEROUTPUT ON SIZE 100000

REM   Body of the PL/SQL procedure examine_chaining.sql

DECLARE
      tbl_name dba_tables.table_name%TYPE;
      num_chains dba_tables.chain_cnt%TYPE;
      nothing BOOLEAN := TRUE;
CURSOR chains IS
      SELECT table_name, chain_cnt FROM dba_tables
        WHERE TABLESPACE_NAME != 'SYSTEM';
--    Display tables with chain count > 0 and then display the
--    ROWID of the first part of each chained row.
BEGIN
      OPEN chains;
      FETCH chains INTO tbl_name, num_chains;

      WHILE chains%FOUND
      LOOP
        FETCH chains INTO tbl_name, num_chains;
        IF num_chains > 0 THEN
        DBMS_OUTPUT.PUT_LINE ('Table ' || tbl_name || ' has '
```

FIGURE 5.28 (*continued*): Script *examine_chaining.sql*

```
--      Call procedure selected_rows_proc ()
--
                || num_chains || ' chained rows.');
               selected_rows_proc (tbl_name);  /* Call procedure */
           nothing := FALSE;
           END IF;
        END LOOP;

        IF (nothing) THEN
           DBMS_OUTPUT.PUT_LINE ('*** CONGRATULATIONS! NO CHAINING AT
           ALL! ***');
           DBMS_OUTPUT.PUT_LINE ('*** NO ROWIDs RETURNED! ***');
        END IF;

        CLOSE chains;
END;
/
```

FIGURE 5.28: (*continued*) Script *examine_chaining.sql*

```
selected_rows_proc.sql
REM    Return chained rows in tables
REM    Script File Name:    My_Directory\selected_rows_proc.sql
REM    Author:              NAME
REM    Date Created:        DATE
REM    Purpose:             For a given table name, return the ROWID
REM                         of the first part of a chained row in the
REM                         table. The table name is passed as a
REM                         parameter to the procedure.
REM

SET serveroutput on size 100000

CREATE OR REPLACE PROCEDURE selected_rows_proc (tbl_name IN
VARCHAR2) AS
        hd_row chained_rows.head_rowid%TYPE;
        time_run chained_rows.analyze_timestamp%TYPE;
```

FIGURE 5.29: Script selected_rows_proc.sql

```
BEGIN
    DECLARE CURSOR selected_rows IS
      SELECT head_rowid, analyze_timestamp FROM chained_rows
      WHERE table_name = tbl_name;
    BEGIN
      OPEN selected_rows;
      FETCH selected_rows INTO hd_row, time_run;
      DBMS_OUTPUT.PUT_LINE ('ROWID of the first part of chained
            row in table ' || tbl_name || ' is ' || hd_row || '
            and table was last ANALYZEd on ' || time_run);
      CLOSE selected_rows;
    END;
END;
/
```

FIGURE 5.29 (*continued*): Script selected_rows_proc.sql

Chaining usually becomes a problem when more than 10% of the rows in a table are chained. Run the following query to return a list of tables with chained rows:

```
select table_name, round ((100*chain_cnt)/num_rows, 2)
    "%Chaining"
from user_tables where num_rows >0 order by 1;
```

For each table with %Chaining > 10, proceed as follows to reduce chaining:

(a) If most of the transactions on the table are UPDATE, increase the value of PCTFREE for the table. The default value of PCTFREE is 10, which usually suffices for most tables. If, however, a table contains many columns with VARCHAR2 data types that are initially NULL but expand subsequently through updates, then the default amount of 10% free space left in each data block may not be sufficient to allow the expansion of the existing rows within that block. In this case, PCTFREE should be set at higher than 10. A higher PCTFREE value leaves more space in an Oracle data block for an updated row to expand within the block, thereby preventing the occurrence of chaining. Start with a new PCTFREE = 30 and run the above query weekly to determine if %Chaining has stopped growing and started decreasing. If chaining still continues to grow, try PCTFREE = 40 and examine if chaining has stopped growing. If it still does not work, export and import the table with PCTFREE = 40.

(b) If most of the transactions on the table are INSERTs, increasing the data block size may help. But that option may cause other problems such as increased block contention on the index leaf blocks. Also, to increase the block size one has to drop and then recreate the database. Hence unless there are other more significant reasons to increase the block size, this option may not be worthwhile to pursue.

(c) If the chained table has a column with the LONG data type, row chaining may be unavoidable. The problem can be minimized by splitting the table into two tables. One table contains all the columns except the column with the LONG data type, and the other table contains only the primary key of the original table and the column with the LONG data type. All programs using the original chained table must be modified to handle the new design involving two tables. See Section 2.3.1 for an actual case study.

Steps (a) and (b) above require that the frequency of INSERTs or UPDATEs on a chained table must be determined. For this purpose the DBA needs to activate auditing on the table and query the view DBA_AUDIT_TRAIL. The four steps listed below describe that process.

- Set the initialization parameter AUDIT_TRAIL to the value TRUE in order to enable auditing.
- Invoke the Server Manager and enter "connect internal" to access the database.
- For each table to be audited, enter the command

    ```
    AUDIT ALL PRIVILEGES ON table_name BY ACCESS;
    ```

    where table_name is the name of the table. The command activates the auditing mechanism on the table. The option BY ACCESS causes an audit record to be written to the table SYS.AUD$ once for each time the table is accessed. For example, if a user performs four update transactions (INSERT, UPDATE, DELETE) on the table, then four separate records are written to SYS.AUD$. The results can be viewed by querying the view DBA_AUDIT_TRAIL.

- Run the following query against DBA_AUDIT_TRAIL:

    ```
    select username, to_char (timestamp, 'dd-mon-yy
    hh24:mi:ss') "Transaction Time", obj_name, action_name
    from dba_audit_trail
    order by username;
    ```

The query returns the list of actions taken on the table. The DBA can determine the frequency of INSERTs and UPDATEs from the list.

5.9.2 Row Migration in Tables

Migration occurs when an UPDATE statement increases the amount of data in a row whereby the updated row can no longer fit into a single Oracle data block. Oracle uses variable length records to store data of VARCHAR2 columns. As a result, if a table contains many columns with VARCHAR2 data types that are initially blank but are subsequently populated through updates, row migration may result by the expansion of existing rows. Oracle tries to find another block with sufficient free space to accommodate the updated row. If such a block is available, Oracle moves the entire row to that block. But it keeps the original row fragment at its old location and sets up a pointer to link this fragment to the new location. The ROWID of a migrated row does not change, nor are the indices, if any, updated. If a new data block to contain the updated row is not available, the row is physically split into two or more fragments stored at different locations. This is row chaining as discussed above.

The scripts listed in Figures 5.28 and 5.29 will detect both chained and migrated rows. Row migration can be addressed by increasing the value of PCTFREE in the affected table, as described above in Section 5.9.1. A more rigorous method to eliminate row migration is given below:

(a) Using the ROWIDs of the affected rows copy them to another table;
(b) Delete the affected rows from the original table;
(c) Insert the rows from Step (a) into the table. This eliminates migration, because migration is caused only by UPDATEs.

5.10 Performance Tuning of Rollback Segments

Although the rollback segments constitute data structures in auxiliary storage, their usage and, therefore, their tuning mechanism are somewhat different from those of tables and indices. For example, rollback segments are always reused. Current transactions overwrite earlier transactions that are now inactive. As a result, the management of rollback segments requires monitoring of their usage by the database transactions. Problems generally surface in two forms:

- Some of the batch jobs take too long to complete; and
- The error message, ORA-01555: snapshot too old (rollback segment too small), appears too often.

It is necessary to perform a planned and detailed investigation of the problem by looking at the transaction sizes and the level of contention among the rollback segments. Delays in executing transactions can be caused by a contention to access the rollback segment header block.

5.10.1 Function of Rollback Segments

Both retrieval and update transactions of a database use rollback segments. An update transaction involves the commands INSERT, UPDATE, and DELETE. The rollback segments store the "before image" version of the data used by such a transaction. A retrieval transaction involves the SELECT command. If a query uses data that another user is updating, Oracle uses the rollback segments to store the data as they existed before the update began.

Each rollback segment belongs to a rollback tablespace that provides its physical storage. As such, each segment consists of multiple extents, which are not necessarily contiguous, and each extent consists of contiguous blocks of storage. A *rollback segment entry* is the set of data blocks that contain the rows that are being modified by an update transaction. If the transaction is committed, the entry is labeled inactive and its storage is available for use by another transaction. If the transaction is rolled back or if the system crashes before a COMMIT occurs, the entry is used for updating the table involved in the transaction. A single rollback segment can contain multiple rollback segment entries, but a single entry cannot span multiple rollback segments. Oracle assigns transactions to rollback segments in a round-robin fashion. This results in an even distribution of the number of transactions in each rollback segment. In order to use the rollback segment, a transaction updates the rollback segment header block, which resides in the data block buffer cache in the SGA.

Three major issues with rollback segments are *wraps*, *extends*, and *waits*. The goal in designing rollback segments is twofold.

- The data for a transaction should fit within a single extent.
- A transaction should not wait to access the rollback segment header block.

When a transaction's rollback segment entry cannot be stored within a single extent, the entry acquires the next extent within that segment if that extent is inactive, i.e., available. This is called a *wrap*. If the next extent is active (i.e., unavailable), the segment *extends* to acquire a new extent from its tablespace. If the current extent is the last extent in the segment and the first extent is inactive, the transaction wraps to the first extent. If the first extent is active, the segment extends to acquire a new extent from its tablespace.

Suppose that a rollback segment has six extents E1, ..., E6. A transaction T currently occupies extents E3 and E4, and needs another extent. If E5 is inactive, then T wraps to E5, as shown in Figure 5.30. If E5 is active, then T extends to a new extent E7, as shown in Figure 5.31.

Rollback segment header activity controls the writing of changed data blocks to the rollback segment. The rollback segment header block resides in the data block buffer cache. If a user process has to wait for access to the rollback segment header block, it is counted as a *wait*. Excessive wraps, extends, and waits indicate problems for the database.

A rollback segment should be created with an optimal size via the OPTIMAL option in the STORAGE clause in the CREATE ROLLBACK SEGMENT command. During regular transactions a rollback segment occasionally grows beyond this optimal size for a particular transaction, but then it shrinks back after the transaction is complete. The dynamic performance views V$ROLLSTAT and V$ROLLNAME provide the statistics on wraps, extends, shrinks, etc., as shown in the SQL script below.

5.10 Performance Tuning of Rollback Segments   117

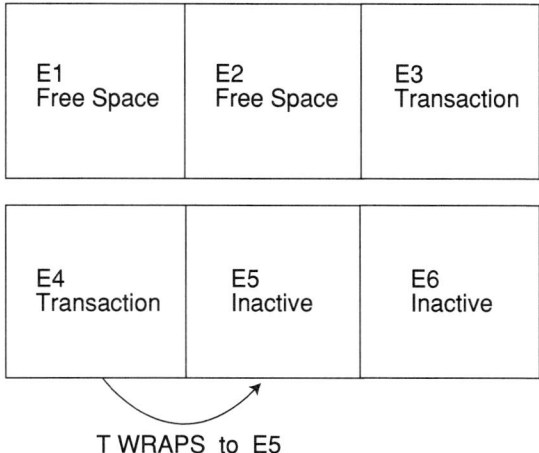

FIGURE 5.30: Transaction WRAPS to Inactive Extent

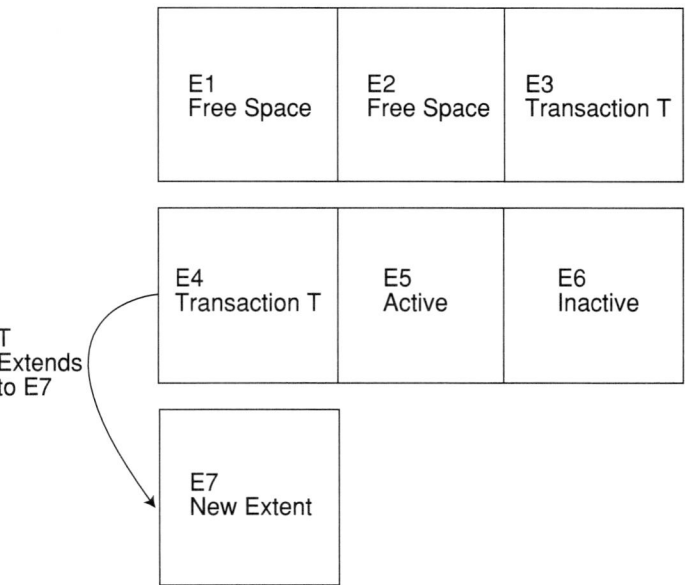

FIGURE 5.31: Transaction EXTENDS to New Extent

5. Tuning of Disk-Resident Data Structures

```
SQL> col name format a10
SQL> select name, optsize, shrinks, aveshrink, wraps, extends
  2  from v$rollstat, v$rollname
  3  where v$rollstat.usn = v$rollname.usn
  4  order by name;
NAME         OPTSIZE      SHRINKS   AVESHRINK     WRAPS   EXTENDS
--------     --------     -------   ---------     -----   -------
RBS1         83886080           0           0      2501         0
RBS2         83886080           0           0      1698         0
RBS3         83886080           0           0      1814         0
RBS4         83886080           1    41984000      1106        10
RBS5         83886080           0           0       172         0
SYSTEM                          0           0         2         0
LARGE_RBS_01 83886080           0           0         1         0
7 rows selected.
```

The column AVESHRINK shows the size by which a rollback segment shrinks. SHRINKS and EXTENDS are exceptional situations and Oracle recommends that they not happen during normal production runs. Each rollback segment listed above has an optimal size of 80 MB.

The statistics on waits are available from the view V$WAITSTAT, as shown below:

```
SQL> select class, count from v$waitstat
  2  order by 1;

CLASS                          COUNT
------------------          --------
bitmap block                       0
bitmap index block                 0
data block                   2309855
extent map                         0
free list                          0
save undo block                    0
save undo header                   0
segment header                    43
sort block                         0
system undo block                  0
system undo header                 0
undo block                      2207
undo header                    14186
unused                             0

14 rows selected.
```

The COUNT for the CLASS "undo header" records the total number of waits to access the rollback segment header block that occurred since the startup of the database.

5.10.2 Problem Symptoms

The following list, although not exhaustive, identifies the major problem areas with the rollback segments:

(a) Large number of WRAPS,
(b) Large number of EXTENDS,
(c) Multiple transactions using the same rollback segment,
(d) High value of WAITS, and
(e) Oracle error message ORA-01555: snapshot too old (rollback segment too small).

Items (a) through (d) have been explained before. Let us examine item (e). Referring to Figure 5.32 we make the following assumptions:

A long running query Q starts at instant x. Subsequently, a transaction T starts at instant $x + a$, say, to update the data, some or all of which are being used by Q. To provide a read-consistent image of the data to Q, Oracle uses the data as they existed before T began. These before image data currently reside in the three extents, E3, E4, and E5, say. Suppose that T finishes execution at instant $x + a + b$. At that instant, extents E3 through E5 are marked inactive and made available for use by other transactions, if needed. But the query Q is not yet complete. Suppose now that at instant $x + a + b + c$, another transaction U starts and acquires extents E1 through E4. Since E1 and E2 are free, no conflict arises from their acquisition by U. However, E3 and E4 contain inactive in-use data still needed by Q. When E3 and E4 are overwritten with new data used by U, Q can no longer resolve the query since its data are partially gone. As a result, Oracle returns the error message ORA-01555: snapshot too old (rollback segment too small). The underlying reason is that the extents of the rollback segment are too small and cause wraps to occur too quickly. Figure 5.32 shows the situation graphically.

The symptoms (a) through (e) listed above arise out of two root causes:

- The size of each extent of a rollback segment is small; and
- The number of rollback segments is low and should be increased.

In order to resolve the problems we need to collect data about the rollback segment usage while the database is running.

120   5. Tuning of Disk-Resident Data Structures

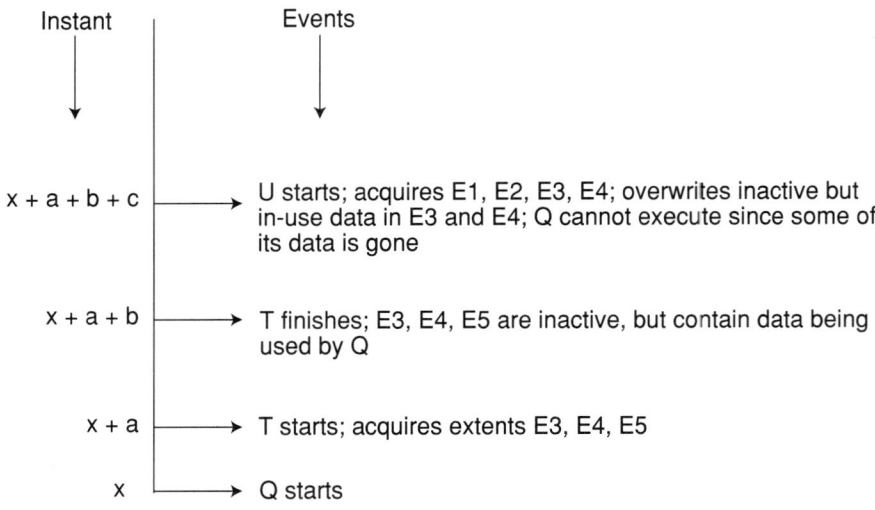

FIGURE 5.32: Scenario for ORA-01555 Error Message

5.10.3 Data Collection

Two categories of data are collected to analyze the problems:

(a) *Usage Data*: For each rollback segment, the data will show the number of blocks used, the number of active transactions, WRAPS, EXTENDS, SHRINKS, blocks shrunk, and WAITS. The information is extracted from the two views, V$ROLLSTAT and V$ROLLNAME. In addition, the data will also show the total count of waits to access the rollback segment header block for each transaction. This information is extracted from the view V$WAITSTAT.

(b) *Transaction Data*: For each active transaction, the data will show its start time, hexadecimal address, the rollback segment name, and the number of blocks used. The information is extracted from the three views, V$TRANSACTION, V$ROLLNAME, and V$SESSION. In addition, for each transaction, the data will also show the session ID, session serial number, Oracle user name, and the SQL text of the query executed by the transaction. This information is extracted from the five views, V$ROLLNAME, V$ROLLSTAT, V$SESSION, V$SQLTEXT, and V$TRANSACTION.

The data should be collected during the period of peak production load such as heavy online user access, long-running batch jobs, etc. Figures 5.33 and 5.34 contain the script files that collect the necessary usage and transaction data from a production database.

5.10 Performance Tuning of Rollback Segments

```
REM     Rollback Segment Usage Data
REM     Script File Name:   /My_Directory/RBS_Usage_Volumes.sql
REM     Spool File Name:    /My_Directory/RBS_Usage_Volumes.lst
REM     Author:             NAME
REM     Date Created:       DATE
REM     Purpose: For each rollback segment, list the number
REM              of blocks used, and numbers of wraps, extends,
REM              and shrinks. Also, show the wait for
REM              'undo header' CLASS.
COLUMN TODAY   NEW_VALUE xTODAY NOPRINT FORMAT A1 TRUNC
TTITLE  LEFT xTODAY -
        RIGHT 'Page ' FORMAT 999 SQL.PNO -
        CENTER 'Rollback Segment Usage Data'    SKIP 4
BTITLE'Script File: /My_Directory/RBS_Usage_Volumes.sql|Spool
File: /My_Directory/RBS_Usage_Volumes.lst'
COLUMN wraps FORMAT 999
COLUMN name HEADING 'Rollback|Segment' FORMAT A10
COLUMN xacts HEADING 'Tran|Count' FORMAT 999

SET LINESIZE 100
SET PAGESIZE 41
SET NEWPAGE 0

REM     SPOOL /My_Directory/RBS_Usage_Volumes.lst

select sysdate RUNTIME, RN.name, RS.xacts, ROUND (RS.writes/4096, 0)
     "Blocks Written", RS.wraps, RS.extends, RS.shrinks,
     ROUND (RS.aveshrink/4096) "Bl.Shr", WAITS,
     TO_CHAR (SysDate, 'fmMonth ddth, YYYY') TODAY
     from v$rollname RN, v$rollstat RS
     where RN.usn = RS.usn
     order by RN.name;

select class, count from v$waitstat where class = 'undo header';

REM     SPOOL OFF

EXIT
```

FIGURE 5.33: Collection of Rollback Segment Usage Data

```
REM    Rollback Segment Data for Active Transactions
REM    Script File Name: /My_Directory/RBS_Transaction_Volumes.sql
REM    Spool File Name:  /My_Directory/RBS_Transaction_Volumes.lst
REM    Author:           NAME
REM    Date Created:     DATE
REM    Purpose:          For each active transaction, list its start
REM                      time, hexadecimal address, number of
REM                      blocks used, rollback segment name, SQL
REM                      text of query, etc.
REM
REM

COLUMN TODAY NEW_VALUE xTODAY NOPRINT FORMAT A1 TRUNC

TTITLE LEFT xTODAY -
    RIGHT 'Page ' FORMAT 999 SQL.PNO -
    CENTER 'Rollback Segment Data for Active Transactions ' SKIP 4
BTITLE 'Script File: name RBS_Transaction_Volumes.sql|Spool File: name
    RBS_Transaction_Volumes.lst'

COLUMN start_time HEADING 'Start Time' FORMAT A20
COLUMN taddr HEADING 'Transaction|Address' FORMAT A12
COLUMN name HEADING 'Rollback|Segment' FORMAT A12
COLUMN used_ublk HEADING 'Blocks|Used' FORMAT 999999
COLUMN username HEADING User format a10
COLUMN sql_text format a25

SET LINESIZE 100
SET PAGESIZE 41
SET NEWPAGE 0

REM    SPOOL name /My_Directory/RBS_Transaction_Volume.lst

select sysdate RUNTIME, T.start_time, S.taddr, RN.name, T.used_ublk,
    TO_CHAR (SysDate, 'fmMonth ddth, YYYY') TODAY
    from v$transaction T, v$rollname RN, v$session S
    where   RN.usn = T.xidusn   AND
            T.addr = S.taddr
    order by 4;

select a.name, b.xacts, c.sid, c.serial#, c.username, d.sql_text
    from v$rollname a, v$rollstat b, v$session c, v$sqltext d,
    v$transaction e
    where a.usn = b.usn
    and    b.usn = e.xidusn
    and    c.taddr = e.addr
    and    c.sql_address = d.address
    order by a.name, c.sid, d.piece;

REM    SPOOL OFF

EXIT
```

FIGURE 5.34: Collection of Rollback Segment Transaction Data

5.10 Performance Tuning of Rollback Segments

The scripts in Figures 5.33 and 5.34 can be run interactively or under the control of command files. For interactive running, it is necessary to remove the REM clauses from the two SPOOL commands in each file. Then spooling will be activated and the output will be spooled to the designated *.lst* files. For running the scripts under the control of command files in a UNIX environment, we can follow one of two paths. We can run both scripts as "cron" jobs under UNIX, or execute two command files for the two scripts. Figure 5.35 contains a sample "crontab" entry. Here both scripts are run every 10 minutes for a 24-hour period and the output is sent to a .lst file in each case.

```
                SAMPLE "crontab file" ENTRY
#ident "@(#)smittra    1.14 97/03/31 SMI"  /* SVr4.0 1.1.3.1   */
#
#Crontab Entry to run RBS_Transaction_Volume.sql on 7/23/99
#
00,10,20,30,40,50 * 23 7 * /My_Directory/RBS_Transaction_Command_crontab
1>> /My_Directory/RBS_Transaction_Volume.lst
#
#Crontab Entry to run RBS_Usage_Volume.sql on 7/23/99
#
00,10,20,30,40,50 * 23 7 *
/My_Directory/RBS_Usage_Command_crontab 1>>
/My_Directory/RBS_Usage_Volume.lst
#
```

FIGURE 5.35: Crontab File Entry

Figures 5.36 and 5.37 contain two UNIX shell scripts to execute the two SQL scripts of Figures 5.33 and 5.34 respectively. In each case, the data collector, say, a DBA, is prompted for the number of iterations to run and the time span between two consecutive runs. For example, the scripts can be run every 15 minutes for a total of 8 hours, every 10 minutes for a 24-hour period, and so on.

```
#!/bin/csh
#
#    File Name:     RBS_Usage_Command
#    Author:        NAME
#    Date Written:  July 22, 1999
#    Purpose:       For each rollback segment, list the number of
#                   blocks used, and numbers of "wraps","extends",
#                    "shrinks"
#    Connect to the production database in Oracle
#    Execute the script file, RBS_Usage_Volume.sql, in Oracle
#
```

FIGURE 5.36: Command File to Collect Usage Data

```
set Usage_ITER_COUNT = 1
echo -n "How many iterations do you want? "
set ITERATIONS_LIMIT = $<
echo The program will loop through $ITERATIONS_LIMIT iterations.

echo -n "Enter in number of seconds the time interval for
         collecting data."
echo -n "For example, to collect data every 2 minutes, enter 120.
         Number of seconds: "
set SLEEP_COUNTER = $<
echo The data will be collected every $SLEEP_COUNTER seconds.

while ($Usage_ITER_COUNT <= $ITERATIONS_LIMIT)
    echo "Usage ITERATION COUNT = "$Usage_ITER_COUNT
    sqlplus supread/supread@database_name @RBS_Usage_Volume 1>>
    RBS_Usage_Volume.lst
    sleep $SLEEP_COUNTER
    @ Usage_ITER_COUNT++
end
echo "Usage Loop terminates."
```

FIGURE 5.36 (*continued*): Command File to Collect Usage Data

```
#!/bin/csh
#
#    File Name:      RBS_Transaction_Command
#    Author:         NAME
#    Date Written:   July 22, 1999
#    Purpose:        For each active transaction, list its start
#                    time, hexadecimal address, number of blocks
#                    used, rollback segment name. SQL text, etc.
#
#
#    Connect to the production database in Oracle
#    Execute the script file, RBS_Transaction_Volume.sql, in Oracle
#
set Tran_ITER_COUNT = 1
echo -n "How many iterations do you want? "
set ITERATIONS_LIMIT = $<
echo The program will loop through $ITERATIONS_LIMIT iterations.

echo -n "Enter in number of seconds the time interval for
         collecting data."
echo -n "For example, to collect data every 2 minutes, enter 120.
         Number of seconds: "
set SLEEP_COUNTER = $<
echo The data will be collected every $SLEEP_COUNTER seconds.
```

FIGURE 5.37: Command File to Collect Transaction Data

```
while ($Tran_ITER_COUNT <= $ITERATIONS_LIMIT)
    echo "Transaction ITERATION COUNT = "$Tran_ITER_COUNT
    sqlplus supread/supread@database_name @RBS_Transaction_Volume 1>>
    RBS_Transaction_Volume.lst
    sleep $SLEEP_COUNTER
    @ Tran_ITER_COUNT++
end
echo "Transaction Loop terminates."
```

FIGURE 5.37 (*continued*): Command File to Collect Transaction Data

5.10.4 Data Analysis

The files, RBS_Usage_Volume.lst and RBS_Transaction_Volume.lst, contain the output from running the script files, RBS_Usage_Volume.sql and RBS_Transaction_Volume.sql respectively. Figures 5.38 and 5.39 display only the first pages from these two output files. The analysis included in Section 5.10.5 is based on the complete output files, however.

```
August 2nd, 1999      Rollback Segment Usage Data         Page 1
RUNTIME              Rollback Tran  Blocks
WAITS                Segment  Count Written  WRAPS  EXTENDS  SHRINKS  Bl.Shr
------------------   -------- ----- -------- ------ -------- -------- ------
02-AUG-1999 122440   RBS1     0     7126     11     0        0        4
02-AUG-1999 122440   RBS2     0     4109     6      0        0        7
02-AUG-1999 122440   RBS3     1     9665     13     0        0        5
02-AUG-1999 122440   RBS4     1     59171    67     0        0        801
02-AUG-1999 122440   RBS5     0     9794     16     0        0        10
02-AUG-1999 122440   SYSTEM   0     2        0      0        0        0
02-AUG-1999 122440   L_RBS_01 0     26343    3      0        0        14
            Script File: /My_Directory/RBS_Usage_Volumes.sql
            Spool File: /My_Directory/RBS_Usage_Volumes.lst
7 rows selected.
August 2nd, 1999     Rollback Segment Usage Data         Page 1
CLASS                            COUNT
------------------               ----------
undo header                      1675
            Script File: /My_Directory/RBS_Usage_Volumes.sql
            Spool File: /My_Directory/RBS_Usage_Volumes.lst
```

FIGURE 5.38: Sample Rollback Segment Usage Data—8/2/99

126   5. Tuning of Disk-Resident Data Structures

```
August 2nd, 1999      Rollback Segment Data for Active Transactions    Page 1
                      Start             Transaction         Rollback   Blocks
RUNTIME               Time              Address             Segment    Used
----------------      ----------------  ---------           --------   ------
02-AUG-1999 124754    08/02/99 11:59:55 1E3339C8            RBS3            2
02-AUG-1999 124754    08/02/99 11:58:37 1E332FC0            RBS4            2
02-AUG-1999 124754    08/02/99 12:46:59 1E333D20            RBS5            2
02-AUG-1999 124754    08/02/99 12:30:21 1E3325B8            L_RBS_01    6,304
02-AUG-1999 124754    08/02/99 12:47:04 1E333318            L_RBS_01        1
        Script File: /My_Directory/RBS_Transaction_Volumes.sql
        Spool File:  /My_Directory/RBS_Transaction_Volumes.lst

August 2nd, 1999     Rollback Segment Data for Active Transactions     Page 1
Rollback
Segment    XACTS    SID    SERIAL#    User           SQL_TEXT
--------   -----    ---    -------    ------         ------------
RBS3          1     33       16       VERTEX         begin DBMS_APPLICATION_IN
           FO.SET_MODULE(:1,NULL);
           end;
RBS4          1     88      1984      VERTEX         begin DBMS_APPLICATION_IN
           FO.SET_MODULE(:1,NULL);
           end;
RBS5          2     18        5       OPS$INVOICE    insert into table
           (column list) values
           (value list);
L_RBS_01      3     65        9       OPS$INVOICE    update table set column
           = value where
           condition(s);
        Script File: /My_Directory/RBS_Transaction_Volumes.sql
        Spool File:  /My_Directory/RBS_Transaction_Volumes.lst

August 2nd, 1999     Rollback Segment Data for Active Transactions     Page 2
Rollback
Segment    XACTS    SID    SERIAL#    User           SQL_TEXT
--------   ------   ----   --------   ---------      ------------
L_RBS_01      3     70        9       OPS$INVOICE    INSERT INTO table
           (column list) values
           (value list);
     Script File: /My_Directory/RBS_Transaction_Volumes.sql
     Spool File:  /My_Directory/RBS_Transaction_Volumes.lst
5 rows selected.
```

FIGURE 5.39: Sample Rollback Segment Transaction Data—8/2/99

5.10.5 Problem Identification and Resolution

In an actual case study done during August 1999 involving a large production database, the two command files were run every 10 minutes over an eight-hour period. The database had six rollback segments, RBS1 through RBS5 and L_RBS_01. The last segment was designed for handling large transactions in batch jobs. The scripts produced two voluminous output files. A careful analysis of the files revealed the following.

1. Large number of WRITES and WRAPS against RBS3, RBS5 and L_RBS_01;
2. Very high WAITS against L_RBS_01;
3. Total of 23 transactions ran in eight hours; #UPDATEs = 12, and #INSERTs = 7 against large tables;
4. Most of the time 5 transactions ran concurrently; at one time there were 6 transactions;
5. The following 5 UPDATE transactions consumed more than one extent in its rollback segment (extent = 1,025 blocks of size 4 K each).

   ```
   Tran ID     StartTime   EndTime (est.)   RBS         Blocks Used
   1E3325B8    12:30:21    16:30:15         L_RBS_01    6,304
   1E334A80    12:55:25    16:30:15         RBS5        14,984
   1E333D20    16:34:31    16:50:18         VL_RBS_01   1,158
   1E3343D0    16:49:39    19:30:43         RBS3        21,676
   1E332910    19:40:43    20:41:12         RBS4        15,296
   ```

6. "undo header" values in V$WAITSTAT view increased from 1,675 to 28,018 in eight hours;
7. The EXTENDS values increased as follows on the segments listed below:

   ```
   RBS         Range of EXTENDS      Time Span
   RBS3        4 to 47               17:46:25 to 20:36:32
   RBS5        3 to 30               14:36:04 to 20:36:32
   L_RBS_01    2 to 98               13:55:53 to 16:26:18
   L_RBS_01    5 to 24               18:46:27 to 20:36:32
   ```

   Based on the above findings I made the following conclusions and recommendations.

(a) The large values of WAITS indicate that there is high contention for accessing the rollback segment header block. This indicates that we need to add more rollback segments.
(b) The high values of EXTENDS for some of the segments indicate that they are improperly sized. The extent size should be increased.
(c) L_RBS_01 should be sized much larger than its current size. Notice the large values of EXTENDS for L_RBS_01 listed above.

In summary, I proposed the following steps to resolve the problems.

- Perform an appropriate sizing of the extents of the rollback segments.
- Determine the number of rollback segments needed for the database.
- Estimate a value for the OPTIMAL parameter of the storage clause.

Compute Size and Number of Rollback Segments

Loney [2, p. 305–314] has given an algorithm to compute the size and number of rollback segments based on a set of assumptions. The C program, RBS_Sizing.c, uses a modification of that algorithm and computes the size and number of rollback segments based on input provided by the user, say, a DBA. The output is sent to a text file, RBS_Sizing.txt, for future reference. Since the file is opened in "append" mode, the user can experiment with different values of the input parameters, compare the results saved in the output file, and then decide on the size of each extent of the rollback segments and the total number of the rollback segments. Figure 5.40 contains the program file RBS_Sizing.c.

```
/*      PURPOSE:
The program prompts the user to enter the values of four
parameters:
Free Space (FS) = percentage of rollback segment reserved as free
     space
Inactive In-use Data (IID) = percentage of rollback segment
     reserved for use by inactive extents containing data being
     used by other queries; this avoids the error message ORA-
     01555: "snapshot too old"
Header Area (HA) = percentage of rollback segment reserved for use
     by rollback segment header block
Commit Frequency (CF) = maximum number of records after which the
     user enters COMMIT or ROLLBACK command
The program uses the following intermediary variables for
computation:
     MPS = Minimum Possible Size
     MTS = Minimum Total Size
     MNRS = Minimum Number of Rollback Segments
     LTS = Largest Transaction Size
     MAX_TS = Maximum Total Size of All Transactions .
The program generates an interactive output, which is saved in a
text file RBS_Sizing.txt for future reference. The output file is
opened in "append" mode to allow the user to experiment with
different parameter values and compare the results.
     PROGRAM FILE NAME: My_Directory\RBS_Sizing.c
     OUTPUT FILE NAME:  My_Directory\RBS_Sizing.txt
     AUTHOR:            NAME
     DATE CREATED:      September 27, 1999
*/
#include     <stdio.h>
#include     <math.h>
```

FIGURE 5.40 : Program File RBS_Sizing.c

```
void main ()
{
    FILE   *fopen (), *out_file;
    int    FS, IID, HA, CF, LTS, MTS_INT, MAX_TS, MNRS;
    float  MPS, MTS;

    out_file = fopen ("RBS_Sizing.txt", "a");

    printf ("\nEnter as an integer the percentage reserved as free
        space: ");
    scanf ("%d", &FS);

    printf ("\nEnter as an integer the percentage reserved for
        inactive in-use extents: ");
    scanf ("%d", &IID);

    printf ("\nEnter as an integer the percentage reserved as
        header area: ");
    scanf ("%d", &HA);

    printf ("\nEnter the maximum number of records processed
        before COMMIT: ");
    scanf ("%d", &CF);

    printf ("\nEnter the largest transaction size in blocks: ");
    scanf ("%d", &LTS);

    printf ("\nEnter the maximum total size of all transactions in
        blocks: ");
    scanf ("%d", &MAX_TS);

    MPS = (CF * LTS) / (100 - (FS + IID + HA));
    MTS = (CF * MAX_TS ) / (100 - (FS + IID + HA));
    MTS_INT = ceil (MTS);
    MNRS = ceil (MTS / MPS);

    printf ("\nYou entered the following parameter values:\n");
    printf ("\nFree Space = %d percent of each extent",FS);
    printf ("\nInactive In-use Data = %d percent of each
        extent",IID);
    printf ("\nHeader Area = %d percent of each extent",HA);
    printf ("\nMaximum Number of Records Processed before COMMIT =
        %d",CF);
    printf ("\nLargest Transaction Size in Blocks = %d", LTS);
    printf ("\nMaximum Total Size of All Transactions in Blocks =
        %d",MAX_TS);

    printf ("\nMPS = %f", MPS);
    printf ("\nMTS = %f", MTS);
    printf ("\nMTS_INT = %d", MTS_INT);
    printf ("\nMNRS = %d", MNRS);
```

FIGURE 5.40 (*continued*): Program File RBS_Sizing.c

```
            printf ("\n\nBased on your input, each extent should be %d
               blocks in size.",MTS_INT);
            printf ("\nThere should be %d rollback segments.\n\n",MNRS);

            fprintf (out_file, "\nYou entered the following parameter
               values:\n");
            fprintf (out_file, "\nFree Space = %d percent of each
               extent",FS);
            fprintf (out_file, "\nInactive In-use Data = %d percent of
               each extent",IID);
            fprintf (out_file, "\nHeader Area = %d percent of each
               extent",HA);
            fprintf (out_file, "\nMaximum Number of Records Processed
               before COMMIT = %d",CF);
            fprintf (out_file, "\nLargest Transaction Size in Blocks =
               %d", LTS);
            fprintf (out_file, "\nMaximum Total Size of All Transactions
               in Blocks = %d",MAX_TS);
            fprintf (out_file, "\nMPS = %f", MPS);
            fprintf (out_file, "\nMTS = %f", MTS);
            fprintf (out_file, "\nMTS_INT = %d", MTS_INT);
            fprintf (out_file, "\nMNRS = %d", MNRS);
            fprintf (out_file, "\n\nBased on your input, each extent
               should be %d blocks in size.",MTS_INT);
            fprintf (out_file, "\nThere should be %d rollback
               segments.\n\n",MNRS);
};
```

FIGURE 5.40 (*continued*): Program File RBS_Sizing.c

I ran the above program with two sets of input values, one for large rollback segments and the other for regular ones. The output file RBS_Sizing.txt is given in Figure 5.41.

```
You entered the following parameter values:

Free Space = 20 percent of each extent
Inactive In-use Data = 15 percent of each extent
Header Area = 5 percent of each extent
Maximum Number of Records Processed before COMMIT = 100
Largest Transaction Size in Blocks = 4200
Maximum Total Size of All Transactions in Blocks = 10952
MPS = 7000.000000
MTS = 18253.000000
MTS_INT = 18253
MNRS = 3
```

FIGURE 5.41: Output File RBS_Sizing.txt

```
Based on your input, each extent should be 18253 blocks in size.
There should be 3 rollback segments.
You entered the following parameter values:

Free Space = 20 percent of each extent
Inactive In-use Data = 15 percent of each extent
Header Area = 5 percent of each extent
Maximum Number of Records Processed before COMMIT = 100
Largest Transaction Size in Blocks = 900
Maximum Total Size of All Transactions in Blocks = 8200
MPS = 1500.000000
MTS = 13666.000000
MTS_INT = 13666
MNRS = 10

Based on your input, each extent should be 13666 blocks in size.
There should be 10 rollback segments.
```

FIGURE 5.41 (*continued*): Output File RBS_Sizing.txt

Niemiec [3, p. 121] offers the following guideline for determining the total number of rollback segments.

```
# Concurrent Transactions           # of Rollback Segments
Less than 16                        4
16 to 32                            8
Greater than 32, say N              N/4, but not more than 50
```

If there is a conflict between the number derived from Figure 5.40 and the above table, always take the greater of the two numbers.

Estimate a Value for the OPTIMAL Parameter of the Storage Clause

The OPTIMAL parameter in the STORAGE clause of the CREATE ROLLBACK SEGMENT command takes its value in bytes, kilobytes (K), or megabytes (M). Oracle tries to maintain this OPTIMAL size of each rollback segment by dynamically deallocating extents from the segment when their data are no longer needed by active transactions. Oracle deallocates as many extents as possible without reducing the total size of the segment below the OPTIMAL value.

Oracle also recommends that MINEXTENTS for a rollback segment be set at 20. This reduces to below 5% the need to extend a segment dynamically. Hence the OPTIMAL size is given by the formula:

```
OPTIMAL = MINEXTENTS x (Extent Size) = 20 x (Extent Size)
```

Since the program above computes the value of Extent Size, OPTIMAL can be calculated accordingly.

132   5. Tuning of Disk-Resident Data Structures

5.10.6 Application of the Algorithm

For the production database in the case study, I ran the program RBS_Sizing.c twice, once for rollback segments to handle very large transactions and then for rollback segments to handle normal transactions. The output in Figure 5.41 has, therefore, two parts. The first part recommends that there be 3 rollback segments with extent size of 18,253 blocks (about 71 MB) for very large transactions. The second part shows that there are 10 rollback segments with extent size of 13,666 blocks (about 53 MB) for regular transactions.

In order to use the designated large segments the programs involving large UPDATE transactions must contain the following block of code before every transaction that must use a designated segment called large_segment.

```
COMMIT;
SET TRANSACTION USE ROLLBACK SEGMENT large_segment;
COMMIT;
```

5.10.7 Follow-up Study

I implemented my recommendations with the new size, number, and types of rollback segments, as listed below.

```
Large Rollback Segments:     Number = 3
                             INITIAL = NEXT = 70 M,
                             MINEXTENTS = 20,
                             OPTIMAL = 1400 M
Regular Rollback Segments:   Number = 10
                             INITIAL = NEXT = 50 M,
                             MINEXTENTS = 20,
                             OPTIMAL = 1000 M
```

Two weeks later I ran the scripts of Figures 5.33, 5.34, 5.36, and 5.37 to collect data. Figures 5.42 and 5.43 contain a sample of rollback segment usage and transaction data for this follow-up study.

```
August 17th, 1999      Rollback Segment Usage Data         Page 1
RUNTIME                Rollback       Tran     Blocks
WAITS                  Segment  Count Written  WRAPS EXTENDS SHRINKS Bl.Shr
-----------------      -------  ----- -------- ----- ------- ------- -------
17-AUG-1999 110309     RBS1       0    227997   131     0       0       0   561
17-AUG-1999 110309     RBS2       0     77180    34     3       1    7680     5
17-AUG-1999 110309     RBS3       0     11985     6     0       0       0    67
```

FIGURE 5.42: Sample Rollback Segment Usage Data—8/17/99

5.10 Performance Tuning of Rollback Segments

```
17-AUG-1999 110309    RBS4      0    10293    5      0    0    0    0
17-AUG-1999 110309    RBS5      0    12460    6      0    0    0    3
17-AUG-1999 110309    RBS6      0     6683    3      0    0    0    0
17-AUG-1999 110309    RBS7      0    39704   18      0    0    0   55
17-AUG-1999 110309    RBS8      1   243754  127      0    0    0   12
17-AUG-1999 110309    RBS9      1    11478    6      0    0    0    2
17-AUG-1999 110309    RBS10     0     5694    3      0    0    0    0
17-AUG-1999 110309    SYSTEM    0        5    1      0    0    0    0
17-AUG-1999 110309    L_RBS_01  0    61166    0      0    0    0  281
17-AUG-1999 110309    L_RBS_02  0     8196    0      0    0    0   79
17-AUG-1999 110309    L_RBS_03  0     1129    0      0    0    0  175
         Script File: /My_Directory/RBS_Usage_Volumes.sql
         Spool File:  /My_Directory RBS_Usage_Volumes.lst
14 rows selected.
August 17th, 1999    Rollback Segment Usage Data       Page 1
CLASS                    COUNT
-----------              -----
undo header              1298
         Script File: /My_Directory/RBS_Usage_Volumes.sql
         Spool File:  /My_Directory RBS_Usage_Volumes.lst
```

FIGURE 5.42 (*continued*): Sample Rollback Segment Usage Data—8/17/99

```
August 17th, 1999    Rollback Segment Data for Active Transactions    Page 1
                     Start              Transaction  Rollback Blocks
RUNTIME              Time               Address      Segment  Used
------------------   ----------------   ----------   -------- ------
17-AUG-1999 114203   08/17/99 11:42:02  1E574BEC     RBS5        2
17-AUG-1999 114203   08/17/99 11:42:03  1E573E8C     RBS8        2
         Script File: /My_Directory/RBS_Transaction_Volumes.sql
         Spool File:  /My_Directory/RBS_Transaction_Volumes.lst
August 17th, 1999    Rollback Segment Data for Active Transactions    Page 1
Rollback
Segment   XACTS   SID  SERIAL#   User          SQL_TEXT
--------  -----   ---  -------   ----------    ----------------
RBS5        1     54      2      OPS$INVOICE   insert into table
                                               (column list) values (value
                                               list);
         Script File: /My_Directory/RBS_Transaction_Volumes.sql
         Spool File:  /My_Directory/RBS_Transaction_Volumes.lst
1 rows selected.
```

FIGURE 5.43: Sample Rollback Segment Transaction Data—8/17/99

An analysis of these data resulted in the following findings.

- WRAPS and WAITS are almost always zero, indicating that the transactions execute within a single extent and that they do not wait for accessing the rollback segment header block.
- "undo header" values in V$WAITSTAT view increase from 1,298 to 2,228 in eight hours, a substantial improvement over the earlier findings reported in Section 5.10.5.
- EXTENDS values are almost always zero.

This indicated that the earlier problems were all gone, at least for the time being. But an ongoing monitoring is necessary to take proactive measures.

One final word of recommendation: If an application involves heavy transaction activities, it may be worthwhile to create two separate rollback tablespaces, each with multiple segments, on two separate drives. This often reduces contention for rollback headers. If this option is selected, then interleaf the order of the segments in the *init.ora* file such that the first segment is in one tablespace, the next one is in the other, and so on. Oracle assigns rollback segments to transactions in the same order as they are listed in the *init.ora* file. By alternating the tablespaces one reduces contention.

Key Words

audit trail
before image
bind variable
block ID
chaining
constraint
contention
crontab
data block buffers
data block header
data dictionary
database transaction
datafile
defragmentation
dictionary cache
export
export via conventional path
export via direct path
EXTENDS
extent

Extent ID
extent map
fragmentation
free space
free space fragmentation index
FREELIST GROUPS
FREELISTS
import
index
initialization parameter
instance
LOB
migration
rollback segment
rollback segment entry
rollback segment header activity
temporary segment
user object
WAITS
WRAPS

References and Further Reading

1. E. Aronoff et al.—*Advanced Oracle Tuning and Administration*, Oracle Press, 1997.
2. K. Loney—*Oracle 8i DBA Handbook*, Oracle Press, 2000.
3. R. J. Niemiec—*Oracle Performance Tuning*, Oracle Press, 1999.
4. W. G. Page et al.—*Using Oracle 8/8i*, Que, 1999.

All the above references have discussed the tuning principles of the disk-resident structures. A clearcut distinction of the instance and the database tuning, as done in this chapter and in Chapter 6, is not found in any of them. Aronoff et al. [1, Chapter 5], Niemic [3, p. 109–114], and Page et al. [4, Chapter 21] discuss the used space fragmentation at the segment level, the chaining of rows in tables, and defragmentation of tables and indices via export/import. Page et al. [4, Chapter 16] offer an excellent treatment of the tuning principles in general and the various tools that are available in Oracle for handling them. Loney [2, Chapter 7] discusses the general management of the rollback segments from the viewpoint of a DBA. In particular, he provides algorithms [2, pp. 305–314] for calculating the size and number of rollback segments and some guidelines for determining the value of the OPTIMAL parameter in creating a rollback segment. Also, Loney [2, Chapter 8] addresses the free space fragmentation in tablespaces.

Exercises

Theoretical exercises are of little value for this chapter since the best practice comes from monitoring the performance of actual production databases and tuning them, as needed. The exercises given below identify some of the areas not specifically covered in Chapter 5 and should be considered an extension of the text.

1. You have been collecting data on extents in tables and tablespaces. You want to generate a report on the trend of extent usage by these objects. Your goal is to be proactive in predicting when an object will fail to extend. Devise an action plan to meet your goal using the following guidelines.

   (a) Write a script to collect the needed data.
   (b) Decide on the frequency of data collection and then collect the data.
   (c) Use a statistical forecasting technique such as linear trend, exponential trend, etc. to forecast future trend usage.
   (d) Write a program using some 3GL such as C, UNIX shell scripting, etc. that prompts the user for a time value, computes the extent sizes for that date, and then returns a message about the need if any for allocating more data files to the objects. *Caution*: You need some understanding of statistical forecasting technique to do the above exercise.

2. Explain why the sizing algorithm of rollback segments (Figure 5.40) is different from that for sizing data and index segments (Section A3 in Appendix A). How

would you size a rollback tablespace given the sizes of its component rollback segments?
3. Do you think that you should be concerned about fragmentation of rollback and temporary tablespaces? Is FSFI (Figure 5.24) a valid measure of their fragmentation? Give reasons for your answer.
4. A table T in an Oracle database under UNIX has over 18 million rows and currently occupies nearly 3 GB of space. Also, T has a column of the LONG data type and is heavily fragmented. You want to defragment T via export/import. List the steps that you want to follow and some potential problems that you will face. (Hint: a UNIX file size cannot exceed 2 GB.)
5. What is the exact difference between row chaining and row migration? Why are both considered potentially harmful? What is the adverse impact of setting PCTFREE too high, say, PCTFREE = 70 and PCTUSED = 30?

6
Tuning of Memory-Resident Data Structures

Outline

6.1 Memory-Resident Data Structures
6.2 Performance Tuning
6.3 Data Block Buffers
6.4 Redo Log Buffer
6.5 Shared SQL Pool
6.6 Background Processes
6.7 Tuning the Memory
6.8 Tuning the CPU
6.9 Pinning Packages in Memory
6.10 Latching Mechanism for Access Control
Key Words
References and Further Reading
Exercises

Overview of the Chapter

The chapter offers an in-depth discussion of the data structures residing in memory, the background processes, and the methods for tuning them. The data structures reside in the System Global Area (SGA) that has three major components, namely, data block buffers, redo log buffer, and shared SQL pool. The background processes operate in the background to keep the database in a consistent state. Since the hardware and the operating system work in conjunction with the Oracle RDBMS, tuning principles of the memory and the CPU are also included in the chapter. It closes with a discussion of several ancillary issues such as latches and pinning packages in memory that help in optimizing the performance of a database.

6.1 Memory Resident Data Structures

As noted in Section 4.2, the Oracle instance consists of the SGA and several background processes. The SGA has three components: data block buffers, redo log buffer, and shared SQL pool. Their respective sizes are determined by the three initialization parameters, DB_BLOCK_BUFFERS, LOG_BUFFER, and SHARED_POOL_SIZE. The background processes are managed by another set of initialization parameters.

6.2 Performance Tuning

The tuning of the Oracle instance involves, at a minimum, the computing optimal values of the initialization parameters, DB_BLOCK_BUFFERS, LOG_BUFFER, and SHARED_POOL_SIZE, and monitoring them on a continuous basis via hit ratios described below. Various metrics are available to guide the tuning process. Sections 6.3 through 6.5 address these issues individually with SQL scripts and their outputs to handle them.

The performance of the SGA components are measured by cache hits, cache misses, and cache reloads. A *cache hit* or *cache get* is the event occurring when data blocks requested by an application are found in the data block buffer cache. When such blocks never resided in the cache and must be fetched from disk file(s) for the first time, the event is called a *cache miss*. If the requested data blocks formerly resided in the cache but have since been swapped to disk under LRU, they are reloaded into the cache. This event is called a *cache reload*. The total counts of each of these three events are used in metrics that are generically called hit ratios. Normally, such hit ratios should be above 90% for a well-tuned instance. Figure 6.1 shows the memory cache areas managed by LRU. Data blocks requested by an application and already residing in the cache result in cache hits. The LRU blocks written to disk files are brought back into the cache as cache reloads. The data blocks that are read into the cache for the first time produce cache misses.

The view V$SYSSTAT contains some 200 distinct parameters that provide valuable information about system statistics. Figure 6.2 contains a script file that generates two lists of these parameters, one sorted alphabetically by their names and the other sorted numerically by their CLASSes and then by their names. The CLASS column of V$SYSSTAT has eight numeric values listed below with their respective meanings.

```
           CLASS             DESCRIPTION
           -----             -----------
             1               User
             2               Redo
             4               Enqueue
             8               Cache
            16               OS
            32               Parallel Server
            64               SQL
           128               Debug
```

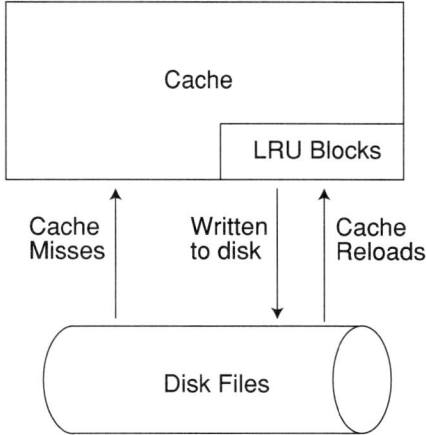

FIGURE 6.1: Cache Areas Managed by LRU Algorithm

The script file is given in Figure 6.2.

```
REM    File Name: Parameter_List_System_Statistics.sql
REM
REM    Purpose: List of Parameters from V$SYSSTAT View
col name format a55
set pagesize 41
set linesize 78
set newpage 0
spool Parameter_List_System_Statistics.lst
select name, value, class from v$sysstat order by name;
select class, name, value from v$sysstat order by class, name;
spool off
```

FIGURE 6.2: Parameters in V$SYSSTAT View

6.3 Data Block Buffers

The size of the data block buffer cache (DBB) in number of blocks is set by the value of the initialization parameter DB_BLOCK_BUFFERS. The larger the value of this parameter, the more memory is available for holding data blocks in memory. The actual size of the DBB in bytes is computed as follows.

```
DBB = DB_BLOCK_BUFFERS x DB_BLOCK_SIZE
```

140   6. Tuning of Memory-Resident Data Structures

For example, if DB_BLOCK_BUFFERS = 75,000 and DB_BLOCK_SIZE = 4 K, then DBB = 75,000 * 4,096 bytes = 307,200,000 bytes = 293 MB. A general guideline is to set DB_BLOCK_BUFFERS to a value such that DBB becomes approximately 25% of the total real memory. Another guideline that often helps is that the size of the DBB should be between 1 and 2% of the total database size.

The efficiency of the cache is measured by the metric called the *data block buffer hit ratio* (DBB-HR) that records the percentage of times a data block requested by an application is available in the cache out of the total number of such requests made. When a data block is read in cache, it is called a *logical read* (LR). When the block is read from disk, it is called a *physical read* (PR). Three specific values of the column V$SYSSTAT.NAME are consistent gets, db block gets, and physical reads. Together they provide the values of LR and PR as follows:

```
LR = consistent gets + db block gets
PR = physical reads
```

The "consistent gets" and "db block gets" represent respectively the number of accesses to a read-consistent image of a block and to the current image of a block residing in the DBB. The "physical reads" represent the number of disk accesses for data not residing in the cache. Each data block request starts as LR. If the block is not in DBB, the LR generates a PR. Thus, the value of LR includes PR. Hence the correct number of times that the requested block is in DBB is given by LR − PR. The formula for DBB-HR is given by:

$$DBB - HR = \frac{LR - PR}{LR}.$$

The more frequently a data block is available in DBB, the higher its cache hit value or LR − PR and, the lower its PR. As a result, the metric DBB-HR approaches 1, which is its ideal value. If the DBB-HR = 1, then PR = 0 implying that all the requested data blocks are in DBB. Figure 6.3 contains the script file for computing the metric DBB-HR.

```
REM  Data Block Buffer Hit Ratio for Example Database
REM  Script File Name: /My_Directory/DBB_HR_value.sql
REM  Spool File Name:  /My_Directory/DBB_HR_value.lst
REM  Author:           NAME
REM  Date Created:     DATE
REM  Purpose:  Compute the hit ratio for data block buffers at
REM           a given instant.
REM           Use the view V$SYSSTAT
REM
REM
COLUMN name FORMAT A30
```

FIGURE 6.3: Computation of Hit Ratio DBB-HR

```
spool DBB_HR_value.lst
select name, value from v$sysstat where name in ('consistent
    gets', 'db block gets', 'physical reads') order by name;
select TO_CHAR (sysdate, 'MM/DD/YY HH:MI:SS') "RunTime",
    a.value + b.value LR, c.value PR,
    ROUND (((a.value + b.value - c.value) / (a.value + b.value)) *
        100)
    "DBB-HR" from v$sysstat a, v$sysstat b, v$sysstat c
    where  a.name = 'consistent gets'
    and    b.name = 'db block gets'
    and    c.name = 'physical reads';
spool off
```

FIGURE 6.3 (*continued*): Computation of Hit Ratio DBB-HR

Figure 6.4 is a sample output from this script file.

```
NAME                        VALUE
---------------             ----------
consistent gets             546345397
db block gets               174344671
physical reads              116061101

RunTime                 LR              PR              DBB-HR
-----------------       ---------       ----------      -----
08/05/99 03:08:53       720690068       116061101       84
```

FIGURE 6.4: Sample Value of DBB-HR

It is recommended that the DBB-HR should exceed 90. This minimizes the impact of the CPU costs for I/O operations. The target value of the DBB-HR should be determined based on the mix of OLTP and batch jobs run against the database. Figure 6.5 contains a script file to compute the DBB-HR for specific Oracle and operating system users.

```
REM  User Mix for Target Data Block Buffer Hit Ratio for Example
REM  Database
REM  Script File Name:    /My_Directory/UserMix_DBB_HR.sql
REM  Spool File Name:     /My_Directory/UserMix_DBB_HR.lst
REM  Author:              NAME
REM  Date Created:        DATE
```

FIGURE 6.5: DBB-HR for Specific Oracle Users

142   6. Tuning of Memory-Resident Data Structures

```
REM  Purpose:   Determine batch and online users for target hit
REM             ratio for data block buffers at a given instant
REM             Use the views V$SESSION and V$SESS_IO
REM
REM

SET PAGESIZE 41
SET NEWPAGE 0
SET FEEDBACK OFF

COLUMN username FORMAT A15
COLUMN osuser FORMAT A10

spool UserMix_DBB_HR.lst

select TO_CHAR (sysdate, 'MM/DD/YY HH:MI:SS') "RunTime", username,
osuser,
     consistent_gets + block_gets LR, physical_reads PR,
     ROUND (((consistent_gets + block_gets - physical_reads) /
(consistent_gets + block_gets)) * 100) "DBB-HR"
     from v$session, v$sess_io
     where v$session.SID = v$sess_io.SID
     and   consistent_gets + block_gets > 0
     and   username is NOT NULL
     order by username, osuser;
spool off
```

FIGURE 6.5 (*continued*): DBB-HR for Specific Oracle Users

Figure 6.6 shows a sample output of this script file.

RunTime	USERNAME	OSUSER	LR	PR	DBB-HR
08/06/99 02:08:04	OPS$INVOICE	invoice	3200	0	100
08/06/99 02:08:04	OPS$INVOICE	invoice	2767	0	100
08/06/99 02:08:04	OPS$INVOICE	invoice	594783	3390	99
08/06/99 02:08:04	OPS$INVOICE	invoice	1062	143	87
08/06/99 02:08:04	OPS$INVOICE	invoice	9443	0	100
08/06/99 02:08:04	OPS$INVOICE	invoice	15862	0	100
08/06/99 02:08:04	OPS$INVOICE	invoice	19371	6	100
08/06/99 02:08:04	OPS$INVOICE	invoice	3945	0	100
08/06/99 02:08:04	OPS$INVOICE	invoice	104	0	100
08/06/99 02:08:04	OPS$INVOICE	invoice	104	0	100
08/06/99 02:08:04	OPS$INVOICE	invoice	169639	8218	95

FIGURE 6.6: Listing of DBB-HR for Specific Oracle Users

The listing in Figure 6.6 shows that the batch users have nearly perfect DBB-HR values. As a guideline, if there are 20 or more users and batch users cause less than 50% of the LRs, then the DBB-HR should be above 94. On the other hand, for less than 20 users, the DBB-HR may range between 91 and 94.

There are two situations where the DBB-HR can be inflated but does not necessarily imply that most of the requested data are available in the DBB.

Rollback Segment Header Activity

The rollback segment header activity controls the writing of changed data blocks to the rollback segments. The rollback segment header is a data block residing in the DBB. It is frequently modified by the update transactions. As such, it normally remains in the cache for long periods of time. Accesses to this block increase the value of the LR used in computing the DBB-HR, although it is not related to data blocks requested by applications. See Section 5.10.1 for additional details.

Page Fault

A data block within the DBB may be moved out to virtual memory when it is associated with an inactive process. If the block is needed later by another process, it is brought into the DBB. That event is called a *page fault* (see Section 6.7). When Oracle brings in the requested block to the DBB, it is recorded as an LR although the data block has been fetched from disk, which is the virtual memory. Thus, DBB-HR increases despite a PR caused by the page fault.

Oracle's system tables x$kcbrbh and x$kcbcbh track respectively the numbers of cache hits and cache misses when the database is running. Figures 6.7 and 6.8 contain the script files that show the changes in cache hits and cache misses respectively as we increase or decrease the DBB by N blocks at a time, where N is a number supplied by the user. You can use different values of N to experiment with the number of additional cache hits (or misses) caused by the increments (or decrements) in the size of the DBB.

```
REM  Additional Cache Hits due to Extra Buffers
REM  Script File Name: My_Directory/DBB_Cache_Hits.sql
REM  Spool File Name:  My_Directory/DBB_Cache_Hits.lst
REM  Author:            NAME
REM  Date Created:      DATE
REM  Purpose:   Explore how many additional cache hits you get as
REM                     you increase the size of DBB
REM                     Use the view x$kcbrbh
REM
REM
COLUMN TODAY    NEW_VALUE xTODAY NOPRINT FORMAT A1 TRUNC
```

FIGURE 6.7: Cache Hits Versus DBB Size

```
TTITLE LEFT xTODAY -
    RIGHT 'Page ' FORMAT 999 SQL.PNO -
    CENTER 'More Cache Hits with Larger DBB Size' SKIP 4
BTITLE  'Script File: My_Directory/DBB_Cache_Hits.sql|Spool File:
    My_Directory/DBB_Cache_Hits.lst'

COLUMN "More Blocks in DBB" FORMAT A30
COLUMN "More Cache Hits" FORMAT 999,999,999

SET LINESIZE 78
SET PAGESIZE 41
SET NEWPAGE 0
SET ECHO OFF
SET VERIFY OFF
SET SQLCASE UPPER

SPOOL   My_Directory/DBB_Cache_Hits.lst

accept interval_span NUMBER prompt 'Enter the number of blocks in
    each interval: '
select &interval_span * TRUNC (indx / &interval_span) + 1 || ' to '
    || &interval_span * (TRUNC (indx / &interval_span) + 1)
    "More Blocks in DBB", sum (count) "More Cache Hits",
    TO_CHAR (SysDate, 'fmMonth ddth, YYYY') TODAY
    from x$kcbrbh
    group by TRUNC (indx / &interval_span);

SPOOL OFF
```

FIGURE 6.7 (*continued*): Cache Hits Versus DBB Size

```
REM  Additional Cache Misses Due to Fewer Buffers
REM  Script File Name: My_Directory/DBB_Cache_Misses.sql
REM  Spool File Name:  My_Directory/DBB_Cache_Misses.lst
REM  Author:           NAME
REM  Date Created:     DATE
REM  Purpose:   Explore how many additional cache misses will occur
REM             as you decrease the size of DBB
REM             Use the view x$kcbcbh.
REM
REM

COLUMN TODAY  NEW_VALUE xTODAY NOPRINT FORMAT A1 TRUNC

TTITLE LEFT xTODAY -
    RIGHT 'Page ' FORMAT 999 SQL.PNO -
    CENTER 'More Cache Misses with Smaller DBB Size' SKIP 4
BTITLE 'Script File: My_Directory/DBB_Cache_Misses.sql|Spool File:
    My_Directory/DBB_Cache_Misses.lst'
```

FIGURE 6.8: Cache Misses Versus DBB Size

```
COLUMN "Fewer Blocks in DBB" FORMAT A30
COLUMN "More Cache Misses" FORMAT 999,999,999

SET LINESIZE 78
SET PAGESIZE 41
SET NEWPAGE 0
SET ECHO OFF
SET VERIFY OFF
SET SQLCASE UPPER

SPOOL  My_Directory/DBB_Cache_Misses.lst

accept interval_span NUMBER prompt 'Enter the number of blocks in
each interval: '
select &interval_span * TRUNC (indx / &interval_span) + 1 || ' to '
    || &interval_span * (TRUNC (indx / &interval_span) + 1)
    "Fewer Blocks in DBB", sum (count) "More Cache Misses",
    TO_CHAR (SysDate, 'fmMonth ddth, YYYY') TODAY
    from x$kcbcbh
    group by TRUNC (indx / &interval_span);
SPOOL OFF
```

FIGURE 6.8 (*continued*): Cache Misses Versus DBB Size

Alternatively, one can experiment with the effect of more or fewer blocks on cache hits or misses by activating the two views, V$RECENT_BUCKET and V$CURRENT_BUCKET. The view V$RECENT_BUCKET is activated by setting the initialization parameter DB_BLOCK_LRU_EXTENDED_STATISTICS to a positive integer N, say, (default being zero). Then Oracle collects N rows of statistics to populate the view, each row reflecting the effect on cache hits of adding one more buffer to the DBB up to the maximum of N buffers. The view V$CURRENT_BUCKET is activated by setting the initialization parameter DB_BLOCK_LRU _STATISTICS to TRUE, the default being FALSE. Then the view V$CURRENT_BUCKET keeps track of the number of additional cache misses that will occur as a result of removing buffers from the DBB. By enabling these two initialization parameters, however, you cause a large performance loss to the system. So, they should be enabled only when the system is lightly loaded. Using the script files in Figures 6.7 and 6.8 to accomplish the same goal is a much more preferable way than enabling these two views. Figures 6.7A and 6.8A contain the SELECT statements that should be used instead of the SELECT statements appearing in Figures 6.7 and 6.8 respectively if the views V$RECENT_BUCKET and V$CURRENT_BUCKET are used instead of the tables x$kcbrbh and x$kcbcbh. The rest of the programs in Figures 6.7 and 6.8 remain the same.

```
select &interval_span * TRUNC (rownum / &interval_span) + 1 || ' to '
   || &interval_span * (TRUNC (rownum / &interval_span) + 1)
   "More Blocks in DBB", sum (count) "More Cache Hits",
   TO_CHAR (SysDate, 'fmMonth ddth, YYYY') TODAY
   from V$RECENT_BUCKET
   group by TRUNC (rownum / &interval_span);
```

FIGURE 6.7A: SELECT Statement for V$RECENT_BUCKET

```
select &interval_span * TRUNC (rownum / &interval_span) + 1 || ' to '
   || &interval_span * (TRUNC (rownum / &interval_span) + 1)
   "Fewer Blocks in DBB", sum (count) "More Cache Misses",
   TO_CHAR (SysDate, 'fmMonth ddth, YYYY') TODAY
   from V$CURRENT_BUCKET
   where rownum > 0
   group by TRUNC (rownum / &interval_span);
```

FIGURE 6.8A: SELECT Statement for V$CURRENT_BUCKET

6.4 Redo Log Buffer

The redo log buffer (RLB) holds the redo log entries in the cache before they are written to a redo log file by the LGWR process. These entries contain the changes that have been made to the database block buffers by the database transactions. The size of the RLB in number of bytes is set by the value of the initialization parameter LOG_BUFFER. The larger the value of this parameter, the lower the redo log file I/O. Oracle recommends a value of 65,536 or more for a busy system. However, for large OLTP production databases the LOG_BUFFER should be 2 to 4 MB in size. A common default value for Oracle databases under UNIX is 163,840 bytes (= 160 KB).

The efficiency of the RLB is measured by the metric called the *redo log buffer hit ratio* (RLB-HR) that measures the ratio of "redo log space requests" to "redo entries." Oracle recommends that the RLB-HR should be ≤ 1/5,000. The view V$SYSSTAT lists 14 parameters under the "Redo" CLASS that provide information about the RLB, redo log files, and the background process LGWR. Three of them are related to RLB-HR and are described below:

- Redo entries = Number of entries made in RLB due to database transactions;
- Redo log space requests = Number of times a user process waits for space in the RLB so that a redo entry can be written there;
- Redo log space wait time = Total elapsed time of waiting for redo log space requests, measured in 1/100ths of a second.

The "redo log space requests" statistic is the most critical for improving the efficiency of the RLB. It should be as close to zero as possible. An increase of the initialization parameter LOG_BUFFER will help decrease this statistic. A positive value of this statistic occurs when both the RLB and the active online redo log file are full so that the LGWR is waiting for disk space in the form of an online redo log file to empty the contents of the RLB. Disk space is made available by performing a log switch that starts a new redo log file. However, for the log switch to occur, Oracle must ensure that all the committed dirty buffers in the data block buffer cache have been written to disk files via the DBWR. If a database has a large data block buffer full of dirty buffers and small redo log files, then a log switch has to wait for the DBWR to write the dirty buffers into disk files before continuing. We can see, therefore, that a chain of events must occur to resolve the situation triggered by a redo log space request.

Since prevention is always better than cure, the metric RLB-HR should be monitored continuously and if it shows an increasing trend toward the value of 1/5,000 (= .0002), the DBA should take corrective action. Figure 6.9 contains the script file to compute RLB-HR and Figure 6.10 shows a sample output from the script file.

```
REM   Redo Log Buffer Hit Ratio for Example Database
REM   Script File Name: /My_Directory/RLB_HR_value.sql
REM   Spool File Name:  /My_Directory/RLB_HR_value.lst
REM   Author:           NAME
REM   Date Created:     DATE
REM   Purpose:          Compute the hit ratio for redo log buffers
                        at a given instant
REM                     Use the view V$SYSSTAT
REM
REM
COLUMN name FORMAT A30
set linesize 120
set pagesize 41
set newpage 0
spool /My_Directory/RLB_HR_value.lst
select name, value from v$sysstat where name in ('redo entries',
'redo log space requests', 'redo log space wait time')
    order by name;
select TO_CHAR (sysdate, 'MM/DD/YY HH:MI:SS') "RunTime", a.value
"Redo Entries",
    b.value "RL Req", ROUND (c.value / 100) "RL Wait in Secs",
    ROUND ((5000 * b.value) / a.value) "RLB-HR"
    from v$sysstat a, v$sysstat b, v$sysstat c
    where a.name = 'redo entries'
    and   b.name = 'redo log space requests'
    and   c.name = 'redo log space wait time';
spool off
```

FIGURE 6.9: Computation of Hit Ratio RLB-HR

6. Tuning of Memory-Resident Data Structures

```
NAME                                              VALUE
------------------------                          --------
redo entries                                      5213968
redo log space requests                                46
redo log space wait time                             1945

RunTime                 Redo Entries  RL Req   RL Wait in Secs   RLB-HR
-----------------       ------------  ------   ---------------   ------
08/12/99 10:08:40       5213970           46                19        0
```

FIGURE 6.10: Sample Value of RLB-HR

6.5 Shared SQL Pool

The shared SQL pool (SSP) consists of three parts: library cache (LC), dictionary cache (DC), and user global area (UGA). We discuss the tuning of the LC and DC here. The UGA has very little impact on the overall performance of a database application.

Library Cache

The LC contains the parse tree and the execution plan for all SQL and PL/SQL statements that are encountered in the course of a transaction, both retrieval and update. Chapter 8 discusses query processing and optimization in detail. For our purpose here, it will suffice to understand that the parsing phase that produces the parse tree is the most time consuming and resource intensive for the following reasons.

- The SQL syntax of the statement is checked.
- All syntax errors are resolved.
- A search is made to determine if an identical SQL statement already resides in the LC.
- The execution plan is prepared.

The metric to measure the efficiency of LC is the *library cache hit ratio* (LC-HR). It uses two statistics, pins and reloads, from the view V$LIBRARYCACHE. A *pin* indicates a cache hit; i.e., the parse tree is available in cache. A *reload* indicates a cache miss, i.e., the parse tree has been flushed from LC under the LRU algorithm and, therefore, must be reloaded from disk. LC-HR represents the ratio

$$\frac{\text{pins}}{\text{pins} + \text{reloads}}$$

and should be >99%. Figure 6.11 provides the script file to compute LC-HR and Figure 6.12 shows a sample output from running the script.

6.5 Shared SQL Pool

```
REM  Library Cache Hit Ratio for Example Database
REM  Script File Name:  /My_Directory/LC_HR_value.sql
REM  Spool File Name:   /My_Directory/LC_HR_value.lst
REM  Author:            NAME
REM  Date Created:      DATE
REM  Purpose:           Compute the hit ratio for library cache at a
REM                     given instant
REM                     Use the view V$LIBRARYCACHE
REM
REM

spool LC_HR_value.lst
select TO_CHAR (sysdate, 'MM/DD/YY HH:MI:SS') "RunTime", sum (pins)
"Total PINS",
    sum (reloads) "Total RELOADS",
    ROUND (sum (pins) / ( sum (pins) + sum (reloads)) ) "LC-HR"
    from v$librarycache;
spool off
```

FIGURE 6.11: Computation of Hit Ratio LC-HR

```
RunTime                  Total PINS      Total RELOADS       LC-HR
-----------------        ----------      -------------       ------
08/16/99 11:08:26        2514995                   611            1
```

FIGURE 6.12: Sample Value of LC-HR

Here we have a perfect value of 1 (or 100%) for the LC-HR. To make the LC-HR approach 1, we need to make "reloads" approach zero, i.e., reduce the number of cache misses. This is the primary goal for tuning the LC. Cache misses can be reduced by keeping parsing to a minimum as follows.

(a) Use as much generic code as possible so that SQL statements can utilize a shared SQL area in SSP.
(b) Use bind variables rather than constants. A *bind variable* in a PL/SQL program is a host variable to which a specific value is bound. The bind variable accepts its value at runtime. Thus, even if its value changes, the parsed form of the SQL statement remains the same and, therefore, the statement is not reparsed.
(c) Increase the size of the LC by increasing the value of the initialization parameter SHARED_POOL_SIZE. The larger LC will be flushed less often by the LRU algorithm.

Figure 6.13 contains a script file to compute SHARED_POOL_SIZE based on the current load and employing a user-supplied padding factor for free space. It is recom-

6. Tuning of Memory-Resident Data Structures

mended that this factor be kept around 33% at start. The following seven-step algorithm is used in this script.

1. Find the primary user of the database. This is usually a generic account representing the application such as OPS$INVOICE, etc.
2. Find the amount of memory utilized by the user in (1).
3. Find the amount of memory in SSP currently in use.
4. Ask for an estimated number of concurrent users accessing the application.
5. Calculate the currently used SSP size as the expression (2) * (4) + (3).
6. Ask for the padding factor for free space, say PF, as a positive decimal number <1.
7. The optimal value of SHARED_POOL_SIZE is (5) * (1 + PF).

```
REM  Shared Pool Size for Example Database
REM  Script File Name:  /My_Directory/Shared_Pool_Size.sql
REM  Spool File Name:   /My_Directory/Shared_Pool_Size.lst
REM  Author:            NAME
REM  Date Created:      DATE
REM  Purpose:           Calculate the size of Shared SQL Pool (SSP)
REM                     based on estimated usage and a padding
REM                     factor for free space.
REM                     Use the views V$PROCESS, V$SESSION,
REM                     V$SESSSTAT, and V$SQLAREA.
REM

SPOOL Shared_Pool_Size.lst

SET ECHO OFF
SET VERIFY OFF
SET HEADING OFF

REM  The script implements a 7-step procedure.

REM  Step 1:  Ask for the primary user of the database. This is
                usually a generic account representing the
REM             application such as INVOICE, MERCHANDISE, etc.

ACCEPT USERNAME PROMPT 'Enter the primary user of the database: '

COLUMN SID NEW_VALUE Primary_User

SELECT SID FROM V$PROCESS A, V$SESSION B
    WHERE A.ADDR = B.PADDR
    AND   B.USERNAME = 'OPS$' || UPPER ('&USERNAME');

REM  Step 2: Find the amount of memory used by the user in Step 1.

COLUMN VALUE NEW_VALUE Memory_Used

SELECT VALUE FROM V$SESSTAT
    WHERE STATISTIC# = 16
    AND   SID = &Primary_User;
```

FIGURE 6.13: Script File to Compute SHARED_POOL_SIZE

```
REM  Step 3: Find the amount of memory in SSP currently in use.
COLUMN SSP_MEMORY NEW_VALUE SSP_Memory_Used
SELECT SUM (SHARABLE_MEM) SSP_MEMORY
    FROM V$SQLAREA;
REM  Step 4:  Ask for an estimated number of concurrent users. This
REM           number will be used to estimate the load on SSP.
ACCEPT  NumUsers PROMPT 'Enter the estimated number of concurrent
        users: '
REM  Step 5: Use the following formula to calculate the size of SSP
REM          as currently used:
REM          Estimated_Current_SSP_Size =
REM          Memory_Used x NumUsers + SSP_Memory_Used
REM          Step 6: Ask for the padding factor for free space as a
             decimal number.
PROMPT  Enter as a decimal number the percentage of SSP that you
        want to reserve as free space:
ACCEPT  Padding_Factor

REM  Step 7:  The optimal value of SHARED_POOL_SIZE is computed by
REM           the formula:
REM           Estimated_SSP_Size = (1 + Padding_Factor) *
              Estimated_Current_SSP_Size
PROMPT
PROMPT
PROMPT

PROMPT
*****************************************************************
PROMPT Final Summary Results:
PROMPT
PROMPT The primary user is &USERNAME
PROMPT
PROMPT Estimated number of concurrent users is &NumUsers
PROMPT
PROMPT Padding factor for free space is &Padding_Factor
SELECT 'Total shared pool based on current user volume is ' ||
    ROUND (((&Memory_Used * &NumUsers + &SSP_Memory_Used)) /
    1048576)   || ' MB' FROM DUAL;
SELECT 'Estimated size of shared pool with ' || &Padding_Factor * 100
    || '% free space allowance is '
    || ROUND ((1 + &Padding_Factor) * (&Memory_Used * &NumUsers +
&SSP_Memory_Used) / 1048576 )
    || ' MB' FROM DUAL;
PROMPT
SPOOL OFF
```

FIGURE 6.13 (*continued*): Script File to Compute SHARED_POOL_SIZE

152   6. Tuning of Memory-Resident Data Structures

FIGURE 6.14 shows a sample output from this script.

```
Enter the primary user of the database: invoice
Enter the estimated number of concurrent users: 49
Enter as a decimal number the percentage of SSP that you want to
reserve as free space:
.3
****************************************************************
Final Summary Results:

The primary user is invoice

Estimated number of concurrent users is 49

Padding factor for free space is .3

Total shared pool based on current user volume is 21 MB

Estimated size of shared pool with 30% free space allowance is 27 MB
```

FIGURE 6.14: Computation of SHARED_POOL_SIZE

There is one phenomenon called invalidation that increases cache misses resulting in a higher value of "reloads". An *invalidation* occurs when a schema object referenced earlier in a SQL statement is modified subsequently. If the object is a table or an index, such modifications occur as a result of ALTER or DROP TABLE, ANALYZE TABLE, ALTER or DROP INDEX, etc. If the object is a PL/SQL package, procedure, or function, it is modified via recompilation. In any such case, the shared SQL area referencing that object becomes invalidated and Oracle marks the area as "invalid." A SQL statement referencing the modified object must be reparsed the next time it is executed and, therefore, the parsed form must be reloaded. Figure 6.15 contains a script file that returns the number of invalidations from V$LIBRARYCACHE. Figure 6.16 contains an Oracle session transcript showing the impact of an ANALYZE command on reloads.

```
REM  Impact of Invalidations on Library Cache Hit Ratio for Example
REM  Database
REM  Script File Name:  /My_Directory/Invalidation.sql
REM  Author:            NAME
REM  Date Created:      DATE
REM  Purpose:           Assess the impact of invalidation on the hit
REM                     ratio for library cache
REM                     Use the view V$LIBRARYCACHE
REM
REM
```

FIGURE 6.15: Script File for Invalidations

6.5 Shared SQL Pool

```
select TO_CHAR (sysdate, 'MM/DD/YY HH:MI:SS') "RunTime", namespace,
pins,
     reloads, Invalidations
     from v$librarycache
     order by namespace;
```

FIGURE 6.15 (*continued*): Script File for Invalidations

```
SQL> @Invalidation
RunTime              NAMESPACE          PINS      RELOADS   INVALIDATIONS
-----------------    ---------------    ------    -------   -------------
08/18/99 12:08:57    BODY                  153          3               0
08/18/99 12:08:57    CLUSTER              5291          3               0
08/18/99 12:08:57    INDEX                  41          0               0
08/18/99 12:08:57    OBJECT                  0          0               0
08/18/99 12:08:57    PIPE                    0          0               0
08/18/99 12:08:57    SQL AREA           302836        287            1312
08/18/99 12:08:57    TABLE/PROCEDURE     38295        563               0
08/18/99 12:08:57    TRIGGER                 0          0               0
8 rows selected.
SQL> analyze table ORDER compute statistics;
Table analyzed.
SQL> @Invalidation
RunTime              NAMESPACE          PINS      RELOADS   INVALIDATIONS
-----------------    ---------------    ------    -------   -------------
08/18/99 12:08:53    BODY                  153          3               0
08/18/99 12:08:53    CLUSTER              5323          3               0
08/18/99 12:08:53    INDEX                  41          0               0
08/18/99 12:08:53    OBJECT                  0          0               0
08/18/99 12:08:53    PIPE                    0          0               0
08/18/99 12:08:53    SQL AREA           303199        294            1359
08/18/99 12:08:53    TABLE/PROCEDURE     38342        570               0
08/18/99 12:08:53    TRIGGER                 0          0               0
8 rows selected.
```

FIGURE 6.16: Oracle Session Transcript for Invalidation

Note that RELOADS and INVALIDATIONS for the SQL AREA are 287 and 1,312 respectively before the ANALYZE command is issued. Subsequently, they increase to 294 and 1,359 respectively.

Dictionary Cache

The dictionary cache (DC) contains relevant data from Oracle's data dictionary pertaining to database objects that are referenced in SQL statements used by applications. If the needed data are available in DC, we have a "gets." If, however, the data have to be brought into DC from disk, we have a "getmisses." After a database has been running for some time, most of the required data are normally found in DC so that the value of "getmisses" becomes low. The efficiency of DC is measured by the *dictionary cache hit ratio* (DC-HR), which is computed by the following formula,

$$\frac{gets}{gets + getmisses}.$$

Ideally, the DC-HR should be 1 implying that all the data dictionary information is available in DC. If DC-HR <90%, the value of the initialization parameter SHARED_POOL_SIZE should be increased using the script in Figure 6.13. Figure 6.17 contains the script file to compute the DC-HR and Figure 6.18 shows a sample output form running this script.

```
REM  Dictionary Cache Hit Ratio for Example Database
REM  Script File Name: /My_Directory/DC_HR_value.sql
REM  Spool File Name:  /My_Directory/DC_HR_value.lst
REM  Author:           NAME
REM  Date Created:     DATE
REM  Purpose:          Compute the hit ratio for dictionary cache
REM                    at a given REM instant
REM                    Use the view V$ROWCACHE
REM
spool DC_HR_value.lst
select TO_CHAR (sysdate, 'MM/DD/YY HH:MI:SS') "RunTime",
    sum (gets) "Total GETS", sum (getmisses) "Total MISSES",
    ROUND (sum (gets) / ( sum (gets) + sum (getmisses)) ) "DC-HR"
    from v$rowcache;
spool off
```

FIGURE 6.17: Script File to Compute DC-HR

```
RunTime            Total GETS    Total MISSES    DC-HR
-----------------  ----------    ------------    ------
08/18/99 04:08:33     2031718           4868         1
1 row selected.
```

FIGURE 6.18: Sample Partial Output

The value of the DC-HR for the three initialization parameters, DC_USERS, DC_USER_GRANTS, and DC_TABLE_GRANTS, should be kept above 95%, because they are used during almost all SQL processing and hence should reside in the DC. Figure 6.19 contains the script file to compute the DC-HR for each initialization parameter with (gets + getmisses) > 0. Figure 6.20 shows a sample output form running this script.

```
REM   Dictionary Cache Hit Ratio for Individual Parameters in
REM   Example Database
REM   Script File Name:    /My_Directory/DC_HR_Parameter_value.sql
REM   Spool File Name:     /My_Directory/DC_HR_Parameter_value.lst
REM   Author:              NAME
REM   Date Created:        DATE
REM   Purpose:             Compute the hit ratio for dictionary cache
REM                        at a given instant
REM                        Use the view V$ROWCACHE
REM
REM

spool DC_HR_Parameter_value.lst
column parameter heading Parameter format a20
select TO_CHAR (sysdate, 'MM/DD/YY HH:MI:SS') "RunTime",
    parameter, gets "Total GETS", getmisses "Total MISSES",
    ROUND ( gets / (gets + getmisses) ) "DC-HR"
    from v$rowcache
    where gets + getmisses > 0
    order by parameter;
spool off
```

FIGURE 6.19: Script File to Compute DC-HR for Specific Parameters

RunTime	Parameter	Total GETS	Total MISSES	DC-HR
08/18/99 04:08:17	dc_files	259	25	1
08/18/99 04:08:17	dc_objects	17034	623	1
08/18/99 04:08:17	dc_profiles	1445	1	1
08/18/99 04:08:17	dc_segments	36459	475	1
08/18/99 04:08:17	dc_sequences	91777	18	1
08/18/99 04:08:17	dc_users	77095	58	1

FIGURE 6.20: Sample Partial Output

6.6 Background Processes

Several initialization parameters interact with the background processes during the database operation. The following table lists alphabetically the more critical parameters along with their default values and the associated background processes.

Parameter	Default Value	Process
ARCH_IO_SLAVES	0	ARCH
DBWR_IO_SLAVES	0	DBWR
LGWR_IO_SLAVES	0	LGWR
LOG_ARCHIVE_BUFFER_SIZE	OS dependent	ARCH
LOG_ARCHIVE_BUFFERS	OS dependent	ARCH
LOG_ARCHIVE_START	FALSE	ARCH
LOG_CHECKPOINT_INTERVAL	OS dependent	LGWR

There are four distinct background processes ARCH, CKPT, DBWR, and LGWR in the above list. They control four areas of Oracle database functions, as listed below.

- ARCH transfers the contents of online redo log files to archived redo log files.
- CKPT triggers the checkpoint event.
- DBWR transfers dirty buffers from the data block buffer cache to disk files.
- LGWR transfers the contents of the redo log buffer cache to the online redo log file groups.

We now examine each background process separately.

6.6.1 DBWR

If an instance has only one DBWR process, it may cause a bottleneck during I/O operations even if data files are properly distributed among multiple devices. It is better to have the effect of running multiple DBWRs for an instance. The following guideline can be used for determining an optimal number of DBWRs.

Rule: Allow one DBWR for every 50 online users performing both retrievals and updates and one DBWR for every two batch jobs performing updates.

We can have the effect of multiple DBWR processes in an instance in two ways by using two different initialization parameters: DBWR_IO_SLAVES or DB_WRITER_PROCESSES. Each procedure is described below.

To determine the number of DBWRs needed for an instance, proceed as follows:

(a) Determine the maximum number of concurrent logins since the database was started. Figure 6.21 contains a script file along with an output to accomplish this task. Note that the columns, SESSIONS_HIGHWATER and SESSIONS_CURRENT in Figure 6.21 have the following meanings.

6.6 Background Processes

```
         SESSIONS_HIGHWATER = highest number of concurrent user
                              sessions since the instance started
         SESSIONS_CURRENT = current number of concurrent user
                            sessions
```

```
select SESSIONS_HIGHWATER "Max #Concurrent Users",
SESSIONS_CURRENT "Current #Concurrent Users"
from v$license;

Sample Output:

Max #Concurrent Users            Current #Concurrent Users
---------------------            -------------------------
          82                                72
```

FIGURE 6.21: Number of Concurrent Users

(b) Determine the distribution of both READ and WRITE I/Os among the datafiles to assess if the database is read-intensive or write-intensive. A write-intensive database should have multiple DBWRs. A read-intensive database may need multiple DBWRs dictated by the number of concurrent online users and batch processes running against the database. Figure 6.22 contains a script file to extract the I/O load information.

```
REM  I/O Load Distribution Among Disk Files
REM  Script File Name:   /My_Directory/IO_Load_Distribution.sql
REM  Spool File Name:    /My_Directory/IO_Load_Distribution.lst
REM  Author:             NAME
REM  Date Created:       DATE
REM  Purpose:            Display list of disk files in descending
REM                      order of
REM                      total I/O operations.
REM

COLUMN TODAY  NEW_VALUE xTODAY NOPRINT FORMAT A1 TRUNC

TTITLE LEFT xTODAY -
    RIGHT 'Page ' FORMAT 999 SQL.PNO -
    CENTER 'I/O Load Distribution among Disk Files ' SKIP 3
BTITLE 'Script File: /My_Directory/IO_Load_Distribution.sql|Spool
File: /My_Directory/IO_Load_Distribution.lst'

COLUMN NAME HEADING 'File|Name' FORMAT A30

SET LINESIZE 120
SET PAGESIZE 41
SET NEWPAGE 0
```

FIGURE 6.22: I/O Load Distribution Among Disks

```
SPOOL IO_Load_Distribution.lst
SELECT NAME, PHYBLKRD, PHYBLKWRT, PHYBLKRD + PHYBLKWRT "I/O Volume",
    ROUND (100 * PHYBLKRD / (PHYBLKRD + PHYBLKWRT)) "%READ Volume",
    ROUND (100 * PHYBLKWRT / (PHYBLKRD + PHYBLKWRT)) "%WRITE Volume",
    TO_CHAR (SysDate, 'fmMonth ddth, YYYY') TODAY
    from V$FILESTAT, V$DATAFILE
    WHERE V$FILESTAT.FILE# = V$DATAFILE.FILE#
    ORDER BY ROUND (100 * PHYBLKWRT / (PHYBLKRD + PHYBLKWRT))
DESC;
SELECT NAME, PHYRDS, PHYWRTS, PHYRDS + PHYWRTS "I/O Count",
    ROUND (100 * PHYRDS / (PHYRDS + PHYWRTS)) "%READ Count",
    ROUND (100 * PHYWRTS / (PHYRDS + PHYWRTS)) "%WRITE Count",
    TO_CHAR (SysDate, 'fmMonth ddth, YYYY') TODAY
    from V$FILESTAT, V$DATAFILE
    WHERE V$FILESTAT.FILE# = V$DATAFILE.FILE#
    ORDER BY ROUND (100 * PHYWRTS / (PHYRDS + PHYWRTS)) DESC;
SPOOL OFF
```

FIGURE 6.22 (*continued*): I/O Load Distribution Among Disks

Figure 6.23 contains a partial output file from running the script shown in Figure 6.22.

May 17th, 2001		I/O Load Distribution among Disk Files			Page 1
File Name	PHYBLKRD	PHYBLKWRT	I/O Volume	%READ Volume	%WRITE Volume
/abc02/temp01.dbf	133182	2049685	2182867	6	94
/abc01/rbs01.dbf	108905	861163	970068	11	89
/abc02/rbs04.dbf	131855	895593	1027448	13	87
/abc02/temp03.dbf	508201	2981511	3489712	15	85
/abc01/rbs02.dbf	140896	585761	726657	19	81
/abc02/temp02.dbf	117277	500856	618133	19	81

FIGURE 6.23: Partial Output of I/O Load Distribution

/abc02/rbs03.dbf	199062	576986	776048	26	74
/abc05/bills.dbf	43676	69088	112764	39	61

```
May 17th, 2001       I/O Load Distribution among Disk Files    Page 1
File                                         I/O       %READ    %WRITE
Name                 PHYRDS    PHYWRTS       Count     Count    Count
--------------       -------   -------       -------   ------   ------
/abc02/temp01.         19943   2049685       2069628        1       99
dbf
/abc02/temp03.         59698   2981511       3041209        2       98
dbf
/abc02/temp02.         17241    500856        518097        3       97
dbf
/abc01/rbs01.         108905    861163        970068       11       89
dbf
/abc02/rbs04.         131855    895593       1027448       13       87
dbf
/abc01/rbs02.         140896    585761        726657       19       81
dbf
/abc02/rbs03.         199062    576986        776048       26       74
dbf
/abc05/billingx02.     43676     69088        112764       39       61
dbf
```

FIGURE 6.23 (*continued*): Partial Output of I/O Load Distribution

(c) Determine the optimal number of DBWRs by using the rule of thumb given at the beginning of this section. This number should be the same or very close to the number of database files or disks as listed in Figure 6.23.

Let us assume that we need to have the effect of running n DBWR processes. We can implement that in two different ways:

- Via the Parameter DBWR_IO_SLAVES—Set the value of the parameter DBWR_IO_SLAVES (called DB_WRITERS in Oracle7) to n;
- Via the Parameter DB_WRITER_PROCESSES—Set the value of the parameter DB_WRITER_PROCESSES to n. Here n must be less than or equal to 10.

The effect of the first option is to have a single DBWR master process spawn n I/O slave processes to parallelize the writing of the contents of the data block buffer cache among these n processes. The effect of the second option is to have n (≤ 10) DBWR processes labeled DBW0 through DBWn to parallelize both the reading and the writing of the contents of the data block buffer cache among these n processes. The only limitation of this latter option is that n must be less than or equal to 10. From the throughput standpoint, n DBWR processes (second option) deliver more throughput than one DBWR process with n I/O slave processes (first option) can. However, if we take the first option, only one DBWR process will be set regardless of the value of the initialization parameter DB_WRITER_PROCESSES.

Let us now apply the above three-step procedure to the database. In doing so we come across several contradictions which are resolved as follows.

- The rule appearing above Step (a) applied to Figure 6.21 suggests two DBWRs to handle the online users. Also, it is known that three to four concurrent batch jobs are run for the application. Hence the rule adds two more DBWRs bringing the total count of DBWRs to four.
- We, therefore, expect to have four or five disks supporting the database, according to Step (c). However, the system uses seven disks, contradicting Step (c).
- Looking at the full output, only a part of which appears in Figure 6.23, we find that only 8 out of a total of 69 rows returned have both %WRITE Volume and %WRITE Count above 60%. So, the application is not write-intensive. This may suggest a smaller number of DBWRs than four.
- But we further notice that the I/O load is not evenly distributed. Disks /abc01 and /abc02 are heavily loaded compared to the remaining five disks in the system. By properly balancing the I/O load among them the total number of disks can be brought down to five.
- Thus, the number of DBWRs is very close to the number of disks, which resolves the contradiction with Step (c).
- Accordingly, we implement this configuration under Oracle 8i *either* by setting the initialization parameter DBWR_IO_SLAVES to the value 4 (default being zero), *or* by setting DB_WRITER_PROCESSES to 4 (default being one).

We now give a five-step procedure to distribute the I/O load evenly among disks. Let us suppose that we need to move the datafile *xyz.dbf* allocated to the tablespace TBS from the disk *disk_1* to the disk *disk_2*. We then proceed as follows.

(a) Bring TBS offline via the following command issued from the Server Manager.

    ALTER TABLESPACE TBS OFFLINE;

(b) Copy the file *xyz.dbf* from *disk_1* to *disk_2* using the operating system command for copying files (e.g., cp /disk_1/xyz.dbf /disk_2/xyz.dbf in UNIX).

(c) Designate the file on disk_2 as the datafile for TBS via the following command.

    ALTER TABLESAPCE TBS
     RENAME /disk_1/xyz.dbf TO /disk_2/xyz.dbf;

(d) Bring TBS online with this new datafile via the following command issued from the Server Manager.

```
    ALTER TABLESPACE TBS ONLINE;
```

(e) Delete the old file /disk_1/xyz.dbf via the operating system command for deleting files when you are sure that the new datafile is working (e.g., `rm /disk_1/xyz.dbf` in UNIX).

6.6.2 LGWR

An instance can be made to run multiple LGWR processes by setting the initialization parameter LGWR_IO_SLAVES to a positive value, the default being zero. There are two cases to consider depending on whether the instance is running in the ARCHIVELOG or in NOARCHIVELOG mode, the latter being the default. In the case of the former, there is an additional background process ARCH that has to be coordinated with LGWR. In the case of the latter, LGWR wakes up periodically and transfers the contents of the redo log buffer into the online redo log files. When one file becomes full, a *log switch* occurs and LGWR starts using the next redo log file. Figure 6.24 gives a script file to show the log switch frequencies over a 24-hour period. Figure 6.25 shows its partial output.

```
REM  Log Switch Frequency List
REM  Script File Name:  /My_Directory/Log_Switch_Frequency.sql
REM  Spool File Name:   /My_Directory/Log_Switch_Frequency.lst
REM  Author:            NAME
REM  Date Created:      DATE
REM  Purpose:           Display the times of log switches during the
REM                     past day
REM                     Use the view V$LOG_HISTORY.
REM

SPOOL Log_Switch_Frequency.lst

SET LINESIZE 78
SET PAGESIZE 41
SET NEWPAGE 0
SELECT TO_CHAR (FIRST_TIME, 'DD-MON-YYYY HH24:MI:SS') "Log Switch
Date/Time"
    FROM V$LOG_HISTORY
    WHERE FIRST_TIME > SysDate - 1
    ORDER BY TO_CHAR (FIRST_TIME, 'DD-MON-YYYY HH24:MI:SS') DESC;
SPOOL OFF
```

FIGURE 6.24: Script File for Log Switch Frequencies

6. Tuning of Memory-Resident Data Structures

```
Log Switch Date/Time
-------------------
25-AUG-1999 16:30:00
25-AUG-1999 16:15:00
25-AUG-1999 16:00:00
25-AUG-1999 15:45:00
25-AUG-1999 15:30:00
25-AUG-1999 15:15:00
25-AUG-1999 15:00:00
25-AUG-1999 14:45:00
25-AUG-1999 14:37:31
25-AUG-1999 14:30:00
25-AUG-1999 14:26:55
25-AUG-1999 14:15:02
25-AUG-1999 14:14:49
25-AUG-1999 14:11:17
25-AUG-1999 14:07:33
25-AUG-1999 14:03:45
25-AUG-1999 14:00:00
25-AUG-1999 13:57:33
25-AUG-1999 13:54:28
25-AUG-1999 13:51:21
25-AUG-1999 13:48:16
25-AUG-1999 13:45:01
25-AUG-1999 13:44:59
25-AUG-1999 13:41:53
```

FIGURE 6.25: Sample Log Switch Frequency Values

Figure 6.25 is a partial list of log switch times. It shows that the first eight switches occurred every 15 minutes. Then the log switches occurred more frequently. The climax was reached when two successive log switches took place only 13 seconds apart, the one at 14:14:49 being followed by the next at 14:15:02. Such a situation usually arises during very large batch jobs running for a long time. Subsequently, the situation improved, however. For a high-activity production database there should be enough redo log files of adequate size so that log switches occur every 20 to 30 minutes. The database in Figure 6.25 has five redo log files of size 50 MB each (see Figure 6.27). The size is too small for the production environment in which the database runs and to start with should be at least tripled.

Figure 6.26 contains a script file that lists the names, sizes, and status of the redo log files and Figure 6.27 shows its output.

```
REM   Redo Log File List
REM   Script File Name:    /My_Directory/Redo_Log.sql
REM   Spool File Name:     /My_Directory/Redo_Log.lst
REM   Author:              NAME
REM   Date Created:        DATE
REM   Purpose:             Display the names, sizes, and status of
REM                        redo log files
REM                        Use the view V$LOG and V$LOGFILE.
REM
REM

SPOOL Redo_Log.lst

COLUMN MEMBER FORMAT A35
select member, a.group#, members, ROUND (bytes / 1048576) "Size in
MB", a.status
     from v$logfile a, v$log b
     where a.group# = b.group#
     order by member;
SPOOL OFF
```

FIGURE 6.26: Script for Redo Log File List

MEMBER	GROUP#	MEMBERS	Size in MB	STATUS
/d01/oradata/INVOICE/redo01b.log	1	2	50	
/d01/oradata/INVOICE/redo02b.log	2	2	50	
/d01/oradata/INVOICE/redo03b.log	3	2	50	
/d01/oradata/INVOICE/redo04b.log	4	2	50	
/d01/oradata/INVOICE/redo05b.log	5	2	50	
/d02/oradata/INVOICE/redo01a.log	1	2	50	
/d02/oradata/INVOICE/redo02a.log	2	2	50	
/d02/oradata/INVOICE/redo03a.log	3	2	50	
/d02/oradata/INVOICE/redo04a.log	4	2	50	
/d02/oradata/INVOICE/redo05a.log	5	2	50	

FIGURE 6.27: Redo Log File List

Note that STATUS = blank in Figure 6.27 indicates that all the files are in use.

6.6.3 CKPT

When a *checkpoint* occurs, two events occur:

- DBWR writes the modified contents of the data block buffer cache, which are called dirty buffers, into the appropriate database files; and
- CKPT updates the control files and the headers in all database files to record the time of the last checkpoint.

A log switch always triggers a checkpoint, but not vice versa. In scheduling a checkpoint we examine two options.

(a) A checkpoint need not occur more frequently than the log switches.

In this case, set the initialization parameter LOG_CHECKPOINT_INTERVAL to a value larger than the size of the online redo log file. This parameter represents the number of redo log file blocks based on the size of the operating system blocks (and not the Oracle blocks) that must be written to the online redo log file by LGWR at each checkpoint. When the value exceeds the size of an online redo log file, a checkpoint occurs only at a log switch. This means that if a system or media crash occurs, data will be lost only since the last log switch occurred. This usually suffices for most production databases. However, databases for a mission-critical application may need more frequent checkpoints so that in case of a crash data will be lost over a much smaller interval of time. This leads us to the second option described below.

(b) A checkpoint must occur more frequently than the log switches.

In this case, set the value of LOG_CHECKPOINT_INTERVAL such that the checkpoints are evenly distributed over the size of the redo log file. For example, if the redo log file consists of 20,000 operating system blocks, set the value of the parameter to a factor of 20,000, say, at 5,000 operating system blocks. This will cause a checkpoint to occur four times as the redo log file fills up to its capacity. The fourth checkpoint will coincide with a log switch. To enforce this option, set the initialization parameter LOG_CHECKPOINT_TIMEOUT to zero, which is the default. This parameter measures the number of seconds elapsed between two consecutive checkpoints. If, for instance, we want a checkpoint every 15 minutes, we set the value of this parameter to 900. By setting it to zero, we disable time-based checkpoints, i.e., no additional checkpoints occur between log switches or between checkpoints forced by LOG_CHECKPOINT_ INTERVAL.

6.6.4 ARCH

ARCH is activated after the database is made to run in ARCHIVELOG mode as follows from the Server Manager,

```
SVRMGR> connect internal
SVRMGR> startup mount database_name;
SVRMGR> alter database archivelog;
SVRMGR> archive log start;
SVRMGR> alter database open;
```

6.6 Background Processes

and then setting the initialization parameter LOG_ARCHIVE_START to TRUE, the default being FALSE. The database can be return to the default mode of NOARCHIVELOG as follows,

```
Svrmgrl
SVRMGR> connect internal
SVRMGR> startup mount database_name;
SVRMGR> alter database noarchivelog;
SVRMGR> alter database open;
```

Once activated, ARCH copies the online redo log files to archived redo log files in a directory defined by the initialization parameter LOG_ARCHIVE_DEST. It is always recommended to run a production database in the ARCHIVELOG mode to save the contents of the online redo log files that have been overwritten by LGWR in a log switch. To avoid contention, the online redo log files and the archived redo log files should reside on different disks. Figure 6.28 shows the interaction of the LGWR and ARCH processes.

The only performance issue related to ARCH arises in the following situation. LGWR wants to do a log switch and write to another online redo log file, but cannot because ARCH is still copying the contents of that file to an archived redo log file. In this case, one or more of the following Oracle wait events triggered by the waiting for a log switch will occur.

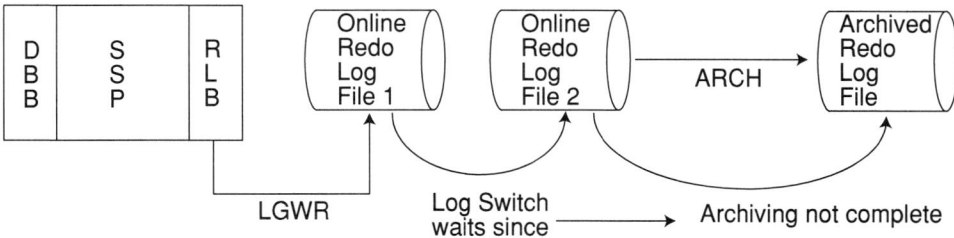

Scenario: LGWR is ready for a log switch. But it enters a wait state since ARCH is still not finished with copying online file to archived file. The entire database enters into a WAIT status.

FIGURE 6.28: ARCH and LGWR Interaction

- Log file switch (archiving needed): The target online redo log file has not been archived yet;
- Log file switch (checkpoint incomplete): Checkpoint is still in progress;
- Log file switch (clearing log file): The target redo log file is to be cleared due to a CLEAR LOGFILE command;

166   6. Tuning of Memory-Resident Data Structures

- Log file switch completion: Waiting for the log switch to complete

The wait time in each case is one second. The root cause of this situation can be one or more of three possibilities.

(a) ARCH works slowly compared to LGWR. To speed it up, set these three initialization parameters to nondefault values:

- ARCH_IO_SLAVES to a positive value such as 3 or 4, the default being zero. This allows multiple ARCH processes to function in parallel;
- LOG_ARCHIVE_BUFFERS, which specifies the number of buffers to be allocated for archiving, to 3 or 4;
- LOG_ARCHIVE_BUFFER_SIZE, which specifies the size of each archival buffer in terms of operating system blocks, to 64. Normally, these three settings work for most production systems.

(b) The online redo log files are small in size so that they wrap too quickly for the LGWR to continue. The remedy is to increase their sizes.
(c) There are too few online redo log files so that the LGWR has to overwrite a file before it has been archived. The solution is to increase the number of these files.

It is recommended that a production database have five to six online redo log file groups with two mirrored files in each group.

6.7 Tuning the Memory

The memory of the database server has two parts: real memory and virtual memory. The SGA resides in memory, preferably in real memory. In Sections 6.3 through 6.5 we have discussed the performance monitoring and tuning of the SGA components. In this section we concentrate on tuning activities of the memory at the operating system level. When Oracle under UNIX uses data files, UNIX reads the data into its own buffer cache, which is a part of the kernel's own memory. Data are then transferred to Oracle's data block buffer cache in the SGA, which is a part of the process memory within UNIX. Both the kernel memory and the process memory come from the same physical memory of the server. Consequently, the memory as a limited resource must be managed as a whole. In general, if all the hit ratios described earlier meet or exceed their target values and the SGA resides within real memory, then the SGA has the correct size and a larger SGA is not needed. Otherwise, a two-step tuning procedure is needed, as described below.

Tune the Memory Allocated to SGA

Figure 6.29 contains a script file showing the size breakdowns of SGA components. Figure 6.30 shows its output.

```
REM  SGA Component Sizes for Example Database
REM  Script File Name:    /My_Directory/SGA_Component_Size.sql
REM  Spool File Name:     /My_Directory/SGA_Component_Size.lst
REM  Author:              NAME
REM  Date Created:        DATE
REM  Purpose:             Display the sizes of the principal
REM                       components of SGA and the percentages of
REM                       the total SGA size occupied by them.
REM                       Use the views V$SGA, V$SGASTAT.
REM
REM
spool /My_Directory/SGA_Component_Size.lst
set heading off
select 'Total SGA Size in megabytes is ' ||
    ROUND (sum (value) / 1048576) || ' MB' from v$sga;
select 'Total SGA Size in bytes is ' || sum (value) from v$sga;
set verify off
ACCEPT Total_Value PROMPT 'Enter Total SGA Size in bytes derived
above: '
select name, bytes, 100 * bytes / &Total_Value "% of Total SGA" from
    v$sgastat where name in
      ('db_block_buffers', 'sql area', 'library cache', 'dictionary
        cache', 'log_buffer', 'free memory')
      order by bytes desc;
spool off
```

FIGURE 6.29 : SGA Components with Size

```
Total SGA Size in megabytes is 415 MB
Total SGA Size in bytes is 434806288
Enter Total SGA Size in bytes derived above: 434806288
NAME                     BYTES              % of Total SGA
----------------         ----------         --------------
db_block_buffers         307200000          70.6521521
sql area                 48674280           11.1944747
library cache            29031016            6.67677005
free memory              16297252            3.74816383
db_block_buffers         15600000            3.5878046
log_buffer                4194304             .964637384
dictionary cache          1448332             .333098219
log_buffer65536          .015072459

8 rows selected.
```

FIGURE 6.30: SGA Components with Size

The value of free memory should be 5% or less of the total SGA size. A higher value indicates that Oracle has aged objects out of the shared SQL pool, which has become fragmented. Figure 6.30 shows that the free memory occupies 3.7% of the SGA indicating very little fragmentation of the shared SQL pool.

Given that the SGA should reside in real memory, the following rule of thumb is often used to compute the required memory for the database server.

Rule: Server memory should be at least three times the sum of the SGA size and the minimum memory required for installing Oracle. If the number of concurrent users is more than 50, then a larger memory is needed.

In some operating systems, the DBA can lock the SGA in real memory so that it is never paged out to disk. If that option is available, use it. Oracle performs better if the entire SGA is kept in real memory.

If the initialization parameter PRE_PAGE_SGA is set to TRUE (default being FALSE), Oracle reads the entire SGA into real memory at instance startup. Operating system page table entries are then pre-built for each page of the SGA. This usually slows down the instance startup time and may also slow down the individual process startup times. But it speeds up the amount of time needed by Oracle to reach its full performance capability after the startup. Therefore, if the database normally runs around the clock and the system does not create and destroy processes all the time (e.g., by doing continuous logon/logoff), then the above setting improves performance. However, it does not prevent the operating system from paging or swapping the SGA after it is initially read into real memory. The issues specific to the operating system are discussed in the next paragraph. To take the full advantage of the PRE_PAGE_SGA setting make the page size the largest possible allowed by the operating system. In general, the page size is operating system specific and cannot be changed. But some operating systems have a special implementation for shared memory that allows the system administrator to change the page size to a larger value.

Tune the Memory at the Operating System Level

In any operating system most of the virtual memory physically resides in auxiliary storage. When the operating system needs real memory to meet a service request but the real memory has fallen below a predefined threshold, blocks are "paged out" from real memory to virtual memory and new processes are "paged into" real memory occupying the space freed up by paging. Paging and swapping are the mechanisms used for managing virtual memory. Thrashing occurs when there is excessive paging and swapping. It causes blocks to be continually transferred back and forth ("thrashed") between real and virtual memory. Paging and swapping impose an overhead on the operating system. The goal for tuning the real memory is to control paging and swapping so that thrashing does not occur.

6.7 Tuning the CPU

Paging occurs when a process needs a page (block) of memory that is no longer in real memory but in virtual memory (disk space). The block must be read from there into real memory. This is called *paging in*. The block that it replaces in real memory may have to be written out to virtual memory. This is called *paging out*. Paging is usually controlled by the LRU algorithm, as with the SGA, and generally involves inactive processes. The disk space in virtual memory where the page is transferred is called the *page space*. *Swapping* is more serious and extensive than paging since an entire active process, instead of only selected pages of a process, is written out from real memory to virtual memory to make room for another process to execute in real memory. The disk space in virtual memory where the process is transferred is called *swap space*. It is strongly recommended that the swap space for an Oracle database server be configured at least two to four times the size of real memory. Insufficient swap space often results in a limited real memory usage since the operating system is unable to reserve swap space for a new process to be loaded into real memory. In the case of swapping, the pages that are written out to virtual memory must later be read back into real memory to continue with their execution, because no process can execute in virtual memory. If there is insufficient real memory, the operating system may have to continuously page in and out of real memory resulting in *thrashing*. Figure 6.31 shows a typical paging and swapping scenario.

Paging is triggered by a page fault, which happens as follows.

Suppose that a page associated with an inactive process has been written out to the page space in the virtual memory under the LRU. A new process now needs that page, but cannot find it. This event is called a *page fault*. Oracle then pages in that page to real memory. Repeated page faults eventually lead to swapping, when an active process is moved from real to virtual memory. These are clear symptoms of system degradation. Consequently, the DBA or the system administrator must monitor very closely both paging and swapping.

The extent of paging and swapping and the amount of free memory can be monitored in a UNIX System V environment via the command *sar* (system activity reporter) run with four switches, -p, -g, -w, and -r. These switches have the following implications:

- -p: Paging in page fault activities,
- -g: Paging out activities,
- -w: System swapping and switching activities, and
- -r: Unused memory pages and disk blocks.

Figure 6.32 contains a script file that prompts the user for two parameters for *sar* and then executes *sar* with those values for each of the four switches described above. Figure 6.33 shows the result of executing the script file of Figure 6.32.

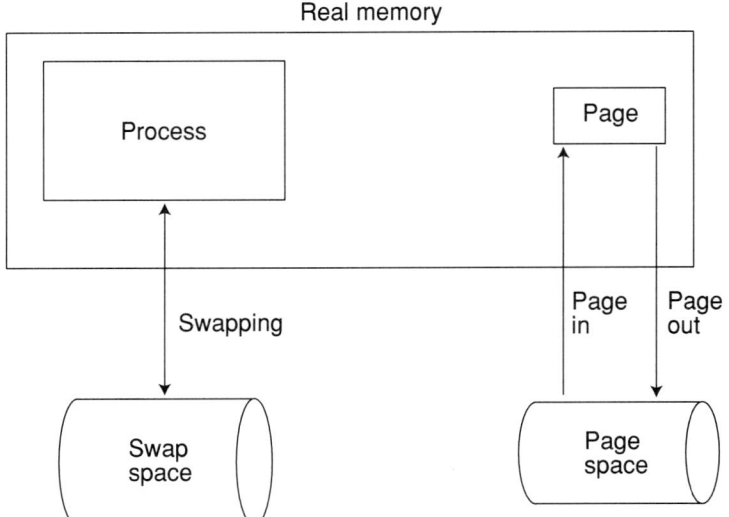

FIGURE 6.31: Paging and Swapping Scenario

```
#!/bin/csh
#
#    File Name:      sar_Switch_Command
#    Author:         NAME
#    Date Written:   DATE
#    Purpose:        Run the 'sar' command with four switches, -p,
#                    -g, -w, and -r.
#                    User enters the frequency of collecting
#                    statistics and the number of such collections.
#
#
printf "\n"
printf "\n"
echo "At what time interval do you want to collect statistics? "
echo -n "Enter the interval in number of seconds: "
set TIME_INTERVAL = $<
printf "\n"
echo "How many times do you want to collect statistics? "
echo -n "Enter the total number of statistics collection that you
want: "
set TOTAL_COUNTER = $<
printf "\n"
```

FIGURE 6.32: Script File for *sar* with User-Supplied Parameters

```
echo "The program will run 'sar' with switches, -p, -g, -w, and -r, "
echo "and will collect statistics every $TIME_INTERVAL seconds for
$TOTAL_COUNTER times."
printf "\n"

printf "\n"
echo sar -p $TIME_INTERVAL $TOTAL_COUNTER
printf "\n"
sar -p $TIME_INTERVAL $TOTAL_COUNTER
printf "\n"
printf "\n"

printf "\n"
echo sar -g $TIME_INTERVAL $TOTAL_COUNTER
printf "\n"
sar -g $TIME_INTERVAL $TOTAL_COUNTER
printf "\n"
printf "\n"

printf "\n"
echo sar -w $TIME_INTERVAL $TOTAL_COUNTER
printf "\n"
sar -w $TIME_INTERVAL $TOTAL_COUNTER
printf "\n"
printf "\n"

printf "\n"
echo sar -r $TIME_INTERVAL $TOTAL_COUNTER
printf "\n"
sar -r $TIME_INTERVAL $TOTAL_COUNTER
printf "\n"
printf "\n"

printf "\n"
echo Statistics collection is complete.
printf "\n"
printf "\n"
```

FIGURE 6.32 (*continued*): Script File for *sar* with User Supplied Parameters

The output from the script shown in Figure 6.32 appears in Figure 6.33.

```
smittra:~ > ./sar_Switch_Command
At what time interval do you want to collect statistics?
Enter the interval in number of seconds: 8

How many times do you want to collect statistics?
Enter the total number of statistics collection that you want: 5
```

FIGURE 6.33: Output from Running *sar* with Four Switches

6. Tuning of Memory-Resident Data Structures

```
The program will run 'sar' with switches, -p, -g, -w, and
-r, and will collect statistics every 8 seconds for 5 times.
sar -p 8 5

SunOS ABCD    5.6 Generic_105181-13 sun4u       08/30/99

11:32:06  atch/s    pgin/s    ppgin/s     pflt/s  vflt/s    slock/s
11:32:14  0.00      0.00      0.00        9.84    12.95     0.00
11:32:22  0.37      0.50      0.50        25.09   119.48    0.00
11:32:30  0.00      0.00      0.00        0.00    0.00      0.00
11:32:38  0.00      0.00      0.00        9.86    9.49      0.00
11:32:46  0.25      0.37      0.37        8.97    12.08     0.00

Average   0.12      0.17      0.17        10.75   30.77     0.00

sar -g 8 5
SunOS ABCD    5.6 Generic_105181-13 sun4u       08/30/99

11:32:46  pgout/s   ppgout/s  pgfree/s    pgscan/s  %ufs_ipf
11:32:54  0.00      0.00      0.00        0.00      0.00
11:33:02  0.00      0.00      0.00        0.00      0.00
11:33:10  0.37      0.37      0.37        0.00      0.00
11:33:18  0.00      0.00      0.00        0.00      0.00
11:33:26  0.00      0.00      0.00        0.00      0.00

Average   0.07      0.07      0.07        0.00      0.00

sar -w 8 5

SunOS ABCD    5.6 Generic_105181-13 sun4u       08/30/99

11:33:26  swpin/s   bswin/s   swpot/s     bswot/s   pswch/s
11:33:34  0.00      0.0       0.00        0.0       587
11:33:42  0.00      0.0       0.00        0.0       581
11:33:50  0.00      0.0       0.00        0.0       573
11:33:58  0.00      0.0       0.00        0.0       625
11:34:06  0.00      0.0       0.00        0.0       626

Average   0.00      0.0       0.00        0.0       598

sar -r 8 5
SunOS  ABCD 5.6 Generic_105181-13 sun4u   08/30/99

11:34:07                      freemem                freeswap
11:34:15                      9031                   13452815
11:34:23                      9031                   13452815
11:34:31                      9032                   13452815
11:34:39                      8924                   13435165
11:34:47                      8760                   13449823

Average                       8956                   13448684

Statistics collection is complete.
```

FIGURE 6.33 (*continued*): Output from Running *sar* with Four Switches

The meanings of the column titles for each switch and potential problem symptoms identified by them are listed below.

Switch -p:

atch/s =	Page faults per second that are satisfied by reclaiming a page currently in memory;
pgin/s =	Number of requests per second for paging in;
ppgin/s =	Number of pages that are paged in per second;
pflt/s =	Page faults per second from protection errors, i.e., illegal access to page, or "copy-on-writes";
vflt/s =	Page faults per second from address translation, i.e., valid page not in memory;
slock/s =	Page faults per second from software lock requests requiring physical I/O.

Problem symptom(s) caused by memory deficiency: A high number of page faults indicated by one or more of *atch/s*, *pflt/s*, *vflt/s*, and *slock/s*.

Switch -g:

pgout/s =	Number of requests per second for paging out;
ppgout/s =	Number of pages that are paged out per second;
pgfree/s =	Number of pages that are placed on free list per second by the page stealing daemon;
pgscan/s =	Pages scanned per second by the page stealing daemon;
%ufs_ipf =	Percentage of UFS *i-nodes* taken off the free list by *iget*s that had reusable pages associated with them. This is the percentage of *iget*s with page flushes.

Problem symptom(s) caused by memory deficiency: A high value of *ppgout/s*

Switch -w:

swpin/s =	Number of transfers per second for swapping in;
bswin/s =	Number of 512-byte blocks transferred per second for swapping in;
swpot/s =	Number of transfers per second for swapping out;
bswot/s =	Number of 512-byte blocks transferred per second for swapping out
pswch/s =	Number of process switches per second.

Problem symptom(s) caused by memory deficiency: High values of one or more of the parameters.

Switch -r:

freemem =	Number of 512-byte blocks of free memory available to user processes;
freeswap =	Number of 512-byte blocks available for page swapping.

Problem symptom(s) caused by memory deficiency: A low value of *freemem*.

The parameter values appearing in Figure 6.33 indicate no problem with the memory size.

Shared Memory and Semaphores

The *shared memory* under UNIX is a data structure residing in real memory and managed by the UNIX kernel. Normally Oracle under UNIX is implemented as a shared resource whereby processes access the Oracle instance and the database through the SGA. All Oracle processes must attach to the SGA. At instance startup the SGA must reside in shared memory, preferably within a single shared-memory segment. Depending on the availability of shared memory the SGA may subsequently be partially paged out to virtual memory. Page faults occur as a result of paging out parts of the SGA. Three parameters control the shared memory situation:

SHMALL   total number of shared-memory segments available in the entire system,
SHMMAX   maximum size in bytes of a single shared-memory segment, and
SHMSEG   maximum number of shared-memory segments that can be attached to a single process.

In order to allow the SGA to stay within a single shared-memory segment, we need to ensure SHMMAX > SGA Size. Proper memory configuration is needed to achieve this goal.

A *semaphore* is an operating system flag used for controlling shared resources. Oracle uses one semaphore for each Oracle process. At the instance start time, Oracle claims all the semaphores that it will use. Given that other concurrent applications use semaphores, the system must have many more semaphores than the total number of Oracle processes and all subprocesses that may be spawned by a process. A system is allocated sets of semaphores, and each set consists of multiple semaphores. Three parameters handle the allocation of semaphores in a UNIX system:

SEMMNI   Maximum number of semaphore sets in the system,
SEMMNS   Maximum number of semaphores available in the system, and
SEMMSL   Maximum number of semaphores in each set in the system.

Hence, the maximum number of available semaphores =

```
MIN (SEMMNS, SEMMNI * SEMMSL)
```

Consequently, the value of MIN (SEMMNS, SEMMNI * SEMMSL) must be much larger than the Oracle initialization parameter PROCESSES. Since semaphores are not system resource intensive, it is advisable to allocate a sufficiently large number of them so as to avoid any potential problem involving creation of Oracle processes.

6.8 Tuning the CPU

The tuning of the CPU belongs more to system administration than to database administration. Hence it is done mostly by the System Administrator instead of the DBA, or at times by them jointly. In this section, we discuss the UNIX command *sar -u* to examine CPU utilization via four statistics:

%usr = Percent of time CPU is running in user mode to handle application tasks,
%sys = Percent of time CPU is running in system mode to handle operating system tasks,
%wio = Percent of time CPU is idle with some process waiting for block I/O, and
%idle = Percent of time CPU is idle.

The following guidelines are used to interpret the output from *sar -u* and identify problem symptoms.

- The less time spent in performing operating system tasks measured by %sys, the better the performance. We strive for:
  —%sys in the range of 25% to 30%
  —%usr in the range of 60% to 75%.
- A high value of %wio shows disk contention problems. A redistribution of I/O load may be in order. We strive for 40% or below for %wio.
- A low value of %idle indicates that the CPU is busy most of the time. If this trend persists, we need to identify the CPU-intensive job(s). A value of 20% or below is a cause of concern.

Figure 6.34 shows a sample output from *sar -u* collecting statistics every eight seconds for five times.

```
sar -u 8 5
SunOS ABCD 5.6 Generic_105181-13 sun4u   09/01/99
12:07:45              %usr           %sys            %wio           %idle
12:07:53               44             25              30              1
12:08:01               43             26              29              2
12:08:09               30             10              54              6
12:08:17               28              9              58              5
12:08:25               31           1054               5
Average                35             16              45              4
```

FIGURE 6.34: Output from "sar –u"

The CPU utilization is poor here due to very low %idle and high %wio.

6.9 Pinning Packages in Memory

When a very large PL/SQL package is compiled, Oracle needs a large number of contiguous blocks in memory. If the shared SQL pool is fragmented to the extent that such a large chunk of contiguous memory area is not available, smaller packages currently residing in memory are aged out via the LRU algorithm to make room for compilation. This delays the execution of the package and thus increases the user response time. To remedy this situation, the DBA can reserve an area within the shared SQL pool to execute such packages. This is called *pinning* a package in the shared SQL pool reserved area. In this case, the necessary blocks of contiguous memory are always made available for compiling them. Smaller objects cannot fragment the reserved area since their sizes do not exceed the threshold to allow using the reserved area.

Two initialization parameters involved in creating the reserved area are:

SHARED_POOL_RESERVED_SIZE   It specifies the percentage of the value of the parameter SHARED_POOL_SIZE that is reserved for requests for large contiguous areas of memory; the default value is 5%; and

SHARED_POOL_RESERVED_MIN_ALLOC   It specifies in number of bytes the threshold for using the SHARED_POOL_RESERVED_SIZE; only memory requirements larger than SHARED_POOL_RESERVED_MIN_ALLOC can allocate space from the reserved area for compiling large packages when a contiguous chunk of memory is not available from the free lists of the shared pool; the default value is 5,000 bytes.

After modifying, if necessary, the init.<instance name>.ora file for the above two parameters, proceed as follows to pin large packages in memory.

(a) Run the script file in Figure 6.35 to identify the PL/SQL objects larger than 10,240 bytes in size and not pinned currently. Note that the size of 10,240 bytes (= 10 K) is arbitrarily chosen. If your needs are different, modify the condition

```
sharable_mem > 10240
```

accordingly before running the script.

```
SET LINESIZE 80
SET PAGESIZE 41
SET NEWPAGE 0
col owner format a10
col name format a30
col type format a20
spool /My_Directory/Pinning_Objects.lst
```

FIGURE 6.35: Script to Identify Large Packages

```
select owner, name, type, sharable_mem from v$db_object_cache
    where kept = 'NO' AND
    type in ('PACKAGE', 'PACKAGE BODY', 'FUNCTION',
        'PROCEDURE')
    AND sharable_mem > 10240
    order by type;
spool off
```

FIGURE 6.35 (*continued*): Script to Identify Large Packages

The output is given as Figure 6.36.

```
OWNER        NAME                    TYPE              SHARABLE_MEM
--------     --------------------    --------------    ------------
SYS          DBMS_STANDARD           PACKAGE              13781
SYS          STANDARD                PACKAGE             165488
SYS          DBMS_UTILITY            PACKAGE              21448
ONESHOT      PKG_ONESHOT_ITEMCREATE  PACKAGE              11414
ONESHOT      PKG_ONESHOT_FETCH       PACKAGE              11593
SYS          DBMS_APPLICATION_INFO   PACKAGE              12805
SYS          DBMS_OUTPUT             PACKAGE              13743
SYS          DBMS_DDL                PACKAGE BODY         10560
ONESHOT      PKG_ONESHOT_LOAD        PACKAGE BODY         34884
SYS          DBMS_UTILITY            PACKAGE BODY         16364
SYS          STANDARD                PACKAGE BODY         23292
11 rows selected.
```

FIGURE 6.36: List of Packages Larger than 10 K

(b) Execute the script DBMSPOOL.sql. For example, under UNIX, run the following command,

```
@$ORACLE_HOME/rdbms/admin/dbmspool
```

This creates a package called dbms_shared_pool consisting of the following procedures.

```
procedure sizes(minsize number)
procedure keep(name varchar2, flag char DEFAULT 'P')
procedure unkeep(name varchar2, flag char DEFAULT 'P')
procedure aborted_request_threshold(threshold_size
number)
```

Note that the list displayed in Figure 6.36 can alternatively be derived by executing the command:

```
EXECUTE dbms_shared_pool.sizes (10);
```

where the argument value of 10 indicates that the package is of size 10 K (= 10,240 bytes) or more.

(c) Decide which objects should be pinned in the shared pool based on an analysis of the list in Figure 6.36.

Then, for each object selected, run the command:

```
EXECUTE dbms_shared_pool.keep ('package_name');
```

to pin the package in memory. Here the argument *'package_name'* is the name of the package to be pinned in memory

(d) Run the command

```
EXECUTE dbms_shared_pool.unkeep ('package_name');
```

to remove pinned objects from the shared pool.

6.10 Latching Mechanism for Access Control

The data structures residing in the SGA are always kept in a consistent state for maintaining database integrity. Consequently, when processes access them, it is imperative that the structures do not change while they are being accessed. The mechanism to control such accesses is called a *latch*. A process must acquire a latch before it can access the SGA. A *contention* arises when multiple processes try to acquire a latch for the same data structure such as the data block buffer cache (DBB) or the redo log buffer cache (RLB). The goal in tuning the latches is to minimize, if not eliminate, the contention among processes. Figure 6.37 contains two queries that return the following,

- SQL statement(s) causing the most latch contention; and
- Session ID(s) and username(s) for sessions waiting for the latch.

```
select a.sid, d.sid, a.name, c.sql_text, d.event from
    V$LATCHHOLDER a, V$SESSION b, V$SQLAREA c, V$SESSION_WAIT d
    where
    a.sid = b.sid and
    b.sql_address = c.address and
    a.laddr = d.p1raw;
```

FIGURE 6.37: Queries on Latch Contention

```
select b.sid, b.username, a.event, a.p1text, a.p1, a.p2text,
    a.p2, a.p3text, a.p3, c.sql_text
    from V$SESSION_WAIT a, V$SESSION b, V$SQLAREA c
    where
    a.event not like 'SQL%' and
    a.sid = b.sid and
    b.sql_address = c.address;
```

FIGURE 6.37 (*continued*): Queries on Latch Contention

There are three areas where a DBA can tune the latches:

(a) RLB via redo allocation latch and redo copy latch,
(b) DBB via LRU latch, and
(c) Free lists for segments.

6.10.1 Latch Contention for RLB

When a process needs to write to the RLB, it acquires a redo allocation latch. The initialization parameter LOG_SMALL_ENTRY_MAX_SIZE specifies the size in bytes of the largest chunk that can be written to the RLB under the redo allocation latch. Its default value is operating system dependent. If the value of this parameter is zero, then all "writes" are considered small and are written to the RLB using this latch. After the writing is complete, the process releases the latch. If the parameter is set to a positive value and the redo entry to be written to the RLB is larger than this value, the process uses the redo allocation latch to allocate space in the RLB for writing and acquires a redo copy latch for doing the actual "write." Once the space is allocated, the process releases the redo allocation latch and uses the redo copy latch to do the actual writing. After the writing is complete, the process releases the redo copy latch.

An instance can have only one redo allocation latch and up to n redo copy latches, where $n = 6 *$ (number of CPUs). The actual value of n is determined by the initialization parameter LOG_SIMULTANEOUS_COPIES. Multiple redo copy latches allow the writing of multiple redo log entries simultaneously, thereby reducing contention among these latches and enhancing performance.

Latches are of two types: willing-to-wait and immediate. The first type requests a latch, waits if the latch is not available, requests again, and waits until the latch is available. The second type requests a latch and if it is not available continues processing. The dynamic performance view V$LATCH contains the statistics for both types of latch contention. The tuning goals for both redo allocation latch and redo copy latch are:

```
WAIT Hit Ratio > .99, NO-WAIT_Hit Ratio > .99, and
    SLEEPS / MISSES ≤ 1.
```

180   6. Tuning of Memory-Resident Data Structures

Figures 6.38 and 6.39 provide respectively the script file and its output showing the above three metrics for the two latches, redo allocation and redo copy.

```
REM  Wait and No-Wait Latch Hit Ratios
REM  Script File Name:   /My_Directory/Redo_Latch_Tuning.sql
REM  Spool File Name:    /My_Directory/ Redo_Latch_Tuning..lst
REM  Author:             NAME
REM  Date Created:       DATE
REM  Purpose:            Compute hit ratios for both wait and
REM                      no-wait latches for redo copy and
REM                      allocation.
REM
COLUMN TODAY    NEW_VALUE xTODAY NOPRINT FORMAT A1 TRUNC
TTITLE    LEFT xTODAY -
    RIGHT 'Page ' FORMAT 999 SQL.PNO -
    CENTER 'Wait and No-Wait Latch Hit Ratios'    SKIP 4
BTITLE    'Script File: /My_Directory/ Redo_Latch_Tuning.sql|Spool
          File: /My_Directory/ Redo_Latch_Tuning.lst'
COLUMN NAME HEADING 'Latch Name' FORMAT A20
SPOOL /My_Directory/Latch_Tuning.lst
select B.name,
    round((gets-misses)/decode(gets,0,1,gets),3) "WAIT Hit Ratio",
    round((immediate_gets/decode((immediate_gets+immediate_misses)
    ,0,1, (immediate_gets+immediate_misses))),3) "NO-WAIT Hit
    Ratio",
    round(sleeps/decode(misses,0,1,misses),3) "SLEEPS/MISSES",
    TO_CHAR (SysDate, 'fmMonth ddth, YYYY') TODAY
    from V$LATCH A, V$LATCHNAME B
    where A.LATCH# = B.LATCH#
    AND B.name in ('redo allocation', 'redo copy')
    order by B.name;
SPOOL OFF
```

FIGURE 6.38 : Script File for Redo Latch Tuning

```
May 17th, 2001    Wait and No-Wait Latch Hit Ratios         Page 1
Latch Name        WAIT Hit Ratio   NO-WAIT Hit Ratio   SLEEPS/MISSES
--------------    --------------   -----------------   -------------
redo allocation        .999                0                 .016
redo copy              .144                1                 .068
        Script File: /My_Directory/Latch_Tuning.sql
        Spool File: /My_Directory/Latch_Tuning.lst
```

FIGURE 6.39: Output for Redo Latch Tuning

Figure 6.39 shows that the WAIT Hit Ratio for redo copy latch and NO-WAIT Hit Ratio for the redo allocation latch do not meet the tuning goals. However, this in itself may not be indicative of problems. The latch contention for redo log buffer access rarely causes any database performance problem. However, if necessary, one can take the following corrective measures.

- For the redo copy latch, increase the value of the initialization parameter LOG_SIMULTANEOUS_COPIES to its maximum allowed value of 6 * (number of CPUs).
- For the redo allocation latch, reduce the value of the initialization parameter LOG_SMALL_ENTRY_MAX_SIZE as noted at the beginning of this section.

6.10.2 Latch Contention for DBB

When new data blocks are read into the DBB, the necessary space must exist there. Otherwise, Oracle removes the least recently used blocks from the DBB via the LRU algorithm to make room for the new data. LRU latches regulate the LRU lists used by the DBB. Each latch controls a minimum of 50 buffers. The initialization parameter DB_BLOCK_LRU_LATCHES determines the number of LRU latches available, default being (Number of CPUs) / 2.

The tuning goal for the LRU latches is to minimize contention among processes that are requesting the latch. The metric used to measure contention is defined by

```
LRU Hit Ratio = SLEEPS / GETS for latch = 'cache buffers
    lru chain'
```

and we need LRU Hit Ratio < .01. If this goal is not met, increase the value of the parameter DB_BLOCK_LRU_LATCHES to the following value,

```
min (6 x (Number of CPUs), (Number of buffers) / 50)
```

Figures 6.40 and 6.41 provide respectively the script file and its output showing the value of the LRU Hit Ratio for the latch "cache buffers lru chain". The LRU Hit Ratio meets the desired goal.

```
REM  LRU Latch Hit Ratio
REM  Script File Name:    /My_Directory/LRU_Latch_Tuning.sql
REM  Spool File Name:     /My_Directory/LRU_Latch_Tuning..lst
REM  Author:              NAME
REM  Date Created:        DATE
REM  Purpose:             Compute hit ratio for LRU latch
REM
REM
```

FIGURE 6.40: Script File for LRU Hit Ratio

```
COLUMN TODAY  NEW_VALUE xTODAY NOPRINT FORMAT A1 TRUNC
TTITLE     LEFT xTODAY -
    RIGHT 'Page ' FORMAT 999 SQL.PNO -
    CENTER 'LRU Latch Hit Ratios'      SKIP 4
BTITLE     'Script File: /My_Directory/LRU_Latch_Tuning.sql|Spool
File: /My_Directory/LRU_Latch_Tuning.lst'
COLUMN NAME HEADING 'Latch Name' FORMAT A20
SPOOL /My_Directory/LRU_Latch_Tuning.lst
select B.name, sleeps, gets,
    round (sleeps / gets) "LRU Hit Ratio",
    TO_CHAR (SysDate, 'fmMonth ddth, YYYY') TODAY
    from V$LATCH A, V$LATCHNAME B
    where A.LATCH# = B.LATCH#
    AND B.name in ('cache buffers lru chain')
    order by B.name;
SPOOL OFF
```

FIGURE 6.40 (*continued*): Script File for LRU Hit Ratio

```
May 17th, 2001     LRU Latch Hit Ratios            Page   1
Latch Name                  SLEEPS       GETS       LRU Hit Ratio
----------------------      ------       -------    ----------
cache buffers lru chain      2580        1327454         0
        Script File: /My_Directory/LRU_Latch_Tuning.sql
        Spool File: /My_Directory/LRU_Latch_Tuning.lst
```

FIGURE 6.41: Output for LRU Hit Ratio

6.10.3 Contention for Free Lists for Segments

For each data and index segment, Oracle maintains one or more free lists. A *free list* is a list of data blocks that have been allocated for the extents of that segment and have free space greater than PCTFREE for that segment. The list is implemented as a linked list to make insertion and deletion of blocks to and from the free list simple. See Section E13 of Appendix E for a discussion of linear linked lists. The blocks of the free list are made available for inserting data into a segment. After a DELETE or an UPDATE statement is executed, Oracle checks to see if the space being used in the block is less than the PCTUSED value for the segment. If it is, the block is placed at the beginning of the free list and becomes the first of the available blocks to be used. When an INSERT occurs in a segment, the free list is used to determine what blocks are available for the INSERT. If multiple processes try to insert data into the same segment, a contention arises for the free lists of that segment. This incurs possible waits for the processes performing the INSERTs. Since there is no initialization parameter setting up the number of free lists, they cannot be created dynamically as needed. Consequently, a sufficient number of them must be set up at the time of creating or altering the segment via the STORAGE clause. This clause is an optional item in any CREATE or ALTER command. Two of the STORAGE options are FREELISTS and FREELIST GROUPS defined below:

```
FREELISTS = number of free lists in each free list group
FREELIST GROUPS = number of groups of free lists,
    default being one
```

The tuning goal in setting up free lists and their groups is to minimize contention among multiple processes inserting data into a segment. The three dynamic performance views V$SESSION_WAIT, V$WAITSTAT, and V$SYSTEM_EVENT are used to identify problems with free list contention. The two data dictionary views DBA_EXTENTS and DBA_SEGMENTS are used to identify the objects that need to be altered to increase the number of their free lists. Figure 6.42 contains a script that executes a three-step procedure to determine if there is free list contention:

(a) Find out if there is wait involved for free lists;
(b) Determine the amount of wait in seconds; and
(c) Determine the segment(s) with free list contention.

```
REM  Free List Tuning to Reduce Contention
REM  Script File Name: /My_Directory/Freelist_Tuning.sql
REM  Spool File Name:  /My_Directory/Freelist_Tuning..1st
REM  Author:           NAME
REM  Date Created:     DATE
REM  Purpose:          Examine contention for free lists and
REM                    resolve contention.
REM
REM

SPOOL /My_Directory/Freelist_Tuning.1st

REM Find out if there is wait involved for free lists
select class, count, time from V$WAITSTAT where
    class = 'segment header' OR
    class = 'free list';
REM Determine the amount of wait in seconds
col event format a20
```

FIGURE 6.42: Script for Determining Free List Contention

```
select event, ROUND (total_waits / 100) "Total Wait in Seconds" from
    V$SYSTEM_EVENT where event = 'buffer busy waits';

REM Determine the segment(s) with free list contention

select segment_name SEGMENT, freelists from dba_segments where
    EXISTS
    (select segment_name, segment_type from dba_extents where
        file_id = (select p1 from V$SESSION_WAIT where
        event = 'buffer busy waits')
        AND
        block_id < (select p2 from V$SESSION_WAIT where
        event = 'buffer busy waits')
        AND
        block_id + blocks > (select p2 from V$SESSION_WAIT where
        event = 'buffer busy waits')
    );
```

FIGURE 6.42 (*continued*): Script for Determining Free List Contention

Figure 6.43 is a sample output. It shows that there is no free list contention.

```
CLASS                  COUNT                      TIME
--------------         -----                      ----
segment header           11                        137
free list                 0                          0

EVENT                             Total Wait in Seconds
------------------                ---------------------
buffer busy waits                           21538

no rows selected
```

FIGURE 6.43: Output for Free List Contention

If one or more segments are returned showing free list contention, then proceed as follows to resolve contention.

- Drop the segment(s) showing contention.
- Recreate the segment(s) with larger value(s) for FREELISTS and FREELIST GROUPS in the STORAGE clause.

Key Words

ARCH
ARCHIVELOG

background process
bind variable

buffer, dirty
cache get
cache hit
cache miss
cache reload
caching algorithm
checkpoint
CKPT
contention
data block buffers
data block header
data dictionary
DBWR
dictionary cache
extent
FREELIST GROUPS
FREELISTS
hit ratio, data block buffer
hit ratio, dictionary cache
hit ratio, library cache
hit ratio, LRU
hit ratio, redo log buffer
index
initialization parameter
invalidation
latch
LGWR
library cache

log switch
logical read
LRU
memory, real
memory, shared
memory, virtual
memory cache
padding factor
page fault
page space
paging
paging in
paging out
physical read
pin
pinning package in memory
redo log buffer
redo log file
reload
rollback segment header activity
semaphore
SGA
shared SQL pool
swap space
swapping
thrashing
UGA

References and Further Reading

1. E. Aronoff et al.—*Advanced Oracle Tuning and Administration*, Oracle Press, 1997.
2. M. R. Ault—*Oracle8 Black Book*, Coriolis Group Books, 1998.
3. S. Bobrowski—*Mastering Oracle7 & Client/Server Computing*, Sybex, 1996.
4. D. K. Burleson—*High-Performance Oracle Database Applications*, Coriolis Group Books, 1998.
5. M.l J. Corey et al.—*Tuning Oracle*, Oracle Press, 1995.
6. J. Dunham—*Database Performance Tuning Handbook*, McGraw-Hill, 1998.
7. K. Loney—*Oracle 8i DBA Handbook*, Oracle Press, 2000.
8. R. J. Niemiec—*Oracle Performance Tuning*, Oracle Press, 1999.

All the above references have discussed the tuning issues along with hit ratios, other performance metrics, and their target values. A clearcut distinction of the instance and the database tuning, as done here, is not found in any of them. A good treatment of hit ratios and their associated benchmark values can be found in Aronoff et al. [1, Chapters 3 and 7] and Ault [2, Chapter 9]. Memory tuning, SGA sizing, and shared SQL pool tuning are discussed in Aronoff et al. [1, Chapter 9], Ault [2, Chapter 11], Corey et al. [5, Chapter 2], and Dunham [6, Chapters 1 and 7]. Burleson [4, Chapter 3] covers memory tuning from a more comprehensive viewpoint of tuning the Oracle architecture. Disk I/O tuning and reducing I/O contention are treated well in Ault [2, Chapter 11] and Bobrowski [3, Chapter 12]. Corey et al. [5, Chapter 4] treat the tuning of CPU in fair detail. Although Aronoff et al. [1], Bobrowski [3], Corey et al. [5], and Dunham [6] cover only up to Oracle7.3, most of the scripts included in their books apply equally well to Oracle 8i. Corey et al. [5, Chapter 9] contain a large number of scripts with nice tuning tips arranged by topics such as space management, table and index sizing, use of buffers in the SGA, etc. The book by Niemiec [8] is almost encyclopedic in nature. Most of its chapters are labeled with the target readers such as Beginner Developer and Beginner DBA, Developer and DBA, DBA, and Advanced DBA.

Exercises

Theoretical exercises are of little value for this chapter since the best practice comes from monitoring the performance of actual production databases and tuning them, as needed. The exercises given below identify some of the areas not specifically covered in Chapter 6 and should be considered an extension of the text.

1. Augmenting the procedures described in Figures 6.7A and 6.8A prepare a report showing the effect of additional cache hits and cache misses as you increase or decrease the size of the DBB by 75 blocks at a time. Analyze the report to determine if there is a peak in additional cache hits and cache misses, or if there is no such visible trend.
2. You need a test database for this exercise. Using the three-step procedure in Section 6.6.1 to estimate the optimal number of DBWRs, determine the number, say, N ($\leq$ 10), of DBWRs needed for an application. Set up this configuration in two different ways by creating two separate instances for the application:

    - One instance has N distinct DBWR processes, and
    - The other instance has N distinct slaves of a single DBWR process.

    Run the application under these two configurations and measure the runtimes of the same batch jobs in the two cases. Do you see any difference in performance between the configurations? Can you explain the difference?

3. Why does the use of bind variables help to reduce the number of "reloads"?
4. An Oracle instance has the following values.
    ```
    Initialization Parameter PROCESSES = P
    V$LICENSE. SESSIONS_HIGHWATER = H
    ```

V$LICENSE. SESSIONS_CURRENT = C

Will there be any inconsistency with the condition

P < min (H, C) ?

5. An Oracle instance is created with the following values:

```
Redo Log File = 24000 KB
LOG_CHECKPOINT_INTERVAL = 6000 KB
LOG_CHECKPOINT_TIMEOUT = 1800
```

It is assumed that a log switch has occurred at 14:00:00 and then occurs every 16 minutes between 14:00:00 and 15:30:00 and that the redo log files fill up uniformly over time. Thus, for example, it takes 8 minutes to write 12,000 KB to the redo log file. Under these assumptions complete the following table.

Checkpoint via INTERVAL	Checkpoint via TIMEOUT	Log Switch
14:00:00		X

(Note that the first row of the table has been completed as the starting point.)

7
Oracle Utility for Tuning and Optimization

Outline

7.1 Scope of Oracle Utilities
7.2 UTLBSTAT and UTLESTAT Utilities
7.3 Location and Function of the Utility Scripts
7.4 Procedure for Running the Utilities
7.5 UTLBSTAT/ESTAT Performance Report Analysis
7.6 Comprehensive Tuning Plan for Internal Level
7.7 Performance Tracking
7.8 Tuning Activities
Key Words
References and Further Reading
Exercises

Overview of the Chapter

The chapter is devoted primarily to a detailed discussion of the two Oracle utilities known as UTLBSTAT and UTLESTAT. The report generated by these utilities consists of 15 sections addressing different areas of performance of the database. The chapter analyzes each section of this report, offers metrics and benchmarks to interpret the results, and offers guidelines for improving performance, as needed. The chapter closes with a checklist of items to help the DBA in the task of ongoing monitoring and tuning of database performance.

7.1 Scope of Oracle Utilities

The performance tracking and tuning of an Oracle database can be done through the variety of scripts that have been discussed in Chapters 5 and 6. They address the performance of specific areas of the database, namely the data structures residing in memory and in auxiliary storage. For a comprehensive performance tuning Oracle provides two utilities called *utlbstat* and *utlestat* that collect systemwide statistics over an interval of time specified by the DBA. The major part of this chapter discusses these two utilities and analyzes the performance report generated by them.

7.2 UTLBSTAT and UTLESTAT Utilities

The dynamic performance views offer a snapshot of the Oracle internal level at a given instant, namely, when they are queried. As such, they are heavily used in SQL scripts to extract necessary performance data as of a given instant. By contrast, the utilities UTLBSTAT and UTLESTAT track the performance of all critical areas of a database over a period of time designated by the DBA and put the findings in a report called REPORT.TXT under 15 distinct categories:

(a) Library Cache: Various hit ratios for the cache;
(b) Systemwide Events: Count of database events related to transactions and logins;
(c) Dirty Buffer Write Queue: Average WRITE queue length;
(d) Systemwide Wait Events for Non-Background Processes: Events causing system bottlenecks and costing CPU time;
(e) Systemwide WAIT Events for Background Processes: Events related to PMON, SMON, DBWR, LGWR, etc.;
(f) Latches with Wait: Latches requested by processes but not available;
(g) Latches with NoWait: Latches requested by processes for immediate acquisition via timeout;
(h) Buffer Busy Wait: Class of buffers not immediately accessible ;
(i) Rollback Segments: Statistics related to active transactions, WRITES, WRAPS, etc.;
(j) Non-Default INIT.ORA Parameters: List of initialization parameters with non-default values;
(k) Dictionary Cache: Data dictionary information pertaining to all database objects;
(l) I/O Operations over Tablespaces: Read and write information for tablespaces;
(m) I/O Load Distribution among Disk Drives: Read and write information for tablespaces by data file names;
(n) Date/Time: Start and stop times for running the utility scripts;
(o) Version of Oracle Products: Version information for each Oracle product used.

7.3 Location and Function of the Utility Scripts

There are two SQL script files, UTLBSTAT.sql and UTLESTAT.sql, that jointly collect the data and generate the report. Their default location under UNIX is in the directory

$ORACLE_HOME/rdbms/admin, and under NT in the directory %ORACLE_HOME%\rdbmsNN\admin, where NN is 73, 80, etc. depending on the version of Oracle. The script UTLBSTAT.sql creates two groups of tables to collect performance data at the beginning and at the end of the data collection period. The tables in the first group contain the word "begin" as a part of their names to signify that they take a snapshot of the database at the start of data collection. Likewise, the tables in the second group contain the word "end" as a part of their names to signify that they take a snapshot of the database at the end of data collection. Figure 7.1 shows the names of the tables and views created by UTLBSTAT.sql and the names of the source tables and views from which they collect the data.

Table/View Name	Source Table/View Name
stats$begin_stats	V$SYSSTAT
stats$end_stats	STATS$BEGIN_STATS
stats$begin_latch	V$LATCH
stats$end_latch	STATS$BEGIN_LATCH
stats$begin_roll	V$ROLLSTAT
stats$end_roll	STATS$BEGIN_ROLL
stats$begin_lib	V$LIBRARYCACHE
stats$end_lib	STATS$BEGIN_LIB
stats$begin_dc	V$ROWCACHE
stats$end_dc	STATS$BEGIN_DC
stats$begin_event	V$SYSTEM_EVENT
stats$end_event	STATS$BEGIN_EVENT
stats$begin_bck_event	none
stats$end_bck_event	STATS$BEGIN_BCK_EVENT
stat$dates	none
stats$file_view	V$FILESTAT, TS$, V$DATAFILE, FILE$
stats$begin_file	STATS$FILE_VIEW
stats$end_file	STATS$BEGIN_FILE
stats$begin_waitstat	V$WAITSTAT
stats$end_waitstat	STATS$BEGIN_WAITSTAT

FIGURE 7.1: Tables and Views Created by UTLBSTAT.sql

The script UTLESTAT.sql creates a set of summary tables that collect statistics during the specified interval of time, generates the output REPORT.TXT, and then drops all the tables created by UTLBSTAT.sql and UTLESTAT.sql. The file REPORT.TXT resides in the default directory of the account from which the script file UTLESTAT.sql is run. Figure 7.2 shows the names of the tables and views created by UTLESTAT.sql and the names of the source tables and views from which they collect the data.

Table/View Name	Source Table/View Name
stats$stats	V$STATNAME, STATS$BEGIN_STATS, STATS$END_STATS
stats$latches	V$LATCHNAME, STATS$BEGIN_LATCH, STATS$END_LATCH
stats$event	STATS$BEGIN_EVENT, STATS$END_EVENT
stats$bck_event	STATS$BEGIN_BCK_EVENT, STATS$END_BCK_EVENT
stats$waitstat	STATS$BEGIN_WAITSTAT, STATS$END_WAITSTAT
stats$roll	STATS$BEGIN_ROLL, STATS$END_ROLL
stats$files	STATS$BEGIN_FILE, STATS$END_FILE
stats$dc	STATS$BEGIN_DC, STATS$END_DC
stats$lib	STATS$BEGIN_LIB, STATS$END_LIB

FIGURE 7.2: Tables and Views Created by UTLESTAT.sql

Figures 7.3 and 7.4 contain respectively the full script files, UTLBSTAT.sql and UTLESTAT.sql.

```
rem
rem $Header: utlbstat.sql 26.feb-96.19:20:51 gpongrac Exp $
    bstat.sql
rem
Rem Copyright (c) 1988, 1996 by Oracle Corporation
Rem NAME
REM    UTLBSTAT.SQL
Rem FUNCTION
Rem NOTES
Rem MODIFIED
Rem    jloaiza    10/14/95 - add tablespace size
Rem    jloaiza    09/19/95 - add waitstat
Rem    jloaiza    09/04/95 - add per second and background waits
Rem    drady      09/09/93 - merge changes from branch 1.1.312.2
Rem    drady      03/22/93 - merge changes from branch 1.1.312.1
Rem    drady      08/24/93 - bug 173918
Rem    drady      03/04/93 - fix bug 152986
Rem    glumpkin   11/16/92 - Renamed from UTLSTATB.SQL
```

FIGURE 7.3: UTLBSTAT.sql

```
Rem     glumpkin   10/19/92 - Renamed from BSTAT.SQL
Rem     jloaiza    01/07/92 - rework for version 7
Rem     mroberts   08/16/91 -        fix view for v7
Rem     rlim       04/29/91 -        change char to varchar2
Rem     Laursen    01/01/91 - V6 to V7 merge
Rem     Loaiza     04/04/89 - fix run dates to minutes instead of months
Rem Martin    02/22/89 - Creation
Rem Jloaiza   02/23/89 - changed table names, added dates, added
param dump
Rem
set echo on;
connect internal;

Rem ************************************************************
Rem                   First create all the tables
Rem ************************************************************
drop table stats$begin_stats;
create table stats$begin_stats as select * from v$sysstat where 0 = 1;
drop table stats$end_stats;
create table stats$end_stats as select * from stats$begin_stats;

drop table stats$begin_latch;
create table stats$begin_latch as select * from v$latch where 0 = 1;
drop table stats$end_latch;
create table stats$end_latch as select * from stats$begin_latch;

drop table stats$begin_roll;
create table stats$begin_roll as select * from v$rollstat where 0 = 1;
drop table stats$end_roll;
create table stats$end_roll as select * from stats$begin_roll;

drop table stats$begin_lib;
create table stats$begin_lib as select * from v$librarycache where 0 = 1;
drop table stats$end_lib;
create table stats$end_lib as select * from stats$begin_lib;

drop table stats$begin_dc;
create table stats$begin_dc as select * from v$rowcache where 0 = 1;
drop table stats$end_dc;
create table stats$end_dc as select * from stats$begin_dc;

drop table stats$begin_event;
create table stats$begin_event as select * from v$system_event where 0 = 1;
drop table stats$end_event;
create table stats$end_event as select * from stats$begin_event;
```

FIGURE 7.3 (*continued*): UTLBSTAT.sql

```
drop table stats$begin_bck_event;
create table stats$begin_bck_event
    (event varchar2(200), total_waits number, time_waited number);
drop table stats$end_bck_event;
create table stats$end_bck_event as select * from
stats$begin_bck_event;

drop table stats$dates;
create table stats$dates (start_time date, end_time date);
drop view stats$file_view;
create view stats$file_view as
    select ts.name  ts,
        i.name name,
        x.phyrds pyr,
        x.phywrts pyw,
        x.readtim prt,
        x.writetim pwt,
        x.phyblkrd pbr,
        x.phyblkwrt pbw,
        round(i.bytes/1000000) megabytes_size
    from v$filestat x, ts$ ts, v$datafile i,file$ f
where i.file#=f.file#
    and ts.ts#=f.ts#
    and x.file#=f.file#;
drop table stats$begin_file;
create table stats$begin_file as select * from stats$file_view where 0 = 1;
drop table stats$end_file;
create table stats$end_file as select * from stats$begin_file;

drop table stats$begin_waitstat;
create table stats$begin_waitstat as select * from v$waitstat where 1=0;
drop table stats$end_waitstat;
create table stats$end_waitstat as select * from stats$begin_waitstat;
Rem *************************************************************
Rem                    Gather start statistics
Rem *************************************************************
insert into stats$dates select sysdate, null from dual;

insert into stats$begin_waitstat select * from v$waitstat;

insert into stats$begin_bck_event
    select event, sum(total_waits), sum(time_waited)
        from v$session s, v$session_event e
        where type = 'BACKGROUND' and s.sid = e.sid
    group by event;

insert into stats$begin_event select * from v$system_event;

insert into stats$begin_roll select * from v$rollstat;
```

FIGURE 7.3 (*continued*): UTLBSTAT.sql

```
insert into stats$begin_file select * from stats$file_view;
insert into stats$begin_dc select * from v$rowcache;
insert into stats$begin_stats select * from v$sysstat;
insert into stats$begin_lib select * from v$librarycache;
insert into stats$begin_latch select * from v$latch;
commit;
```

FIGURE 7.3 (*continued*): UTLBSTAT.sql

```
rem
rem $Header: utlestat.sql 12-jan-98.13:50:59 kquinn Exp $ estat.sql
rem
Rem Copyright (c) 1988, 1996, 1998 by Oracle Corporation
Rem NAME
REM    UTLESTAT.SQL
Rem FUNCTION
Rem    This script will generate a report (in "report.txt") which
Rem    will contain usefull information for performance
Rem    monitoring. In particular information from v$sysstat,
Rem    v$latch, and v$rollstat.
Rem NOTES
Rem    Don't worry about errors during "drop table"s, they are
Rem    normal.
Rem MODIFIED
Rem    kquinn    01/12/98 - 607968: Correct nowait latch hit ratio calc
Rem    jklein    08/23/96 - bug 316570 - fix typo
Rem    akolk     08/09/96 - #387757: fix latch hitratios
Rem    akolk     07/19/96 - #298462: correcting latch miss rate
           (Fixing)
Rem    akolk     07/19/96 - #298462: correcting latch miss rate
Rem    akolk     07/12/96 - #270507: remove db_block_write_batch
Rem    jloaiza   10/14/95 - add vtcsh 5.18 (BBN) 2/20/90 Patch
           level 0
Rem    jloaiza   09/19/95 - add waitstat
Rem    jloaiza   09/04/95 - per second stats, split background
           waits
Rem    drady     09/09/93 - merge changes from branch 1.1.312.2
Rem    drady     04/26/93 - Stat name changes for 7.1
Rem    drady     03/22/93 - merge changes from branch 1.1.312.1
Rem    drady     08/24/93 - bug 173918
Rem    drady     03/04/93 - fix bug 152986
Rem    glumpkin  11/23/92 - Creation
Rem    glumpkin  11/23/92 - Renamed from UTLSTATE.SQL
```

FIGURE 7.4: UTLESTAT.sql

```
Rem     glumpkin   10/20/92 - Renamed from ESTAT.SQL
Rem     jloaiza    03/26/92 - add write queue query
Rem     jloaiza    02/24/92 - fix latch stats
Rem     jloaiza    01/17/92 - improve output
Rem     jloaiza    01/07/92 - rework for version 7
Rem Laursen  01/01/91 - V6 to V7 merge
Rem Trabosh  09/27/89 - added order by and group by to stats$files
Rem Loaiza   04/04/89 - fix run dates to do minutes instead of
        months
Rem Loaiza   03/31/89 - add kqrst usage column
Rem Jloaiza  03/16/89 - improve names and formats
Rem Jloaiza  03/09/89 - make kqrst columns intelligible
Rem Jloaiza  02/23/89 - changed table names, added dates
Rem Martin   02/22/89 - Creation
set echo on;
connect internal;

Rem **************************************************************
Rem                  Gather Ending Statistics
Rem **************************************************************
insert into stats$end_latch select * from v$latch;
insert into stats$end_stats select * from v$sysstat;
insert into stats$end_lib select * from v$librarycache;
update stats$dates set end_time = sysdate;
insert into stats$end_event select * from v$system_event;
insert into stats$end_bck_event
    select event, sum(total_waits), sum(time_waited)
        from v$session s, v$session_event e
        where type = 'BACKGROUND' and s.sid = e.sid
        group by event;
insert into stats$end_waitstat select * from v$waitstat;
insert into stats$end_roll select * from v$rollstat;
insert into stats$end_file select * from stats$file_view;
insert into stats$end_dc select * from v$rowcache;

Rem **************************************************************
Rem                  Create Summary Tables
Rem **************************************************************
drop table stats$stats;
drop table stats$latches;
drop table stats$roll;
drop table stats$files;
drop table stats$dc;
drop table stats$lib;
drop table stats$event;
drop table stats$bck_event;
drop table stats$bck_event;
drop table stats$waitstat;
```

FIGURE 7.4 (*continued*): UTLESTAT.sql

```
create table stats$stats as
select e.value-b.value change , n.name
    from v$statname n , stats$begin_stats b , stats$end_stats e
      where n.statistic# = b.statistic# and n.statistic# =
      e.statistic#;
create table stats$latches as
    select  e.gets-b.gets gets,
            e.misses-b.misses misses,
            e.sleeps-b.sleeps sleeps,
            e.immediate_gets-b.immediate_gets immed_gets,
            e.immediate_misses-b.immediate_misses immed_miss,
            n.name
      from v$latchname n , stats$begin_latch b , stats$end_latch e
        where n.latch# = b.latch# and n.latch# = e.latch#;
create table stats$event as
    select  e.total_waits-b.total_waits event_count,
            e.time_waited-b.time_waited time_waited,
            e.event
      from stats$begin_event b , stats$end_event e
        where b.event = e.event
    union all
    select  e.total_waits event_count,
            e.time_waited time_waited,
            e.event
      from stats$end_event e
        where e.event not in (select b.event from
        stats$begin_event b);
Rem background waits
create table stats$bck_event as
    select  e.total_waits-b.total_waits event_count,
            e.time_waited-b.time_waited time_waited,
            e.event
      from stats$begin_bck_event b , stats$end_bck_event e
        where b.event = e.event
    union all
    select  e.total_waits event_count,
            e.time_waited time_waited,
            e.event
      from stats$end_bck_event e
        where e.event not in (select b.event from
        stats$begin_bck_event b);
Rem subtrace background events out of regular events
update stats$event e
    set (event_count, time_waited) =
        (select  e.event_count - b.event_count,
                 e.time_waited - b.time_waited
          from stats$bck_event b
```

FIGURE 7.4 (*continued*): UTLESTAT.sql

```
         where e.event = b.event)
      where e.event in (select b.event from stats$bck_event b);
create table stats$waitstat as
select   e.class,
         e.count - b.count count,
         e.time - b.time time
      from stats$begin_waitstat b, stats$end_waitstat e
         where e.class = b.class;
create table stats$roll as
select   e.usn undo_segment,
         e.gets-b.gets trans_tbl_gets,
         e.waits-b.waits trans_tbl_waits,
         e.writes-b.writes undo_bytes_written,
         e.rssize segment_size_bytes,
         e.xacts-b.xacts xacts,
         e.shrinks-b.shrinks shrinks,
         e.wraps-b.wraps wraps
      from stats$begin_roll b, stats$end_roll e
         where e.usn = b.usn;
create table stats$files as
select   b.ts table_space,
         b.name file_name,
         e.pyr-b.pyr phys_reads,
         e.pbr-b.pbr phys_blks_rd,
         e.prt-b.prt phys_rd_time,
         e.pyw-b.pyw phys_writes,
         e.pbw-b.pbw phys_blks_wr,
         e.pwt-b.pwt phys_wrt_tim,
         e.megabytes_size
      from stats$begin_file b, stats$end_file e
         where b.name=e.name;
create table stats$dc as
select   b.parameter name,
         e.gets-b.gets get_reqs,
         e.getmisses-b.getmisses get_miss,
         e.scans-b.scans scan_reqs,
         e.scanmisses-b.scanmisses scan_miss,
         e.modifications-b.modifications mod_reqs,
      e.count count,
      e.usage cur_usage
      from stats$begin_dc b, stats$end_dc e
         where b.cache#=e.cache#
         and nvl(b.subordinate#,-1) = nvl(e.subordinate#,-1);
```

FIGURE 7.4 (*continued*): UTLESTAT.sql

```
create table stats$lib as
select    e.namespace,
          e.gets-b.gets gets,
          e.gethits-b.gethits gethits,
          e.pins-b.pins pins,
          e.pinhits-b.pinhits pinhits,
          e.reloads - b.reloads reloads,
          e.invalidations - b.invalidations invalidations
       from stats$begin_lib b, stats$end_lib e
         where b.namespace = e.namespace;
Rem *********************************************************
Rem                      Output statistics
Rem *********************************************************
spool report.txt;

set    charwidth 12
set    numwidth 10
Rem    Select Library cache statistics. The pin hit rate should be high.
select    namespace library,
          gets,
          round(decode(gethits,0,1,gethits)/decode(gets,0,1,gets),3)
             gethitratio,
          pins,
          round(decode(pinhits,0,1,pinhits)/decode(pins,0,1,pins),3)
             pinhitratio,
          reloads, invalidations
       from stats$lib;

set    charwidth 27;
set    numwidth 12;
Rem The total is the total value of the statistic between the time
Rem bstat was run and the time estat was run. Note that the estat
Rem script logs on as "internal" so the per_logon statistics will
Rem always be based on at least one logon.
select    n1.name "Statistic",
          n1.change "Total",
          round(n1.change/trans.change,2) "Per Transaction",
          round(n1.change/logs.change,2) "Per Logon",
          round(n1.change/(to_number(to_char(end_time, 'J'))*60*60*24 -
                    to_number(to_char(start_time, 'J'))*60*60*24 +
                 to_number(to_char(end_time, 'SSSSS')) -
                 to_number(to_char(start_time, 'SSSSS')))
             , 2) "Per Second"
       from stats$stats n1, stats$stats trans, stats$stats logs,
       stats$dates
       where trans.name='user commits'
         and logs.name='logons cumulative'
         and n1.change != 0
       order by n1.name;
```

FIGURE 7.4 (*continued*): UTLESTAT.sql

```
set numwidth 27
Rem Average length of the dirty buffer write queue. If this is larger
Rem than the value of:
Rem 1. (db_files * db_file_simultaneous_writes)/2
Rem or
Rem 2. 1/4 of db_block_buffers
Rem which ever is smaller and also there is a platform specific limit
Rem on the write batch size (normally 1024 or 2048 buffers). If
    the average length of the dirty buffer write queue is larger
Rem than the value calculated before, increase
Rem db_file_simultaneous_writes or db_files.
Rem Also check for disks that are doing many more IOs than other
    disks.
select queue.change/writes.change "Average Write Queue Length"
     from stats$stats queue, stats$stats writes
    where queue.name = 'summed dirty queue length'
      and writes.name = 'write requests';
set charwidth 32;
set numwidth 13;
Rem System wide wait events for non-background processes (PMON,
Rem SMON, etc). Times are in hundreths of seconds. Each one of
Rem these is a context switch which costs CPU time. By looking at
Rem the Total Time you can often determine what is the bottleneck
Rem that processes are waiting for. This shows the total time
Rem spent waiting for a specific event and the average time per
Rem wait on that event.
select    n1.event "Event Name",
          n1.event_count "Count",
       n1.time_waited "Total Time",
       round(n1.time_waited/n1.event_count, 2) "Avg Time"
    from stats$event n1
   where n1.event_count > 0
   order by n1.time_waited desc;
Rem System wide wait events for background processes (PMON, SMON, etc)
select    n1.event "Event Name",
          n1.event_count "Count",
       n1.time_waited "Total Time",
       round(n1.time_waited/n1.event_count, 2) "Avg Time"
    from stats$bck_event n1
   where n1.event_count > 0
   order by n1.time_waited desc;
set charwidth 18;
set numwidth 11;
Rem Latch statistics. Latch contention will show up as a large
Rem value for the 'latch free' event in the wait events above.
Rem Sleeps should be low. The hit_ratio should be high.
```

FIGURE 7.4 (*continued*): UTLESTAT.sql

```
select name latch_name, gets, misses,
       round((gets-misses)/decode(gets,0,1,gets),3)
         hit_ratio,
       sleeps,
       round(sleeps/decode(misses,0,1,misses),3) "SLEEPS/MISS"
    from stats$latches
      where gets != 0
      order by name;
set numwidth 16
Rem Statistics on no_wait gets of latches. A no_wait get does not
Rem wait for the latch to become free, it immediately times out.
select name latch_name,
       immed_gets nowait_gets,
       immed_miss nowait_misses,
       round((immed_gets/(immed_gets+immed_miss)), 3)
         nowait_hit_ratio
    from stats$latches
      where immed_gets + immed_miss != 0
      order by name;
Rem Buffer busy wait statistics. If the value for 'buffer busy
Rem wait' in the wait event statistics is high, then this table
Rem will identify which class of blocks is having high contention.
Rem If there are high 'undo header' waits then add more rollback
Rem segments. If there are high 'segment header' waits then adding
Rem freelists might help. Check v$session_wait to get the
Rem addresses of the actual blocks having contention.
select * from stats$waitstat
    where count != 0
    order by count desc;
set numwidth 19;
Rem Waits_for_trans_tbl high implies you should add rollback
    segments.
select * from stats$roll;
set charwidth 39
Rem The init.ora parameters currently in effect:
select name, value from v$parameter where isdefault = 'FALSE'
    order by name;
set charwidth 15;
set numwidth 8;
Rem get_miss and scan_miss should be very low compared to the requests.
Rem cur_usage is the number of entries in the cache that are being
    used.
select * from stats$dc
    where get_reqs != 0 or scan_reqs != 0 or mod_reqs != 0;
```

FIGURE 7.4 (*continued*): UTLESTAT.sql

```
set charwidth 80;
set numwidth 10;
Rem Sum IO operations over tablespaces.
select
      table_space||' '
         table_space,
      sum(phys_reads) reads, sum(phys_blks_rd) blks_read,
      sum(phys_rd_time) read_time, sum(phys_writes) writes,
      sum(phys_blks_wr) blks_wrt, sum(phys_wrt_tim) write_time,
      sum(megabytes_size) megabytes
    from stats$files
    group by table_space
    order by table_space;
set charwidth 48;
set numwidth 10;
Rem I/O should be spread evenly accross drives. A big difference
    between
Rem phys_reads and phys_blks_rd implies table scans are going on.
select   table_space, file_name,
         phys_reads reads, phys_blks_rd blks_read, phys_rd_time
         read_time,
         phys_writes writes, phys_blks_wr blks_wrt, phys_wrt_tim
write_time,
         megabytes_size megabytes
    from stats$files order by table_space, file_name;
set charwidth 25
Rem The times that bstat and estat were run.
select   to_char(start_time, 'dd-mon-yy hh24:mi:ss') start_time,
         to_char(end_time,   'dd-mon-yy hh24:mi:ss') end_time
    from stats$dates;
set charwidth 75
Rem Versions
select * from v$version;

spool off;

Rem ************************************************************
Rem                       Drop Temporary Tables
Rem ************************************************************

drop table stats$dates;

drop table stats$begin_stats;
drop table stats$end_stats;
drop table stats$stats;

drop table stats$begin_latch;
drop table stats$end_latch;
drop table stats$latches;
```

FIGURE 7.4 (*continued*): UTLESTAT.sql

```
drop table stats$begin_roll;
drop table stats$end_roll;
drop table stats$roll;

drop table stats$begin_file;
drop table stats$end_file;
drop table stats$files;
drop view  stats$file_view;

drop table stats$begin_dc;
drop table stats$end_dc;
drop table stats$dc;

drop table stats$begin_lib;
drop table stats$end_lib;
drop table stats$lib;

drop table stats$begin_event;
drop table stats$end_event;
drop table stats$event;

drop table stats$begin_bck_event;
drop table stats$end_bck_event;
drop table stats$bck_event;

drop table stats$begin_waitstat;
drop table stats$end_waitstat;
drop table stats$waitstat;
```

FIGURE 7.4 (*continued*): UTLESTAT.sql

7.4 Procedure for Running the Utilities

The initialization parameter TIMED_STATISTICS must be set to TRUE (default being FALSE) for collecting the full set of statistics. Figures 7.1 and 7.2 show that the V$ views constitute the basis of the data collected by the two utilities. Since the V$ views collect performance data from the instant of the database startup, allow the database and all its accompanying applications to run for a period of time before running the scripts. The time interval during which the scripts collect data must be chosen to reflect the worst performance issues so that the statistics such as hit ratios can identify problem points. For example, one may run these scripts during the peak production hours or during heavy batch activities. At the beginning of the selected time interval run the script UTLBSTAT.sql from the Server Manager and at the end of that time interval run UTLESTAT.sql from the Server Manager. The output file REPORT.TXT resides in the default directory of the account from which the Server Manager is invoked. For a stable database run the two scripts every three to four weeks and take corrective actions, as needed.

Figures 7.5 and 7.6 contain respectively the commands to run the two scripts.

```
smittra:~ > svrmgrl
Oracle Server Manager Release 3.0.5.0.0 - Production
(c) Copyright 1997, Oracle Corporation. All Rights Reserved.
Oracle8 Enterprise Edition Release 8.0.5.1.0 - Production
PL/SQL Release 8.0.5.1.0 - Production
SVRMGR> @utlbstat
```

FIGURE 7.5: Command to Run UTLBSTAT.sql

```
smittra:~ > svrmgrl
Oracle Server Manager Release 3.0.5.0.0 - Production
(c) Copyright 1997, Oracle Corporation. All Rights Reserved.
Oracle8 Enterprise Edition Release 8.0.5.1.0 - Production
PL/SQL Release 8.0.5.1.0 - Production
SVRMGR> @utlestat
```

FIGURE 7.6: Command to Run UTLESTAT.sql

7.5 UTLBSTAT/ESTAT Performance Report Analysis

The performance report REPORT.TXT consists of 15 parts listed in Section 7.2 containing statistics about the Oracle internal level. In Subsections 7.5.1 through 7.5.15 we discuss each part separately.

7.5.1 Library Cache Statistics

Figure 7.7 contains data showing the performance of the library cache, which is a part of the shared SQL pool in the SGA (see Section 4.2.1). The data help us to determine if the shared SQL statements are being reparsed due to insufficient memory being allocated to the library cache. The crucial data to look for in Figure 7.7 are SQL AREA under LIBRARY and its accompanying statistics under GETHITRATIO, PINHITRATIO, and RELOADS. These are defined below:

$$\text{GETHITRATIO} = \frac{\text{number of times that a requested object was found in cache}}{\text{total number of requests made}};$$

$$\text{PINHITRATIO} = \frac{\text{number of times that a pinned object was in cache}}{\text{total number of pin requests made}};$$

RELOADS = number of cache misses during execution of a SQL statement.

The guidelines for library cache statistics are as follows.

1. GETHITRATIO should be greater than .9.
2. PINHITRATIO should be greater than .99.
3. The ratio RELOADS / PINS should be less than .01, and preferably zero.

If any one or more of the above three guidelines are not met, the size of the shared SQL pool may be too small and may need to be increased. See Section 6.5 for further details on tuning the shared SQL pool.

Figure 7.7 shows that

```
GETHITRATIO = .9, PINHITRATIO = .928, RELOADS / PINS = 0.
```

Hence guidelines (1) and (2) are not met, but (3) is. If this trend continues, the shared SQL pool size should be increased.

```
SVRMGR>
SVRMGR> set charwidth 12
Charwidth                              12
SVRMGR> set numwidth 10
Numwidth                               10
SVRMGR> Rem Select Library cache statistics. The pin hit rate
should be high.
SVRMGR> select namespace library,
     2> gets,
     3> round(decode(gethits,0,1,gethits)/decode(gets,0,1,gets),3)
     4> gethitratio,
     5> pins,
     6> round(decode(pinhits,0,1,pinhits)/decode(pins,0,1,pins),3)
     7> pinhitratio,
     8> reloads, invalidations
     9> from stats$lib;
LIBRARY          GETS    GETHITRATI   PINS    PINHITRATI   RELOADS   INVALIDATI
------------     ----    ----------   ----    ----------   -------   ----------
BODY                2           .5       2           .5          0            0
CLUSTER             0            1       0            1          0            0
INDEX               0            1       0            1          0            0
OBJECT              0            1       0            1          0            0
PIPE                0            1       0            1          0            0
SQL AREA          170           .9     502         .928          0            1
TABLE/PROCED      133         .842     133         .752          0            0
TRIGGER             0            1       0            1          0            0
8 rows selected.
```

FIGURE 7.7: Library Cache Statistics

7.5.2 Systemwide Events Statistics

Figure 7.8 contains a partial output of systemwide events statistics. It lists only those statistics that are used for our discussion here. This part of REPORT.TXT covers a wide range of performance areas for the database. For each statistic, it displays the total number of operations, the total number of operations per user commit, per user logon, and per second. "Per logon" will always be based on at least one logon since the script UTLESTAT.sql logs on as "internal." We discuss only five major performance statistics here.

(a) *Buffer Hit Ratio*: This has been discussed in Section 6.3. Figure 7.8 shows that

consistent gets = 1,013; db block gets = 460; physical reads = 216.

Therefore,

Logical reads = consistent gets + db block gets = 1,013 + 460 = 1,473
Buffer hit ratio = (logical reads–physical reads) / logical reads = .85.

Since the ratio < .9, the data block buffer cache should be increased in size.

(b) *Number of DBWR Processes*: The following three statistics determine if we need to increase the number of DBWR background process.

Dirty buffers inspected = Number of modified (dirty) buffers that were aged out via the LRU algorithm (see Section 4.2.1).
Free buffer inspected = Number of buffers that were skipped by foreground processes to find a free buffer.
Free buffer requested = Number of times a free buffer was requested.

The guidelines here are as follows.

1. The value of "dirty buffers inspected" should be zero. If the value is positive, then DBWR is not working fast enough to write all the dirty buffers to the data files before they are removed from the data block buffer cache under LRU.
2. The ratio (free buffer inspected/free buffer requested) should be ≤.04. If this ratio is greater than .04, then there may be too many unusable buffers in the data block buffer cache. It may mean that checkpoints are occurring too frequently so that DBWR cannot keep up.

If the guidelines above are not met, set the initialization parameter DBWR_IO_SLAVES to a positive value, the default being zero.
From Figure 7.8 we get

```
dirty buffers inspected = 3,
free buffer inspected/free buffer requested
    = 4 / 237 = .02
```

Here we get ambiguous results in that (1) does not hold, but (2) holds. The value of DBWR_IO_SLAVES is zero for the database. Further investigation is needed before we set this parameter to a positive value.

(c) *Redo Log Buffer Hit Ratio*: This has been discussed in Section 6.4.

Figure 7.8 shows that

```
redo log space requests = 805, redo entries = 387,815
```

Therefore, redo log buffer hit ratio

```
= (redo log space requests)/(redo entries)
= 805/387,815 = .002
```

This exceeds the guideline that the ratio should be $\leq .0002$, as noted in Section 6.4. Hence the value of the initialization parameter LGWR_IO_SLAVES should be increased from its current default value of zero.

(d) *Sorting Area Size*: It is recommended that all the sorts be done in memory instead of through the creation of temporary segment(s) in the TEMP tablespace.

Figure 7.8 shows that

```
sorts(memory) = 447, sorts (disk) = 16
```

The guideline is as follows: sorts (disk) should be <5% of sorts(memory). Otherwise, increase the initialization parameter SORT_AREA_SIZE. Since 5% of 447 = 22.35, the guideline is satisfied here.

(e) *Dynamic Extension of Segments*: Rollback segments created with an OPTIMAL clause are dynamically extended if needed. Too much dynamic extension is bad for performance. The following guideline involving the two statistics, recursive calls and user calls, can be used to detect if any dynamic extension is occurring.

If recursive calls/user calls > 30, too much dynamic extension is occurring. In this case, resize the extents of rollback segments resulting in fewer but larger extents. See Section 5.10 for further details about rollback segments.

From Figure 7.8 we find that the ratio

```
(recursive calls/user calls) = 1975 / 111 = 17.8
```

indicating that the dynamic extension is not an issue here.

```
SVRMGR>
SVRMGR> set charwidth 27;
Charwidth                 27
SVRMGR> set numwidth 12;
Numwidth                  12
SVRMGR> Rem   The total is the total value of the statistic between
              the time
SVRMGR> Rem   bstat was run and the time estat was run. Note that
              the estat
SVRMGR> Rem   script logs on as "internal" so the per_logon
              statistics will
SVRMGR> Rem always be based on at least one logon.
SVRMGR> select n1.name "Statistic",
     2> n1.change "Total",
     3> round(n1.change/trans.change,2) "Per Transaction",
     4> round(n1.change/logs.change,2) "Per Logon",
     5> round(n1.change/(to_number(to_char(end_time, 'J'))*60*60*24 -
     6> to_number(to_char(start_time, 'J'))*60*60*24 +
     7> to_number(to_char(end_time, 'SSSSS')) -
     8> to_number(to_char(start_time, 'SSSSS')))
     9> , 2) "Per Second"
    10> from stats$stats n1, stats$stats trans, stats$stats logs,
         stats$dates
    11> where trans.name='user commits'
    12> and logs.name='logons cumulative'
    13> and n1.change != 0
    14> order by n1.name;
```

Statistic	Total	Per Transact	Per Logon	Per Second
consistent gets	1013	1013	101.3	.18
db block gets	460	460	46	.08
dirty buffers inspected	3	3	.3	0
free buffer inspected	4	4	.4	0
free buffer requested	237	237	23.7	.04
physical reads	216	216	21.6	.04
recursive call	1975	1975	197.5	.35
redo entries	387815	387815	3878.15	65.27
redo log space requests	805	805	80.5	.13
sorts(disk)	16	16	1.6	0
sorts(memory)	447	447	44.7	.07
user calls	111	111	11.1	.02

```
74 rows selected
SVRMGR>
```

FIGURE 7.8: Partial Listing of Systemwide Events Statistics

7.5.3 Dirty Buffer Write Queue

Figure 7.9 contains the output for this part. The value of this statistic should be very close to zero. The "Rem" statements in Figure 7.9 provide the following guideline:

```
dirty buffer write queue ≤
min ((db_files * db_file_simultaneous_writes)/2,
db_block_buffers/4).
```

If this guideline is not met, increase the initialization parameter DB_FILES or DB_FILE_SIMULTANEOUS_WRITES.

For this database, the values of the above three parameters are:

```
DB_FILES = 256, DB_FILE_SIMULTANEOUS_WRITES = 4,
DB_BLOCK_BUFFERS = 200
```

Since

```
0 = dirty buffer write queue ≤ 50 = min (512, 50),
```

the guideline is satisfied here.

```
SVRMGR>
SVRMGR> set numwidth 27
Numwidth                        27
SVRMGR> Rem Average length of the dirty buffer write queue. If
            this is larger
SVRMGR> Rem than the value of:
SVRMGR> Rem 1. (db_files * db_file_simultaneous_writes)/2
SVRMGR> Rem or
SVRMGR> Rem 2. 1/4 of db_block_buffers
SVRMGR> Rem which ever is smaller and also there is a platform
            specific limit
SVRMGR> Rem on the write batch size (normally 1024 or 2048
            buffers). If the average
SVRMGR> Rem length of the dirty buffer write queue is larger than
            the value
SVRMGR> Rem calculated before, increase
            db_file_simultaneous_writes or db_files.
SVRMGR> Rem Also check for disks that are doing many more IOs than
            other disks.
SVRMGR> select queue.change/writes.change "Average Write Queue Length"
     2> from stats$stats queue, stats$stats writes
     3> where queue.name = 'summed dirty queue length'
     4> and writes.name = 'write requests';
Average Write Queue Length
--------------------------
                         0
1 row selected.
SVRMGR>
```

FIGURE 7.9: Dirty Buffer Write Queue

7.5.4 Systemwide Wait Events for Non-Background Processes

Figure 7.10 contains the output for this part. Each wait event is a context switch that costs CPU time. By looking at the Total Time column in Figure 7.10 we can determine the bottleneck for processes. Total Time and Avg Time represent respectively the total amount of time and the average amount of time that processes had to wait for the event. Both times are computed over the period of time during which the statistics were collected. The time is measured in 1/100ths of a second.

The general guideline in interpreting the statistics is to regard all "waits" as bad. The waits for non-background processes discussed in this section directly affect the user processes. The following events are of interest for performance tuning.

```
free buffer waits = wait because a buffer is not available
buffer busy waits = wait because a buffer is either being read
                    into the data block buffer cache by another
                    session or the buffer is in memory in an
                    incompatible mode; i.e., some other session
                    is changing the buffer
log buffer space = wait for space in the log buffer
log file synch = wait of COMMIT or ROLLBACK foreground
                    processes in redo log buffers to be written to
                    the online redo log files
log file switch (checkpoint incomplete) = wait for the next
                                            redo log file since
                                            the checkpoint for
                                            that file is still
                                            incomplete
```

The following guidelines can be used with respect to the above events.

1. If (buffer busy waits)/(logical read) > .04, we need to examine the specific CLASS of data blocks that are involved in high contention. This is discussed in Section 7.5.8. Also, see Section 7.5.2, (a), for a definition of "logical read" used in the metric.
2. The two events, free buffer waits and log file switch (checkpoint incomplete), indicate one or more of the following,

    - DBWR cannot keep up with the update transaction activities;
    - Checkpoints are occurring too frequently.

    To remedy the situation,

    - Create additional DBWR_IO_SLAVES process. See Section 6.6.1 for additional details;
    - Check if the size of the online redo log files is too small. See Section 6.6.2 for additional details;

- Check the values of the initialization parameters LOG_CHECKPOINT_INTERVAL and LOG_CHECKPOINT_TIMEOUT.

3. A high value of the event "log buffer space" indicates that the LGWR cannot keep up with recording transactions from the redo log buffers into the online redo log files. To resolve the issue, first increase the initialization parameter LOG_BUFFER by 5% and examine the effect. If problems continue, further increase the value of the initialization parameter LGWR_IO_SLAVES.
4. A high value of the event "log file synch" indicates possible I/O problems.

```
SVRMGR>
SVRMGR> set charwidth 32;
Charwidth                               32
SVRMGR> set numwidth 13;
Numwidth                                13
SVRMGR> Rem System wide wait events for non-background Times are
in SVRMGR> hundreths of seconds. Each one of these is a context
switch
SVRMGR> Rem which costs CPU time. By looking at the Total Time you can
SVRMGR> Rem often determine what is the bottleneck that processes are
SVRMGR> Rem waiting for. This shows the total time spent waiting for a
SVRMGR> Rem specific event and the average time per wait on that event.
SVRMGR> select n1.event "Event Name",
    2> n1.event_count "Count",
    3> n1.time_waited "Total Time",
    4> round(n1.time_waited/n1.event_count, 2) "Avg Time"
    5> from stats$event n1
    6> where n1.event_count > 0
    7> order by n1.time_waited desc;
Event Name                        Count        Total Time     Avg Time
-----------------------------     -----        ----------     --------
SQL*Net message from client       140          0              0
SQL*Net message from dblink       17           0              0
SQL*Net message to client         140          0              0
SQL*Net message to dblink         17           0              0
control file sequential read      17           0              0
db file sequential read           163          0              0
file open                         18           0              0
log file sync                     2            0              0
refresh controlfile command       4            0              0
9 rows selected.
SVRMGR>
```

FIGURE 7.10: Systemwide Wait Events for Non-Background Processes

7.5.5 Systemwide WAIT Events for Background Processes

Figure 7.11 contains the output for this part. The comments of Section 7.5.4 apply equally well to this section. If ARCH, DBWR, or LGWR cannot keep up with the operation activities, increase respectively the values of the initialization parameters, ARCH_IO_SLAVES, DBWR_ IO_SLAVES, or LGWR_ IO_SLAVES. See Sections 6.6.1, 6.6.2, and 6.6.4 for further details about these three parameters pertaining to the background processes.

```
SVRMGR>
SVRMGR> Rem System wide wait events for background processes
(PMON, SMON, etc)
SVRMGR> select n1.event "Event Name",
    2> n1.event_count "Count",
    3> n1.time_waited "Total Time",
    4> round(n1.time_waited/n1.event_count, 2) "Avg Time"
    5> from stats$bck_event n1
    6> where n1.event_count > 0
    7> order by n1.time_waited desc;
Event Name                    Count      Total Time    Avg Time
--------------------------    ------     ----------    --------
control file parallel write   1882           0            0
control file sequential read     8           0            0
db file parallel write          10           0            0
db file scattered read          11           0            0
db file sequential read         17           0            0
log file parallel write          6           0            0
pmon timer                    1896           0            0
rdbms ipc message             5691           0            0
smon timer                      19           0            0
9 rows selected.
SVRMGR>
```

FIGURE 7.11: Systemwide Wait Events for Background Processes

7.5.6 Latches with Wait

Figure 7.12 contains the output for this part. Oracle defines a *latch* as a "low level serialization mechanism to protect shared data structures in the SGA," i.e., the data block buffer cache, the redo log buffer cache, the library cache, and the dictionary cache. In essence, a latch is a lock on a part of the SGA to control accesses to data structures in the SGA. A server or a background process acquires a latch for very short time while manipulating or looking at one of these structures. The number of latches on the data block buffer cache is given by the formula:

    2 x (number of CPUs), in Oracle 7.0
    6 x (number of CPUs), in Oracle 8i

The library cache has only one latch. Latch contention occurs when multiple Oracle processes concurrently attempt to obtain the same latch. See Section 6.10 for an additional discussion of the latch.

Three of the columns, gets, misses, and sleeps, in Figure 7.12 are described below:

Gets = Number of times a latch was requested and was available;
Misses = Number of times a latch was requested and was not available initially;
Sleeps = Number of times a latch was requested, was not available, and was requested again.

The two metrics that are used as guidelines for managing latch contention are:

$$\text{hit ratio} = \frac{\text{gets} - \text{misses}}{\text{gets}}, \text{sleeps/miss} = \frac{\text{sleeps}}{\text{misses}}.$$

We can now provide the following guidelines.

1. The hit ratio should be >.99 for latch_names = cache buffers chain, library cache, redo copy, and redo allocation. Otherwise, take the following steps.

   Cache buffers chain: increase the value of the initialization parameter DB_BLOCK_BUFFERS by 10%.
   Library cache: increase the value of the initialization parameter SHARED_POOL_SIZE; or pin large SQL and PL/SQL packages in memory via DBMS_SHARED_POOL.KEEP procedure (see Section 6.9 for details).
   Redo copy: increase the value of the initialization parameter LOG_SIMULTANEOUS_COPIES to 2 * (number of CPUs) in Oracle 7.0, and to 6 * (number of CPUs) in Oracle 8i.
   Redo allocation: decrease the value of the initialization parameter LOG_SMALL_ENTRY_MAX_SIZE; this parameter controls the maximum size of a redo entry that can be copied to the redo log using the redo allocation latch.

2. The ratio sleeps/miss should not exceed one. Otherwise, it implies that some processes had to sleep more than once before acquiring the latch.

In general, contention for redo log buffer access via the two latches, redo copy and redo allocation, rarely inhibits database performance. However, in the case where some of the metrics do not comply with the guidelines, the above measures can be taken. For Figure 7.12 all the hit ratios are one and all the sleeps/miss ratios are zero indicating no contention. Section 6.10 discusses the contention issues in more detail.

```
SVRMGR>
SVRMGR> set charwidth 18;
Charwidth                         18
SVRMGR> set numwidth 11;
Numwidth                          11
SVRMGR> Rem Latch statistics. Latch contention will show up as a
large value for
SVRMGR> Rem the 'latch free' event in the wait events above.
SVRMGR> Rem Sleeps should be low. The hit_ratio should be high.
SVRMGR> select name latch_name, gets, misses,
     2> round((gets-misses)/decode(gets,0,1,gets),3)
     3> hit_ratio,
     4> sleeps,
     5> round(sleeps/decode(misses,0,1,misses),3) "SLEEPS/MISS"
     6> from stats$latches
     7> where gets != 0
     8> order by name;
LATCH_NAME          GETS    MISSES   HIT_RATIO    SLEEPS   SLEEPS/MISS
------------------  -----   ------   ---------    ------   -----------
Active checkpoint   1896      0         1           0          0
Checkpoint queue l  4219      0         1           0          0
Token Manager          9      0         1           0          0
cache buffer handl     1      0         1           0          0
cache buffers chai  2871      0         1           0          0
cache buffers lru     24      0         1           0          0
dml lock allocatio    11      0         1           0          0
enqueue hash chain   657      0         1           0          0
enqueues            1298      0         1           0          0
global transaction   477      0         1           0          0
global tx free lis     6      0         1           0          0
global tx hash map    32      0         1           0          0
ktm global data       19      0         1           0          0
library cache       2654      0         1           0          0
library cache load    70      0         1           0          0
list of block allo     1      0         1           0          0
messages           11397      0         1           0          0
modify parameter v   100      0         1           0          0
multiblock read ob    38      0         1           0          0
ncodef allocation     90      0         1           0          0
process allocation     9      0         1           0          0
redo allocation     1925      0         1           0          0
redo writing        3794      0         1           0          0
row cache objects   2080      0         1           0          0
sequence cache        27      0         1           0          0
```

FIGURE 7.12: Statistics for Latches with Wait

```
session allocation      138     0     1     0     0
session idle bit        263     0     1     0     0
session switching        90     0     1     0     0
shared pool            1067     0     1     0     0
sort extent pool         19     0     1     0     0
transaction alloca       46     0     1     0     0
transaction branch      119     0     1     0     0
undo global data        468     0     1     0     0
user lock                14     0     1     0     0
34 rows selected.
SVRMGR>
```

FIGURE 7.12 (*continued*): Statistics for Latches with Wait

7.5.7 Latches with NoWait

Figure 7.13 contains the statistics for this part. As with Section 7.5.6, the metric NOWAIT_HIT_RATIO should exceed .99. For Figure 7.13 this guideline is met.

```
SVRMGR> set numwidth 16
Numwidth                      16
SVRMGR>   Rem Statistics on no_wait gets of latches. A no_wait get
          Rem does not
SVRMGR>   Rem wait for the latch to become free, it immediately
          Rem times out.
SVRMGR> select name latch_name,
    2>   immed_gets nowait_gets,
    3>   immed_miss nowait_misses,
    4>   round((immed_gets/(immed_gets+immed_miss)), 3)
    5>   nowait_hit_ratio
    6>   from stats$latches
    7>   where immed_gets + immed_miss != 0
    8>   order by name;
LATCH_NAME              NOWAIT_GETS   NOWAIT_MISSES   NOWAIT_HIT_RATIO
-----------------       -----------   -------------   ----------------
cache buffers chai          483             0               1
cache buffers lru           612             1             .998
process allocation            9             0               1
redo copy                    28             0               1
4 rows selected.
```

FIGURE 7.13: Latches with NoWait

7.5.8 Buffer Busy Wait

Figure 7.14 contains the statistics for this part. Unfortunately, no statistics are shown since there is no wait involved here. However, we discuss below the guidelines that Oracle offers in handling these statistics when they appear.

The output has three columns, CLASS, COUNT, and TIME, explained below:

CLASS   Class of the latch; there are 14 of them altogether: bitmap block, bitmap index block, data block, extent map, free list, save undo block, save undo header, segment header, sort block, system undo block, system undo header, undo block, undo header, and unused.
COUNT   Number of times a request for a latch was made, but it was busy.
TIME   Amount of time that the process waited.

It was noted in Section 7.5.4 that if (buffer busy waits) / (logical read) > .04, we need to examine the specific CLASSes of data blocks that are involved in high contention. In such cases, the output of this section lists CLASSes with positive values under COUNT and TIME. We are listing below the corrective actions to take for some of the CLASSes where contention is more frequent:

1. *Data Blocks*: Occurs when DBWR cannot keep up; increase the value of DBWR_IO_SLAVES parameter.
2. *Free List*: May occur when multiple data loading programs performing multiple INSERTs run at the same time; try to stagger the runtimes to avoid simultaneous execution; otherwise, increase the value of FREELISTS in the STORAGE clause of the affected segment(s). See Section 6.10.3 for more detail.
3. *Segment Header*: Occurs when there is free list contention; proceed as in paragraph (2) above. See Section 6.10.3 for more detail.
4. *Undo Header*: Occurs when there are not enough rollback segments so that there is contention for accessing the rollback segment header block; increase the number of rollback segments. See Section 5.10 for a discussion of rollback segments.

```
SVRMGR>
SVRMGR> Rem    Buffer busy wait statistics. If the value for 'buffer
                busy wait' in
SVRMGR> Rem    the wait event statistics is high, then this table
                will identify
SVRMGR> Rem    which class of blocks is having high contention. If
                there are high
SVRMGR> Rem    'undo header' waits then add more rollback segments.
                If there are
SVRMGR> Rem    high 'segment header' waits then adding freelists
                might help. Check
```

FIGURE 7.14: Buffer Busy Wait

7.5 UTLBSTAT/ESTAT Performance Report Analysis

```
SVRMGR> Rem    v$session_wait to get the addresses of the actual
               blocks having
SVRMGR> Rem contention.
SVRMGR> select * from stats$waitstat
    2> where count != 0
    3> order by count desc;
CLASS                       COUNT                     TIME
--------------              --------------            --------------
0 rows selected.
SVRMGR>
```

FIGURE 7.14 (*continued*): Buffer Busy Wait

7.5.9 Rollback Segments

Figure 7.15 contains the statistics for this part. The only guideline that Oracle provides is the following.

  If TRANS_TBL_WAITS is high, add more rollback segments.

Refer to Section 5.10 for much more detailed discussions about how to identify and resolve problems related to the sizes and numbers of the rollback segments.

```
SVRMGR>
SVRMGR> set numwidth 19;
Numwidth                       19
SVRMGR> Rem   Waits_for_trans_tbl high implies you should add
              rollback segments.
SVRMGR> select * from stats$roll;
UNDO_SEGMENT         TRANS_TBL_GETS          TRANS_TBL_WAITS
UNDO_BYTES_WRITTEN SEGMENT_SIZE_BYTES       XACTS              SHRINKS
WRAPS
--------------       ----------------        ----------------   ---------
---------            --------------          -------------      ---------   ---------
                                   0                       20            0
0                             407552                        0            0
0
                                   1                       21            0
0                            3151872                        0            0
0
                                   2                       20            0
0                            3151872                        0            0
0
                                   3                       27            0
```

FIGURE 7.15: Rollback Segments

```
2330                    3151872                          -1              0
0
                              4                          24              0
54                      3143680                           0              0
0
                              5                          26
                                                          0
2382                    3149824                           1              0
0
                              6                          20              0
0                       3143680                           0              0
0
                              7                          20              0
0                       3149824                           0              0
0
                              8                          20              0
0                       3149824                           0              0
0
                              9                          20              0
0                       3149824                           0              0
0
                             10                          20              0
0                       3143680                           0              0
0
                             11                          20              0
0                      10483712                           0              0
0
12 rows selected.
SVRMGR>
```

FIGURE 7.15 (*continued*): Rollback Segments

7.5.10 Non-Default INIT.ORA Parameters

Figure 7.16 contains the data for this part. This is a list of those initialization parameters that have been modified from their respective default values.

```
SVRMGR> set charwidth 39
Charwidth                               39
SVRMGR> Rem The init.ora parameters currently in effect:
SVRMGR> select name, value from v$parameter where isdefault =
'FALSE'
     2> order by name;
```

FIGURE 7.16: Non-Default INIT.ORA Parameters

```
NAME                              VALUE
--------------------------------  --------------------------------
audit_file_dest                   /oracle/EXAMPLE/adump
background_dump_dest              /oracle/EXAMPLE/bdump
compatible                        8.0.5
control_files                     /oradata/EXAMPLE/control01.ctl,
                                  /oradata/EXAMPLE/control02.ctl
core_dump_dest                    /oracle/EXAMPLE/cdump
db_block_buffers                  200
db_block_size                     2048
db_file_multiblock_read_count     16
db_files                          256
db_name                           EXAMPLE
dml_locks                         100
global_names                      FALSE
log_archive_dest                  /oracle/EXAMPLE/arch
log_archive_start                 FALSE
log_buffer                        65536
log_checkpoint_interval           5000
log_files                         255
max_dump_file_size                10240
max_enabled_roles                 35
max_rollback_segments             100
nls_date_format                   DD-MON-YYYY HH24MISS
open_links                        20
open_links_per_instance           20
processes                         100
rollback_segments                 RBS1, RBS2, RBS3, L_RBS_01
sequence_cache_entries            10
sequence_cache_hash_buckets       10
shared_pool_size                  10000000
user_dump_dest                    /oracle/EXAMPLE/udump
29 rows selected.
SVRMGR>
```

FIGURE 7.16 (*continued*): Non-Default INIT.ORA Parameters

7.5.11 Dictionary Cache

Figure 7.17 contains the statistics for this part. The columns of interest are GET_REQS, GET_MISS, SCAN_REQ, and SCAN_MIS, explained below:

GET_REQS Number of requests for objects in the dictionary cache;
GET_MISS Number of object information not in cache;
SCAN_REQ Number of scan requests;
SCAN_MIS Number of times a scan failed to find the data in the cache.

The following guidelines are used for interpreting the data dictionary statistics.

1. GET_MISS and SCAN_MIS should be very low compared to GET_REQS.
2. The following ratio

$$\Sigma\,(GET\_MISS)/\Sigma\,(GET\_REQS)$$

should be less than .15. Otherwise, if there is an increasing trend of this ratio, then increase the size of the dictionary cache by increasing the value of the initialization parameter SHARED_POOL_SIZE.

From Figure 7.17 we find that the above ratio is 36/743 = .05, which complies with the guideline (2). Guideline (1) is clearly satisfied.

```
SVRMGR> set charwidth 15;
Charwidth                       15
SVRMGR> set numwidth 8;
Numwidth                        8
SVRMGR> Rem   get_miss and scan_miss should be very low compared to
              the requests.
SVRMGR> Rem   cur_usage is the number of entries in the cache that
              are being used.
SVRMGR> select * from stats$dc
  2> where get_reqs != 0 or scan_reqs != 0 or mod_reqs != 0;
NAME            GET_REQS  GET_MISS  SCAN_REQ  SCAN_MIS  MOD_REQS  COUNT  CUR_U
--------------  --------  --------  --------  --------  --------  -----  -----
dc_tablespaces         4         0         0         0         0      2      1
dc_free_extents       82         2         2         0         6     10      5
dc_segments            7         2         0         0         2     68     61
dc_rollback_seg      456         0         0         0         0     28     13
dc_used_extents        2         2         0         0         2     29     24
dc_users              53         3         0         0         0     26     11
dc_user_grants        30         2         0         0         0     58      9
dc_objects            65        17         0         0         0    184    182
dc_synonyms            6         2         0         0         0     12      8
dc_usernames          26         4         0         0         0     21     10
dc_object_ids          3         1         0         0         0     99     97
dc_profiles            7         0         0         0         0      2      1
dc_database_lin        2         1         0         0         0      4      3
13 rows selected.
SVRMGR>
```

FIGURE 7.17: Dictionary Cache Statistics

7.5.12 I/O Operations over Tablespaces

Figure 7.18 contains the statistics for this part. The four columns, READS, BLKS_READ, WRITES, and BLKS_WRT, show the I/O operations for the database. They are described below:

READS   Total number of physical reads from the disk files;
BLKS_READ Total number of data blocks read from the disk files;
WRITES   Total number of physical writes to the disk files;
BLKS_WRT   Total number of data blocks written to the disk files.

The performance of I/O operations improves when a single "read" (or "write") can read (or write) multiple data blocks from a disk file (or to a disk file). This leads us to the following guidelines:

1. If READS and BLKS_READ are very close in value, increase the value of the initialization parameter DB_FILE_MULTIBLOCK_READ_COUNT, the default being eight.
2. If WRITES and BLKS_WRT are very close in value, increase the value of the initialization parameter DB_FILE_SIMULTANEOUS_WRITES, the default being four.

The column MEGABYTES shown as MB in Figure 7.18 represents the total number of megabytes allocated to a tablespace. If the tablespace has multiple data files, the sizes of all of the data files are added to derive the value of MEGABYTES for that tablespace. But the formula to compute MEGABYTES has an error. Since 1 MB = 1,048,576 bytes and not 1,000,000 bytes, the formula below in the file UTLBSTAT.sql

```
round (i.bytes / 1000000) megabytes_size
```

should be changed to read

```
round (i.bytes / 1048576) megabytes_size
```

to produce the correct result.

```
SVRMGR>
SVRMGR> set charwidth 80;
Charwidth                            80
SVRMGR> set numwidth 10;
Numwidth                             10
SVRMGR> Rem Sum IO operations over tablespaces.
SVRMGR> select
    2> table_space||'                    '
    3> table_space,
    4> sum(phys_reads) reads, sum(phys_blks_rd) blks_read,
    5> sum(phys_rd_time) read_time, sum(phys_writes) writes,
    6> sum(phys_blks_wr) blks_wrt, sum(phys_wrt_tim) write_time,
    7> sum(megabytes_size) megabytes
    8> from stats$files
    9> group by table_space
   10> order by table_space;
```

FIGURE 7.18: I/O Operations over Tablespaces

```
TABLE_SPACE   READS   BLKS_READ   READ_TIME   WRITE   BLKS_WRT   WRITE_TIME   MB
-----------   -----   ---------   ---------   -----   --------   ----------   --
DATA            1         1           0         0        0           0        10
IDX             1         1           0         0        0           0        10
RLBK            9         9           0        32       32           0        44
SYSTEM        173       220           0       107      107           0        84
TEMP            0         0           0         0        0           0        10
5 rows selected.
SVRMGR>
```

FIGURE 7.18 (*continued*): I/O Operations over Tablespaces

7.5.13 I/O Load Distribution Among Disk Drives

Figure 7.19 contains the statistics for this part. It includes the data of Figure 7.18 along with the datafile names of the tablespaces, which is unique to this output. Hence the output shown in Figure 7.19 has been reformatted to display only the first five columns of the output. It omits the remaining four columns, WRITES, BLKS_WRT, WRITE_TIME, and MEGABYTES, which are available from Figure 7.18. The I/O load should be evenly distributed among the disk drives. This has been discussed in detail in Section 6.6.1.

```
SVRMGR>
SVRMGR> set charwidth 48;
Charwidth                      48
SVRMGR> set numwidth 10;
Numwidth                       10
SVRMGR> Rem   I/O should be spread evenly accross drives. A big
              difference between
SVRMGR> Rem   phys_reads and phys_blks_rd implies table scans are
              going on.
SVRMGR> select table_space, file_name,
     2> phys_reads reads, phys_blks_rd blks_read, phys_rd_time
     3> read_time, phys_writes writes, phys_blks_wr blks_wrt,
     4> phys_wrt_tim write_time, megabytes_size megabytes
     5> from stats$files order by table_space, file_name;
TABLE_SP   FILE_NAME                         READS   BLKS_READ   READ_TIME
--------   -------------------------         -----   ---------   ---------
DATA       /abc01/EXAMPLE/data01.dbf           1         1            0
IDX        /abc07/EXAMPLE/idx01.dbf            1         1            0
RLBK       /abc10/EXAMPLE/rlbk01.dbf           9         9            0
SYSTEM     /abc06/EXAMPLE/system01.dbf       173       220            0
TEMP       /abc09/EXAMPLE/temp01.dbf           0         0            0
5 rows selected.
SVRMGR>
```

FIGURE 7.19: I/O Load Distribution Among Disk Drives

7.5.14 Date/Time

Figure 7.20 contains the output for this part. It shows the start time and the end time of the period during which the two utility scripts collected the data.

```
SVRMGR>
SVRMGR> set charwidth 25
Charwidth                 25
SVRMGR> Rem The times that bstat and estat were run.
SVRMGR> select to_char(start_time, 'dd-mon-yy hh24:mi:ss') start_time,
     2> to_char(end_time,   'dd-mon-yy hh24:mi:ss') end_time
     3> from stats$dates;
START_TIME                        END_TIME
-----------------                 -----------------
13-sep-99 12:57:48                13-sep-99 14:32:56
1 row selected.
SVRMGR>
```

FIGURE 7.20: Date/Time of Data Collection

7.5.15 Versions of Oracle Products

Figure 7.21 contains the output of this part. It shows the versions of all the Oracle products that were running at the time of generating the report.

```
SVRMGR>
SVRMGR> set charwidth 75
Charwidth                 75
SVRMGR> Rem Versions
SVRMGR> select * from v$version;
BANNER
----------------------------------------------------------------
Oracle8 Enterprise Edition Release 8.0.5.1.0 - Production
PL/SQL Release 8.0.5.1.0 - Production
CORE Version 4.0.5.0.0 - Production
TNS for Solaris: Version 8.0.5.0.0 - Production
NLSRTL Version 3.3.2.0.0 - Production
5 rows selected.
SVRMGR>
```

FIGURE 7.21: Versions of Oracle Products

7.6 Comprehensive Tuning Plan for Internal Level

We have explored in Chapters 5 through 7 a large repertoire of techniques to monitor the performance of all the components of the internal level and provided a large number of scripts with output to handle the tuning issues. This section synthesizes these guidelines and offers a comprehensive tuning plan to help a DBA to be proactive rather than reactive in tuning the internal level.

The internal level consists of two distinct parts: instance and database. The instance consists of memory-resident data structures in the form of cache buffers and the background processes. The database consists of datafiles residing in the auxiliary storage. For each part, the DBA must pursue an ongoing two-pronged attack as described below:

- *Performance Tracking*: Monitor daily activities for problem symptoms and identify the root cause(s) of each symptom. This is regarded as proactive performance tracking.
- *Tuning Activity*: Resolve each root cause and monitor its impact via the performance tracking activity. In case of any adverse side effect, take corrective action. This is regarded as the ongoing tuning activity.

The above two activities are interdependent in that the effect of any tuning activity is measured by the continuous performance tracking.

7.7 Performance Tracking

The performance tracking tasks are discussed below under two categories, disk-resident data structures and memory-resident data structures.

7.7.1 Disk-Resident Data Structures

1. Establish the baseline of the database using the scripts in Figures 5.1, 5.3, 5.5, 5.7, 5.9, 5.11, and 5.13.
2. Run the script in Figure 5.15 to identify any user having SYSTEM as its default or temporary tablespace. Assign TOOLS as the default tablespace and TEMP as the temporary tablespace for these users.
3. Monitor all changes to the database at the schema level and update the conceptual level accordingly. The conceptual and the internal levels must always match on schema, i.e., tables, indices, views, constraints, procedures, functions, packages, package bodies, sequences, and synonyms.
4. Monitor used space fragmentation in data and index tables with the script in Figure 5.16. Examine the contiguity of extents using the algorithm given in Section 5.6.

5. Monitor free space fragmentation in tablespaces with the scripts in Figures 5.18, 5.19, 5.21, 5.24, and 5.26. Examine the contiguity of extents using the algorithm given in Section 5.8.
6. Monitor the chaining of tables with the scripts in Figures 5.28 and 5.29.
7. Monitor the contention and sizing of rollback segments with the scripts in Figures 5.33, 5.34, 5.36, and 5.37. Create two rollback tablespaces, if appropriate, as described in Section 5.10.7.

7.7.2 Memory-Resident Data Structures

1. Establish the baseline of the instance via its init<instance name>.ora file.
2. Monitor the performance of SGA components via the various hit ratios and other performance metrics discussed in Sections 6.3 through 6.5.
3. Monitor the performance of the background processes by checking the adequacy of DBWRs, LGWRs, and ARCHs. Also, monitor the efficiency of checkpoints and log switches. Use the scripts given in Figures 6.3, 6.5, 6.9, 6.11, 6.17, 6.19, 6.22, 6.24, 6.26, 6.29, and 6.32 to help you in executing Steps (2) and (3).
4. Monitor the change of the initialization parameter values and ensure that the changed values are taking effect. For example, in many cases you need to shut down and then start up the database after any changes made to the init<instance name>.ora file.
5. Monitor ongoing database performance by using the V$ views.
6. For a stable database, run the UTLBSTAT/ESTAT utility scripts every three to four weeks. Analyze REPORT.TXT generated by the scripts to identify problem areas. See Sections 7.5 and its subsections for more details.

7.8 Tuning Activities

The tuning activities are discussed below under two categories, disk-resident data structures and memory- resident data structures.

7.8.1 Disk-Resident Data Structures

1. If the used space in tables or indices shows fragmentation, take appropriate corrective action by resizing their extents. See Section 5.6 for further details. Refer to Appendix A for sizing algorithms with examples.
2. If the free space in tablespaces shows fragmentation, take appropriate corrective action using the measures in Section 5.8.
3. If tables indicate excessive chaining, take corrective action with the measures in Section 5.9.
4. If the rollback segments show contention, use the program in Figure 5.40 to estimate their correct size and number.

7.8.2 Memory-Resident Data Structures

1. If any of the hit ratios or performance metrics do not meet the target values, take appropriate corrective actions. See Sections 6.3 through 6.5.
2. Through performance tracking assess the impact of Step (1). If the problem persists, repeat Step (1) until the problem is resolved.
3. Experiment with the sizing of the data block buffer cache and shared SQL pool using the scripts in Figures 6.7, 6.8, and 6.13.

Key Words

background process	LGWR
data block buffers	library cache
data block header	memory cache
data dictionary	redo log buffer
DBWR	redo log file
dictionary cache	REPORT.TXT
hit ratio, data block buffer	rollback segment
hit ratio, dictionary cache	SGA
hit ratio, library cache	shared SQL pool
hit ratio, LRU	UTLBSTAT
hit ratio, redo log buffer	UTLESTAT
initialization parameter	V$ view
instance	WAITS
latch	WRAPS

References and Further Reading

1. D. K. Burleson—*High-Performance Oracle Database Applications*, Coriolis Group Books, 1998.
2. M. J. Corey et al—*Tuning Oracle*, Oracle Press, 1995.
3. K. Loney—*Oracle 8i DBA Handbook*, Oracle Press, 2000.

Corey et al. [2, Chapter 8] offers an integrated coverage of performance tuning under the title "Putting it All Together: A Wholistic Approach," which is helpful for junior DBAs. Loney [3, Chapter 6] recommends that a separate database be created to monitor the performance of one or more production databases, because otherwise the scripts run against the production databases may skew the statistical findings. Burleson [1, Chapter 11] suggests creating an Oracle performance database with Oracle utilities for a comprehensive performance tracking and tuning plan. The database will be populated by a modified UTLESTAT utility that will dump the collected data into this database after REPORT.TXT is created. The unmodified UTLESTAT utility currently deletes all the tables that were created to collect statistical data (see the last section, Drop Temporary Tables, of Figure 7.4).

Exercises

No exercises are provided here since this chapter discusses almost exclusively the two Oracle utilities, UTLBSTAT and UTLESTAT. Running them on a regular basis and following the checklists of Sections 7.7 and 7.8 for performance tracking and tuning of databases will be the appropriate exercises.

8
Optimization of the External Level of a Database

Outline

8.1 Contents of the External Level
8.2 Principles of Query Optimization
8.3 Query Optimization in Oracle
8.4 Optimal Indexing Guidelines
8.5 Methodology for Optimal Indexing
8.6 Implementation of Indices in Oracle
8.7 Tools for Tracking Query Performance
Key Words
References and Further Reading
Exercises

Overview of the Chapter

The chapter offers an in-depth discussion of the external level of an Oracle database. The external level consists of the queries run against the database. The chapter contains the tools and techniques for tracking query performance and methods for optimizing queries. As such, the developers are the prime users of this chapter.

The chapter starts with a theoretical discussion of query optimization along with an introduction to Oracle's cost-based and rule-based optimizers. Indexing plays a crucial role in query performance. Selectivity of columns is the deciding factor for determining the correct type of indexing for the columns. Oracle offers six types of indexing, all of which are described with examples. The chapter closes with a discussion of four Oracle tools to track query performance via execution plans and runtime statistics.

8.1 Contents of the External Level

An external level of a database is regarded as a window into its conceptual level from a user viewpoint. Since different users have different information needs, a database has many external levels. All of them extract data from the single internal level and process them to produce the necessary information for the users. Thus, each external level originates as a set of one or more queries and may result in a report. If necessary, additional formatting software can be used to put the report in a nice readable format.

A query can involve data retrieval or update. Thus, the SQL commands used in an external level are SELECT, INSERT, UPDATE, and DELETE. But mostly the SELECT command is used since the majority of users retrieve information from a database rather than update it. Also, since an update operation is potentially destructive, users with update privilege are far fewer than those with retrieval privilege.

The tuning of an external level, therefore, consists of the tuning of SQL queries. The major tuning effort involves the tuning of SELECT statements however, because often update operations or creation of database objects use the SELECT statement. For example, an update operation such as SELECT FOR UPDATE OF includes a SELECT statement, the creation of a view or of a table using CREATE TABLE AS SELECT involves a SELECT statement, and so on.

8.2 Principles of Query Optimization

A query, especially a complex one, can usually be formulated in multiple ways using SQL. Although all of them will return the same result, not all of them will execute equally efficiently. Consequently, a relational DBMS such as Oracle transforms the query into an equivalent query which can be executed most efficiently. The efficiency can be measured by the response time or throughput. In a generic sense, the criterion for efficiency is called the *cost* of processing the query. The process by which a query is executed such that its cost is minimized is called *query optimization* and the software that optimizes a query is called the *query optimizer.* Any relational DBMS has a query optimizer that plays a crucial role in performance tuning of the external levels.

The processing of a query consists of three phases: parse, execute, and fetch.

Parse Phase

- The optimizer checks the syntax of the query for accuracy.
- It then identifies the database objects that are referenced in the query.
- It refers to the data dictionary to resolve all these references. The referred objects must exist in the schema accessible by the user entering the query.
- It reports all errors encountered in the above steps.
- The cycle repeats until all the errors are rectified.

Execute Phase

- The optimizer performs the necessary read and write operations to support the parsed query.

Fetch Phase

- The optimizer retrieves all data, if any, that are returned by the execute phase, sorts them if necessary, and displays the final information to the user.

The parse phase is usually the most resource intensive and time consuming, because during this phase the optimizer examines alternative execution plans for the query and selects the one with the least cost. Consequently, the query optimizer concentrates on the parse phase to optimize performance. The process of query optimization consists of the following steps.

Step 1: Formulate an internal representation of the query.

Before the query processing starts, the query optimizer translates the query into a usable form. The relational algebra, or the tuple relational calculus, or the domain relational calculus is used for this conversion. See Appendix E for a discussion of these three alternative but equivalent mathematical representations. Since SQL is primarily relational algebra-based, the internal representation is made using the relational algebra.

Step 2: Convert the internal representation into an equivalent canonical form.

During this step the query optimizer finds an expression that is equivalent to the relational algebra expression but is more efficient for execution purposes. This form is called the *canonical form* of the query. The query optimizer derives this canonical form by using a variety of rules such as performing selections and projections first, reducing the sizes of the component tables in a join operation before performing the join, etc.

Step 3: Select an optimal access path.

The query optimizer examines a set of alternative implementation plans for the canonical form and then selects the one that has the least "cost." Using this "cheapest" path the query is executed and the output displayed.

There are three types of cost involved in query processing:

- *I/O cost* is the cost of transferring data from disk files to memory.
- *CPU cost* is the cost of processing the data residing in memory.
- *Network cost* is the cost of transferring information from one node to another along a network. This cost applies only to distributed databases.

For queries against centralized databases, the I/O cost is predominant since memory speed is much faster than data transfer speed from disks. The network cost becomes predominant when a query accesses remote databases or fetches data from different nodes in a distributed database.

Of the three phases of query processing mentioned earlier, the parse phase corresponds to Steps (1) and (2), and the execute and fetch phases together correspond to Step (3).

The basic ingredient of any query processing is table search. The search can be *unqualified* as in

```
SELECT column(s) FROM table;
```

or *qualified* as in

```
SELECT column(s) FROM table(s) WHERE condition(s);
```

The search can be implemented as a sequential access or indexed access of the table. In a *sequential access* of a table, all its rows are accessed; in the case of an unqualified search all of them are returned, whereas in a qualified search zero or more rows matching the selection criteria specified in the WHERE clause are returned. In an *indexed access* to a table, a two-step search is made: first, a binary search of the index table to retrieve the addresses (ROWIDs in Oracle) of the matching rows, and, then, a direct access of the rows via their retrieved addresses.

An index can be unique or nonunique. For a unique index, each index value is distinct. For a nonunique index, duplicate values can exist. If an index consists of a single column, it is called a single index. If an index includes two or more columns, it is called a concatenated or a composite index.

8.3 Query Optimization in Oracle

The query optimizer in Oracle follows the theoretical procedure outlined above with its own unique implementation mechanisms. Two issues in this regard deserve special mention.

Row Operation Versus Set Operation

The output generated during the execute phase is displayed during the fetch phase. Oracle uses two alternative approaches to control the timing of display of the output. If all the rows returned by the execute phase are generated first before being displayed, the operation is called a *set operation*. If, on the other hand, as soon as the first row is generated it is displayed, the operation is called a *row operation*. Thus the set operation optimizes the throughput and hence is appropriate for batch jobs. The row operation optimizes the response time and hence is appropriate for online users of OLTP applications.

Oracle allows the use of hints under its cost-based query optimizer to improve the performance of a query. See Sections 9.3.1 and 9.3.2 for details. By default, Oracle strives for best throughput and hence leans on set operations. The query formulator can try to override this choice by including a hint as a part of the SELECT statement to suggest that the query optimizer use the hint in executing the query. But the query optimizer may ignore the hint. Some of these hints enforce a set operation and some others a row operation. For example, the hint ALL_ROWS ensures that the output is displayed only after all the returned rows are ready and is, therefore, a set operation. On the other hand, the hint FIRST_ROWS ensures that the output starts to be displayed as soon as the first row is returned and is thus a row operation. For a join, the hint MERGE_JOIN is a set operation, and NESTED_LOOPS is a row operation.

Optimizer Modes

Starting with Oracle7 two query optimizer modes are available: rule-based and cost-based. The mode can be set at any one of three levels: instance, session, and statement.

- *Instance level*: This is set by the value of the initialization parameter OPTIMIZER_MODE. Its default value is CHOOSE and its other possible values are RULE, FIRST_ROWS, and ALL_ROWS.
- *Session level*: This is set by the ALTER SESSION command as follows,

  ```
  ALTER SESSION SET OPTIMIZER_GOAL = value,
  ```

  where *value* is any one of the four settings: CHOOSE, RULE, FIRST_ROWS, and ALL_ROWS. The setting remains valid only during the session.
- *Statement level*: This is set by including hints as part of the query. See Sections 9.3.1 and 9.3.2 for a discussion of hints.

The query optimizer operates as follows under the four settings mentioned above:

Rule

Rule-based optimization is syntax driven in that it uses the query syntax to evaluate the alternative access paths that a query can follow. Each path is assigned a score based on the rank that Oracle assigns to that path for data retrieval. The ranks range from 1 to 15, as listed in Figure 8.1. Rank 1 is the best and rank 15 the worst.

```
Rank          Access Path
 1            Single row by ROWID
 2            Single row by cluster join
 3            Single row by hash cluster key with unique or
              primary key
 4            Single row by unique or primary key
 5            Cluster join
 6            Hash cluster key
 7            Indexed cluster key
 8            Composite key
 9            Single-column indices
10            Bounded range search on indexed columns
11            Unbounded range search on indexed columns
```

FIGURE 8.1: Ranking of Access Paths Under Rule-Based Optimization

12	Sort-merge join
13	MAX or MIN of indexed column
14	ORDER BY on indexed columns
15	Full table scan

FIGURE 8.1 (*continued*): Ranking of Access Paths Under Rule-Based Optimization

The success of rule-based optimization depends on how well the query has been tuned.

Choose

This is the default setting. If at least one of the tables used in a query has been ANALYZEd with the COMPUTE STATISTICS or ESTIMATE STATISTICS option, then CHOOSE enforces the cost-based optimizer for optimizing that query. Also, queries against partitioned tables always use the cost-based optimizer irrespective of the presence of statistics. In all other cases, the rule-based optimizer is used. In order to optimize a query the cost-based optimizer uses statistical data about the tables used in the query. For example, the optimizer knows how many rows the tables have, how selective the indices are, how the data values are distributed within each table, etc. All of these statistics are used in evaluating alternative execution plans and selecting the one with the least cost. The cost of a full table scan of *table* is computed by the formula:

$$\text{Cost} = \frac{\text{Value of BLOCKS column for table in DBA\_TABLES}}{\text{DB\_FILE\_MULTIBLOCK\_READ\_CNT}}.$$

The cost of an indexed search by *index* is computed by the formula:

$$\text{Cost} = \frac{\text{Selectivity of } index}{\text{Clustering Factor of } index \text{ in DBA\_INDEXES}}.$$

See Section 8.4.1 for the definition of selectivity and Section 8.6.1 for the definition of clustering factor.

If the statistics are not up to date, the cost computation will be wrong and, as a result, the path chosen may not be optimal. Hence it is essential to ANALYZE all the tables in a database and to reANALYZE a table if it has undergone some significant update activities. Each time a table is ANALYZEd, the statistics pertaining to itself and all of its index tables are updated. Also, if some of the tables in a database are ANALYZEd and the rest are not, the cost-based optimizer may perform full table scans on the latter. This often defeats the purpose of query optimization. Therefore, tables should be ANALYZEd regularly.

Oracle recommends that all queries use the cost-based optimizer since it is more reliable. Also, Oracle no longer enhances the rule-based optimizer. The role of the rule-based optimizer will diminish over time. If, for some reason, one wants to use both the cost-based and the rule-based optimizers, then the DBA should set OPTIMIZER_MODE to its default value of CHOOSE. A developer can override the cost-based optimizer for a query by explicitly using the hint RULE in its formulation. But such a hybrid approach should be taken only if there is a strong justification for it.

FIRST_ROWS, ALL_ROWS

By setting the parameter to FIRST_ROWS or ALL_ROWS one can enforce the cost-based optimizer. However, FIRST_ROWS is a row operation. Hence it causes the optimizer to choose execution plans that minimize the response time. On the other hand, ALL_ROWS is a set operation. Hence it causes the optimizer to choose execution plans that maximize the throughput.

In conclusion, we recommend that the default setting of CHOOSE be used for a database. All the tables must be ANALYZEd to start with and be reANALYZEd whenever major updates occur. For OLTP applications with plenty of update transactions by the users it is advisable to ANALYZE the updated tables on a weekly basis. All index tables associated with a data table are then automatically reANALYZEd.

8.4 Optimal Indexing Guidelines

We have discussed some general principles of indexing at the conceptual level in Section 3.4. Here we explore that topic further from an implementation viewpoint. Irrespective of the optimizer mode selected, indexed search of tables via indexed columns has the greatest impact on query performance. Since indexing speeds up retrieval via indexed columns but slows down the update of an indexed table when the update includes the indexed column(s), one should not create indices on columns indiscriminately. A systematic plan of action is needed to implement an optimal indexing technique in a database. We address this issue in two stages. First, we provide a set of general criteria in Sections 8.4.1 through 8.4.4 to guide the developers in deciding on an optimal indexing strategy. Next, we provide a four-step methodology in Sections 8.5.1 through 8.5.4 for

- Identifying tables and columns to be indexed and
- Determining the types of indices to be used such as unique or nonunique and single or concatenated.

8.4.1 Selectivity of Columns

Step 1: The column(s) targeted for indexing must have high selectivity.

The *selectivity* of a set of column(s) in a table is defined as the ratio m/n, where

m = number of distinct values of the set, often called its *cardinality*;
n = total number of rows in the table.

The selectivity of a set of columns is a measure of the usefulness of that set in reducing the I/O required by queries against the table using that set. The maximum value of selectivity is 1 when every value of the set is distinct so that $m = n$. For example, the column(s) used as the primary key of a table have selectivity 1.

Given two columns C_1 and C_2 with respective selectivities s_1 and s_2, say, the selectivity of $C_1 \Psi C_2$ is given by

$s_1 + s_2$, if Ψ is AND operator

$s_1 + s_2 - s_1 * s_2$, if Ψ is OR operator

Figure 8.2 contains a script with a partial output that lists all indices in all tables with their respective selectivities. Before using this script the following command must be run for each table in the database,

ANALYZE TABLE *table_name* COMPUTE STATISTICS;

```
PROMPT
PROMPT
PROMPT    Before running this script you must ANALYZE each table
          in the PROMPT database with COMPUTE STATISTICS option.
PROMPT
PROMPT    List of all indices with their selectivities
PROMPT

SELECT A.TABLE_NAME, A.INDEX_NAME,
       ROUND ((A.DISTINCT_KEYS/DECODE(B.NUM_ROWS, 0, 1,
       B.NUM_ROWS)), 2) SELECTIVITY
       FROM USER_INDEXES A, USER_TABLES B
       WHERE A.TABLE_NAME = B.TABLE_NAME
       ORDER BY A.TABLE_NAME, A.INDEX_NAME;

PARTIAL OUTPUT:

Before running this script you must ANALYZE each table in the
database with COMPUTE STATISTICS option.

List of all indices with their selectivities

TABLE_NAME          INDEX_NAME              SELECTIVITY
----------          ----------              -----------
TABLE_1             PK_TABLE_1                        1
TABLE_2             IND_TABLE_2                    0.44
TABLE_3             PK_TABLE_3                        1
TABLE_4             PK_TABLE_4                      .98
TABLE_5             PK_TABLE_5                     1.09
TABLE_6             UNQ_TABLE_6                     .92
TABLE_7             IND_TABLE_7                     .88
TABLE_8             UNQ_TABLE_8                      .8
```

FIGURE 8.2: Script with Output for Computing Selectivity of Indices

Figure 8.3 contains a script with partial output to compute the selectivity of individual columns of any table designated by the user.

```
PROMPT
PROMPT
PROMPT  Enter the name of the table for which you want the
        selectivity of
PROMPT its columns
PROMPT
ACCEPT TARGET_TABLE
PROMPT
PROMPT Table name is &TARGET_TABLE
PROMPT
SELECT B.COLUMN_NAME, NUM_DISTINCT, NUM_ROWS,
    ROUND ( (NUM_DISTINCT/DECODE(NUM_ROWS, 0, 1, NUM_ROWS)), 2 )
SELECTIVITY
    FROM USER_INDEXES A, USER_TAB_COL_STATISTICS B
    WHERE B.TABLE_NAME = '&TARGET_TABLE'
    AND A.TABLE_NAME = B.TABLE_NAME
    ORDER BY NUM_DISTINCT DESC;

PARTIAL OUTPUT:

Enter the name of the table for which you want the selectivity of
its columns
TABLE_X
Table name is TABLE_X
old    4:   WHERE B.TABLE_NAME = '&TARGET_TABLE'
new    4:   WHERE B.TABLE_NAME = 'TABLE_X'
COLUMN_NAME            NUM_DISTINCT         NUM_ROWS         SELECTIVITY
-----------            ------------         --------         -----------
COLUMN_1                       2430             2430                1.00
COLUMN_2                       2225             2430                 .92
COLUMN_3                       1623             2430                 .67
COLUMN_4                       1053             2430                 .43
COLUMN_5                       1031             2430                 .42
COLUMN_6                        867             2430                 .36
COLUMN_7                        708             2430                 .29
COLUMN_8                        327             2430                 .13
COLUMN_9                        252             2430                  .1
COLUMN_10                        59             2430                 .02
COLUMN_11                        27             2430                 .01
COLUMN_12                        12             2430                   0
COLUMN_13                         7             2430                   0
COLUMN_14                         5             2430                   0
```

FIGURE 8.3: Script with Output for Computing Selectivity of Columns

The script in Figure 8.3 computes the selectivity of individual columns only. If we need the selectivity of concatenated columns in a table, we need to query that table with the specific concatenation of columns. For example, suppose that a three-column concatenated index is created on the three columns (COLUMN_X, COLUMN_Y, COLUMN_Z). Then the selectivity of the concatenated columns is determined as follows.

```
COLUMN A HEADING 'Count of              |Concatenated Columns'
COLUMN B HEADING 'Selectivity of        |Concatenated Columns'
SELECT COUNT(DISTINCT COLUMN_X||'%'||COLUMN_Y||'%'||COLUMN_Z) A
    FROM TABLE_NEEDED;
SELECT ROUND (COUNT(DISTINCT
COLUMN_X||'%'||COLUMN_Y||'%'||COLUMN_Z)
    / DECODE (COUNT (1), 0, 1, COUNT (1)), 2)
    B FROM TABLE_NEEDED;
```

The output from the above code appears below.

```
Count of
Concatenated Columns
--------------------
                 257

Selectivity of
Concatenated Columns
--------------------
                 .86
```

8.4.2 Selectivity of Concatenated Indices

Step 2: The leading column of a concatenated index must have high selectivity.

The first column of a concatenated index is called its leading column. This column should be used in the predicates of the WHERE clause of a query. To make the indexed search efficient, it is necessary that the leading column have high selectivity. The second most used and most selective column should be the second column in the concatenated index, and so on. If such columns are not available, the application design should be revisited. The selectivity of the leading column of a concatenated index plays a major role in the selectivity of the entire index.

8.4.3 Concatenated Indices Versus Single Indices

Step 3: A multicolumn concatenated index is usually preferable to multiple separate single-column indices.

Figure 8.1 shows that a rule-based optimizer assigns a rank of 8 to retrieval of rows via a concatenated index and a rank of 9 to that by separate single-column indices. This indicates that the multicolumn concatenated index is marginally better than multiple separate single-column indices. The cost-based optimizer computes the cost of query processing based on selectivity and the ranks of various possible access paths. As a result, the decision in either case goes in favor of a multicolumn concatenated index. In reality, however, this desired option can offer substantial improvement over the other option, especially in the case of AND-EQUAL operation (see Section 8.7.1 under the paragraph "OPERATION with OPTIONS"). If necessary, in addition to creating a multicolumn concatenated index, one or more separate single-column indices may be created on some of the component columns of the concatenated index.

It is possible to combine several single columns each with low selectivity into one concatenated column set with high selectivity. In that case, creating a concatenated index on the column set improves performance. As an example, consider a report that lists employees by gender belonging to each department of a company. The column "Sex" has only two values, M and F, say. The column "Department" also has a low selectivity. However, the pair (Department, Sex) has a relatively high selectivity. We put "Department" as the leading column in the index (Department, Sex) since its cardinality is higher than that of 'Sex' whenever a company has three or more departments.

8.4.4 Level of Indexing

Step 4: The application type determines the level of indexing needed.

An online transaction processing (OLTP) application has very different structure and access patterns than a decision support system (DSS). The latter includes reporting databases and data warehouses. An OLTP involves a lot of online updates, whereas a DSS rarely has such activities since its data are less sensitive to time. Given that indexing slows down updates involving the indexed columns, overindexing or improper indexing is less harmful for a DSS than for an OLTP application. Sometimes creating more indices on tables can be beneficial for the DSS to improve the performance of its queries.

8.5 Methodology for Optimal Indexing

Using the four guidelines described in Sections 8.4.1 through 8.4.4 we can lay down the following four-step methodology to create indices in such a way that query processing is optimized without sacrificing too much of the performance for update operations. An index should be created only if it is justified by the principles below.

8.5.1 Potential Targets for Indexing

Step 1: Identify the columns and tables that may need to be indexed.

As described in Section 8.1, each external level of a database involves a query using one or more column(s) in one or more table(s). Make a complete list of these items in a format as follows:

- Query Name: Use a name representative of the purpose of the query;
- Column Name: (Self-explanatory);
- Table Name: (Self-explanatory).

Sorting this list by table name, query name, and column name one gets a list of queries with their component columns for each table. Identify the columns that are used as predicates in the WHERE clauses, or are used in the ORDER BY or GROUP BY clauses. These are the potential candidates for indexing. However, a query benefits from an indexed search if at most 15% of the rows are returned by the search. Also, we have to exclude from this list all those columns that are used for full table scans alone. These considerations must be used to prepare the final list of columns to be indexed.

8.5.2 Minimal Indexing at Startup

Step 2: Start with the minimum level of indexing of all tables.

As noted in Section 3.4, a table does not need an index. But such a table will have no protection against inserting duplicate rows. Consequently, we should start with indexing the primary (PK) and foreign keys (FK) in tables. Oracle automatically creates a unique index on each PK. So, no separate indexing is needed for them. Since FKs are mostly used in join conditions among tables, create a nonunique index on each FK in each table. Note that in general FKs with the same value appear multiple times in a child table matching a single value of the corresponding PK in its parent table and, therefore, a unique index cannot be created on an FK. The only exception arises when two tables linked via PK-FK connection are in a 1:1 relationship. But this relationship is undesirable and should be avoided at the conceptual level.

In enforcing referential integrity via a PK–FK or a UK–FK relationship, Oracle allows a NULL FK-column to match a NOT NULL PK-column and a NOT NULL FK-column to match a NULL UK-column. In other words, Oracle enforces an exact matching of the referencing and the referenced columns in referential integrity only when all of the referencing and the referenced columns are NOT NULL. Note that a PK-column is, by definition, NOT NULL, but a UK-column is not. Unless created as NOT NULL, a UK-column remains NULL. The following annotated session transcript describes this situation.

Annotated Session Transcript

PK-FK Relationship:

SQL> create table X
    2 (a number,
    3 b char (4),
    4 c varchar2 (10),
    5 d number (8,2),
    6 e date);

8.5 Methodology for Optimal Indexing

Table created.

SQL> alter table X add constraint X_PK primary key (a, b, c);

Table altered.

SQL> desc X

Name	Null?	Type
A	NOT NULL	NUMBER
B	NOT NULL	CHAR(4)
C	NOT NULL	VARCHAR2(10)
D		NUMBER(8,2)
E		DATE

NOTE: The PK-columns are made NOT NULL.

SQL> create table Y
    2 (aa number,
    3 bb char (4),
    4 cc varchar2 (10),
    5 f date,
    6 g number (7,3),
    7 h varchar2 (22));

Table created.

SQL> alter table Y add constraint Y_FK
  2 FOREIGN KEY (aa, bb, cc) references X (a, b, c);

Table altered.

SQL> insert into X (a, b, c, d)
2 values (1, 'JOHN', 'MA', 68.23);

1 row created.

SQL> insert into Y (aa, bb, cc, g)
2 values (NULL, NULL, 'MA', 77.231);

1 row created.

SQL> insert into Y (aa, bb, cc, g)
2 values (NULL, NULL, NULL, 65);

1 row created.

NOTE: Y(NULL, NULL, 'MA') and Y(NULL, NULL, NULL) both match X(1, 'JOHN', 'MA').

8. Optimization of the External Level of a Database

UK-FK Relationship:

SQL> edit
Wrote file afiedt.buf

```
1  create table P
2     (p number,
3     q char (4),
4     r varchar2 (10),
5     s number (8,2),
6*    t date)
```
SQL> /

Table created.

SQL> alter table P add constraint P_UK unique (p, q, r);

Table altered.

SQL> desc P

Name	Null?	Type
P		NUMBER
Q		CHAR(4)
R		VARCHAR2(10)
S		NUMBER(8,2)
T		DATE

NOTE: The UK-columns remain NULL.

SQL> edit
Wrote file afiedt.buf

```
1  create table Q
2     (pp number,
3     qq char (4),
4     rr varchar2 (10),
5     u date,
6     v number (7,3),
7*    w varchar2 (22))
```
SQL> /

Table created.

SQL> alter table Q add constraint Q_FK
  2 FOREIGN KEY (pp, qq, rr) references P (p, q, r);

Table altered.

SQL> insert into P (p, q, r, s)
2 values (NULL, NULL, 'MA', 68.23);

1 row created.

SQL> insert into Q (pp, qq, rr, v)
2 values (1, 'JOHN', 'MA', 68.23);

1 row created.

SQL> insert into Q (pp, qq, rr, v)
2 values (1, NULL, 'MA', 68.23);

1 row created.

NOTE: Q(1, 'JOHN', 'MA') and Q(1, NULL, 'MA') both match P (NULL, NULL, 'MA').

8.5.3 Incremental Indexing for Single-Table Queries

Step 3: Extend indexing incrementally in each table for single-table queries.

Let Q be a query based on a single table T. We assume that T has been uniquely indexed on its PK and nonuniquely indexed on each FK, if any. But T has no other indices. The syntax for Q is as follows,

```
SELECT col_1, ..., col_n FROM T WHERE
cond_1Ψcond_2Ψ...Ψcond_k;
```

Here $k \geq 0$, $n \leq$ (total number of columns in T), and Ψ is the logical operator AND or OR. Then we note the following facts.

(a) If $k = 0$ and $n <$ (total number of columns in T), then the WHERE clause is empty and Q is an unqualified query; i.e., Q returns all the rows of T but only a subset of the columns of T. In this case, Q takes the form

```
SELECT col_1, ..., col_n FROM T;
```

Here Q is an *unqualified* query.

(b) If $k > 0$ and $n =$ (total number of columns in T), then Q takes the form

```
SELECT * FROM T WHERE cond_1Ψcond_2Ψ...Ψcond_k;
```

Here Q is a *qualified* query.

(c) If both $k = 0$ and $n =$ (total number of columns in T), then Q takes the simplest form

```
SELECT * FROM T;
```

and Q is an *unqualified* query; i.e., Q returns all the rows and columns of T.

When $k = 0$ irrespective of the value of n, as in cases (a) and (c), Q is *unqualified*. Oracle then performs a full table scan of T and no indexing is needed. When $k > 0$ irrespective of the value of n, Q is *qualified*. The predicates *cond_1*, ..., *cond_k* are called *qualifying* or *limiting* conditions on the columns of T. A qualifying condition cond_i, $1 \le i \le k$, has the general form (col_r Φ expression), $1 \le r \le n$, where Φ is a relational operator and takes any of six possible values, ($<, >, \le, \ge, =, !=$). Columns in T should then be indexed depending on the qualifying conditions. Now proceed as follows.

- Make a list of all the columns that are used in qualifying conditions in Q.
- Repeat this step for every query on T using qualifying conditions.
  (We now have a complete list of all columns in T that are used in one or more qualified queries on T.)
- Determine the retrieval pattern of the columns, e.g., retrieved as a single column, as a set of columns, etc.
- Using the script in Figure 8.3 or the preceding SELECT statements, compute the selectivity of each column or set of columns identified above.
- Each column or column set with high selectivity, say, selectivity >.75, is a candidate for indexing, single or concatenated. But exclude column(s), if any, that are used with built-in functions such as AVG, SUBSTR, TO_DATE, etc. since indices are not used on columns that are modified by such functions unless function-based indices are created on them. See Section 10.9 to determine if function-based indices should be created in this case.
- Consider creating a concatenated index on a set of columns in a table when those columns are frequently used together in mutiple qualifying conditions connected by AND, especially if their combined selectivity is greater than their individual selectivities.

8.5.4 Incremental Indexing for MultiTable Queries

Step 4: Extend indexing incrementally in each table for multitable queries.

Let Q be a query based on m tables $T_1, ..., T_m$. The syntax of Q differs from that for a single-table query only with respect to the join conditions involving the tables $T_1, ..., T_m$. Any join condition has the form $T_i.col\_r = T_j.col\_s$, where often col_r is the PK of T_i and col_s is the matching FK in T_j. In that case, they are already indexed. If col_r and col_s are not in a (PK, FK) relationship, then compute the selectivity of col_r to decide if it should be indexed. As we show in Section 9.5, Oracle uses a driving table to start processing a join. This table may undergo a full table scan and, therefore, should be small in size.

8.6 Implementation of Indices in Oracle

Oracle offers three types of indices: B*-tree, bitmap, and reverse key. In each case, a separate index table exists for each index created on a data table. In addition, one can use index organized tables, clusters, and histograms. The first two contain data that can be retrieved faster than if they were stored in regular tables. Histograms represent statistics collected by the ANALYZE command. They are stored in data dictionary views and are used by the cost-based optimizer to tune the execution of SQL statements. These are now described in the subsections below.

8.6.1 B*-Tree Index

Structure of B-Tree Index*

The index table of a very large data table becomes very large itself when there is a one-to-one correspondence between the rows of the index table and those of the data table. To alleviate this problem, multilevel indices are created. Here the index table itself is treated as a data table and an index table is built to the first index table. The process can be carried to any number of levels desired, but rarely do we need more than four levels of indexing. This technique is known as building a multi-level or *tree structured* index. The data structure known as a B*-tree is a particular type of the tree structured index. Oracle uses this mechanism for implementing certain types of indices, namely, those on columns with high selectivity. A B*-tree consists of nodes and arcs connecting the nodes. One special node is called the *root* of the tree and the terminal nodes are called *leaf nodes*. A B*-tree is balanced ("B" stands for "balanced") so that the time to access any leaf node is always approximately the same. The nodes at all levels except the leaf level contain index data pointing to indices at the next lower level. Only the leaf nodes contain indexed data values and their respective ROWIDs for locating the corresponding rows in the data table. The leaf nodes are doubly linked.

Let us suppose that a table T has its primary key on column C with the data type NUMBER (4). Hence Oracle creates a single unique index on C. Figure 8.4 shows a B*-tree with four levels implementing this index. Suppose that we want to retrieve the record that has C = 7,500. The search process starts at the root. Since 7,500 > 6,500, the search traverses the pointer from 6,500 to the second level. Since 7,500 > 7,000 and 7,500 < 9,000, the next search traverses the pointer from 7,000 to the third level. Here it finds the node containing 7,500. Finally, the search follows the pointer to the leaf node containing the data (7,500, ROWID). Using the ROWID the row with C = 7,500 is accessed and retrieved.

In a B*-tree index, all but the leaf nodes contain index values that are called *nondense* because they are not in a one-to-one correspondence with the data values. The index values at the leaf nodes are, therefore, called *dense*. Using the binary search process as described above the target row(s) are retrieved. If no match is found among the leaf nodes, Oracle returns a message "no rows selected."

We have discussed above the case of a unique index where a ROWID exists for every data value. For a nonunique index, the ROWID is included in the key in sorted order so that such indices are sorted by the index key value and the ROWID. Key values containing all NULLs are not indexed except for cluster indices (see Section 8.6.5). Two rows can both contain all NULLs and still not violate a unique index constraint. For a concatenated index, the key value consists of the concatenation of individual component values of the index.

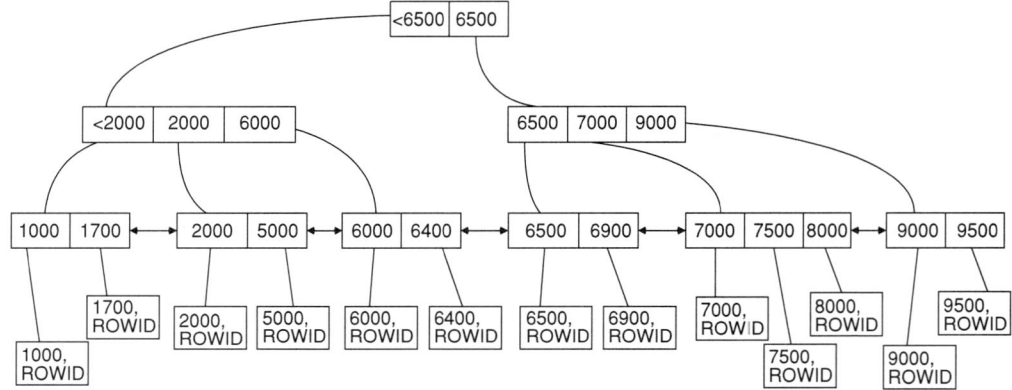

FIGURE 8.4: B*-Tree Index Diagram

The B*-tree index has the following advantages.

- All leaf nodes are at the same depth from the root so that the access time remains about the same irrespective of the breadth of the tree.
- All nodes of the tree are 75% full on the average.
- This data structure provides excellent retrieval performance for indexed searches, both exact match and range scans, for columns with high selectivity.
- INSERT, UPDATE, and DELETE operations are efficient, maintaining key order for fast retrieval.

Maintenance of B*-Tree Index

The B*-tree indices grow from the leaf nodes upwards. For the convenience of our discussion let us assume a three-level B*-tree and let us label the root node as level 0 and the leaf node as level 2. Usually indices with monotonically increasing key values cause the leaf nodes to increase. As rows are inserted into the indexed table, the new index entries are added to the right side of the tree at each level starting with level 2. When the rightmost leaf node becomes full, Oracle splits it into two nodes at the same level and puts 50% of the data in the original node and 50% in the newly created leaf node. A new pointer is now inserted into the rightmost branch node at level 1, which is immediately above the split leaf node, to point to the new leaf node. This process is repeated as new rows are inserted into the indexed table until the rightmost branch node at level 1 becomes full and has to split in two. This pattern is repeated until the root node at level 0 can no longer contain the pointers to the nodes at level 1. Since Oracle does not split the root node, it adds a new level of branch nodes immediately above the level containing the leaf nodes. Then we get a four-level B*-tree where the leaf nodes now appear as level 3 and the branch levels above it are labeled as levels 2 and 1 pointing upward. The deeper an index is, the less efficient it becomes. Oracle recommends that a B*-tree should not extend to more than four levels. The performance of a B*-tree index degrades when the tree contains more than four levels. In such cases, a rebuilding of the index is needed. See Section 9.2.4 for more details about rebuilding indices.

Figure 8.5 shows an example of the statistics for a B*-tree index and Figure 8.6 contains a sample output from the script.

```
REM  B*-Tree Index Structure for a Database
REM  Script File Name: My_Directory\INDEX_STRUCTURE.sql
REM  Spool File Name:  My_Directory \INDEX_STRUCTURE.lst
REM  Author:           NAME
REM  Date Created:     DATE
REM  Purpose:          Information on B*-tree index structures used
REM                    in the database
REM
REM

COLUMN TODAY  NEW_VALUE xTODAY NOPRINT FORMAT A1 TRUNC

TTITLE       LEFT xTODAY -
    RIGHT 'Page ' FORMAT 999 SQL.PNO -
    CENTER 'B*-tree Index Structure '    SKIP 4
BTITLE 'Script File: My_Directory\ INDEX_STRUCTURE.sql|Spool File:
    My_Directory\ INDEX_STRUCTURE.lst'

COLUMN TABLE_NAME HEADING 'Table|Name' FORMAT A10
COLUMN INDEX_NAME HEADING 'Index|Name' FORMAT A15
COLUMN BLEVEL HEADING ' Depth ' FORMAT 999
COLUMN LEAF_BLOCKS HEADING 'Leaf|Block|Count' FORMAT 999999
COLUMN AVG_LEAF_BLOCKS_PER_KEY HEADING 'Avg|Lf|Bl' FORMAT 999
COLUMN AVG_DATA_BLOCKS_PER_KEY HEADING 'Avg|Data|Bl' FORMAT 999
COLUMN CLUSTERING_FACTOR HEADING ' CF ' FORMAT 999,999,999
COLUMN DISTINCT_KEYS HEADING 'Distinct|Values' FORMAT 999,999,999

BREAK ON TABLE_NAME SKIP 1 ON INDEX_NAME SKIP 0

SET LINESIZE 78
SET PAGESIZE 39
SET NEWPAGE 0
```

FIGURE 8.5: Script for Displaying Structure of B*-Tree Index

```
SPOOL My_Directory\INDEX_STRUCTURE.lst
SELECT TABLE_NAME, INDEX_NAME, BLEVEL, DISTINCT_KEYS, LEAF_BLOCKS,
    AVG_LEAF_BLOCKS_PER_KEY, AVG_DATA_BLOCKS_PER_KEY, CLUSTERING_FACTOR,
    TO_CHAR (SysDate, 'fmMonth ddth, YYYY') TODAY
    FROM DBA_INDEXES
    WHERE TABLE_NAME NOT LIKE '%$' AND TABLE_NAME NOT LIKE '%#'
    AND TABLE_NAME NOT LIKE '%#%#' AND TABLE_NAME NOT LIKE '%$%'
    ORDER BY TABLE_NAME, INDEX_NAME;
SPOOL OFF
```

FIGURE 8.5 (*continued*): Script for Displaying Structure of B*-tree Index

The script contains column names from DBA_INDEXES, some of which are explained below.

BLEVEL	B*-Tree level; depth of the index from its root block to its leaf blocks. A depth of zero indicates that the root node and the leaf node are the same. Even for very large indices the BLEVEL should not exceed three. Each BLEVEL represents an additional I/O that must be performed against the B*-tree.
LEAF_BLOCKS	Number of leaf blocks in the tree.
DISTINCT_KEYS	Number of distinct keys in the index, also called the cardinality of the index; if this value is less than 15 or so, a bitmap index may perform better.
AVG_LEAF_BLOCKS_PER_KEY	Average number of leaf blocks per key; this is always 1 except for nonunique indices.
AVG_DATA_BLOCKS_PER_KEY	Average number of data blocks per key; this measures the size of the index; its value is high for indices with low cardinality (e.g., gender, status, etc.) and for very large indices.
CLUSTERING_FACTOR	It represents the total count of the indexed table blocks that have to be fetched if all the I/O is done via the leaf block records. If the clustering factor is close to the number of blocks in the table, then the index is considered to be well clustered. This yields a low cost for the query. If the clustering factor is close to the rowcount of the indexed table, then for every leaf record a different block of the table has to be fetched. This yields a high cost for the query.

```
May 17th, 2001         B*-tree Index Structure            Page 9
                                 Leaf      Avg    Avg
Table      Index      Distinct   Block     Lf     Data
Name       Name       Depth      Values    Count  Bl     Bl     CF
------     ---------  --------   ------    -----  ----   ---    ------
TABLE1     PK_TABLE1      1       9,793      79    1      1      9,787
TABLE2     PK_TABLE2      1       2,206      29    1      1        119
TABLE3     PK_TABLE3      0           0       0    0      0          0
TABLE4     PK_TABLE4      1       2,538      24    1      1         36
TABLE5     PK_TABLE5      0          12       1    1      1          1
TABLE6     PK_TABLE6      1         479       3    1      1         12
TABLE7     PK_TABLE7      0         144       1    1      1          2
TABLE8     PK_TABLE8      0         130       1    1      1          2
TABLE9     PK_TABLE9      3   1,863,877   30040    1      1  1,422,533
TABLE10    PK_TABLE10     2      56,126     504    1      1      5,718
TABLE11    PK_TABLE11     2     119,072     488    1      1      9,715
           Script File: My_Directory\INDEX_STRUCTURE.sql
           Spool File: My_Directory\INDEX_STRUCTURE.lst
```

FIGURE 8.6: Sample Listing of Structure of B*-Tree Index

Looking at Figure 8.6 we find that the depth of the tree is mostly 0 or 1, which is good. Since all the indices are PKs, their distinct values equal the rowcounts of the underlying indexed tables. Hence the clustering factors of TABLE1 and TABLE9 are very close to their respective rowcounts. So, queries involving PK_TABLE1 and PK_TABLE9 will have high costs.

The mathematical theory of B*-trees and the general tree traversal algorithm are discussed in Section E14, Appendix E.

8.6.2 Bitmap Index

Structure of Bitmap Index

B*-tree indices do not perform well for columns with low selectivity. Oracle recommends that if more than 15% of the rows are returned by a query, a full table scan is better than an indexed search. For example, an indexed search of a table by a column labeled "Gender" is very inefficient since that column has an average selectivity of .5 or so. Starting with version 7.3 Oracle introduced the bitmap index to handle indices with low selectivity. Of course, the concept is not new. It has been used successfully in non-relational DBMSs such as Model 204 since the 1960s. However, their use in a relational DBMS was ignored until the mid-1990s when the data warehouses became widely used. Such applications are characterized by having no update transactions and involving complex queries against very large tables. Users typically perform ad hoc queries against data warehouses making it virtually impossible for the developers or the DBAs to anticipate them and then index the columns appropriately. Bitmap indices are especially suitable for handling such situations where columns have low selectivity. Oracle was the first to apply this principle to a relational DBMS.

A bitmap index for a column is useful under the following circumstances.

(a) The column has low selectivity.
(b) The table is very infrequently updated.
(c) The table is very large, say over 500,000 rows.
(d) The query involves one or more columns connected by AND or OR.

Internally a bitmap index maps the distinct values of the bitmap indexed column to each record. One row is stored in the index table for each distinct value of the column. The number of bits (0 or 1) in each row equals the number of rows in the indexed table. When a new row is inserted in the table, an extra bit is added to each row in the index table. The value of this bit depends on the value of the indexed column in the new row. When an existing row in the table is updated or deleted, the bit in its corresponding position in the bitmap index table is changed accordingly. During this transaction the entire bitmap segment is locked, making it a costly operation. Hence bitmap indices are recommended only for tables that are not frequently updated. The following example shows how a query on a bitmap indexed table is performed.

Example of Bitmap Index

Suppose that an insurance company with offices nationwide maintains an archived table CLAIM_HISTORY with the structure:

```
CLAIM_HISTORY (ClientID, Policy_Type, Client_Type,
Region, Claim_Status)
```

ClientID is the primary key and is implemented via a B*-tree index. The other four columns have the distinct values:

- Policy_Type = 10, 20, 30, 40, 50 (coded values reflecting different policy categories);
- Client_Type = Individual, Institutional;
- Region = East, West, North, South; and
- Claim_Status = Active, Closed.

All of these columns are suitable candidates for bitmap indexing. Suppose that the table has the following sample data.

ClientID	Policy_Type	Client_Type	Region	Claim_Status
912	20	Institutional	East	Closed
299	10	Institutional	North	Closed
1001	10	Individual	West	Active
1500	30	Individual	West	Closed
2123	10	Individual	South	Active
2129	20	Institutional	North	Closed

8.6 Implementation of Indices in Oracle

The bitmap index tables for the four columns have the following values.

```
Policy_Type  10:     <011010>   Client_Type   Individual:    <001110>
             20:     <100001>                 Institutional: <110001>
             30:     <000100>
             40:     <000000>
             50:     <000000>
Region       East:   <100000>   Claim_Status  Active:        <001010>
             West:   <001100>                 Closed:        <110101>
             North:  <010001>
             South:  <000010>
```

Suppose now that the following row is inserted into the table: (1301, 50, Individual, South, Active). Then an extra bit is added to each row of each bitmap index table as follows.

```
Policy_Type  10:     <0110100>  Client_Type   Individual:    <0011101>
             20:     <1000010>                Institutional: <1100010>
             30:     <0001000>
             40:     <0000000>
             50:     <0000001>
Region       East:   <1000000>  Claim_Status  Active:        <0010101>
             West:   <0011000>                Closed:        <1101010>
             North:  <0100010>
             South:  <0000101>
```

Suppose that we run the following query against the table CLAIM_HISTORY:

```
select * from CLAIM_HISTORY where
   Policy_Type = 20  AND
   Client_Type = 'Institutional'  AND
   (Region = 'East' OR Region = 'North')  AND
   Claim_Status = 'Closed';
```

As shown below, the query is processed by first selecting the rows that have "1" for each condition separately and then returning those that have "1" for all four conditions together. The query optimizer quickly compares the bitmap values for each qualifying condition in the query and returns the final result.

```
Policy_Type = 20                        returns      rows 1 and 6
Client_Type = 'Institutional'           returns      rows 1, 2,
and 6
(Region = 'East' OR Region = 'North')   returns      rows 1, 2,
and 6
Claim_Status = 'Closed'                 returns      rows 1, 2, 4, and 6
```

Therefore, rows 1 and 6 are returned by the query. Thus, the output appears as follows.

ClientID	Policy_Type	Client_Type	Region	Claim_Status
912	20	Institutional	East	Closed
2129	20	Institutional	North	Closed

As shown above, the bitmap indices perform very fast Boolean operations on columns with low selectivity. Complex AND and OR logic are performed within the index table without accessing the underlying data table. The latter is accessed only to retrieve the rows returned by the complete set of qualifying conditions. Without a bitmap index many such queries would be processed via full table scans. The higher the number of columns used in the qualifying conditions, the more valuable the bitmap indices are. Also, because of the high number of repeating "1"s and "0"s in the index table, bitmap indices can be compressed very effectively for storage and then decompressed at execution time. The lower the selectivity, the better the compression. Thus, in the above example, the compression of Client_Type and Claim_Status, each with only two distinct values, is better than that for Region with four distinct values and Policy_Type with five distinct values. In decompressed form, the index files for Client_Type and Claim_Status are each half in size of the index file for Region.

Creation and Maintenance of Bitmap Index

Figure 8.7 contains the command showing the creation of a bitmap index and the resulting output. The syntax is the same as that of CREATE INDEX with the addition of the keyword BITMAP.

```
SQL> CREATE BITMAP INDEX BITIND#CTRY_CODE_C ON CUSTOMER_ACCOUNT
(CTRY_CODE_C);
Index created.
SQL> SELECT INDEX_NAME, TABLE_NAME, TABLESPACE_NAME FROM
USER_INDEXES
   2* WHERE INDEX_TYPE = 'BITMAP'
INDEX_NAME               TABLE_NAME            TABLESPACE_NAME
-----------------        ----------------      ----------------
BITIND#CTRY_CODE_C       CUSTOMER_ACCOUNT      INDEX_1
```

FIGURE 8.7: Creation of Bitmap Index

Given that bitmap indices are suitable for columns with low selectivity, use the script in Figure 8.3 and the SELECT statements appearing below Figure 8.3 to identify the potential candidates for bitmap indexing. A column with selectivity below .5 may benefit from bitmap indexing. The ideal method is to create both B*-tree and bitmap indices on such a column and then test the runtime for queries on that column under both situations. The index that runs faster should be selected.

Update transactions treat B*-tree and bitmap indices differently. Suppose that n indexed rows in a table T are being updated. If T is B*-tree indexed, then the tree itself is restructured after each row is updated so as to keep it balanced. As a result, the B*-tree is modified n times, thereby slowing down the updates. But if T is bitmap indexed, then the index table is updated after all the n rows have been updated. During the update of each row of T the updated bitmap column and the ROWID of each updated row are stored temporarily in the sort buffer in memory. Hence the initialization parameter SORT_AREA_SIZE must be sized properly for good performance with INSERTs and UPDATEs on bitmap indices. In addition, two other initialization parameters must be properly set to yield good performance on bitmap indices.

(a) CREATE_BITMAP_AREA_SIZE: This parameter measures the amount of memory allocated for bitmap indices. Its default value is 8 MB, although a larger value leads to faster index creation. If the selectivity of the indexed column is very low, say .2 or .3, the parameter may be set at KB level. As a general rule, the higher the selectivity, the larger the value of the parameter to yield good performance.

(b) BITMAP_MERGE_AREA_SIZE: This parameter measures the amount of memory needed to merge bitmaps retrieved from a range scan of the index. Its default value is 1 MB. A larger value improves performance since the bitmap segments must be sorted before being merged into a single bitmap.

Neither of these two parameters can be altered at the session level.

8.6.3 Reverse Key Index

A *reverse key index* reverses the bytes of each column key value when storing them in the index leaf nodes, but maintains the column order for a concatenated index. For example, suppose that an Order_ID has been generated by Oracle's sequence mechanism and contains the following five values: 10001, 10002, 10003, 10004, and 10005. If an index is created on Order_ID as a B*-tree index, the five sequential values are stored as adjacent leaf nodes on the B*-tree. As the index continues to grow, the BLEVEL starts to degrade due to repetitive splitting of the branch nodes. But if a reverse key index is created on Order_ID, the index values are stored as 10001, 20001, 30001, 40001, and 50001. Thus the values spread the leaf nodes more evenly and reduce the repetitive splits of the branch nodes.

In general, a reverse key index is beneficial when a sequential key value is used to populate the index. Figure 8.8 shows the commands for creating or altering a reverse key index. The key word "reverse" tells Oracle to create the index as a reverse key. To alter an existing index, the "rebuild" option is necessary. After altering the index it is advisable to rename the altered index so as to contain the word "revkey" as a part of its name. This helps to identify the reverse key indices by name when retrieved from the DBA_INDEXES view.

```
SQL> create index revkey_Order_ID on ORDERS (Order_ID) reverse;
Index created.
SQL> alter index CONTRACTS_PK rebuild reverse;
Index altered.
SQL> alter index CONTRACTS_PK rename to revkey_CONTRACTS_PK;
Index altered.
```

FIGURE 8.8: Creation and Modification of Reverse Key Index

8.6.4 Index Organized Table

An *index organized table* appears the same as a regular table with a B*-tree index on the primary key (PK). But instead of maintaining a data table and a B*-tree index table separately, Oracle maintains one single B*-tree index structure that contains both the PK values and the other column values for each row. Since a separate data table is not stored, an index organized table uses less storage than a regular table. Also, it provides faster PK-based access for queries involving an exact match or a range scan of the PK. The rows in the table do not have ROWIDs, but instead are stored as ordered by the PK. No secondary indices can be created on the table.

The storage space for an index organized table is divided into two portions: index and overflow. The index portion is stored in an index tablespace and the overflow portion in a separate data tablespace. The splitting of rows in the table between the two areas is governed by two clauses in the CREATE TABLE command for the table:

- PCTTHRESHOLD p, where p is an integer and $0 \leq p \leq 50$; and
- INCLUDING *column_name*, where *column_name* is a column in the table.

For a given value of p, PCTTHRESHOLD p returns a value that equals $p\%$ of the data block size for the database. Whenever the size of a new or an updated row exceeds this value, the row is split into two parts for storage. The column in the INCLUDING clause and all the columns that are listed before that column in the CREATE TABLE command for the table are stored in the index tablespace. The remaining column(s), if any, are stored in a different tablespace called the overflow area.

Figure 8.9 shows the command for creating an index organized table and a sample output from running the command. Note that although the storage structure for the table is a B*-tree index and it is stored in an index tablespace, it is created via the CREATE TABLE command rather than the CREATE INDEX command.

```
CREATE TABLE ORDER_LINE_ITEMS
     (ORDER_ID NUMBER (4),
       LINE_NUM NUMBER (3),
       QTY_SOLD NUMBER,
       ITEM_NAME VARCHAR2 (30),
       SHIP_DATE DATE,
       CONSTRAINT pk#ORDER_LINE_ITEMS
       PRIMARY KEY (ORDER_ID, LINE_NUM) )
ORGANIZATION INDEX TABLESPACE INDEX_2
PCTTHRESHOLD 25
INCLUDING QTY_SOLD
OVERFLOW TABLESPACE DATA_2;
```

FIGURE 8.9: Creation of Index Organized Table

The PCTTHRESHOLD for the table is 25. Thus, if the data block size is 8 K, any row larger than 2,048 bytes (= 2 K) is split into two parts for storage. The first three columns, OREDER_ID, LINE_NUM, and QTY_SOLD, of the row are stored in INDEX_2, and the remaining two columns, ITEM_NAME and SHIP_DATE, are stored in DATA_2. The clause ORGANIZATION INDEX signifies that the rows of the table are stored in the order of the PK. The default clause is ORGANIZATION HEAP, which indicates that the rows are stored in the order of their physical entry into the table.

8.6.5 Cluster

A *cluster* is a group of two or more tables that are physically stored together in the same disk area. Tables benefit from clustering when the following three conditions hold.

(a) The tables have common column(s).
(b) They are related by a PK–FK relationship.
(c) The tables are frequently joined via the (PK, FK) columns.

The physical proximity of the data in a cluster improves the performance of join queries involving the clustered tables. The common column(s) of the tables stored in a cluster constitute the *cluster key*, which refers to the rows in every table. The cluster key can be the PK or a part of the PK of one or more of the tables. As an example, consider two tables, ORDER and LINE_ITEM, with the following structures.

```
ORDER (OrderID, other columns)
LINE_ITEM (OrderID, Line_Num, other columns)
Here    ORDER.PK = OrderID
        LINE_ITEM.PK = OrderID, Line_Num
        LINE_ITEM.FK = OrderID = ORDER.PK
```

If ORDER and LINE_ITEM are frequently joined via the column OrderID, they are good candidates for being stored as clustered tables with OrderID as the cluster key. Note that the cluster key is the PK of ORDER and a part of the PK of LINE_ITEM. Figure 8.10 shows the storage arrangement of ORDER and LINE_ITEM as unclustered tables and Figure 8.11 shows the same when the tables are stored in a cluster.

```
ORDER:                        LINE_ITEM:
OrderID   Other Columns       OrderID    Line_Num    Other Columns
2153       ........           6195        001         ........
1694       ........           6195        002         ........
1188       ........           1694        001         ........
6195       ........           3244        001         ........
3244       ........           3244        002         ........
                              3244        003         ........
                              1188        001         ........
                              2153        001         ........
                              2153        002         ........
                              2153        003         ........
                              2153        004         ........
```

FIGURE 8.10: ORDER and LINE_ITEM in Unclustered Form

```
Cluster Key
(OrderID)
1188            LINE_ITEM              Other Columns
                001                     ........
1694            LINE_ITEM              Other Columns
                001                     ........
2153            LINE_ITEM              Other Columns
                001                     ........
                002                     ........
                003                     ........
                004                     ........
3244            LINE_ITEM              Other Columns
                001                     ........
                002                     ........
                003                     ........
6195            LINE_ITEM              Other Columns
                001                     ........
                002                     ........
```

FIGURE 8.11: ORDER and LINE_ITEM in Clustered Form

Each distinct value of the cluster key is stored only once in a clustered table configuration regardless of whether it occurs once or many times in the tables, thereby resulting in less storage space. However, clustered tables require more storage space than unclustered tables. The sizing algorithm for clustered tables and indices is much more complex than that for unclustered tables and indices. See Loney [6, pp. 193–197] for the former and Appendix A for the latter. When retrieving data from the clustered tables, each table appears as if it contains all its rows including duplication, if any. When two clustered tables are joined via their cluster key, the response time is generally reduced since the returned data are stored mostly in physically contiguous data blocks. However, full table scans are generally slower for clustered tables than for unclustered tables. Clustering is not recommended in the following situations.

- At least one of the clustered tables is frequently used for full table scans. Such a table uses more storage than if it were stored as an unclustered table. As a result, Oracle has to read more data blocks to retrieve the data than if the table were unclustered. This increases the time for full table scans.
- The data from all the tables with the same cluster key value uses more than two data blocks. Here again Oracle has to read more data blocks to retrieve the data than if the table were unclustered.
- Partitioning is not compatible with clustering.

Creation of Clusters

A cluster of two or more tables is created via the CREATE CLUSTER command. Each table in a cluster is created via the CREATE TABLE command with the CLUSTER clause. The maximum length of all the cluster columns combined for a single CREATE CLUSTER command is 239 characters. At least one cluster column must be NOT NULL. Tables with LONG columns cannot be clustered. Figure 8.12 shows the commands to create the cluster ORDER_PROCESS with two tables, ORDER and LINE_ITEM, in that cluster.

```
SQL>      CREATE CLUSTER ORDER_PROCESS
  2       (OrderID NUMBER (10))
  3       PCTFREE 5    PCTUSED 90
  4       SIZE 500
  5       TABLESPACE DATA_2
  6       STORAGE       (INITIAL 1M NEXT 1M
  7       MINEXTENTS 2 MAXEXTENTS 505
  8       PCTINCREASE 0 );
Cluster created.
SQL>      CREATE TABLE NEW_ORDER
  2       (OrderID NUMBER (10) PRIMARY KEY,
  3       Order_Date DATE,
  4       Special_Requirement VARCHAR2 (20))
  5       CLUSTER ORDER_PROCESS (OrderID);
```

FIGURE 8.12: Creation of Cluster with Two Tables

```
Table created.
SQL>      CREATE TABLE LINE_ITEM
  2       (OrderID NUMBER (10),
  3       LINE_NUM NUMBER (3),
  4       Item_Price NUMBER (8,2),
  5       PRIMARY KEY (OrderID, LINE_NUM))
  6       CLUSTER ORDER_PROCESS (OrderID);
Table created.
```

FIGURE 8.12 (*continued*): Creation of Cluster with Two Tables

The clause SIZE used in Figure 8.12 represents the average size of a row in the cluster. Thus, the size of a row in the cluster ORDER_PROCESS is estimated as 500 bytes.

Cluster Types: Index and Hash

Oracle allows two types of clusters: index and hash.

An *index cluster* uses an index to maintain the clustered data via the cluster key. The index created on the key is called a *cluster index*. It must be created before any data can be put into the cluster. This is the default option. It works on the principle of storing together all the rows from all the clustered tables having the same value of the index. This index is searched for retrieving data from the cluster. The performance gain that a cluster offers arises from the reduced number of disk I/Os. Figure 8.13 shows the creation of an index cluster.

```
SQL>      CREATE INDEX IND_ORDER_PROCESS
  2       ON CLUSTER ORDER_PROCESS
  3       TABLESPACE ODTRANIS002
  4       STORAGE    (INITIAL 1M NEXT 1M
  5                  MINEXTENTS 2 MAXEXTENTS 505
  6                  PCTINCREASE 0);
Index created.
```

FIGURE 8.13: Creation of Index Cluster

An index cluster can be dropped via the DROP CLUSTER command. When the clause INCLUDING TABLES accompanies this command, all tables and indices included in the cluster are also dropped. Figure 8.14 shows this feature.

```
SQL> DROP CLUSTER ORDER_PROCESS INCLUDING TABLES;
Cluster dropped.
SQL> SELECT * FROM USER_INDEXES WHERE INDEX_NAME = 'IND_ORDER_PROCESS';
no rows selected
```

FIGURE 8.14: Dropping of Index Cluster

A *hash cluster* uses a hash function to calculate the location of a row by using the value of the cluster key for that row. When a row is inserted into the cluster, the hash function converts the value of the hash key for that row into the address of the row. The hash function can be user defined or system generated. If it is user defined, the hash cluster is created with a special clause HASH IS, which designates one column of the cluster for storing the hash value. This clause is optional. It should be used only when the cluster key is a single numeric column and its value is uniformly distributed. If it is omitted, Oracle uses a system generated hash function. Another specific clause, which is mandatory for creating a hash cluster, is HASHKEYS. It represents the maximum number of cluster key entries allowed for the cluster. Its value should be a prime number. Otherwise, Oracle rounds it up to the nearest prime number. The reason for making HASHKEYS a prime lies in the hashing algorithm used for computing the address of a row based on its cluster key. See Section E6, Appendix E, for the mathematical theory underlying hashing. Figure 8.15 shows the creation of a hash cluster in two flavors: user supplied hash function and system generated hash function.

```
SQL>     CREATE CLUSTER ORDER_PROCESS
  2      (OrderID NUMBER (10) )
  3      PCTFREE 5 PCTUSED 90
  4      SIZE 500
  5      HASHKEYS 1003
  6      TABLESPACE ODTRANTS002
  7      STORAGE    (INITIAL 2M NEXT 1M
  8                  MINEXTENTS 2 MAXEXTENTS 505
  9                  PCTINCREASE 0);
Cluster created.
SQL>     DROP CLUSTER ORDER_PROCESS;
Cluster dropped.
```

FIGURE 8.15: Creation of Hash Cluster—Two Flavors

```
SQL>       CREATE CLUSTER ORDER_PROCESS
  2        (OrderID NUMBER (10) )
  3        PCTFREE 5 PCTUSED 90
  4        SIZE 500
  5        HASH IS OrderID
  6        HASHKEYS 1003
  7        TABLESPACE ODTRANTS002
  8        STORAGE    (INITIAL 2M NEXT 1M
  9                   MINEXTENTS 2 MAXEXTENTS 505
 10        PCTINCREASE 0);
Cluster created.
```

FIGURE 8.15 (*continued*): Creation of Hash Cluster—Two Flavors

In Figure 8.15, the cluster ORDER_PROCESS is created first without the HASH IS clause so that Oracle uses a system generated hash function. Then the cluster is dropped and recreated with the HASH IS clause so that Oracle now uses the data in the column OrderID, which is numeric, to compute the address of the corresponding row.

Decision Tree for Using Clusters

As with other indexing options discussed so far, a cluster is beneficial only under certain circumstances. Three alternative options are available in this respect: indexed unclustered table, index cluster, and hash cluster. One needs to assess these two factors to make an informed decision:

- Type of the tables: static (validation) versus dynamic (transaction); and
- Nature of qualifying conditions in a query: exact match, range scan, other.

Figure 8.16 shows a decision tree describing the selection process that considers the above two factors. Since a dynamic table undergoes frequent updates, clustering is not recommended there. For static tables, the choice is clear for exact match and range scan. The category of "Other" is vague, as always. The developer has to exercise his or her judgment to make a decision.

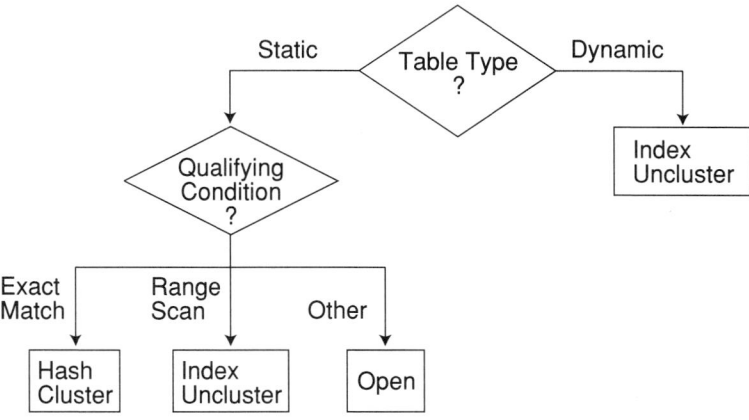

FIGURE 8.16: Decision Tree for Selection of Clustering

8.6.6 Histogram

Histograms are statistical entities that are used for describing the distribution of data. We can have a histogram of the data in any column of a table, not just an indexed column. However, Oracle uses them to determine the distribution of the data of an indexed column, especially when the data are not uniformly distributed. The cost-based optimizer can accurately estimate the execution cost of an indexed query if the data in the indexed column are uniformly distributed. But if the data are skewed, the query optimizer benefits from using a histogram for estimating the selectivity of an indexed column. If the selectivity is low due to the skewed distribution of data, the query optimizer may decide to use a full table scan. As an example, consider a table EMPLOYEE containing personnel data of a large Boston-based company. Although some of the employees may live in New Hampshire, Maine, or Rhode Island, a large majority would reside in Massachusetts. Consequently, the data of the column EMPLOYEE.State will be severely skewed in favor of State = MA. A histogram of the data in State tells the query optimizer that an indexed search by State is undesirable.

A histogram consists of a set of buckets. Each bucket contains information from the same number of rows and has a starting point and an ending point. These two points display respectively the starting and ending values of the indexed column for the given number of rows. The data dictionary views, DBA_HISTOGRAMS and DBA_TAB_COLUMNS, contain information about histograms. Figure 8.17 contains the code to generate histograms and a partial list of the accompanying statistics. Note that only the columns ENDPOINT_NUMBER and ENDPOINT_VALUE are stored in the view DBA_HISTOGRAMS, because the starting value of bucket N, say, immediately follows the ending value of bucket $N - 1$. The parameter SIZE determines the maximum number of buckets allocated to the column.

8. Optimization of the External Level of a Database

```
SQL>  ANALYZE TABLE CUSTOMER COMPUTE STATISTICS FOR COLUMNS CUST_ID
      SIZE 100;
Table analyzed.
SQL>  ANALYZE TABLE CUSTOMER COMPUTE STATISTICS FOR ALL INDEXED
      COLUMNS;
Table analyzed.
SQL>  DESC DBA_HISTOGRAMS
      Name                    Null?            Type
      ----------------        -----            --------------
      OWNER                                    VARCHAR2(30)
      TABLE_NAME                               VARCHAR2(30)
      COLUMN_NAME                              VARCHAR2(4000)
      ENDPOINT_NUMBER                          NUMBER
      ENDPOINT_VALUE                           NUMBER
SQL>  COL COLUMN_NAME FORMAT A20
SQL>  COL TABLE_NAME FORMAT A20
SQL>  COL OWNER FORMAT A10
SQL>  SELECT TABLE_NAME, COLUMN_NAME, ENDPOINT_NUMBER, ENDPOINT_VALUE
      FROM DBA_HISTOGRAMS WHERE TABLE_NAME = 'CUSTOMER' AND
      COLUMN_NAME = 'CUST_ID';
TABLE_NAME       COLUMN_NAME       ENDPOINT_NUMBER      ENDPOINT_VALUE
----------       -----------       ---------------      --------------
CUSTOMER         CUST_ID                  0                   1
CUSTOMER         CUST_ID                  1                  34
CUSTOMER         CUST_ID                  2                  68
         .   .   .   .   .   .   .   .   .   .
CUSTOMER         CUST_ID                 73                2520
CUSTOMER         CUST_ID                 74                2546
75 rows selected.
SQL>  SELECT MAX (CUST_ID) FROM CUSTOMER;
MAX(CUST_ID)
------------
    2546
SQL>  SELECT TABLE_NAME, COLUMN_NAME, NUM_BUCKETS, LAST_ANALYZED,
      SAMPLE_SIZE
   2  FROM DBA_TAB_COLUMNS WHERE
   3  TABLE_NAME = 'CUSTOMER' AND COLUMN_NAME = 'CUST_ID';
TABLE_NAME       COLUMN_NAME     NUM_BUCKETS     LAST_ANAL     SAMPLE_SIZE
----------       -----------     -----------     ---------     -----------
CUSTOMER         CUST_ID              74         29-DEC-99        2507
```

FIGURE 8.17 : Generation of Histogram

Figure 8.17 shows that CUST_ID uses only 74 buckets out of the 100 allocated and 2,546 is the largest value of CUST_ID. On an average each bucket stores 34.4 (= 2,546/74 rounded) values of CUST_ID.

8.6.7 In Conclusion

As discussed in Sections 8.6.1 through 8.6.6, Oracle offers six different options to create indices and get the benefit of indexed search. In conclusion, we ask: which index do we use and when? The answer is an obvious cliche: it depends. In this section we list the features of each type of index so that the developers and the DBAs can decide which types of indices to use and how to create them in an optimal fashion.

The qualifying condition of a query involves a search based on an exact match or a range scan. The following list summarizes the search feature of each of the six types of indices.

Index Type	Features
B*-tree	Exact match, range scan for columns with high selectivity
Bitmap	Exact match, range scan for columns with low selectivity
Reverse Key	Sequential key value used to populate the index
Index Organized	Exact match, range scan using PK-based access
Cluster	Tables related via PK–FK link and frequently used together in joins
Histogram	Exact match, range scan for nonuniformly distributed data

In general, B*-tree indices are used most widely followed by bitmap indices. Clusters help join queries, but have their drawbacks too. One major problem with clusters is to size them properly. Clusters, especially hash clusters, often waste storage. Also, we need to keep in mind that creating a bad index is almost as harmful for performance as not creating an index at all. When multiple columns are candidates for an index, we must weigh the two possible alternatives: one concatenated index on all the columns versus separate single column indices on each separate column. Use the selectivity of the columns as the guiding factor in both cases. Section 8.4 contains further details on optimal indexing.

8.7 Tools for Tracking Query Performance

Oracle offers four distinct tools for tracking query performance:

- EXPLAIN PLAN
- SQLTRACE
- TKPROF
- AUTOTRACE.

EXPLAIN PLAN is invoked within a session running a query, determines the execution plan of the query, and puts the steps of the plan to a table called the PLAN_TABLE. This table is created by running an Oracle script called UTLXPLAN.sql. SQLTRACE provides detailed information regarding the execution of a query. But the output is difficult to read and interpret. TKPROF is an operating system utility that takes this output and puts it into a readable format. Finally, AUTOTRACE generates the execution plan for a query like the EXPLAIN PLAN utility and provides statistics for processing the query.

AUTOTRACE tracks I/O-based statistics, and SQLTRACE tracks time-based statistics. There is, however, some overlap in the information provided by the two tools. Both of them return statistics on logical and physical reads. The advantage in using AUTOTRACE is that we do not need TKPROF to format the output. But AUTOTRACE takes longer to run, because it first parses the query to provide the execution plan and then executes the query to derive the related statistics. On the other hand, EXPLAIN PLAN only parses the query to derive the execution plan, but does not execute it. As a result, it saves on the execution time of the query, but does not provide any related statistics. If a query takes too long to run, then AUTOTRACE will take at least equally long to produce its output. But EXPLAIN PLAN run alone will return the execution plan much more quickly. Noting from Section 8.2 that the parse phase of query processing is the most resource intensive and time consuming, the information available from the EXPLAIN PLAN is mostly sufficient for tuning the query. For highly complex queries both AUTOTRACE and SQLTRACE should be used to identify areas where tuning can be done.

8.7.1 EXPLAIN PLAN

This utility allows the developer to examine the access path selected by a query optimizer to execute a query. Its real benefit lies in the fact that the execution plan is displayed without actually executing the query. The developer can view the plan, examine a set of alternative plans, and then decide on an optimal plan to execute. The utility works as follows.

(a) Run the script file UTLXPLAN.sql to create a table named PLAN_TABLE in your account. This script and a whole set of additional UTL*.sql scripts are usually found in the Oracle home directory listed below:

```
$ORACLE_HOME/rdbms/admin   (for UNIX)
orant\rdbms80\admin   (for NT)
```

Figure 8.18 shows the structure of PLAN_TABLE so that you can create it via the CREATE TABLE command, if necessary:

```
SQL> desc plan_table
    Name                        Null?           Type
    ---------------             -------         -------
    STATEMENT_ID                                VARCHAR2(30)
    TIMESTAMP                                   DATE
```

FIGURE 8.18: Structure of PLAN_TABLE

```
REMARKS                         VARCHAR2(80)
OPERATION                       VARCHAR2(30)
OPTIONS                         VARCHAR2(30)
OBJECT_NODE                     VARCHAR2(128)
OBJECT_OWNER                    VARCHAR2(30)
OBJECT_NAME                     VARCHAR2(30)
OBJECT_INSTANCE                 NUMBER(38)
OBJECT_TYPE                     VARCHAR2(30)
OPTIMIZER                       VARCHAR2(255)
SEARCH_COLUMNS                  NUMBER
ID                              NUMBER(38)
PARENT_ID                       NUMBER(38)
POSITION                        NUMBER(38)
COST                            NUMBER(38)
CARDINALITY                     NUMBER(38)
BYTES                           NUMBER(38)
OTHER_TAG                       VARCHAR2(255)
PARTITION_START                 VARCHAR2(255)
PARTITION_STOP                  VARCHAR2(255)
PARTITION_ID                    NUMBER(38)
OTHER                           LONG
```

FIGURE 8.18 (*continued*): Structure of PLAN_TABLE

(b) Type the following command at the "SQL>" prompt.

```
explain plan
set Statement_Id = 'TEST'
for
(query statement);
```

SQL returns a rather cryptic message, "Explained." This means that the utility has created in PLAN_TABLE one record for each operation used by the query and identified by the identifier Statement_ID = "TEST".

Figure 8.19 describes the columns of PLAN_TABLE.

```
STATEMENT_ID = The value of the optional STATEMENT_ID parameter
  specified in the EXPLAIN PLAN statement.
TIMESTAMP = The date and time when the EXPLAIN PLAN statement was
  issued.
REMARKS = Any comment (up to 80 bytes) can be associated with each
  step of the explained plan. To add or change a remark on any row
  of the PLAN_TABLE, the UPDATE statement must be used to modify
  the rows of the PLAN_TABLE.
```

FIGURE 8.19: Columns of PLAN_TABLE

> OPERATION = The name of the internal operation performed in this step. In the first row generated for a statement, the column contains one of the following values: DELETE STATEMENT, INSERT STATEMENT, SELECT STATEMENT, UPDATE STATEMENT.
> OPTIONS = A variation on the operation described in the OPERATION column.
> OBJECT_NODE = The name of the database link used to refer to the object (a table name or view name). For local queries using the parallel query option, this column describes the order in which output from operations is consumed.
> OBJECT_OWNER = The name of the user who owns the schema containing the table or index.
> OBJECT_NAME = The name of the table or index.
> OBJECT_INSTANCE = A number corresponding to the ordinal position of the object as it appears in the original statement. The numbering proceeds from left to right, outer to inner with respect to the original statement text. A view expansion results in unpredictable numbers.
> OBJECT_TYPE = A modifier that provides descriptive information about the object; for example, NONUNIQUE for indices.
> OPTIMIZER = The current mode of the optimizer.
> SEARCH_COLUMNS = Not currently used.
> ID = A number assigned to each step in the execution plan.
> PARENT_ID = The ID of the next execution step that operates on the output of the ID step.
> POSITION = The order of processing for steps that all have the same PARENT_ID.
> COST = The cost of the operation as estimated by the cost-based optimizer. For statements that use the rule-based optimizer, this column is null. Cost is not determined for table access operations. The value of this column does not have any particular unit of measurement; it is merely a weighted value used to compare costs of execution plans of a given query.
> CARDINALITY = The number of rows accessed by the operation, as estimated by the cost-based optimizer.
> BYTES = The number of bytes accessed by the operation, as estimated by the cost-based optimizer.
> OTHER_TAG = Describes the contents of the OTHER column.
> PARTITION_START = The start partition of a range of accessed partitions.
> PARTITION_STOP = The stop partition of a range of accessed partitions.
> PARTITION_ID = The step that has computed the pair of values of the PARTITION_START and PARTITION_STOP columns.
> OTHER = Other information that is specific to the execution step that a user may find useful.

FIGURE 8.19 (*continued*): Columns of PLAN_TABLE

The possible values of OTHER_TAG are

    Blank = Serial execution.

SERIAL_FROM_REMOTE = Serial execution at a remote site.
SERIAL_TO_PARALLEL = Serial execution; output of step is partitioned or broadcast to parallel query servers.
PARALLEL_TO_PARALLEL = Parallel execution; output of step is repartitioned to second set of parallel query servers.
PARALLEL_TO_SERIAL = Parallel execution; output of step is returned to serial "query coordinator" process.
PARALLEL_COMBINED_WITH_PARENT = Parallel execution; output of step goes to next step in same parallel process. No interprocess communication is available to parent.
PARALLEL_COMBINED_WITH_CHILD = Parallel execution; input of step comes from prior step in same parallel process. No interprocess communication is available from child.

The query execution plan is determined by querying PLAN_TABLE using the columns Statement_ID, Operation, Options, Object_Name, ID, Parent_ID, and Position. figures 8.20 and 8.21 contain two SELECT statements that put the execution plan of a query in a tabular format and a nested format respectively. The tabular format displays each operation and each option separately, whereas the nested format improves readability of the plan, labels each step of the plan with a number, and assigns a cost for executing the query under the cost-based optimizer.

```
SQL> explain plan
     set statement_id = 'Query'
     for
     select Cust_name, Acct_Name, Status from Customer A,
     Account B where A.Cust_ID = B.Cust_ID
     order by Cust_name, Acct_Name;
Explained.

SQL> SELECT operation, options, object_name, id, parent_id, position
     FROM plan_table
     WHERE statement_id = 'Query'
     ORDER BY id;
OPERATION            OPTIONS      OBJECT_NAME    ID   PARENT_ID   POSITION
----------------     --------     -----------    --   ---------   --------
SELECT STATEMENT                                 0                88
SORT                 ORDER BY                    1    0           1
HASH JOIN                                        2    1           1
TABLE ACCESS         FULL         CUSTOMER       3    2           1
TABLE ACCESS         FULL         CUSTOMER       4    2           2
```

FIGURE 8.20: Execution Plan in Tabular Format

```
SQL>   explain plan
       set statement_id = 'Query'
       for
       select Cust_name, Acct_Name, Status from Customer A,
       Account B
       where A.Cust_ID = B.Cust_ID
       order by Cust_name, Acct_Name;
Explained.
SQL> SELECT DECODE(ID,0,'',
     LPAD(' ',2*(LEVEL-1))||LEVEL||'.'||POSITION)||' '||
     OPERATION||' '||OPTIONS||' '||OBJECT_NAME||' '||
     OBJECT_TYPE||' '||
     DECODE(ID,0,'Cost = '||POSITION) "Execution Plan"
     FROM PLAN_TABLE
     CONNECT BY PRIOR ID = PARENT_ID
     AND STATEMENT_ID = 'Query'
     START WITH ID = 0 AND STATEMENT_ID = 'Query'
Execution Plan
-----------------------------------------------------------
SELECT STATEMENT      Cost = 88
  2.1 SORT ORDER BY
    3.1 HASH JOIN
      4.1 TABLE ACCESS FULL CUSTOMER
      4.2 TABLE ACCESS FULL ACCOUNT
```

FIGURE 8.21: Execution Plan in Nested Format

Figures 8.20 and 8.21 show that the cost of the query is 88. The cost is not absolute. It is meaningful only with respect to a given query. Thus, two queries with the same cost C, say, do not necessarily perform equally well. But if a given query has n execution plans with respective costs C_i, $i = 1, 2, \ldots, n$, then the plan with the cost = min (C_i, $i = 1, 2, \ldots, n$) performs the best. Both figures display the types of operations the database must perform to resolve the query irrespective of whether the query has been run already. Thus, the output helps the developer to experiment with alternative versions of a query to decide on the best access path that the developer wants.

The execution plan in the nested format is read from innermost to outermost steps and from top to bottom. We start at the highest step number and move towards the lowest. Two steps labeled as $m.n_1$ and $m.n_2$, say, are read in the order $m.n_1$ followed by $m.n_2$ if $n_1 < n_2$. Let us now interpret the execution plan in Figure 8.21.

The query optimizer executes the plan steps in the following order.

```
      4.1 TABLE ACCESS FULL CUSTOMER
      4.2 TABLE ACCESS FULL ACCOUNT
```

Each operation involves a full table scan and returns rows from a table when the ROWID is not available for a row search. Since the query does not contain any qualifying conditions on the columns of either table, the query optimizer performs a full table scan of CUSTOMER followed by the same of ACCOUNT until all rows have been read. It then returns them to Step 3.1 for further processing.

    3.1 HASH JOIN

This operation joins two tables by creating an in-memory bitmap of one of the tables and then using a hash function to locate the matching rows of the other table. When one table is significantly smaller than the other table and fits into the available memory area, a hash join is performed instead of the traditional NESTED LOOPS join. Even if an index is available for the join, a hash join may be preferable to a NESTED LOOPS join. Since CUSTOMER is significantly smaller than ACCOUNT, it is read into memory. Then a hash function is used to retrieve all the matching rows of ACCOUNT. The result is then returned to Step 2.1.

    2.1 SORT ORDER BY

This operation is used for sorting results without elimination of duplicate rows. The rows returned by step 3.1 are sorted first by Cust_name, and then by Acct_Name. The sorted rows are then stripped of duplicates and the final result is returned to the user.

    SELECT STATEMENT

This is the final statement of the execution plan. It merely indicates that the query involves a SELECT statement as opposed to INSERT, UPDATE, or DELETE.

The two columns, OPERATION and OPTIONS, are most important for analyzing the execution plan. Oracle offers 23 operations. An operation can have one or more OPTIONS, as described below.

OPERATION with OPTIONS

1. AND-EQUAL		Accepts multiple sets of ROWIDs and returns the list of ROWIDs that are common to all the sets.
2. BITMAP		Has five OPTIONS listed below:
	a. CONVERSION	TO ROWIDS converts the bitmap representation to actual ROWIDs that can be used to access the table. FROM ROWIDS converts the ROWIDs to a bitmap representation. COUNT returns the number of ROWIDs if the actual values are not needed.
	b. INDEX	SINGLE VALUE looks up the bitmap for a single key value in the index. RANGE SCAN retrieves bitmaps for a key value range. FULL SCAN: a bitmap index full scan is performed if there is no start or stop key.
	c. MERGE	Merges several bitmaps resulting from a range scan into one bitmap.

    d. MINUS   Subtracts the bits of one bitmap from another. This row source is used for negated predicates and can be used only if there are some nonnegated predicates yielding a bitmap from which the subtraction can take place.

    e. OR   Computes the bitwise OR of two bitmaps.

3. CONCATENATION   An operation that accepts multiple sets of rows and returns the union of all the sets.

4. CONNECT BY   A retrieval of rows in a hierarchical order for a query containing a CONNECT BY clause.

5. COUNT   An operation that counts the number of rows selected from a table. It offers the following OPTION.

    STOPKEY   A count operation where the number of rows returned is limited by the ROWNUM expression in the WHERE clause.

6. FILTER   An operation that accepts a set of rows, eliminates some of them, and returns the rest.

7. FIRST ROW   A retrieval on only the first row selected by a query.

8. FOR UPDATE   An operation that retrieves and locks the rows selected by a query containing a FOR UPDATE clause.

9. HASH JOIN   An operation that joins two sets of rows, and returns the final result. It offers two OPTIONS:

    a. ANTI   A hash antijoin.

    b. SEMI   A hash semijoin.

10. INDEX   This is an access method. It offers three OPTIONS:

    a. UNIQUE SCAN   A retrieval of a single ROWID from an index.

    b. RANGE SCAN   A retrieval of one or more ROWIDs from an index. Indexed values are scanned in ascending order.

    c. RANGE SCAN DESCENDING   A retrieval of one or more ROWIDs from an index. Indexed values are scanned in descending order.

11. INLIST ITERATOR   It offers the OPTION:

    CONCATENATED   Iterates over the operation below it, for each value in the "IN" list predicate.

12. INTERSECTION   An operation that accepts two sets of rows and returns the intersection of the sets, eliminating duplicates.

13. MERGE JOIN   This is a join operation that accepts two sets of rows, each sorted by a specific value, combines each row from one set with the matching rows from the other, and returns the result. It offers three OPTIONS:

    a. OUTER   A merge join operation to perform an outer join statement.

	b. ANTI	A merge antijoin.
	c. SEMI	A merge semijoin.
14. MINUS		An operation that accepts two sets of rows and returns rows that appear in the first set but not in the second, eliminating duplicates.
15. NESTED LOOPS		This is a join operation that accepts two sets of rows, an outer set and an inner set. Oracle compares each row of the outer set with each row of the inner set and returns those rows that satisfy the join condition. It offers the OPTION:
	OUTER	A nested loops operation to perform an outer join statement.
16. PARTITION		It offers the OPTION:
	CONCATENATED	Iterates over the operation below it, for each partition in the range given by the PARTITION_START and PARTITION_STOP columns.
17. PROJECTION		An internal operation.
18. REMOTE		A retrieval of data from a remote database.
19. SEQUENCE		An operation involving accessing values of a sequence.
20. SORT		It offers five OPTIONS:
	a. AGGREGATE	A retrieval of a single row that is the result of applying a group function to a group of selected rows.
	b. GROUP BY	An operation that sorts a set of rows into groups for a query with a GROUP BY clause.
	c. JOIN	An operation that sorts a set of rows before a merge-join.
	d. ORDER BY	An operation that sorts a set of rows for a query with an ORDER BY clause.
	e. UNIQUE	An operation that sorts a set of rows to eliminate duplicates.
21. TABLE ACCESS		This operation provides an access method. It offers four OPTIONS:
	a. FULL	A retrieval of all rows from a table.
	b. CLUSTER	A retrieval of rows from a table based on a value of an indexed cluster key.
	c. HASH	Retrieval of rows from a table based on hash cluster key value.
	d. BY ROWID	A retrieval of a row from a table based on its ROWID.
22. UNION		An operation that accepts two sets of rows and returns the union of the sets, eliminating duplicates.
23. VIEW		An operation that executes the query defining the view and then returns the resulting rows to another operation.

As noted in Section 8.3, an operation can be a row or a set operation. A row operation returns one row at a time, whereas a set operation processes all the rows and then returns the entire set. We list below the 23 operations grouped under these two categories.

```
Row Operations                  Set Operations
AND-EQUAL                       FOR UPDATE
BITMAP                          HASH JOIN (hybrid of row
CONCATENATION                       and set)
CONNECT BY                      INTERSECTION
COUNT                           MERGE JOIN
FILTER                          MINUS
FIRST ROW                       REMOTE (can be row or set)
HASH JOIN (hybrid of            SORT
row and set)                    UNION
INDEX                           VIEW
INLIST ITERATOR
NESTED LOOPS

PROJECTION
PARTITION
REMOTE (can be row or set)
SEQUENCE
TABLE ACCESS
```

8.7.2 SQLTRACE

The SQLTRACE utility both parses and executes a query, whereas the EXPLAIN PLAN utility only parses it. As a result, SQLTRACE provides more information than EXPLAIN PLAN, but also takes longer to run. The following two steps are performed for enabling SQLTRACE and displaying its output.

(a) Set three initialization parameters as follows.:

- TIMED_STATISTICS = TRUE.
- MAX_DUMP_FILE_SIZE = *your estimated size*.
- USER_DUMP_DEST = *designated directory*.

The default value of TIMED_STATISTICS is FALSE. By setting it to TRUE, we allow Oracle to collect runtime statistics such as CPU and elapsed times, various statistics in the V$ dynamic performance views, etc.

When the SQL trace facility is enabled at the instance level, every call to the server produces a text line in a file using the file format of the operating system. The parameter MAX_DUMP_FILE_SIZE provides the maximum size of these files in operating system blocks. Its default value is 10,000 operating system blocks. It can accept a numerical value or a number followed by the suffix K or M, where K means that the number is multiplied by 1,000 and M means a multiplication by 1,000,000. The parameter can also assume the special value of UNLIMITED, which means that there is no upper limit on the dump file size. In this case, the dump files can grow as large as the operating system permits. This is an undesirable option due to its potential adverse impact on disk space and hence should be used with extreme caution. If the trace output is truncated, increase the value of this parameter.

The parameter USER_DUMP_DEST specifies the pathname for a directory where the server writes debugging trace files on behalf of a user process. The default value for this parameter is the default destination for system dumps on the operating system.

(b) Enable SQLTRACE at a session level or at the instance level as follows.

Session Level

Type the command ALTER SESSION SET SQL_TRACE TRUE; Then enter the query to be traced. At the end of the session, disable the utility by typing ALTER SESSION SET SQL_TRACE FALSE;

Instance Level

Set the initialization parameter SQL_TRACE = TRUE in the init<instance name>.ora file. This causes Oracle to TRACE every query in the database resulting in degradation of performance. Consequently, this option is not recommended. Alternatively, this option may be activated for a short time, if needed, and then be deactivated at the instance level by setting SQL_TRACE = FALSE, which is the default.

The output file of a SQLTRACE session under UNIX is named in the format SID_ora_PID.trc, where SID is the instance name and PID is the server process ID. The file consists of three sections described below.

SQL Statement

This section consists of the query that was executed. It allows the developer or the DBA to examine the query when analyzing the rest of the output.

Statistical Information

This section has two parts. The first part is tabular in form and the second part is a list of items. The tabular part has eight columns and four rows. The first column is labeled "call" and has four values: parse, execute, fetch, and totals, which is the sum of the first three columns. For each value of call, the remaining seven columns provide the corresponding statistics. These eight columns are described below:

CALL	Type of call made to the database, i.e., parse, execute, or fetch;
COUNT	Number of times a statement was parsed, executed, or fetched;
CPU	Total CPU time in seconds for all parse, execute, or fetch calls for the Statement;
ELAPSED	Total elapsed time in seconds for all parse, execute, or fetch calls for the statement;
DISK	Total number of data blocks physically read from the datafiles on disk for all parse, execute, or fetch calls;
QUERY	Total number of buffers retrieved from the data block buffer cache for all

	parse, execute, or fetch calls. These buffers are said to be retrieved in consistent mode for SELECT statements;
CURRENT	Total number of buffers retrieved from the data block buffer cache for all parse, execute, or fetch calls. These buffers are said to be in current mode for INSERT, UPDATE, and DELETE statements;
ROWS	Total number of rows processed by the SQL statement. This total does not include rows processed by subqueries of the SQL statement. For SELECT statements, the number of rows returned appears for the fetch step. For INSERT, UPDATE, and DELETE statements, the number of rows processed appears for the execute step.

The second part of this section consists of the three lines of output:

- Number of library cache misses resulting from parse and execute steps for each SQL statement;
- Optimizer hint, if applicable (see Section 9.3.1 for optimizer hints);
- User ID of the user issuing the SQL statement. If the SQL trace input file contains statistics from multiple users and the statement was issued by more than one user, then only the ID of the last user to parse is listed. Note that the user IDs of all database users appear in the data dictionary in the column ALL_USERS.USER_ID.

EXPLAIN PLAN

This section describes the execution plan of the query under two headers, rows and execution plan. The latter displays the steps of the plan in a nested format as in Figure 8.21 without the step numbers and the former displays the number of rows returned by each step of the plan. Figure 8.22 shows the transcript of a SQLTRACE session.

```
ALTER SESSION SET SQL_TRACE TRUE;
select Cust_name, Acct_Name, Status from Customer A, Account B
   where A.Cust_ID = B. Cust_ID
   and rownum < 21
   order by Cust_name, Acct_Name;
ALTER SESSION SET SQL_TRACE FALSE;
OUTPUT FROM SESSION:
Session altered.
```
(Display of data of the 20 rows omitted here)
```
20 rows selected.
Session altered.
```

FIGURE 8.22: Transcript of a SQLTRACE Session

8.7.3 TKPROF

TKPROF is an operating system utility that converts the output file from a SQLTRACE session into a readable format. Its syntax is as follows.

```
TKPROF filename1 filename2 [PRINT=number] [AGGREGATE=NO]
    [INSERT=filename] [SYS=YES/NO] [TABLE=filename]
    [RECORD=filename] [EXPLAIN=username/password]
    [SORT=parameters]
```

The arguments and their respective values are explained below.

filename1: Name of the input file containing statistics produced by SQLTRACE; it can be a trace file for a single session or a file produced by concatenating individual trace files from multiple sessions.

filename2: Name of the output file to which TKPROF writes its formatted output

[PRINT=*number*]: Number of statements to be included in the output file; if omitted, TKPROF lists all traced SQL statements.

[AGGREGATE=NO]: If specified as AGGREGATE = NO, TKPROF does not aggregate multiple users of the same SQL text.

[INSERT=*filename*]: Creates a SQL script labeled *filename* that stores the trace statistics in the database; the script creates a table and inserts a row of statistics for each traced SQL statement into the table.

[SYS=*YES/NO*]: Enables (YES) or disables (NO) the listing of recursive SQL statements issued by the user SYS into the output file. The default is YES. Regardless of the value selected for this parameter, the statistics for all traced SQL statements, including recursive SQL statements, are inserted into the output file.

[TABLE=*filename*]: The value of *filename* specifies the schema and name of the table into which TKPROF temporarily places execution plans before writing them to the output file. If the specified table already exists, TKPROF deletes all rows in the table, uses it for the EXPLAIN PLAN command (which writes more rows into the table), and then deletes those rows. If this table does not exist, TKPROF creates it, uses it, and then drops it. The specified user must be able to issue INSERT, SELECT, and DELETE statements against the table. If the table does not already exist, the user must also be able to issue CREATE TABLE and DROP TABLE statements.

[RECORD=*filename*]: Creates a SQL script with the specified *filename* for storing all of the nonrecursive SQL in the trace file.

[EXPLAIN=*username/password*]: Prepares the execution plan for each SQL statement in the trace file and writes these execution plans to the output file. TKPROF produces the execution plans by issuing the EXPLAIN PLAN command after connecting to Oracle with the specified *username/password*. TKPROF takes longer to process a large trace file if the EXPLAIN option is used. This option is related to the option [TABLE=*filename*] listed above. If this option is used without the option [TABLE=*filename*], TKPROF uses the table PROF$PLAN_TABLE in the schema of the user specified by the EXPLAIN option. If, on the other hand, the TABLE option is used without the EXPLAIN option, TKPROF ignores the TABLE option.

[SORT=*parameters*]: Oracle provides a large number of sorting choices under this option. The traced SQL statements are sorted in descending order of the specified sort options before listing them in the output file. If more than one sort option is specified, the output is sorted in descending order by the sum of the values specified in the sort options. If this parameter is omitted, TKPROF lists statements in the output file in order of first use. The available sort options are listed below:

  PRSCNT = Number of times parsed;
  PRSCPU = CPU time spent in parsing;
  PRSELA = Elapsed time spent in parsing;
  PRSDSK = Number of physical reads from disk during parse;
  PRSQRY = Number of consistent mode block reads during parse;
  PRSCU = Number of current mode block reads during parse;
  PRSMIS = Number of library cache misses during parse;
  EXECNT = Number of executes;
  EXECPU = CPU time spent in executing;
  EXEELA = Elapsed time spent in executing;
  EXEDSK = Number of physical reads from disk during execute;
  EXEQRY = Number of consistent mode block reads during execute;
  EXECU = Number of current mode block reads during execute;
  EXEROW = Number of rows processed during execute;
  EXEMIS = Number of library cache misses during execute;
  FCHCNT = Number of fetches;
  FCHCPU = CPU time spent in fetching;
  FCHELA = Elapsed time spent in fetching;
  FCHDSK = Number of physical reads from disk during fetch;
  FCHQRY = Number of consistent mode block reads during fetch;
  FCHCU = Number of current mode block reads during fetch;
  FCHROW = Number of rows fetched;

We describe below the procedure to generate an output file under TKPROF. Let us assume that

- Trace file = Ora00118.TRC,
- USER_DUMP_DEST = G:\oradba\admin\ordr\udump, and
- Oracle Home directory = E:\orant\RDBMS80\TRACE.

Hence the trace file Ora00118.TRC resides in the directory G:\oradba\admin\ordr\udump. Now proceed as follows.

- Run the query.
- From the Oracle Home directory run the command

8.7 Tools for Tracking Query Performance

```
tkprof80 G:\oradba\admin\ordr\udump\Ora00118.TRC
C:\Ora00118_TRC.out
```

The output file C:\Ora00118_TRC.out is now available for analysis.

Figure 8.23 shows the result of using TKPROF with default options.

```
TKPROF: Release 8.0.5.0.0 - Production on Fri Jan 14 13:51:28 2000
(c) Copyright 1998 Oracle Corporation. All rights reserved.
Trace file: G:\ORADBA\admin\ordr\udump\Ora00118.trc
Sort options: default
****************************************************************
count    = number of times OCI procedure was executed
cpu      = cpu time in seconds executing
elapsed  = elapsed time in seconds executing
disk     = number of physical reads of buffers from disk
query    = number of buffers gotten for consistent read
current  = number of buffers gotten in current mode (usually for
             update)
rows     = number of rows processed by the fetch or execute call
****************************************************************
select Cust_name, Acct_name, Status from Customer A, Account B
    where A.Cust_ID = B. Cust_ID
    and rownum < 41
    order by Cust_name, Acct_name

call      count    cpu     elapsed   disk    query   current   rows
-------   -----    ----    --------  -----   -----   -------   ----
Parse       2      0.00    0.00        0       0        0        0
Execute     2      0.02    0.02        0       0        0        0
Fetch       6      0.02    0.89       44      32       12       40
-------   -----   -----   --------  -----   ------   -------   ----
total      10      0.04    0.91       44      32       12       40

Misses in library cache during parse: 1
Optimizer goal: CHOOSE
Parsing user id: 18
****************************************************************
```

FIGURE 8.23 : Sample TKPROF Session

8.7.4 AUTOTRACE

AUTOTRACE produces the execution plan without using TKPROF to format the output. To activate AUTOTRACE, we issue the following command within SQL*Plus

```
sql> SET AUTOTRACE ON TIMING ON
```

278   8. Optimization of the External Level of a Database

and then enter the query statement to be AUTOTRACEd. The output consists of four parts:

(a) Result of executing the query;
(b) Execution time of the query measured in realtime, not the CPU time; the unit of time is the millisecond, i.e., 1/1,000th of a second;
(c) Execution plan of the query;
(d) Statistics of system resources used such as logical and physical reads, sorts done, number of rows returned, etc.

However, the output is less detailed than that produced by SQLTRACE and TKPROF. Figure 8.24 contains the transcript of an AUTOTRACE session.

```
SET AUTOTRACE ON TIMING ON
select Cust_Name, Account_Name, Status from Customer A, Account B
    where A.Cust_ID = B.Cust_ID
    and rownum < 21
    order by Cust_Name, Account_Name;
PARTIAL OUTPUT:
CUST_NAME                ACCOUNT_NAME                STATUS
-------------            ----------------------      -------
Customer One             Customer Account One          T
Customer Two             Customer Account Two          T
Customer Three           Customer Account One          A
Customer Four            Customer Account Three        A
        . . . . . . . . . . . . . . . . . . . . .
20 rows selected.
    real: 1903
Execution Plan
----------------------------------------------------------------
    0        SELECT STATEMENT Optimizer=CHOOSE (Cost=88 Card=2382
             Bytes=507366)
    1    0      SORT (ORDER BY) (Cost=88 Card=2382 Bytes=507366)
    2    1        COUNT (STOPKEY)
    3    2          HASH JOIN (Cost=12 Card=2382 Bytes=507366)
    4    3            TABLE ACCESS (FULL) OF 'CUSTOMER' (Cost=1 Card=9
             52 Bytes=65688)
    5    3            TABLE ACCESS (FULL) OF 'ACCOUNT' (Cost=4 Card=
             2430 Bytes=349920)
```

FIGURE 8.24: Transcript of an AUTOTRACE Session

```
Statistics
----------------------------------------------------------
          0  recursive calls
          6  db block gets
         11  consistent gets
          0  physical reads
          0  redo size
       2586  bytes sent via SQL*Net to client
        908  bytes received via SQL*Net from client
          5  SQL*Net roundtrips to/from client
          2  sorts (memory)
          0  sorts (disk)
         20  rows processed
```

FIGURE 8.24 (*continued*): Transcript of an AUTOTRACE Session

If we issue the command SET AUTOTRACE TRACEONLY EXPLAIN, then we get the query execution plan with the cost of each step. On the other hand, EXPLAIN PLAN alone returns only the total cost of the query without any step-by-step breakdown.

Key Words

access, indexed
access, sequential
AND logic
AUTOTRACE
B*-tree
B*-tree index
bitmap index
BLEVEL
bucket
cluster
cluster join
CLUSTERING_FACTOR
concatenated index
cost of query processing
decision tree
dense index
driver
driving table
dynamic performance view
ending point
equijoin

exact match
execute phase
EXPLAIN PLAN
fetch phase
hash cluster
hash function
hash function, system generated
hash function, user supplied
hash join
hashing
hint
index cluster
index organized table
internal representation
leaf node
LEAF_BLOCKS
least cost
limiting condition
nested loops join
nondense index
optimization, cost-based

optimization, rule-based
optimizer mode
optimizer, cost-based
optimizer, rule-based
OR logic
parse phase
PLAN_TABLE
qualifying condition
query, qualified
query, unqualified
query optimizer
range scan
relational algebra
relational calculus, domain

relational calculus, tuple
reverse key index
row operation
set operation
sort–merge join
SQLTRACE
starting point
storage space, index
storage space, overflow
tabular format
throughput
TKPROF
tree-structured index

References and Further Reading

1. E. Aronoff et al.—*Advanced Oracle Tuning and Administration*, Oracle Press, 1997.
2. M. R. Ault—*Oracle8 Black Book*, Coriolis Group Books, 1998.
3. S. Bobrowski—*Mastering Oracle7 & Client/Server Computing*, Sybex, 1996.
4. D. K. Burleson—*High-Performance Oracle Database Applications*, Coriolis Group Books, 1998.
5. M. J. Corey et al—*Tuning Oracle*, Oracle Press, 1995.
6. K. Loney—*Oracle 8i DBA Handbook*, Oracle Press, 2000.
7. S. S. Mittra—*Principles of Relational Database Systems*, Prentice-Hall, 1991.
8. R. J. Niemiec—*Oracle Performance Tuning*, Oracle Press, 1999.

All of the above books except [7] discuss query tuning under both rule-based and cost-based optimizers in Oracle. But none of them offers the unified view of addressing the database performance tuning problems at all three levels jointly, i.e., conceptual (Chapter 3), internal (Chapters 4 through 7), and external (Chapters 8 and 9), as discussed here. Mittra [7, Chapter 5] discusses the theoretical issue of query optimization using relational algebra and relational calculus. Corey et al. [5, p. 173–174] discuss the three phases of query processing. Aronoff et al. [1, pp. 264–269], Ault [2, Chapter 10], Bobrowski [3, p. 458–465], Burleson [4, pp. 191–196], Corey et al. [5, pp. 188–193], and Niemiec [8, Chapter 8] treat the topic of optimal indexing and selectivity from various viewpoints with many examples. In particular, we mention Bobrowski [3, pp. 465–472] for examples of clustering, and Aronoff et al. [1, Chapter 13] for good examples of histograms and an extensive treatment of the row and set operations with plenty of examples of their EXPLAIN PLAN output.

Exercises

Theoretical exercises are of little value for this chapter since the best practice comes from optimizing the performance of queries in your own development environment before they migrate to the test or production databases. The exercises given below identify some of the areas not specifically covered in Chapter 8 and should be considered an extension of the text.

1. Refer to Figure 8.3. Write a program using some procedural language such as Pro*C, UNIX shell scripting, etc. according to the following specifications:

    (a) Ask the user to enter a column name for computing its selectivity.
    (b) Ask the user if more column(s) need to be added to the set before computing the selectivity.
    (c) Repeat Step (b) until the user is finished with input.
    (d) Connect to the Oracle database, and compute the selectivity of the column(s) entered by the user.
    (e) Format an output to display the result nicely.

2. A database contains the following objects.
    ```
    CUSTOMER (Cust_ID, Cust_Name, Cust_Type, Cust_Region, ....)
    ORDER (Order_ID, …)
    LINE_ITEM (Order_ID, Line_Number, Line_Amount, …)
    CUST_ORDER (Cust_ID, Order_ID, …)

    CUSTOMER.PK = Cust_ID;        ORDER.PK = Order_ID;
    LINE_ITEM.PK = (Order_ID, Line_Number);
    CUST_ORDER.PK = (Cust_ID, Order_ID)
    ```

    In addition, two nonunique B*-tree indices are created on the two columns CUSTOMER.Cust_Type and CUSTOMER.Cust_Region.

    You want to produce a report with the specification:

    - Headers: Customer Name, Region, Type, Total Order Amount;
    - Region = East or North;
    - Type = Residential.

    Note that each order has one or more line items, each of which has a corresponding line amount. You must add all the line amounts for a given order to get the order amount for that order. Also, Region has four values: East, West, North, South. Type has two values: Industrial, Residential.

    (a) Run the query to generate the report specified above.
    (b) Use EXPLAIN PLAN to find the execution plan of the query and interpret the plan. In particular, find the driver of the query and determine if that table is indeed the best candidate for the driver.

(c) Get runtime statistics in two ways: using SQLTRACE with TKPROF, and using AUTOTRACE with TIMING ON.
(d) Verify that you get the same execution plan in both cases.

3. Redo Exercise 2 with the change:

   Drop the B*-tree indices on the two columns, CUSTOMER.Cust_Type and CUSTOMER.Cust_Region and create two bitmap indices on them. What differences do you notice in the execution plan and the runtime statistics under the new indices?

4. Refer to Exercises 2 and 3 above. You have collected runtime statistics in both cases using SQLTRACE with TKPROF, and using AUTOTRACE with TIMING ON. List the statistics collected in both cases under the three headers:

   - Common to both SQLTRACE with TKPROF, and AUTOTRACE with TIMING ON;
   - Unique to SQLTRACE with TKPROF;
   - Unique to AUTOTRACE with TIMING ON.

9
Query Tuning and Optimization Under Oracle 8i

Outline

9.1 Oracle Query Performance
9.2 Query Tuning in Oracle: General Principles
9.3 Query Tuning in Oracle: Cost-based Optimizer
9.4 Query Tuning in Oracle: Rule-based Optimizer
9.5 Tuning of Join Queries
9.6 Statistical Forecasting for Tracking Performance
Key Words
References and Further Reading
Exercises

Overview of the Chapter

The chapter starts with an overview of query performance issues as a continuation of Chapter 8. It then provides a set of general guidelines for tuning poorly performing queries. This is followed by specific guidelines for cost-based and rule-based optimizers under Oracle 8i. Since joining usually poses a single challenge to write an optimal query, a separate section discusses this topic. The chapter closes with a brief introduction to using statistical forecasting methods to handle the prediction of critical metrics for both external and internal levels of an Oracle database.

9.1 Oracle Query Performance

Chapter 8 discussed the theoretical basis of query optimization and sound indexing principles to lead to optimal queries. Oracle 8i contains a repertoire of tools to tune a non-optimal query on the basis of its execution plan and runtime statistics. The tools can be grouped under two categories: cost-based and rule-based. Although there are some general guidelines that apply to both categories, the specific tools for the cost-based optimizer are different from those for the rule-based optimizer. We discuss the general principles in Section 9.2 and the principles specific to an optimizer in Sections 9.3 and 9.4.

9.2 Query Tuning in Oracle: General Principles

A query is designed for external users and can be formulated in multiple ways. The objective of query tuning is to select the formulation that performs the best. The performance is measured by the response time for interactive queries and by the throughput for batch jobs. As discussed in Section 8.7.1, there are 23 operations, some of which come with multiple options, that are used by Oracle's query optimizer to parse a query. These operations fall into three categories:

- row operation,
- set operation, and
- hybrid of row and set operations.

The row operations improve the response time of a job, whereas the set operations increase its throughput. As such, these two categories benefit respectively the interactive and the batch queries. The hybrid operations can benefit both and must be selected properly by the query developer. If the cost-based optimizer is used, the execution plan returned by the EXPLAIN PLAN utility assigns a cost to each version of the plan. Then the query developer needs to select the one with the least cost. If, on the other hand, the rule-based optimizer is used, no cost is assigned to the execution plan. Consequently, the query developer has to select the best plan based on his or her experience.

9.2.1 Poorly Performing Queries

A query performs poorly when its data have to be retrieved from disks via physical reads. The higher the number of physical reads, the worse the performance. On the other hand, if a query uses too much of the data block buffer cache in SGA, there may not be enough left for use by other queries running simultaneously. If the latter situation persists, the DBA should increase the value of the initialization parameter DB_BLOCK_BUFFERS. Therefore, to identify the poorly performing queries we need to follow a three-step methodology:

(a) Identify queries using high amount of physical reads;
(b) Identify queries using high amount of logical reads;
(c) Identify the user running queries that need tuning.

Figure 9.1 contains a script that displays queries, the numbers of physical and logical reads for each query, and their respective users. Figure 9.2 contains a sample output from running the script. Some of the columns from V$SQLAREA used in the script are explained below:

DISK_READS   Total number of physical reads made by a query; select a threshold of your choice;
BUFFER_GETS   Total number of logical reads made by a query; select a threshold of your choice;
SQL_TEXT   Full text of the query statement being processed.

The two ratios, Logical Reads to Executions and Physical Reads to Executions, represent respectively the rates at which a given query hits the data block buffer cache and data files on disks.

```
REM  Listing of poorly performing queries
REM  Script File:       My_Directory\Bad_Queries.sql
REM  Spool File Name:   My_Directory\Bad_Queries.lst
REM  Author:            NAME
REM  Date Created:      DATE
REM  Purpose:           Information on queries with their physical
and logical REM          reads
REM
REM
COLUMN TODAY      NEW_VALUE xTODAY NOPRINT FORMAT A1 TRUNC

TTITLE     LEFT xTODAY -
           RIGHT 'Page ' FORMAT 999 SQL.PNO -
           CENTER 'Listing of Poorly Performing Queries'    SKIP 4
BTITLE     'Script File: My_Directory\Bad_Queries.sql|
           Spool File: My_Directory\Bad_Queries.lst'
COLUMN USERNAME HEADING 'User' FORMAT A6
COLUMN DISK_READS HEADING 'Physical|Reads' FORMAT 999,999
COLUMN P_RATIO HEADING 'Physical Reads|to Executions'
COLUMN SQL_TEXT HEADING 'Query|Statement' FORMAT A80
COLUMN BUFFER_GETS HEADING 'Logical|Reads' FORMAT 999,999,999
COLUMN L_RATIO HEADING 'Logical Reads|to Executions'

BREAK ON USERNAME SKIP 1

SET LINESIZE 132
SET PAGESIZE 41
SET NEWPAGE 0

PROMPT
PROMPT
PROMPT Enter the directory for spool file:
PROMPT
ACCEPT SPOOL_DIR
PROMPT
PROMPT Enter the name of spool file:
PROMPT
```

FIGURE 9.1: Script Showing Queries with Physical and Logical Reads

```
ACCEPT SPOOL_NAME
PROMPT
PROMPT Enter threshold for physical reads
PROMPT
ACCEPT P_READS_THRESHOLD
PROMPT
PROMPT Enter threshold for logical reads
PROMPT
ACCEPT L_READS_THRESHOLD
PROMPT
SPOOL &SPOOL_DIR\&SPOOL_NAME
SELECT B.USERNAME, A.DISK_READS, A.EXECUTIONS Executions,
    ROUND (A.DISK_READS / DECODE (A.EXECUTIONS, 0, 1, A.EXECUTIONS),
4)
    P_RATIO, A.SQL_TEXT, TO_CHAR (SysDate, 'fmMonth ddth, YYYY')
TODAY
    FROM V$SQLAREA A, DBA_USERS B
    WHERE A.PARSING_USER_ID = B.USER_ID
    AND A.DISK_READS > &P_READS_THRESHOLD
    AND USERNAME != 'SYS'
    ORDER BY A.DISK_READS DESC;
SELECT B.USERNAME, A.BUFFER_GETS, A.EXECUTIONS Executions,
    ROUND (A.BUFFER_GETS/DECODE(A.EXECUTIONS, 0, 1, A.EXECUTIONS), 4)
    L_RATIO, A.SQL_TEXT, TO_CHAR (SysDate, 'fmMonth ddth, YYYY')
TODAY
    FROM V$SQLAREA A, DBA_USERS B
    WHERE A.PARSING_USER_ID = B.USER_ID
    AND A.BUFFER_GETS > &L_READS_THRESHOLD
    AND USERNAME != 'SYS'
    ORDER BY A.BUFFER_GETS DESC;
```

FIGURE 9.1 (*continued*): Script Showing Queries with Physical and Logical Reads

A sample output appears in Figure 9.2.

```
Enter the directory for spool file:
My_Directory
Enter the name of spool file:
Bad_Queries.lst
Enter threshold for physical reads
30000
```

FIGURE 9.2: Output Showing Queries with Physical and Logical Reads

```
Enter threshold for logical reads
1000000
old    6:      AND A.DISK_READS > &P_READS_THRESHOLD
new    6:      AND A.DISK_READS > 30000
May 17th, 2001       Listing of Poorly Performing Queries      Page 1
        Physical  Physical Reads   Query
User    Reads     EXECUTIONS       to Executions   Statement
----    -------   ----------       -------------   ----------------
APPL    61,900    1                61900           BEGIN :rv :=
                                                   ACCOUNT_CLEANUP (:1 ) ;
                                                   END;
        47,513    134783           .3525           UPDATE CUSTOMER SET
                                                   SHR_N = :1, CUST_ID =
                                                   :2, MKT_VAL = :3,
                                                   PMT_DATE = :4 WHERE
                                                   ACCT_ID = :5
        41,576    7041             5.9048          DELETE FROM CREDIT
                                                   WHERE CREDIT_CODE =
                                                   :b1
        Script File: My_Directory\Bad_Queries.sql
        Spool File: My_Directory\Bad_Queries.lst
old    6:      AND A.BUFFER_GETS > &L_READS_THRESHOLD
new    6:      AND A.BUFFER_GETS > 1000000
May 17th, 2001  Listing of Poorly Performing Queries   Page 1
        Logical                    Logical Reads    Query
User    Reads     EXECUTIONS       to Executions    Statement
----    -------   ----------       -------------    ----------------
APPL    93,712,442   1             93712442         BEGIN :rv :=
                                                    ACCOUNT_CLEANUP (:1 ) ;
                                                    END;
        90,655,107   7041          12875.317        DELETE FROM CUSTOMER
                                                    WHERE   CUST_ID =
                                                    :b1;
        2,963,414    7041          420.8797         DELETE FROM ACCOUNT
                                                    WHERE ACCT_ID = :b1;
        Script File: My_Directory\Bad_Queries.sql
        Spool File: My_Directory\Bad_Queries.lst
```

FIGURE 9.2 (*continued*): Output Showing Queries with Physical and Logical Reads

Once we identify queries that need tuning, we need to contact the users running these queries and ask them to take corrective action as described in Sections 9.3 and 9.4. This is often an iterative process that needs close monitoring by the DBA.

9.2.2 Frequency of COMMITs

During an update transaction involving the INSERT, UPDATE, or DELETE commands, system resources remain engaged until the data are committed. For example, in the case of UPDATEs and DELETEs the rollback segments containing the before image data are freed only after the transaction is committed or rolled back. Thus, when COMMITs are issued frequently, these system resources are released:

- Rollback segments containing before image data,
- All locks acquired on rows located within blocks that reside in the data block buffer cache, and
- Space in the redo log buffer cache.

This minimizes the resource requirements of queries and results in an improved query performance. The frequency of COMMITs can be enforced by placing either of the following two commands at the beginning of a transaction:

```
SET AUTOCOMMIT n /* Issues COMMIT after every n records */
SET AUTOCOMMIT ON /* Issues COMMIT after every record */
```

The value of "n" in the command "SET AUTOCOMMIT n" depends on the database transaction activities. I have used $n = 10,000$ for active OLTP databases with good performance. A larger value of n often ties up rollback segments too long. The command "SET AUTOCOMMIT ON" should be used only for small transactions since it degrades performance. If a system is volatile, this command helps by committing every updated record. In general, one should not use this command.

9.2.3 Full Table Scan

Full table scans are mostly time consuming operations. Since they are heavily used by batch transactions, tuning queries involving full table scans benefit the batch jobs. The data blocks read by a full table scan are always marked as least recently used and are, therefore, removed quickly from the data block buffer cache in the SGA under the LRU algorithm. This is known as *buffer aging*. As a result, if a subsequent query needs the same data, the corresponding data blocks have to be fetched again into the data block buffer cache. This phenomenon slows down the execution of queries using full table scans. The problem can be addressed by using the hint CACHE (see Section 9.3 for full details) in queries involving full table scans. This causes Oracle to retain the data blocks used by full table scans in the data block buffer cache in the SGA so that subsequent queries can access those blocks via logical reads. In addition, full table scans can be parallelized by using the hint PARALLEL (see Section 9.3).

9.2.4 Rebuilding Indices

It was noted in Section 8.6.1 that the number of levels in a B*-tree should not exceed four. As a new level is added to the tree, an extra data block has to be read to retrieve the ROWID of the desired row. Since the data blocks are not read sequentially, they each require an extra disk I/O. The level of a B*-tree increases due to three factors; the size of the table, a very narrow range of the index values, and a large number of deleted rows in the index. This situation may arise due to continuous usage and update of the table. Niemiec [3, pp. 76–78] recommends that if the number of deleted rows in an index approaches 20 to 25 % of the total rowcount of the index table, rebuilding the index is appropriate. This will reduce the number of levels and the amount of empty space that is being read during a disk I/O. The command for rebuilding an index is given below:

```
ALTER INDEX index REBUILD PARALLEL
TABLESPACE tablespace
STORAGE (storage clause);
```

The REBUILD option allows the index to be rebuilt using the existing index and without using the underlying table. There must be enough disk space to store both indices during the operation.

See Section 10.11 for rebuilding indices online.

9.2.5 Explicit Versus Implicit Cursors in PL/SQL

PL/SQL is Oracle's proprietary procedural language that augments SQL, which is non-procedural. PL/SQL provides the three programming structures, assignment, decision, and iteration, allowing a developer to write structured programs and use embedded SQL to interface with an Oracle database. One major difference between a structured program and a SQL query is that the former works on one record at a time, and the latter works with a group of records returned by the query. As a result, any database procedural language such as PL/SQL needs a mechanism to process one record at a time from a group of records returned by a SQL query. The *cursor* of a PL/SQL program provides this mechanism. The program manages a cursor by using four commands:

- DECLARE CURSOR cursor_name IS (select STATEMENT);
- OPEN CURSOR cursor_name;
- FETCH CURSOR cursor_name INTO variable(s);
- CLOSE CURSOR cursor_name;

A cursor can be *explicit* or *implicit*. An explicit cursor is created by the developer as a part of a PL/SQL program and is handled with the four commands listed above. An implicit cursor is any SQL statement issued by a user. It can involve SELECT, INSERT, UPDATE, or DELETE. It is an unnamed address where the SQL statement is processed by SQL or by the cursor handler of PL/SQL. Every time a SQL operation is requested by the user, an implicit cursor is used. It can be introduced in a PL/SQL program through a query that does not identify the cursor by name, but instead contains the SQL statement that defines the scope of the cursor. Figures 9.3 and 9.4 contain examples of an explicit and an implicit cursor respectively.

```
DECLARE CURSOR CUSTOMER_TYPE_CUR IS              -- Cursor DECLAREd
    SELECT CUST_TYPE.TYPE_DESCR FROM
    CUSTOMER CUST, CUSTOMER_TYPE CUST_TYPE
    WHERE CUST.TYPE_CODE = CUST_TYPE.TYPE_CODE;
IF NOT CUSTOMER_TYPE_CUR%ISOPEN
    THEN OPEN CUSTOMER_TYPE_CUR;                 -- Cursor OPENed
END IF;
FETCH CUSTOMER_TYPE_CUR INTO :CUST.TYPE_DESCR;   -- Cursor FETCHed
CLOSE CUSTOMER_TYPE_CUR;      -- Cursor CLOSEd
```

FIGURE 9.3: Explicit Cursor Example

```
SELECT CUST_TYPE.TYPE_DESCR INTO :CUST.TYPE_DESCR
    FROM CUSTOMER CUST, CUSTOMER_TYPE CUST_TYPE
    WHERE CUST.TYPE_CODE = CUST_TYPE.TYPE_CODE;
```

FIGURE 9.4: Implicit Cursor Example

Although functionally both explicit and implicit cursors are equivalent, the former is preferable for query tuning. An explicit cursor as in Figure 9.3 is not only easy to read, but also performs better. It issues a single call to the database for data. An implicit cursor as shown in Figure 9.4 does not mention the cursor in the code. Consequently, Oracle generates two calls to the database: first, to fetch the required data, and, second, to check for any error condition that the first call may have detected. Therefore, it is preferable to use explicit cursors in the PL/SQL programs.

9.2.6 Denormalization

We discussed denormalization in Section 3.3.1 from the viewpoint of the conceptual level of a database. When the denormalization takes place, the queries using the changed tables will be affected. For example, if computed columns such as TOTAL_SALE, REVENUE_BY_REGION, etc. are added to a table, the query formulation will change. If some lookup tables are dropped and pulled into a transaction table, join queries will be affected. All such queries must then be examined via EXPLAIN PLAN for performance and must be retuned, if necessary.

9.2.7 Integration of Views into Queries

We discussed integration of views into queries in Section 3.5 from the viewpoint of the conceptual level of a database. Here we address it from a query tuning viewpoint. If a query includes a view, the query optimizer has two options for processing the query:

- Resolve the view first and then resolve the query by integrating the result set returned by the view into the query;
- Integrate the definition of the view into the rest of the query and then execute the resulting query.

Usually, the second option performs better with respect to response time, because the view as a set operation is replaced with a row operation. In particular, if the view returns a large set or if the result of the view is subjected to additional filtering conditions, the query benefits from using the second option above. But if the view includes a grouping operation such as SUM, COUNT, DISTINCT, GROUP BY, etc., the second option is not available. In this case, the grouping operation may be transferred from the view to the body of the query, the view redefined without the grouping operation, and then the query reformulated to yield the same result. However, if such a reformulation is not possible due to the nature of the operation, then the first option is the only one available.

9.2.8 Query Tuning Checklist

We close this section with a checklist for tuning queries.

(a) Find the query that performs poorly.
(b) Run EXPLAIN PLAN to find its execution plan.
(c) Examine the plan in Step (b) to determine if the objects in the query are properly indexed and if the indices are being used in the plan. See Sections 8.5 and 8.6 for optimal indexing guidelines.
(d) If the indexing is not optimal, create new indices or alter the existing indices to improve query performance. Then repeat Steps (b) and (c) until you are satisfied that the indexing is optimal for the objects used by the query.
(e) If the query is time critical, use SQLTRACE with TKPROF (Sections 8.7.2 and 8.7.3), or AUTOTRACE (Section 8.7.4) to determine its execution time.
(f) If the execution time is acceptable, then the query is properly tuned. If the execution time is not acceptable, examine possible options discussed in Sections 9.2.1 through 9.2.6.
(g) Repeat Steps (a) through (f) for every query that needs to be tuned.

Figure 9.5 contains a flowchart describing the query tuning process graphically.

292   9. Query Tuning and Optimization Under Oracle 8i

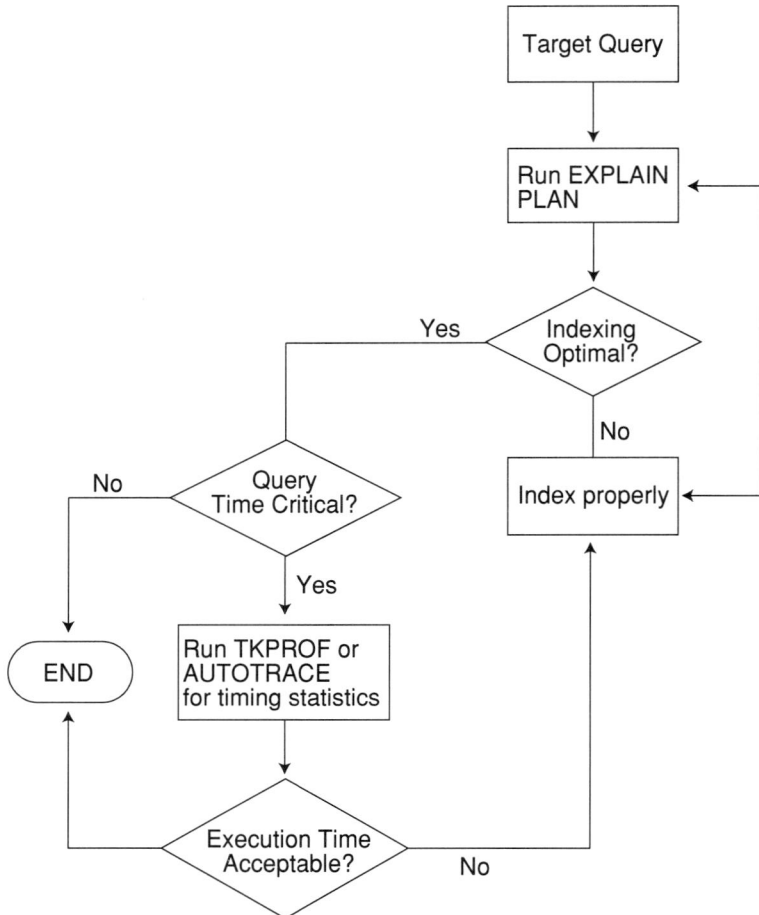

FIGURE 9.5: Flowchart of Query Tuning Procedure

9.3 Query Tuning in Oracle: Cost-based Optimizer

We saw in Section 8.3 that Oracle offers two modes of optimizers, cost-based and rule-based. The former is the default and is recommended by Oracle for query optimization. This option is enforced by setting the initialization parameter OPTIMIZER_MODE to its default value of CHOOSE. Based on information about the data that the optimizer does not know, the developer can influence the query optimization by specifying as part of the query the direction to process it. This is called a *hint*, which is included in the query statement. But a hint is only a direction for the optimizer to process the query in a particular way. It is not mandatory and the optimizer may elect to ignore the hint.

9.3.1 Categories of Hints

A variety of hints is available for query optimization. The hints belong to six distinct categories. They are described below with a brief description of each along with the categories to which they belong:

- Optimization approach and goal for a SQL statement,
- Access path for a table accessed by the statement,
- Join order for a join statement,
- Join operation in a join statement,
- Parallel execution, and
- Other.

Optimization Approaches and Goals

Hints belonging to this category cause the optimizer to use the designated approach regardless of the presence or absence of statistics, the value of the initialization parameter OPTIMIZER_MODE, and the value of the same parameter used in an ALTER SESSION command. Hints belonging to this group apply only to queries submitted directly as opposed to queries contained in PL/SQL programs. There are four hints in this category.

ALL_ROWS Uses the cost-based approach to optimize a query with a goal of maximum throughput, i.e., minimum total resource consumption.

FIRST_ROWS Uses the cost-based approach to optimize a query with a goal of minimum response time. This hint causes the optimizer to make the following choices when an index scan is available.

- Use index scan instead of a full table scan;
- Use a nested loops join over a sort–merge join whenever the associated table is the potential inner table of the nested loops; and
- Use sorting made available by an ORDER BY clause to avoid a sort operation.

CHOOSE Causes the optimizer to choose between the rule-based approach and the cost-based approach for a SQL statement based on the presence of statistics for the tables accessed by the statement. If the data dictionary contains statistics for *at least one* of these tables, the optimizer uses the cost-based approach and optimizes with the goal of maximum throughput. If the data dictionary contains no statistics for any of these tables, the optimizer uses the rule-based approach.

RULE Specifically uses rule-based optimization for a query and ignores any other hints specified for the query.

Note that this group of hints was discussed earlier in Section 8.3.

Access Path

Hints belonging to this category cause the optimizer to use the specified access path only if the access path is available based on the existence of an index or a cluster and the syntax of the query. If a hint specifies an unavailable access path, the optimizer ignores it. There are 15 hints in this category:

FULL (*table*)	Uses a full table scan of *table*.
ROWID (*table*)	Uses a table scan by ROWID of *table*.
CLUSTER (table)	Uses a cluster scan of table; applies only to clustered objects.
HASH (table)	Uses a hash scan of table; applies only to tables stored in a cluster.
HASH_AJ	Transforms a NOT IN subquery into a hash antijoin.
HASH_SJ	Transforms a correlated EXISTS subquery into a hash semijoin.
INDEX (table *index...index*)	Uses an index scan of table by index and may optionally specify one or more indices as listed below.

- If a single available index is specified, the optimizer performs a scan on the index. It does not consider a full table scan or a scan on another index on the table.
- If a list of available indices is specified, the optimizer considers the cost of a scan on each index in the list and then performs the index scan with the least cost. The optimizer may also choose to scan multiple indices from this list and merge the results, if such an access path has the lowest cost. The optimizer does not consider a full table scan or a scan on an index not listed in the hint.
- If no indices are specified, the optimizer considers the cost of a scan on each available index on the table and then performs the index scan with the least cost. The optimizer may also choose to scan multiple indices and merge the results, if such an access path has the least cost. The optimizer does not consider a full table scan.

INDEX_ASC (*table index*)	Chooses an index scan of *table* by *index* for the specified table. If the query uses an index range scan, Oracle scans the index entries in ascending order of their indexed values.
INDEX_DESC (table *index*)	Same as INDEX_ASC except that Oracle scans the index entries in descending order of their indexed values.
INDEX_COMBINE (*table index*)	If no indices are given as arguments for the hint, the optimizer uses the Boolean combination of bitmap indices that has the best cost estimate. If certain indices are given as arguments, the optimizer tries to use some Boolean combination of those particular bitmap indices.
INDEX_FFS (table *index*)	Performs a fast full index scan of *table* by *index* instead of a full table scan. It accesses only the index and not the corresponding table. So, this hint is used only when all the information needed by the query resides in the index as in an index-organized table. See Section 8.6.4 for more detail.

MERGE_AJ	Transforms a NOT IN subquery into a merge antijoin.
MERGE_SJ	Transforms a correlated EXISTS subquery into a merge semijoin.
AND_EQUAL (table index...index)	Uses an access path that merges the scans on several single-column indices index...index on table.
USE_CONCAT	Forces combined OR conditions in the WHERE clause of a query to be transformed into a compound query using the UNION ALL set operator. Normally, this transformation occurs only if the cost of the query using the concatenations is cheaper than the cost without them. It turns off inlist processing and OR-expands all disjunctions, including inlists.

Join Order

Hints belonging to this category cause the optimizer to use the join order specified in the hint. There are two hints in this category.

ORDERED	Joins tables in the order in which they appear in the FROM clause. If this hint is omitted, the optimizer chooses the order in which to join the tables. This hint benefits the optimization if the developer knows something about the number of rows selected from each table that the optimizer does not. For example, if the tables have not been ANALYZEd recently, the statistics become misleading. Here the developer can choose an inner and outer table better than the optimizer.
STAR	Forces a star query plan to be used if possible. A star plan places the largest table in the query last in the join order and joins it with a nested loops join on a concatenated index. This hint applies when there are at least three tables, the concatenated index of the large table has at least three columns, and there are no conflicting access or join method hints. The optimizer also considers different permutations of the small tables. The most precise method is to order the tables in the FROM clause in the order of the keys in the index, with the large table last.

Join Operation

Hints belonging to this category cause the optimizer to use the join operation specified in the hint. Oracle recommends that USE_NL and USE_MERGE hints be used with the ORDERED hint for optimizing performance. There are four hints in this category:

USE_NL (*table*)	Joins each specified *table* to another row source with a nested loops join using the specified table as the inner table. By default, the inner table is the one that appears immediately after the FROM clause.

USE_MERGE (*table*)	Joins each specified *table* with another row source with a sort–merge join.
USE_HASH	Joins each specified table with another row source with a hash (table) join.
DRIVING_SITE	Executes the query at a different site than that selected by the (table) optimizer using table as the driver. This hint can be used with both rule-based and cost-based optimization.

Parallel Execution

Hints belonging to this category cause the optimizer to decide how statements are parallelized or not parallelized when using parallel execution. There are six hints in this category.

PARALLEL (table integer integer)	Specifies the desired number of concurrent servers that can be used for a parallel operation on table. The first integer specifies the degree of parallelism for the given table; the second integer specifies how the table is to be split among the instances of a parallel server. It applies to INSERT, UPDATE, and DELETE statements in addition to SELECT. If any parallel restrictions are violated, the hint is ignored.
NOPARALLEL (table)	Overrides a PARALLEL specification in the table clause for table. In general, hints take precedence over table clauses.
APPEND	When used with INSERT, data ARE appended to a table without using the existing free space in the block. If INSERT is parallelized using the PARALLEL hint or clause, the append mode is used by default. The NOAPPEND hint can be used to override the append mode. The APPEND hint applies to both serial and parallel inserts.
NOAPPEND	Overrides APPEND hint.
PARALLEL_INDEX (table index integer integer)	Specifies the desired number of concurrent servers that can be used to parallelize index range scans for partitioned indices
NOPARALLEL_INDEX (table index)	Overrides a PARALLEL attribute setting on an index.

Other Hints

This is a catch-all category that includes eight hints listed below.

CACHE (*table*)	Specifies that the blocks retrieved for this *table* are placed at the most recently used end of the LRU list in the buffer cache when a full table scan is performed. This option is useful for small lookup tables. See Section 9.2.3 for additional details.

NOCACHE (table)	Specifies that the blocks retrieved for this table are placed at the least recently used end of the LRU list in the buffer cache when a full table scan is performed. This is the default behavior of blocks in the data buffer cache in SGA.
MERGE (table)	Works in conjunction with the setting of the initialization parameter COMPLEX_VIEW_MERGING. When this parameter is set to TRUE, complex views or subqueries are merged for processing. When set to its default value FALSE, this parameter causes complex views or subqueries to be evaluated before the referencing query is processed. In this case, the MERGE hint causes a view to be merged on a per-query basis.
NO_MERGE (table)	Prevents the merging of mergeable views, thereby allowing the developer to have more control over the processing of views. When the initialization parameter COMPLEX_VIEW_ MERGING is set to TRUE, the NO_MERGE hint within the view prevents a designated query from being merged.
PUSH_JOIN_PRED (*table*)	Works in conjunction with the setting of the initialization parameter PUSH_JOIN_PREDICATE. When this parameter is set to TRUE, the optimizer can evaluate, on a cost basis, , whether pushing individual join predicates into the view will benefit the query. This can enable more efficient access paths and join methods, such as transforming hash joins into nested loop joins, and full table scans to index scans. If the initialization parameter PUSH_JOIN_PREDICATE is set to FALSE, the PUSH_JOIN_ PRED hint forces the pushing of a join predicate into the view.
NO_PUSH_JOIN _PRED (table)	Prevents the pushing of a join predicate into the view when the initialization parameter PUSH_JOIN_PREDICATE is set to TRUE.
PUSH_SUBQ	Causes nonmerged subqueries to be evaluated at the earliest possible place in the execution plan. Normally, such subqueries are executed as the last step in the execution plan. But if the subquery is relatively inexpensive and reduces the number of rows significantly, performance improves if the subquery is evaluated earlier. The hint has no effect if the subquery is applied to a remote table or one that is joined using a merge join.
STAR_TRANS- FORMATION	Causes the optimizer to use the best plan in which the transformation has been used. Without the hint, the optimizer makes a cost-based decision to use the best plan generated without the transformation, instead of the best plan for the transformed query. Even if the hint is given, there is no guarantee that the transformation will occur. The optimizer will generate the subqueries if it seems reasonable to do so. If no subqueries are

generated, there is no transformed query, and the best plan for the untransformed query is used regardless of the hint.

9.3.2 Hint Syntax and Examples

A hint is included in a query by using any one of the following two syntax.

```
SELECT    /*+ hint_name        */    column(s)
FROM table(s) WHERE condition(s);

SELECT    --+ hint_name        column(s)
FROM table(s) WHERE condition(s);
```

The slash asterisk (/*) or a pair of hyphens (--) can be used to signify a hint. The plus sign (+) must *immediately* follow * or -- without an intervening space. If /* is used, the hint must be closed with */. No such closing punctuation is needed for the -- version. The *hint_name* can be any one of the hints described above. If multiple hints are used, each must be separated from the next with a space. But multiple hints are not recommended since the query optimizer may get confused by them and may even ignore some or all of them. If an alias is used for a table, the alias must be used in the hint instead of the table name. When using a hint it is advisable to run the hinted query with the EXPLAIN PLAN or AUTOTRACE (see Sections 8.7.1 and 8.7.4) option to ensure that the hint has been properly formulated and has indeed been used by the optimizer.

We now give below several examples of queries using some of the hints listed above.

```
FULL:           SELECT /*+ FULL (A) */ Name, Balance
                FROM CUST_ACCOUNT A WHERE Cust_ID = 1846;

INDEX_DESC:     SELECT /*+ INDEX_DESC (ORDER PK_ORDER) */
                Order_ID, Cust_Name, Order_Amount FROM ORDER;

ORDERED:        SELECT --+ ORDERED ORDER.Order_ID, Line_Num,
                Item_Name FROM ORDER, LINE_DETAIL WHERE
                ORDER.Order_ID = LINE_DETAIL. Order_ID
                AND Order_Amount > 10000;

DRIVING_SITE:   SELECT  /*+ DRIVING_SITE (A) */
                * FROM ORDER, LINE_DETAIL@CHICAGO A WHERE
                 ORDER.Order_ID = A.Order_ID;

PUSH_SUBQ:      SELECT   --+ PUSH_SUBQ  ORDER.Order_ID, Line_Num,
                Item_Name FROM ORDER, LINE_DETAIL WHERE
                ORDER.Order_ID = LINE_DETAIL. Order_ID AND
                Name IN
                (SELECT Name FROM ORDER WHERE
                Order_Amount > 10000);
```

9.4 Query Tuning in Oracle: Rule-based Optimizer

The rule-based optimizer can be enforced in three possible ways at two different levels.

Instance Level: There are two possible options:

- Set the initialization parameter OPTIMIZER_MODE to RULE.
- Accept the default value CHOOSE of the initialization parameter OPTIMIZER_MODE, but do not ANALYZE any table. Then CHOOSE reverts to RULE.

Query Level: Follow the two steps below:

- Set the initialization parameter OPTIMIZER_MODE to CHOOSE.
- Use the hint RULE in the body of the query.

The rule-based optimizer uses the ranking of different operations used in processing a query and selects the execution plan with the lowest rank. There are 15 operations, each having an assigned rank. Table access by ROWID is fastest with rank 1 and full table scan is slowest with rank 15. Figure 8.1 lists all 15 operations with their respective ranks.

The rule-based and cost-based optimizers use different criteria for query optimization. The former uses the rank of operations, and the latter uses the cost of execution with maximum throughput as the default goal. As a result, the same query can have two different execution plans under the two different optimizers. FIGURE 9.6 shows an example of this situation. The query has been run with AUTOTRACE ON TIMING ON EXPLAIN options.

```
select Cust_Name, Account_Name, Status from Customer A, Account B
    where A.Cust_ID = B.Cust_ID
    and rownum < 21
    order by Cust_Name, Account_Name;
OUTPUT from Cost-based Optimizer:
20 rows selected.
  real: 1922
Execution Plan
----------------------------------------------------------
  0       SELECT STATEMENT Optimizer=CHOOSE (Cost=88 Card=2382
          Bytes=5
          07366)
  1   0     SORT (ORDER BY) (Cost=88 Card=2382 Bytes=507366)
  2   1       COUNT (STOPKEY)
  3   2         HASH JOIN (Cost=12 Card=2382 Bytes=507366)
  4   3           TABLE ACCESS (FULL) OF 'CUSTOMER' (Cost=1 Card=9
                  52 Bytes=65688)
  5   3           TABLE ACCESS (FULL) OF 'ACCOUNT' (Cost=4 Card=
                  2430 Bytes=349920)
```

FIGURE 9.6: Execution Plans Under Cost- and Rule-based Optimizers

```
Statistics
----------------------------------------------------------
          0        recursive calls
          6        db block gets
         11        consistent gets
          0        physical reads
          0        redo size
       2587        bytes sent via SQL*Net to client
        908        bytes received via SQL*Net from client
          5        SQL*Net roundtrips to/from client
          2        sorts (memory)
          0        sorts (disk)
         20        rows processed

select  /*+ RULE */  Cust_Name, Account_Name, Status
    from Customer A, Account B
    where A.Cust_ID = B.Cust_ID
    and rownum < 21
    order by Cust_name, Account_Name;

OUTPUT from Rule-based Optimizer:

20 rows selected.
   real: 1903

Execution Plan
----------------------------------------------------------
      0          SELECT STATEMENT Optimizer=HINT: RULE
      1    0       SORT (ORDER BY)
      2    1         COUNT (STOPKEY)
      3    2           NESTED LOOPS
      4    3             TABLE ACCESS (FULL) OF 'ACCOUNT'
      5    3             TABLE ACCESS (BY INDEX ROWID) OF 'CUSTOMER'
      6    5               INDEX (UNIQUE SCAN) OF 'PK_CUSTOMER' (UNIQUE)

Statistics
----------------------------------------------------------
          0        recursive calls
          3        db block gets
         43        consistent gets
          2        physical reads
          0        redo size
       2588        bytes sent via SQL*Net to client
        929        bytes received via SQL*Net from client
          5        SQL*Net roundtrips to/from client
          2        sorts (memory)
          0        sorts (disk)
         20        rows processed
```

FIGURE 9.6 (*continued*): Execution Plans Under Cost- and Rule-based Optimizers

Note that the two plans are not identical. The cost-based optimizer uses a hash join of CUSTOMER and ACCOUNT, and the rule-based optimizer uses a nested loops join of those two tables. Also, the runtime statistics are close but not identical. The real time is slightly different, 1,922 (= 1.922 seconds) for cost versus 1,903 (= 1.903 seconds) for rule.

9.5 Tuning of Join Queries

A join query involves n (≥ 2) tables linked via common columns. Its complexity increases as n increases and the predicates of the qualifying conditions become progressively difficult with a variety of relational and logical operators. A join is a binary operation. Hence when n (>2) tables are joined, the optimizer uses $n - 1$ join operations as follows:

- The first and the second tables are joined producing result set 1.
- Result set i is then joined with table $i + 2$ yielding result set $i + 1$, where $i = 1, 2, \ldots, n-2$.
- Result set $n - 1$ is the final result from the n-table join query.

The performance of a join depends on the following four main factors.

Selection of the First Table in the Join, Which Is Called the Driving Ttable or the Driver

This table may undergo a full table scan. Hence its size is crucial for the performance. Under *rule-based optimization* the driver is selected as follows.

- If one table is indexed and the other is not, then the driving table is the one without an index.
- If both tables are indexed, then the table having the index with a lower rank becomes the driving table.
- If both tables are indexed and the indices have the same rank, then the table on the right becomes the driving table.

Under *cost-based optimization* with an ORDERED hint the driver is the first table listed under the FROM clause. If no hint is used, the cost-based optimizer selects the driver according to the available statistics on the table and the associated cost of the query.

Access Path Selected by the Query Optimizer to Resolve the Individual Joins

For an n-table join, there are $n(n - 1)/2$ possible permutations of the table set leading to as many possible access paths. When n is large, say, $n > 6$, the number of permutations exceeds 15.

Level of Indexing and Their Selectivity for the Component Tables

Lack of indexing or poor indexing can have significant effects.

Use of Hints to Suggest a Specific Access Path

Here the experience of the developer is very critical for using the correct hint. The cost-based optimizer offers six hints under two categories to handle the join queries (see Section 9.3.1):

```
Join Order        ORDERED, STAR
Join Operation:   USE_NL, USE_MERGE, USE_HASH,
DRIVING_SITE
```

Both rule and cost-based optimizers provide four types of join, namely, nested loops, sort–merge, hash, and cluster. Since the driver table of a join usually undergoes a full table scan, always try to make the smallest table in the join be the driver. Also, ensure that all the columns used in the join conditions are indexed. The scanning time of a table under full table scan depends on the initialization parameter DB_FILE_MULTIBLOCK_READ_COUNT. It determines how many blocks will be read from the disk in a sequential read operation as in a full table scan. Setting it to an appropriate value benefits the join operation.

Let us now assume that the join handles the following query Q.

```
SELECT A.column_1, A.column_2, B.column_3
FROM table_1 A, table_2 B
WHERE
A.column_1 = B.column_1;
```

For the sake of discussion we assume that A is the driver.

Nested Loops

The optimizer

1. Reads the first row of A;
2. Retrieves the value of A.column_1;
3. Finds all rows in B for which B.column_1 matches A.column_1;
4. If no match is found, reads the next row in A;
5. If a match is found, sends A.column_1, A.column_2, B.column_3 from the matching rows in A and B to the result set;
6. Reads the next row of A;
7. Repeats Steps (2) through (6) until all rows in A are read and processed via a full table scan of A.

Figure 9.7 contains a flowchart of a nested loops join.

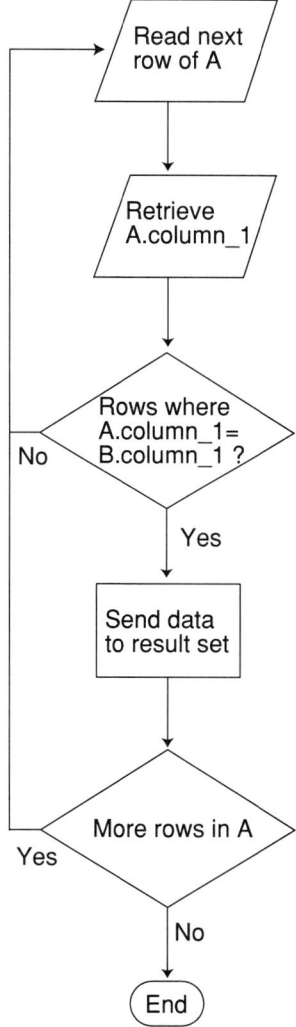

FIGURE 9.7: Nested Loops Join

The nested loops join works with any join condition, not necessarily just an equijoin, i.e., where the join condition is an equality. It is very efficient when A is a small table related to B in a 1:N relationship and B.column_1 is uniquely indexed or is highly selective in a nonunique index. Otherwise, this join can cause a performance drag.

Sort–Merge Join

The optimizer

1. Sorts all the rows of A by A.column_1 to SORTED_A, say;
2. Sorts all the rows of B by B.column_1 to SORTED_B, say;
3. If SORTED_A.column_1 does not match SORTED_B.column_1, continues to read the next row(s) of SORTED_A until SORTED_A.column_1 matches SORTED_B.column_1;
4. When a match is found between SORTED_A.column_1 and SORTED_B.column_1, continues to read all succeeding rows of SORTED_B for which SORTED_A.column_1 matches SORTED_B.column_1;
5. Sends A.column_1, A.column_2, B.column_3 from the matching rows found above to the result set;
6. Reads next row of SORTED_A;
7. Repeats steps 3 through 6 until all rows in SORTED_A are read and processed via a full table scan of SORTED_A.

Figure 9.8 contains a flowchart of a sort–merge join.

The sort–merge join is effective when the index on the joined column is not highly selective or when the join condition returns more than 10% of the rows in the driver. But this join works only with equijoins. Its performance depends on the initialization parameter SORT_AREA_SIZE, because the tables involved in the join are sorted first. This parameter specifies the maximum amount, in bytes, of the Program Global Area (PGA) in memory that can be used for a sort. The PGA is an area in memory that is used by a single Oracle user process. The memory in the PGA is not shareable. If multithreaded servers (MTS) are enabled, the sort area is allocated from the SGA. After the completion of the sort but before the fetching of the sorted rows to the user area, the memory is released down to the size specified by the initialization parameter SORT_AREA_RETAINED_SIZE. After the last row is fetched, all of the memory is released back to the PGA, not to the operating system.

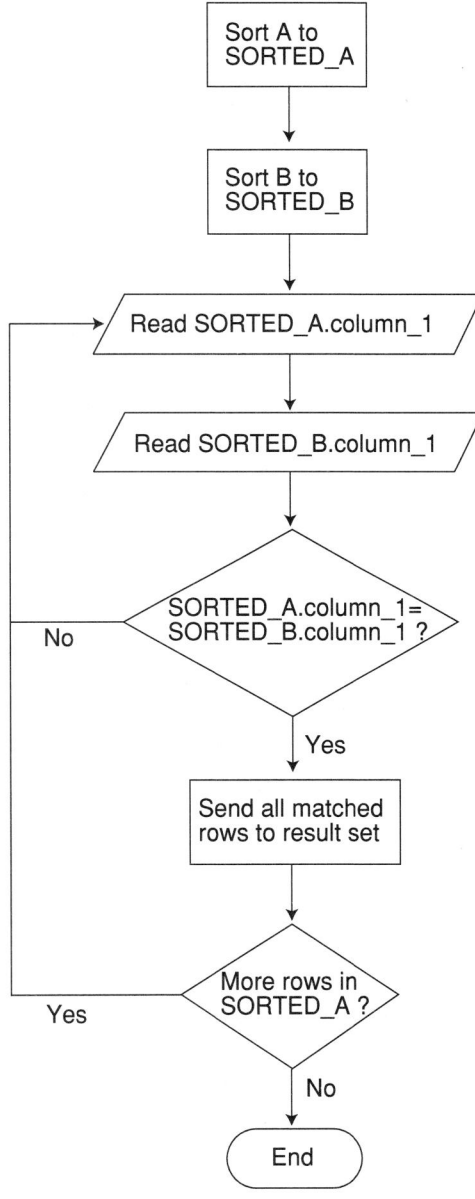

FIGURE 9.8: Sort–Merge Join

If an entire sort cannot be performed in the amount of space in memory allocated by this parameter, then the sorting space is split between the memory and a temporary segment in the temporary tablespace. The sort is performed in parts by doing as much sort as possible in memory at a time, then storing the result in a temporary segment, and continuing this process until the sort is complete. If this parameter is set too low, excessive disk I/O will be needed to transfer data between the temporary segment on disk and the sort area in the PGA in memory for performing sorts. If this parameter is set too high, the operating system may run out of physical memory and start swapping. The sizing of the parameter SORT_AREA_SIZE is somewhat tricky. The default value, which is operating system dependent, usually suffices for most OLTP applications. But the value may need to be adjusted to 2 MB or more for decision support systems, batch jobs, or large CREATE INDEX operations. Multiple allocations of the sorting space never exist. Hence there is only one memory area of SORT_AREA_SIZE for each user process at any time. This parameter can be set dynamically at the session level via the ALTER SESSION command.

If necessary, the DBA and the developers can jointly determine the largest sorting space needed for an application and compute an appropriate value for this parameter. Remember that the SGA should not exceed 40% of the total physical memory and the sorting space size determined by the value of SORT_AREA_SIZE must fit within the SGA. See Section 6.7 for further details about tuning memory.

Hash Join

The hash join involves the concept of a hash table and hashing. A *hash table* data structure is an array of some fixed size containing the values of a variable and their respective addresses. *Hashing* means searching the hash table for a specific value and, if found, accessing the full record via its address stored in the table. Section E15 in Appendix E discusses the hashing concepts in detail.

The optimizer

1. Reads all the values of B.column_1;
2. Builds in memory a hash table of all these values;
3. Reads the first row of A
4. Retrieves the value of A.column_1;
5. Finds from the hash table the addresses of all rows in B for which B.column_1 matches A.column_1;
6. If no match is found, reads the next row in A;
7. If a match is found, sends A.column_1, A.column_2, B.column_3 from the matching rows in A and B to the result set;
8. Reads the next row of A;
9. Repeats Steps (4) through (8) until all rows in A are read and processed via a full table scan of A.

As such, a hash join is similar to a nested loops join except that the optimizer first builds a hash table of the values of B.column_1. Figure 9.9 contains the flowchart of a hash join.

A hash join is effective when table B does not have a good and highly selective index on B.column_1. But it needs sufficient memory space so as to fit the hash table of

B.column_1 entirely in memory. The performance of hash joins depends on three initialization parameters: HASH_AREA_SIZE, HASH_JOIN_ENABLED, and HASH_MULTIBLOCK_IO_COUNT. All of them can be modified dynamically via the ALTER SESSION command. HASH_AREA_SIZE determines the amount of memory, in bytes, that is made available for building a hash table. Its default value is 2 * SORT_AREA_SIZE. If HASH_AREA_SIZE is too small, a part of a large hash table may have to be stored in a temporary segment in a temporary tablespace causing performance degradation. If it is too big, it may use up the physical memory. HASH_JOIN_ENABLED specifies whether the optimizer should consider hash join as an option. Its default value is TRUE, which allows the cost-based optimizer to use it. If it is set to FALSE, hash join is not available as a join method. HASH_MULTIBLOCK_IO_COUNT specifies how many sequential blocks a hash join reads and writes in one I/O. Its default value is 1. If the multithreaded server mode is activated, this parameter is set at 1 regardless of the value assigned to it. The maximum value of this parameter depends on the operating system, but is always less than the maximum I/O size allowed by the operating system. As such, its role for hash joins is similar to the role of DB_FILE_MULTIBLOCK_READ_COUNT for sort–merge joins. Oracle provides formulas for estimating the value of HASH_MULTIBLOCK_IO_COUNT.

Cluster Join

A cluster join is a special case of a nested loops join. If both of the tables A and B are members of a cluster and if the join is an equijoin between the cluster keys A.column_1 and B.column_1, then the optimizer can use a cluster join. This join is very efficient since both A and B reside in the same data blocks. But since the clusters have certain restrictions (see Section 8.6.5), cluster joins are not that popular.

308   9. Query Tuning and Optimization Under Oracle 8i

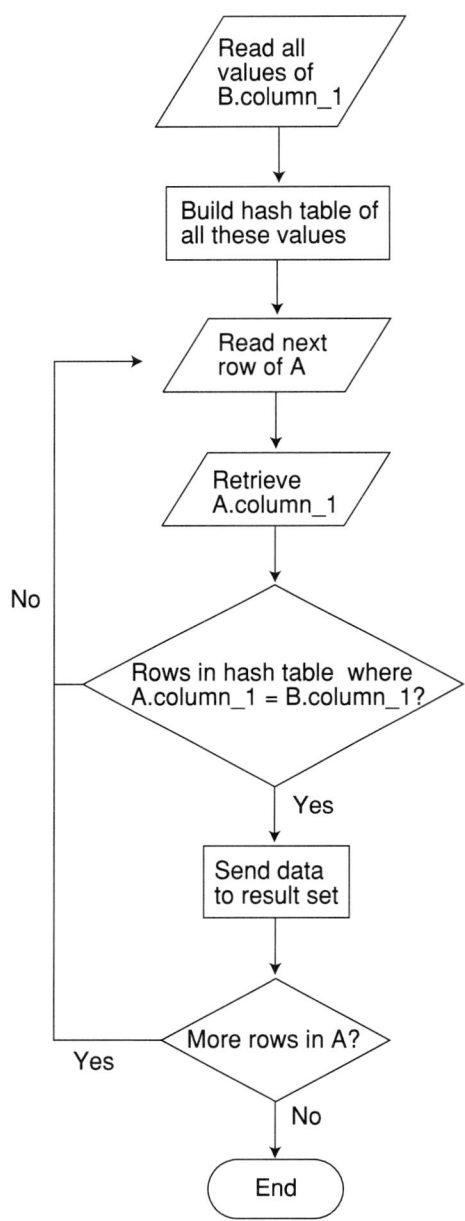

FIGURE 9.9: Hash Join

An Actual Case Study

This involved a join query joining two tables CUSTOMER and ACCOUNT from two different databases. ACCOUNT was a small table with 10,000+ rows residing at a local database. CUSTOMER was a large table with 5+ million rows residing on a remote database. The query Q is given below.

```
Q:   select
        a.Cust_Acct_Code, a.Cust_Credit_Code, a.Balance_Due_Date,
        a.Balance_Amt from V_CUSTOMER@CHICAGO a, ACCOUNT b
     where
        a.Cust_Acct_Code = b.Cust_Acct_Code and
        a.Cust_Credit_Code = b.Cust_Credit_Code;
```

Here V_CUSTOMER is a view based on the table CUSTOMER at the remote database and runs as follows.

```
SELECT * FROM CUSTOMER;
```

When Q was run as formulated above, it took several hours to fetch the result. We then reformulated Q as Q_ with the view replaced by its underlying table as follows:

```
Q':  select
        a.Cust_Acct_Code, a.Cust_Credit_Code, a.Balance_Due_Date,
        a.Balance_Amt from CUSTOMER@CHICAGO a, ACCOUNT b
     where
        a.Cust_Acct_Code = b.Cust_Acct_Code and
        a.Cust_Credit_Code = b.Cust_Credit_Code;
```

Q' took only 8 seconds to run. We ran Q and Q_ with TIMING and AUTOTRACE ON to find their execution plans. Since Q included a view that executed as a set operation done on a very large table at the remote site, the execution time was understandably very high. The optimizer used a HASH JOIN for processing Q. But Q_ was executed with a NESTED LOOPS join with the local table ACCOUNT as the driver. As a result, Q_ took only 8 seconds to run. The IT policy necessitated that the query be run with a view instead of a table. We experimented with two hints, ORDERED and USE_NL, to see if the local table could be used as the driver. The first hint ORDERED did not work since one of the access operations was REMOTE. We then used the hint USE_NL along with ORDERED to force a nested loops join using the local table as the driver. It worked and we were able to avoid a hash join. The final formulation of Q took 8 seconds to run and is given below.

```
Q:   select /*+ ORDERED USE_NL(a) */
        a.Cust_Acct_Code, a.Cust_Credit_Code, a.Balance_Due_Date,
        a.Balance_Amt from ACCOUNT b, V_CUSTOMER@CHICAGO a
     where
        a.Cust_Credit_Code = b.Cust_Credit_Code and
        a.Cust_Acct_Code = b.Cust_Acct_Code;
```

9.6 Statistical Forecasting for Tracking Performance

Forecasting is a systematic process to predict the future by an analysis of the past data. The forecaster studies the past through historical data to determine any trend that may exist and then uses that trend to forecast future values of the data. The underlying assumption in forecasting is that the past trend will continue into the future. Some basic characteristics of forecasting are:

- Forecasts are accurate within a margin of error;
- A forecast gives the predicted value with a range indicating the estimated error involved in the forecast; and
- Forecasts become less and less accurate as they move farther and farther into the future.

Chapters 4 through 9 provide a variety of techniques to track the performance of an Oracle database at the internal and the external levels. When a DBA collects data periodically, say, once a week every Tuesday at 7 A.M., a high volume of historical data gradually builds up. They can be used to make predictions about the future such as usage of free space in tablespaces, depletion of available storage in disk files, error trend by type and number, volume of throughput for batch jobs, response times of queries under specific data volumes, etc. The tools of forecasting become very handy in addressing these situations.

Mathematical Tools for Forecasting

Regression analysis or *trend analysis* is the tool used for forecasting the value of a variable that depends on another variable. For example, based on a set of past data values, we can predict the run time of a query depending on the size of the table involved, or the growth rate of extents used by a segment over time, etc. In the first case, the size of a table in bytes, say, is called the independent variable and the runtime of the query is called the dependent variable since it changes as the size of the table changes. Similarly, in the second case, time is the independent variable and the number of extents of the segment is the dependent variable. Mathematically, this relationship is expressed by the equation $y = f(x)$, where x is the independent variable and y the dependent variable. Given a value for x, the equation determines a unique value of y and is said to represent the trend of y as x changes. The nature of the trend depends on the form of the function $f(x)$. The methodology of forecasting runs as follows.

Let us suppose that we have a set of n past data value pairs (x_1, y_1), (x_2, y_2), ..., (x_n, y_n), where x_i is the independent variable and y_i is the dependent variable, for $i = 1, 2, \ldots, n$. For specific forms of the regression function $f(x)$, formulas are available to compute values of $f(x)$ from the data set (x_i, y_i), where $i = 1, 2, \ldots, n$. We discuss below three forms of the trend function $f(x)$.

(a) *$f(x)$ is a linear function* i.e., $f(x) = a + bx$, where a and b are constants. The trend is called *linear*.

(b) <u>*f(x) is a quadratic function*</u>, i.e., $f(x) = a + bx + cx^2$, where a, b, and c are constants. The trend is called *quadratic*.

(c) *f(x) is an asymptotic growth curve*, for example,

$f(x) = k / (1 + 10^{a+bx})$ logistic curve,
$\log(f(x)) = \log k + (\log a) b^x$ Gompertz curve,
$f(x) = k + ab^x$ modified exponential curve.

The linear trend mostly suffices for trend prediction in performance tracking. Spreadsheets such as EXCEL provide the capability of predicting linear trends based on given (x, y) values.

Example of Linear Trend

Assume that the number of extents allocated to a table over a 10-week period of data collection are as follows.

Week	Number of Extents
1	3
2	10
3	15
4	19
5	35
6	38
7	44
8	61
9	100
10	105

Here we have 10 pairs (x, y), where x-values represent weeks and y-values represent number of extents. Figure 9.10 shows the result from an EXCEL spreadsheet giving the forecast value of y for $x = 11$, i.e., for the eleventh week.

```
       x                                          y
       1                                          3
       2                                         10
       3                                         15
       4                                         19
       5                                         35
       6                                         38
       7                                         44
       8                                         61
       9                                        100
      10                                        105
Forecast value of y for x = 11         104.8666667
```

FIGURE 9.10: Spreadsheet with Forecast Value

For $x = 11$, we get $y = 104.867$. This means that for week 11, the number of extents will remain the same at 105.

Key Words

access, indexed
access, sequential
asymptotic growth curve
AUTOTRACE
B*-tree index
bitmap index
buffer aging
cluster
cluster join
concatenated index
driver
driving table
equijoin
exact match
execute phase
EXPLAIN PLAN
explicit cursor
fetch phase
filtering condition
hash cluster
hash function
hash join
hashing
hint
implicit cursor

index cluster
linear trend
MTS
multithreaded server
nested format
nested loops join
optimization, cost-based
optimization, rule-based
optimizer mode
optimizer, cost-based
optimizer, rule-based
parse phase
PGA
PLAN_TABLE
Program Global Area
quadratic trend
query optimizer
range scan
row operation
runtime statistics
set operation
sort–merge join
SQLTRACE
temporary tablespace

References and Further Reading

1. E. Aronoff et al.—*Advanced Oracle Tuning and Administration*, Oracle Press, 1997.
2. S. S. Mittra—*Decision Support Systems: Tools and Techniques*, John Wiley & Sons, Inc., 1986.
3. R. J. Niemiec—*Oracle Performance Tuning*, Oracle Press, 1999.

Niemiec [3] offers an extensive treatment of using hints in queries under cost-based optimization in Chapter 7 and the tuning of join queries in Chapter 8. In addition, Niemiec [3, p. 398–412] discusses some statistical techniques for predicting query execution times based on table sizes. The mathematical tools for forecasting can be found in Mittra [2, Chapter 5].

We now describe some special features of two of the above references. Aronoff et al. [1, Chapter 11] contain a set of 10 SQL tuning tips that are helpful for the developers. Niemiec's work [3] is encyclopedic in nature, offering a large variety of tuning guidelines with examples for DBAs and developers. He provides two PL/SQL programs [3], pp. 669–671] to identify offensive queries. The DBAs and developers will find them quite handy for tuning their applications.

Exercises

Theoretical exercises are of little value for this chapter since the best practice comes from optimizing the performance of queries in your own development environment before they migrate to the test or production databases. Therefore, no exercises are provided in this chapter.

10
Special Features of Oracle 8i and a Glimpse into Oracle 9i

Outline

10.1 Scope of the Chapter
10.2 Evolution of Oracle Through Versions 8 and 8i
10.3 Partitioning of Tables and Indices
10.4 Materialized Views
10.5 Defragmentation via Local Tablespace Management
10.6 LOB Data Type Versus LONG Data Type
10.7 Multiple Buffer Pools in the SGA
10.8 Query Execution Plan Stability via Stored Outlines
10.9 Index Enhancements
10.10 Query Rewrite for Materialized Views
10.11 Online Index Creation, Rebuild, and Defragmentation
10.12 ANALYZE Versus DBMS_STATS
10.13 Optimization of Top_N Queries
10.14 Glimpse into Oracle 9i
Key Words
References and Further Reading

Overview of the Chapter

The chapter covers several special features of Oracle 8i pertaining to performance tuning and optimization that were not covered in the earlier chapters. The topics are grouped under three categories: conceptual, internal, and external levels of a database. An overview of some of the features of Oracle 9i is also included.

10.1 Scope of the Chapter

Chapters 3 through 9 covered the performance tuning techniques for the conceptual, internal, and external levels of an Oracle 8i database. Many of those features were already available under Oracle8. Oracle Corporation released Oracle 8i with the primary focus on Web-enabled applications. As we know, the "i" in 8i stands for Internet. But Oracle 8i offers a variety of new features that are useful for any Oracle database irrespective of a Web component. Most of these features that are directly applicable to performance tuning and optimization have been discussed in Chapters 3 through 9. In this chapter we discuss a few additional capabilities of Oracle 8i not covered earlier.

We first provide a brief history of the evolution of Oracle RDBMS through the various incarnations of versions 8 and 8i. We then list a set of performance tuning topics that are available from Oracle 8i and group them under three separate categories, conceptual level, internal level, and external level. The rest of the chapter involves a discussion of these topics with examples and SQL scripts, as needed. The chapter closes with a section on an overview of some selected features of Oracle 9i.

10.2 Evolution of Oracle Through Versions 8 and 8i

Oracle8 covered through version 8.0.5. Oracle 8i started with version 8.1, the initial release, which went up to version 8.1.5. It was then upgraded to version 8.1.6 as Release 2, and then to version 8.1.7 as Release 3. Currently, Release 3 is the latest version of Oracle 8i. Oracle Corporation labels version 8.1.7 as the "terminal release of the Oracle 8i," stating that this version "is an extremely stable and thoroughly tested release and will be supported longer than the initial versions of Oracle 8i" (see [6]). The main features of Oracle 8i are listed below (see [7] for details).

Version 8.1.5

- Content Management for Internet,
- InterMedia, Spatial, Time Series, and Visual Image Retrieval,
- Java Support,
- Date Wrehousing and Very Large Data Bases (VLDB),
- Partitioning Enhancements,
- System Management,
- Oracle Parallel Server,
- Distributed Systems, and
- Networking Features and Advanced Security,

Version 8.1.6

- Improvements of Existing Oracle Features,
- Java Enhancements,

- Enhanced Support of Internet Computing,
- Enhancements of Networking Features and Advanced Security,
- Advanced New Functionality, and
- New Features of Object Relational Databases.

Version 8.1.7

- Additional Java Enhancements,
- Oracle Internet File Systems (iFS),
- Enhanced XML Support,
- Oracle Integration Server,
- Additional Enhancements of Security, InterMedia, and Spatial Features, and
- Improved Management of Standby Databases.

We list below a set of topics embodying some special features of Oracle 8i that pertain to the performance tuning and optimization issues of an Oracle database. As indicated in Section 10.1, they are grouped under three separate categories: conceptual, internal, and external levels.

Conceptual Level

(a) Partitioning of Tables and Indices, and
(b) Materialized Views.

Internal Level

(a) Defragmentation via Local Tablespace Management,
(b) LOB Data Type Versus LONG Data Type, and
(c) Multiple Buffer Pools in the SGA.

External Level

(a) Query Execution Plan Stability via Stored Outlines,
(b) Index Enhancements,
(c) Query Rewrite for Materialized Views,
(d) Online Index Creation, Rebuild, and Defragmentation,
(e) ANALYZE Versus DBMS_STATS, and
(f) Optimization of Top_N Queries.

Sections 10.3 through 10.13 cover these topics.

10.3 Partitioning of Tables and Indices

In Section 3.6 we discussed the partitioning of tables and indices as a tool for tuning the conceptual level. When a very large nonpartitioned table, say one with multimillion rows, is partitioned, its management for performance becomes easier to handle and data retrieval from the table becomes quicker. A partitioned table allows the DBA to manage each partition of the table independently of the other partitions. Thus the availability of data on a large partitioned table is higher than that on a comparably sized nonpartitioned table. Also, if a disk failure damages only one partition of an object, the remaining partitions can still be used while the DBA repairs the damaged partition.

Partitioning was first introduced in Oracle8 and only range partitioning (see Section 3.6.2) was available. Oracle 8i made several enhancements to partitioning that are summarized below:

(a) Hash Partitioning,
(b) Composite Partitioning,
(c) Data Dictionary Views for Partitioned Objects, and
(d) ANALYZE Command for Partitioned Objects.

Sections 10.3.1 to 10.3.4 describe these four features.

10.3.1 Hash Partitioning

When a table is partitioned by range, it is generally assumed that the DBA knows how much data will fit into each partition. However, this information may not always be available when the DBA wants to create a partition. Hash partitions alleviate this problem. They allow Oracle 8i to manage the dynamic distribution of data into the partitions. Figure 10.1 contains the SQL command for creating a table using hash partitions.

```
SQL>
Wrote file afiedt.buf
    1    create table cust_order
    2    (order_id number (4),
    3    order_description varchar2 (50),
    4    order_date date,
    5    customer_id number (4),
    6    invoice_id number (4))
    7    storage (initial 2M next 1M pctincrease 0)
    8    partition by hash (order_id) partitions 8
    9*   store in (perf_data1, perf_data2, perf_data3, perf_data4)
SQL> /
Table created.
```

FIGURE 10.1: Hash Partitioning of a Table with STORE IN Clause

In creating a table with hash partitioning one must comply with the following requirements.

- Indicate that the hash method of partitioning is used.
- Specify the partition key column, the number of partitions for the table, and the tablespaces in which the hash partitions will be stored. This last item is indicated with the STORE IN clause. It ensures that the data of the partitioned table are spread across multiple disks to reduce I/O contention. For example, the table CUST_ORDER created in Figure 10.1 has eight partitions spread over four tablespaces, PERF_DATA1, PERF_DATA2, PERF_DATA3, PERF_DATA4, all of which are dynamically managed by Oracle 8i. Unlike range partitioning, it is not known which row belongs to which partition.
- Ensure that the number of partitions defined with the partitions clause is 2^n, where n is a positive integer.
- Ensure that the number of tablespaces specified in the STORE IN clause is a factor of the number of partitions. Thus, the number of tablespaces must be 2^m, where m ($\leq n$) is a positive integer.

Alternatively, one can omit the number of partitions and the STORE IN clause and explicitly define the partition names and their respective tablespaces. Figure 10.2 contains an example of this option.

```
SQL>
Wrote file afiedt.buf
    1      create table new_order
    2      (order_id number (4),
    3      order_description varchar2 (50),
    4      order_date date,
    5      customer_id number (4),
    6      invoice_id number (4))
    7      storage (initial 2M next 1M pctincrease 0)
    8      partition by hash (order_id)
    9      (partition p1 tablespace perf_data1,
   10      partition p2 tablespace perf_data2,
   11      partition p3 tablespace perf_data3,
   12      partition p4 tablespace perf_data4,
   13      partition p5 tablespace perf_data1,
   14      partition p6 tablespace perf_data2,
   15      partition p7 tablespace perf_data3,
   16*     partition p8 tablespace perf_data4)
SQL> /
Table created.
```

FIGURE 10.2: Hash Partitioning of a Table Without STORE IN Clause

10.3.2 Composite Partitioning

Hash partitioning as described above can be combined with range partitioning to create subpartitions by hash on the partitions by range. Although slightly more complex than hash or range partitioning, the composite partitioning increases the overall potential for parallelism. Figure 10.3 contains an example of composite partitioning. The table COMP_ORDER is partitioned by range on the ORDER_DATE column and then subpartitioned by hashing on the ORDER_ID column.

```
SQL>
Wrote file afiedt.buf
  1    create table comp_order
  2    (order_id number (4),
  3    order_description varchar2 (50),
  4    order_date date,
  5    customer_id number (4),
  6    invoice_id number (4))
  7    partition by range (order_date)
  8    subpartition by hash (order_id) subpartitions 8
  9    store in (perf_data1, perf_data2, perf_data3, perf_data4)
 10    (partition co1 values less than (TO_DATE('10-NOV-2000',
       'DD-MON-YYYY')),
 11    partition co2 values less than (TO_DATE('10-JAN-2001', 'DD-
       MON-YYYY')),
 12    partition co3 values less than (TO_DATE('10-MAR-2001', 'DD-
       MON-YYYY')),
 13*   partition co4 values less than (MAXVALUE))
SQL> /
Table created.
```

FIGURE 10.3: Composite Partitioning of a Table

10.3.3 Data Dictionary Views for Partitioned Objects

The Oracle 8i data dictionary contains several new views that provide information about the partitioned tables and indices. They provide additional information beyond what was already available from the Oracle8 data dictionary views such as DBA_TABLES, DBA_INDEXES, DBA_TAB_COLUMNS, and DBA_OBJECTS. The new views along with their descriptions are listed below.

DBA_PART_TABLES	Partition basis of tables including the partition keys
DBA_PART_INDEXES	Partition basis of indices including the partition keys
DBA_PART_KEY_COLUMNS	Partition keys used for all tables and indices
DBA_TAB_PARTITIONS	Partitions of all tables in the database
DBA_IND_PARTITIONS	Partitions of all indices in the database

DBA_PART_COL_STATISTICS	Statistics for cost-based optimization for the partition columns for all tables and indices
DBA_PART_HISTOGRAMS	Distribution of data in partitions for all partitions in the database
DBA_TAB_SUBPARTITIONS	Description of subpartitions for each composite partitioned table
DBA_SUBPART_KEY_COLUMNS	Key columns on subpartitioned composite tables and their local indices

Figures 10.4A and 10.4B contain two sample listings from DBA_PART_TABLES and DBA_TAB_PARTITIONS respectively involving the three partitioned tables created above.

```
SQL> COL TABLE_NAME FORMAT A11
SQL> COL PARTITION_COUNT HEADING "P_CNT" FORMAT 999
SQL> COL DEF_SUBPARTITION_COUNT HEADING "SP_CNT" FORMAT 99
SQL> COL PARTITIONING_KEY_COUNT HEADING "PKEY_CNT" FORMAT 99
SQL> COL SUBPARTITIONING_KEY_COUNT HEADING "SPKEY_CNT" FORMAT 99
SQL>
Wrote file afiedt.buf
  1  select TABLE_NAME, PARTITIONING_TYPE, SUBPARTITIONING_TYPE, PARTITION_COUNT,
  2  DEF_SUBPARTITION_COUNT, PARTITIONING_KEY_COUNT, SUBPARTITIONING_KEY_COUNT
  3  from dba_part_tables
  4  where owner = 'SEKHAR'
  5* ORDER BY 1
SQL> /

TABLE_NAME   PARTITI   SUBPART  P_CNT    SP_CNT   PKEY_CNT  SPKEY_CNT
----------   -------   -------  -----    ------   --------  ---------
COMP_ORDER   RANGE     HASH     4        8        1         1
CUST_ORDER   HASH      NONE     8        0        1         0
NEW_ORDER    HASH      NONE     8        0        1         0
```

FIGURE 10.4A: Listing from DBA_PART_TABLES

```
SQL> COL PARTITION_NAME HEADING "P_NAME" FORMAT A10
SQL>
Wrote file afiedt.buf
  1  select TABLE_NAME, composite, PARTITION_NAME, SUBPARTITION_COUNT, PARTITION_POSITION,
  2  TABLESPACE_NAME from dba_tab_partitions
  3  where table_owner = 'SEKHAR'
  4* ORDER BY 1
SQL> /
```

FIGURE 10.4B: Listing from DBA_TAB_PARTITIONS

TABLE_NAME	COM	P_NAME	SUBPARTITION_COUNT PARTITION_POSITION	TABLESPACE_NAME
COMP_ORDER	YES	CO1	8	1 USERDATA
COMP_ORDER	YES	CO2	8	2 USERDATA
COMP_ORDER	YES	CO3	8	3 USERDATA
COMP_ORDER	YES	CO4	8	4 USERDATA
CUST_ORDER	NO	SYS_P9	0	1 PERF_DATA1
CUST_ORDER	NO	SYS_P10	0	2 PERF_DATA2
CUST_ORDER	NO	SYS_P11	0	3 PERF_DATA3
CUST_ORDER	NO	SYS_P12	0	4 PERF_DATA4
CUST_ORDER	NO	SYS_P13	0	5 PERF_DATA1
CUST_ORDER	NO	SYS_P14	0	6 PERF_DATA2
CUST_ORDER	NO	SYS_P15	0	7 PERF_DATA3
CUST_ORDER	NO	SYS_P16	0	8 PERF_DATA4
NEW_ORDER	NO	P1	0	1 PERF_DATA1
NEW_ORDER	NO	P2	0	2 PERF_DATA2
NEW_ORDER	NO	P3	0	3 PERF_DATA3
NEW_ORDER	NO	P4	0	4 PERF_DATA4
NEW_ORDER	NO	P5	0	5 PERF_DATA1
NEW_ORDER	NO	P6	0	6 PERF_DATA2
NEW_ORDER	NO	P7	0	7 PERF_DATA3
NEW_ORDER	NO	P8	0	8 PERF_DATA4

20 rows selected.

FIGURE 10.4B (*continued*): Listing from DBA_TAB_PARTITIONS

10.3.4 ANALYZE Command for Partitioned Objects

The ANALYZE command provides these capabilities for a table or an index:
- COMPUTE or ESTIMATE STATISTICS,
- LIST CHAINED ROWS, and
- VALIDATE STRUCTURE.

All of them are available for partitioned tables and partitioned indices as well. In addition, the DBA can perform the tasks.

- Collect statistics for individual table partition or index partition;
- Validate the structure of individual table partition or index partition; and
- Perform the list chained rows feature on individual table partition or index partition.

If a specific partition is not specified, ANALYZE performs its analysis on all the partitions of a table or an index. This is the default functionality of the command. The relevant commands are listed below:

```
ANALYZE INDEX CUST_ORDER_idx
COMPUTE STATISTICS FOR ALL COLUMNS;

ANALYZE TABLE COMP_ORDER PARTITION (co2)
LIST CHAINED ROWS;

ANALYZE TABLE NEW_ORDER PARTITION (p6)
VALIDATE STRUCTURE INTO INVALID_ROWS;
```

10.4 Materialized Views

In Section 3.7 we briefly discussed replication as a tool for performance tuning of the conceptual level. The two types of replication described there were basic or snapshot replication and advanced or multimaster replication. Oracle 8i introduced the materialized views to replace the snapshot replications. A *materialized view* stores the view definition along with the data resulting from executing the definition. As such, it is different from a regular view which stores only the view definition. Thus, a materialized view is both a named database object representing a SQL statement (like a regular view) and a stored object containing the data from the execution of that SQL statement at the time the view was created. Materialized views make queries that contain summary data or that use large or multiple join operations run faster, because the query is processed only once and the data are stored for later reuse. Figure 10.5 contains the SQL commands to create a materialized view and its associated log.

```
SQL>
Wrote file afiedt.buf
  1     create materialized view links_view
  2     tablespace perf_data
  3     storage (initial 100K next 50K pctincrease 0)
  4     refresh complete
  5     start with SYSDATE
  6     next SYSDATE + 7
  7     as
  8*    select * from links_copy
SQL> /

Snapshot created.

SQL> create materialized view log on links_copy
  2     tablespace perf_data
  3     storage (initial 100K next 50K pctincrease 0)
  4     with ROWID;
Snapshot log created.
```

FIGURE 10.5: Creation of a Materialized View

Oracle 8i provides four options for the REFRESH clause for updating the data of a materialized view by executing the view definition. Each option repopulates the view by using the contents of the base table(s), which may have changed. The options are listed below.

REFRESH COMPLETE	Replace the data completely. This option is used when the materialized view is first created as in Figure 10.5.
REFRESH FAST	Replace only the data that have changed since the last refresh. Oracle 8i uses the materialized view logs or ROWID ranges to determine which rows have changed.
REFRESH FORCE	Use REFRESH FAST, if possible; otherwise, use REFRESH COMPLETE.
REFRESH NEVER	Never refresh the view data.

If the data changes account for less than 25% of the rows in the base table, the REFRESH FAST option is generally better than the REFRESH COMPLETE option.

In addition to the REFRESH options, the DBA must specify the intervals at which the data will be refreshed. This can be done in two ways: automatic and manual. The *automatic refreshing* occurs either when the underlying base table data changes are committed, or at regular intervals specified by the DBA. *Manual refreshing* is done manually by the DBA by executing the view definition.

See Section 10.10 for the QUERY REWRITE option of materialized views related to query optimization.

10.5 Defragmentation via Local Tablespace Management

It was noted in Section 5.8 that the free space in a tablespace gets fragmented as more and more segments are created and continue to grow in the tablespace. An effective way to manage the space is to size properly the extents of individual segments in a tablespace and then track their growth and fragmentation via data dictionary views such as DBA_SEGMENTS, DBA_EXTENTS, and DBA_FREE_SPACE. Oracle 8i introduced the locally managed tablespaces to alleviate this problem by letting Oracle internally manage the space. The goal is to reduce or eliminate the free space fragmentation.

The space in a tablespace under Oracle 8i can be managed in two ways: through data dictionary views and through local management. The former is the default. The traditional techniques of space management using data dictionary views such as DBA_SEGMENTS, DBA_EXTENTS, and DBA_FREE_SPACE were discussed in Chapter 5. There we saw that the DBA has to track the fragmentation of free space via scripts and take necessary steps to defragment the tablespaces, as needed. A locally managed tablespace, on the other hand, is managed internally by Oracle. It maintains a bitmap in each of its datafiles to keep track of the free or used status of the data blocks in that datafile. Each bit in the bitmap corresponds to a block or a group of data blocks. When an extent is allocated or freed for reuse, Oracle changes the bitmap values to show the new status of the blocks belonging to that extent. These changes do not generate any rollback data, because they do not update any tables in the data dictionary. Local management also automatically tracks adjacent free space so that the DBA does not need to coalesce the adjacent free extents for tablespace defragmentation.

10.5.1 Methods of Local Management

Oracle provides two methods for allocating extents in a locally managed tablespace:
- Autoallocate, and
- Uniform.

Autoallocate Method

Under the *autoallocate* method, which is the default, one can specify the size of the initial extent and then Oracle determines the optimal sizes of the subsequent extents from a selection of 64 KB, 1 MB, 8 MB, and 64 MB. When a segment is created in such a tablespace, Oracle assigns 64 KB to the next extents until the segment reaches 1 MB in size. At that point, the subsequent extents are sized at 1 MB each. When the segment reaches a size of 64 MB, the subsequent extent sizes are increased to 8 MB each. Finally, if the table reaches a size of 1 GB, the subsequent extent size is increased for the last time to 64 MB.

Uniform Method

Under the *uniform* method, one can specify an extent size when the tablespace is created or use the default extent size, which is 1 MB. All the extents of the tablespace and of the segments created in that tablespace will be of that uniform size. No segment can be created in such a tablespace with a different extent size. See Section 10.5.2 below for the impact of the STORAGE clause at the segment level.

Figure 10.6 shows two locally managed tablespaces created with the uniform and the autoallocate options.

```
SVRMGR>         create tablespace loc_manage_data
  2>    datafile
  3>    '/home/oracle/oradata/invoice/group03/loc_manage_data01.dbf'
  4>    size 100M
  5>    EXTENT MANAGEMENT LOCAL UNIFORM SIZE 8M;
Statement processed.
SVRMGR> commit;
Statement processed.
SVRMGR>         create tablespace loc_manage_data_auto
  2>    datafile
  3>
  '/home/oracle/oradata/invoice/group03/loc_manage_data_auto01.dbf'
  4>    size 100M
  5>    EXTENT MANAGEMENT LOCAL AUTOALLOCATE;
Statement processed.
```

FIGURE 10.6: Creation of Locally Managed Tablespaces

The data dictionary view DBA_TABLESPACES contains two columns, EXTENT_MANAGEMENT and ALLOCATION_TYPE, to display the management mechanism of tablespaces. The column EXTENT_MANAGEMENT tells us whether the extents of a tablespace are managed via data dictionary ("DICTIONARY") or locally ("LOCAL"). The column ALLOCATION_TYPE tells us whether the extent sizes are uniform ("UNIFORM") or determined automatically ("SYSTEM") by Oracle. Figure 10.7 shows a fragment of a listing of the tablespaces with these two columns.

```
SQL> col ALLOCATION_TYPE heading "Allocation|Type" format a12
SQL> col TABLESPACE_NAME format a21
SQL> col INITIAL_EXTENT format 999,999,999
SQL> col NEXT_EXTENT format 999,999,999
SQL> col EXTENT_MANAGEMENT heading "Extent|Management" format a12
SQL>
```

FIGURE 10.7: Listing of Locally Managed and Dictionary Managed Tablespaces

```
Wrote file afiedt.buf
  1 select TABLESPACE_NAME, INITIAL_EXTENT, NEXT_EXTENT,
  2 EXTENT_MANAGEMENT, ALLOCATION_TYPE
  3 from dba_tablespaces
  4* order by 1
SQL>/

                                              Extent       Allocation
TABLESPACE_NAME       INITIAL_EXTENT NEXT_EXTENT Management Type
--------------------- -------------- ----------- ---------- ----------
USERDATA                    102,400     102,400  DICTIONARY USER
USERINDEX                   102,400     102,400  DICTIONARY USER
INDEXDATA                   102,400     102,400  DICTIONARY USER
LOC_MANAGE_DATA           8,388,608   8,388,608  LOCAL      UNIFORM
LOC_MANAGE_DATA_AUTO         65,536              LOCAL      SYSTEM
PERF_DATA                    20,480      20,480  DICTIONARY USER
```

FIGURE 10.7 (*continued*): Listing of Locally Managed and Dictionary Managed Tablespaces

10.5.2 STORAGE Clause in Locally Managed Tablespaces

The extent sizes of a locally managed tablespace are managed at the tablespace level and not at the segment level. The STORAGE clause of a segment in such a tablespace has practically no impact on the space allocated for that segment. More precisely, the situation is as follows.

If the STORAGE clause of a segment specifies the parameters (INITIAL, NEXT, MINEXTENTS), then Oracle computes the total space determined by these three parameters and allocates that amount to the INITIAL EXTENT of the segment. But the NEXT EXTENT is determined differently, as noted below.

(a) If the extent management is uniform, then NEXT EXTENT equals the value specified by the UNIFORM SIZE clause of the tablespace.
(b) If the extent management is autoallocate, then NEXT EXTENT and, therefore, PCTINCREASE are ignored.

Figure 10.8 contains a session transcript showing the following steps.

- Two tables, TEST01 and TEST02, are created in two locally managed tablespaces, one uniform (LOC_MANAGE_DATA) and the other autoallocate (LOC_MANAGE_DATA_AUTO) respectively.
- The two tables have an identical STORAGE clause.
- Oracle creates an INITIAL EXTENT of both TEST01 and TEST02 that equals the total space computed from the INITIAL, NEXT, and MINEXTENTS values of the STORAGE clause.
- Oracle assigns the value of 8 MB to the NEXT EXTENT of TEST01, but does not assign any value to the NEXT EXTENT of TEST02.

```
SESSION TRANSCRIPT
SQL> edit
Wrote file afiedt.buf

  1  CREATE TABLE TEST01
  2  (ABC NUMBER,
  3  DEF CHAR (7),
  4  TEST_DATE DATE)
  5  TABLESPACE LOC_MANAGE_DATA
  6* STORAGE (INITIAL 40K   NEXT 2M MINEXTENTS 6   PCTINCREASE 0)
SQL> /

Table created.

SQL> edit
Wrote file afiedt.buf

  1  CREATE TABLE TEST02
  2  (GHI NUMBER,
  3  JKL CHAR (7),
  4  NEW_DATE DATE)
  5  TABLESPACE LOC_MANAGE_DATA_AUTO
  6* STORAGE (INITIAL 40K   NEXT 2M MINEXTENTS 6   PCTINCREASE 0)
SQL> /

Table created.

SQL> COL TABLESPACE_NAME FORMAT A22
SQL> COL SEGMENT_NAME HEADING "SEGMENT|NAME" FORMAT A20
SQL> COL INITIAL_EXTENT HEADING "INITIAL|EXTENT"
SQL> COL NEXT_EXTENT HEADING "NEXT|EXTENT"
SQL> COL PCT_INCREASE HEADING "%INCR." FORMAT 99
SQL> select tablespace_name, segment_name, initial_extent, next_extent,
  2  pct_increase from dba_segments where owner = 'SEKHAR' AND TABLESPACE_NAME IN
  3  ('LOC_MANAGE_DATA', 'LOC_MANAGE_DATA_AUTO')
  4  ORDER BY 1, 2;

TABLESPACE_             SEGMENT_      INITIAL_    NEXT_        %INCR.
NAME                    NAME          EXTENT      EXTENT
------------------      -------       --------    --------     -------
LOC_MANAGE_DATA         TEST01        10526720    83886080          0
LOC_MANAGE_DATA_AUTO    TEST02        10526720
```

FIGURE 10.8: Impact of STORAGE Clause of Segments

Note that INITIAL_EXTENT (= 10526720) for TEST01 and TEST02 is computed as follows.

INITIAL = 40 K = 40,960 bytes, NEXT = 2 M = 2,097,152, MINEXTENTS = 6.

10.5 Defragmentation via Local Tablespace Management

Hence total storage = INITIAL + (MINEXTENTS−1) x NEXT
= 40,960 + 5 x 2,097,152
= 10,526,720.

However, the extent counts of TEST01 and TEST02 are different, as shown in Figure 10.9.

```
SQL> edit
Wrote file afiedt.buf
  1   SELECT TABLESPACE_NAME, SEGMENT_NAME, EXTENTS FROM dba_segments
  2   where owner = 'SEKHAR' AND TABLESPACE_NAME IN
  3   ('LOC_MANAGE_DATA', 'LOC_MANAGE_DATA_AUTO')
  4*  ORDER BY 1, 2
SQL> /
TABLESPACE_NAME               SEGMENT_NAME              EXTENTS
-------------------           --------------            --------
LOC_MANAGE_DATA               TEST01                       2
LOC_MANAGE_DATA_AUTO          TEST02                      11
```

FIGURE 10.9: Extent Counts of TEST01 and TEST02

For TEST01, the total space of 10,526,720 bytes (= 10.4 MB) is provided by 2 extents of size 8 MB each, which is the UNIFORM SIZE value for its holding tablespace. For TEST02, the total space of 10,526,720 bytes (= 10.4 MB) is provided by 11 extents of size 1 MB each. Since the segment TEST02 needs over 1 MB of space, the extent size becomes 1 MB each (see the paragraph, Autoallocate Method, in Section 10.5.1 above). Therefore, 10.4 MB is provided by 11 extents.

From this point on, as we allocate additional extents to TEST01 and TEST02, the extent count increases accordingly. Figure 10.10 shows the result of adding four extents to each table. Note that the column EXTENTS has increased by 4 for each table beyond their earlier values in Figure 10.9.

```
SQL> ALTER TABLE TEST01 ALLOCATE EXTENT;
Table altered.
SQL> /
Table altered.
SQL> /
Table altered.
```

FIGURE 10.10: Impact of Allocating Additional Extents

```
SQL> /
Table altered.
SQL> ALTER TABLE TEST02 ALLOCATE EXTENT;
Table altered.
SQL> /
Table altered.
SQL> /
Table altered.
SQL> /
Table altered.
SQL>  SELECT TABLESPACE_NAME, SEGMENT_NAME, EXTENTS FROM dba_segments
  2   where owner = 'SEKHAR' AND TABLESPACE_NAME IN
  3   ('LOC_MANAGE_DATA', 'LOC_MANAGE_DATA_AUTO')
  4   ORDER BY 1, 2;

TABLESPACE_NAME              SEGMENT_NAME         EXTENTS
-------------------          --------------       --------
LOC_MANAGE_DATA              TEST01                     6
LOC_MANAGE_DATA_AUTO         TEST02                    15
```

FIGURE 10.10 (*continued*): Impact of Allocating Additional Extents

10.5.3 DBMS_SPACE_ADMIN Package

This built-in package consists of a set of PL/SQL procedures and functions that help the DBA to maintain the integrity of the locally managed tablespaces. For example, using the procedure SEGMENT_VERIFY the DBA can verify the consistency of the extent map of the segment, i.e., that the bitmaps properly reflect the way in which the extents are allocated and that no two segments claim the same extent. There are two procedures in this package called TABLESPACE_MIGRATE_TO_LOCAL and TABLESPACE_MIGRATE_FROM_LOCAL that take a tablespace name as an argument and allow respectively the migration of a dictionary managed tablespace to a locally managed tablespace and vice versa. Figures 10.11 and 10.12 contain the commands showing the execution of these two procedures and subsequent verification that the tablespaces indeed migrated as desired. Note that the segment PERF_DATA is migrated from dictionary managed to locally managed. Also note that the segment PERF_DATA is migrated to dictionary managed from locally managed autoallocate.

10.5 Defragmentation via Local Tablespace Management

```
SQL> select tablespace_name, extent_management, allocation_type
  2  from dba_tablespaces
  3  order by 1;
TABLESPACE_NAME              EXTENT_MAN           ALLOCATIO
----------------             ----------           ---------
LOC_MANAGE_DATA              LOCAL                UNIFORM
LOC_MANAGE_DATA_AUTO         LOCAL                SYSTEM
PERF_DATA                    DICTIONARY           USER
SQL> begin
  2  DBMS_SPACE_ADMIN.TABLESPACE_MIGRATE_TO_LOCAL ('PERF_DATA');
  3  end;
  4  /
PL/SQL procedure successfully completed.
SQL> select tablespace_name, extent_management, allocation_type
  2  from dba_tablespaces
  3  order by 1;
TABLESPACE_NAME              EXTENT_MAN           ALLOCATIO
----------------             ----------           ---------
LOC_MANAGE_DATA              LOCAL                UNIFORM
LOC_MANAGE_DATA_AUTO         LOCAL                SYSTEM
PERF_DATA                    LOCAL                USER
```

FIGURE 10.11: Use of TABLESPACE_MIGRATE_TO_LOCAL

```
SQL> begin
  2  DBMS_SPACE_ADMIN.TABLESPACE_MIGRATE_FROM_LOCAL ('PERF_DATA');
  3  end;
  5  /
PL/SQL procedure successfully completed.
SQL> select tablespace_name, extent_management, allocation_type
  2  from dba_tablespaces
  3  order by 1;
TABLESPACE_NAME              EXTENT_MAN           ALLOCATIO
----------------             ----------           ---------
LOC_MANAGE_DATA              LOCAL                UNIFORM
LOC_MANAGE_DATA_AUTO         LOCAL                SYSTEM
PERF_DATA                    DICTIONARY           USER
```

FIGURE 10.12: Use of TABLESPACE_MIGRATE_FROM_LOCAL

The DBMS_SPACE_ADMIN package requires that the initialization parameter COMPATIBLE be set to 8.1.6 or higher. Starting with Oracle 8.1.6, when a tablespace is migrated from dictionary management to local management, the bitmap header block that stores the free and used extent information of the datafile underlying a locally managed tablespace is stored in the location previously occupied by the start of the first free extent in the datafile.

For further details about the DBMS_SPACE_ADMIN package run the following SQL commands,

```
SET HEADING OFF
SET NEWPAGE 0
SELECT TEXT FROM DBA_SOURCE
    WHERE NAME = 'DBMS_SPACE_ADMIN'
    AND TYPE = 'PACKAGE';
```

10.5.4 Impact on Defragmentation

When a segment is created in a locally managed tablespace under the UNIFORM SIZE option, it does not get fragmented at all. Any isolated free extent in the tablespace matches the uniform extent size and, therefore, gets reused when more space is needed. In addition, the locally managed tablespaces offer several advantages over the dictionary managed tablespaces, as listed below.

- Local management of extents automatically tracks adjacent free space, thereby eliminating the need to coalesce adjacent free extents manually.
- A dictionary managed tablespace may incur recursive space management operations. This happens when consuming or releasing space in an extent in the tablespace results in another operation that consumes or releases space in a rollback segment or a data dictionary table. This scenario does not apply to locally managed tablespaces, because they do not use rollback segments and do not update data dictionary tables. Changes to the bitmaps representing the free or used status of extents in a locally managed tablespace are not propagated to the data dictionary tables.
- Since a locally managed tablespace does not record free space information in the data dictionary tables, it reduces contention on these tables.

10.6 LOB Data Type Versus LONG Data Type

A column defined as a LONG data type can take values up to 2 GB. As a result, a table having a LONG column often leads to row chaining. See Section 2.3.1 for an example and Section 5.9 for a discussion of row chaining and row migration in tables. The LOB data type, by contrast, avoids this problem. Oracle recommends that we migrate from LONG columns to LOB columns in a table. We list below the main differences between a LONG column and a LOB column.

1. A table can have only one LONG column, but multiple LOB columns, because the underlying storage mechanisms of the two data types are different. The data of a LONG column are stored inline. On the other hand, if the data of a LOB column ex-

ceed 4,000 bytes, then only the pointer to the data for the LOB column is stored inline with the table data. In other words, no LOB column will ever require more than 4,000 bytes of space inline with other table data. As a result, SELECT statements on the LONG column return the actual data, whereas the same statements on a LOB column return only the pointer to the data if the data value exceeds 4,000 bytes.
2. LOB columns can assume values up to 4 GB, whereas LONG columns can be up to 2 GB. Thus, LOB columns are larger than LONG columns.
3. LOB data can be accessed piecewise, whereas LONG access is sequential. Only the entire value of a LONG column can be obtained unless one defines a procedure to retrieve the LONG column a chunk at a time. Even then, the procedure must read through the contents of the LONG column sequentially. On the other hand, parts of the LOB column can be obtained at random. This offers more flexibility in handling LOB columns compared to LONG columns.
4. A LOB column can be included in partitioned tables as long as the LOB column is not the partition key. LONG columns do not support that feature.
5. LOB columns can be distributed and replicated, but LONG columns cannot.

Oracle recommends that LONG columns be migrated to LOB columns since the LONG data type will not be supported in the future. The function TO_LOB can be used to convert a LONG data type column to a LOB data type column as part of an operation INSERT AS SELECT.

10.7 Multiple Buffer Pools in the SGA

In Chapter 6 we discussed the System Global Area (SGA) and its three major components:

- Data block buffers,
- Redo log buffer, and
- Shared SQL pool.

In particular, Section 6.3 dealt with the data block buffer (DBB) cache in detail. It was noted there that all data blocks requested by user processes are stored for use in the single DBB cache irrespective of the time span during which the cached objects were needed. The space in the DBB cache is managed by the least recently used (LRU) algorithm to determine which buffers to recycle when user processes need to allocate space and the DBB cache is full. This is done by the mechanism of paging and swapping (see Section 6.7 in the paragraph "Tune the Memory at the Operating System Level").

Under Oracle 8i the DBB cache has been restructured so as to address the needs of different user processes accessing different database objects with different time demands on retaining the objects in the cache. This is accomplished by dividing the DBB cache into three separate buffer pools:

- Keep pool,
- Recycle pool, AND

- Default pool.

The underlying principle in assigning objects to a specific buffer pool is to reduce or eliminate physical reads.

10.7.1 Three Types of Buffer Pools

The *keep buffer pool* is used for storing data blocks of database objects that are needed to stay in the pool for a long time. This pool is never flushed and consists of buffers that need to be pinned in memory indefinitely. Objects in the keep pool are not removed from memory, meaning that references to objects in the keep pool will not result in a physical read. This pool should be used only for small tables that are frequently accessed and need to stay in memory at all times.

The *recycle buffer pool* is used for storing data blocks of database objects that need not stay in the pool for any length of time. These might include data blocks read in as part of full table scans or blocks read in order to update a row, followed quickly by a commit. The recycle pool is instantly flushed in order to reduce contention and waits in the pool by leaving the LRU list empty at all times. This pool should be used for large and less important tables that are usually accessed only once in a long time.

The space left in the DBB cache after the keep and the recycle pools get their own allocated space is assigned to the *default pool*. The DBB cache is the set-theoretic union of the three pools. If the keep and the recycle pools are not set up for an instance via initialization parameters, the default pool spans the entire DBB cache.

10.7.2 Initialization Parameters for Buffer Pools

The overall DBB cache storage and LRU latch allocation are set at instance startup time by two initialization parameters, DB_BLOCK_BUFFERS and DB_BLOCK_LRU_LATCHES. As noted in Section 6.10, a *latch* is an Oracle internal resource that governs access to other resources. A user process must acquire a latch before it can access any structure in the SGA such as the DBB cache. The LRU latch controls access to the DBB cache by server processes acting on behalf of user processes.

The number of latches determined by the initialization parameter DB_BLOCK_LRU_LATCHES for an instance must be proportional to the number of buffers in the DBB cache determined by the initialization parameter DB_BLOCK_BUFFERS. The ratio

```
DB_BLOCK_BUFFERS / DB_BLOCK_LRU_LATCHES
```

must be ≥ 50. Otherwise, the instance will not start.

In order to set up the keep and recycle buffer pools we need the following two initialization parameters:

```
BUFFER_POOL_KEEP = (BUFFERS:n₁, LRU_LATCHES: n₂)
BUFFER_POOL_RECYCLE = (BUFFERS: n₃, LRU_LATCHES: n₄),
```

where $n_1, \ldots, n_4$ are integers satisfying the two conditions:

$$n_1 / n_2 \geq 50; \text{ and } n_3 / n_4 \geq 50$$

We note that each parameter has two components, BUFFERS and LRU_LATCHES, which determine respectively the size of the pool and the number of latches dedicated to managing access to the pool. The space left in the DBB cache after configuring the keep and recycle pools is allocated to the default pool. Thus, if DBB cache size = n, then THE default pool size = $n - (n_1 + n_3)$.

10.7.3 Assigning Tables to Buffer Pools

A table is assigned to the keep or the recycle buffer pool via the command

```
ALTER TABLE table STORAGE (BUFFER_POOL KEEP);
```

or

```
ALTER TABLE table STORAGE (BUFFER_POOL RECYCLE);
```

Since each partition of a partitioned table can have its own STORAGE clause, each partition can be assigned to different buffer pools, if necessary. A table that is not explicitly assigned to the keep or the recycle buffer pool is assigned to the default buffer pool. Figure 10.13 shows that the table CUST_ORDER is assigned to the keep pool.

```
SQL> select table_name, initial_extent, next_extent, pct_increase
from dba_tables where
  2   table_name = 'CUST_ORDER';

TABLE_NAME         INITIAL_EXTENT    NEXT_EXTENT    PCT_INCREASE
----------         --------------    -----------    ------------
CUST_ORDER                  20480        1937408               0

SQL>  ALTER TABLE CUST_ORDER
  2   STORAGE (BUFFER_POOL KEEP);
Table altered.
SQL> col buffer_pool format a15
SQL> edit
Wrote file afiedt.buf
  1  select table_name, initial_extent, next_extent, pct_increase,
buffer_pool
  2* from dba_tables where table_name = 'CUST_ORDER'
SQL> /
TABLE_NAME   INITIAL_EXTENT   NEXT_EXTENT   PCT_INCREASE  BUFFER_POOL
----------   --------------   -----------   ------------  -----------
CUST_ORDER            20480       1937408              0         KEEP
```

FIGURE 10.13: Table Assignment to KEEP Pool

Note that when a table is assigned to a particular buffer pool, its data are not actually loaded into the pool. The data remain as usual in the tablespace in which the table has been created. But when the data of the table need to be fetched into the DBB cache for processing, they are stored in the buffer pool to which the table has been assigned.

10.7.4 Computation of Sizes of Buffer Pools

The keep pool is sized with three somewhat conflicting goals.
- It is large enough to store all database objects that should be kept in memory.
- It is adequate for accommodating the growth of the objects kept there.
- It is small enough in the context of the overall DBB cache so that infrequently used objects are not kept there while more frequently used objects are removed from the default and recycle pools unnecessarily.

The recycle pool is sized to ensure that objects are not removed from that pool so quickly that Oracle has to perform extra I/O to load, unload, and reload data to memory.

Sizing the Keep Pool

Use the following three-step process to size the keep pool.
- Identify the tables that will be assigned to the keep pool.
- For each identified table, run the following command.

   ```
   ANALYZE TABLE table COMPUTE STATISTICS;
   ```
- Run the following query.

   ```
   select sum (BLOCKS) BUFFERS,
   decode(floor(sum(BLOCKS)/50), 0, 1, floor(sum(BLOCKS)/50))
   LRU_LATCHES from dba_tables
   where table_name in (table_list);
   ```

Here *table_list* consists of the names of the tables to be placed in the keep pool.

The keep pool will reduce the physical reads associated with the use of the tables in the pool, but will not eliminate it entirely. The tables will need to be read into the pool initially before they are kept there. If a table grows in size, it may no longer fit in the keep pool. In this case, the table will begin to lose blocks out of the pool. Also, it is important that the access method is not a full table scan.

Figure 10.14 contains the query that returns the sizes of the buffers and the lru_ latches for the table INVOICE targeted for the keep pool. Note that BUFFERS / LRU_ LATCHS = 699/13 = 53.8 > 50, as required.

```
SQL> select sum (blocks) Buffers,
  2    round (decode (floor (sum (blocks) / 50), 0, 1, floor (sum
(blocks) / 50)), 0)
  3    lru_latches
  4    from dba_tables where table_name = 'INVOICE';
BUFFERS              LRU_LATCHES
-------              -----------
    699                   13
```

FIGURE 10.14: Sizing the KEEP Pool

Sizing the Recycle Pool

The recycle pool is sized through stepwise refinement using the tools SQLTRACE and TKPROF (see Sections 8.7.2 and 8.7.3), as described below.

1. Assign tables to the recycle pool as needed by the application.
2. Enable SQLTRACE at the session level.
3. Run the SQL statements that the application would typically run against these tables.
4. Process the trace file through TKPROF, and open the output file.
5. Record the value in the cell at the intersection of the column "disk" and row "total" for each SQL statement run in Step (3). This represents the total number of data blocks physically read from disk for the corresponding SQL statement.
6. Now, ALTER the tables so that they are no longer assigned to the recycle pool.
7. Repeat Steps (2) through (4).
8. Record the value in the cell at the intersection of the column "disk" and row "total" for each SQL statement run this second time.
9. If the value in Step (5) is larger than the corresponding value in Step (8), then decrease the size chosen for the recycle pool, because with the current size of the pool Oracle is removing and then reloading buffers before the SQL statement finishes execution.

10.7.5 Performance Monitoring of Buffer Pools

The performance information about multiple buffer pools can be found in the dynamic performance view V$BUFFER_POOL_STATISTICS. The hit ratios for objects in the buffer pools are determined by using this performance view. This view is created by running the script file catperf.sql located in the directory $ORACLE_HOME/rdbms/admin in UNIX. It is quite possible that the DBB cache hit ratio (see Figures 6.3 and 6.4) for the keep pool approaches but does not achieve the value 100.

10.8 Query Execution Plan Stability via Stored Outlines

The execution plan of a query can be viewed via the EXPLAIN PLAN utility, as discussed in Section 8.7.1. But when the same query is processed under different environments such as a different server, a different version of Oracle, etc., there is no guarantee that the same execution plan will be used in all cases. Oracle 8i offers a feature called stored outline whereby an execution plan of a query can be stored and used in all cases. This makes the query execution plans stable under changed environments.

A *stored outline* is an object consisting of the text of the query, other attributes such as the name of the outline and the hash value for the text of the query, and any hint(s) indicating how the query should be processed. This feature allows the developers to stabilize the way in which Oracle 8i processes the query across different environments. Regardless of the type of change to the environment such as any reconfiguration of the init.ora file, an upgrade of Oracle to a new version, a reorganization of the database, or any change of object statistics, etc., the stored outline suggests to the query optimizer that the query be processed in exactly the same way each time. In order to utilize this feature, the query must be formulated in exactly the same way including cases each time. Otherwise, Oracle 8i treats the query as a different statement. However, we need to remember that since a stored outline consists of hints, there is no absolute guarantee that the query optimizer will follow these hints.

A stored outline is identified by a unique name given to the outline, a category to which the outline belongs, and the query statement. The category name can be DEFAULT, which is the default option, or any other name assigned by the DBA or the developer. Any number of unique category names can be used to store outlines pertaining to different functional areas or usage. One must first create an outline and then instruct Oracle to use that outline. Oracle does not use an existing outline automatically.

10.8.1 Creation of Stored Outlines

There are two ways by which a stored outline can be created for a query, as described below.

Via CREATE Command

Use the command CREATE [OR REPLACE] OUTLINE for a named category. A *category* is a named collection of queries for each of which Oracle saves the execution plan to be used whenever the query is processed. Figure 10.15 contains the script to create a stored outline for a category called BATCH.

10.8 Query Execution Plan Stability via Stored Outlines

```
SQL> create outline invoice_listing for category BATCH on
  2 SELECT ORDER_ID, INV_DATE, ACCT_NAME from INVOICE
       WHERE ACCT_NAME = 'LITTLE ROCK CORP';
Operation 180 succeeded.
```

FIGURE 10.15: Creation of Stored Outline via CREATE

The CREATE OUTLINE statement creates a stored outline, which contains a set of attributes that the optimizer uses to create an execution plan. The data dictionary views, DBA_OUTLINES and DBA_OUTLINE_HINTS, provide information about stored outlines. The information about the stored outline created above is recorded in the data dictionary view DBA_OUTLINES as shown in Figure 10.16.

```
SQL> set long 6000
SQL> select * from dba_outlines where owner = 'SEKHAR';
NAME                 OWNER              CATEGORY
--------             --------------     -----------------
USED       TIMESTAMP         VERSION
---------  ----------        ----------
SQL_TEXT
-------------------------------------------------------------
INVOICE_LISTING      SEKHAR                         BATCH
UNUSED     05-OCT-01 8.1.7.1.0
SELECT ORDER_ID, INV_DATE, ACCT_NAME from INVOICE
WHERE ACCT_NAME = 'LITTLE ROCK CORP'
```

FIGURE 10.16: Listing of Stored Outline in DBA_OUTLINES

Figure 10.17 contains the corresponding information from the data dictionary view DBA_OUTLINE_HINTS.

```
SQL> select * from dba_outline_hints where owner = 'SEKHAR';
NAME                         OWNER                   NODE
STAGE    JOIN_POS
------------------           ---------------------   ---------
HINT
-------------------------------------------------------------
INVOICE_LISTING              SEKHAR                    1
3          0
NO_EXPAND
```

FIGURE 10.17: Listing of Stored Outline in DBA_OUTLINE_HINTS

```
INVOICE_LISTING              SEKHAR                    1
3            0
ORDERED
INVOICE_LISTING              SEKHAR                    1
3            0
NO_FACT(INVOICE_LISTING)
INVOICE_LISTING              SEKHAR                    1
3            1
FULL(INVOICE_LISTING)
INVOICE_LISTING              SEKHAR                    1
2            0
NOREWRITE
INVOICE_LISTING              SEKHAR                    1
1            0
NOREWRITE

6 rows selected.
```

FIGURE 10.17 (*continued*): Listing of Stored Outline in DBA_OUTLINE_HINTS

Via ALTER Command

The same effect as in the CREATE command discussed above can be achieved by running the following sequence of commands

```
ALTER SESSION SET CREATE_STORED_OUTLINE = BATCH;
SELECT ORDER_ID, INV_DATE, ACCT_NAME from INVOICE
       WHERE ACCT_NAME = 'LITTLE ROCK CORP';
ALTER SESSION SET CREATE_STORED_OUTLINE = FALSE;
```

Oracle creates the stored outline for the query, gives it a system-generated name, and stores it under the category BATCH. If multiple queries are issued between the two ALTER SESSION commands, then Oracle generates stored outlines for all of them and stores all of them under the category BATCH. Instead of assigning a specific category name such as BATCH one can run the command

```
ALTER SESSION SET CREATE_STORED_OUTLINE = TRUE;
```

In that case, Oracle stores all the outlines under the category called DEFAULT.

There is no initialization parameter to set up stored outlines at the instance level. But the feature can be set up globally for a database via the statement

```
ALTER SYSTEM SET CREATE_STORED_OUTLINE = TRUE;
```

10.8.2 Using Stored Outlines

After creating the outlines, we need to specify that Oracle use them. By default, Oracle does not use a stored outline. Oracle can be enforced to use stored outlines by running the command.

    ALTER SESSION SET USE_STORED_OUTLINES = value;

Here *value* can be TRUE or FALSE or a predefined category name. If the *value* is TRUE, then Oracle uses the outlines stored under the DEFAULT category. If the *value* is a category name, then the outlines in that category are used. If no outline exists in that category for a query, Oracle 8i checks the DEFAULT category for an outline. If none is found, Oracle 8i simply generates an execution plan for the query and uses that plan. If the *value* is FALSE, then Oracle does not use the stored outlines.

10.8.3 Management of Stored Outlines

Oracle creates a user OUTLN with DBA privilege for managing the execution plan stability with stored outlines. The directory $ORACLE_HOME/rdbms/admin in UNIX contains the script catproc.sql that calls two scripts, dbmsol.sql and prvtol.plb. The script dbmsol.sql creates the package OUTLN_PKG and the script prvtol.plb creates the body of OUTLN_PKG. Using the package OUTLN_PKG the user OUTLN centrally manages the stored outlines and their outline categories. This user is created automatically during the installation of Oracle 8i. There are other tables (base tables), indices, grants, and synonyms related to this package. In the case of upgrade, it is necessary to run the Installer again or the manual upgrade script c0800050.sql located in the directory $ORACLE_HOME/rdbms/admin in UNIX.

Figure 10.18 shows the attributes of OUTLN as a user.

```
SQL> select * from dba_users where username = 'OUTLN';
USERNAME                          USER_ID          PASSWORD
------------------                ----------       ------------
ACCOUNT_STATUS       LOCK_DATE    EXPIRY_DA        DEFAULT_TABLESPACE
------------------   ---------    ---------        ------------------
TEMPORARY_TABLESPACE              CREATED          PROFILE
--------------------              -------          ------------------
INITIAL_RSRC_CONSUMER_GROUP
---------------------------
EXTERNAL_NAME
---------------------------
OUTLN                             1726             8281BBEB9997A666
OPEN                                               SYSTEM
SYSTEM                            17-FEB-01 DEFAULT
DEFAULT_CONSUMER_GROUP
```

FIGURE 10.18: Attributes of OUTLN User

The tablespace SYSTEM is assigned both as the default and the temporary tablespace for OUTLN. But one can change one or both to other tablespaces, if desired. Figure 10.19 shows that both tablespaces have been changed for the user OUTLN.

```
SQL>  ALTER USER OUTLN
  2     DEFAULT TABLESPACE USERDATA
  3     TEMPORARY TABLESPACE TEMP;
User altered.
SQL> select * from dba_users where username = 'OUTLN';
USERNAME                     USER_ID            PASSWORD
------------------           ---------          ----------
ACCOUNT_STATUS               LOCK_DATE    EXPIRY_DA   DEFAULT_TABLESPACE
------------------           ---------    ---------   ------------------
TEMPORARY_TABLESPACE                      CREATED     PROFILE
--------------------                      -------     --------------
INITIAL_RSRC_CONSUMER_GROUP
---------------------------
EXTERNAL_NAME
------------------------------------------------------------------
OUTLN                            1726            8281BBEB9997A666
OPEN                                                    USERDATA
TEMP                                      17-FEB-01   DEFAULT
DEFAULT_CONSUMER_GROUP
```

FIGURE 10.19: OUTLN User with Altered Tablespaces

10.9 Index Enhancements

Oracle 8i introduced several enhancements to indexing. We discuss these two topics in this section.

- Function-based index, and
- Descending index.

Function-Based Index

If a query uses an indexed column that is modified by an Oracle built-in function (e.g., UPPER, ROUND, SUM, etc.) or by a computational formula, then the query optimizer performs a full table scan instead of an indexed search. For example, let us suppose that a table INVOICE has an index on a column named ACCT_NAME. Then, the following query will perform an indexed search on ACCT_NAME.

```
SELECT ORDER_ID, INV_DATE, DELETE_FLAG FROM INVOICE
WHERE ACCT_NAME = 'LITTLE ROCK CORP';
```

But when we modify ACCT_NAME by a function such as UPPER, a full table scan will be made of the INVOICE table. Thus, the query below will not use the index on ACCT_NAME:

```
SELECT ORDER_ID, INV_DATE, ACCT_NAME FROM INVOICE
WHERE UPPER (ACCT_NAME) = 'LITTLE ROCK CORP';
```

Similarly, the query below will perform a full table scan due to the function SUM:

```
SELECT SUM (INVOICE_AMT) FROM INVOICE;
```

Oracle 8i introduced the *function-based index* whereby an index can be created on one or more columns that are modified by a computational formula or by a built-in Oracle function. This improves the query performance by making it possible to perform an indexed search on column(s) that have been modified.

To enable the use of function-based indices, we must issue the following two commands at the session level.

```
ALTER SESSION SET QUERY_REWRITE_ENABLED = TRUE;
ALTER SESSION SET QUERY_REWRITE_INTEGRITY=TRUSTED;
```

Figure 10.20 contains a session transcript showing that a B*-tree index on ACCT_NAME uses a full table scan of INVOICE, while a function-based index on UPPER (ACCT_NAME) performs an indexed search.

```
SESSION TRANSCRIPT:
SQL>  create index ACCT_NAME_idx on INVOICE (ACCT_NAME)
  2   tablespace perf_data;
Index created.
SQL>
Wrote file afiedt.buf
  1   explain plan
  2     set statement_id = 'TEST_QUERY_20'
  3     for
  4     select ORDER_ID, INV_DATE, ACCT_NAME from INVOICE
  5     where
  6     upper (ACCT_NAME) = 'LITTLE ROCK CORP'
  7*    order by 1
SQL> /
Explained.
SQL>  SELECT DECODE(ID,0,'',
  2      LPAD(' ',2*(LEVEL-1))||LEVEL||'.'||POSITION)||' '||
  3      OPERATION||' '||OPTIONS||' '||OBJECT_NAME||' '||
  4      OBJECT_TYPE||' '||
```

FIGURE 10.20: B*-Tree Index Versus Function-Based Index

```
     5     DECODE(ID,0,'Cost = '||POSITION) "Execution Plan"
     6     FROM PLAN_TABLE
     7     CONNECT BY PRIOR ID = PARENT_ID
     8     AND STATEMENT_ID = 'TEST_QUERY_20'
     9     START WITH ID = 0 AND STATEMENT_ID = 'TEST_QUERY_20';

Execution Plan
----------------------------------------------------------------
SELECT STATEMENT              Cost = 73
   2.1 SORT ORDER BY
       3.1 TABLE ACCESS FULL INVOICE

SQL>  create index ACCT_NAME_function_idx on
   2  INVOICE (UPPER (ACCT_NAME))
   3  tablespace perf_data;

Index created.

SQL> alter session set QUERY_REWRITE_ENABLED = TRUE;

Session altered.

SQL> alter session set QUERY_REWRITE_INTEGRITY = TRUSTED;

Session altered.

SQL>  explain plan
   2  set statement_id = 'TEST_QUERY_6'
   3  for
   4  select ORDER_ID, INV_DATE, ACCT_NAME from INVOICE
   5  where
   6  upper (ACCT_NAME) = 'LITTLE ROCK CORP';

Explained.

SQL>  SELECT DECODE(ID,0,'',
     2     LPAD(' ',2*(LEVEL-1))||LEVEL||'.'||POSITION)||' '||
     3     OPERATION||' '||OPTIONS||' '||OBJECT_NAME||' '||
     4     OBJECT_TYPE||' '||
     5     DECODE(ID,0,'Cost = '||POSITION) "Execution Plan"
     6     FROM PLAN_TABLE
     7     CONNECT BY PRIOR ID = PARENT_ID
     8     AND STATEMENT_ID = 'TEST_QUERY_6'
     9     START WITH ID = 0 AND STATEMENT_ID = 'TEST_QUERY_6';

Execution Plan
----------------------------------------------------------------
SELECT STATEMENT              Cost = 2
   2.1 TABLE ACCESS BY INDEX ROWID INVOICE
       3.1 INDEX RANGE SCAN ACCT_NAME_FUNCTION_IDX NON-UNIQUE
```

FIGURE 10.20 (*continued*): B*-Tree Index Versus Function-Based Index

Bitmap indices can be function based. Function-based indices can also be partitioned.

Descending Index

The data in a B*-tree index are stored in ascending order, ordered from the lowest column value to the highest. But in Oracle 8i we can categorize data in a B*-tree index in descending order by creating an index on column(s) and specifying DESC as the order in which the indexed data are stored. This feature becomes very useful in queries where sorting operations are mixed, some ascending and some descending. For example, let us consider the following table.

   STUDENT (Student_id, Last_Name, First_Name, Grade, ...)

We issue the following query on STUDENT.

   SELECT LAST_NAME, FIRST_NAME, GRADE FROM STUDENT
   ORDER BY LAST_NAME, FIRST_NAME, GRADE DESC;

If the STUDENT table is large, then without descending indices Oracle may need a large amount of sort space to retrieve the indexed data for LAST_NAME and FIRST_NAME in the ascending sort order and the GRADE data in the descending order. But if we create a descending index on GRADE, then its B*-tree index will store the indexed data in descending order. As a result, a large sort space will not be needed. Figure 10.21 shows the creation of a descending index on the column STUDENT.GRADE.

```
SQL>  create index desc_grade_idx on
  2     STUDENT (grade desc)
  3     tablespace perf_data;
Index created.
```

FIGURE 10.21: Descending Index

It is possible to create a concatenated index on multiple columns with mixed sort order, i.e., some columns in ascending order and the rest in descending order. Figure 10.22 shows an example of such an index.

```
SQL>  create index mixed_name_grade_idx on
  2     STUDENT (last_name asc, first_name asc, grade desc)
  3     tablespace perf_data;
Index created.
```

FIGURE 10.22: Concatenated Index with Mixed Sort Order

Finally, a function-based index can be combined with the descending index feature to create a function-based descending index.

10.10 Query Rewrite for Materialized Views

Let us suppose that Q is a query based on tables $T_1, T_2, \ldots, T_n$. If a materialized view is defined on the tables $T_1, T_2, \ldots, T_n$ and the *query rewrite* option is enabled for the materialized view, then Oracle 8i allows an automatic rewrite of the query to use the materialized view instead of the base tables in order to improve performance. For this option, the cost-based optimizer must be used. The following two steps are needed to enable the query rewrite option.

- Set the initialization parameter QUERY_REWRITE_ENABLED to TRUE either in the init.ora file for the instance, or via the ALTER SESSION or ALTER SYSTEM command for the session or the system. To enable query rewrite, one must have either the global query rewrite or query rewrite privileges enabled on the system.
- Set the initialization parameter QUERY_REWRITE_INTEGRITY to one of three possible values to identify the desired level of integrity for query rewrites:
  - ENFORCED allows query rewrites if the materialized view is updated regularly and all constraints are validated. This is the default setting.
  - TRUSTED allows query rewrites on constraints that may not have been validated when enabled.
  - STALE_TOLERATED allows query rewrites even when the materialized view has not been refreshed and when constraints are not necessarily validated when enabled.

It is recommended that the materialized view and the base table(s) that it uses be in the same schema. Otherwise, the creator of the view needs the GLOBAL QUERY REWRITE system privilege. Figure 10.23 contains the SQL command to enable query rewrite.

```
SQL>
Wrote file afiedt.buf
  1  create materialized view invest_option_view
  2  tablespace perf_data
  3  storage (initial 100K next 50K pctincrease 0)
  4  refresh complete
  5  start with SYSDATE
  6  next SYSDATE + 7
  7  as
  8* select * from invest_option
SQL> /
Snapshot created.
```

FIGURE 10.23: Materialized View with QUERY REWRITE

```
SVRMGR>  alter materialized view invest_option_view
    2>   enable query rewrite;
Statement processed.
SVRMGR> commit;
Statement processed.
```

FIGURE 10.23 (*continued*): Materialized View with QUERY REWRITE

The optimizer hints, /*+rewrite */ and /*+norewrite */, can be used for specifying that the query rewrite option be used on SELECT statements.

Several dictionary views are available for materialized view information. They are listed below.

ALL_REFRESH_DEPENDENCIES	List of tables used by materialized views.
DBA_MVIEW_AGGREGATES	Information about grouping functions used by materialized views.
DBA_MVIEW_ANALYSIS	Information about materialized views supporting query rewrites.
DBA_MVIEW_DETAIL_RELATIONS	List of all objects referenced in a materialized view.
DBA_MVIEW_JOINS	List of columns joined from base tables in materialized views.
DBA_MVIEW_KEYS	More information about the relationships between objects identified in DBA_MVIEW_DETAIL_RELATIONS.

10.11 Online Index Creation, Rebuild, Defragmentation

In Section 9.2.4 we discussed the rebuilding of indices for reducing fragmentation of the index table and achieving better performance. However, up to Oracle8 the rebuilding of an index required that no DML operation (insert, update, delete) could be performed on the table while the index was being rebuilt, because Oracle placed an exclusive lock on the table. Oracle 8i introduced a new method for building or rebuilding indices using a less restrictive locking mechanism that allows other users to make changes to data in the table while the index is being rebuilt. These user-made changes, however, continue to be recorded in the rebuilt index. Oracle accomplishes this as follows.

(a) Oracle obtains exclusive locks on the table for a very short time to define the structure of the index and to update the data dictionary.
(b) When these operations are complete, Oracle releases the exclusive locks on the table. As a result, users can change the data of the table again.

(c) Oracle continues to rebuild the index by populating the index with data from the table.
(d) Oracle also creates an index-organized copy of the table called a *journal table*. The journal table stores data changes made by users while the index is being rebuilt.
(e) When the rebuild using the data from the original table is complete, Oracle compares the data in the rebuilt index with changes recorded in the journal table, if any. Each change is then merged into the index, and the row is simultaneously deleted from the journal table as long as no user is making changes to that row.
(f) If it takes too many iterations through the journal table to clean out all the data, Oracle places an exclusive lock on the journal table until the cleaning operation is complete. This is the only time other than at the very beginning of the build or rebuild operation when other users cannot change data of the table.

Figure 10.24 shows the command to rebuild an index online.

```
SQL> alter index FACILITIES_LIDFAC_UK rebuild online;
Index altered.
```

FIGURE 10.24: Rebuild Index Online

The above process applies primarily to the B*-tree indices and their variants such as function based, descending, and reverse key indices, and for partitioned indices. It does not apply to the bitmap, cluster, and secondary indices in index organized tables.

10.12 ANALYZE versus DBMS_STATS

The ANALYZE command generates statistics at three levels, tables, indices, and columns. Under Oracle 8i the relevant statistics for each level can be retrieved via SELECT statements against the appropriate data dictionary views as listed below.

Level	Data Dictionary Views
Table	DBA_ALL_TABLES, DBA_OBJECT_TABLES, DBA_TABLES, DBA_TAB_PARTITIONS, DBA_TAB_SUBPARTITIONS
Index	DBA_INDEXES, DBA_IND_PARTITIONS, DBA_IND_SUBPARTITIONS
Column	DBA_TAB_COLUMNS, DBA_TAB_COL_STATISTICS, DBA_PART_COL_STATISTICS, DBA_SUBPART_COL_STATISTICS

As an alternative to ANALYZE, Oracle 8i offers the DBMS_STATS package to generate statistics for the cost-based optimizer. This package provides a mechanism for users to view and modify optimizer statistics gathered for database objects. It also allows the gathering of some statistics in parallel. The statistics can reside in two different locations:

- Specific data dictionary views such as DBA_TABLES, DBA_INDEXES, etc.;
- A table created in the user's schema for this purpose.

However, the cost-based optimizer uses only the statistics stored in the data dictionary views. The statistics stored in a user's table have no impact on the optimizer.

The package is divided into three main sections, each section consisting of a set of procedures.

Section 1: Procedures that gather certain classes of optimizer statistics and have either improved or equivalent performance characteristics compared to the ANALYZE command.

The following procedures belong to this section.

- GATHER_DATABASE_STATS—Collects statistics for all database objects,
- GATHER_SCHEMA_STATS—Collects statistics for all objects owned by a particular user;
- GATHER_INDEX_STATS—Collects statistics for a specified index;
- GATHER_TABLE_STATS—Collects statistics for a specified table.

Section 2: *Procedures that enable the storage, retrieval, and removal of the statistics related to individual columns, indices, and tables, and removal of statistics related to a schema and an entire database.*

The following procedures belong to this section.

- SET_COLUMN_STATS—Sets column-related statistics;
- SET_INDEX_STATS— Sets index-related statistics;
- SET_TABLE_STATS— Sets table-related statistics;
- GET_COLUMN_STATS—Gets column-related statistics;
- GET_INDEX_STATS—Gets index-related statistics;
- GET_TABLE_STATS—Gets table-related statistics;
- DELETE_COLUMN_STATS—Deletes column-related statistics;
- DELETE _INDEX_STATS—Deletes index-related statistics;
- DELETE _TABLE_STATS—Deletes table-related statistics ;
- DELETE_SCHEMA_STATS—Deletes statistics for a schema;
- DELETE_DATABASE_STATS—Deletes statistics for an entire database.

Section 3: *Procedures THAT create and drop the statistics table and transfer statistics between the data dictionary views and the statistics table.*

The following procedures belong to this section.

- CREATE_STAT_TABLE—Creates the statistics table;
- DROP_STAT_TABLE—Drops the statistics table;

- UPDATE_STAT_TABLE—Upgrades the statistics table from an older version;
- EXPORT_'level'_STATS—Transfers statistics from the data dictionary views to the statistics table, where 'level' can be substituted with COLUMN, INDEX, TABLE, SCHEMA, or DATABASE;
- IMPORT_'level'_STATS—Populates statistics from the statistics table into the data dictionary views, where 'level' can be substituted with COLUMN, INDEX, TABLE, SCHEMA, or DATABASE.

Most of the procedures in DBMS_STATS include three common input parameters: STATTAB, STATOWN, and STATID. These parameters allow the users to store statistics in their own tables instead of the data dictionary views. These externally stored statistics do not affect the cost-based optimizer. Users can thereby maintain and experiment with different sets of statistics without permanently changing the good statistics stored in the data dictionary views. The functions of the three input parameters are described below.

- STATTAB: This parameter identifies the user statistics table where the statistics are stored. If STATTAB is NULL, the statistics are stored directly in the data dictionary views.
- STATOWN: If the schema that contains the object for which statistics are collected is different from the schema in which the user statistics table resides, then this parameter specifies the owner of the schema in which the user statistics table resides.
- STATID: If users maintain separate sets of statistics within a single table identified by a STATTAB, then this parameter identifies each separate set of statistics.

For all of the SET/GET/DELETE procedures, if STATTAB is not provided (i.e., NULL), the procedures directly update the statistics collected in the data dictionary views. Therefore, if the users plan to modify the data dictionary views directly, they need not create these statistics tables. However, if STATTAB is NOT NULL, then the SET/GET/DELETE procedures update the user-specified statistics table identified by the parameter STATTAB. The user-created statistics table can also be managed through the use of DBMS_STATS. Finally, one can use DBMS_STATS to populate statistics to be used in conjunction with stored outlines.

Oracle initially claimed that DBMS_STATS collects statistics faster than ANALYZE. But this was found to be wrong. Subsequently, Oracle recognized that there was a bug in the DBMS_STATS package causing the slow performance of the package. This bug was fixed in Oracle 8i version 8.1.6.

For further details about the DBMS_STATS package run the following SQL commands.

```
SET HEADING OFF
SET NEWPAGE 0
SELECT TEXT FROM DBA_SOURCE WHERE NAME = 'DBMS_STATS'
    AND TYPE = 'PACKAGE';
```

10.13 Optimization of Top_N Queries

The definition of a top-*N* query depends on two items: ROWNUM pseudocolumn and inline view.

As we have seen before, every table in an Oracle database contains a hidden column called ROWNUM that can be used to limit the number of rows returned by a query. For example, the query

```
SELECT * FROM CUST_ORDER WHERE ROWNUM <= 50;
```

returns 50 rows from the table CUST_ORDER due to the selection criterion of "ROWNUM <= 50".

An *inline view* is characterized by three properties.

- It is a subquery used in the FROM clause of a query to construct the view at runtime.
- It may contain an ORDER BY clause.
- It can be given an alias in the main query where it appears, but it cannot be given a name and saved as a database object.

A *top-N query* is a query that obtains the *N* largest or smallest values of a column by using the ROWNUM pseudocolumn in its selection criteria and an ORDER BY clause in an inline view that returns the main result set of the query. The ORDER BY clause of the inline view sorts the data of the desired column in the proper order before returning the resulting data. The final selection is made in the main query for the *N* largest or smallest values via a condition in the WHERE clause of the form ROWNUM <= N. The ascending order is used for the *N* smallest values, and the descending order is used for the *N* largest values. Figure 10.25 contains an example of a top-20 query that returns 20 rows with the largest values of the Application Version.

```
SQL> col APPLICATION_ID heading "Application|ID"
SQL> col APPLICATION_VERSION heading "Application|Version"
SQL> col EQUIP_STATUS heading "Hardware|Status" format a10
SQL> edit
Wrote file afiedt.buf

  1  select rownum RANK, APPLICATION_ID, APPLICATION_VERSION,
EQUIP_STATUS
  2  from
  3  (select APPLICATION_ID, APPLICATION_VERSION, EQUIP_STATUS
from APPLICATION_LIST
  4  where APPLICATION_VERSION is NOT NULL
  5  and EQUIP_STATUS is NOT NULL
  6  order by APPLICATION_VERSION desc, EQUIP_STATUS)
  7* where ROWNUM <= 20
SQL> /
```

FIGURE 10.25: Example of Top-*N* Query

```
                Application      Application     Hardware
RANK            ID               Version         Status
-----           -----------      -----------     ---------
    1           38857            4               LEASE
    2           38857            4               OTHER
    3           38857            4               OTHER
    4           38857            4               OTHER
    5           38857            4               OTHER
    6           38857            4               OTHER
    7           38857            4               OWN
    8           38857            4               OWN
    9           38857            3               LEASE
   10           38857            3               OTHER
   11           38857            3               OTHER
   12           38857            3               OTHER
   13           38857            3               OTHER
   14           38857            3               OTHER
   15           38857            3               OWN
   16           38857            3               OWN
   17           20007            2               LEASE
   18           37453            2               LEASE
   19           38857            2               LEASE
   20           38857            2               OTHER

20 rows selected.
```

FIGURE 10.25 (*continued*): Example of Top-*N* Query

Note that the inline view is defined by the following query.

```
select APPLICATION_ID, APPLICATION_VERSION, EQUIP_STATUS
from APPLICATION_LIST
where APPLICATION_VERSION is NOT NULL
and EQUIP_STATUS is NOT NULL
order by APPLICATION_VERSION desc, EQUIP_STATUS;
```

However, this view is not saved as a regular view in the database and cannot be referenced outside the top-*N* query. Through the support of the ORDER BY clause in inline view operations and an enhanced sorting algorithm Oracle 8i supports much faster processing of top-*N* queries than did the previous releases. These combined new features allow Oracle 8i to discard data that are not in the top-*N* set before sorting the data.

10.14 Glimpse into Oracle 9i

Oracle 9i continues the focus on the Internet introduced with Oracle 8i. It provides a series of special features de4signed for an e-business environment. In addition, Oracle 9i offers new capabilities that extend the existing features of Oracle 8i aimed at the traditional relational database environment. In this section we discuss a set of features of Oracle 9i relevant to the performance tuning and optimization issues.

Tablespace Management

When a tablespace is created via the CREATE TABLESPACE command with the clause SEGMENT SPACE MANAGEMENT, two options are available: MANUAL and AUTO. The option MANUAL is the default that creates the dictionary managed tablespaces as in Oracle 8i. The option AUTO creates the locally managed tablespaces as discussed in Section 10.5. However, the default for the EXTENT MANAGEMENT clause depends on the setting of the initialization parameter COMPATIBLE, as noted below.

- If COMPATIBLE is set to 8.1.7 or lower, then the tablespace is created as dictionary managed.
- If COMPATIBLE is set to 9.0.0.0 or higher, then the tablespace is created as locally managed. A permanent locally managed tablespace cannot be assigned as a user's temporary tablespace.

Flashback Query

This feature allows the user to retrieve data via SQL query from a point of time in the past. The user first needs to specify the date and time for which he or she wants to query the data. Subsequently, any SELECT statement issued by the user as the flashback query operates on the data as they existed at the specified date and time. The underlying mechanism is known as Oracle's multiversion read consistency capability, which is achieved by restoring data by applying undo operations as needed. The DBA needs to specify how long undo should be kept in the database. When a flashback query is executed, a snapshot of the data is created via undo operations on the data. The DBA must size the rollback segments large enough to contain the undo information for executing a flashback query.

The performance of a flashback query as measured by its response time depends on two factors:

- Amount of data being queried and retrieved, and
- Number of changes made to the data between the current time and the user specified flashback time.

There are several restrictions on the use of flashback queries, as noted below.

- They cannot be issued by the user SYS. In order to use such queries on data dictionary tables owned by SYS, it is necessary to grant the SELECT privilege on these tables to a non-SYS user who then issues these queries.
- These queries do not work with the QUERY REWRITE option of the materialized views (see Section 10.10). This option must be disabled when using the flashback queries.

When a query is executed for a time in the past, a snapshot of the data as they existed at that time is recreated using the undo operation on the data saved in the rollback segments. For every piece of data that has changed since the time requested by the flashback query, the corresponding undo data need to be retrieved and compiled. Hence the performance of the flashback query can degrade significantly as the volume of data which need to be recreated increases. As a result, a flashback query works best when it is used to select a small set of data, preferably using indices. If a flashback query has to perform a full table scan, its performance will depend on the amount of DML activities performed on that table between the present time and the time of the data that the flashback query is retrieving. Sometimes parallel query slaves can be used to improve the performance of such full table scans.

It is necessary to set up the database for using the flashback query feature. The init.ora file contains four "undo" initialization parameters with the following default values:

```
NAME                        VALUE
--------------------        --------
undo_management             MANUAL
undo_retention              900
undo_suppress_errors        FALSE
undo_tablespace             UNDOTBS
```

Now proceed as follows.

- Set undo_management to AUTO.
- The default value of 900 for undo_retention establishes a retention period of 900 seconds or 15 minutes. That means that all committed undo information in the system is retained for at least 15 minutes. It ensures that all queries running for 15 minutes or less do not get the error message "snapshot too old" under normal circumstances. If the default value is inadequate, set undo_retention to a new value.
- If the default tablespace name UNDOTBS is unsatisfactory, provide a new name for the undo_tablespace parameter.

FIRST_ROWS Hint

The FIRST_ROWS (n) hint is an improvement over the FIRST_ROWS hint (see Section 9.3.1) and is fully cost-based. Oracle recommends that this new hint be used in place of the previous FIRST_ROWS hint which might give suboptimal results for "first n" queries with a very selective CONTAINS clause. The FIRST_ROWS (n) hint is used like the FIRST_ROWS hint in cases where we want the shortest response time. For example, to obtain the first eight rows in the shortest possible time, use the new hint as follows.

```
select /* FIRST_ROWS(8) */ account_id from INVOICE
where contains (account_name, 'Little Rock Corp') > 0
order by invoice_date desc;
```

Dynamic SGA

The System Global Area (SGA) consists of several memory-resident data structures that constitute an Oracle instance (see Section 4.2.1). The size of the SGA is static in the sense that it is allocated at the start of an instance and cannot be changed dynamically while the instance is running. Oracle 9i offers a new feature called the *dynamic SGA* that allows a DBA to modify the SGA size dynamically. This provides an SGA that can grow and shrink in response to a DBA command depending on the operational performance needs of the database. The Oracle Server process can modify the physical address space use in response to the need of physical memory for the operating system.

Under the dynamic SGA infrastructure the DBA can

- Size the buffer cache, the shared pool, and the large pool without having to shut down the instance; and
- Allow the limits to be set at runtime on how much physical memory will be used for the SGA. The instance will be started under-conFigured and will use as much memory as the operating system gives it.

The dynamic SGA creates a new unit of memory allocation called a *granule*, which is a unit of contiguous virtual memory that can be allocated dynamically while the instance is running. The size of a granule is calculated as follows depending on the estimated total SGA size.

```
granule = 4 MB if SGA size < 128 MB,
granule = 16 MB otherwise
```

The buffer cache, the shared pool, and the large pool are allowed to grow and shrink depending on granule boundaries. When the instance is started, Oracle allocates the granule entries, one for each granule to support an address space of size SGA_MAX_SIZE bytes. Subsequently, each component acquires as many granules as it requires. The minimum SGA size is three granules resulting from an allocation of one granule each to the fixed SGA including the redo buffers, the buffer cache, and the shared pool.

The DBA can alter the granules allocated to components by using the ALTER SYSTEM command. This command interchanges free granules among the three components of the SGA, namely, the buffer cache, the shared pool, and the large pool. But the granules are never automatically deallocated from one component of the SGA and allocated to another. The granules are rounded up to the nearest default granule size (4 or 16 MB). Adding a number of granules to a component with the ALTER SYSTEM command succeeds only if Oracle has sufficient free granules to satisfy the request. Oracle cannot automatically allocate granules from one component to another. Instead, the DBA must ensure that the instance has enough free granules to satisfy the increase of a component's granule use. If the current size of the SGA memory is less than SGA_MAX_SIZE, then Oracle can allocate more granules until the SGA size reaches the limit of SGA_MAX_SIZE. The Oracle Server that invokes the ALTER SYSTEM command reserves a set of granules for the corresponding SGA component. The foreground process then hands the completion to the background process. The background process completes the operation by taking the reserved granules and adding them to the component's granule list. This is referred to as growing the SGA memory area of a component.

SGA memory is tracked in granules by SGA components. One can monitor the tracking via the V$BUFFER_POOL view.

Enhanced Cost Optimization

The cost-based optimizer of Oracle 8i determines the processing cost of a query primarily on the basis of time spent in retrieving data, i.e., logical and physical reads (see Section 8.3, Optimizer Modes, under "CHOOSE"). Oracle 9i has added the memory and CPU costs to the I/O-based cost of Oracle 8i. The enhanced algorithm for cost calculation results in better cost optimization plans, less resource usage, and faster overall performance. Latch contention (see Section 6.10) in several areas has been reduced or even eliminated.

Automatic Management of Rollback Segments

The management of rollback segments involves three main tasks for the DBA, namely, to determine:

- Sizes of the segments,
- Number of the segments, and
- Categories of the segments so as to allocate one category to large batch jobs handling long running queries and the other category for handling other jobs.

The goal here is to minimize the Oracle error ORA-01555: snapshot too old. See Section 5.10 for an actual case study.

Oracle 9i introduces the feature of automatic management of rollback segments. As a result, a database can manage its own rollback segments without any extensive DBA intervention. The DBA needs to allocate a rollback tablespace called UNDO to retain the undo information and specify the length of time that the undo information needs to be retained in the rollback segments. Then, Oracle takes care of issues such as undo block contention, consistent read retention which is the root cause of the error ORA-01555, and space utilization.

Miscellaneous Features

- Index Coalesce: Defragments free space in B*-tree index leaf blocks while the associated table remains online for user access.
- Resumable Space Allocation: If a large operation such as a batch update or bulk data load encounters too many "out of space" errors, the DBA can suspend the operation temporarily, fix the problem by allocating additional datafiles as needed, and then restart the operation from the point where it was suspended. This can be done without interrupting the normal database operation.

- Caching Query Execution Plans: These plans are cached in the shared pool so that the DBA can investigate any reported performance problem without reexecuting the offending queries.
- Basic Replication: Provides bidirectional replication with automated conflict detection and resolution; supports configurations that include a single updatable master site with multiple updatable or read-only snapshot sites
- Unused Index Maintenance: Allows the database server to track unused indices.
- DB_CACHE_SIZE: Specifies the size of the DEFAULT buffer pool for buffers created with the block size determined by the DB_BLOCK_SIZE parameter. Oracle recommends that DB_CACHE_SIZE be used to size the DEFAULT buffer pool instead of DB_BLOCK_BUFFERS.

Key Words

buffer pool
buffer pool sizing
category
composite partitioning
DBMS_SPACE_ADMIN
DBMS_STATS
default pool
descending index
dictionary managed tablespace
dynamic SGA
flashback query
function-based index
granule
hash partitioning
index coalesce
inline view
journal table
keep pool
LOB data type
locally managed tablespace
locally managed tablespace, autoallocate
locally managed tablespace, uniform
LONG data type
materialized view
materialized view, QUERY REWRITE
materialized view, REFRESH clause
OUTLN user
OUTLN_PKG
rebuilt index
recycle pool
snapshot replication
STORE IN clause
stored outline
subpartition
top_N query
undo initialization paramaeters

References and Further Reading

1. J. S. Couchman—*Oracle8 Certified Professional Exam Guide*, Oracle Press, 1999.
2. R. Greenwald, R. Stackowiak, and J. Stern—*Oracle Essentials: Oracle 9i, Oracle 8i, Oracle8*, O'Reilly, 2001.
3. K. Loney and G. Koch—*Oracle 8i: The Complete Reference*, Oracle Press, 2000.
4. K. Loney and M. Theriault—*Oracle 8i DBA Handbook*, Oracle Press, 2000.

5. R. J. Niemiec—*Oracle Performance Tuning Tips & Techniques*, Oracle Press, 1999.
6. Oracle Corporation—*Oracle 8i Release 3 New Features Summary*, August 2000.
7. Oracle Corporation—*Getting to Know Oracle8i—Release 2 (8.1.6)*, December 1999.
8. Oracle Corporation—*Oracle 9i Database README Release Notes*, June 2001.
9. Oracle Corporation—*Oracle 9i New Features Summary*, May 2001.
10. D. Scherer, W. Gaynor, A. Valentinsen, and X. Cursetjee—*Oracle 8i Tips & Techniques*, Oracle Press, 2000.

The chapter covers a set of topics embodying new features in Oracle 8i and Oracle 9i related primarily to database performance tuning and optimization. The best source of information on these topics is Oracle MetaLink which contains numerous papers dealing with actual issues and case studies raised by Oracle DBAs and developers related to these features. I have drawn heavily from many of these papers published in the MetaLink. The site can be accessed at the URL http://metalink.oracle.com and searched for the relevant topics. In addition, the references cited above contain more information on some of the topics.

References [6] and [7] constitute the primary source of the contents of Section 10.2. Couchman [1, Chapters 25–28] discusses a large set of topics dealing with features that are unique to Oracle 8i, not all of which, however, pertain to database performance tuning and optimization. Greenwald et al. [2] offer a comprehensive coverage of Oracle database internals. In particular, [2, Chapters 2, – 4, and 6] addresses Oracle 9i features. Loney and Koch [3] provide an in-depth discussion of snapshots and materialized views in Chapter 23, and LOB data types in Chapter 30. Loney and Theriault [4, pp. 175–177] provide some additional insights for creating and altering stored outlines. Niemiec [5, Chapter 13] provides a few topics on Oracle 8i features. Scherer et al. [10, Chapter 5] contain a comprehensive discussion of the DBMS_STATS package and the process of automatic statistics gathering for cost-based optimization. References [8] and [9] constitute the primary source of the contents of Section 10.14. As of June 9, 2001 Oracle has published a list of open bugs not all of which, however, pertain to performance tuning and optimization issues. See [8, § 43] for full details.

Part 3
Contemporary Issues

Part 3 consists of two chapters that discuss two contemporary issues, namely, the tuning principles of data warehouses and of Web-based databases. The tuning principles of an OLTP database are substantially the same as those for a data warehouse or a Web-based database. In this part we capture only those tools and techniques that are unique to these two special types of databases.

Chapter 11 starts with a discussion of the design principles of a data warehouse and identifies the structural differences between a transactional database and a data warehouse. It then introduces the data loading principles for a data warehouse. The chapter closes with a discussion of the tuning principles for a data warehouse at the internal and external levels.

Chapter 12 starts with an introduction to the three-tier and n-tier architectures of client server applications with emphasis on Web-based applications. The Oracle product OAS is discussed in detail and an overview is offered of the new product iAS. The chapter closes with a discussion of the tuning principles for a Web-based database at the internal and external levels.

11
Tuning the Data Warehouse at All Levels

Outline

11.1 Advent of Data Warehouse
11.2 Features of Data Warehouse
11.3 Design Issues of Data Warehouse
11.4 Structure of Data Warehouse
11.5 Proliferation from Data Warehouse
11.6 Metadata
11.7 Implementation and Internal Level
11.8 Data Loading in Warehouse
11.9 Query Processing and Optimization
Key Words
References and Further Reading
Exercises

Overview of the Chapter

The chapter discusses the performance tuning of a data warehouse at all three levels, i.e., conceptual, internal, and external. In order to put the discussion in the proper context the chapter starts with the general design features and the structure of a data warehouse. The concept of the star schema plays a central role in the conceptual level and the star queries provide a unique mechanism to tune the external levels. Both receive an in-depth treatment in the chapter. Sections 11.2 through 11.6 discuss a variety of topics dealing with the conceptual level. Sections 11.7 and 11.8 deal with the internal level and data loading tools for bulk data load. Section 11.9 treats the external level, especially star queries and star transformation.

11.1 Advent of Data Warehouse

Data warehouses came into the market during the early 1990s as a unique data processing and reporting mechanism. But THEIR origin can be traced to the late 1970s when Visicalc was introduced by THE Digital Equipment Corporation as a spreadsheet software allowing its users the "What If" capabilities in a very rudimentary form. Gradually the spreadsheets became more sophisticated and evolved into the decision support system or DSS by the early to mid-1980s. Since then the DSSs have been used primarily for strategic and tactical planning, and the transactional databases have satisfied the information needs for daily operations. Due to their distinctly different functionality the underlying database of a DSS is structured differently from that of a transactional system. In a broad sense, a data warehouse can be regarded as the database underlying a DSS.

As we saw in Chapter 1, relational databases came into the market in 1979. Initially, the same databases were used for both a transactional system and a DSS. This led to several problems, primarily from the database performance and tuning viewpoint, because of the differences in data needs and query processing mechanisms of these two distinct types of application. As a result, during the early 1990s a different structure emerged for the database of a DSS in the form of a data warehouse. This structure is often called a reporting database, because that is its primary function. Inmon, who is often called the "father of the data warehouse," introduced the term and the concept of a data warehouse in the early 1990s. He built the concept around the IBM architecture that addresses enterprisewide data access needs. Inmon's role in creating the concept of a data warehouse is somewhat similar, though to a lesser degree, to Codd's role in introducing the relational databases. A data warehouse accepts data from diverse and disparate data sources ranging from legacy applications on mainframes to the modern three-tier Web-based applications and stores them in a central repository for generating a wide variety of business reports. These reports are used by management for short- and long-range planning. As such, the data warehouse works as the backbone of an enterprisewide DSS. Its data are used both for report generation and as input to forecasting and optimizing models such as time series analysis, queueing models, linear and nonlinear programming, etc.

The database underlying a data warehouse has to be kept tuned at all times at all three levels, i.e., conceptual, internal, and external. For this purpose, the database has to be properly designed, implemented, and maintained. In the rest of this chapter we discuss these topics. We include only those issues that are unique to a data warehouse and, therefore, were not addressed in the earlier chapters.

11.2 Features of Data Warehouse

Four features characterize a data warehouse.

- It is subject oriented instead of transaction oriented.

- Data are collected from various sources and integrated into the warehouse structure. As a result, inconsistencies among data sources are resolved before the data are loaded into the warehouse.
- Data are less detailed and are often summarized through rollups.
- Data are nonvolatile since they are loaded in bulk from the source feeds and snapshots of transactional databases. End users do not change the data through online transactions.

The development life cycle of a data warehouse is the opposite of that of transactional systems. Somewhat dramatically, Inmon [6, p. 24] calls it CLDS, which is SDLC (system development life cycle) read backwards. While SDLC is driven by requirements, CLDS is data driven and works as follows.

- Start with the data in transactional databases and legacy file systems.
- Combine multiple data sources through extraction programs, rollups, and denormalization.
- Generate reports to analyze the data collected so far.
- Identify user requirements and decide on the final data models needed.

The hardware usage of a data warehouse is different from that of transactional systems. There are peaks and valleys in transactional processing, but ultimately a fairly predictable pattern emerges comprising batch jobs and interactive user transactions. For a data warehouse, however, the usage pattern is ad hoc and mostly unpredictable except for scheduled batch jobs that populate the data warehouse and prescheduled reports that run at designated times. Consequently, a data warehouse and a transactional database should not run on the same machine. A server can be optimized for a transactional application or for a data warehouse, but not for both.

11.3 Design Issues of Data Warehouse

Although a data warehouse is implemented as a relational database, many of the general design issues for a transactional relational database do not apply here. Consequently, we list below a few specific guidelines that are followed in the design of a data warehouse.

Granularity

Granularity refers to the level of detail via aggregation captured by the data elements in the warehouse. A high level of granularity means a low level of detail, which is the characteristic of the warehouse. On the other hand, transactional databases exhibit a low level of granularity, i.e., a high level of detail that is needed for day-to-day operations. As a result, an insurance warehouse can provide answers to questions such as: What is the average dollar value of auto insurance claims during the last 12 months. But it cannot answer the question: What is the claim amount settled for client James Arnold. Often a middle ground is followed based on time. Thus, the insurance warehouse may retain data with low granularity for a sliding window of 30 days, say, while retaining only high granularity for data older than 30 days. This is called *multiple levels of granularity*.

Determining the correct level of granularity poses a unique challenge for the designers of data warehouses. Usually this is accomplished through stepwise refinement as follows.

- Build a small subset of the target warehouse and generate reports.
- Allow users to use these reports and collect their feedback.
- Modify the design to incorporate the feedback and adjust the levels of granularity.
- Ask users to use reports from the modified design and collect their feedback.
- Repeat the above incremental development until you achieve the correct level(s) of granularity.

Partitioning

Partitioning represents the breaking up of large blocks of detailed data into smaller physical units. Data can be partitioned by a combination of one or more of such attributes as date, line of business, geographical region, organizational units, etc. If granularity and partitioning are handled properly, the other design issues become easy to manage.

Denormalization

Denormalization is the mechanism by which data in the 3NF tables in transactional databases are combined for inclusion in warehouse tables. As a result, both primitive and derived data elements appear in a data warehouse. This situation introduces transitive dependency in data warehouse tables. For example, a CUSTOMER ORDER table may contain columns, Customer Name, Address, . . . , Monthly Order appearing 12 times during one year, and Annual Average Monthly Order. The last column is derived from the 12 primitive columns, the Monthly Orders for 12 months. As such, the CUSTOMER ORDER table is not in 3NF. It is quite common to have tables in 2NF or even in 1NF in a data warehouse.

Various methods are used to denormalize data. Aggregation is one technique that has been discussed above under granularity. A second strategy is to introduce data redundancy in tables. For example, the two-character STATE CODE may be used in multiple tables in a warehouse. Rather than creating a separate lookup table with STATE CODE and STATE NAME and then enforcing a join operation each time the STATE NAME is needed, we include the two columns, STATE CODE and STATE NAME, together in every table where STATE CODE appears. This brings in data redundancy, but avoids multiple joins.

We know that data redundancy causes multiple update problems to keep data synchronized in a transactional database. Since tables in a data warehouse are updated only through batch jobs but never via online user transactions, such multiple update problems are handled in a warehouse through appropriate processing logic in the batch update programs.

Resolution of Data Inconsistencies

The data elements in a warehouse are gathered from diverse sources such as relational databases, nonrelational databases, file systems, Data Divisions of COBOL programs, etc. The data name, data type, and field size for the same data element can be different in different sources. It is the responsibility of the designer to resolve all inconsistencies before data can be loaded into the target tables. Four major types of inconsistency are described below.

- *Synonyms*: Multiple names for the same data element; e.g., SSNO, SS#, SOC_SEC_NUM, etc. all refer to the same element, the social security number.
- *Homonyms*: Same name for different data elements; e.g., NAME can mean the customer name in CUSTOMER table, the part name in the PART table, the supplier name in the SUPPLIER table, etc.
- *Type Mismatch*: Same data with different data types; e.g., the social security number may be a character string in one data source and a numeric field in another data source.
- *Size Mismatch*: Same data with different sizes; e.g., the social security number may be a 9-digit field in one data source and a character string of length 11 in another data source.

Wrinkle of Time

There is a time lag between record updates in a transactional database and those in a data warehouse. This time lag is called the *wrinkle of time*. A wrinkle of 24 hours is normal. The wrinkle implies that transactional data and warehouse data are loosely coupled. Data in the former must settle down before they are transferred to the latter. This does not, however, affect the usability of the warehouse data, because the warehouse does not need instantaneous updates as does a transactional database.

11.4 Structure of Data Warehouse

The design issues described in Section 11.3 indicate that a data warehouse often uses denormalized tables from transactional databases as its basic structure. Typically a data warehouse focuses on a specific subject area such as insurance claims, investment accounts, market niche, etc. As a result, the warehouse contains a few very large denormalized tables which are supported by a set of small normalized lookup tables for data validation. The large tables are in essence postjoins of 3NF tables from transactional databases. They are called *fact* tables. The small lookup tables are called *dimension* tables. This structure is called a *star schema* where the fact tables represent the kernel of the star and the dimension tables resemble the spokes of the star. The term star schema was coined by Dr. Ralph Kimball, the founder of Red Brick Systems, and has since been used industrywide. Figure 11.1 shows the structure of a star schema consisting of n fact tables supported collectively by m dimension tables.

Each dimension table represents an attribute of a fact table. The queries supported by a warehouse involve several dimensions related to a fact. Hence they are called multidimensional and a data warehouse is often called a multidimensional database (MDDB). The process of extracting information about the various dimensions of a fact is called *dimensional analysis*. For example, the following query may be posed to an insurance claims data warehouse.

What is the average claim amount for auto insurance during the calendar year 1999 for the six New England states?

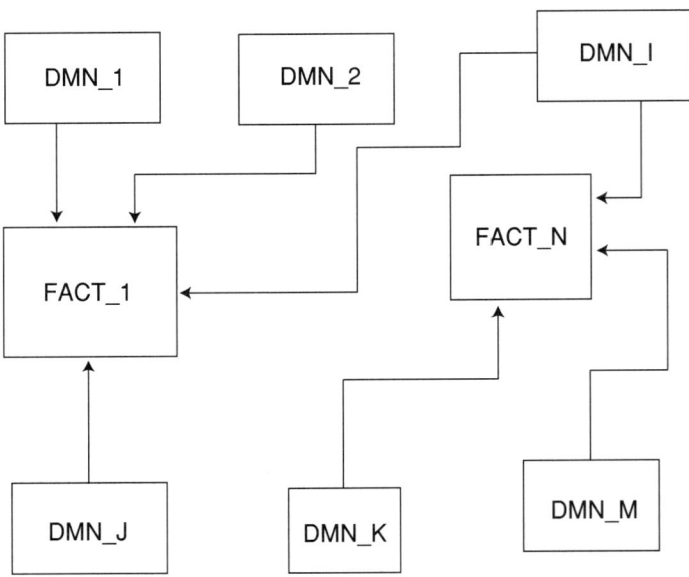

FIGURE 11.1: Star Schema

The query involves three dimensions: insurance type (auto), time (1999), and region (New England states). A fact table contains the basic summarized data such as claimant name, total monthly claim, insurance type, month, state, etc. The four dimension tables, insurance type, month, year, and state, provide the lookup data for the query.

11.5 Proliferation from Data Warehouse

During the last five to seven years the data warehouse has generated several new paradigms. Two of them, namely, datamart and data mining, deserve special mention. We discuss them in the next two subsections.

11.5.1 Datamart

The data warehouse supports the DSS requirements of a large organization and handles several different but related subject areas. Its fact tables may range from four to six in number along with an even larger number of dimension tables. For example, an insurance data warehouse may deal with three separate subject areas such as customer transactions, insurance claims, and new market venture. As discussed in Section 11.2, a data warehouse is built via CLDS in stepwise refinements. Thus, the warehouse may start with the customer transactions component at first, then build the insurance claims piece, and finally complete the warehouse with the new market venture segment. Each component is called a datamart. Thus, a *datamart* can be regarded as a subset of a data warehouse dealing with a single subject area. Several datamarts focusing on several related subject areas comprise a data warehouse. The above example shows that the insurance data warehouse consists of three related datamarts. However, we must keep in mind that each time a new datamart is added to the existing one(s), some data modeling and restructuring will be needed.

The real appeal of a datamart over a data warehouse lies in two factors.

- Cost: A datamart is less costly to build than a data warehouse. Corey and Abbey [4, pp. 193] report that a data warehouse comes with a price tag of three to five million dollars and takes up to three years for delivery.
- Ease of Use: Tools can handle datamarts more easily due to their smaller size allowing end users to retrieve data and produce reports more easily and perhaps quickly.

Datamarts are really the stepping stones to a data warehouse. However, in the rest of the chapter we use the term data warehouse collectively to refer to a datamart and a data warehouse.

In collaboration with many other vendors Oracle established a consortium called Warehouse Technology Initiative (WTI). The members of WTI offer a variety of tools that augment the functionality of Oracle warehousing and help customers to build a robust environment for their DSSs.

11.5.2 Data Mining

Users of a data warehouse access it to run ad hoc queries and generate predesigned reports. Except for the DBAs and developers, the rest of the user community does not access it via the command line using the SQL prompt. Instead a GUI front-end is provided for the end users that allows them to formulate their queries or select reports from some available lists under various categories. The underlying software converts the user requests into appropriate SQL code and executes them or invokes some report executables to return the results to the users. The goal of the software is to search the data warehouse, drill down as far as necessary to retrieve and assemble the requested information, and then display it for the users. An integral part of this search process is to understand the relationships among different pieces of data, to discern trends or patterns among the data elements, and to bring it out for the benefit of the users. *Data mining* is defined as the discovery and pattern recognition process for data elements in a data warehouse.

The fact and dimension tables of a data warehouse contain information about a related set of data belonging to a subject area. The discovery process of data mining explores the hidden underlying relationships among them that are not clearly visible to end users. For example, consider two fact tables, Customer Transaction (CT) and Insurance Claim (IC) in an insurance data warehouse. IC may contain a relatively large volume of auto insurance claims tied to a small set of zip codes. On exploring CT one may find that these zip codes represent three cities each of which contains a large number of colleges and universities. Further data mining may lead to the discovery of the relationship between the high number of auto accidents in these cities and the ages of the young students attending the educational institutions there.

Pattern recognition involves the correlation between two sets of data such that a change in one triggers a corresponding change in the other, either in the same direction or in the opposite. The statistical theory of correlation and chi-square tests have been used to handle pattern recognition in many areas. The process works in two steps. First, a hypothesis is formulated claiming the existence of a pattern. Next, data are collected over a period of time to validate or refute the hypothesis. Depending on the outcome we confirm or deny the existence of the pattern. If a pattern exists, additional reports may be generated utilizing it for the benefit of the organization. For example, a company knows that by advertising a product it can increase its sale. The data warehouse of the company contains volumes of data supporting this hypothesis. However, the data on the surface may not indicate that consumers with a specific level of education and a specific income range can be targeted by advertising only in certain specific media. Data mining can uncover this pattern. Although using software for data mining can indeed benefit a company, the expense incurred in such use has to be justified on a cost benefit analysis method.

Refer to any college-level statistics book for further details on hypothesis testing, chi-square test, and correlation and other related statistical methods.

11.6 Metadata

Metadata is described as a database about a database. Often the terms *meta database* or simply *metabase* are used. It consists of a set of text descriptions of all the columns, tables, views, procedures, etc. used in a database, the schema diagrams at the logical level, business rules implemented through various data validation algorithms such as declarative integrity and triggers, sizing algorithms used for the physical database, etc. Section 1.4.4 describes the metadata for an OLTP relational database. Oracle's data dictionary views and the V$ dynamic performance views are two examples of built-in metadata. They collect realtime data and statistics about all the database objects, the components of the SGA, background processes, and user transactions among others. The metadata for a data warehouse contains all of the above data needed for an OLTP database and, in addition, includes data about all the mappings needed for extracting data from the raw data sources and sending them to the target data tables in the warehouse.

The metadata is created, maintained, and processed through CASE tools such as Oracle Designer 2000, ERwin, Power Designer, etc. Any such software must have the ability to allow the users to run ad hoc queries and generate predesigned reports including diagrams. The users fall into two categories, technical and nontechnical. Technical users include DBAs and developers. Nontechnical users include business analysts.

Metadata for Technical Users

The DBAs extract information from the metadata dealing with sizes of database objects, availability of free space, trend of allocation of next extents to segments, data file sizes, disk space allocation, etc. Recall that all this information is available from the Oracle data dictionary, as described in Chapter 4. The DBA can utilize the scripts given in Chapters 4 to 6 or can reverse engineer the logical model from the data warehouse and then use some metadata tool to extract the information.

The developers' needs are different from those of a DBA and lean more towards the applications using the data warehouse. They may want to know the index structure on the fact and dimension tables, logical versus physical data models, schema diagrams, details of mappings between the source and target data stores, data validation as enforced by the metadata, etc. Although the scripts included in Chapters 8 through 10 provide some help, the use of a CASE tool is highly recommended.

Metadata for Nontechnical Users

These users are primarily business analysts who are subject area experts from a business viewpoint, but are not necessarily technically competent. They use the metadata to ensure that the warehouse can adequately provide data to support the DSS of the organization. Their primary focus is on the schema diagrams, descriptions of data elements at table and view levels, data validation routines enforcing the business rules, verification of source and target for individual data elements, etc. They should use a CASE tool to get the desired information.

11.7 Implementation and Internal Level

The warehouse database can be implemented by following the methodology described in Section 1.6. We describe below a set of issues specific to a warehouse.

Initialization Parameters

As discussed in Chapter 4, the initialization parameters control the settings of an instance. A database is started up by identifying its parameter file (pfile) via the command: startup pfile='*pfile_path*'. The parameters along with the guidelines listed below pertain to both internal and external levels of a data warehouse.

- *db_block_buffers*: It represents the number of data blocks cached in the memory (see Sections 4.2.1 and 6.3). Set this parameter to 30% of the total memory.
- *db_file_multiblock_read_count*: It represents the number of data blocks that are read in one I/O operation during a full table scan. Since I/O is a major activity in a data warehouse, set this parameter between 16 and 32. For a heavily accessed warehouse, set the value to the high end of the range.
- *db_files*: It represents the maximum number of database files that can remain open concurrently. This number should be around 1,020 for a warehouse with partitioning and with separate tablespaces for its fact and dimension tables and their respective indices.
- *log_buffer*: It represents the size of the redo log buffer cache in bytes (see Sections 4.2.1 and 6.4). Set it to a large value such as 4 MB to handle large transactions during warehouse updates. This will reduce the number of log switches and hence fewer I/Os.
- *open_cursors*: It represents the maximum number of cursors that can remain open simultaneously. Set this parameter to a value between 400 and 600.
- *processes*: It represents the maximum number of concurrent processes that can connect to the Oracle server. Set this parameter between 200 and 300. For the UNIX operating system, the number of semaphores must be set much higher than this parameter (see Section 6.7).
- *rollback_segments*: It specifies one or more rollback segments by name that are assigned to an instance. Due to the large volume of updates during the data load phase of the warehouse allocate six to eight segments of size 100 MB each with MINEXTENTS = 20.
- *shared_pool_size*: It represents the size in bytes of the shared SQL pool in SGA (see Sections 4.2.1 and 6.5). Set its value to 20 MB or more.
- *sort_area_size*: It represents in bytes the amount of memory allocated to do sorts for user requested operations. Since warehouse users often perform large sorts, set its value between 2 and 4 MB.
- *star_transformation_enabled*: If it is set to TRUE, the cost-based optimizer uses the star transformation for processing a star query via the best execution plan.

User Accounts

In a production database we normally create three categories of user accounts:

- SELECT privilege on all database objects;
- SELECT, INSERT, UPDATE, and DELETE privileges on all database objects; and
- CREATE, ALTER, DROP privileges on all database objects.

In general, the first category is assigned to developers, the second to end users, and the third to DBAs.

Various other combinations including the DBA privilege are possible. In a data warehouse, however, users do not make online updates. Instead data are loaded into the warehouse via nightly batch jobs (see Section 11.8 below). As a result, the user accounts are created primarily of the first category, i.e., with SELECT privilege only.

11.8 Data Loading in Warehouse

The data in a data warehouse come from different sources that are diverse in nature. The sources can be data files of legacy applications, Data Divisions of COBOL programs, nonrelational databases, Oracle and non-Oracle relational databases, etc. It is necessary to define a complete set of mappings that describe the source of each data element in the warehouse. The mapping defining the source of a column C in a table T, say, in the warehouse can be of the types:

- A single field in a source file;
- A single column in a source table in a relational or a nonrelational database;
- Aggregation of multiple columns in a single source table via group functions such as SUM, COUNT, AVG, etc.
- Combination of multiple columns in multiple source tables processed through some predefined algorithm. For example, suppose that a manufacturing company maintains four regional databases, each containing monthly sales data on customer orders. The column T.C in the warehouse represents the maximum average monthly sale taken over the four regions. The algorithm to compute the value of T.C will then be as follows.

  — Compute the moving average of 12 distinct monthly sales data for each region. It yields four monthly average figures for the four regions;
  — Select the maximum of these four average figures for the four regions.

All such mappings belong to the metadata for the warehouse (see Section 11.6). The data inconsistencies, if any, discussed in Section 11.3 are resolved through these mappings.

The data loading for the warehouse is accomplished by implementing the set of mappings through some tools. However, the update operation of a warehouse differs from that of a transactional database. The latter is updated through two types of data loading:

- Online interactive data entry by the online users with update privilege, and
- Prescheduled batch jobs moving large data feeds into the database.

For a data warehouse, the first type of update does not apply, because the online users of a data warehouse access it only for generating reports and running ad hoc queries. Consequently, the data warehouse is updated through regularly scheduled, usually nightly, bulk data loading batch jobs. The source data for the mappings can be prepared in two stages. First, the raw data from a variety of sources are brought into a temporary staging area which should preferably be an Oracle database. The aggregation and extraction algorithms reflecting the desired level of granularity and other design requirements are applied to the staging database. Next, the processed data are loaded into the fact and dimension tables of the data warehouse as the targets of the mappings. Due to the wrinkle of time discussed in Section 11.3, the data finally loaded into the warehouse are not up to date, and are not meant to be either. Figure 11.2 shows a schematic of the data loading process for a data warehouse via the mappings.

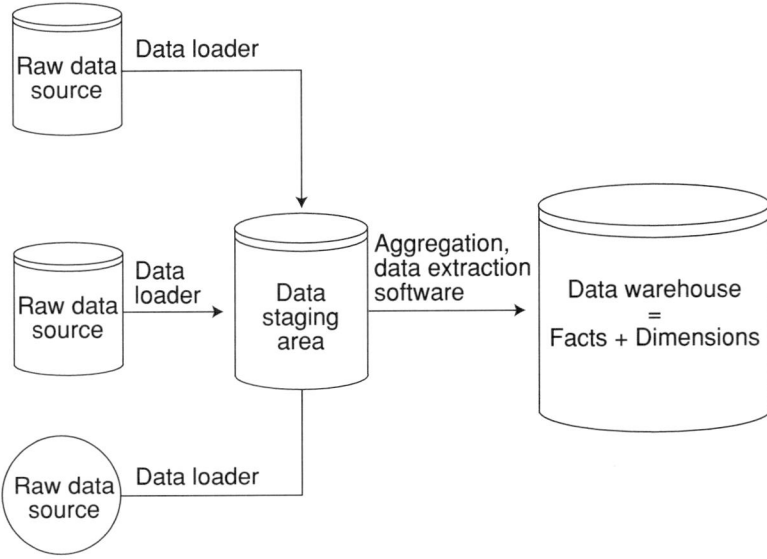

FIGURE 11.2: Schematic of Data Loading Process

Various tools are available for implementing the mappings to load data from raw data sources into a warehouse. We describe below two Oracle tools and make some comments about third party tools in general.

SQL*Loader

SQL*Loader is used to load data from operating system files into the tables of an Oracle database. Such files are mostly used in mainframe-based legacy applications. Thus, SQL*Loader is helpful in the first stage of data loading where data from diverse sources are collected in a staging area such as an intermediate Oracle database. The loader session needs two inputs:

- The source data to be moved into the Oracle tables, and
- A set of command line parameters that provide the details of the mapping such as the format and location of the source data, and the location of the target data.

The SQL*Loader has the features:

- Accept data from disk or tape,
- Allow one or more filtering criteria,
- Provide a variety of data types,
- Support both fixed length and variable length records, and
- Provide a wide range of error trapping routines and error reports to allow error recovery.

A detailed discussion of SQL*Loader is beyond the scope of this book. Corey and Abbey [4, Chapter 5] offers a good coverage of the technical details of SQL*Loader.

Export and Import

These two utilities in Oracle complement each other in scope. Export copies data in Oracle database objects into a compressed binary file called the export dump file that is readable by Oracle only. The default name of the dump file is expdat.dmp, although the name can be changed by the user performing the export. Import then copies the contents of the dump file into one or more Oracle tables. Export and import can be used for implementing mappings that connect data in transactional Oracle databases and an Oracle data warehouse.

Export and import operate in three modes:

- FULL: The entire database,
- USER: Database objects owned by a particular user, and
- TABLE: Data and data definitions of individual tables.

Both utilities can be invoked in one of three possible ways:

- Interactive dialogue between the user and Oracle,
- Command line parameters entered at the command line, and
- A set of parameters entered via the *parfile*.

As with SQL*Loader, a detailed discussion of export and import is beyond the scope of this book. Corey and Abbey [4, Chapter 5] offer a good coverage of the technical details of these two utilities.

Third Party Tools

Many third party tools are available for loading data into Oracle databases. Oracle's WTI (see Section 11.5.1) includes Power Mart, which is a GUI-based data loading tool marketed by Informatica. It consists of three components:

- Informatica Designer, which has three parts:
  — Source Analyzer,
  — Warehouse Designer,
  — Transformation Designer;

- Informatica Repository Manager; and
- Informatica Server Manager.

The tool connects to a repository via ODBC, which can be an Oracle database. The Source Analyzer stores extracted information from raw data sources in the Informatica Repository, which is managed by the Informatica Repository Manager. The Warehouse Designer prepares the logical and physical data models. The Transformation Designer prepares a set of mappings connecting the data sources to the target tables and columns in the warehouse. The mappings are designed by the "drag and drop" mechanism and can be changed easily whenever the data model changes. The Informatica Server Manager is used for configuring and running specific data loading sessions. Each session executes a set of mappings to transform data from sources to targets. When a session completes successfully, the target table(s) become populated.

Power Mart manuals available from Informatica should be used for additional details about the product.

11.9 Query Processing and Optimization

The general principles of query optimization described in Chapters 8 and 9 apply to a data warehouse. However, a warehouse often uses a special type of query known as the *star query*. Such a query utilizes the star schema structure of a data warehouse that consists of fact and dimension tables discussed in Section 11.4. Oracle 8i provides a special query optimization plan called the *star query execution plan* to handle star queries formulated against a star schema. A star query SQ, say, has the following structure.

SQ consists of a set of SELECTed columns from a fact table, say, FT, that are equi-joined to several dimension tables, say, DT1, ..., DTn, via PK–FK relationships. Each DTi, $i = 1, \ldots, n$, has a PK that matches an FK in FT and FT has a concatenated index that includes each of these FKs. The WHERE clause of SQ consists of two parts. One part contains qualifying conditions on columns of DTi, $i = 1, \ldots, n$. The other part contains the join conditions connecting the PK of each DTi, $i = 1, \ldots, n$, with the corresponding FK in FT. The star query execution plan requires that the following conditions hold.

- $n = 3$, i.e., there must be at least three dimension tables.
- There must be no USE_MERGE or USE_HASH hint on the fact table.
- The only allowed hint on the fact table is INDEX or INDEX_COMBINE.

In general, DT1, ..., DTn have many fewer columns and rows than FT. If the smallest dimension table from the set can be used as the driver for SQ and be joined with the remaining dimension tables in the query before the result set is joined with FT, then the processing time for SQ is minimized. Without loss of generality we can assume that DT1 is the smallest table in the query. The star query execution plan causes the fact table FT in the query to be joined at last with the prior result set as follows.

- Retrieve those rows from DT1, ..., DTn that satisfy the qualifying conditions of SQ.
- Create a table constituting a Cartesian product of these retrieved rows.
- Store this table in memory for fast processing of SQ.
- Join this table with FT as the last step of executing SQ and displaying the result set.

The star query execution plan requires that the following two conditions hold:

- FT must be much greater in size than each DTi, $i = 1, \ldots, n$.
- The qualifying conditions return only a few rows from DT1, ..., DTn so that the Cartesian product becomes a small table that can be stored in memory.

One must use proper hints in the query formulation to enforce this plan. It joins the fact table with the prior result set by means of a nested loops join on a concatenated index. It is advisable to verify with EXPLAIN PLAN that indeed the nested loops join is used. The optimizer also considers different permutations of the small tables. If the tables are ANALYZEd regularly, the optimizer will choose an efficient star query execution plan. Oracle offers two alternative ways to process star queries:

- Using hints, and
- Using star transformation.

11.9.1 Using Hints

There are two options under this category, as described below.

Combination of Three Hints

Using the query SQ described above, order the tables DTi, $i = 1, \ldots, n$, in the FROM clause in the order of the keys in the concatenated index of FT and place FT last. Then use the three hints:

```
/*+ ORDERED USE_NL(FT) INDEX(IND_CONCAT) */
```

where IND_CONCAT is the concatenated index of FT.

Example:

The warehouse maintains data about a financial investment application. Its star schema contains a fact table ACCT_FACT and four dimension tables, ACCT_DIMN, CRNC_DIMN, PERIOD_DIMN, and PERF_DIMN. The fact table contains computed data about the performance of individual accounts. The four dimension tables contain reference data for accounts, currency, investment period, and performance types. Each dimension table has a PK that appears as an FK in the fact table. The fact table has a four-column concatenated index on the four FKs. The detailed structure is as follows (see Figure 11.3).

```
ACCT_FACT        (ACCT_ID, CRNC_CODE, PERIOD_ID, PERF_ID,
                  TOT_FISCAL_PERF, AVG_FISCAL_PERF)
ACCT_DIMN        (ACCT_ID, ACCT_NAME, CUST_NAME, PLAN_NAME)
CRNC_DIMN        (CRNC_CODE, CRNC_NAME)
PERIOD_DIMN      (PERIOD_ID, PERIOD_END_DATE, MONTH, QUARTER)
PERF_DIMN        (PERF_ID, PERF_NAME)
```

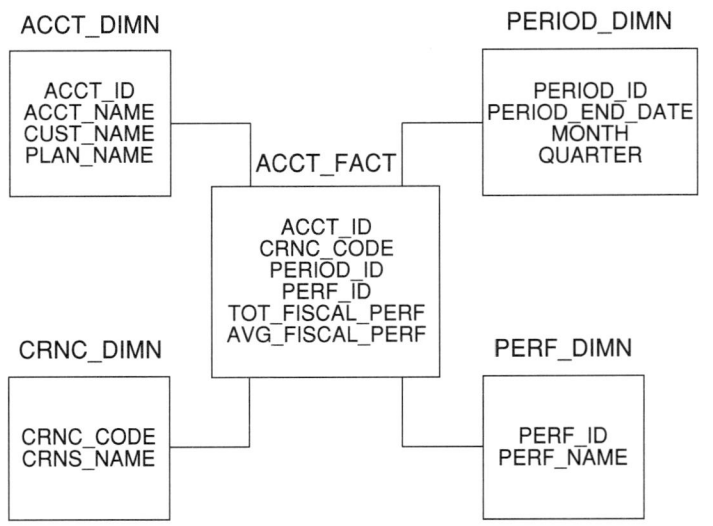

FIGURE 11.3: Star Schema of Five Tables

The table ACCT_FACT has a four-column concatenated index on the set (ACCT_ID, CRNC_CODE, PERIOD_ID, PERF_ID). We run the following query SQ against the warehouse.

```
SQ:   SELECT  /*+ ORDERED USE_NL(E) INDEX(IND_CONCAT) */
      TOT_FISCAL_PERF, AVG_FISCAL_PERF
      from
      ACCT_DIMN A, CRNC_DIMN B, PERIOD_DIMN C, PERF_DIMN D,
      ACCT_FACT E
      WHERE
      A. CUST_NAME = 'value1'  AND
      B. CRNC_NAME = 'value2'  AND
      C. QUARTER = 3  AND
      D. PERF_NAME = 'value3'  AND
      A. ACCT_ID = E. ACCT_ID  AND
      B. CRNC_CODE = E. CRNC_CODE  AND
      C. PERIOD_ID = E.PERIOD_ID     AND
      D. PERF_ID = E. PERF_ID;
```

11.9 Query Processing and Optimization

The star query SQ represents a star join. Its first part after the WHERE clause consists of four qualifying conditions on the four dimension tables. The second part contains four join conditions. The concatenated index IND_CONCAT on the four FK columns facilitates this type of join. The order of the columns in this index must match the order of the tables in the FROM clause and the fact table must appear at last. This is critical to performance. Figure 11.4 shows the execution plan for SQ under this version.

```
SQL> SELECT /*+ ORDERED USE_NL(E) INDEX(IND_CONCAT) */
  2    TOT_FISCAL_PERF, AVG_FISCAL_PERF
  3    from
  4    ACCT_DIMN A, CRNC_DIMN B, PERIOD_DIMN C, PERF_DIMN D,
  5    ACCT_FACT E where
  6    A.CUST_NAME = 'value1' and
  7    B.CRNC_NAME = 'value2' and
  8    C.QUARTER = 1 AND
  9    D.PERF_NAME = 'value3' and
 10    A.ACCT_ID = E.ACCT_ID and
 11    B.CRNC_CODE = E.CRNC_CODE AND
 12    C.PERIOD_ID = E.PERIOD_ID AND
 13    D.PERF_ID = E.PERF_ID;
61 rows selected
SQL> EXPLAIN PLAN
  2    SET STATEMENT_ID = 'FIGURE 11.4'
  3    FOR
  4    SELECT /*+ ORDERED USE_NL(E) INDEX(IND_CONCAT) */
  5    TOT_FISCAL_PERF, AVG_FISCAL_PERF
  6    from
  7    ACCT_DIMN A, CRNC_DIMN B, PERIOD_DIMN C, PERF_DIMN D,
  8    ACCT_FACT E where
  9    A.CUST_NAME = 'value1' and
 10    B.CRNC_NAME = 'value2' and
 11    C.QUARTER = 1       AND
 12    D.PERF_NAME = 'value3' and
 13    A.ACCT_ID = E.ACCT_ID and
 14    B.CRNC_CODE = E.CRNC_CODE AND
 15    C.PERIOD_ID = E.PERIOD_ID AND
 16    D.PERF_ID = E.PERF_ID;
Explained.
```

FIGURE 11.4: Star Query Execution Plan—Version 1

```
SQL>  SELECT DECODE(ID,0,'',
  2   LPAD(' ',2*(LEVEL-1))||LEVEL||'.'||POSITION)||' '||
  3   OPERATION||' '||OPTIONS||' '||OBJECT_NAME||' '||
  4   OBJECT_TYPE||' '||
  5   DECODE(ID,0,'Cost = '||POSITION) "Execution Plan"
  6   FROM PLAN_TABLE
  7   CONNECT BY PRIOR ID = PARENT_ID
  8   AND STATEMENT_ID = 'FIGURE 11.4'
  9   START WITH ID = 0 AND STATEMENT_ID = 'FIGURE 11.4';
Execution Plan
------------------
 SELECT STATEMENT      Cost = 20130
    2.1 NESTED LOOPS
       3.1 MERGE JOIN CARTESIAN
          4.1 MERGE JOIN CARTESIAN
             5.1 MERGE JOIN CARTESIAN
                6.1 TABLE ACCESS FULL ACCT_DIMN
                6.2 SORT JOIN
                   7.1 TABLE ACCESS FULL CRNC_DIMN
             5.2 SORT JOIN
                6.1 TABLE ACCESS FULL PERIOD_DIMN
          4.2 SORT JOIN
             5.1 TABLE ACCESS FULL PERF_DIMN
       3.2 TABLE ACCESS FULL ACCT_FACT
13 rows selected.
```

FIGURE 11.4 (*continued*): Star Query Execution Plan—Version 1

STAR Hint

An alternative method to process a star query such as SQ is to use the STAR hint /*+ STAR */. This version of SQ reads as follows.

```
SQ:  SELECT   /*+ STAR */
     TOT_FISCAL_PERF, AVG_FISCAL_PERF
     FROM
     ACCT_DIMN A, CRNC_DIMN B, PERIOD_DIMN C, PERF_DIMN D,
     ACCT_FACT E
     WHERE
     A.CUST_NAME = 'value1'  AND
     B.CRNC_NAME = 'value2'  AND
     C.QUARTER = 3  AND
     D.PERF_NAME = 'value3'  AND
     A.ACCT_ID = E.ACCT_ID  AND
     B.CRNC_CODE = E.CRNC_CODE AND
     C.PERIOD_ID = E.PERIOD_ID  AND
     D.PERF_ID = E.PERF_ID;
```

Figure 11.5 shows the execution plan for SQ under this version.

```
SQL> SELECT /*+ STAR */
  2      TOT_FISCAL_PERF, AVG_FISCAL_PERF
  6      from
  7      ACCT_DIMN A, CRNC_DIMN B, PERIOD_DIMN C, PERF_DIMN D,
  8      ACCT_FACT E where
  9      A.CUST_NAME = 'value1' and
 10      B.CRNC_NAME = 'value2' and
 11      C.QUARTER = 1       AND
 12      D.PERF_NAME = 'value3' and
 13      A.ACCT_ID = E.ACCT_ID and
 14      B.CRNC_CODE = E.CRNC_CODE AND
 15      C.PERIOD_ID = E.PERIOD_ID AND
 16      D.PERF_ID = E.PERF_ID;
61 rows selected
SQL> EXPLAIN PLAN
  2      SET STATEMENT_ID = 'FIGURE 11.5'
  3      FOR
  4      SELECT /*+ STAR */
  5      TOT_FISCAL_PERF, AVG_FISCAL_PERF
  6      from
  7      ACCT_DIMN A, CRNC_DIMN B, PERIOD_DIMN C, PERF_DIMN D,
  8      ACCT_FACT E where
  9      A.CUST_NAME = 'value1' and
 10      B.CRNC_NAME = 'value2' and
 11      C.QUARTER = 1       AND
 12      D.PERF_NAME = 'value3' and
 13      A.ACCT_ID = E.ACCT_ID and
 14      B.CRNC_CODE = E.CRNC_CODE AND
 15      C.PERIOD_ID = E.PERIOD_ID AND
 16      D.PERF_ID = E.PERF_ID;
Explained.
SQL> SELECT DECODE(ID,0,'',
  2      LPAD(' ',2*(LEVEL-1))||LEVEL||'.'||POSITION)||' '||
  3      OPERATION||' '||OPTIONS||' '||OBJECT_NAME||' '||
  4      OBJECT_TYPE||' '||
  5      DECODE(ID,0,'Cost = '||POSITION) "Execution Plan"
  6      FROM PLAN_TABLE
  7      CONNECT BY PRIOR ID = PARENT_ID
  8      AND STATEMENT_ID = 'FIGURE 11.5'
  9      START WITH ID = 0 AND STATEMENT_ID = 'FIGURE 11.5';
```

FIGURE 11.5: Star Query Execution Plan—Version 2

```
Execution Plan
------------------------------
 SELECT STATEMENT        Cost = 9
  2.1 NESTED LOOPS
    3.1 NESTED LOOPS
      4.1 NESTED LOOPS
        5.1 MERGE JOIN CARTESIAN
          6.1 TABLE ACCESS FULL PERF_DIMN
          6.2 SORT JOIN
            7.1 TABLE ACCESS FULL CRNC_DIMN
        5.2 TABLE ACCESS FULL ACCT_FACT
      4.2 TABLE ACCESS BY INDEX ROWID ACCT_DIMN
        5.1 INDEX UNIQUE SCAN PK_ACCOUNT UNIQUE
    3.2 TABLE ACCESS BY INDEX ROWID PERIOD_DIMN
      4.1 INDEX UNIQUE SCAN PK_PERIOD_DIMN UNIQUE
13 rows selected.
```

FIGURE 11.5 (*continued*): Star Query Execution Plan—Version 2

11.9.2 Star Transformation

The star transformation is an alternative way for executing star queries efficiently under the cost-based query optimizer. The methods described in Section 11.9.1 work well for star schemas with a small number of dimension tables and dense fact tables. The star transformation provides an alternative method when one or more of the following conditions hold.

- The number of dimension tables is large.
- The fact table is sparse.
- There are queries where not all dimension tables have qualifying predicates.

The star transformation does not compute a Cartesian product of the dimension tables. As a result, it is better suited for those star queries where the sparsity of the fact table and/or a large number of dimension tables would lead to a large Cartesian product with few rows having actual matches in the fact table. In addition, rather than relying on concatenated indices, the star transformation is based on combining bitmap indices on individual FK-columns of the fact table. Hence it is necessary to create a bitmap index on each FK-column in the fact table. These columns have low cardinality and, therefore, are ideal candidates for bitmap indexing. The star transformation can thus choose to combine indices corresponding precisely to the constrained dimensions. There is no need to create many concatenated indices where the different column orders match different patterns of constrained dimensions in different queries.

The two hints, STAR and STAR_TRANSFORMATION, are mutually exclusive in the sense that a query can use only one of these two hints. If a query does not mention either of these two hints explicitly, then the query optimizer uses the STAR path when the number of tables involved in the FROM clause of the query exceeds the value of the initialization parameter OPTIMIZER_SEARCH_LIMIT.

To use the hint STAR_TRANSFORMATION the query must satisfy the conditions:

- No bind variable(s) in the SELECT statement,
- No CONNECT BY or START WITH clause, and
- No hint FULL on the fact table.

The fact table must satisfy these conditions:

- Has more than 15,000 rows,
- Is not a view or a remote table, and
- Has three or more bitmap indexed FK-columns.

The dimension tables can be views, however.

The star transformation is enabled for query processing as follows.

- Set the initialization parameter STAR_TRANSFORMATION_ENABLED to TRUE. The default is FALSE. A third allowable value for this parameter is TEMP_DISABLE, which means that the query optimizer does not use temporary tables in the star transformation.
- Use the STAR_TRANSFORMATION hint to suggest to the optimizer to use the execution plan in which the transformation is used.

As with any hint, the query optimizer may choose to ignore the star transformation hint if it regards an alternative path as better. In general, the queries for the star transformation have to be very selective (i.e., restrictive WHERE clause) for the query optimizer to choose a star transformation join. Otherwise, it usually does parallel hash joins. Oracle does not allow the use of star transformation for tables with any of the characteristics:

- Tables with a table hint that is incompatible with a bitmap access path,
- Tables with too few bitmap indices,
- Remote tables,
- Antijoined tables,
- Tables that are already used as a dimension table in a subquery,
- Tables that have a good single-table access path, and
- Tables that are too small for the transformation to be worthwhile.

The hint STAR works well if the Cartesian product produces few rows. The hint STAR_TRANSFORMATION works well if equijoin predicates produce few rows. In other situations one must use a trial and error method to determine the best formulation of a star query.

Key Words

aggregation
ANALYZE
Cartesian product
data mining
data redundancy
datamart
decision support system
denormalization
dimension table
dimensional analysis
DSS, see decision support system
EXPLAIN PLAN
export
extraction programs
fact table
homonym
import
life cycle
log switch
meta database
metabase

metadata
multidimensional database
parameter file
qualifying condition
redo log buffer
repository
rollback segment
schema diagram
semaphore
SGA
shared SQL pool
SQL*Loader
star query
star query execution plan
star schema
star transformation
synonym
transitive dependency
Warehouse Technology Initiative
wrinkle of time
WTI

References and Further Reading

1. E. Aronoff, K. Loney, and N. Sonawalla—*Advanced Oracle Tuning and Administration*, Oracle Press, 1997.
2. D. K. Burleson—High-Performance *Oracle Database Applications*, Coriolis Group Books, 1996.
3. D. K. Burleson—*High-Performance Oracle Data Warehousing*, Coriolis Group Books, 1997.
4. M. J. Corey and M. Abbey—*Oracle Data Warehousing*, Oracle Press, 1997.
5. M. M. Gorman—*Managing Data Base*, QED Information Sciences, 1984.
6. W.. H. Inmon—*Building the Data Warehouse*, John Wiley & Sons, 1993.
7. S. S. Mittra—*Decision Support Systems: Tools and Techniques*, John Wiley & Sons, 1986.
8. S. S. Mittra—*Principles of Relational Database Systems*, Prentice-Hall, 1991.
9. S. G. Schur—*Database Factory*, John Wiley & Sons, 1994.
10. E. Sparley—*The Enterprise Data Warehouse*, Volume 1, Prentice-Hall—Hewlett-Packard Professional Books, 1999.

Burleson [3, Chapters 1–3], Corey and Abbey [4, Chapters 1 and 2], Inmon [6, Chapters 1–4), and Schur [9, Chapter 9] have discussed the evolution of the concept of a data warehouse and the characteristics and design issues resulting from them. Sparley

[10] offers a very comprehensive coverage of warehouse building methodology, data modeling, and metadata design. Mittra [7, Chapters 1 and 2] provides a good introduction to decision support systems including their architecture. Corey and Abbey [4, Chapters 7 and 8, and Appendices A and B] is a good source for information on datamarts and data mining including some URLs for information sources. Burleson [3, Chapter 15] contains a good treatment of data mining and includes a list of principal data mining products available in the market. Gorman [5] discusses metadata from a general data management viewpoint, and Mittra [8, Chapter 9] and Corey and Abbey [4, Chapter 9] offer a more database- and warehouse-oriented treatment. The issues dealing with warehouse implementation and the tuning of its internal level can be found in Burleson [3, Chapters 11 and 14] and Corey and Abbey [4, Appendix C]. Star queries are discussed in detail in Aronoff et al. [1, Chapter 11], Burleson [2, Chapter 10], Burleson [3, Chapter 12], and Corey and Abbey [4, Chapter 6].

Exercises

1. Refer to Exercise 3, Chapter 9. Assume that you want to design a datamart with ORDER and LINE_ITEM combined into a single fact table and with CUSTOMER and CUST_ORDER as two dimension tables. Remove Cust_Type and Cust_Region from CUSTOMER and introduce them as dimension tables such as TYPE and REGION. Make additional changes, as needed, to make the new structure represent the conceptual level of a datamart.

    (a) Run the query specified in the exercise against the datamart and record the execution plan and runtime.
    (b) Run the same query using the hints described in Section 11.9.1 under "Combination of Three Hints" and record the execution plan and runtime.
    (c) Run the same query again using the STAR hint described in Section 11.9.1 and record the execution plan and runtime.
    (d) Compare your findings in parts (a), (b), and (c) above to determine which execution plan is the best for your query.

2. Record the values of the initialization parameters listed in Section 11.7 except star_transformation_enabled for an operational database and a data warehouse in your workplace.

    (a) Identify the differences in their values and try to justify the differences.
    (b) If you are not convinced that the values are indeed appropriate, talk with your DBA to explore further. If you are the DBA, then either satisfy yourself that the values are justified or change the values as needed.

3. Explore the data loading tools that are used in a data warehouse environment with which you are familiar.
   (a) Prepare a metadata listing of all the mappings used in bulk data loading.
   (b) For each mapping, identify the source, the target, and the transformation being done to derive the target from the source.
   (c) Describe how data inconsistencies are resolved during the transformation. Specifically, examine the four types of inconsistencies listed in Section 11.3.
4. Explore the wrinkle of time for a data warehouse with which you are familiar.
   (a) Is there a single uniform wrinkle for all tables in the warehouse, or are there different wrinkles for different tables?
   (b) In the latter case, determine the reason for the difference and examine if any data inconsistency enters the warehouse due to the different wrinkles for different tables.
   (c) Explore the possibility of setting up a single wrinkle equal to the maximum value of all the different wrinkles. Will it introduce any operational difficulty?

12
Web-Based Database Applications

Outline

12.1 Advent of Web-Based Applications
12.2 Components of Web-Based Applications
12.3 Oracle Application Server (OAS)
12.4 Database Transaction Management Under OAS
12.5 Oracle Internet Application Server (iAS)
12.6 Performance Tuning of Web-Based Databases
12.7 Tuning of Internal Level
12.8 Tuning of External Level
Key Words
References and Further Reading
Exercises

Overview of the Chapter

The chapter provides performance tuning guidelines for Web-based database applications. After introducing the three-tier architecture of such applications the chapter guides the reader through the different layers of the architecture. The major concepts of web browser, application server, and nonpersistent HTTP protocols are discussed. The architecture of the Oracle Application Server (OAS) and its Transaction Management services are reviewed since OAS offers a robust platform for building Web-based applications with high performance. An overview of Oracle's new Internet Application Server (iAS) is also presented.

The database tuning principles of Web-based applications are no different from those for non-Web database applications. As such, the principles discussed in Chapters 3 through 10 apply equally well to Web-based applications. The chapter closes with an overview of tuning tools available in Oracle 8i.

12.1 Advent of Web-Based Applications

Since the mid-1990s a new application paradigm emerged as a three-tier client-server architecture with the World Wide Web as its basis. The *world wide web* can be defined as a collection of Web sites connected by the Internet. Each Web site consists of a computer that acts as a server performing a variety of functions to meet the information needs of end users. The Internet works as the backbone for this new paradigm. The two-tier client-server architecture of the late 1980s was replaced by this three-tier architecture with a potential of extension to an n-tier architecture. The functionality of each tier is described below.

Tier 1: This is the client tier. Its primary component is a Web browser such as the Netscape Navigator or Microsoft Internet Explorer. It is often called a *thin client* to distinguish it from the client of a two-tier architecture. The latter client is *fat* since it houses the entire client-side software.

Tier 2: This is the application tier that consists of a suite of software that accepts requests from the client (tier 1), communicates with the database (tier 3) for the required data, processes them, and returns the information to the client.

Tier 3: This tier contains the database and performs all database management functions. It is the remote tier that is not accessed directly by the end users.

In an n-tier architecture, where $n > 3$, the functionality of tier 2 is distributed over tiers 2 through $n - 1$. The nth tier houses the database for the application along with the supporting RDBMS.

This new paradigm has several unique features, as listed below.

(a) The client is completely portable across platforms.

Thin clients comprising Common Gateway Interface (CGI) compliant programs can run on any machine under any operating system. This makes the application independent of any specific platform. As a result, system-specific installation is not needed. The end users need a Web browser in addition to the client-side software to utilize the application.

(b) The processing intelligence of the application resides primarily on the middle tier.

This makes application upgrading fairly centralized at the middle tier. In this respect, the three-tier architecture resembles a mainframe model. The main difference between the two models is that whereas the client in the latter is a dumb terminal without any processing capability, the client in the former offers a rich GUI with considerable processing power.

(c) The connection to the third tier comprising the database is nonpersistent.

Each connection made by the application to the third tier ends as soon as the database transaction generated by the user request is complete. If the same user issues another request resulting in another database transaction, a second connection ensues. Hence the connection is labeled as *nonpersistent*. By contrast, in a two-tier application the end user logging at the client level accesses the database on the server via the connection established by the user request. As long as the user remains logged in, the connection is maintained. Hence the connection is labeled as *persistent*. Once a persistent connection is opened, it stays opened and results in quick response time. But idle user sessions waste such resources. A nonpersistent connection, on the other hand, releases the resource as soon as the transaction is complete, thereby allowing many more users to share this limited resource. No one user holds up a connection.

A Web-based database application optimizes database connectivity to achieve quick response time with nonpersistent connections.

12.2 Components of Web-Based Applications

We start with a rather simplistic operational scenario of a Web-based application that allows prospective candidates to register online for courses. We first describe the user's view of the application. We then analyze the individual steps in the registration process to identify the underlying tools for designing and implementing these applications.

(a) Using a Web browser the prospective candidate calls for a registration form.
(b) The Web browser transmits the request to the application server.
(c) The application server transmits the data entry form to the Web browser for display.
(d) The candidate completes the form online and submits it.
(e) The Web browser transmits the submitted form to the application server for processing.
(f) The application server opens up a connection to the database server and transmits the form data for updating the database.
(g) The RDBMS updates the appropriate table(s) with the form data, commits the transaction, and sends an acknowledgment to the application server.
(h) The application server transmits the acknowledgment to the Web browser for display.
(i) The candidate finds that he or she is enrolled in the course.

These nine steps involve the following tasks from a user's viewpoint.

- The Web browser displays some contents called *pages* in response to user requests. A page typically displays text, pictures, and possibly some other animation.
- A page may contain *links* to other pages in the same or different applications. The user can access these remote pages by activating the links.
- During this time the user is connected to the Web browser alone and is totally oblivious of the locations and structures of the linked pages.
- The Web server establishes a nonpersistent connection with other Web and database servers for each request and returns the result to the user's Web browser. For this reason the Web browser is often called the *universal desktop*.

388   12. Web-Based Database Applications

In order to perform the functions listed above we need the following set of tools that serve as props for designing a Web-based application.

1. *Web browser* to provide end user interface;
2. *Application server* to establish nonpersistent connections and to process user requests;
3. *Database server* running one or more RDBMSs such as Oracle, SQL Server, Informix, etc. to provide SQL as the nonprocedural query language and some procedural languages such as PL/SQL (Oracle), Transact SQL (SQL Server), etc. for supporting the database tier;
4. *HTTP* (Hyper Text Transport Protocol), which is a stateless request/response protocol, to transmit objects back and forth between the Web browser and the application server. An HTTP transaction consists of a request from the client directed to the server and a response to the request returned by the server;
5. *HTML* (Hyper Text Markup Language) to code display objects. HTML pages contain texts interspersed with tags that cause the Web browser to display these pages with formats as directed by the tags. The pages are static in that they cannot change their behavior in response to user generated events.
6. *Compiled or interpreted programming languages* such as Perl, C++, Java, UNIX shell languages, etc. to code CGI-compliant application programs residing on the application server that makes pages dynamic. These server-resident executable programs generate customized results in response to a user's request.

Figure 12.1 contains a schematic of a Web-based database application.

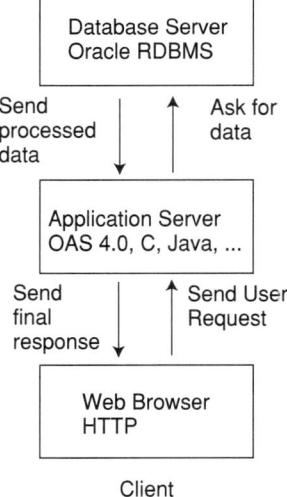

FIGURE 12.1: Architecture of Web-Based Database Application

12.3 Oracle Application Server (OAS)

The Oracle Application Server (OAS) consists of a suite of software residing on tier 2 (see Section 12.1) that provides a robust platform for building a Web-based application. OAS 4.0 can work with Oracle 7.3.4 and higher as the RDBMS residing on tier 3 [1, pp.27]. OAS 4.0.8 evolved through four versions that were marketed with different names. To start with, Oracle introduced Oracle Web Server (OWS) to enter the Web market. Versions 1 and 2 used the name OWS. It was changed to Oracle Web Application Server (OWAS) in version 3. Then it was changed to Oracle Application Server (OAS) in version 4. The architecture has fairly stabilized by now. OAS consists of the three principal layers shown in Figure 12.2. They are described below.

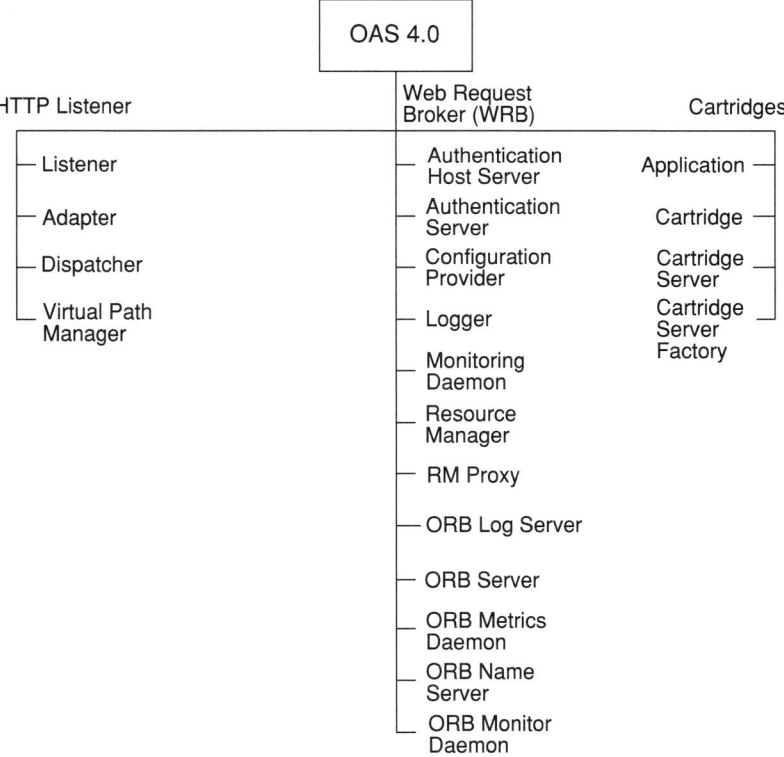

FIGURE 12.2: Architecture of OAS 4.0

HTTP Listener

This layer offers the universal front-end for all Web-based applications. End users enter their requests via a Web browser at this layer. They can request static pages or invoke server-side programs to activate and display dynamic pages. The four components of this layer perform the following functions.

- *Listener*: Handles incoming requests and routes them to the Dispatcher.
- *Adapter*: Embodies a common application programming interface (API) used by Oracle and other third party listeners to connect to the Dispatcher.
- *Dispatcher*: Accepts a request from Listener and dispatches it to an appropriate cartridge instance (see the paragraph "Cartridges and Components" below).
- *Virtual Path Manager*: Provides the Dispatcher with cartridge mapping and authentication requirements for the cartridge instance.

Web Request Broker (WRB)

This layer has 12 components that perform 12 functions to invoke and execute cartridge instances that are requested by the Dispatcher in Layer 1. Such requests normally ask for specific services such as executing a PL/SQL program, displaying an HTML page, etc. A single WRB instance can be used by multiple HTTP listeners. WRB works with an *Object Request Broker* (ORB), which is compliant with the *Common Object Request Broker Architecture* (CORBA). The 12 functions performed by the WRB are listed below.

- *Authentication Host Server*: Authenticates users via available schemes.
- *Authentication Server*: Completes the authentication process using one authentication broker and several authentication providers.
- *Configuration Provider*: Provides configuration information to local or remote system components.
- *Logger*: Enables components to write warnings or error messages to a log file or the database.
- *Monitoring Daemon*: Monitors the status of OAS objects and processes.
- *Resource Manager*: Performs overall resource management such as watching Cartridge Server processes, evaluating and responding to requests, etc.
- *RM Proxy*: Obtains object references from JCORBA and EJB objects and returns them to clients.
- *ORB Log Server*: Allows ORB processes to write status and error messages to a log file.
- *ORB Server*: As the main ORB process, facilitates the distribution of object requests.
- *ORB Metrics Daemon*: Collects statistics for the OAS monitoring daemon for enhanced load balancing.
- *ORB Name Server*: Contains the registry for OAS processes including ORB, OAS components, cartridges, and listeners except the Node Manager.
- *ORB Monitor Daemon*: Brings up and monitors the ORB components.

12.3 Oracle Application Server (OAS)

The ultimate goal of WRB is to activate the cartridges and components to service end user requests. The above 12 processes collectively accomplish that goal. The individual steps involved in this activation are described below. The responsible processes are listed within parentheses.

1. End user request arrives at Web browser.
2. HTTP listener identifies the cartridge instance, say, CART, needed by the request.
3. HTTP listener transmits the request to ORB services provided by Oracle Media Net (ORB Server, ORB Name Server, ORB Log Server, ORB Metrics Daemon, ORB Monitor Daemon).
4. If CART is available, then

    (a) WRB is invoked (Configuration Provider, Logger, OAS Monitoring Daemon).

    (b) CART instance is authenticated and provided (Authorization Host Server and Authorization Server).

    (c) WRB is started and CART instance is created in the cartridge factory (Resource Manager, RM Proxy).

5. If CART is not available, then

    (a) HTTP listener requests WRB that a new CART instance be created (Configuration Provider, Logger, OAS Monitoring Daemon).

    (b) Steps (b) and (c) are repeated.

Figure 12.3 shows the above sequence of steps graphically.

392   12. Web-Based Database Applications

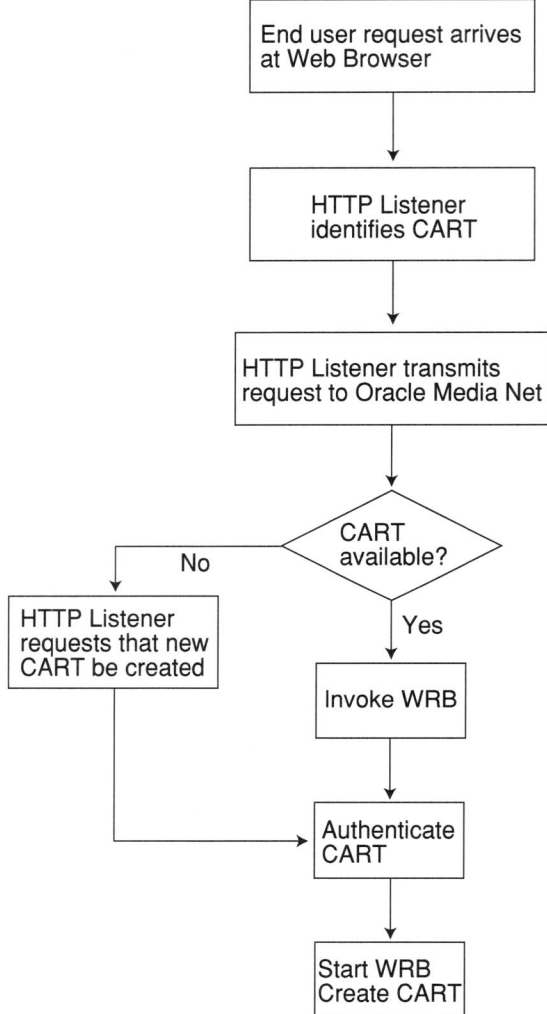

FIGURE 12.3: Cartridge Activation Process for WRB

Cartridges and Components

Cartridges are C programs that reside on the application server and implement the functionality of the application. Being executable programs cartridges perform specific services or functions for end users such as implementing requests sent to the HTTP listener by the Web browser. A cartridge can invoke or execute programs written in other languages such as PL/SQL, Perl, Java, etc. These latter programs are called *components*. Together cartridges and components can be utilized as reusable code implementing specialized functions such as computation of sales tax, estimation of inventory reorder level, projection of human resource for a given level of customer needs and operating budget, etc.

This layer performs four functions as listed below:

- *Application*: Controls cartridges executing application code;
- *Cartridge*: Uses configuration data and passed parameters to execute code in the server;
- *Cartridge Server*: Manages and runs the cartridges as part of the application; and
- *Cartridge Server Factory*: Instantiates a cartridge when the Cartridge Server first starts up and when requests for cartridges come in.

12.4 Database Transaction Management Under OAS

In addition to activating cartridge instances in response to end user requests WRB performs a variety of services. An important one from a database viewpoint is the Transaction Management service. Since HTTP is a stateless or nonpersistent protocol, a problem arises in handling user requests that depend on earlier actions initiated by the same user. In such a case, it is necessary to group database operations into separate transactions, where each transaction consists of a collection of retrieval and update operations and spans multiple HTTP requests and/or cartridges written in PL/SQL, C, Java, JWeb, LiveHTML, and JCORBA and EJB objects. These transactions are called distributed. The cartridges used by distributed transactions are called *stateful*, because they keep track of the database operations invoked by a specific user request.

A transaction invoked as a result of an end user request is a batch process executing against the database. As such, it may consist of several update requests such as, say, two inserts, one delete, and three changes. Oracle ensures that each transaction is executed as a group under the application control to maintain the database integrity. With this end in view the OAS Transaction Management services implement the following three features.

(a) Atomic Property

The transaction execution follows an all-or-none approach. If at least one of the component steps does not complete successfully, the entire transaction is rolled back. This returns the database to the pretransaction stage so that it remains internally consistent. In particular, it ensures that referential integrity constraints are not violated as a result of partial updates.

(b) Single Source Update

By implementing row-level exclusive locks on tables that are being updated by a transaction, Oracle ensures that such updates are not overwritten by other updates made by other concurrent users. Once the full transaction is committed, Oracle releases the lock to make the updated table(s) available for other users.

(c) Permanency of Update

Once rows are updated, they are written to the data block buffer and labeled as "dirty" buffers. Subsequently, the DBWR background process transfers them to the appropriate tables on disk files. In case of a system or media crash Oracle restores the full database to a consistent state through its recovery mechanism.

Transaction Management services within the WRB cause transactions to start explicitly by accessing a particular URL. The transaction ends when either the commit URL or the rollback URL is accessed.

12.5 Oracle Internet Application Server (iAS)

OAS 4.0.8.2 was the terminal release of OAS. Subsequently Oracle marketed a new Web server called Internet Application Server (iAS) based on the Apache server and targeted as the next generation platform for Web applications. iAS allows an application to retrieve data from the Oracle database, static HTML, as well as Java-based applications. It offers the ability to have frequently used data (table, Java, EJB, etc.) stored on a middle tier for faster response time. It offers the features:

- A deployment model with multiple deployment options;
- A variety of methods for generating Web content including PL/SQL and PSP, Java servlets and JSP, and Perl;
- Partial conformance to existing and evolving standards such as Java, J2EE, and CORBA.

iAS is a middle-tier application server designed for the Intranet and Internet. It provides a set of installed services so that a complete middle tier becomes easy to conFigure and manage. iAS is compatible with Oracle8 and above. More specifically, iAS 1.0.0 is certified by Oracle to be compatible with Oracle 8.0.6 and iAS 1.0.22 with Oracle 8.1.7.

12.6 Performance Tuning of Web-Based Databases

The database in a Web-based application resides on the remote tier (tier 3) where the server version of the RDBMS such as Oracle is installed. The Web application may or may not use OAS or other Oracle Web application development tools. As noted in Section 12.3, OAS 4.0 requires Oracle 7.3.4 or higher versions on tier 3. In order to make OAS work efficiently with Oracle, the minimum and maximum number of cartridge instances should be estimated and set accordingly at the time of installation of the OAS. A heuristic approach to estimate these values is given below.

- Estimate the peak number N, say, of concurrent requests that will be handled by each type of cartridge, say, PL/SQL, C, Java, etc.

- Set the minimum and the maximum number of cartridges at $0.7N$ and $1.5N$ respectively, assuming that these limits do not impose excessive paging. Oracle recommends that when all cartridge instances are running, no more than 75% of the available swap space should be consumed.

The structure of the database on tier 3 and its tuning principles are the same irrespective of the application. To optimize the database performance it is necessary to monitor and tune each level, i.e., conceptual, internal, and external. Therefore, the tools and principles discussed in Chapters 3 through 10 for Oracle 8i apply equally well to the database of a Web-based application. We discuss the tuning principles briefly in Sections 12.7 and 12.8.

12.7 Tuning of Internal Level

As noted in Section 12.4, distributed transactions under OAS span multiple HTTP requests and/or cartridges. For such transactions involving large workloads one can improve the transaction performance by setting up multiple nodes at the site. A typical configuration can run Listeners and Dispatchers on the primary node and Cartridge Servers on remote nodes as shown in Figure 12.4. It is assumed in the diagram that the application is a heavy user of cartridges; i.e., the majority of end user requests involves dynamic pages. As such, this configuration is quite different from one where end users predominantly use static HTML pages. By distributing the workload among multiple nodes one minimizes processor contention between OAS components and the database.

A primary benefit and function of an application server is to load balance users across persistent connections. Thus, for example, 100 users connected to an application server may share 10 connections pooled by it. The application server may indeed persist with the pooled connections on behalf of its anticipated user workload to reduce the response time for users.

396   12. Web-Based Database Applications

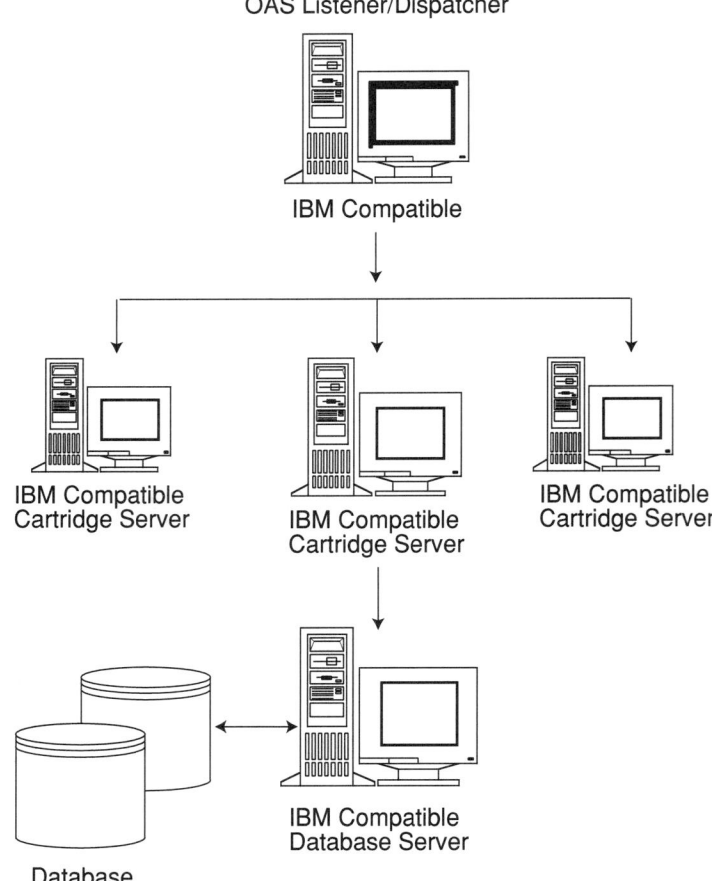

FIGURE 12.4: Sample Configuration of OAS

Oracle 8i offers a set of built-in packages that help in running a well-tuned application against the database. The list below gives an overview of some of these packages. Brown [1, Chapter 9] contains a detailed discussion of these packages with sample code fragments.

(a) DBMS_ALERT: Provides support for asynchronous notification of database events. It allows the monitoring of database changes occurring from the start to the end of a procedure.

(b) DBMS_APPLICATION_INFO: Provides a mechanism for registering the name of the application module currently running and its current action within the database. Using this package the DBA can determine usage and performance of real users and take corrective action, if needed.

(c) DBMS_DDL: Allows the DBA to execute DDL commands from within a stored procedure. Such commands include CREATE, ALTER, and ANALYZE.
(d) DBMS_SESSION: Provides access to the command ALTER SESSION and other session information from within stored procedures. The DBA can alter session-specific parameters dynamically with this package.
(e) DBMS_UTILITY: Contains a large number of procedures that help tuning both the internal and the external levels. In particular, DBAs can use procedures and functions such as analyze_schema, analyze_database, is_parallel_server, get_time, get_parameter_value, db_version, etc. for their tasks.

12.8 Tuning of External Level

The following is a partial list of packages available from Oracle 8i to help tune the external level. Brown [1, Chapter 9] provides further descriptions of these packages.

(a) DBMS_SQL: Provides a means to use Dynamic SQL for accessing the database. The package contains a large repertoire of procedures and functions that can be used in writing PL/SQL code.
(b) DBMS_TRACE: Allows one to turn on and off the tracing of all SQL statements (see Section 8.7.4) at a session level. The output from tracing can be analyzed to identify poorly performing queries.

Key Words

3-tier architecture	nonpersistent connection
application server	persistent connection
cartridge	thin client
Common Gateway Interface	Transaction Management
component	universal desktop
HTTP Listener	Web browser
Hyper Text Markup Language	Web server
Hyper Text Transport Protocol	World Wide Web
n-tier architecture	

References and Further Reading

1. B. D. Brown—*Oracle 8i Web Development*, Oracle Press, 2000.
2. Dynamic Information Systems—*Oracle Web Application Server Handbook*, Oracle Press, 1998.
3. P. Ju—*Databases on the Web*, M&T Books, 1997.

4. Oracle Corporation—*Analytic Functions for Oracle 8i, An Oracle Technical White Paper*, October 1999.
5. J. Rodley—*Developing Databases for the Web & Intranets*,Coriolis Group Books, 1997.

Ju [3, Chapter 2] and Rodley [5, Chapter 1] provide a nice introduction to the new paradigm of Web-based database applications. Dynamic Information Systems [2, Chapter 2] and Rodley [5, Chapter 4] offer good descriptions of the architecture of Web-based applications, primarily of the Web browser and the application server functions. Dynamic Information Systems [2, Chapters 3, 10] discusses OWAS 3.0, which is the version prior to OAS 4.0. Brown [1, Chapter 10] gives a comprehensive coverage of the features of the four different versions of OAS. Transaction Management services constitute an important feature of both OWAS 3.0 and OAS 4.0. Dynamic Information Systems [2, Chapter 10] and Brown [1, Chapters 10, 14] discuss this feature of OWAS and OAS respectively. Brown [1, Chapter 4] discusses the use of UNIX "sar" utility and the principle of load balancing among nodes as tools for tuning the internal level of the Web database. Both of them have been discussed earlier in Chapter 6 of the present book. Brown [1, Chapter 9] gives a detailed treatment of Oracle 8i built-in packages for tracking database performance at both internal and external levels under Oracle 8i.

Exercises

This chapter does not introduce any new tools for performance tuning. Instead it refers to Chapters 4 through 10 for the corresponding tools and methods. Hence the exercises below involve the use of those tools in a Web-based database environment. The exercises also assume that you have access to Web-based database applications as a DBA and that these applications are built with Oracle8 and/or Oracle 8i.

1. Apply the tuning principles and tools for the internal level of a database as discussed in Chapters 4 through 7 and 10 to a Web-based application built with Oracle 8i. Assess the effect of your tuning by using metrics such as hit ratios, shared SQL pool size, "sar" utility for measuring the extent of paging and swapping, SGA size versus real memory size, etc.
2. Use the tuning principles and tools for the external level of a database as discussed in Chapters 8 through 10 to a Web-based application built with Oracle 8i. Compare the results with those derived by using the built-in packages for tuning as discussed in Section 12.7.
3. If you have experience with using OAS 4.0 under Oracle8 and Oracle 8i, describe the differences in performance of OAS 4.0, if any, between these two versions of the Oracle RDBMS.

Appendices

The five appendices included here discuss several DBA issues, although not directly related to performance tuning and optimization.

Appendix A provides a sizing methodology for estimating the storage space needed for tables, indices, and tablespaces. Two C programs are included to implement the sizing algorithms.

Appendix B contains a step-by-step methodology to create an instance and its associated database. A large number of scripts are included in the appendix to help a DBA perform this task.

Appendix C offers a similar step-by-step methodology to drop an instance and its associated database.

Appendix D provides a methodology for refreshing an existing database with data from another database with identical structure. The transportable tablespaces introduced in Oracle 8i are used for this purpose.

Appendix E contains the mathematical foundation of relational database systems. It is designed for mathematically inquisitive readers who are interested in the theory underlying relations, normalization principles, query languages, and the search process.

Appendix A
Sizing Methodology in Oracle 8i

Outline

    A1. Transition from Logical to Physical Database Design
    A2. Space Usage via Extents
    A3. Algorithms for Sizing Tables, Indices, Tablespaces
    A4. STORAGE Clause Inclusion: Table and Index Levels
    A5. Sizing Methodology
    A6. RBS, SYSTEM, TEMP, and TOOLS Tablespace Sizing
    Key Words
    References and Further Reading

Overview of the Appendix

The appendix contains a semiautomated step-by-step methodology for sizing database objects in a relational database under Oracle. The methodology can be easily automated. The transition from logical to physical database design is the starting point of any sizing. The appendix describes how the five crucial parameters for sizing are computed based on the rowsize and rowcount of each table and the type and composition of each index. Two C programs are included to perform the actual sizing of tables and indices. Tablespaces are sized on the basis of the sizes of their component objects. The appendix contains three spreadsheets that show the actual computation of the STORAGE parameters for database objects.

A1. Transition from Logical to Physical Database Design

The sizing of database objects such as tables, indices, and tablespaces constitutes a crucial component of physical database design. It estimates the amount of disk space needed to store the entire database. The goal for sizing is threefold:

- Provide an accurate estimate of disk storage needed,
- Ensure that the nondata and nonindex tablespaces (e.g., SYSTEM, ROLLBACK, etc.) are properly designed, and
- Minimize tablespace fragmentation and row chaining in tables.

To avoid confusion, I assume that the following logical data structure information already exists as the end product of a prior logical database design effort:

(a) Complete table structure including names, data types, and sizes of the columns;
(b) Full set of PKs and FKs with identification of each FK and its matching PK in table.column format;
(c) All CHECK constraints, as far as known at this stage;
(d) NOT NULL and UNIQUE constraints, as applicable; and
(e) Additional indexing requirements besides the PKs in table.column format, if known.

The transition from logical to physical database design involves the mapping of the logical data structures onto physical disk storage so that CREATE TABLE, CREATE INDEX, etc. commands can be written readily. This requires the sizing of tables, indices, and tablespaces for the STORAGE clauses. The internal storage requirements of these database objects are properly estimated in order to assign values to their storage components called initial and next extents. If a data modeling tool such as Oracle Designer 2000 or ERwin is used, the scripts for creating tables and indices with appropriate storage clauses are generated automatically from the logical specifications.

Besides the tablespaces for tables and indices, an Oracle database contains the SYSTEM tablespace, the rollback tablespace, usually referred to as the RBS, and the temporary tablespace, usually called the TEMP. Each of these should also be sized properly, as explained in Section A6.

A2. Space Usage via Extents

The STORAGE clause for a tablespace and a segment (table, index, rollback, and temporary) consists of five parameters: INITIAL, NEXT, MINEXTENTS, MAXEXTENTS, and PCTINCREASE. Their respective default values are listed below:

INITIAL = 5 data blocks;
NEXT = 5 data blocks;
MINEXTENTS = 1 for all segments except rollback; 2 for rollback segments;
MAXEXTENTS = variable (see Section 1.5.1);
PCTINCREASE = 50.

When a segment is created, its extents are allocated according to the value of MINEXTENTS. If MINEXTENTS = 1, then only the INITIAL extent is allocated. If MINEXTENTS > 1, then besides the INITIAL extent, (MINEXTENTS − 1) number of NEXT extents are also allocated. Subsequently, each NEXT extent is allocated when the current extent becomes full. The NEXT extent is sized according to the following formula,

```
NEXT = NEXT * (1 + PCTINCREASE / 100).
```

Oracle sets the default value of PCTINCREASE to 50. We can see right away that PCTINCREASE = 50 will lead to a combinatorial explosion of the size of the NEXT extents, because then each NEXT EXTENT will be 1.5 times the size of the current NEXT EXTENT. Therefore, one should make PCTINCREASE = 0. However, see the caveat in Section A4. The default value of MAXEXTENTS has already been listed in Section 1.5.1. The option MAXEXTENTS = UNLIMITED, which assigns the value of 2,147,483,645 to MAXEXTENTS, should be used with caution and with regular monitoring of the storage space in the tablespaces, because it may lead to a system crash when a disk becomes full during an unusually long update transaction.

A3. Algorithms for Sizing Tables, Indices, Tablespaces

Oracle stores new data in the free space available within a data block, which can be of size 2, 4, 8, 16, 32, or 64 K. The block header consisting of fixed and variable block headers consumes about 90 bytes. Next, the PCTFREE (default value is 10%) area is set aside to allow existing records to expand through updates. The remaining space in the data block is available for inserting new records. Thus, the available free space in a data block of size 2 K (= 2,048 bytes) with PCTFREE = 10 is estimated as follows.

```
Block = 2048
Block Header = 90
PCTFREE Area = 10% * (2048-90) = 196 (rounded up)
```

So, available free space = 1,958–196 = 1,762 bytes.

A larger value of the block size provides more free space since the block header remains constant at 90 bytes. See Figure A.1.

Appendix A. Sizing Methodology in Oracle 8i

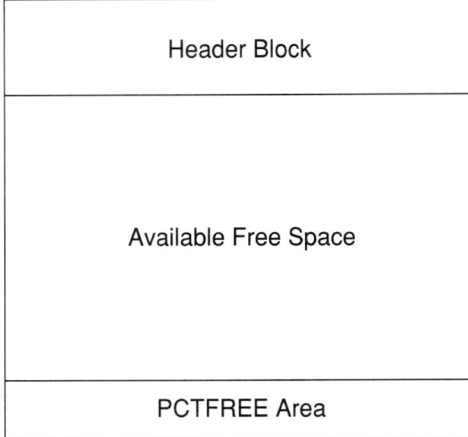

FIGURE A.1: ORACLE Data Block

Various algorithms are available to estimate the storage space needed for storing the rows of a table. All of them need the rowcount of a table as one of the input parameters. Usually, this is difficult to obtain. Also, overestimation is always recommended. I use two C programs, one for tables and the other for indices.

Table

```
/*      PURPOSE: This program reads the name of a table in the
        database, its rowsize, and its rowcount from a text file.
        Then it computes the number of Oracle blocks needed to store
        the data of the table and prints the result in the output
        file.

        PROGRAM FILE NAME:   tablsize.c
        INPUT FILE NAME:     tbls.txt
        OUTPUT FILE NAME:    tbls_size.txt
        AUTHOR:              NAME
        DATE CREATED: DATE
*/

#include        <stdio.h>

#define         BLOCK_SIZE      8192
#define         HEADER 90
#define         PCTFREE         10.0
void main ()
{
        FILE    *fopen (), *in_file, *out_file;
        int     num_blocks_needed, num_rows_per_block, block_space,
                rowsize, num_rows;
        float   available_block_space, rows_per_block,
```

```
                blocks_needed, rowcount;
        char    line [81], table_name [50];
        /*      Open the input file tbls.txt in READ mode and
                the output file tbls_size.txt in APPEND mode    */
        in_file = fopen ("tbls.txt", "r");
        out_file = fopen ("tbls_size.txt", "a");
/*      Read each record in the file tbls.txt, disassemble it into
                three separate fields, TABLE_NAME, ROWSIZE, and
                ROWCOUNT, and compute the number of Oracle blocks
                needed to store the records of the table        */
        while ( fgets (line, 81, in_file) != NULL )
        {  sscanf (line, "%s  %d  %f", table_name, &rowsize,
           &rowcount);
        num_rows = rowcount;
        block_space = BLOCK_SIZE - HEADER;
        available_block_space = block_space * (1 - PCTFREE / 100);
        rows_per_block = available_block_space / rowsize;
        num_rows_per_block = rows_per_block;
        blocks_needed = rowcount / num_rows_per_block;
        num_blocks_needed = blocks_needed + 1.0;

        fprintf (out_file, "%-50s%d\n", table_name, num_blocks_needed);
        }
}
```

Index

```
/*      PURPOSE:        This program reads from input file the
                        following parameters:
                        -- an index name,
                        -- total length of indexed columns,
                        -- total number of indexed columns,
                        -- the number of columns exceeding 127
                           characters,
                        -- uniqueness,
                        -- and rowcount of the table.
                Then it computes the number of Oracle blocks needed to
                store the index data and prints the result in the output
                file.
                PROGRAM FILE NAME:      indxsize.c
                INPUT FILE NAME:        indx.txt
                OUTPUT FILE NAME:       indx_size.txt

                AUTHOR:         NAME
                DATE CREATED:           DATE
*/
#include<stdio.h>

#define     BLOCK_SIZE          8192
#define     HEADER              161
```

```c
#define    HEADER_SPACE    8
#define    PCTFREE         10.0
void main ()
{
        FILE   *fopen (), *in_file, *out_file;
        int    num_blocks_needed, num_indices_per_block,
               block_space,tot_length_ind_cols;
        int    tot_num_ind_cols, tot_num_long_cols, num_rows,
               index_space, unq_ind;
        float  available_block_space, indices_per_block,
               blocks_needed, rowcount;
        char   line [81], index_name [50];
        /* Open the input file indx.txt in READ mode and the
              output file indx_size.txt in APPEND mode.        */
        in_file = fopen ("indx.txt", "r");
        out_file = fopen ("indx_size.txt", "a");
        /*   Read each record in the file indx.txt, disassemble it
             into six separate fields, INDEX_NAME,
             TOT_LENGTH_IND_COLS, TOT_NUM_IND_COLS,
             TOT_NUM_LONG_COLS, UNQ_IND, and ROWCOUNT; then
             compute the total number of Oracle blocks needed to
             store the index, and print the result in the output
             file indx_size.txt.   */
        while ( fgets (line, 81, in_file) != NULL )
        {       sscanf (line, "%s %d %d %d %d %f",
                    index_name, &tot_length_ind_cols,
                    &tot_num_ind_cols, &tot_num_long_cols, &unq_ind,
                    &rowcount);
            num_rows = rowcount;
            block_space = BLOCK_SIZE - HEADER;
            available_block_space = block_space * (1 - PCTFREE / 100);
            index_space = tot_length_ind_cols + tot_num_ind_cols +
                    tot_num_long_cols + HEADER_SPACE + unq_ind;
            indices_per_block = available_block_space / index_space;
            num_indices_per_block = indices_per_block;
            blocks_needed = rowcount / num_indices_per_block;
            num_blocks_needed = blocks_needed + 1.0;
            fprintf (out_file, "%-50s%d\n", index_name, num_blocks_needed);
        }
}
```

Tablespace

A tablespace for tables or indices holds all the tables or indices respectively that are created in that tablespace. The size of a tablespace, therefore, is calculated using the sizes of its contents as follows.

```
DATA TABLESPACE = Σ {(INITIAL + NEXT * (MAXEXTENTS-1)) + 1K}
     Table ∈ Tablespace
INDEX TABLESPACE = Σ {(INITIAL + NEXT * (MAXEXTENTS-1)) + 1K}
     Index ∈ Tablespace
```

The component 1 K is used for overhead.

The above formulas apply only when MAXEXTENTS is assigned a finite value instead of the value UNLIMITED.

A4. STORAGE Clause Inclusion: Table and Index Levels

The algorithms given above indicate that database objects such as tables and indices should be sized bottom up. The STORAGE clause of a table or an index should be constructed as follows.

INITIAL = Oracle blocks needed to store a fully populated table or index in Production.
NEXT = Oracle blocks needed to store the incremental growth at some regular frequency (e.g., monthly, quarterly, etc.).
PCTINCREASE = 0.

These are only guidelines and should be adjusted depending on the situation. Also, development and test databases are usually in a state of flux and are much smaller in size than a production database. Properly scaled down sizes of the objects in a production database usually suffice as estimates of sizes of objects in a development or a test database.

There is one caveat, though, for setting PCTINCREASE = 0. If PCTINCREASE is positive, the background process SMON (system monitor) automatically coalesces contiguous free extents in a tablespace into a single extent. This helps in keeping the free space in tablespaces defragmented. A compromise can be made by setting PCTINCREASE = 1, the smallest positive integer, so that SMON can operate and, at the same time, the NEXT EXTENT sizes increase very slowly. Thereby a combinatorial explosion of NEXT EXTENT sizes does not occur.

A5. Sizing Methodology

The methodology consists of the following steps.

(a) Run the program *tablsize.c* to determine the number of blocks needed for storing data of each table. The file *tbls_size.txt* contains this information.
(b) Run the program *indxsize.c* to determine the number of blocks needed for storing data of each index. The file *indx_size.txt* contains this information.
(c) Create a spreadsheet *Table Sizing.xls* as shown in Figure A.2.

(d) Create a spreadsheet *Index Sizing.xls* as shown in Figure A.3.
(e) Create a spreadsheet *Tablespace Sizing.xls* as shown in Figure A.4.

		Table Sizing Spreadsheet		
Table Name	Tablespace	Initial Extent (= 6 months of data in Kbytes)	Next Extent (= 1 month of data in Kbytes)	Blocks
AAAA	Data	608	101	152
BBBB	Data	2780	463	695
CCCC	Data	1820	303	455
DDDD	Data	200004	33334	50001
	Total	205212	34201	51303

FIGURE A.2: Table Sizing.xls

A6. RBS, SYSTEM, TEMP, and TOOLS Tablespace Sizing

These four tablespaces grow differently than the data and index tablespaces. Hence their INITIAL and NEXT extents are sized differently, as described below.

RBS

We assume that RBS stores two rollback segments, RBS1 and RBS2. A rollback segment stores the before image data for rows marked for update and delete. Oracle allocates extents for rollback segments in a round-robin fashion. Extents whose data have been committed or rolled back are marked inactive and are available for reuse. If a long query using the data marked for update or delete started before the update or delete occurred and is still continuing, it may look for data in these inactive extent(s). But when the data in some of these extent(s) are overwritten with new data, the query can no longer find the data it needs. In such a case, Oracle returns a rather cryptic message, "snapshot too old." To remedy such situations, I have designated RBS2 as the rollback segment to be used for long transactions via the SET TRANSACTION command given below.

```
commit;    /* clear prior rollback segment assignment */
set transaction use rollback segment RBS2
(Oracle long update transaction statements appear here)
commit;    /* clear assignment of current rollback segment RBS2 */
```

The initial and next extents of RBS2 are, therefore, much larger than those of RBS1.

Index Sizing Spreadsheet			
Index Name	Tablespace	Initial Extent (= 6 months of data)	Next Extent (in Kbytes)	Blocks
IND_1	Index	860	143	215
IND_2	Index	892	149	223
IND_3	Index	180	30	45
IND_4	Index	21336	3556	5334
IND_5	Index	85840	14307	21460
IND_6	Index	8684	1447	2171
IND_7	Index	14816	2469	3704
	Total	132608	22101	33152

FIGURE A.3: Index Sizing.xls

SYSTEM

It stores only the data dictionary, V$ tables, and several tables pertaining to stored objects such as SOURCES$, TRIGGERS$, etc. But it must never store any user tables, indices, constraints, etc.

TEMP

Its segment sizes change continually depending on the space needed by a sorting operation. Always designate the TEMP tablespace as "temporary" as follows.

   create tablespace TEMP temporary;

Then, only the temporary segments can be stored there. This allows each sorting operation that uses TEMP to continue without dropping and then claiming a new segment, thereby reducing fragmentation.

TOOLS

It stores database objects created by any Oracle or third party tools. By default such tools use SYSTEM as the database account and, therefore, any objects created by them use SYSTEM as the tablespace. This should never be done. To enforce this policy, designate TOOLS as the default tablespace for the SYSTEM account and reduce the quota of this account on SYSTEM tablespace to zero as follows.

```
alter user SYSTEM
quota 30M on TOOLS
quota 0 on SYSTEM
default tablespace TOOLS
temporary tablespace TEMP;
```

Tablespace Sizing Spreadsheet					
Tablespace Name	Tablespace Type	Datafile size (= 3 years data in Mbytes)	Initial Extent (= 6 months data in Mbytes)	Next Extent (= 1 month data in Mbytes)	Max Extents
Data	Data in Transaction Tables	1221	201	34	31
Index	Index for Transaction Tables	790	130	22	31
		Datafile Size in Mbytes	Initial Extent in Mbytes	Next Extent in Mbytes	Max Extents
RBS	Rollback Tablespace	975	25	25	31
RBS1	Rollback Segment 1	255	5	5	31
RBS2	Rollback Segment 2	720	20	20	31
System	Oracle Data Dictionary, V$ tables, and SYSTEM Rollback Segments	350	5	5	50
Temp	Temporary Segments	350	5	5	50
Tools	Database Objects Created by Oracle and 3rd Party Tools	200	2	2	50-
	Total Storage for 3 years	3886			

FIGURE A.4: Tablespace Sizing.xls

As a result, no database objects can be created by the SYSTEM account on the SYSTEM tablespace. The size of the TOOLS tablespace is an unknown at the beginning.

If one uses Oracle's data replication option, more storage in TOOLS will be needed to store the catalog tables REPCAT$ and the error tables needed by replication. This should be taken into consideration in sizing the TOOLS tablespace.

Key Words

block header, fixed
block header, variable
round-robin
SMON

References and Further Reading

1. E. Aronoff et al.—*Advanced ORACLE Tuning and Administration*, Oracle Press, 1997.
2. K. Loney—*Oracle 8i DBA Handbook*, Oracle Press, 2000.
3. S. S. Mittra—"Sizing Database Objects for an Oracle Database", *Intelligent Enterprise Oracle View*, 5/17/1999.

Loney [2, Chapter 5] discusses an algorithm to compute the sizes of tables and indices. The C programs included in Section A3 use a slight variation of them. In addition, Loney provides valuable information about the sizing of database objects and the space management mechanism used by Oracle. Mittra [3] contains an earlier version of the sizing algorithm used here.

Appendix B
Instance and Database Creation

Outline

B1. Preparation
B2. Instance Startup
B3. Database Creation
B4. Creation of Users, Roles, Privileges, Schema
B5. Miscellaneous Informational Items
Attachments 1 to 15

Overview of the Appendix

The appendix provides a complete checklist and a set of step-by-step instructions to create an instance and the underlying database under UNIX. It is assumed that ABCD is the name of the instance and the database and that Oracle 8.1.7 is the RDBMS. The 15 attachments contain various script files and system files related to the instance and database creation process.

B1. Preparation

I recommend that the UNIX shell command *script* be used to create a complete transcript of the sessions to create the full database. It helps the beginner DBAs to keep track of their actions including errors during the creation of the database. For example, type at UNIX prompt:

    script –a *scriptfile*

The file *scriptfile* will contain everything that is displayed on the screen. The option "-a" will continue to append to the same *scriptfile* all the transactions from all sessions in case the database creation spans multiple sessions.

Oracle requires a number of directories and files to be placed in certain specific locations before it starts the instance and creates the database. This section describes these preparatory steps. The names and locations of these files and directories are dependent on the installation. Change the steps below, as needed, to match your specific installation.

Oracle first starts the instance in the NOMOUNT state from the specifications of the parameter file ("pfile"). It allocates memory to the SGA and activates the required background processes. Then it creates the database via the command CREATE DATABASE, creates the data dictionary views, and all the tablespaces.

(a) Login as oracle/oradba or some other highly privileged account.

(b) cd $ORACLE_HOME/dbs

(This directory contains the file initABCD.ora or contains a link to another directory containing that file. In the latter case, type cd (link to that directory); e.g., type "cd /oracle/admin/ABCD/pfile". See Attachment 1 for the initABCD.ora file.

(c) Edit the file initABCD.ora, as needed. This file sets up the updatable initialization parameters. For example, you may want to assign nondefault values to certain initialization parameters such as PROCESSES, DB_FILES, etc.

(d) Ensure that the file /oracle/admin/ABCD/pfile/configABCD.ora exists. This file sets up the Oracle configuration for the instance ABCD. See Attachment 2 for the configABCD.ora file.

(e) cd /etc

(f) Find the file "oratab" and ensure that the file contains the line:

```
ABCD:/oracle/product/8.1.7:Y
```

(This causes Oracle to recognize the new instance ABCD. The field value "Y" indicates to the *dbstart* utility that the database will be brought up at the system boot time.) See Attachment 3 for the oratab file.

(g) Edit the file /etc/listener.ora to include the following blocks.

```
(ADDRESS=
(PROTOCOL=IPC)
(KEY= ABCD)
)
(SID_DESC =
(SID_NAME = ABCD)
(ORACLE_HOME = /oracle/product/8.1.7)
 )
```

This ensures that the Oracle listener will run when the instance and the database are created. See Attachment 4 for the listener.ora file.

(h) cd /oradata

Normally the datafiles for the tablespaces in the database are created in one or more subdirectories of this directory, although different locations are not uncommon. For this appendix, it is assumed that 10 directories named u01a, u01b, u02a, u02b, ..., u05a, u05b are created as subdirectories of this directory. Next, ensure that a subdirectory named ABCD exists under each of u01a through u05b. All datafiles, control file, and redo log files will be stored in these 10 subdirectories.

```
/oradata/u01a/ABCD
/oradata/u01b/ABCD
/oradata/u02a/ABCD
/oradata/u02b/ABCD
/oradata/u03a/ABCD
/oradata/u03b/ABCD
/oradata/u04a/ABCD
/oradata/u04b/ABCD
/oradata/u05a/ABCD
/oradata/u05b/ABCD
```

(i) cd /usr/lbin/oracle/bin

(j) ls –l

This displays the contents of this directory, which should include the file db_prms. This file is the *parameter file* for the instance ABCD. Verify that the directory also contains the file db_util, which must contain the line

```
prm_file=/usr/lbin/oracle/bin/db_prms
```

to signify that ABCD recognizes db_prms as its parameter file. See Attachment 5 for the db_prms file and Attachment 6 for the db_util file.

(k) Insert the following line for ABCD in db_prms.

```
:ABCD:system:manager:applmgr:apps:fnd:/dev/rmt/5mn:Y:N:Y:Y:fn
snetdev
```

(This allows the Oracle listener to be started on ABCD.)

(l) cd /oratmp

This directory contains several subdirectories including arch, dbstats, log, and dump. Create a subdirectory ABCD under each of these four directories. Oracle puts various alert log files, trace files, dump files, etc. here as follows.

Archived log files	in	/oratmp/arch/ABCD
Alert log files	in	/oratmp/log/ABCD
Process trace files	in	/oratmp/log/ABCD
Dump files	in	/oratmp/dump/ABCD

(m) cd /oratmp/dump/ABCD

(n) Create three subdirectories bdump, cdump, and udump under /oratmp/dump/ABCD. They function respectively as

```
background dump destination    =    /oratmp/dump/ABCD/bdump,
user dump destination          =    /oratmp/dump/ ABCD/udump,
core dump destination          =    /oratmp/dump/ ABCD/cdump
```

You are now ready to run the scripts for starting the instance ABCD.

B2. Instance Startup

An Oracle instance consists of the ystem global area (SGA) and up to 11 background processes such as DBWR, LGWR, CKPT, PMON, etc., described in Section 4.2. The script file *create1_ABCD.sql* creates the instance ABCD. The present section describes the steps for instance startup.

(a) Log in your home directory or subdirectory that contains the script file create1_ABCD.sql. This file creates the instance ABCD, two groups of redo log files, and the datafile for SYSTEM tablespace.
(b) Export ORACLE_HOME and ORACLE_SID to their respective destinations as follows.
- ORACLE_SID=ABCD; export ORACLE_SID= ABCD
- ORACLE_HOME=*value*, where *value* represents the designated directory for ORACLE_HOME (e.g., /home/oracle/product/8.1.7)
  export ORACLE_HOME=*value*
(c) To ensure that you are indeed pointing to the ORACLE_SID= ABCD, type at UNIX prompt:

```
env | grep ABCD
```

This displays, as a minimum, the following set of lines.

```
dba_udump=/oratmp/dump/ABCD/udump
dba_cdump=/oratmp/dump/ABCD/cdump
dba_bdump=/oratmp/dump/ABCD/bdump
ORACLE_SID=ABCD
dba_log=/oratmp/log/ABCD
dba_stats=/oratmp/dbstats/ABCD
dba_arc=/oratmp/arch/ABCD
```

These lines indicate that

- You are indeed pointing to the correct instance ABCD; and
- The "dump" directories are properly set up underneath ABCD for alert log files, trace files, dump destination files, and archived log files.

(d) Type   svrmgrl
(Invokes Server Manager in line mode. The prompt appears as svrmgr>)
(e) Type   connect internal
(A message appears "Connected".)
(f) Type   @ create1_ ABCD.sql
See Attachment 7 for create1_ ABCD.sql file.

A successful execution of this script file starts the instance ABCD and displays the following message.

```
Connected
Total System Global Area        13409004 bytes
Fixed Size                         47852 bytes
Variable Size                   11649024 bytes
Database Buffers                 1638400 bytes
Redo Buffers                       73728 bytes
Statement processed
```

B3. Database Creation

An Oracle database consists of the datafiles, tablespaces, redo log files, control files, and parameter file, as described in Section 4.3. In order to create the database ABCD after you have created the instance ABCD, proceed as follows:

(a) Follow Steps B2(a) through B2(d) given above.
(b) Type @create2_ ABCD.sql
    (Creates the database ABCD, its tablespaces, datafiles, and rollback segments.)
    See Attachment 8 for the create2_ ABCD.sql file.
(c) Type @SYS_MOD.sql
    (This script file designates TEMP as the temporary tablespace for SYS and SYSTEM accounts so that no other tablespace can be used by SYS or SYSTEM as its temporary tablespace. Also, TOOLS is designated as the default tablespace for the SYSTEM user account so that no database objects created by Oracle or any third party tools/utilities can be created in SYSTEM tablespace.) See Attachment 9 for the SYS_MOD.sql file.

B4. Creation of Users, Roles, Privileges, Schema

(a) Type @CREATE_USER_ROLE.sql
    (Creates two user accounts, one with username/password as ABCD_OWNER/EXPLORE having DBA privilege and the other with username/password as ABCD_USER/EXPLORE having SELECT, INSERT, UPDATE, DELETE, and EXECUTE ANY PROCEDURE privileges.)
    See Attachment 10 for the CREATE_USER_ROLE.sql file.
(b) Login as ABCD_OWNER/EXPLORE in the ABCD database and run the schema creation script called ABCD_Schema_Creation.sql. This creates the tables and indices in the ABCD database. All the objects created by this script are owned by the user ABCD_OWNER. See Attachment 11 for the script file ABCD_Schema_Creation.sql.
(c) Type @PUBL_SYN.sql
    (This creates a spool file SYNON_cr.sql to create public synonyms as "object name"

418   Appendix B.   Instance and Database Creation

for all database objects owned by ABCD_OWNER so that any other user can access these objects without putting a prefix ABCD_OWNER to each object name.) See Attachment 12 for the PUBL_SYN.sql file.
(d) Type   @SYNON_cr.sql
(This creates all the requisite public synonyms mentioned in Step (c) above.) See Attachment 13 for the SYNON_cr.sql file.
(e) Run all the appropriate scripts for creating views, triggers, procedures, etc.

B5. Miscellaneous Informational Items

(a) $ORACLE_HOME is the root directory for Oracle files. It has several subdirectories including: bin, dbs, jdbc, lib, network, nlsrtl, ocommon, oracore, orainst, ord, otrace, plsql, precomp, rdbms, slax, sqlplus, svrmgr, and unixdoc.
(b) $ORACLE_HOME/rdbms/admin has all the UTL*.sql files. You need to run UTLXPLAN.sql to create PLAN_TABLE for using the EXPLAIN PLAN utility.
(c) See Attachment 14 for the UTLXPLAN.sql file.
(d) $ORACLE_HOME/sqlplus/admin has the file pupbld.sql that must be run from the SYSTEM/MANAGER account to avoid the message:

"Warning: Product user profile information not loaded!"

This is only a warning and will not cause any problem even if you do not run *pupbld.sql*. See Attachment 15 for pupbld.sql file.

Attachments

ATTACHMENT 1: initABCD.ora

```
# $Header: initx.orc 12-jun-97.09:14:56 hpiao Exp $ Copyr (c) 1992
Oracle
#
# include database configuration parameters
ifile              = /oracle/admin/ABCD/pfile/configABCD.ora
rollback_segments  = (RBS1,RBS2,RBS3,RBS4,RBS5)

################################################################
###
##
# Example INIT.ORA file
#
# This file is provided by Oracle Corporation to help you
# customize your RDBMS installation for your site. Important
# system parameters are discussed, and example settings given.
#
```

```
# Some parameter settings are generic to any size installation.
# For parameters that require different values in different size
# installations, three scenarios have been provided: SMALL,
# MEDIUM, and LARGE. Any parameter that needs to be tuned
# according to installation size will have three settings, each
# one commented according to installation size.
#
# Use the following table to approximate the SGA size needed for
# the three scenarios provided in this file:
#
#                -------Installation/Database Size------
#                SMALL           MEDIUM          LARGE
# Block   2K     4500K           6800K           17000K
# Size    4K     5500K           8800K           21000K
#
# To set up a database that multiple instances will be using,
# place all instance-specific parameters in one file, and then
# have all of these files point to a master file using the IFILE
# command. This way, when you change a public parameter, it will
# automatically change on all instances. This is necessary, since
# all instances must run with the same value for many parameters.
# For example, if you choose to use private rollback segments,
# these must be specified in different files, but since all gc_*
# parameters must be the same on all instances, they should be in
# one file.
#
# INSTRUCTIONS: Edit this file and the other INIT files it calls
# for your site, either by using the values provided here or by
# providing your own. Then place an IFILE= line into each
# instance-specific INIT file that points at this file.
################################################################
####
###
# tuning parameters
db_files = 254
db_name = ABCD
# db_file_multiblock_read_count = 8             # SMALL
# db_file_multiblock_read_count = 16            # MEDIUM
  db_file_multiblock_read_count = 32            # LARGE

# db_block_buffers = 200                        # SMALL
# db_block_buffers = 550                        # MEDIUM
  db_block_buffers = 3200                       # LARGE

# shared_pool_size = 3500000                    # SMALL
# shared_pool_size = 6000000                    # MEDIUM
  shared_pool_size = 50000000                   # LARGE

log_checkpoint_interval = 10000

  processes = 350                               # LARGE
# processes = 100                               # MEDIUM
# processes = 250                               # LARGE
```

```
dml_locks = 100                             # SMALL
# dml_locks = 200                           # MEDIUM
# dml_locks = 500                           # LARGE

# log_buffer = 8192                         # SMALL
# log_buffer = 32768                        # MEDIUM
 log_buffer = 163840                        # LARGE

sequence_cache_entries = 10                 # SMALL
# sequence_cache_entries = 30               # MEDIUM
# sequence_cache_entries = 100              # LARGE

sequence_cache_hash_buckets = 10            # SMALL
# sequence_cache_hash_buckets = 23          # MEDIUM
# sequence_cache_hash_buckets = 89          # LARGE

# audit_trail = true            # if you want auditing
# timed_statistics = true       # if you want timed statistics
max_dump_file_size = 10240      # limit trace file size to 5 Meg
each

# log_archive_start = true      # if you want automatic archiving

global_names = TRUE

# mts_dispatchers="ipc,1"
# mts_max_dispatchers=10
# mts_servers=1
# mts_max_servers=10
# mts_service=ORCL
# mts_listener_address="(ADDRESS=(PROTOCOL=ipc)(KEY=PNPKEY))"

# needed if running OPS
# PARALLEL_SERVER=TRUE
```

ATTACHMENT 2: configABCD.ora

```
#
# $Header: cnfg.orc 1.1 95/02/27 12:14:25 wyim Osd<unix> $ Copyr
(c) 1992 Oracle
#
# cnfg.ora - instance configuration parameters

control_files        = (/oradata/u01b/ABCD/ctl_001.ctl,
                        /oradata/u02b/ABCD/ctl_002.ctl,
                        /oradata/u03b/ABCD/ctl_003.ctl)

# Below for possible future use...
#init_sql_files      = (?/dbs/sql.bsq,
#                       ?/rdbms/admin/catalog.sql,
#                       ?/rdbms/admin/expvew.sql)

background_dump_dest       = /oratmp/dump/ABCD/bdump
core_dump_dest             = /oratmp/dump/ABCD/cdump
user_dump_dest             = /oratmp/dump/ABCD/udump
log_archive_dest           = /oratmp/arch/ABCD/ABCD
db_block_size              = 8192
```

```
# checkpoint_process        = true
db_name                     = ABCD
db_files                    = 254
compatible                  = 8.1.5
open_cursors                = 500
nls_date_format             = DD-MON-RR
nls_language                = AMERICAN
nls_territory               = AMERICA
nls_numeric_characters      = ".,"
nls_sort                    = binary
optimizer_mode              = CHOOSE
_optimizer_undo_changes     = true
hash_join_enabled           = false
row_locking                 = always
OS_AUTHENT_PREFIX           = "OPS$"

# unlimited_rollback_segments  = true
```

ATTACHMENT 3: ORATAB

```
ORCL:/oracle/product/8.1.7:N
ABCD:/oracle/product/8.1.7:Y
```

ATTACHMENT 4: listener.ora

```
################
# Filename......: listener.ora
# Date.........: 10-NOV-00 13:38:20
################
LISTENER =
    (ADDRESS_LIST =
        (ADDRESS=
            (PROTOCOL=IPC)
            (KEY= ORCL.world)
        )
        (ADDRESS=
            (PROTOCOL=IPC)
            (KEY= ORCL)
        )
        (ADDRESS=
            (PROTOCOL=IPC)
            (KEY= ABCD)
        )
        (ADDRESS =
        (COMMUNITY = FNS2)
        (PROTOCOL = TCP)
        (Host = abcnetde)
        (Port = 1521)
        )
    )
STARTUP_WAIT_TIME_LISTENER = 0
CONNECT_TIMEOUT_LISTENER = 10
```

```
TRACE_LEVEL_LISTENER = OFF
SID_LIST_LISTENER =
  (SID_LIST =
    (SID_DESC =
       (SID_NAME = ORCL)
       (ORACLE_HOME = /oracle/product/8.1.7)
    )
    (SID_DESC =
       (SID_NAME = ABCD)
       (ORACLE_HOME = /oracle/product/8.1.7)
    )
  )
```

ATTACHMENT 5:   db_prms

```
#****************************************************************
#: Parameter  Description                    Example
#: ---------  -----------                    -------
#: $1         active or inactive SID         " ":active, #:inactive
#: $2         Oracle SID name                XXX_D, XXX_P
#: $3         database system username       sysusername
#: $4         database system password       syspassword
#: $5         AP manager password            apmanager
#: $6         AP username                    apusername
#: $7         AP password                    appassword
#: $8         tape device name               /dev/rmt/1m
#: $9         concurrent manager flag        Y or N
#:            (financials)
#: $10        turn nightly export on/off     Y or N
#: $11        turn nightly physical backup   Y or N
#:            on/off
#: $12        restart database after backup  Y or N
#:            flag
#: $13        UNIX system node name          development:develop
#:            production:waltham
#:****************************************************************
#:
  :ORCL:system:manager::::/dev/rmt/5mn:Y:N:Y:Y:abcnetdev
  :ABCD:system:manager::::/dev/rmt/5mn:Y:N:Y:Y:abcnetdev
```

ATTACHMENT 6:   db_util

```
#!/bin/sh
#
#     Input: $1 is the Oracle SID name
#
#     Definition:
#         Set Oracle SID specific UNIX environment
#         variables for use in database maintenance scripts.
#         SID specific parameters are maintained in
```

```
#              file db_prms.
#
in1=$
#
in2=$1
# input parameter is ORACLE SID name
prm_file=/usr/lbin/oracle/bin/db_prms
# data base parameter file
#
# verify input parameter is a valid SID
# if input parameter is blank or an invalid SID then exit
#
if [ "$in1" -ne 1 -o "`grep "$in2" /etc/oratab`" = "" ]
then
    echo ""
    echo "db_envs : Invalid Oracle SID - $in2 "
    echo "db_envs : Aborting db_envs"
    echo ""
    sleep 5
    exit 1
else    # exit if SID not found or not active in the db_prms
file
  if [ "`grep "$in2" $prm_file | awk -F: '{print $2}'`" = "" -o
"`grep "$in2" $prm_file | awk -F: '{print $1}'`" = "#" ]
   then
     echo ""
     echo "db_envs : Inactive Oracle SID - $in2"
     echo "db_envs : Verify Oracle SID in db_prms"
     echo "db_envs : Aborting db_envs"
     echo ""
     sleep 5
      exit 1
   fi
fi
#
# extract all administration parameters and
# assign them to global environment variables
#
db_excl=`grep ${in2} $prm_file | awk -F: '{print $1}'`
db_dsid=`grep ${in2} $prm_file | awk -F: '{print $2}'`
db_smgr=`grep ${in2} $prm_file | awk -F: '{print $3}'`
db_spas=`grep ${in2} $prm_file | awk -F: '{print $4}'`
db_amgr=`grep ${in2} $prm_file | awk -F: '{print $5}'`
db_ausr=`grep ${in2} $prm_file | awk -F: '{print $6}'`
db_apas=`grep ${in2} $prm_file | awk -F: '{print $7}'`
db_tdev=`grep ${in2} $prm_file | awk -F: '{print $8}'`
db_cflg=`grep ${in2} $prm_file | awk -F: '{print $9}'`
db_eflg=`grep ${in2} $prm_file | awk -F: '{print $10}'`
db_bflg=`grep ${in2} $prm_file | awk -F: '{print $11}'`
db_sflg=`grep ${in2} $prm_file | awk -F: '{print $12}'`
db_node=`grep ${in2} $prm_file | awk -F: '{print $13}'`
```

```
export db_excl db_dsid db_smgr db_spas db_amgr db_ausr
export db_apas db_tdev db_cflg db_eflg db_bflg db_sflg export db_node
```

ATTACHMENT 7:   create1_ABCD.SQL

```
spool $HOME/ABCD/create1_ABCD.log;
connect INTERNAL
startup nomount pfile=$ORACLE_HOME/dbs/initABCD.ora
CREATE DATABASE ABCD
LOGFILE  GROUP 1 ('/oradata/u01a/ABCD/log_a01.dbf',
                  '/oradata/u04a/ABCD/log_a02.dbf') size 50M reuse,
         GROUP 2 ('/oradata/u01a/ABCD/log_b01.dbf',
                  '/oradata/u04a/ABCD/log_b02.dbf') SIZE 50M reuse
MAXLOGFILES 32
MAXLOGMEMBERS 3
MAXLOGHISTORY 1
DATAFILE '/oradata/u03a/ABCD/sys_001.dbf' SIZE 300M
MAXDATAFILES 254
MAXINSTANCES 1
CHARACTER SET WE8ISO8859P1
NATIONAL CHARACTER SET WE8ISO8859P1;

spool off;
```

ATTACHMENT 8:   create2_ABCD.sql

```
spool $HOME/ABCD/create2_ABCD.log;

set echo on
connect INTERNAL

CREATE ROLLBACK SEGMENT SYSROL TABLESPACE "SYSTEM"
STORAGE (INITIAL 100K NEXT 100K);

ALTER ROLLBACK SEGMENT "SYSROL" ONLINE;

@$ORACLE_HOME/rdbms/admin/catalog.sql;
@$ORACLE_HOME/rdbms/admin/catproc.sql;
@$ORACLE_HOME/rdbms/admin/catexp.sql;
@$ORACLE_HOME/rdbms/admin/catexp7.sql;
@$ORACLE_HOME/sqlplus/admin/pupbld.sql;

REM ***    Create tablespace for rollback segments       ***

CREATE TABLESPACE RBS DATAFILE '/oradata/u03b/ABCD/rbs_001.dbf'
SIZE 1000M
DEFAULT STORAGE (INITIAL 10M  NEXT 10M MINEXTENTS 5 MAXEXTENTS 31
PCTINCREASE 0);

REM ***    Alter SYSTEM tablespace        ***

ALTER TABLESPACE SYSTEM
DEFAULT STORAGE (INITIAL 50M NEXT 5M MINEXTENTS 1 MAXEXTENTS 51
PCTINCREASE 0);

REM ***    Create tablespace for data in transaction tables     ***
```

```
CREATE TABLESPACE DATA_A DATAFILE
'/oradata/u01a/ABCD/data_a01.dbf' SIZE 2000M
DEFAULT STORAGE (INITIAL 1000M NEXT 50M MINEXTENTS 1 MAXEXTENTS
151 PCTINCREASE 0);

ALTER TABLESPACE DATA_A ADD DATAFILE
'/oradata/u02a/ABCD/data_a02.dbf' SIZE 2000M;

REM ***   Create tablespace for data in validation tables     ***

CREATE TABLESPACE DATA_B DATAFILE '/oradata/u05a/ABCD/dat_b01.dbf'
SIZE 200M
DEFAULT STORAGE (INITIAL 1M NEXT 1M MINEXTENTS 1 MAXEXTENTS 151
PCTINCREASE 0);

REM ***   Create tablespace for temporary segments      ***

CREATE TABLESPACE TEMP DATAFILE '/oradata/u01b/ABCD/tmp_001.dbf'
SIZE 200M
DEFAULT STORAGE (INITIAL 5M NEXT 5M MINEXTENTS 1 MAXEXTENTS 31
PCTINCREASE 0) TEMPORARY;

REM ***   Create tablespace for indices for transaction tables  ***

CREATE TABLESPACE INDEX_A DATAFILE
'/oradata/u05b/ABCD/idx_a01.dbf' SIZE 1500M
DEFAULT STORAGE (INITIAL 100M NEXT 10M MINEXTENTS 1 MAXEXTENTS 141
PCTINCREASE 0);

REM ***   Create tablespace for indices for validation tables   ***

CREATE TABLESPACE INDEX_B DATAFILE
'/oradata/u04b/ABCD/idx_b01.dbf' SIZE 200M
DEFAULT STORAGE (INITIAL 1M NEXT 1M MINEXTENTS 1 MAXEXTENTS 180
PCTINCREASE 0);

REM ***   Create TOOLS tablespace              ***

CREATE TABLESPACE TOOLS DATAFILE '/oradata/u02b/ABCD/tls_001.dbf'
SIZE 40M
DEFAULT STORAGE (INITIAL 1M NEXT 1M MINEXTENTS 1 MAXEXTENTS 31
PCTINCREASE 0);

REM ***   Create rollback segments RBS1,RBS2,RBS3,RBS4,RBS5    ***
REM ***   in the rollback tablespace RBS      ***
create rollback segment RBS1 tablespace RBS
      storage(initial 5M next 5M minextents 20 optimal 100M);

create rollback segment RBS2 tablespace RBS
      storage(initial 5M next 5M minextents 20 optimal 100M);

create rollback segment RBS3 tablespace RBS
      storage(initial 5M next 5M minextents 20 optimal 100M);

create rollback segment RBS4 tablespace RBS
      storage(initial 5M next 5M minextents 20 optimal 100M);

create rollback segment RBS5 tablespace RBS
      storage(initial 20M next 20M minextents 20 optimal 400M);

alter rollback segment RBS1 online;
```

```
alter rollback segment RBS2 online;
alter rollback segment RBS3 online;
alter rollback segment RBS4 online;
alter rollback segment RBS5 online;

REM ***   Take temporary rollback segment SYSROL offline     ***

alter rollback segment SYSROL offline;
spool off
```

ATTACHMENT 9: SYS_MOD.sql

```
REM Script for Altering SYS and SYSTEM Users
REM Script File:   My_Directory\SYS_MOD.sql
REM Spool File:    My_Directory\SYS_MOD.log
REM Author:        NAME
REM Date Created:  DATE
REM Purpose:       Alter SYS and SYSTEM users for their default
                   tablespaces

SPOOL /users/oracle/ABCD/SYS_MOD.log

ALTER USER SYS TEMPORARY TABLESPACE TEMP;
ALTER USER SYSTEM
    QUOTA UNLIMITED ON TOOLS
    QUOTA 0 ON SYSTEM
    DEFAULT TABLESPACE TOOLS
    TEMPORARY TABLESPACE TEMP;

SPOOL OFF
```

ATTACHMENT 10: CREATE_USER_ROLE.sql

```
REM Create users with roles and privileges for ABCD database
REM Script File Name:  My_Directory\CREATE_USER_ROLE.sql
REM Author:            NAME
REM Date Created:      DATE
REM Purpose:           Create two user accounts, ABCD_OWNER with
REM                    DBA privilege and ABCD_USER with SELECT,
REM                    INSERT, UPDATE, DELETE, and EXECUTE ANY
REM                    PROCEDURE privileges.
REM

REM ABCD_OWNER has DBA privileges.

CREATE USER ABCD_OWNER IDENTIFIED BY EXPLORE
    DEFAULT TABLESPACE DATA_A
    TEMPORARY TABLESPACE TEMP
    QUOTA UNLIMITED ON DATA_A
    QUOTA UNLIMITED ON TEMP;

GRANT DBA TO ABCD_OWNER;

REM ABCD_USER has SELECT, INSERT, UPDATE, DELETE and EXECUTE ANY
REM PROCEDURE privileges.

CREATE USER ABCD_USER IDENTIFIED BY EXPLORE
```

```
        DEFAULT TABLESPACE DATA_A
        TEMPORARY TABLESPACE TEMP
        QUOTA UNLIMITED ON DATA_A
        QUOTA UNLIMITED ON TEMP;

CREATE ROLE ABCD_USER_ROLE;

GRANT  CREATE SESSION, ALTER SESSION, EXECUTE ANY PROCEDURE,
       SELECT ANY TABLE, INSERT ANY TABLE, UPDATE ANY TABLE,
       DELETE ANY TABLE
TO     ABCD_USER_ROLE;

GRANT  ABCD_USER_ROLE TO ABCD_USER;
```

ATTACHMENT 11: ABCD_Schema_Creation.sql

```
REM  First run the script My_Directory\CREATE_USER_ROLE.sql to
REM  create the account ABCD_OWNER with DBA privilege. Then, run
REM  the schema creation script from ABCD_OWNER account to create
REM  all database objects such as tables, constraints, indices,
REM  etc. This will make ABCD_OWNER account the owner of all these
REM  objects. The schema creation script is given in pseudocode
REM  using symbolic names instead of actual object names. SQL
REM  commands are written in uppercase, and entries to be
REM  provided by the DBA appear in lowercase italics.

REM  DROP/CREATE TABLE syntax; a table can have multiple constraints
REM  Repeat the code for each table in the ABCD database

DROP TABLE table_name CASCADE CONSTRAINTS;

CREATE TABLE table_name
    (column_1 datatype constraint (e.g., NOT NULL, UNIQUE),
     ...
     column_n datatype constraint (e.g., NOT NULL, UNIQUE)
    )

    CONSTRAINT constraint_name PRIMARY KEY (column_name(s)) USING
    INDEX
        PCTFREE value
        INITRANS value
        MAXTRANS value
        STORAGE (INITIAL value  NEXT value  PCTINCREASE value
                MAXEXTENTS value  MINEXTENTS value )
        TABLESPACE tablespace_name,

    CONSTRAINT constraint_name FOREIGN KEY (column_name(s))
        REFERENCES table_name.column_name(s),
    CONSTRAINT constraint_name CHECK (condition),

TABLESPACE tablespace_name;

REM  DROP/CREATE INDEX syntax; a table can have multiple indices
REM  Repeat the code for each index in the ABCD database

CREATE [UNIQUE] INDEX index_name ON table_name (column_name(s))
       PCTFREE value
       INITRANS value
```

```
            MAXTRANS value
            STORAGE (INITIAL value  NEXT value  PCTINCREASE value
                     MAXEXTENTS value  MINEXTENTS value )
            TABLESPACE tablespace_name;
REM Create other objects such as triggers, functions, procedures,
REM packages after running the above script.
```

ATTACHMENT 12:   PUBL_SYN.sql

```
REM Creation of public synonyms for database objects
REM Script File Name:   My_Directory\PUBL_SYN.sql
REM Spool File Name:    My_Directory \SYNON_cr.sql
REM Author:             NAME
REM Date Created:       DATE
REM Purpose:            Create public synonyms for all database
REM                     objects in any database
REM
REM

SPOOL     My_Directory\SYNON_cr.sql

SET HEADING OFF
SET FEEDBACK OFF

SELECT 'DROP PUBLIC SYNONYM ' || OBJECT_NAME || ';' FROM
USER_OBJECTS
     WHERE OBJECT_TYPE = 'TABLE' OR OBJECT_TYPE = 'VIEW' OR OBJECT_TYPE
     = 'INDEX'
     ORDER BY OBJECT_TYPE, OBJECT_NAME;

SELECT 'CREATE PUBLIC SYNONYM ' || OBJECT_NAME || ' FOR
ABCD_OWNER.' ||
     OBJECT_NAME || ';' FROM USER_OBJECTS
     WHERE OBJECT_TYPE = 'TABLE' OR OBJECT_TYPE = 'VIEW'
     ORDER BY OBJECT_TYPE, OBJECT_NAME;

SPOOL OFF
```

ATTACHMENT 13:   SYNON_cr.sql

```
REM    Only four sample DROP and CREATE statements are shown below.

DROP PUBLIC SYNONYM ACTIVE_MAILING;
DROP PUBLIC SYNONYM AGENT_BILLING;
DROP PUBLIC SYNONYM APPLICATION_LOG;
DROP PUBLIC SYNONYM ATTRIBUTE_LIST;

CREATE PUBLIC SYNONYM ACTIVE_MAILING FOR ABCD_OWNER.ACTIVE_MAILING;
CREATE PUBLIC SYNONYM AGENT_BILLING FOR ABCD_OWNER.AGENT_BILLING;
CREATE PUBLIC SYNONYM APPLICATION_LOG FOR ABCD_OWNER.APPLICATION_LOG;
CREATE PUBLIC SYNONYM ATTRIBUTE_LIST FOR ABCD_OWNER.ATTRIBUTE_LIST;
```

ATTACHMENT 14: UTLXPLAN.sql
(Taken from $ORACLE_HOME/rdbms/admin directory)

```
Rem
Rem $Header: utlxplan.sql big_dev/0 11-aug-95.14:02:45 achaudhr
Rem Exp $ xplainpl.sql
Rem
Rem Copyright (c) 1988, 1995, 1996 by Oracle Corporation
Rem NAME
Rem    UTLXPLAN.SQL
Rem FUNCTION
Rem NOTES
Rem MODIFIED
Rem    ddas       05/17/96 - change search_columns to number
Rem    achaudhr   07/23/95 - PTI: Add columns partition_{start, stop,
Rem                          id}
Rem    glumpkin   08/25/94 - new optimizer fields
Rem    jcohen     11/05/93 - merge changes from branch 1.1.710.1 - Rem
Rem                          9/24
Rem    jcohen     09/24/93 - #163783 add optimizer column
Rem    glumpkin   10/25/92 - Renamed from XPLAINPL.SQL
Rem    jcohen     05/22/92 - #79645 - set node width to 128 (M_XDBI in
Rem                          gendef)
Rem    rlim       04/29/91 - change char to varchar2
Rem    Peeler     10/19/88 - Creation
Rem
Rem This is the format for the table that is used by the EXPLAIN
Rem PLAN statement. The explain statement requires the presence
Rem of this table in order to store the descriptions of the row
Rem sources.

create table PLAN_TABLE (
    statement_id            varchar2(30),
    timestamp               date,
    remarks                 varchar2(80),
    operation               varchar2(30),
    options                 varchar2(30),
    object_node             varchar2(128),
    object_owner            varchar2(30),
    object_name             varchar2(30),
    object_instance numeric,
    object_type             varchar2(30),
    optimizer               varchar2(255),
    search_columns          number,
    id                      numeric,
    parent_id               numeric,
    position                numeric,
    cost                    numeric,
    cardinality             numeric,
    bytes                   numeric,
    other_tag               varchar2(255),
    partition_start         varchar2(255),
    partition_stop          varchar2(255),
```

```
                  partition_id            numeric,
                  other                   long);
```

ATTACHMENT 15:   pupbld.sql
(Taken from $ORACLE_HOME/sqlplus/admin directory)

```
rem
rem $Header: /plus/v4/spam/precious/files/ACTIVE/pupbld.sql,v 1.2
rem 1996/06/21 02:25:41 cjones Exp $
rem Copyright (c) Oracle Corporation 1988, 1994, 1996. All Rights
rem Reserved.
rem
rem +----------------------------------------------------------+
rem | PUPBLD.SQL -- CREATE PRODUCT AND USER PROFILE TABLES     |
rem |                                                          |
rem | Connect as SYSTEM before running this script             |
rem |                                                          |
rem | This script is used by the DBA to create the             |
rem | product_user_profile                                     |
rem | synonym in the SYSTEM account                            |
rem +----------------------------------------------------------+
rem
rem +----------------------------------------------------------+
rem | If PRODUCT_USER_PROFILE existed, use its values and drop it |
rem +----------------------------------------------------------+

drop synonym product_user_profile;

create table sqlplus_product_profile as
   select product, userid, attribute, scope, numeric_value, char_value,
   date_value from product_user_profile;

drop table product_user_profile;
alter table sqlplus_product_profile add (long_value long);

rem +----------------------------------------------+
rem | Create SQLPLUS_PRODUCT_PROFILE from scratch  |
rem +----------------------------------------------+

create table sqlplus_product_profile
(
 product            varchar2 (30) not null,
 userid             varchar2 (30),
 attribute          varchar2 (240),
 scope              varchar2 (240),
 numeric_value      decimal (15,2),
 char_value         varchar2 (240),
 date_value         date,
 long_value         long
);

rem
rem Remove SQL*Plus V3 name for sqlplus_product_profile
rem
```

```
drop table product_profile;

rem +-----------------------------------------------------------+
rem | Create the view PRODUCT_PRIVS and grant access to that    |
rem +-----------------------------------------------------------+

drop view product_privs;
create view product_privs as
    select product, userid, attribute, scope,
           numeric_value, char_value, date_value, long_value
    from sqlplus_product_profile
    where userid = 'PUBLIC' or user like userid;

grant select on product_privs to public;
drop public synonym product_profile;
create public synonym product_profile for system.product_privs;
drop synonym product_user_profile;
create synonym product_user_profile for
system.sqlplus_product_profile;
drop public synonym product_user_profile;
create public synonym product_user_profile for
system.product_privs;

rem +-------------------+
rem | End of pupbld.sql |
rem +-------------------+
```

Appendix C
Instance and Database Removal

Outline

C1. Preparation
C2. Locating the Components
C3 Removing the Components
C4. Verification

Overview of the Appendix

The appendix provides a methodology for dropping an instance and its associated database.

C1. Preparation

In order to drop an instance and its associated database it is necessary to remove these components:

(a) Data files, log files, and control files constituting the database;
(b) Parameter file init<SID>.ora and configuration file config<SID>.ora;
(c) Destination files for bdump, cdump, udump, archive, and audit;
(d) Database links referencing the database ;
(e) References to ORACLE_SID for the instance in the ORATAB file;
(f) References to the database in the files TNSNAMES.ora and LISTENER.ora, and
(g) References to the background processes.

Section C2 contains the steps along with SQL scripts to identify and locate the above components so that they can be subsequently removed from the system. The database must be running to allow extracting the relevant location information. Therefore, if nec-

434   Appendix C. Instance and Database Removal

essary, run the following command from Server Manager after connecting as "connect internal".

    startup pfile='*pfile path*'

Also, it is recommended that you make a full cold backup of the database.

C2. Locating the Components

Locate Data Files, Log Files, and Control Files Constituting the Database

Obtain a Listing of the Datafiles

```
SVRMGR> select name from v$datafile;
NAME
------------------------------------------------------------------
/home/oracle/oradata/ABCD/system/SYSTEM01.dbf
/home/oracle/oradata/ABCD/system/PREVIEW01.dbf
. . . . . . . . . . . . .
/home/oracle/oradata/ABCD/indexes/group03/INVOICE_INDEX01.dbf
/home/oracle/oradata/ABCD/tables/group03/INVOICE_LOCM_DATA01.dbf
/home/oracle/oradata/ABCD/indexes/group03/INVOICE_LOCM_INDEX01.dbf

90 rows selected.
```

Obtain a Listing of the Log Files

```
SVRMGR> select member from v$logfile;
MEMBER
------------------------------------------------------------------
/home/oracle/oradata/ABCD/admin/system/redoA05.log
/home/oracle/admin/ABCD/system/redoB05.log
/home/oracle/oradata/ABCD/admin/system/redoA04.log
. . . . . . . . . . . . . . . . . . . . .
10 rows selected.
```

Obtain a Listing of the Control Files

```
SVRMGR> select name from v$controlfile;
NAME
------------------------------------------------------------------
/home/oracle/oradata/ABCD/admin/system/cntrlA01.ctl
/home/oracle/oradata/ABCD/admin/system/cntrlA02.ctl
/home/oracle/admin/ABCD/system/cntrlB01.ctl
/home/oracle/admin/ABCD/system/cntrlB02.ctl

4 rows selected.
```

Locate the Parameter File init<SID>.ora and Configuration File config<SID>.ora

These two files can be located by means of an appropriate directory search in the server.

Locate the Destination Files for bdump, cdump, udump, archive, and audit

```
SVRMGR> show parameters dest
NAME                            TYPE      VALUE
------------------------        ------    --------------------
audit_file_dest                 string    ?/rdbms/audit
background_dump_dest            string    /home/oracle/admin/ABCD/bdump
core_dump_dest                  string    /home/oracle/admin/ABCD/cdump
log_archive_dest                string    /home/oracle/oradata/ABCD/admi
log_archive_dest_1              string
log_archive_dest_2              string
log_archive_dest_3              string
log_archive_dest_4              string
log_archive_dest_5              string
log_archive_dest_state_1        string    enable
log_archive_dest_state_2        string    enable
log_archive_dest_state_3        string    enable
log_archive_dest_state_4        string    enable
log_archive_dest_state_5        string    enable
log_archive_duplex_dest         string
log_archive_min_succeed_dest    integer   1
standby_archive_dest            string    ?/dbs/arch
user_dump_dest                  string    /home/oracle/admin/ABCD/udump
```

Locate the Database Links Referencing the Instance

```
SQL> col username format a10
SQL> col host format a15
SQL> edit
Wrote file afiedt.buf

    1* select * from dba_db_links
SQL> /

OWNER     DB_LINK          USERNAME    HOST             CREATED
------    -------------    --------    -------------    ---------
PUBLIC    DEV01.MASTER1                dev01.master1    23-JUL-99
PUBLIC    FERNO.MASTER1                ferno.master1    23-JUL-99
PUBLIC    ABCD.TRNSRV                  ABCD.trnsrv      23-JUL-99
```

Locate References to ORACLE_SID for the Instance in the ORATAB File

This file is located either in the /etc or in the /var/opt/oracle directory. The location of this file is operating system dependent.

Locate the Files TNSNAMES.ora and LISTENER.ora

These two files can be located by means of an appropriate directory search in the server.

Identify the Background Processes of the Instance

This can be done by the UNIX command "ps –ef | grep ORACLE_SID," where the actual value of ORACLE_SID must be used when running the command.

C3. Removing the Components

Having located all the components of the database we now remove them one at a time and, if necessary, recursively.

(a) Use the UNIX command "rm" to remove all data files, log files, control files, init.ora file, and config.ora file identified above.
(b) Use the SQL command "drop public database link *link_name*" to drop each link identified above.
(c) Remove the lines referencing the ORACLE_SID for all instances using this database in the ORATAB file identified above. A sample entry that must be deleted is of the form

```
ORACLE_SID:/home/oracle/product/8.1.7:Y
```

(d) Delete all blocks in TNSNAMES.ora and LISTENER.ora files that refer to this database. Since Oracle uses the first file found, delete the referenced blocks from all copies of these two files in case multiple copies of these files exist in the system.
(e) Remove all background processes related to the instance as follows.

```
prdesrv% ps -ef | grep ORACLE_SID > background_processes.txt
prdesrv% more background_processes.txt
 oracle   376    1 0   Nov 17 ?       0:00
/home/oracle/product/8.1.7/bin/tnslsnr ABCD.prdesrv -inherit
 oracle 16863    1 0   Dec 17 ?       0:00 ora_lgwr_ABCD
 oracle 16867    1 0   Dec 17 ?       0:07 ora_smon_ABCD
 oracle 16872    1 0   Dec 17 ?       0:00 ora_i201_ABCD
 oracle 16865    1 0   Dec 17 ?       0:16 ora_ckpt_ABCD
 oracle 16884    1 0   Dec 17 ?       0:00 ora_i101_ABCD
 oracle 16886    1 0   Dec 17 ?       0:00 ora_i102_ABCD
 oracle 16890    1 0   Dec 17 ?       0:00 ora_i104_ABCD
 oracle 16888    1 0   Dec 17 ?       0:00 ora_i103_ABCD
 oracle 16861    1 0   Dec 17 ?       0:00 ora_dbw0_ABCD
 oracle 16869    1 0   Dec 17 ?       0:00 ora_reco_ABCD
ABCDdba 17914          17912 0 09:22:40 pts/1   0:00 -csh
 oracle 16859    1 0   Dec 17 ?       0:00 ora_pmon_ABCD
 oracle 17712    1 0 08:36:52 ?       0:00 oracleABCD (LOCAL=NO)
ABCDdba 18062  155 0 09:30:34 ?       0:00 in.ftpd
prdesrv% kill -9 process_ID
```

Here *process_ID* refers to the individual process numbers listed above. Repeat the "kill –9" command for each process.

(f) Remove all the directories recursively that are related to the instance(s) using this database. But if any other instances exist that refer to the files in these directories, then do not proceed with this step.

C4. Verification

By removing all the files that are associated with the database we have eliminated all references to the instance and freed up all resources tied to this database and all the instances that reference it. Also, all the storage space has been reclaimed. To be on the safe side, it is better to try starting up the instance with the init<SID>.ora file that was deleted in Step C3(a). Oracle should return an error message that the instance cannot be started. But if the instance starts even partially, then the steps described in Sections C2 and C3 should be rechecked and repeated until the instance and its associated database are totally removed.

Appendix D
Database Refresh with Transportable Tablespaces

Outline

D1   Database Refresh Process
D2. Detailed Methodology with Scripts
D3. Time Estimates
D4   Internal Inconsistency
Key Words

Overview of the Appendix

The appendix provides a methodology and its implementation with scripts for refreshing a database using transportable tablespaces. It addresses the issue of possible internal inconsistency that may arise during the process and a way to rectify it.

D1. Database Refresh Process

In a multienvironment database installation a nonproduction database such as a test, development, or training is refreshed periodically with up-to-date data from the production database. During the refresh access to the source and the destination databases is restricted. Oracle 8i introduced the transportable tablespaces as a mechanism for reducing the duration of such restricted access and allowing the refresh process to be automated fairly easily.

A *transportable tablespace* is a tablespace whose segments can be exported from a source database to a destination database if it belongs to a set of self-contained tablespaces. A set of tablespaces is *self-contained* if the segments belonging to the set do not contain any references to tablespaces outside the set. For example, an index on a table belonging to the set cannot reside on a tablespace outside that set. Oracle 8i provides a PL/SQL procedure to test whether a set of tablespaces is self-contained.

The set of transportable tablespaces used in the refresh must satisfy the following conditions.

- They must be identical in name and number on both the source and the destination databases.
- The source and the destination database must be on the same hardware platform. For example, one can transport a tablespace from a Sun Solaris platform to another Sun Solaris platform, but not to an HP-UX platform.
- The source and the destination database must have the same block size; i.e., the initialization parameter db_block_size must be identical in value on both the source and the destination databases.
- A tablespace on the source database cannot be transported to a destination database if the latter already contains a tablespace with the same name.

Conceptually, the refresh process consists of the following steps.

- Identify a set of self-contained tablespaces in the source database that will be used in the refresh process.
- Export the metadata, i.e., the structural information, of these tablespaces to an export dump file.
- Copy the disk files comprising these tablespaces to the destination database file system.
- Import the metadata into the destination database so as to be plugged into the copied datafiles.

D2. Detailed Methodology with Scripts

We assume that a set S consisting of four tablespaces, DATA01, DATA02, INDEX01, and INDEX02, in the source database X will be used as transportable tablespaces to refresh a destination database Y. The refresh process can be divided into two stages: physical export from X and physical import into Y.

D2.1 Physical Export from Source Database X

During this stage the metadata of the self-contained tablespaces of X is exported to an export dump file and the disk files of these tablespaces are copied to Y via an operating system level copy command.

(a) Determine if S is self-contained. Figure D.1 contains the detailed procedure with output for this step. We find that S is self-contained.

```
SQL> execute sys.dbms_tts.TRANSPORT_SET_CHECK
('DATA01,DATA02,INDEX01,INDEX02', TRUE);
PL/SQL procedure successfully completed.
SQL> SELECT * FROM SYS.TRANSPORT_SET_VIOLATIONS;
no rows selected
```

FIGURE D.1: Set of Self-Contained Tablespaces

If, on the other hand, S is not self-contained, then Oracle displays a set of violations as shown in Figure D.2. In that case, S cannot be used as a set of transportable tablespaces for the database refresh.

```
SQL> execute sys.dbms_tts.TRANSPORT_SET_CHECK
('DATA01,DATA02,USERDATA,INDEX01,INDEX02,USERINDEX', TRUE);
PL/SQL procedure successfully completed.
SQL> SELECT * FROM SYS.TRANSPORT_SET_VIOLATIONS;
VIOLATIONS
-----------------------------------------------------------
Constraint INVOICE_PK between table INVOICE in tablespace
INVDATA and table CUST_INVOICE in tablespace USERDATA
Constraint SO_NUM_VER_UK between table INVOICE in tablespace
INVDATA and table CUST_INVOICE in tablespace USERDATA
Constraint FTI_SR_RTS_FK between table INVOICE in tablespace
INVDATA and table CUST_INVOICE in tablespace USERDATA
. . . . . . . . . . . . . . . . . . . . . . . . . . . . . .
12 rows selected.
```

FIGURE D.2: Set of Non-Self-Contained Tablespaces

(b) Assuming S to be self-contained, put the four tablespaces in READ ONLY mode as follows.

```
alter tablespace DATA01 read only;
alter tablespace DATA02 read only;
alter tablespace INDEX01 read only;
alter tablespace INDEX01 read only;
```

Verify the altered status of the tablespaces by running the following command.

```
Select tablespace_name, status from dba_tablespaces
order by 1;
```

The four tablespaces, DATA01, DATA02, INDEX01, and INDEX02, will have their status as READ ONLY. The segments in the above four tablespaces will be available only for data retrieval until the tablespaces are altered again to the READ WRITE mode.

(c) Use a copy utility at the operating system level to copy all the datafiles comprising these four tablespaces of X to appropriate locations on Y. For example, under UNIX one can use "cp" to copy files on the same server or "ftp" to copy files to a different server. Ensure that there is enough space on Y to hold the copied files. If such space is not available, proceed as follows.

- Execute Steps (a) and (b) of Section D2.2 (see below) so that the datafiles of Y corresponding the four tablespaces, DATA01, DATA02, INDEX01, and INDEX02, are no longer in use. The space occupied by them now becomes available.
- Copy the datafiles on X to their respective locations on Y that have just been freed up.

After the copying is finished, verify that the size of each copied file exactly matches the size of its source file. If a copied file is smaller than its source, then the copying did not complete successfully. In that case, repeat the copying process for the file until the size of the copied file equals that of the source file.

(d) Export the metadata of the four tablespaces using Oracle's export utility for transportable tablespaces.

```
exp parfile=exp_transp_tblspc.txt
```

Figure D.3 contains the code of the export parameter file ("parfile") for performing the export.

```
userid='sys as sysdba'
TRANSPORT_TABLESPACE=Y
TABLESPACES=DATA01,DATA02,INDEX01,INDEX02
file=X_tblspc.dmp
log= X_tblspc.log
```

FIGURE D.3: Export Parameter File "exp_transp_tblspc.txt"

Oracle prompts for the password when the export is run. Enter "sys as sysdba" in response.

D2.2 Physical Import into Destination Database Y

During this stage the tables and the tablespaces of Y matching the set S are dropped, the metadata of the tablespaces are imported from the export dump file to Y, and each tablespace is matched with its disk file(s) already copied from X.

(a) Drop all tables cascading their constraints from the tablespaces DATA01 and DATA02 on Y by running a series of statements of the form

```
drop table table_name cascade constraints;
```

for every table belonging to the tablespaces DATA01 and DATA02.

(b) Drop the four tablespaces on Y including their contents by running the following series of commands.

```
drop tablespace DATA01 including contents;
drop tablespace DATA02 including contents;
drop tablespace INDEX01 including contents;
drop tablespace INDEX02 including contents;
```

(c) Stop the instance by issuing the following command.

```
SVRMGR> shutdown immediate
```

(d) Start the instance by issuing the following command.

```
SVRMGR> startup pfile='pfile_path'
```

The database Y no longer contains the four tablespaces DATA01, DATA02, INDEX01, and INDEX02. Hence their metadata can be imported from the export dump file created in Step (d), Section D2.1.

(e) Import the metadata of the four tablespaces using Oracle's import utility for transportable tablespaces.

```
imp parfile=imp_transp_tblspc.txt
```

Figure D.4 contains the code of the import parameter file ("parfile") for performing the import.

```
userid='sys as sysdba'
TRANSPORT_TABLESPACE=Y
TABLESPACES=DATA01,DATA02,INDEX01,INDEX02
DATAFILES=('copied disk file(s) for DATA01','copied disk
file(s) for DATA02', 'copied disk file(s) for INDEX01',
'copied disk file(s) for INDEX02')
file=X_tblspc.dmp
log= Y_tblspc.log
```

FIGURE D.4: Import Parameter File "imp_transp_tblspc.txt"

The string '*copied disk file(s) for DATA01*' stands for the full absolute path on Y of each datafile copied from X comprising DATA01. A similar interpretation applies to DATA02, INDEX01, and INDEX02.

(f) Put the four tablespaces DATA01, DATA02, INDEX01, and INDEX02 on X back to READ WRITE mode by issuing the following commands:

```
alter tablespace DATA01 READ WRITE;
alter tablespace DATA02 READ WRITE;
alter tablespace INDEX01 READ WRITE;
alter tablespace INDEX02 READ WRITE;
```

Verify the altered status of these tablespaces by issuing the following command.

```
select tablespace_name, status from dba_tablespaces
order by 1;
```

Check that the four tablespaces DATA01, DATA02, INDEX01, and INDEX02 have their status changed to ONLINE.

D3. Time Estimates

This section contains some time estimates to run the individual steps. They are included here to provide some timing guidelines for DBAs for scheduling the database refresh jobs with the least possible impact on the end users. These estimates are based on my own experience in running these scripts in a large database installation with one production database and five nonproduction databases supporting development, test, training, and performance. I have run the scripts about once a month for each nonproduction database in a staggered schedule. The database statistics are as follows:

- The instances run Oracle 8.1.7 under Sun Solaris 2.6.
- In each database, eight self-contained tablespaces contain nearly 500 tables and 800 indices and span 30 datafiles. These tablespaces are used as the transportable tablespaces for the refresh.
- Total storage space used by the datafiles is approximately 60 GB.
- The export dump file takes about 20 MB in storage.

The time estimates given below are slightly overestimated. Only the steps that take longer than five minutes are listed.

Section/Step	Time Estimate
D2.1/c	4 hours (copying three files in parallel at a time)
D2.1/d	30 minutes
D2.2/a	20 minutes
D2.2/b	10 minutes
D2.2/e	30 minutes

Including preparation and ancillary tasks the total refresh procedure for a database of size 60+ GB takes about 6 hours. During this time the source and the destination databases remain unavailable except that the source database can be accessed for data retrieval only. This does not always sit well with the business users. As a compromise, the DBA can put the tablespaces on the source database X to READ WRITE mode after executing Step (d), Section D2.1. Then, Step (f), Section D2.2 is not needed. X becomes fully available to the users after about 4 1/2 hours instead of 6 hours. But this shortcut may cause a problem as discussed in Section D4 below.

D4. Internal Consistency

Let us consider the following scenario involving a database refresh process starting with Step (b), Section D2.1 and ending with Step (f), Section D2.2. The time instant in each step represents the instant when the step is completed.

Time Instant	Section/Step
t_1	D2.1/b
t_2	D2.1/c
t_3	D2.1/d
t_4	D2.2/a
t_5	D2.2/b
t_6	D2.2/c
t_7	D2.2/d
t_8	D2.2/e
t_9	D2.2/f

Since the steps are sequential, we assume that $t_i < t_{i+1}$, where $i = 1, \ldots, 8$.

As a result of Step (b), Section D2.1, the datafiles of the four tablespaces cannot be updated after the instant t_1. Step (c), Section D2.1 produces the copied datafiles during the time interval ($t_1 < t \le t_2$). Hence the time stamp on any of the copied datafiles does not exceed t_2. Step (d), Section D2.1 produces the export dump file X_tblspc.dmp containing the metadata of the four tablespaces at instant t_3. If the dump file gets corrupted for some reason (it has happened to me a few times), then Step (e), Section D2.2 will fail. In that case, Step (d), Section D2.1 must be repeated and be followed by Step (e), Section D2.2. This loop must be repeated until Step (e), Section D2.2 succeeds with a complete import. Since the four tablespaces of the source database X are still in READ ONLY mode, the time-stamps of the copied datafiles on Y match those of the source datafiles of X. Consequently, no internal inconsistencies occur.

Suppose now that to make X available earlier for both retrieval and update by the end users, the four tablespaces of X are ALTERed into the READ WRITE mode after Step (d), Section D2.1. Then, the source datafiles on X start getting updated at instants subsequent to t_2. Thereby the copied datafiles on the destination database Y become "out of synch" with their sources. If now an export is taken of the four tablespaces of X, then an internal inconsistency will arise between the timestamps of the source datafiles on X and the time stamps of their copies made earlier on Y. In fact, the timestamps of the datafiles on Y will be less than the new timestamps of the datafiles on X. When Step (e), Section D2.2 is run with the new export dump file, Oracle detects the violation of internal consistency due to the timestamp mismatch and returns the following error message.

```
IMP-00017: following statement failed with ORACLE error 19722:
 "BEGIN
sys.dbms_plugts.checkDatafile(NULL,2385892692,6,256000,4,6,0,0,1970"
 "6,72926999,1,NULL, NULL, NULL, NULL); END;"
IMP-00003: ORACLE error 19722 encountered
ORA-19722: datafile DATA01_a.dbf is an incorrect version
ORA-06512: at "SYS.DBMS_PLUGTS", line 1594
ORA-06512: at line 1
IMP-00000: import terminated unsuccessfully
```

Figure D.5 shows the violation of internal consistency graphically. We assume that at instant $t_{3.1}$, where $t_3 < t_{3.1} < t_4$, the four tablespaces on X are put back into READ WRITE mode. Then at instant $t_{8.1}$, where $t_8 < t_{8.1}$, the export causes internal inconsistency.

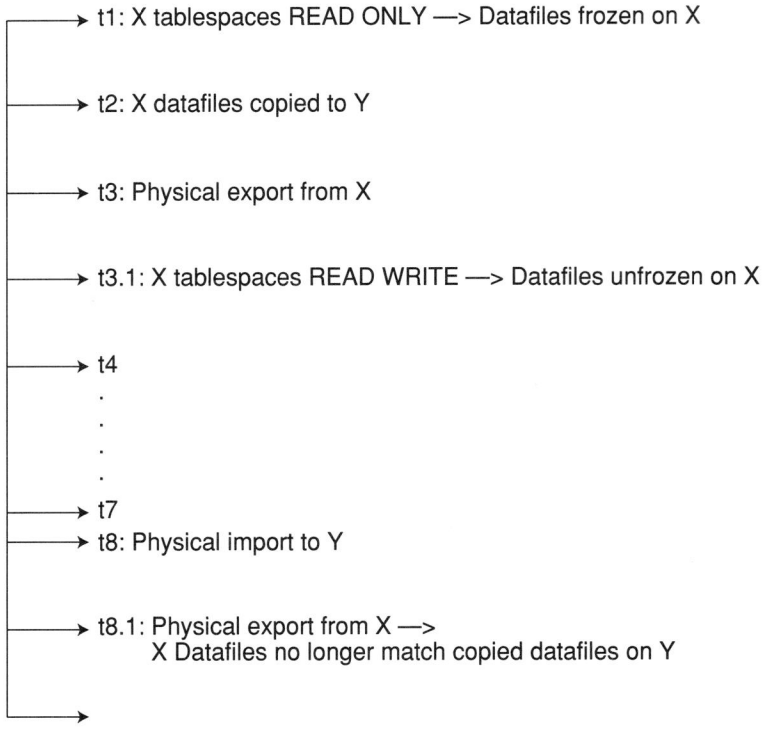

LEGEND: At instant t8.1, export of DATA01's datafile has a different time stamp from its copy taken at the earlier instant t3.

FIGURE D.5: Graphic Representation of Internal Inconsistency

Key Words

export parameter file
import parameter file

self-contained tablespaces
transportable tablespaces

Appendix E
Mathematical Foundation of Relational Databases

Outline

E1. Relational Database Systems Foundation Pillars
E2. Relation
E3. Functional Dependency
E4. Query Languages
E5. Relational Algebra: Prescriptive Query Languages
E6. Primitive and Derived Operations
E7. Closure Property for Relational Algebra
E8. Relational Calculus: Descriptive Query Languages
E9. Tuple Relational Calculus
E10. Domain Relational Calculus
E11. Equivalence Theorem for Algebra and Calculus
E12. Data Structures for Search Algorithms
E13. Linear Linked List
E14. Search Tree
E15. Hash Table
E16. Performance Metrics
Key Words
References and Further Reading

Overview of the Appendix

The appendix discusses four major mathematical topics that form the foundation of relational database systems. Functional dependency forms the basis of normalization principles used in logical database design. Relational algebra, tuple relational calculus, and domain relational calculus provide three alternative but mathematically equivalent paradigms for building query languages. SQL uses relational algebra primarily along with the

EXISTS command based on relational calculus. The three data structures used for designing efficient search algorithms are described with some discussions of search times in each case. Search algorithms constitute an active research area of theoretical computer science which is based on mathematics.

E1. Relational Database Systems Foundation Pillars

Dr. Codd established the theory of relational databases on four fundamental concepts, each of which has its root in mathematics:

- Relation,
- Functional Dependency,
- Query Language, and
- Search Algorithm.

Relation is the central concept underlying a relational database. In common database parlance a relation is called a table. Functional dependency is at the root of the principle of normalization, which drives the design of the conceptual level of a relational database. Queries are used for both retrieval and update, i.e., insert, modify, and delete, operations on a database. Queries are written in a query language. Dr. Codd proposed two distinct but mathematically equivalent formalisms to design a query language. They are called relational algebra and relational calculus, although the latter has no connection with differential or integral calculus. A query is executed via one of three types of search algorithm:

- Sequential search,
- Indexed search, or
- Direct access.

The respective data structures for these algorithms are:

- Sequential search: Linear linked list,
- Indexed search: B-Tree and B*-Tree, and
- Direct access: Hash table.

E2. Relation

The *Cartesian product* of n sets $A_1, \ldots, A_n$ is written as $A_1 \times \ldots \times A_n$ and is defined as a set of n-tuples $(a_1, a_2, \ldots, a_n)$ such that $a_i \in A_i$, $i = 1, 2, \ldots, n$. We use the notation $A_1 \times \ldots \times A_n = \{(a_1, a_2, \ldots, a_n) \mid a_i \in A_i, i = 1, 2, \ldots, n\}$.

An *n-ary relation* $R(A_1, \ldots, A_n)$ defined on n sets $A_1, \ldots, A_n$ is a subset of the Cartesian product $A_1 \times \ldots \times A_n$. Each a_i is called an *attribute* of R defined on the *domain* A_i, $i = 1, 2, \ldots, n$. The integer n is called the *degree* or *arity* of the relation R.

In database terminology a relation is called a table, an attribute is a column of the table, and an n-tuple is a row of the table. The domain of an attribute is the set of all possible values of the attribute although the attribute may not actually take all those values.

Example

Consider the table CUSTOMER defined below.

```
Cust_ID         NUMBER(5),
Name            VARCHAR2 (20),
Balance         NUMBER (10,2),
Credit_Status   CHAR (10)
```

CUSTOMER is a quaternary or 4-ary relation with four attributes, Cust_ID, Name, Balance, and Credit_Status. The respective domains of these attributes are given by:

```
Cust_ID    {5-digit numbers}
Name       {character strings of variable length up to 20}
Balance    {10-digit numbers with two digits to the right
            of the decimal}
Status     {character strings of fixed length 10}
```

Obviously, none of the columns assumes all possible values from its domain.

E3. Functional Dependency

A *function* is a mapping or correspondence between the elements of two sets. Thus, the function $f: X \rightarrow Y$ is a mapping between the elements of two sets X and Y such that given an element $x \in X$, there exists a single element $y \in Y$ to which x is mapped. We write $y = f(x)$ and call y the image of x under the mapping f. X is called the domain of f and $f(X) = \{ y \in Y \mid y = f(x) \} \subseteq Y$ is called the range of f. We call x the independent variable and y the dependent variable. If x is a scalar variable, then f is called a function of a single variable. If x is a vector variable, then f is called a function of multiple variables. For example, if $x = (x_1, x_2, \ldots, x_n)$, then f is a function of n variables and is written as $y = f(x_1, x_2, \ldots, x_n)$.

The statistical measures used in performance tuning are examples of functions. Metrics such as selectivity and cardinality of columns, num_rows of a table, etc., can be written as functions as shown below:

- Selectivity of a column set C at a given instant t = selectivity (C, t), where C can be a set of one or more columns of a table;
- Cardinality of a column set C at a given instant t = cardinality (C, t), where C can be a set of one or more columns of a table;
- Number of rows in a table T at a given instant t = num_rows (T,t), etc.

Then, we note that for any given value of t, we have:

$$\text{selectivity}(C, t) = \text{cardinality}(C, t) / \text{num\_rows rows}(T,t).$$

Given a relation R, an attribute y of R is functionally dependent (FD) on another attribute x of R if and only if each x-value in R has associated with it exactly one y-value in R, irrespective of any insertions, modifications, or deletions at any given time. We also say that x functionally determines y. In symbols we write $R.x \to R.y$. Here x can be a composite attribute of R consisting of two or more columns. We note that functional dependency is an extension of the concept of a single-valued mathematical function. If we assume that X and Y are the domains of the attributes x and y respectively, then the functional dependency $R.x \to R.y$ is represented by the function $f\colon X \to Y$ such that each $x \in X$ has a unique image $f(x) = y \in Y$. If x is a single attribute of R, then f is a function of a single variable. If x is a composite attribute of R, then f is a function of multiple variables. In the latter case, y is fully functionally dependent (FFD) on x if $R.x \to R.y$ holds, but $R.z \to R.y$ does not hold for any proper subset z of x in R. Clearly, FFD implies FD, but the converse is not true.

For the relation CUSTOMER described above, the attributes, Name, Balance, and Credit_Status, are functionally dependent on Cust_ID.

Consider now the relation GRADE given below:

```
GRADE (Student_ID, Course_Number, Letter_Grade)
```

The attribute Letter_Grade is fully functionally dependent on the composite attribute (Student_ID, Course_Number) since neither Student_ID nor Course_Number alone can uniquely determine Letter_Grade.

In order to design the conceptual level of a database in an efficient manner it is necessary to determine the full set of FDs among the attributes, although this may not always be a feasible task for large databases.

In 1974 W. W. Armstrong introduced a set of axioms, which are often referred to as *Armstrong's Axioms*, to generate the complete set of FDs from a given starter set. These axioms use the notion of closure of a set. Given a set S of FDs for a set of attributes, the set of all FDs logically deducible from S is called the *closure of S* and is denoted by CL(S). We can derive CL(S) from S by using the rules listed below.

1. *Reflexivity*: If X is a set of attributes and $Y \subset X$, then $X \to Y$ holds.
2. *Augmentation*: If $X \to Y$ and W is a set of attributes, then $W \wedge X \to W \wedge Y$ holds, where $\wedge$ is the conjunction operator (see Section E5.2).
3. *Transitivity*: If $X \to Y$ and $Y \to Z$, then $X \to Z$.
4. *Union*: If $X \to Y$ and $X \to Z$, then $X \to Y \wedge Z$.
5. *Decomposition*: If $X \to Y \wedge Z$, then $X \to Y$ and $X \to Z$.
6. *Pseudotransitivity*: If $X \to Y$ and $W \wedge Y \to Z$, then $X \wedge W \to Z$.

Rules 1 to 3 are called Armstrong's axioms. They are regarded as *sound* since they can generate a set of accurate FDs. They are also labeled *complete* since they can determine the entire closure CL (S) of S. Korth and Silberschatz [3, pp. 187 and 223] have given two algorithms in pseudo Pascal language to compute CL (S) from a given S.

E4. Query Languages

Programming languages have undergone changes through four generations since their creation in the late 1940s when computers first came into the market, ENIAC in 1949 soon followed by EDVAC. The four generations are defined as follows.

- First Generation (1GL): Machine languages using bits;
- Second Generation (2GL): Assembler languages;
- Third Generation (3GL): Procedural languages such as FORTRAN, COBOL, C, Pascal, Ada, PL/SQL, etc.;
- Fourth Generation (4GL): Nonprocedural languages such as SEQUEL, ISBL, QUEL, SQL, etc.

The main distinctions between 3GLs and 4GLs are the following.

(a) In a 3GL program the programmer has to specify both WHAT information is needed and HOW the information is to be retrieved. Therefore, the program must include such housekeeping tasks as opening and closing files, fetching cursors explicitly, etc. A 4GL program, on the other hand, merely describes WHAT information is needed, but not HOW the information is to be retrieved. The built-in query optimizer takes care of those tasks.

(b) A 3GL program allows the programmer to use the three programming structures, namely, assignment, decision, and iteration. But a 4GL does not provide any of these capabilities. As a result, for complex reports that cannot be generated through 4GL, the programmer has to use a 3GL such as C, C++, Ada, etc. or a host language interface program such as PL/SQL, Pro*C, Pro*Ada, etc. in Oracle.

Codd introduced query languages as nonprocedural 4GLs to extract information from a database. Prior to the advent of relational databases the 4GLs did not exist. The query languages accompanying nonrelational DBMSs such as IMS, IDMS, etc. used proprietary 3GLs as their own query languages. Codd first built the 4GLs as a new kind of query language. He proposed two alternative mechanisms to design query languages and called them relational algebra and relational calculus. The latter was formulated in two flavors, tuple relational calculus and domain relational calculus. Codd proved mathematically that relational algebra, tuple relational calculus, and domain relational calculus are equivalent with respect to their expressive power. But query languages based on relational algebra are *prescriptive* in nature since the query syntax requires that the operations in the query be performed in a definite order. On the other hand, the query languages based on tuple or domain relational calculus are *descriptive* since the query syntax only specifies the operations to be performed but does not impose any order in which they are to be executed.

We pursue further this topic in Section E11 after discussing the relational algebra and calculus.

E5. Relational Algebra: Prescriptive Query Languages

Codd [1] introduced eight n-ary set-theoretic operations as the basis for his theory of relational algebra. They can be grouped into two categories with four in each category:

(a) Set-Theoretic Operations: Union, intersection, difference, and Cartesian product
(b) Special Relational Algebra Operations: Selection, projection, join, and division.

E5.1 Set-Theoretic Operations

Two relations R_1 and R_2 are said to be *union compatible* if R_1 and R_2 have the same degree, say n, and the kth attribute of R_1 has the same domain as the kth attribute of R_2, where $k = 1, \ldots, n$. However, the corresponding attributes need not have the same name.

Let $f_1, \ldots, f_n$ be n distinct operations on a set S and let $f_{i1}, \ldots, f_{ik}, k < n$, be a proper subset of these n operations. If each of the remaining $n - k$ operations of the total set of n operations can be written in terms of the k operations $f_{i1}, \ldots, f_{ik}$, then we say that these k operations are *primitive*, and the remaining $n - k$ are *derived*.

Two sets S_1 and S_2 are *isomorphic* if there exists a one-to-one and onto mapping between the elements of S_1 and S_2. Two finite sets with the same number of elements are always isomorphic. An example of two isomorphic infinite sets is the following.

$$S_1 = \{n \mid n \text{ is a positive integer}\}; \quad S_2 = \{n \mid n \text{ is a squared integer}\}.$$

The mapping $n \in S_1 \leftrightarrow n^2 \in S_2$ establishes the isomorphism between S_1 and S_2.

We now describe the four set-theoretic operations below.

Union

Given two union compatible relations R_1 and R_2 of degree n each, the *union* of R_1 and R_2 is a relation of degree n, which is written as $R_1 \cup R_2$ and is defined as follows.

$$R_1 \cup R_2 = \{r \mid r \text{ is an } n\text{-tuple}, r \in R_1 \text{ or } r \in R_2 \text{ or } r \in (\text{both } R_1 \text{ and } R_2)\}.$$

Example: Let $R_1 = \{\text{all rows in CUSTOMER} \mid \text{Balance} > 10{,}000\}$
$R_2 = \{\text{all rows in CUSTOMER} \mid \text{Credit\_Status} = \text{"Excellent"}\}$
Then, $R_1 \cup R_2$ consists of all rows in CUSTOMER for which
Balance > 10,000 or Credit_Status is "Excellent" or both.

Although defined as a binary operation, union can be extended to m (>2) union compatible relations as follows:

$$R_1 \cup R_2 \cup \ldots \cup R_m = \{r \mid r \text{ is an } n\text{-tuple}, r \in R_i \text{ for at least one } i = 1, 2, \ldots, m\}$$

Intersection

Given two union compatible relations R_1 and R_2 of degree n each, the *intersection* of R_1 and R_2 is a relation of degree n, which is written as $R_1 \cap R_2$ and is defined as follows.

$$R_1 \cap R_2 = \{r \mid r \text{ is an } n\text{-tuple}, r \in R_1 \text{ and } r \in R_2\}$$

Example: Let R_1 = {all rows in CUSTOMER | Balance > 10,000}
R_2 = {all rows in CUSTOMER | Credit_Status = "Excellent"}
Then, $R_1 \cap R_2$ consists of all rows in CUSTOMER for which both Balance > 10,000 and Credit_Status is "Excellent".

Although defined as a binary operation, intersection can be extended to m (> 2) union compatible relations as follows.

$$R_1 \cap R_2 \cap \ldots \cap R_m = \{r \mid r \text{ is an } n\text{-tuple}, r \in R_i \text{ for all } i = 1, 2, \ldots, m\}.$$

Difference

Given two union compatible relations R_1 and R_2 of degree n each, the *difference* of R_1 and R_2 is a relation of degree n, which is written as $R_1 - R_2$ and is defined as follows:

$$R_1 - R_2 = \{r \mid r \text{ is an } n\text{-tuple}, r \in R_1 \text{ but } r \notin R_2\}$$

Example: Let R_1 = {all rows in CUSTOMER | Balance > 10,000}
R_2 = {all rows in CUSTOMER | Credit_Status = 'Excellent'}
Then, $R_1 - R_2$ consists of all rows in CUSTOMER for which Balance > 10,000 but Credit_Status is not "Excellent".

Cartesian Product

Given two relations R_1 and R_2 of degree m and n respectively, the Cartesian product of R_1 and R_2 is a relation of degree $m + n$, which is written as $R_1 \times R_2$ and is defined as follows.

$$R_1 \times R_2 = \{r \mid r \text{ is an } (m+n)\text{-tuple of the form } (a_1, \ldots, a_m, b_1, \ldots, b_n) \text{ such that } (a_1, \ldots, a_m) \in R_1 \text{ and } (b_1, \ldots, b_n) \in R_2\}$$

If R_1 and R_2 have respectively p and q rows, then $R_1 \times R_2$ has pq rows.

Example: Let R_1 = CUSTOMER, as defined above
R_2 = ORDER (Order_ID, Order_Amount, Order_Date).
Then, $R_1 \times R_2$ is a relation of degree 7 with the structure:
$R_1 \times R_2$ = (Cust_ID, Name, Balance, Status, Order_ID, Order_Amount, Order_Date).
Every tuple of CUSTOMER is concatenated with every tuple of ORDER to produce the Cartesian product CUSTOMER × ORDER. If CUSTOMER has 100 rows, say, and ORDER has 1,000 rows, then CUSTOMER × ORDER has 100,000 rows.

E5.2 Special Relational Algebra Operations

Four operations belonging to this category are described below.

Selection

Let R be a relation of degree n, a_1 and a_2 be two attributes of R, and Θ be a relational operator; i.e., Θ takes any one of six possible values, $<, \leq, >, \geq, =, \neq$. Then, the Θ-*selection* of R on a_1 and a_2 is defined to be the following set of tuples t of R: $\{t \mid t \in R, \text{ and } a_1 \Theta a_2 \text{ holds}\}$.

In particular, a_2 can be a constant c, say. In that case, the Θ-selection is defined by $\{t \mid t \in R, \text{ and } a_1 \Theta c \text{ holds}\}$.

The Θ-selection of R is a unary operation and returns a horizontal subset of R, i.e., the set of all tuples of R that are related by the relational operator Θ. Hence the Θ-selection is implemented by a WHERE clause in SQL such as (R WHERE $a_1 \Theta a_2$). The expression $a_1 \Theta a_2$ is called the *predicate* of the Θ-selection. The predicate can be extended from a single relational operator Θ to a Boolean combination of such operators by using the three primitive Boolean operations, conjunction ($\land$), disjunction ($\lor$), and negation ($\sim$). These compound predicates are defined as follows in terms of the Θ-selection and the three set-theoretic operations, union, intersection, and difference.

- R WHERE $p_1 \land p_2 \equiv (R$ WHERE $p_1) \cap (R$ WHERE $p_2)$
- R WHERE $p_1 \lor p_2 \equiv (R$ WHERE $p_1) \cup (R$ WHERE $p_2)$
- R WHERE $\sim p \equiv R - (R$ WHERE $p)$

Note that p, p_1, and p_2 are simple predicates of the form $a_1 \Theta a_2$. Also, the binary combinations $p_1 \land p_2$ and $p_1 \lor p_2$ can be extended to k-ary combinations such as $p_1 \land p_2 \land \ldots \land p_k$ and $p_1 \lor p_2 \lor \ldots \lor p_k$ respectively, since union and intersection can be so extended.

The relational algebraic operation of Θ-selection is different from the command SELECT of SQL. SELECT is a much more powerful operation than the Θ-selection and is, in fact, used to implement the relational algebraic operations.

Projection

Let R be a relation of degree n with attributes $a_1, \ldots, a_n$. Let $a_{i1}, \ldots, a_{ik}$, $k < n$, be a subset of these n attributes. The *k-projection* of R on the k attributes $a_{i1}, \ldots, a_{ik}$ is written as $R[a_{i1}, \ldots, a_{ik}]$ and is defined by

$$R[a_{i1}, \ldots, a_{ik}] = \{t \mid t \in R, t = (t_1, \ldots, t_k) \text{ such that } t_j \text{ is the value assumed by } t \text{ for the attribute } a_{ij}, j = 1, \ldots, k\}$$

Clearly, $R[a_{i1}, \ldots, a_{ik}]$ is a vertical subset of R. The projection is a unary operation.

Join

Let R_1 and R_2 be two relations of degree m and n respectively and let Θ be a relational operator, i.e., $\Theta = (<, \leq, >, \geq, =, \neq)$. If x and y are two attributes of R_1 and R_2 respectively, then the Θ-*join* of the relation R_1 on x with the relation R_2 on y is defined as follows:

$\{t \mid t$ is a concatenation of tuples $t_1 \in R_1$ and $t_2 \in R_2$ such that $t_1.x \Theta t_2.y$ holds$\}$

The Θ-join is a relation of degree $m + n$. If R_1 has p rows and R_2 has q rows, then their Θ-join will have at most pq rows, because the join condition will eliminate those rows that do not satisfy the condition $t_1.x \Theta t_2.y$. We can express a Θ-join in terms of a Cartesian product and a Θ-selection as follows.

1. Let $R = R_1 \times R_2$ so that R is of degree $m + n$.
2. Perform the Θ-selection of R such that $R.x \Theta R.y$ holds.

We can define six possible types of Θ-join corresponding to the six different values of the operator Θ. If Θ is the equality operator, the Θ-join is called an *equijoin*. An equijoin by definition has two identical columns since R has the condition $t_1.x = t_2.y$. Therefore, we take a projection of an equijoin to remove one of the two identical columns. The resulting relation is called a *natural join*, or simply a *join*. Therefore, the algorithm to compute a join of R_1 on x with R_2 on y consists of Steps (1) and (2) above along with Step (3) stated below:

3. Perform the projection of R on all its attributes except $R.x$ or $R.y$.

We note that when R_1 and R_2 are of degree m and n respectively, the degree of their join is at most $m + n - 1$.

Division

The *division* operation divides a *dividend* relation R of degree $m + n$ by a *divisor* relation S of degree n to yield a *quotient* relation R / S of degree m. The $(m + i)$th attribute of R and the ith attribute of S must be defined on the same domain for $i = 1, \ldots,$ n. Let us write the tuples r and s of R and S as follows.

$$R = \{r \mid r = (r_1, \ldots, r_m, r_{m+1}, \ldots, r_{m+n})\}, S = \{s \mid s = (s_1, \ldots, s_n)\}.$$

Then the quotient R/S consists of tuples t such that the following condition holds:

$$R/S = \{t \mid t = (t_1, \ldots, t_m), \text{ and } (t_1, \ldots, t_m, s_1, \ldots, s_n) \in R \text{ for all tuples } (s_1, \ldots, s_n) \in S\}.$$

Note that R is the Cartesian product of T and S. This resembles the arithmetical notation of multiplication and division. For example, if A, B, and C are real numbers and $C = A / B$, then we write $A = B \times C$. The same notation is used in relational algebra for describing the division operation. For any two relations R and S, if $T = R / S$ is the quotient relation, then we can write $R = T \times S$, where $T \times S$ is the Cartesian product of T and S.

Example of a Query in Relational Algebra

Refer to the relation CUSTOMER of Section E2. Assume that the relation contains the following five tuples.

Cust_ID	Name	Balance	Credit_Status
11111	XYZ Corporation	101665.36	Excellent
22222	Acme Corporation	62400.00	Good
33333	John Kartofski	245.88	Poor
44444	Sheila Majumder	3949.00	Good
55555	Commerce Magnet	0.00	Unknown

Query: select name, balance for all CUSTOMERs with balance < 10000 and with credit_status other than 'Poor' and 'Unknown'

Relational Algebra Version

Let us suppose

1. $(CUSTOMER)_1 = \{t \mid t \in CUSTOMER, Balance < 10000\}$.
2. $(CUSTOMER)_2 = \{t \mid t \in CUSTOMER, Credit\_Status \neq ("Poor", "Unknown")\}$.
3. $(CUSTOMER)_3 = \{t \mid t \in (CUSTOMER)_1\} \cap \{t \mid t \in (CUSTOMER)_2\}$.
4. $(CUSTOMER)_4 = (CUSTOMER)_3$ [Name, Balance].

Then, $(CUSTOMER)_4$ is the final result that returns the following tuple.

    Sheila Majumder   3949.00

E 6. Primitive and Derived Operations

Five of the eight relational algebra operations discussed in Section E5 are primitive and the remaining three are derived. The five primitive operations are: union, difference, Cartesian product, selection, and projection. The three derived ones are: join, intersection, and division. This means that

- None of the five primitive operations can be expressed in terms of the other four;
- The three derived operations can all be expressed in terms of one or more of the five primitive operations.

The first statement is quite difficult to prove mathematically. Ullman [6, Volume 1, Chapter 2] gives an outline of a formal mathematical proof. The second statement can be proved as follows.

Join: Join is defined in terms of Cartesian product, selection, and projection, as shown in Section E5.

Intersection: Intersection can be defined in terms of difference as follows:
$$R_1 \cap R_2 = R_1 - (R_1 - R_2)$$

Division: $R / S = R[X] - ((R[X] \times S) - R)[X]$, where $R[X]$ represents the projection of R on its composite attribute X.

E7. Closure Property for Relational Algebra

A set S with an n-ary operation F is said to be closed with respect to F if for every set of elements $(s_1, \ldots, s_n) \in S$, the element $F(s_1, \ldots, s_n) \in S$. This property is called the *closure* property of S with respect to F. For example, the set of all integers is closed with respect to addition, subtraction, and multiplication, but not with respect to division, because the quotient of two integers is not necessarily an integer.

The closure property plays a significant role in executing retrieval and update operations on a relational database. It is necessary to ensure that any such operation will always return a member of the database. Since retrievals and updates are done through query languages which are based on relational algebra, it is sufficient to show that a relational database is always closed with respect to the eight operations of relational algebra. This means that if we perform one or more of these eight operations on a relational database, we get back a result set that belongs to the same database. We can write nested relational expressions such as subqueries using the relations of the database and be assured that the results will belong to the database. It is enough to prove this closure property for the five primitive operations only.

Let R_i represent a relation of degree d_i, $i = 1, \ldots, n$, in a relational database Ω containing n relations $R_1, \ldots, R_n$. Let $D_{i1}, \ldots, D_{idi}$ be the domains of the d_i attributes of R_i. Then, the rows of R_i, which are d_i-tuples, mathematically constitute a subset of the Cartesian product set $D_{i1} \times \ldots \times D_{idi}$. This is true for all the n relations $R_1, \ldots, R_n$ of Ω. Let us now consider a Cartesian product set Γ defined as follows:

$$\Gamma = D_{11} \times \ldots \times D_{1d1} \times D_{21} \times \ldots \times D_{2d2} \times \ldots \times D_{n1} \times \ldots \times D_{ndn} = \Pi (D_{i1} \times \ldots \times D_{idi})$$

Then, the relation R_i is isomorphic to the subset of Γ that consists of those tuples that have zeros for all entries except those at positions $(i1, \ldots, idi)$, where they coincide with the tuples of R_i, $i = 1, \ldots, n$. Hence the tuples of Ω are isomorphic to the tuples of Γ. The closure of Ω consists of Ω and the results of relational algebraic operations performed on Ω. The closure of Ω is thus a subset of Γ. Therefore, we need to prove that Γ is closed with respect to the five primitive operations of relational algebra.

Given any two relations R_j and R_k in Ω, each is isomorphic to a subset of Γ. Their union $R_j \cup R_k$ returns a set of tuples that belong to at least one of them. Hence the union is also isomorphic to a subset of Γ. The difference $R_j - R_k$ returns a subset of R_j and hence is isomorphic to a subset of Γ. A selection and a projection of a relation R in Ω are unary operations that return respectively a horizontal and a vertical subset of R. Since R is isomorphic to a subset of Γ, so are its selection and projection. Finally, consider the Cartesian product $R_j \times R_k$ of the two relations R_j and R_k of Ω. Each of them is isomorphic to a subset of Γ. Their Cartesian product $R_j \times R_k$ consists of tuples t whose components are concatenations of tuples in R_j and R_k and, as such, are isomorphic to subsets of Γ.

This completes the proof that Γ and, therefore, Ω are closed with respect to the operations of relational algebra.

E8. Relational Calculus: Descriptive Query Languages

Relational calculus provides an alternative mechanism for formulating the query languages. It differs from relational algebra in its level of abstraction for writing the query. The theory was first introduced in 1967 by J. L. Kuhns. Codd later proposed two versions of relational calculus, namely, tuple and domain. We discuss them in Sections E9 and E10 respectively.

A word on the terminology: relational calculus is based on first-order predicate logic, which is often called predicate calculus. But it is totally different from differential or integral calculus of mathematics. The term is merely a carryover from past usage.

Relational calculus uses a predicate as its basic element and is based on three primitive operations:

- A unary operation of negation, written as NOT or $\sim$,
- A binary operation of conjunction, written as AND or $\wedge$, and
- A binary operation of disjunction, written as OR or $\vee$.

In terms of them we define two derived operations and two quantifiers:

- IF ... THEN, or $\Rightarrow$,
- IF AND ONLY IF, or $\Leftrightarrow$,
- FOR ALL, or $\forall$, known as the universal quantifier, and
- EXISTS, or $\exists$, known as the existential quantifier.

The first five operations are defined by their respective truth tables given below. In each table, p and q are two symbolic predicates and T and F represent the truth values of "true" and "false" respectively.

Truth Tables of Primitive Operations

NOT or $\sim$

p	$\sim$ p
T	F
F	T

AND or $\wedge$

p	q	p $\wedge$ q
T	T	T
T	F	F
F	T	F
F	F	F

OR or ∨

p	q	p ∨ q
T	T	T
T	F	T
F	T	T
F	F	F

Truth Tables of Derived Operations

IF ... THEN, or ⇒

p	q	p ⇒ q
T	T	T
T	F	F
F	T	T
F	F	T

Implication is defined in terms of negation and conjunction as follows.

$\quad$ p ⇒ q $\quad$ means $\quad$ ~ p ∨ q.

Its truth table is derived by using the above definition, although the plain English meaning of implication does not make the above truth table self evident.

IF AND ONLY IF, or ⇔

p	q	p ⇔ q
T	T	T
T	F	F
F	T	F
F	F	T

Equivalence is defined in terms of implication as follows.

$\quad$ p ⇔ q $\quad$ means $\quad$ (p ⇒ q) ∧ (q ⇒ p).

Its truth table is derived by using the above definition.

Universal and Existential Quantifiers

The universal quantifier, FOR ALL or ∀, asserts that a property is true for all values of a variable.

Example: $\quad$ If $a > b$ and $b > c$, then $a > c$
$\quad\quad\quad\quad$ can be written as
$\quad\quad\quad\quad$ $(\forall a, b, c)\ ((a > b) \land (b > c)) \Rightarrow (a > c)$

The existential quantifier, EXISTS or ∃, asserts that a property is true for at least one value of a variable.

Example: "For any two numbers a and b, there always exists at least one number c between them" can be written as
$$(\forall\, a, b)\, (\exists\, c)\, ((a < c) \wedge (c < b))$$

De Morgan's laws connect conjunction, disjunction, and negation as follows.

$\sim (p \wedge q)$	means	$\sim p \vee \sim q$
$\sim (p \vee q)$	means	$\sim p \wedge \sim q$

The universal and the existential quantifiers are connected as follows.

$\sim (\forall\, x\, P(x))$	means	$\exists\, y\, (\sim P(y))$
$\sim (\exists\, x\, P(x))$	means	$\forall y\, ((\sim P(y)))$,

where $P(x)$ and $P(y)$ are predicates with arguments x and y respectively.

E9. Tuple Relational Calculus

The basic element of tuple relational calculus is the *tuple variable*, which represents the tuple of a relation. The notation $R(t)$ means that t is a tuple of the relation R. In relational database terminology this means that t is a row of the table R. For the purpose of defining a query language we need to consider only the *safe* tuple relational calculus expressions. These four terms are basic to the definition of safe expressions:

- Atom,
- free variable,
- bound variable, and
- formula.

Atom

An *atom* is of three types:

(a) $R(t)$, as defined above, to mean that t is a tuple of the relation R.
(b) $s(i)\, \Theta\, u(j)$, where s and u are tuple variables and Θ is a relational operator, to mean that the ith component of s is related to the jth component of u by the operator Θ. For example, $s(3) > u(5)$ means that the third component of s is greater than the fifth component of u.
(c) $s(i)\, \Theta\, c$, where c is a constant and $s(i)$ is defined as in type (b) above, to mean that the ith component of s is related to the constant c by the operator Θ. For example, $s(2) \mathrel{!=} 6$ means that the second component of s is not equal to 6.

Free and Bound Variables

If a variable is introduced by the quantifier $\forall$ or $\exists$, it is called *bound*. Otherwise, it is *free*. A free variable resembles a global variable in a programming language like C. A bound variable is like a local variable. The quantifiers play the role of declarations in C.

Formula

A *formula* is defined recursively as follows.

(a) Every atom is a formula. All occurrences of tuple variables mentioned in the atom are free in the formula.
(b) If ψ_1 and ψ_2 are formulas, so are $\psi_1 \wedge \psi_2$, $\psi_1 \vee \psi_2$, and $\sim \psi_1$. Occurrences of tuple variables are free or bound in $\psi_1 \wedge \psi_2$, $\psi_1 \vee \psi_2$, and $\sim \psi_1$ accordingly as they are free or bound in the individual components ψ_1 and ψ_2.
(c) If ψ is a formula, then so is $(\exists s \mid \psi(s))$. The formula means that there exists a value of s such that when we substitute this value for all free occurrences of s in ψ the formula becomes true. Occurrences of s that are free in ψ are bound to $\exists s$ in $(\exists s \mid \psi(s))$.
(d) If ψ is a formula, then so is $(\forall s \mid \psi(s))$. The formula means that whatever value we substitute for all free occurrences of s in ψ the formula becomes true. Occurrences of s that are free in ψ are bound to $\forall s$ in $(\forall s \mid \psi(s))$.
(e) Parentheses may be placed around formulas, as needed, to override the default order of precedence. The default order is: relational operators ($<, \leq, >, \geq, =$, and $!=$) the highest, the quantifiers $\forall$ and $\exists$ the next, and then the three operators $\sim$, $\wedge$, and $\vee$, in that order.
(f) Nothing else is a formula.

Safe Tuple Relational Calculus Expressions

We are now ready to define a safe tuple relational calculus expression. The definition ensures that such an expression returns only finite relations.

Let R be a relation of degree n with attributes $r_1, \ldots, r_n$ that have the respective domains $D_1, \ldots, D_n$. Then, by definition, each tuple of R belongs to the Cartesian product $D_1 \times \ldots \times D_n$. The tuple relational calculus expression $\{t \mid t \in D_1 \times \ldots \times D_n, \sim R(t)\}$ returns all those n-tuples that belong to $D_1 \times \ldots \times D_n$, but do not belong to R. If one or more D_k, $k = 1, \ldots, n$, are infinite sets, the above expression returns an infinite set of n-tuples, which is meaningless. For example, we cannot store or print such expressions. Consequently, it is necessary to restrict the calculus to yield only finite sets of tuples. This leads us to the concept of safe tuple relational calculus expressions.

Given a formula ψ, let us define a set $\Delta(\psi)$ to consist of all symbols that either appear explicitly in ψ or are components of a tuple in some relation R used by ψ. We call $\Delta(\psi)$ the *domain* of ψ. $\Delta(\psi)$ is a function of the actual relations to be substituted for the relation variables in ψ. Since each relation has only a finite set of tuples, $\Delta(\psi)$ is a finite set.

A tuple relational calculus expression $\{t \mid \psi(t)\}$ is defined to be safe if the following three conditions hold.

(a) Each component of the tuple t belongs to $\Delta(\psi)$.
(b) For each existentially quantified subformula of ψ of the form $(\exists\, s \mid \psi_1(s))$, the subformula is true if and only if there is a tuple s with values from $\Delta(\psi_1)$ such that $\psi_1(s)$ holds.
(c) For each universally quantified subformula of ψ of the form $(\forall s \mid \psi_1(s))$, the subformula is true if and only if $\psi_1(s)$ holds for all tuples s with values from the domain $\Delta(\psi_1)$.

The purpose of the notion is to ensure that only values from $\Delta(\psi)$ appear in the result and to ensure that we can test for existentially quantified and universally quantified subformulas without having to test infinitely many possibilities.

Example of a Query in Tuple Relational Calculus

Consider the relation CUSTOMER and the query described in Section E5.2. We give below the formulation of the query in tuple relational calculus:

Query: Select name, balance for all CUSTOMERs with balance < 10000 and with credit_status other than "Poor" and "Unknown"

Tuple Relational Calculus Version:

$\{t^{(2)} \mid (\exists\, u^{(4)})\, (\text{CUSTOMER}(u)) \wedge (u(3) < 10{,}000) \wedge (u(4) \neq \text{"Poor"}) \wedge (u(4) \neq \text{"Unknown"}) \wedge (t(1) = u(2)) \wedge (t(2) = u(3)))\}$,

where

$t^{(n)}$ means that t is an n-tuple with components $(t(1), \ldots, t(n))$,
$u(1) = \text{Cust\_ID}$
$u(2) = \text{Name}$
$u(3) = \text{Balance}$
$u(4) = \text{Credit\_Status}$.

E10. Domain Relational Calculus

The basic element of domain relational calculus is the domain variable, which represents individual components of a tuple variable, and uses the same operations and quantifiers as in tuple relational calculus. An *atom* in domain relational calculus takes either of the two forms:

(a) $R(r_1 \ldots r_n)$, where R is an n-ary relation and every r_i is either a constant or a domain variable
(b) $r \Theta s$, where r and s are constants or domain variables and Θ is a relational operator

$R(r_1...r_n)$ asserts that the values of those r_is must be selected that make $(r_1...r_n)$ a tuple in R. The meaning of $r \Theta s$ is that r and s must make $r \Theta s$ true.

Formulas in domain relational calculus use the five operators, $\sim$, $\wedge$, $\vee$, $\Rightarrow$, $\Leftrightarrow$, and the two quantifiers, $\exists$ and $\forall$. But in each case the arguments must be domain variables instead of tuple variables. Free and bound variables and the scope of a bound variable are defined the same way as in tuple relational calculus. A domain relational calculus expression is of the form $\{r_1...r_n \mid \psi(r_1, \ldots, r_n)\}$, where ψ is a formula whose only free domain variables are the distinct variables $r_1, \ldots, r_n$. The domain relational calculus expression $\{r_1...r_n \mid \psi(r_1, \ldots, r_n)\}$ is defined to be *safe* if the following three conditions hold.

(a) $\psi(r_1...r_n)$ is true implies that each r_i is in $\Delta(\psi)$.
(b) If $(\exists s)(\varphi(s))$ is a subformula of ψ, then $\varphi(s)$ is true implies that $s \in \Delta(\varphi)$.
(c) If $(\forall s)(\varphi(s))$ is a subformula of ψ, then $\varphi(s)$ is true implies that $s \in \Delta(\varphi)$.

Example of a Query in Domain Relational Calculus

Consider the relation CUSTOMER and the query described in Section E5.2. We give below the formulation of the query in domain relational calculus:

Query: Select name, balance for all CUSTOMERs with balance < 10000 and with credit_status other than "Poor" and "Unknown"

Domain Relational Calculus Version:

$\{t_1 t_2 \mid (\exists u_1)(\exists u_2)(\exists u_3)(\exists u_4) (\text{CUSTOMER}(u_1 u_2 u_3 u_4) (u_3 < 10,000) \wedge (u_4) \neq \text{"Poor"}) \wedge (u_4) \neq \text{"Unknown"}) \wedge (t_1 = u_2) \wedge (t_2 = u_3)\}$,

where

u_1 = Cust_ID,
u_2 = Name,
u_3 = Balance,
u_4 = Credit_Status.

E11. Equivalence Theorem for Algebra and Calculus

It was noted in Section E4 that query languages based on relational algebra are prescriptive, and those based on relational calculus are descriptive. The three examples given in Sections E5.2 (relational algebra), E9 (tuple relational calculus), and E10 (domain relational calculus) illustrate that concept. The query of Section E5.2 shows that although Steps (1) and (2) can happen in any order, both Steps (1) and (2) must be completed before Step (3) and then Step (4) can execute. Thus there is a prescribed order in which the component steps need to be executed. But the queries in Sections E9 and E10 do not require such a sequential order of execution. Despite this difference query languages based on algebra and calculus are equivalent in their expressive power.

Codd [1, pp. 78–85] first proposed the tuple relational calculus in a formulation slightly different from that described in Section E9. His objective was to use the calculus as a benchmark for evaluating query languages. In [1] he introduced a query language named ALPHA, which was never implemented commercially, as an example of a query language based on tuple relational calculus. He established that a query language that does not at least have the expressive power of the safe formulas of tuple or domain relational calculus, or of the five primitive operations of relational algebra is inadequate for retrieval and update operations of relational database systems. SQL, which is the ANSI 4GL for relational databases, is a hybrid of relational algebra and calculus. SQL is predominantly relational algebra based, but it uses the existential quantifier of relational calculus in its command EXISTS.

The equivalence of relational algebra and calculus is proved mathematically as follows.

- If E is a relational algebra expression, then E can be written as a safe tuple relational calculus expression E', say. The proof uses the principle of finite induction on the number of relational algebra operations used in E.
- If E is a safe tuple relational calculus expression, then E can be written as a safe domain relational calculus expression.
- If E is a safe domain relational calculus expression, then E can be written as a relational algebra expression.

The above three theorems together prove that the three alternative formulations of query languages are mathematically equivalent. A detailed formal proof can be found in Mittra [4, Chapter 4], Ullman [5, Chapter 5], and Yang [8, Chapter 3]. Ullman [6, Volume 1, Chapter 4] provides several examples of query languages including SQL that are based on algebra or calculus.

A query language is said to be *relationally complete* if it is at least as powerful in its expressive capability as the tuple relational calculus. Due to the equivalence theorem discussed above, a query language can be proved to be relationally complete if it can emulate the five primitive operations of relational algebra. SQL can be proved to be relationally complete by writing five SQL expressions to implement the five primitive operations of relational algebra, as shown below.

Union:	SELECT × FROM R
	UNION
	SELECT × FROM S;
Difference:	SELECT × FROM R
	WHERE NOT EXISTS
	(SELECT × FROM S WHERE
	all-columns-of R = all-columns-of S);
Cartesian Product:	SELECT × FROM R, S;

Selection: SELECT × FROM *R* WHERE *p*;
                  (*p* is the predicate of the selection)
Projection: SELECT DISTINCT col_1, ... , col_n
                  FROM *R*;
                  (*R* has more than *n* columns).

It is easier to prove relational completeness by using relational algebra than by using tuple or domain relational calculus. Due to the recognition of SQL as the ANSI 4GL, calculus-based languages such as QUEL or QBE have become obsolete. Their study is motivated now primarily by theoretical research reasons.

E12. Data Structures for Search Algorithms

Three distinct types of search are used in database transactions: sequential, indexed, and direct. The three corresponding data structures that are used for implementing these search algorithms are respectively: linear linked list, search tree, and hash table. As subjects of theoretical computer science their basis is rooted in mathematics. We describe them in the next three sections.

E13. Linear Linked List

A *linear linked list* consists of a set of *nodes* that are not necessarily contiguous in memory. Each node has two parts, data and pointer. In the C language, for example, a node can be implemented as the STRUCT data type where the last element of the STRUCT is a pointer variable that contains the address of the next node in the list. A linear linked list provides a convenient mechanism for creating and maintaining a continually changing data object such as a relation in a database without the need to reorder and restructure the list with every update. For example, in Oracle a node represents a row of a table, the data part of the node contains the data values of the row, and the pointer part contains the ROWID of the next row. The header node of the list contains the ROWID of the first row. The pointer part of the *n*th node contains the ROWID of the (*n* + 1)st row. The pointer part of the last node is NULL signifying the end of the list. Figure E.1 represents a linear linked list.

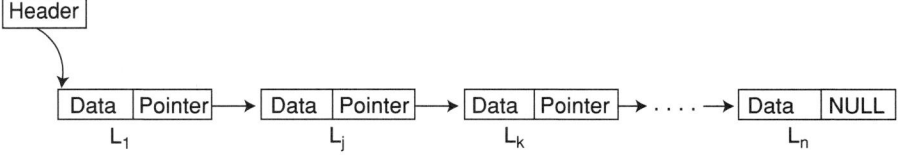

FIGURE E.1: Linear Linked List

The advantage of a linear linked list is that the insertion of a new node or the deletion of an existing node can be accomplished by merely resetting the pointer part of the affected node.

Insertion

Suppose that a list L contains n nodes $l_1, \ldots, l_n$ and that we want to insert a new node l between the nodes l_j and l_k. We proceed as follows (see Figure E.2).

- Replace the pointer part of node l with the pointer part of l_j;
- Replace the pointer part of node l_j with the starting address of node l.

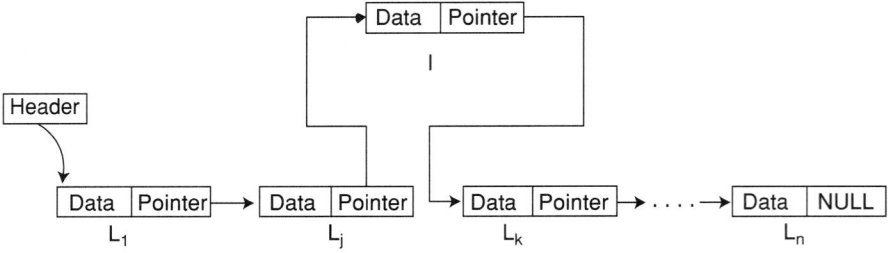

FIGURE E.2: Insertion into a List

Deletion

Suppose that we want to delete a node l_j currently placed between the nodes l_1 and l_k. We proceed as follows (see Figure E.3).

- Replace the pointer part of l_1 with the starting address of l_k.

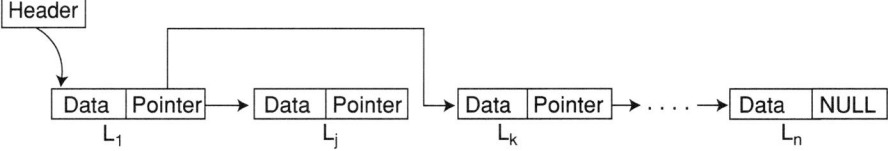

FIGURE E.3: Deletion from a List

Modification

A modification of a node l is implemented as a deletion of l followed by an insertion of the modified data part of l.

Search Algorithm

A linear linked list can be searched to return nodes whose data parts match given selection criteria. The search consists of the following steps.

- Start with the first node of the list.
- Return the data part of each matching node.
- Continue the search until you reach the last node.
- Terminate the search.

Figure E.4 shows the flowchart of the search algorithm. Clearly it represents a sequential search.

Thus, if a relation is implemented as a linear linked list, the update, i.e., insertion, deletion, and modification, and retrieval transactions are implemented as outlined above. The retrieval via a linear linked list involves a full table scan.

E14. Search Tree

A *tree T* is defined recursively as follows.

(a) T is a collection of nodes, which can be empty.
(b) If T is nonempty, T has a distinguished node r called the *root* of T and zero or more subtrees $T_1, \ldots, T_k$. The root of each subtree is connected to r by a directed *edge*.
(c) The root of each subtree is called a *child* of r and r is called the *parent* of each subtree root.

Thus, T consists of k nodes one of which is called its root. The root is connected to the remaining $(k-1)$ nodes by $(k-1)$ directed edges. Each of these nodes can be the root of a subtree. Nodes with no children are called *leaves* or *terminal nodes*. Nodes with the same parent are called *siblings*. Figure E.5 shows a tree.

470　Appendix E. Mathematical Foundation of Relational Databases

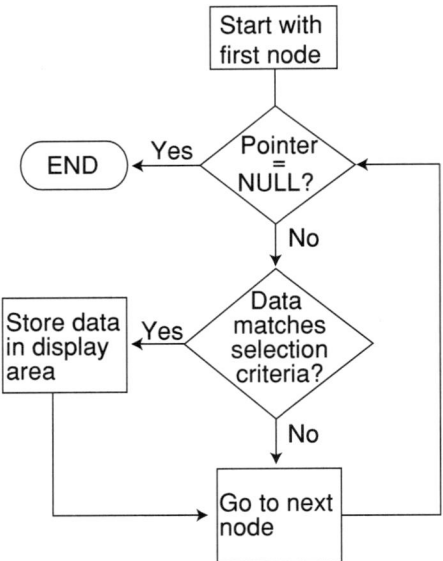

FIGURE E.4: Search Algorithm of a Linear Linked List

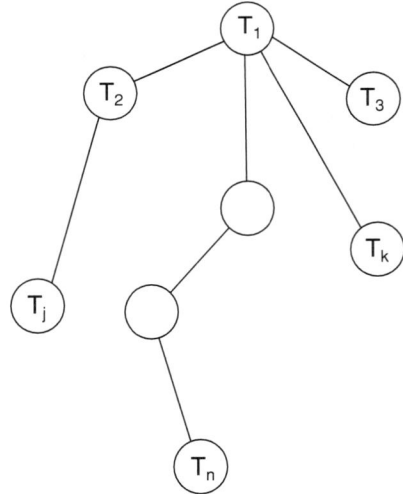

FIGURE E.5: Example of a Tree

A *B-tree of order n* is a special type of tree that is always *balanced*. This means that the tree satisfies the following four conditions.

- The root is either a leaf or has between 2 and n children.
- All nonleaf nodes except the root have between $\lceil n/2 \rceil$ and n children.
- All leaves are at the same depth n.
- All leaves have between $\lceil n/2 \rceil$ and n data values.

The notation $\lceil n/2 \rceil$, called the *ceiling* of $n/2$, is defined as follows.

$$n = 2m \Rightarrow \lceil n/2 \rceil = m;\ n = 2m + 1 \Rightarrow \lceil n/2 \rceil = m + 1.$$

All key values along with pointers for the data indexed by the keys are stored in the leaves. Each nonleaf node contains pointers to the nodes at the next lower level. For any two nodes p and q, the data contained in p is always less than the data contained in q if p lies to the left of q.

Search Algorithm

To search for data indexed by a given key value in a B-tree of order n we proceed as follows.

- Start at the root of the tree.
- Branch down in at most n directions at each succeeding lower level until you reach the leaves.
- Search each leaf node to find the pointer to the data indexed by the given key value. If the data do not exist, a NULL pointer is returned.

Insertion

To insert a new key into a B-tree of order n we proceed as in the search process described above. When we reach the leaf nodes, we insert the key into a leaf node so as to maintain the order of key values in the leaf nodes. However, this process may pose a problem, because a leaf can contain at most n keys. If the target node is already full, the new key cannot be inserted. In this case, we split the node into two nodes and adjust the pointers from their parents. This process may lead to an increase in the height of the tree causing an increase in the search time.

B-trees are widely used in implementing indices in a relational database. The index B-tree is kept in auxiliary storage such as a disk file. During the execution of a database transaction such as retrieval via indexed search or updating an indexed table the relevant portion of the tree is brought into the memory. As we know, the disk access speed is several orders of magnitude slower than accessing the memory. The order n of an index B-tree is chosen such that a nonleaf node fits into one database block, which is always a multiple of the operating system block size. Usually when n belongs to the range $32 \leq n \leq 256$, this condition is satisfied. The maximum number of elements that are stored in a leaf node is chosen so that a full leaf fits into one database block. This means that a record can be found via an indexed search in a very few disk accesses since the level of a B-tree usually does not exceed 4. The root and possibly the first level of nodes can even be kept in memory.

Based on algorithm analysis it is found that a B-tree is mostly 69% (= ln 2) full. To utilize this fact a special type of B-tree, called B*-tree, is defined which requires that for a B*-tree of order n, each node must have between $2n/3$ and n children. This means that each node of a B*-tree is at least 67% full. It leads to a better storage utilization. Oracle uses the B*-tree mechanism to implement its indices.

E15. Hash Table

The search techniques used by linear linked lists and B-trees involve searching a set of nodes to find and return those whose data match the selection criteria. Obviously, the fewer the number of searches, the more efficient the search technique. Ideally, therefore, we would like to have a data structure that does not need any unnecessary comparisons of the selection criteria with the data part of each node. This requires that the location of a key depend only on the key value itself. Hash tables provide such a data structure.

A *hash table* is an array of some fixed size N, say, that stores the key values along with their addresses for a database relation. A key, by definition, is a string consisting of single or multiple column values according to whether the key is single or composite. Each key is mapped onto its location or address by means of a *hash function H*, say, defined as follows,

$$H: \{keys\} \rightarrow \{addresses\}$$

such that H (key) = address of the key and $0 \leq H$ (key) $\leq N - 1$, where N is the size of the hash table and is selected as a large prime number. The *division remainder algorithm* is a commonly used form of hash function. It uses the mechanism known as the *modulo arithmetic*. N is called the *modulus*. The algorithm is defined as follows.

(a) The hash table consists of N buckets, each bucket containing zero or more key values.
(b) Let v be a key value, which must be numeric. Divide v by the modulus N.
(c) The remainder r, which can be zero, derived in Step (b) satisfies the condition $0 \leq r \leq N - 1$ and is written as v mod (N). The key value v then belongs to the bucket r.

If v is a character string, it is converted to a number by means of some suitable transformation. A commonly used transformation is the following.

Let v consist of m characters and let k_i be the ASCII code for the $(i + 1)$st character in v, where $i = 0, 1, \ldots, m-1$. Then, the numeric transform λ, say, of v is given by the expression

$$\lambda = \sum_{i=0}^{m-1} k_{m-i-1} \times (32)^i.$$

Steps (b) and (c) are now applied to λ to compute the bucket number of v.

When an integer v is divided by a modulus N, it leaves N possible remainders 0, 1, 2, ..., $N - 1$. The infinitely many integers of the form $kN + r$, where k is any integer, leave the same remainder r when divided by N. The set $\{\ kN + r \mid k$ is any integer$\}$ is called an *equivalence class* of integers modulo N. Any modulus N partitions the set of integers into N disjoint equivalence classes of congruent elements such that any two elements of the same class leave the same remainder when divided by the modulus. Each bucket in a hash table is an equivalence class of key values. Since we can map a virtually endless set of keys onto a finite number of buckets given by the modulus N, multiple keys can and do map onto the same bucket. This leads to the problem of collision, which is resolved in two ways:

- Open hashing (also called separate chaining), and
- Closed hashing (also called open addressing)

We now describe each method of resolution.

Open Hashing

For each bucket in the hash table we maintain a linear linked list of all keys that hash to the same bucket. Let us suppose that

N = size of hash table = number of buckets in the hash table
r = bucket number, where $r = 0, 1, 2, \ldots, N - 1$

Then, bucket r consists of the key value of r and a pointer to a linear linked list containing all key values of the type $kN + r$, where k is an integer. Figure E.6 shows an example where $N = 7$, a prime number.

To search for a given key value v, say, in a hash table with modulus N, we proceed as follows.

- Let $r = v \bmod N$
- Access bucket r for the key $= v$
- Search the linear linked list originating at r until you find v
- If a NULL pointer is returned, then v is not in the hash table

Closed Hashing

Open hashing has the disadvantage of requiring pointers and a second data structure, namely, the linear linked list. This tends to slow down the search time slightly due to the time required to allocate new cells. *Closed hashing*, which is also known as *open addressing*, is an alternative method that does not use the linked lists.

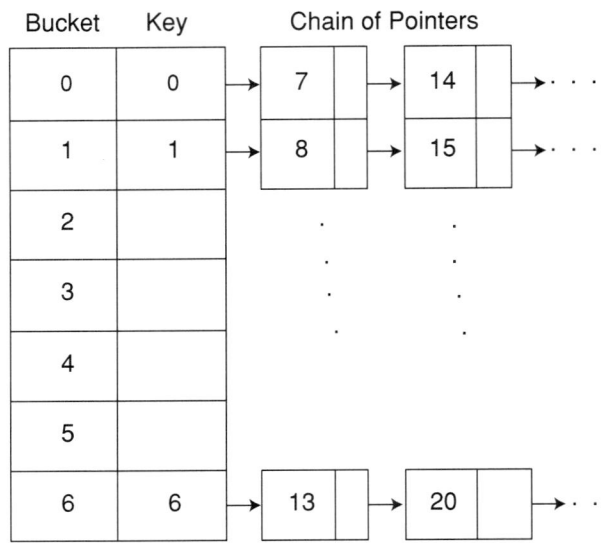

FIGURE E.6: Open Hash Table

Let
  N = size of the hash table, i.e., N = modulus
  N = key value that must be stored in a bucket
  $H(v) = v \bmod (N)$, where H is the hash function, i.e., $H(v)$ is the bucket where v is hashed via the hash function of modulo arithmetic.

If the bucket $H(v)$ is already occupied, a collision arises. Under closed hashing all the remaining buckets located after the bucket $H(v)$ are tried sequentially until an empty one is found to place v. The search can wrap around the hash table if the end of the table is reached. The mathematical procedure is given below.

Let
  $h_i(v)$ = bucket to store v under closed hashing, where $i = 0, 1, 2, \ldots, N-1$.

Define
  $h_i(v) = (H(v) + f(i)) \bmod (N)$, where $i = 0, 1, 2, \ldots, N-1$

Then, $f(i)$ is called the *probing function* and is used for resolving the collision. We define $f(0) = 0$. Buckets $h_0(v), h_1(v), \ldots, h_{N-1}(v)$ are tried until a free bucket is found for storing v.

Two forms of the probing function are commonly used:

- Linear probing where we set $f(i) = i$
- Quadratic probing where we set $f(i) = i^2$

Example of Linear Probing

Let $N = 17$, and $v = 5, 2042, 123, 36, 1753, 372, 50, 1222$. We assume that these key values arrive in that order to be stored in the hash table via the hash function H defined by $H(v) = v \bmod (17)$. If a collision arises, then v is hashed to a bucket determined by the sequence of linear probing functions $h_i(v)$ defined as follows.

$$h_i(v) = (v \bmod (17) + i) \bmod (17), \text{ where } i = 0, 1, 2, \ldots, 16.$$

Hence 5 hashes to bucket 5 mod (17) = 5.
2042 hashes to bucket 2042 mod (17) = 2.
123 hashes to bucket 123 mod (17) = 4.
36 hashes to bucket 36 mod (17) = 2, which leads to a collision.

To resolve the collision we compute the sequence of functions

$$h_0(36) = (36 \bmod (17) + 0) \bmod (17) = 2 \bmod (17) = 2.$$
$$h_1(36) = (36 \bmod (17) + 1) \bmod (17) = 3 \bmod (17) = 3.$$

Since bucket 3 is free, the key 36 is placed in bucket 3. Next comes $v = 1753$ which hashes to bucket 2. Since this bucket is already occupied, we compute the sequence of functions

$$h_i(1753) = (1753 \bmod (17) + i) \bmod (17), \text{ where } i = 0, 1, 2, \ldots, 16.$$

Successive computation yields the following results.

$$h_0(1753) = 2, h_1(1753) = 3, h_2(1753) = 4, h_3(1753) = 5, h_4(1753) = 6.$$

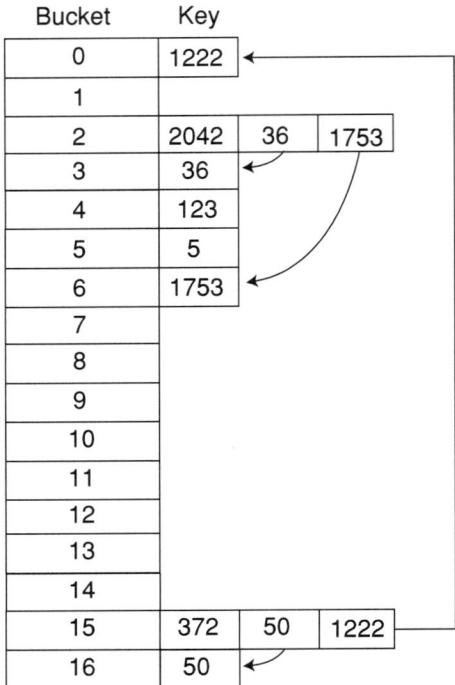

FIGURE E.7: Closed Hash Table with Linear Probing

Since bucket 6 is not occupied, key 1753 is placed there. Proceeding similarly we find the following hash locations for the remaining keys: 372 → 15, 50 → 16, and 1222 → 0. Figure E.7 shows the hash table configuration with all these keys. We note that the search for key 1222 starts at the computed hash location of bucket 15, then goes to bucket 16, and then wraps around the hash table to find the ultimate location of bucket 0 where the key 1222 is stored.

Since in closed hashing all keys are ultimately stored inside the table instead of being stored in separate linked lists, the size of the hash table must be sufficiently large. Normally, the size N is taken as at least double the number of key values. The linear probing amounts to trying buckets sequentially with wraparound until an empty bucket is located. As a result, blocks of occupied buckets start to form clusters. This phenomenon is known as *primary clustering*. It means that it will take longer to find an empty bucket to place a key value that hashes into a bucket in the cluster area. Two examples of primary clustering can be found in Figure E.7 at the buckets 2 and 15. Under linear probing the hash table should not be allowed to get more than 70% full. Under quadratic probing that number dwindles to below 50%. In fact, the following theorem can be proved mathematically.

Under quadratic probing with a prime modulus a key value can always be inserted if the table is at least half empty.

Rehashing

As a hash table gets too full, the execution time of storing a key gets longer and empty buckets become harder to find. In this case, the following strategy known as *rehashing* is adopted.

(a) Build another hash table that is at least double the size of the original table.
(b) Design a new hash function.
(c) Scan the entire original hash table to compute the new hash value of each key.
(d) Insert each key into the new table according to the value computed in Step (c).

According to the division remainder algorithm using modulo arithmetic the new hash function is defined as follows. Let $H(v) = v \bmod (p_1)$, where p_1 is a prime, be the original hash function. We define the rehash function $RH(v)$ as follows.

$$RH(v) = v \bmod (p_2), \text{ where } p_2 \text{ is a prime} > 2p_1$$

E16. Performance Metrics

We have discussed three types of search algorithms based on three separate data structures:

- Sequential search via linear linked lists,
- Indexed search via B*-trees, and
- Direct search via hash tables.

The performance of each search technique is measured by its search time. In this section we discuss various estimates of search times as functions of the number of elements, say n, being searched. In other words, we assume that the table being searched has n elements.

Given two functions $f(n)$ and $g(n)$, where n is a non-negative integer, we define $g(n)$ to be of *order* $f(n)$ if there exists some nonnegative integer N such that $g(n) \leq c f(n)$, for all $n \geq N$, where c is a constant. We write $g(n) = O(f(n))$. It can be proved easily that $O(f(n))$ is linear in its argument, i.e.,

$$O(f_1(n) + f_2(n)) = O(f_1(n)) + O(f_2(n)), \text{ for any two functions } f_1(n), f_2(n).$$

Linear Linked List

The maximum search time for a linear linked list with n elements is $O(n^2)$ since in a worst case scenario the desired element can be at the end of the list and each node is accessed in constant time of $O(1)$.

B-tree

Let the set of n elements be arranged in a B-tree of order m. Then the average search time for an element is $O(\log_m(n))$. The same estimate applies to a B*-tree, which is a special case of a B-tree.

Hash Table

Given a hash table T with m buckets and n keys, we define the *load factor* μ of T as $\mu = n/m$. Thus the load factor represents the average number of keys that can be stored in each bucket. Note that μ can be less than, equal to, or greater than 1. It is assumed that μ remains fixed as both n and $m \to \infty$, i.e., in real terms, both n and m grow arbitrarily large.

Since the address, i.e., the bucket number, of a key element in a hash table is computed from the value of the key, the access time of any key is constant, i.e., $O(1)$. Based on this fact the following theorems hold.

1. In open hashing the search time for a key irrespective of whether the key exists in the table is $O(1 + \mu)$, where μ is the load factor.
2. In closed hashing with $\mu < 1$, the expected number of probes in an unsuccessful search, i.e., where the key does not reside in the hash table, is at most $1/(1 - \mu)$.
3. In closed hashing with $\mu < 1$, the expected number of probes in a successful search, i.e., where the key resides in the hash table, is at most
$$(1/\mu) * \log_e(1/(1 - \mu)) + 1/\mu$$

Theorems (2) and (3) assume that the keys are uniformly distributed over the hash table.

Key Words

Armstrong's axioms
atom
B-tree
bound variable
bucket
Cartesian product
closed hashing
closure property
collision
conjunction
De Morgan's laws
difference
disjunction
division remainder algorithm
domain

domain relational calculus
equijoin
equivalence class
equivalence theorem
existential quantifier
formula
free variable
fully functionally dependent
function
functional dependency
generation of languages
hash function
hash table
intersection
isomorphic

language, descriptive
language, prescriptive
leaf
linear linked list
linear probing
load factor
modulo arithmetic
modulus
n-ary relation
negation
open hashing
primary clustering
probing function
projection
quadratic probing
rehashing

relation, arity of
relation, degree of
relational algebra
relational calculus
relationally complete
safe tuple relational calculus
search algorithm
selection
sibling
theta-join
tree
truth table
tuple relational calculus
union compatible
universal quantifier

References and Further Reading

1. E. F. Codd—*Relational Completeness of Data Base Sublanguages*, Data Base Systems, Courant Computer Science Symposia Series, Volume 6, Prentice-Hall, 1972.
2. T. H. Cormen, C. E. Leiserson, and R. L. Rivest—*Introduction to Algorithms*, MIT Press, 1996.
3. H. F. Kortz and A. Silberschatz—*Database System Concepts*, McGraw-Hill, 1986.
4. S. S. Mittra—*Principles of Relational Database Systems*, Prentice-Hall, 1991.
5. J. D. Ullman—*Principles of Database Systems*, Computer Science Press, 1982.
6. J. D. Ullman—*Principles of Database and Knowledge-Base Systems*, Volumes 1 and 2, Computer Science Press, 1988 and 1989.
7. M. A. Weiss—*Data Structures and Algorithm Analysis in C*, Benjamin/Cummings, 1993.
8. C. C. Yang—*Relational Databases*, Prentice-Hall, 1986.

Codd's paper [1] is the classical source of the mathematical foundation of relational databases. He introduced the basics of relational algebra and relational calculus in this paper. Mittra [4, Chapter 4], Ullman [5, Chapter 5] and Yang [8, Chapter 3] contain mathematical proof of the equivalence of relational algebra and calculus. Ullman [6, Volume 1, Chapter 4] discusses several query languages as examples of languages based on relational algebra and calculus. Cormen et al. [2, Chapters 11, 12, and 19] and Weiss [7, Chapters 3 to 5] are good sources for additional materials on data structures and algorithm analysis. In particular, Cormen et al. [2, Chapter 12] contains proofs of the three theorems cited at the end of Section E16.

Index

A

acceptance test, 6, 42, 52
access
   indexed, 232
   sequential, 232
access path, 33, 37–38, 231, 233–234, 238, 264, 268, 293–295, 297, 301, 381–382
advanced replication, 52
aggregation, 363, 372, 382
alert log file, 69, 79, 80, 415, 416
alternate key, 8, 25
ANALYZE, 35, 110–111, 152,–153, 234–236, 245, 262, 299, 315, 317–318, 323, 337, 349, 350, 351, 375, 382, 397
AND logic, 279
application server, 7, 385, 387–388, 392, 394–395, 397–398
ARCH, 58, 63, 65–66, 79, 156, 161, 164–166, 184, 212
ARCHIVELOG, 65–66, 68, 79–80, 161, 164–165, 184
archiving, 18, 25, 65, 165, 166, 420
Armstrong's axioms, 452, 477
asymptotic growth curve, 311–312
atom, 462–464, 477
atomic concept, 7–8, 25
attribute, 8–10, 25, 27, 296, 364, 366, 430–431, 450–452, 454, 456–457, 459
AUTOTRACE, 34, 55, 263–264, 277–279, 282, 291, 298–299, 309, 312
auxiliary storage, 36–38, 57–59, 64, 67, 82–83, 115, 168, 190, 224, 471

B

B-tree, 47, 79, 470–471, 477
B*-tree, 37, 245–250, 252–254, 263, 279, 281–282, 289, 312, 344, 346, 349, 472, 477–478
B*-tree index, 245–247, 249–250, 253–254, 263, 279, 281–282, 312, 344, 346, 349, 356
background process, 30, 55, 57–61, 63, 65, 67, 69, 79, 106, 137–138, 146, 156, 161, 184, 190, 200, 206, 210–212, 224–226, 355, 368, 394, 407, 414, 416, 433, 436
balanced tree, *see* B-tree
basic replication, 42, 52
before image, 115, 119, 134, 288, 408
bind variable, 134, 149, 184, 186, 381
bitmap index, 118, 216, 248–253, 269, 279, 312, 380–381
BLEVEL, 247–248, 253, 279
bound variable, 462–465, 478
bucket, 261, 263, 279, 472–475, 477
buffer
   dirty, 147, 156, 164, 200, 206, 208, 209
   free, 206, 208, 210

C

cache get, 138, 185
cache hit, 138, 140, 143, 145, 148, 185, 186, 338
cache memory, 38, 61
cache miss, 138, 143–145, 148–149, 152, 185–186, 205

cache reload, 138, 185
caching algorithm, 58, 185
candidate key, 8, 25
canonical form, 33, 38, 231
cardinality, 25, 235, 239, 248, 380, 429, 451–452
Cartesian product, 375, 380–381, 382, 450, 454–455, 457–459, 463, 477
cartridge, 18, 390–395, 397
cascading, 14, 25, 443
CASE, 14, 21, 28, 30, 38–39, 43, 369
CGI, *see* Common Gateway Interface
chaining, 20, 25, 31, 33, 35–38, 82, 110–115, 134–136, 225, 333, 402, 473
CHECK (constraint), 13, 15, 21, 28, 51–52, 93, 402, 427, 441
checkpoint, 58, 63–66, 79–80, 156, 163–165, 185, 210, 214, 219, 419, 421
CKPT, 58, 63, 65–66, 79, 156, 163–164, 185, 416
class, 6, 25, 118, 121, 139, 183, 198, 201, 216, 473
client-server application, 6, 25, 28
client-server architecture, 30, 38, 386
closed hashing, 473–474, 476, 478
closure property, 449, 459, 478
cluster, 74, 233, 246, 255–260, 271, 279, 294, 302, 307, 312, 348, 476
cluster index, 258
cluster join, 233, 279, 307, 312
CLUSTERING_FACTOR, 247–248, 279
collision, 473–475, 478
Common Gateway Interface, 386, 397
component, 7–8, 22, 46, 48, 49, 58, 71, 136, 231, 239–240, 246, 316, 355–356, 367–368, 386–387, 390–393, 395, 397, 401–402, 407, 433–434, 436, 459, 462–465
concatenated index, 238–239, 244, 246, 253, 263, 279, 295, 312, 345, 374–377
conceptual level, 1, 20, 25, 29–32, 34, 38, 41–44, 46–49, 52–54, 82, 96, 224, 230, 235, 240, 290–291, 316, 318, 323, **361**, 383, 450, 452
conjunction, 137, 297, 452, 456, 460–462, 478
constraint, 47, 49–51, 93, 134, 241–242, 246, 393, 402, 409, 441, 443, 427
contention, 49–50, 52, 64, 66, 113, 115, 127, 134, 165, 175, 178–179, 181, 183–186, 200–201, 210, 213–214, 216–217, **225**, 319, 333, 335, 357, 395
control file, 65, 68, 79, 164, 211–212, 415, 417, 433–434, 436
crontab, 123, 134

D

data
 mining, 366, 368, 382–383
 redundancy, 364, 382
 replication, 20, 32, 38, 42, 52–53, 411
 retrieval, 6, 36, 47, 52, 60, 97, 230, 233, 318, 442, 445
 transfer rate, 37, 38
 update, 52
 validation, 13, 19, 25, 28, 42, 365, 368–369, 425
 warehouse, 28, 46, 53, 239, 249, 361–374, 382–384
data block buffers, 60–61, 64, 77, 134, 137–138, 140, 142, 185, 226
data block header, 134, 185, 226
data consistency, 41, 52
Data Definition Language, 4, 25, 38
data dictionary, 14, 24–25, 28, 30, 32, 35, 37–38, 48, 52, 57, 60, 62, 64, 70, 74, 76, 79, 80, 82, 134, 154, 183, 185, 219, 226, 230, 245, 261, 274, 293, 320, 326–327, 333, 340, 348–351, 354, 368–369, 409–410, 414
data integrity, 14–15, 20, 47, 52, 60
Data Manipulation Language, 4, 25
database transaction, 8, 25, 36, 60, 64, 68, 79, 102, 115, 134, 146, 288, 385–386, 393, 467, 471

datafile, 18, 38, 49, 65, 67, 79, 84–85, 89, 104, 134, 160–161, 194, 222, 326, 327, 333, 410, 414–417, 424–425, 434, 440, 442–446
datamart, 366–367, 382–383
DBWR, 58, 61, 64–65, 79, 147, 156, 159–160, 164, 185–186, 190, 206–207, 210, 212, 216, 226, 394, 416
DDL, *see* Data Definition Language
De Morgan's laws, 462, 478
decision support system, 46, 53, 239, 306, 362, 382–383
decision tree, 260, 279
declarative constraint, 13, 26
defragmentation, 97, 105, 107, 134–135, 326
denormalization, 13, 20, 26, 32, 34, 38, 41, 43–44, 46–47, 52–54, 290, 363, 382
dense index, 279
descriptive query language, 449, 460
dictionary cache, 62, 64, 134, 148, 154–155, 167, 185, 212, 219–220, 226
difference (relational algebraic operation), 6, 80, 102, 105, 136, 186, 202, 222, 289, 386, 388, 454–456, 458–459, 465, 478
dimension table, 365–370, 372, 374, 375, 377, 380–383
dimensional analysis, 366, 382
disjunction, 456, 460, 462, 478
distributed database, 28, 32, 42, 52, 66, 231–232
division remainder algorithm, 472, 477–478
domain relational calculus, 231, 449, 453, 464–467, 478
driver, *see* driving table
driving set, 43, 52
driving table, 35, 38, 44, 53, 244, 279, 301, 312
DSS, *see* decision support system,
dynamic performance view, 57, 70, 116, 179, 183, 190, 272, 279, 338, 368

E

ending point (of a histogram), 261, 279
entity, 8–9, 11–12, 26, 28, 39
equijoin, 279, 303, 307, 312, 374, 381, 457, 478
equipartitioned, 50–51, 53
equivalence class, 473, 478
equivalence theorem, 449, 465–466, 478
ERwin, 14, 21, 43, 369, 402
execute phase, 231–232, 279, 312
execution plan, 33–34, 38, 47, 55, 62, 148, 229, 231, 234–235, 263–264, 266–269, 274–275, 277, 279, 281–284, 291, 297, 299, 309, 339, 340, 342, 370, 374–375, 377–383
existential quantifier, 460–462, 466, 478
EXPLAIN PLAN, 20, 34, 37, 55, 263–265, 272, 274–275, 279–281, 284, 291, 298, 312, 339, 375, 377, 379, 382, 418
explicit cursor, 289–290, 312
export, 100, 110, 113, 134–136, 373, 382, 416, 422, 424, 439–440, 442–447
export parameter file, 442, 447
extends, 42, 52, 116, 118, 121, 123
extent
 initial, 16, 95, 96, 105, 326
 next, 16–17, 39, 85, 95–96, 99, 103, 104–105, 116, 326, 369, 402–403, 407–409
extent map, 216
external level, 20, 26, 30–34, 38–39, 55, 229–230, 239, 310, 315–317, 361, 370, 385, 397–398
extraction programs, 363, 382

F

fact table, 365–369, 374–375, 377, 380–383
fetch phase, 232, 279, 312
filtering condition, 291, 312
first normal form, 26
FK, 14–15, 19, 22–23, 26, 35, 240–244, 255, 374–375, 377, 380–381, 402, 441
foreign key, 13–14, 26, 34, 93, 95, 240

formula, 96, 131, 140, 151, 154, 212, 221, 234, 343, 344, 403, 407, 462–466, 478
fragmentation, 20, 36–38, 82–83, 99, 101, 106–107, 134–136, 168, 224–225, 326, 348, 402, 409
free space, 33, 36, 81–82, 96–97, 101–108, 110, 113–114, 134–135, 149–152, 182, 225, 296, 310, 326, 333, 357, 369, 403, 407
free space fragmentation index, 106, 134
free variable, 462–463, 478
FREELIST GROUPS, 134, 183–185
FREELISTS, 97, 134, 183–185, 216
full table scan, 35, 37–38, 43–44, 47–48, 53, 234, 240, 244, 249, 252, 257, 261, 268, 288, 293–294, 297, 299, 301–302, 304, 306, 335, 337, 343–344, 355, 370, 469
fully functionally dependent, 452, 478
function, 6, 26, 59, 65, 152, 166, 259, 269, 271, 310–311, 334, 343–345, 349, 362, 371, 386, 388, 390, 393, 395, 397–398, 428–429, 451–452, 463
functional dependency, 26–27, 449–452, 478
functionally dependent, 11, 26, 452, 478

G
generation of languages, 478

H
hash cluster, 233, 259–260, 263, 271, 279, 312
hash
  function, 72, 259, 269, 279, 312, 472–474–475, 477–478
  join, 269, 279, 297, 301, 306, 309, 312, 381
  table, 62, 306, 449–450, 467, 472–478
hashing, 62, 259, 279, 306, 312, 320, 473–474, 476
hint, 55, 232, 235, 274, 279, 288, 292–299, 301–302, 309, 312, 339, 355, 374, 378, 380–381, 383

hit ratio
  data block buffer, 140
  dictionary cache, 154
  library cache, 148
  redo log buffer, 146, 207
homonym, 365, 382
host language interface, 13, 33, 38, 453
HTML, *see* Hyper Text Markup Language
HTTP, *see* Hyper Text Transport Protocol
HTTP Listener, 390–392, 397
Hyper Text Markup Language, 388, 397
Hyper Text Transport Protocol, 388, 397

I
I/O load, 49, 53, 157, 160, 175, 222
implicit cursor, 290, 312
import parameter file, 443, 447
index organized table, 245, 254, 279, 349
indexed search, 35, 37–38, 43–44, 47, 50, 53, 234–235, 238, 240, 246, 249, 261, 263, 343–344, 450, 471, 477
initialization parameter, 20, 57–59, 61–62, 64–66, 69, 74, 77, 79–80, 114, 134, 138–139, 145–147, 149, 154–156, 160–161, 164–166, 168, 174, 176, 179, 181, 183, 185, 190, 203, 206–207, 209, 211–213, 218, 220–221, 225–226, 233, 253, 272–273, 284, 292–293, 297, 299, 302, 304, 307, 332, 335, 341, 347, 354–355, 369, 381, 383, 414, 440
instance, 18, 47, 55, 57–60, 62–67, 69–70, 74, 77–80, 134, 135, 138, 156, 157, 161, 164, 168, 174, 176, 179, 185–187, 219, 224–226, 233, 272–273, 335, 341, 347, 356, 369–370, 390–391, 393–394, 399, 413–417, 419–420, 429, 433, 435–437, 443–444
Integrity Enhancement Feature, 4, 26
internal level, 20, 26, 30–33, 38, 44, 47, 55, 57–59, 70, 77, 82, 190, 204, 224, 230, 283, 316, 361, 369, 383, 385, 395, 398
internal representation, 33, 231, 279
intersection, 270, 338, 454–456, 458, 478

invalidation, 152, 185
isomorphic, 454, 459, 478

J

join, 35, 38, 43–45, 79, 231, 233–234, 240, 244, 255, 263, 269–271, 280, 291, 293, 295–297, 301–304, 306–307, 309, 312, 323, 364, 374–378, 380–381, 421, 454, 457, 458

K

key, 8, 11, 14, 26, 31, 38, 47, 49, 50, 93, 233, 245–246, 248, 253, 255–259, 263, 269, 271, 319, 334, 349, 375, 414, 420–421, 427, 471–478

L

latch, 178–179, 181, 185, 191, 193, 195–197, 200–202, 212–216, 226, 335
leaf, 113, 245–246, 248, 253, 279, 357, 471, 478
leaf node, 245–246, 248, 253, 279, 471
LEAF_BLOCKS, 247–248, 279
least cost, 231, 234, 279, 284, 294
LGWR, 58, 61–66, 68, 79, 146–147, 156, 161, 164–166, 185, 190, 207, 211–212, 226, 416
library cache, 62, 79, 148–149, 152, 167, 185, 204–205, 212–214, 226, 274, 276–277
life cycle, 4, 363, 382
limiting condition, 244, 279
linear linked list, 182, 449–450, 467–470, 472–473, 477, 479
linear probing, 474–476, 479
linear trend, 135, 311–312
load factor, 478–479
LOB, 50, 110, 134, 315, 317, 333–334, 358–359
log switch, 66, 69, 79–80, 147, 161–162, 164–166, 185, 187, 225, 370, 382
logical data independence, 31, 38
logical design, 5, 11, 30, 38
logical read, 140, 185, 206, 210, 216, 284–287, 289
logical record, 26, 30–31, 38
LRU algorithm, 62, 148, 169, 176, 181, 206, 288

M

mapping
    conceptual to internal level, 31, 38
    external to conceptual level, 31, 38
maxextent, 16, 26
memory
    real, 140, 166, 168–169, 174, 370, 398
    shared, 168, 174
    virtual, 143, 166, 168–169, 174, 356
memory cache, 58, 79, 138, 185, 226
message, 26, 31, 34, 115, 119, 128, 135, 211–212, 245, 265, 355, 390, 408, 416, 418, 437, 446
meta database, 14, 368, 382
metabase, 368, 382
metadata, 361, 368–369, 371, 382–384, 440, 442–443, 445
migration, 33, 36–37, 82, 110, 114–115, 134, 136, 331, 333
modulo arithmetic, 472–474, 477, 479
modulus, 472–474, 476, 479
MRU, 58
MTS, *see* multithreaded server
multidimensional database, 366, 382
multithreaded server, 58, 62, 66, 304, 307, 312

N

n-ary relation, 450, 454, 459, 464, 479
n-tier, 6, 30, 361, 386, 397
n-tier architecture, 361, 386, 397
natural join, *see* equijoin
negation, 456, 460–462, 479
nested format, 267–268, 274, 312
nested loops join, 279, 293, 295–296, 301–303, 306–307, 309, 312, 375
network traffic, 32, 42, 53

nondense index, 279
nonpersistent connection, 387–388, 397
nonprocedural language, 4
normalization, 11, 26, 32, 46, 399, 449–450

O

OFA, *see* Optimal Flexible Architecture, 67, 68
OLTP, *see* On Line Transaction Processing
On Line Transaction Processing, 43, 46–47, 53, 77, 100, 141, 146, 232, 235, 239, 288, 306, 361, 368–369
1:1, *see* relationship, one to one
1:N, *see* relationship, one to many
1NF, *see* first normal form
open addressing, *see* closed hashing
open hashing, 478–479, 473
Optimal Flexible Architecture, 67, 79–80, 94
optimal indexing, 41, 235, 263, 280, 291
optimization
    cost-based, 296, 301, 312, 321, 359
    rule-based, 234, 294, 301
optimizer mode, 235, 280, 312
optimizer
    cost-based, 55, 234–235, 238, 245, 261, 266–267, 280, 284, 299, 301–302, 307, 347, 349–351, 357, 370
    rule-based, 229, 234, 238, 266, 283–284, 299, 301
OR logic, 252, 280
overflow storage space, *see* index organized table

P

package, 26, 82, 152, 176–178, 185, 224, 331–333, 342, 349–351, 359, 396–398, 428
page fault, 143, 169, 173, 185
page space, 169, 185
paging, 168–169, 173–174, 185, 334, 395, 398
paging in, 169, 173, 185
paging out, 169, 173–174, 185
parallel processing, 32, 38, 42, 53
parameter file, 47, 57, 77–79, 371, 382, 414–415, 417, 423, 433, 435, 442, 443
parse phase, 231–232, 264, 280, 312
partition, 49–51, 53, 266, 271, 318–319, 320, 321, 323, 334, 336, 364, 370, 429–430, 473
PARTITION BY RANGE, 49–51, 53
partitioned table, 49–51, 53, 234, 318, 319–321, 323, 334, 336
persistent connection, 387–388, 395, 397
PGA, *see* Program Global Area
physical data independence, 31, 38
physical design, 27, 30, 38
physical read, 140–141, 185, 206, 208, 221, 264, 276–279, 284–286, 300, 335, 337, 357
physical record, 26, 30–31, 38
pin, 148, 176, 178, 185, 199, 205, 213
PK *see* primary key
PLAN_TABLE, 263, 264, 265, 266, 267, 268, 276, 280, 312, 345, 378–379, 418, 429
PMON, 58, 64, 190, 200, 212, 416
prescriptive query language 449, 454
primary clustering, 476, 479
primary key, 8, 10–11, 13–14, 25–26, 35, 38, 41, 47, 53, 93, 114, 233, 236, 241, 245, 250, 254
privilege, 25–26, 76, 230, 342, 347, 354, 370–371, 413–414, 417, 426–427
probing function, 474–475, 479
procedure, 6, 18, 26, 58, 76, 82, 100, 106, 110–112, 150, 152, 156, 160, 166, 177, 183, 186, 213, 232, 276–277, 331–332, 334, 368, 396–397, 417–418, 426–428, 440–441, 445, 474
process, 1, 3, 5–7, 9, 16, 20, 26–27, 28, 30, 32, 34, 37, 42, 44, 52, 55, 58–60, 62–65, 68–69, 79, 96, 100, 114, 116, 138, 143, 146, 156, 159, 166, 168–169,

173–175, 178–179, 186, 210, 214–216, 230–231, 245, 247, 260, 267, 273, 275, 288–289, 292, 304, 306, 310, 335, 337, 349, 356, 359, 366–372, 375, 378, 386–388, 390–394, 399, 407, 413–417, 421, 436–437, 439–440, 442, 445, 471
Program Global Area, 304, 312
projection, 393, 454, 456–459, 467, 479
pseudocode, 30, 38, 39, 51, 427

Q

quadratic probing, 474, 476, 479
quadratic trend, 312
qualified query, 243
qualifying condition, 244, 251–252, 260, 263, 269, 280, 301, 374–375, 377, 382
query optimization, 33, 38, 55, 229–231, 234, 280, 283, 292–293, 299, 325, 374
query optimizer, 33, 62, 230–233, 251, 261, 264, 268–269, 280, 284, 291, 298, 312, 339, 343, 380–381, 453

R

range scan, 246, 253–254, 260, 263, 269, 280, 294, 296, 312
rebuild index, 349
recursive relationship, 9, 26, 28
redo log buffer, 60–62, 64–65, 68, 79, 137–138, 146–147, 156, 161, 178, 181, 185, 207, 210–213, 226, 288, 333, 370, 382
redo log file, 18, 61–62, 64–66, 68, 79, 146–147, 156, 161–166, 185, 187, 210–211, 226, 415–417
referential integrity, 13–14, 19, 26, 35, 38, 42, 46–47, 53, 240, 393
rehashing, 477, 479
relation
    arity of, 450, 479
    degree of, 61, 296, 457, 479
relational algebra, 4, 33, 231, 280, 449–450, 453–454, 456–460, 465–467, 479
relational calculus, 4, 33, 280, 449–450, 453, 460, 462–467, 479

relationally complete, 466, 479
relationship,
    many to many, 8, 26
    one to many, 8, 26
    one to one, 8, 26
reload, 138, 148, 185, 337
REPORT.TXT, 20, 190–191, 203–204, 206, 225–226
repository, 14, 30, 364, 374, 382
response time, 31, 33–34, 36, 38, 41–44, 46–47, 53–54, 176, 230, 232, 235, 257, 284, 291, 293, 310, 354–355, 387, 394–395
reverse key index, 253, 280
role, 3, 13, 26, 72, 229, 230, 234, 238, 307, 361–362, 413, 417, 426–427, 459, 463
rollback segment entry, 116, 134
rollback segment header activity, 134, 143, 185
round-robin, 116, 408, 411
row operation, 232–233, 235, 272, 280, 284, 291, 312
runtime statistics, 77, 229, 272, 282–283, 301, 312

S

safe tuple relational calculus, 462–463, 466, 479
schema diagram, 368–369, 382
SDLC, 3, 4–7, 26–28, 42, 53, 363
search algorithm, 449–450, 467, 469–471, 477, 479
second normal form, 26
selection, 232, 260, 326, 352, 454, 456, 458–459, 467, 469, 472, 479
selectivity, 37–38, 44, 47, 53, 234–239, 244–246, 249–250, 252–253, 261, 263, 280–281, 453–454
self-contained tablespaces, 441–442, 446, 449
semaphore, 174, 185, 382
separate chaining, *see* open hashing

set operation, 232, 235, 272, 280, 284, 291, 309, 312
SGA, 20, 26, 58–62, 79, 116, 137–138, 166–169, 174, 178, 185–186, 204, 212, 225–226, 284, 288, 297, 304, 306, 315, 317, 334–335, 356–357, 368, 370, 382, 398, 414, 416, 419
shared SQL pool, 60, 62, 77, 79, 137–138, 148, 168, 176, 185–186, 204–205, 226, 370, 382, 398
sibling, 469, 479
SMLC, *see* software maintenance life cycle
SMON, 58, 64, 80, 106, 190, 200, 212, 407, 411
software development life cycle, 3, 5, 26
software maintenance life cycle, 3, 5, 26
sort–merge join, 234, 280, 293, 296–297, 304–305, 307, 312
SQL*Loader, 19, 372–373, 382
SQLTRACE, 55, 263–264, 272–275, 278, 280, 282, 291, 312, 338
star query, 295, 370, 374–375, 377–382
star query execution plan, 374–375, 382
star schema, 361, 365–366, 374–376, 380, 382
star transformation, 361, 370, 375, 380–382
starting point, 7, 10, 32, 187, 261, 280, 401
stored procedure, 46, 53, 397
subtype, 10, 26, 28
supertype, 10, 26, 28
swap space, 169, 185, 395
swapping, 168–169, 173, 185, 306, 334, 398
system generated hash function, 259–260
System Global Area, *see* SGA

T

tabular format, 267, 280
Θ-join, 457
theta-join, 479
Θ-selection, 456–457
thin client, 7, 386, 397
third normal form, 11, 13, 26, 43, 46

thrashing, 168–169, 185
3NF, *see* third normal form
three-tier architecture, 385–386, 397
throughput, 33, 160, 230, 232, 235, 280, 284, 293, 299, 310
TKPROF, 55, 263–264, 275–278, 280, 282, 291, 338
trace file, 69, 80, 273, 275–276, 338, 415–416, 420
Transaction Management, 385, 393–394, 397–398
transitive dependency, 13, 26–27, 44, 46, 364, 382
transportable tablespaces, 399, 439–444, 447
tree, 62, 79, 148, 245–246, 248–249, 253, 289, 469, 471–473, 480
tree structured index, 245
trigger, 26
truth table, 460–461, 479
tuple relational calculus, 231, 449, 453, 462–466, 479
2NF, *see* second normal form

U

UGA, 62, 80, 148, 185
union compatible, 454–455, 479
universal desktop, 387, 397
universal quantifier, 460–461, 479
unqualified query, 243
update anomaly, 44, 53
user object, 80, 94, 134
user supplied hash function, 259
UTLBSTAT, 55, 70, 74, 77, 189–195, 203–204, 221, 225–227
UTLESTAT, 20, 55, 70, 74, 77, 189–192, 195–204, 206, 226–227

V

V$ view, 24, 57, 68, 70, 74–76, 80, 82, 203, 225–226
validation table, 14, 24, 26, 45, 425
vector-valued attribute, 9–10, 26

W

Waits, 116, 118–121, 125, 127, 132, 134, 146, 179, 183–184, 194–198, 201, 203, 210, 216–217, 226, 235
Warehouse Technology Initiative, 367, 382
Web browser, 7, 385–388, 390–392, 397–398
Web server, 387, 389, 394, 397
World Wide Web, 386, 397
wraps, 116, 118–119, 121, 123, 198, 476
wrinkle of time, 365, 372, 382, 384
WTI, 367, 374, 382

Z

X$ table, 57, 74, 76, 80